MW00995929

A Memorial

for

Shirley Madrigrano

who loved the

Opera

The Politics of Opera

The POLITICS *of* OPERA

A *History from*
Monteverdi to Mozart

MITCHELL COHEN

Princeton University Press
PRINCETON AND OXFORD

Copyright © 2017 by Mitchell Cohen

Requests for permission to reproduce material from this
work should be sent to Permissions, Princeton University Press

Published by Princeton University Press,
41 William Street, Princeton, New Jersey 08540

In the United Kingdom: Princeton University Press,
6 Oxford Street, Woodstock, Oxfordshire OX20 1TR

press.princeton.edu

Jacket art: Jean Antoine Watteau (1684–1721), *The Union of Comedy and Music*,
oil on canvas, Private Collection © Christie's Images / Bridgeman Images.

Jacket design by Karl Spurzem.

Library of Congress Cataloging-in-Publication Data

Names: Cohen, Mitchell, 1952–
Title: The politics of opera : a history from Monteverdi to Mozart / Mitchell Cohen.
Description: Princeton : Princeton University Press, 2017. | Includes
bibliographical references and index.
Identifiers: LCCN 2017005887 | ISBN 9780691175027 (hardcover : alk. paper)
Subjects: LCSH: Opera—Political aspects—History.
Classification: LCC ML3918.O64 C65 2017 | DDC 782.109—dc23 LC record
available at https://lccn.loc.gov/2017005887

British Library Cataloging-in-Publication Data is available

This book has been composed in Janson Text LT Std and Bodoni Std

Printed on acid-free paper. ∞

Printed in the United States of America

1 3 5 7 9 10 8 6 4 2

Remembering
IRVING HOWE

CONTENTS

PART 4: ANCIENTS IN MODERNITY

PART 5: ". . . AND ALTHOUGH I AM NO COUNT . . ."

ILLUSTRATIONS

. . . for it cannot be that these
vast movements should take place
in silence . . .

—CICERO, "Scipio's Dream"

Humanism does not mean "What I do, no animal
could do," but that we refused what the beast within
us urged and we want to retrieve man from anything
that has crushed him anywhere. No doubt [the] long
dialogue of metamorphoses and resurrections unites
the believer to a divine voice. Man becomes man only
when he pursues what is highest in himself. But it is
grand that an animal who knows he must die wrests
the music of the constellations from the nebuli and
casts it into future centuries suggesting to them voices
as yet unknown (des paroles inconnues).

—ANDRÉ MALRAUX, *The Voices of Silence*

PROLOGUE: MIXTURES, BOUNDARIES, PARALLELS

Early operas began usually with prologues.

One or several figures would appear before the audience, personifying a principle ("Virtue" or "Constancy") or a genre ("Tragedy") or even "Music" itself. Perhaps ancient deities would materialize; gods and goddesses also embodied principles or feelings (love, for example, in the case of Venus). Perhaps a celebrity from antiquity such as Ovid would step forth. The viewers-listeners might be addressed directly, or there might be an exchange among those on stage. Pointers and foreshadows were thus provided for themes and passions, concerns and ideas (often contesting) of the coming performance. There could also be bows—sometimes metaphorical, sometimes obvious and deep—to the powers-that-were. Then the scenario would change and a story would begin. Motifs would become increasingly more audible and visible.

Operagoers note often how politics weaves frequently through or even animates what they behold on stage. Those weavings and animations are the concern of this book. It speaks of "political operas" in a broad sense: operas that address politics and political ideas directly or indirectly; or that harbor important political implications; or that say or suggest something important about the politics of the times in which they were written (and sometimes about our own times—or apparently so). These pages try to place operas within politics and to situate politics within operas, all while bearing in mind that politics is only one aspect of an opera, as it is only one aspect of life. The book is framed by a striking historical detail—or perhaps it is better called a suggestive parallel—that I noticed some years ago. Opera was born of the same era—its tail end—that gave birth to the notion of the "modern" state or, more expansively, modern politics. It was an epoch of metamorphoses in many domains.

And so I started an investigation that began in the later Renaissance, and I teased from history a fragmentary story that began with the earliest operas and their political world and continued on to Mozart's last operas, which were written two years after an old regime in a modernizing world exploded in the French Revolution. Sometimes I discerned simple ideological purpose in operas or manifest acclaim for this or that ruler or a kind of rule. Sometimes ideology was below the surface, a subtext of what some critics would call deeper structures at work—subterranean mental categories that shaped what was to happen on stage. Sometimes I detected very subtle points or even defiance advanced either in words or music or both. Frequently, I perceived in operas elucidating reflections of or revealing questions posed to the political times, and not always consciously. Often enough, I found in operas a mix, not always an even one by any means, of all these features and more. Politics, then, appeared in opera in a variety of ways: ideological claims, applause, subversive suggestions, embedded worldviews and categories, elucidating reflections, revealing or combative probes. A mix—synthesis is a better description only sometimes—has many values. It allows one thing to be said obviously in order to permit something quite different to be said in delicate or more cautious tones elsewhere in the same work. Yet, alas, a mix can also be just a jumble.

Opera is by definition an art of diversity. Among the most obvious of varied elements it brings together are words and music, story and voice, staging and audience. The individual merit or bearing of each of these components within a whole can be the source of disagreement or simply be incongruous. There is, as one scholar stresses, always an "operatic compromise," and the movement of ideas "from one medium to another"—the principal media here being words and music—"often takes place incrementally and invisibly, making it difficult to notice."[1] But the movement can also be delineated more distinctly since a composer has a range of musical means with which to engage words and ideas. For example, altering keys can suggest that something important is changing in the story on stage. But it can also suggest that you ought to think differently about what you are viewing. The use of musical motifs—a pattern of notes associated with an idea or a person or an event—can serve as reminiscences or anticipations and may even challenge words being sung at a particular moment, as if to say, "remember that as you are listening to this." Still, a commonplace remains true: librettos of clumsy quality or trifling concerns have been legion, and while a few of them survive, it is usually only by the graces of music. Conversely, librettos with fine poetry and interesting ideas will rarely outlive mediocre composers. An attentive survey of opera history will find a good many formidable librettos suffused with sophisticated notions and suggestions together with daunting depictions of human dilemmas and foibles, many of which engaged, animated, and inspired the imagination of composers. They ought to be explored, even some of those that were not privileged to be in great musical partnership. Their contexts need special consideration if the goal is a larger picture of politics in opera. It is a widespread but anachronistic notion, largely a product of the nineteenth century, that words and their meanings must always be secondary considerations in operas—that they are nothing at all except vehicles for a composer's imagination to bring out what is truly important, which is our feelings.

The problem is captured neatly by the decision of a prominent midtwentieth-century British historian to choose opera as an explanatory metaphor in a nonoperatic context. (We will often come across these curious phenomena: musical or operatic metaphors used to aid in political arguments and political metaphors deployed to clarify musical explanations.) Lewis Namier, seeking to distinguish appearance from reality in politics, proposed that principles extolled by politicians are rarely more than masks for other motives. "What matters most," he contended, "is the underlying emotions, the music, to which ideas are a mere libretto, often of inferior quality." Should those feelings ebb, all that is left are doctrinal assertions "or at best innocuous clichés."[2] Had Namier been speaking directly of opera he would have missed the point—or rather the mix—that was there from opera's initial stages. In the beginning music was supposed to bring out and even shape and not just prettify what was in words. Politicians certainly don disguises, but a closer look at politics in opera can disclose much more than clichés.

A nineteenth-century philosopher who was notorious for believing somewhat too much in rationality provides a useful contrast to Namier's remark. Hegel's points, made in the 1820s and with aesthetic questions specifically in mind, don't apply to all operas or at all times. They are, however, worth keeping in mind because they raise so many key issues and difficulties of exploring politics in opera. Hegel thought it essential to ask if an artwork fostered judgments—more precisely, intelligent judgments. Did it do more than simply entertain? A text that is to be set to music, he thought, should on one hand have substance and on the other should not be so weighty and complicated that the composer's imagination had no scope for artistic creativity. "The chief thing to be demanded of a good libretto," he thought, "is that its contents shall have an inherent and true solidity." While beautiful melody can, he conceded, render a verbal text "less decisive," music would still "crave" words with "some real meaning." Musical "profundity" can never be "conjured" out of something flat or out of "trumpery," for a composer "can add what seasoning and spices he likes, but a roasted cat will never make a hare-pie."[3] His allusion is to a parable by Goethe. In it a cook tries in vain to prove his hunting acumen. But, alas, he shoots a cat instead of a hare. Having done this, he sets it "before the company, dressed with plenty of ingenious herbs."[4] Yet on the eating, it is still a cat. Put another way, music that is not only decorative brings out content in a libretto.[5]

One way to conceive the place of ideas in opera history, particularly in political opera, is as the site of ongoing struggles over making Hegel's hare-pie: how do ingredients like words and music, animated in different ways by ideas and emotions, come together? While good music does indeed tend to survive bad librettos, it is when libretto and music have comparable qualities that opera, especially political opera, is at its most successful. Mozart's greatest operas were wholes made up of plots, ideas, words, and his extraordinary music. What words and ideas and dramatic situations suit which music? How do words and music balance off or shape or animate each other in order to fulfill successfully a dramatic purpose? To what extent does one become a function of the other? These questions are especially acute if an opera has a political theme or purpose. After all, what happens if the idea within a well-spiced opera is the political equivalent of a roasted cat? Or what if a real hare is so overseasoned that it turns unsavory?

II.

Here is a sketch of the historical route of my explorations—an anticipatory map of where this book goes.

I looked first to Florence, Mantua, and Venice in the late sixteenth and seventeenth centuries. In Florence, the center of Tuscan life and perhaps the most celebrated city of the Renaissance, I found circles of humanists, mostly aristocrats, discussing relations among words and music. Their exchanges and experiments led to what became early opera. Tuscany was then under the firm rule of Medici dukes, who had imposed relative quiet after a period of political turmoil. Even had they wanted to do so, those aristocratic humanists didn't and couldn't say much aloud about politics. They were, however, concerned with a question that can be taken easily as a substitute: how can or should things be said (or sung) to an audience? The resulting operas by their hands were interesting and (at least partly) attractive although not persistently compelling.

The first great exemplars of opera took form a little later in Mantua and Venice in works by Claudio Monteverdi. This remarkable composer—astonishing in the wide-ranging resourcefulness of his inventive imagination—was a true reformer of his art. He made his musical marks first under one kind of regime (in Mantua where, as in Florence, a Duke's solo voice spoke aloud to politics) but spent his last decades within a very different type of political order. The commercial patricians who ruled the Venetian republic to which he moved were especially proud of their constitutional regime (or what they claimed it to be) as of their musical world. In Monteverdi's day, however, Venetian politics was very troubled. He was a musician and not a political philosopher; his relocation to Venice was for professional reasons. Yet his librettists in the Mantuan duchy as well as in Venice's republic were always shrewd men living in proximity to power. Not only were they well placed to observe its workings, so was he.

I then considered Paris in the second half of the seventeenth century. French opera emerged as an ongoing enterprise, mostly during Louis XIV's famously absolutist reign, thanks in particular to Florence-born Giovanni Battista Lulli, better known as Jean-Baptiste Lully. His works were filled with ingenious engagements of music and the French language, but usually without much political subtlety. The political universe had an obvious center in the Sun King's realm. Yet in the eighteenth century, matters became more complicated. After a period whose spirit seemed to move in a different direction—both power and music needed some softer tones after the fanfares of a *"grand siècle"*—came various transitions, contrasts, and then especially Jean-Philippe Rameau. This composer and theorist of music believed in something stable: the cosmos had a clear arrangement and its rationality could be found in the structure of harmony (Plato, long before him, thought similarly). Yet Rameau's operas also captured expanding horizons and sensibilities of a world in motion—of Europe going out into the world. His French world mixed baroque style, "gallant" elegance, and a growing multifaceted movement known in summary form subsequently as the Enlightenment. All this was within the context of an opulent Old Regime that was sometimes soft and ofttimes brittle. Rameau faced chastisement by implacable champions of Lully; his novelty and originality, for them, threatened their order of things—whatever Rameau's own sense of order. And Rameau also had to contend with a notably complicated and restless man who was his jealous admirer and antagonist and who is most remembered for his political theories.

This was Geneva-born Jean-Jacques Rousseau, eloquent advocate of the radical idea that government was legitimate only if the People, a collectivity, was its sovereign. He was, however, also famous in Rameau's day as a quarrelsome critic of music and as an opera composer. Against Rameau this intellectual harbinger of political change insisted that melody, whose notes cross a musical score horizontally, is prior to harmony, whose vertical structure on paper is translated usually into multiple notes sounded at once. If we allow ourselves to project from a musical argument about melodic expressiveness and acoustical structures to one about the human condition—some musicologists would object to this as an inappropriate leap—it is as if Rousseau were making a claim for the priority of romantic individuality in movement to chords of a rationally and hierarchically regulated cosmos. But while one of Rousseau's operas, *Le Devin du Village* ("The Village Soothsayer"), achieved extraordinary popularity, there are good reasons why it is now mostly an object of curiosity. Rousseau's unexceptional talent as a composer could not compare, whether he imagined harmony or melody, to that of Rameau.

Finally, my journey continued to Vienna, home of the "Imperial Poet" (or "Caesarean Poet") of the Holy Roman Empire. Pietro Metastasio—his last name, an adopted one, means "transformation"—wrote librettos that presented the ways and troubles of rulers. They articulated and extolled a regime's ideology, that of his Habsburg patrons. (Many prominent composers set them.) Metastasio's influence, once great, had already been challenged and was fading when Mozart settled in Vienna in 1781. The following decade was full of political transformations in the imperial capital and there were cataclysms across Europe, the most enormous one in Paris. Nothing suggests that Mozart composed while thinking of the latest news. Yet artists never exist outside human history, as if swimmers in some ethereal, aesthetic inner equivalent of deep space. Even the greatest or singular of them—and few compare to Mozart—are situated in the human world and engage it. Consciously or not, they inhale their times and exhale them creatively. While it would be obviously absurd and incongruous to subsume Mozart's achievements under political categories, an interpretation of his operas must account for the fact that most of them spoke to major issues of his century—not as tracts but as artistic engagements with the world. And Mozart, together with his various librettists, lived in a world thick with political and social drama, at an era's trembling end. The French state cracked.

So I began in an age characterized by political and artistic reconfigurations—those represented by the state's and (a little later) opera's formation. I concluded in an age of political challenges and gigantic commotions that were contemporaries of operas composed with particular genius and versatility. Locks and keys and politics changed in the interim. So too did meanings and doings.

Ovid's *Metamorphoses* was a steady companion throughout my voyage. I had read it many decades earlier and returned to it as the source of so many operas. Going back and forth from it to the operas—an elevating experience—was inevitable to understand better what was on early modern minds. One reason why Ovid's retelling of Greek myths spoke to his own Roman times, to the Renaissance, to early modernity, and speaks to our own era is his presentation of transformations of one reality into another, of one age into another, of one order into another, of one kind of being into another. These are recurrent human and natural realities, although they are never a matter of the same ages, the same orders, or the same human beings, and there is no reason to pretend that they are such. Ovid's tales are immediate and allusive. It is often only after looking back and forth to earlier and later tales that a reader recognizes the distance gone—that he or she has arrived in the midst of something else, with feet on a new path (even as older routes seem to reemerge underfoot too). All this needs to be kept in mind, backstage as it were, when engaging the dialectic of change and constancy of our variegated human condition—and the politics and arts that come of it.

I am not a poet; Ovid was a great one. I have nonetheless allowed myself to be inspired by his need to tell stories. They, like those marking out the history of political opera, are elucidating and puzzling, obvious and ambiguous, often seeming to slip slyly one into another. They are also filled with juxtapositions that push you to look backward and forward when engaging what is in front of you. Political ideas in opera cannot be divorced from the stories in which they are embedded and those stories, even when they return from another time and seem to transcend a particular moment, are no less embedded in historical contexts. The stories need retelling and the history needs recognizing as we engage political operas; change is a constant.

III.

Opera's birth is usually dated to Carnival time in 1597–98, when an experimental drama by Florentine humanists was presented to a small audience in a count's palazzo. *Dafne* recounted a well-known myth about the failed pursuit by Apollo, a god associated with the sun and the arts, of a Nymph. Love and laws, especially laws of nature, were among the obvious themes as it showed that there are impassable frontiers, even for a deity. Greek and Roman antiquity provided the myth's sources, but its music was called "new" because of how it came together with words; the drama was sung through in its entirety by a kind of musicalized declamation. *Dafne's* music is lost but we do have both music and the libretto for *Euridice*, which was staged two years later. The same humanists collaborated on it, retelling how Greek mythology's most famous musician descended to hell in the hope of retrieving Eurydice, his love. *Euridice's* music aimed to bring out sentiments and notions in the librettist's poetry. Rhetoric, especially ancient writings about rhetoric—the invention of the printing press in the fifteenth century made them more widely accessible than ever before—was one of the great preoccupations of Renaissance humanists, and a musical rhetoric was at work in these innovative efforts. The "new music" drew on what those Florentines believed to be characteristic of ancient music in fabled Athens. In other words, antiquity inspired what they called "new"— which they also contrasted to what they called "modern." One of them, Vincenzo Galilei, father of Galileo, wrote a *Dialogue on Ancient and Modern Music.*[6]

That word "modern" is, of course, a notorious source of contention. Its use is almost always in some way arbitrary. While some twentieth-century philosophers identified "modern" with their own times (or with the nineteenth century), it was musically speaking especially identified by the Florentine humanists with polyphonic madrigals. Multiple vocal lines overlay and underlay each other in this popular form of secular musical entertainment. Multiplicity created beauty and charm in sound, though at the expense of the comprehensibility of the words. Those humanists were perturbed about this incomprehensibility. The alternative was at first deemed by them to be monody, that is, a single vocal line with accompaniment. Music could by this means help to bring out what was being said; it was thus amenable to stage drama as well as song. The turn toward monody was not motivated politically but it had an interesting, if unavoidably inexact, political counterpart in latter sixteenth-century Florence: one voice commanded there, that of the duke. Most everyone else was an adjutant or simply impotent. (The role of the clergy did, however, add significant wrinkles of power in the social hierarchy.)

In broader context, the Florentine experiments took place as European borders and authorities were being shuffled and reshuffled. Often a result of bloody combat, the changes almost always came with weighty implications for the continent's populations (most of which also had no voice at all in what was happening). Political power expanded all while it concentrated and as the many-layered and diffuse feudal world began to fade. (It never did fully.) Politics, one could say, increasingly channeled and became more focused, anticipated in a way by painters who had earlier, in the fifteenth century, used "single-point perspective" to organize what viewers saw on canvas. Later, in seventeenth-century France, Descartes sought a single, irrefutable standpoint from which to deduce truth. Oneness rang loudly amidst multiple clangs in these centuries and in different domains. Political order—"the state"—was perceived increasingly to be a centralizing organization over territory with its own distinct dynamics. An attentive ruler could ill afford to ignore them if he wanted to sustain his dominion.

Europe's larger picture was complicated further because the Reformation had shattered Christianity's unity in the sixteenth century. Religious wars ensued between Catholics and Protestants (and among them) all while Christian conflicts with "the Turk" continued (Ottoman troops stood at the gates of Vienna in 1529 and, after a century and a half of wars, again in 1683). So too did perennial jurisdictional disputes persist among anxious ecclesiastical and assertive lay authorities. In the meantime, the "Age of Exploration," also known as one of imperialism, opened vistas and led to conquests and competition across the globe. And European political domains—empires, realms, fiefdoms—vied with one another. In the seventeenth century, more war came and then found a resolution (only temporarily) by the 1648 Peace of Westphalia, which outlined, more or less, the future system of states. It was a critical moment. Nonetheless, modern politics in Europe can hardly be assigned a precise birth date and is best seen as a series of configurations that materialized over two to three centuries.

The configuring was perhaps best captured in writings by a multitalented Florentine—a diplomat, theorist, historian, and playwright. He died decades before opera was born but his ideas and the issues they raised lurked on and resonated powerfully (indeed, they still do). This was Niccolò Machiavelli, a humanist who looked backward and forward as he scrutinized the present. He idealized the virtues of the ancient Roman republic, served as an official in a Florentine one, and after it fell had to face renewed Medici rule. Some think his most famous work, *The Prince* of 1513, was written in self-interest by a man who understood that reality (the Medici) precluded, at least then, any return to a republic, which was the regime he favored. Whatever his personal motivations—*The Prince* was not published during his lifetime—Machiavelli had an uncanny ability to evaluate how politics worked. He had unsettling suggestions—especially for Christians of his day—about how rulers or leaders, if they want to be successful politically, ought to play different roles and take on different appearances at different times. Perhaps because he was also a playwright, he thought perspicaciously about simulation and dissimulation on the political stage. And while proffering advice about how a prince could best sustain "his" own realm, Machiavelli spoke simultaneously of the "state" as if it had its own self-constituting rubric—a "majesty" apart from whoever happened to be the ruler and apart from heaven's designs (the preoccupation of another power, the church). So he posed distinctive questions about what strengthens or weakens states. The needs of "*patria*," to which he was devoted before anything else, served to focus his perspective in a singular way.

By the last decades of the century and then well into the next one, men who wrote about politics pressed on with or challenged these lines of thought. "What gave legitimacy to a state's demand for obedience?" they asked. What was the role of law in "the state"? In the bloody sixteenth century few lions and lambs lay down with each other. Might political logic, which seemed so often brutal, contradict religious precepts? Might Christian compassion be morally laudatory but politically foolhardy? Theologians were disturbed greatly by the notion that politics had its own brutal logic, "reason of state," and pondered how—or if—it suited a Christian cosmos. This was also a matter of considerable weight for dukes or princes or emperors (but also popes), who justified and presented themselves as, or at least feigned being, men of faith while they had sometimes, often more than sometimes, to break moral codes to this or that "realistic" political purpose. Florentine midwives of opera bent knees to dukes and were not political philosophers. Yet controversies about "reasons of state" were mightily present in the discursive universe around them, often taking form as reconsiderations of Tacitus, the ancient Roman historian. We will find him looming in the backdrop to opera's early development, but not for musical reasons. His works and their style had come into vogue and he was, like Machiavelli, plainspoken and hardheaded. Wrote Machiavelli himself: "There is in fact a golden saying voiced by Cornelius Tacitus who says that men have to respect the past but to submit to the present, and while they should be desirous of having good princes, should put up with them of whatever sort they may turn out to be." He went further: "those who act otherwise usually bring disaster both upon themselves and upon their country."[7] Ironically, this Florentine political theorist wrote these words to summarize the greatest lesson he took from Tacitus in a book (his *Discourses on Livy*) that laid out for posterity why Machiavelli preferred republican government to monarchies or princedoms. Later in the sixteenth century, aristocrats in Medici Florence might have observed that Tacitus matured at a time when one political voice, that of Rome's emperor, counted, while society's elite sported titles but little power. Talking about rhetoric or being a poet or writing history can substitute for politics, and can be much safer.

Central issues of politics are heard in early opera, sometimes sotto voce, sometimes expressed robustly. Sometimes ideas are intimated with canniness, and sometimes politics are woven into stage events without apparent self-consciousness. For one instance, to which I will return, take how early operas recounted the myth of Orpheus. This young musician-prince (Apollo's son) crosses boundaries of two worlds, from sunlight into darkness, from the land of the living to that of the dead. His purpose is to convince Pluto, monarch of the Underworld, to bend his domain's basic law. Orpheus asks him to allow a recent immigrant (Eurydice), who arrived in Pluto's realm unwillingly, to emigrate for compassion's sake. Pluto contemplates aloud: if this law—one that I willed—is not maintained firmly, won't the entire foundation of the kingdom crumble? After all, if we expand Pluto's reasoning we arrive at one of the most important of political issues: determining a state's jurisdictions, deciding who can be inside or outside of it and who (or what) stands as the final authority within it. Pluto's dilemma, which Machiavelli would have appreciated, captures the difficulties of the transition to modern politics. (Machiavelli, like mythology's Pluto, would not have spoken of immigration and emigration policies, although he knew a good deal about their contemporary equivalents since political émigrés and exiles have populated all recorded history, much including his own.)

"The surest sign that a group or a society has entered into a self-conscious possession of a new concept is that a corresponding vocabulary will be developed . . . which can then be used to pick out and discuss the concept in question with consistency." So writes Quentin Skinner, whose influential scholarship has focused especially on how "the state" and similar political terms (such as "sovereignty") were reimagined in the Renaissance and after. Machiavelli, for instance, spoke of the state "not simply as a concept but as an actually existing entity."[8] The sure sign is also a notice that things are being done in novel ways. A similar claim may be made of "opera," a word that simply means a "work" in Italian. But this can be said with reasonable surety about what we now recognize as "opera": in its beginning there was not this word as we use it, only the priority among opera's inventors of words to music. The word "opera" came into its more common usage mostly in the seventeenth and early in the eighteenth centuries. It might be said that this word—like "the state" in its own domain, somewhat earlier—caught up with what was already being done. What began under assorted names or descriptive terms took on an identity, although this identity would, in turn, take on many shapes, much as "the state" did. Earlier, in Italy, there had been "dramas in music" or "fables in music." In France there would be "lyric tragedies." The generic designation of "opera" took hold first in England, France, and then German-speaking lands for Italian works presented in them. A late seventeenth-century German critic spoke of a new art form called "opera," which he turned into "*Werck*" in German. "Opera," wrote another of its proponents, came from Latin for "work" and ought to be used for a theatrical mix of words and music that Italians characterized as "*dramma per musica*" or "*melodramma*." It was also often called "*Singspiel*," or song-play, in German (this name would take on an additional more specific connotation of stage works with alternating songs and spoken dialogue). "Operetta" was also used by the turn of the century.[9] By the mid-eighteenth century someone who went to an "opera" in Italy or other countries knew, more or less, to expect on stage a combination of words and music telling some kind of story, accompanied often by engaging, perhaps quite extravagant staging and sometimes by dance.* Still, the words "more or less" are important. There is much (although hardly the whole) truth in philosopher R.W. Collingwood's assertion that "no 'work of art' is ever finished." He elaborated: "Work ceases upon the picture or manuscript not because it is finished, but because sending-in day is at hand, or because the printer is clamorous for copy, or because 'I am sick of working at this thing' or 'I can't see what more I can do to it.'" Some artists would, undoubtedly, dispute this—"I won't hand it in (or display it) until I know it is just right"—but if we extend Collingwood's claim to stage works, which obviously include operas, we are reminded that every production brings inevitable change, however "faithful" a director or conductor or performers try to be to a composer or librettist's initial concept (or to an understanding of that concept).[10]

The flux of time and place that we have described concerning "the state" and "opera" can be compared, albeit with a certain prudence, to a technical aspect of music. (Comparing flux requires as much caution as comparing imagined absolutes.) Although a tuning fork was invented in the early eighteenth century, there was no standard for musical pitch throughout

---

*For simplicity's sake, I will, most of the time, use "opera" in a generic sense throughout this book, while recognizing that it is anachronistic in some cases and at times blurs different genres of opera. For the same reason, I use "Italy" and "Italian" generically. Italy was not a unified country until the nineteenth century and local dialects predominated in different regions of the peninsula, all while Tuscan developed eventually as its literary (then national) language.

Europe until the nineteenth century. The pitch of a note depends on the speed of sound waves, that is, the frequency of cycles of their vibrations produced, say, on a string of a violin or within a column of air in, say, an oboe or a flute. Faster vibrations create higher pitches; slower, lower. A common pitch must be established for instruments for an ensemble to play together "in tune." Historically speaking, an absence of standardization was of modest consequence when performances did not go beyond localities. However, when they did go to other places and times, or when musicians or singers from different places played or sang together, an anchor or reference for musical notes became increasingly desirable—indeed, necessary. The state, opera, and pitch were not terms of absolutism. Designations needed to catch up with what was being done.

In fact, as instrumental music became increasingly significant in European art music there was "pitch inflation" (pitch levels rose), to the chagrin of vocalists, who were compelled to adjust to what was in effect a change in aesthetic hierarchy. The issue drifted into politics. A French government charged a commission with responsibility to formulate a law standardizing pitch in 1859. In technical terms, it was set at 435 Hz (Hz being a unit of cyclical frequency) for an A note above middle C. An international conference in 1939 set the standard at 440 Hz and this became "concert pitch" for musical ensembles (although not all of them). Musical pitch identifies the place of a tone within a scale and, consequently, it is essential for harmonizing different notes. An analogy can be made to justice. Political philosophers have compared it since antiquity to "harmony." Plato characterized a just state as one in which three classes of people played roles appropriate to their distinct aptitudes. Yet the meaning of social or political harmony varies significantly according to time and place, especially given diversity of mores and religions throughout history. So one might go so far as to say that political and social harmony, representing a kind of order, resonated differently in various times and places as, for example, A-major chords might sound differently—while still having the same internal relations among tones—according to locale due to distinctions in the pitch of A—the latter being a means to musical order.

IV.

Historical birth dates never indicate this or that instant, but are markers of developments, convergence, and confluences. Longer, multiple processes are always complicated by, indeed dependent on, contingencies that come together in some way. This is so whether the newborn is an art form, a political formation, an economic system, or something else. And after a life enters the world, it moves in diverse ways. While we now know of DNA's imprint, a life still changes as it takes in different aspects of the surrounding world all while it acts on it. Lives interact with environments through the mental, emotional, and physical tools individuals develop. By using the word "tool" here I do not intend a hard and fixed utensil but something at once supple and simple. I mean by it various means and resources—those available within individuals, those that are better construed, to use Lucien Goldmann's term, as transindividual (that is, shared by and within people) and those that are accessible, but sometimes imposed—from outside them. Individual, transindividual, outside—none of these is entirely separate from the others. And they inevitably alter. Much as you might know the physical principles of swimming, Hegel once observed, you only learn to swim by actually jumping into the water. Having done so, however, you apprehend many things anew, not least about your body and its movements but also about what surrounds it. You learn what of the outside world is within you and what you have internalized of it.

As opera changed and grew in many ways so too did its audiences. At first, they were viewers of private, aristocratic, or court entertainments; they became broader publics attending displays that were parts of this or that ducal celebration (usually a wedding); and finally they were ticket buyers at a commercial enterprise. Opera's bearings on the surrounding world have been both variable and real. Still, comparisons of its impact with the stage in Athenian antiquity lend themselves easily to exaggeration, implying that all the arts have decisive, direct, and huge public functions. This is sometimes so as part of the more general leavening effect of culture but the arts, and certainly opera, always have had limits (although film and new technologies create larger prospects). We have no record telling us that the man who sang sad Apollo left the palazzo after *Dafne*'s performance to lead a campaign, accompanied by irate members of the audience and cast, to demand in Florence's streets that borders between gods and nymphs, princes and subjects, or aristocrats and commoners be effaced, lest life be tragic. (Social distinctions would have been the norm in his world anyway.)

However great the values of art, and while political actions—ranging from demonstrations to assassinations—at opera houses did become periodic staples of opera history, it is evident that many more lives are encompassed by political, economic, and social transformations than by operas. Some circumspection is needed nowadays when lazy attempts at "cultural criticism," a much-abused phrase, substitute for political, economic, or social thinking. Culture and criticism need to be saved from these; art and metamorphoses in culture tell us a great deal and signify too many important things about lives and events, actions and their meanings. It is an old notion: political perceptions, ideas, moods, and reflexes are—or can be—embedded within or suggested by imaginative works. If, sometimes, staged works can be propagandistic, at other times they may—and often do —allow for or provoke better understandings of portentous developments than those proffered by participants in them. Opera's means are musicalized fictions or musicalized myths or musicalized reinventions of history (these can be close to the same thing). When operas have historical settings, they are never literal; they comprise illusory historical mimesis in which events as they "actually happened" are usually of token importance at best. It has long been pointed out that affairs of state don't normally take place by means of arias with an orchestra. Should political demonstrators sing in the streets and create a spectacle, perhaps accompanied by a guitar or drum, they do not usually do so following a scenario mapped out in advance by a librettist and composer (although some political events are in their own ways choreographed). Politics in opera, as in other arts, must work through illusions and allusion, no matter how much an aria, for one example, aims to imitate emotions or suggest ideas through movements of a human voice.

Yet a familiar danger always lurks when opera and politics are explored together. Call it an interpretative conceit: the imposition without a second (or third) thought of our own concerns on those expressed initially in another time and place. My point is not to protest the interpretation of a seventeenth-century work, whether a political essay or an artwork, by our own lights. It is to insist that when we do so we recall (and never forget) that electric bulbs are more recent inventions. Even a luminous interpretation of an illusion—and even the most realistic art is illusion or it would not be art—requires intellectual self-regulation. A crucial means for that, I think, is considered knowledge of or an expansive familiarity with the world in which the opera (or a poem or painting or novel or essay) came into being. Otherwise an interpreter may be talking principally of him- or herself, which may or may not be interesting. The point is not to reduce all meanings to their origins. It is to recognize that without adequate knowledge of a work's genesis, as well as its structures, an interpreter may have no grasp of its meanings except what his or her own head imputes to them. A twenty-first-century interpreter's concerns may be, or may partly be, or may not at all be immanent in an opera (or a poem or a painting or a novel). "Consider the following questions again and again," urged Beatus Rhenanus (a scholarly friend of Erasmus and a student of Tacitus's works), "When was the text you are reading written, by whom and on what; then [only] compare recent times with old ones."[11] And then, I would add, ambiguity and knowledge can engage each other.

In short, interpretations of illusions can be elucidating or illusory. It is better, I think, to go to and fro between then and now as best we can, always cognizant that we are doing so—rather than to impress unawares our now on the then. This is one reason why grasping political ideas in operas needs external references of time and of place. Immanuel Kant once distinguished between judgments of beauty that are "free"—by which he meant governed solely by formal aesthetic criteria—and those that are "dependent" on something outside art, say, ethics or politics. My concerns in this book are heavily "dependent." It is self-evident that it is the music that makes an opera an opera rather than a play; it is obvious that music's roles in an opera are multiple. Music can drive the work and give life to it; it can, if it is mediocre music, turn a compelling libretto into a roaring bore. Music can draw out emotions and convictions and point to ideas and meanings; it can disguise or complicate all these by misleading us intentionally in its interactions with words and plots; and politics, some would argue, can be embedded in the material of music itself (the extent to which this is so and how—and its significance—is the source of considerable disagreement).

Here is an example (to which we will return). When Monteverdi gives Seneca, a philosopher and advisor to a crazed Roman emperor, bass tones in *The Coronation of Poppea*, they suggest his wisdom and those of the words he sings. Those words speak directly to the importance of rationality in political decision-making. Yet bass tones with very different words might convey that a philosopher or ruler should have deep patriotic feelings—which are not always so reasonable. Or, to change registers: when the voice of the Queen of the Night in Mozart's *The Magic Flute* bounds up and down, it suggests that she lacks self-mastery. The more her furies, the greater the leaps. Yet these might mean little beyond beautifully constructed acrobatics in sound if we don't know why she is infuriated. Or they could signify simply that the composer imagined that the person singing would have unusual, powerful reach, never to be stymied. But that is obviously not the case in the context of the story told in *The Magic Flute*. And—for a contrary possibility—consider that words can take to one course (saying something directly) while music moves in a contradictory way. A composer may be hinting deliberately that something happening on stage is not quite right or simply wrong or that a character is not as he or she appears to be.

By contrast, powerfully imagined music can also obscure odious political ideas or even make them deceptively enthralling. Recall Hegel's roasted cat. If the importance of political meanings in words is bracketed, if the words are considered not truly relevant because the music alone matters, particularly as means to a drama, then it is hard to see why a libretto is needed in the first place. It is also difficult to imagine why there should be an opera rather than a tone poem or, alternatively, a play (with, perhaps, some background music). And it is certainly hard to see why there should be a political opera if inspired music doesn't need the politics. It wouldn't matter then if a libretto and the ideas in it are good or bad or revealing or obtuse. A musical motif may animate political words, but without a sufficient grasp of what those words implied in a given time and place—and in that context as part of a story with interacting characters—it is virtually impossible to discern what meanings music may have brought out in or to them (except, perhaps, by the interpreter's conceit). "Justice" or "politics" as well as all sorts of mores don't always imply the same things or resonate in the same ways in different eras. The words or keys may be the same, while the pitch is not. This is one reason why lesser operas, those that are not outstanding or not so attractive—perhaps by long-forgotten figures, perhaps by a Rousseau who is remembered mostly for nonmusical reasons—can nonetheless convey a great deal about politics, the world, and art. They also help us understand what was important at the time in which they appeared (even if we might not want to see them too often). When it comes to political matters, it is possible for them to tell us important things about key questions and terms of debate—together with but not in place of master works.

Drama, wrote Joseph Kerman in one of the twentieth century's most influential essays on opera, "is not, exclusively, a matter of the effective deployment of plot. Skillfully contrived situations, clever exits and entrances, and violent *coups de théâtre* do not compose the soul of a drama. Neither does strict naturalism in character, locale, or detail . . ." Instead, he argued, drama receives its most "serious" creative articulation through a medium—poetry, or in the case of opera, music. "Each art," he elaborates, "has the final responsibility for the success of the drama, for it is within their capacity to define the response of characters to deeds and situations. Like poetry, music can reveal the quality of action, and thus determine dramatic form in the most serious sense."[12] "Form" is the key word in this passage and within limits Kerman made a commanding formulation. Yet if the quality of action has anything to do with what unfolds on stage, then content must intrude—rudely, perhaps, if one prefers only aesthetic considerations narrowly conceived, but necessarily *if the concern is political*. For then it is necessary to understand the political whys and wherefores as much as how the shape of words or music makes them compelling. We have to know—or try to know—what words and music (and plot, actions, and political setting) are doing to understand and explain them.

Samuel Johnson wrote famously that Shakespeare addressed his own era and its tastes along with "the common reader of all time."[13] The politics of political opera is best engaged by first questioning this claim for opera but then by going constantly to and fro between the two apparent alternatives. Each—one time-bound (Shakespeare's era), the other transcending temporal restriction (the common reader of all time)—ought to be used to correct or to challenge our appreciation, aesthetically and intellectually, along with our political grasp of the other. But such corrections can never reach a sole or definitive interpretation. Indeed, that imaginary reader of all time does not really exist except ambiguously or heuristically. When it comes to understanding politics you have to know something about temporal questions and the language of an era. The same is so if you want to grasp politics within an artwork. Otherwise, you may just imagine that you know what you are talking about or interpreting. In writing this book I sometimes tried to imagine what Hegel called "the Whole"—including both the "then" and the "now" in the back of my mind. I tried to do this heuristically to grasp particulars in history. I make no claim to having actually captured it. This is not only because I am a student of political thought and not a musicologist. For the sake of manageability, I limited the geography of this book to Italy, France, and the Habsburg Empire. This regionalization allows for focus in the transmission of various ideas and is not intended as devaluation of a plethora of engaging questions about politics and opera in, say, Britain, Prussia, or Russia.

But even were a quest for "the Whole" plausible, I fear I lack the requisite reach. I have never met anyone who has it. This is to say, to insist, that something vital is missing in attempts to explain politics within operas absent adequate historical prisms that help us to facilitate perceptions of and distinctions between hare-pies and roasted cats—whether they come of our own times or of others.

ACKNOWLEDGMENTS

Authors who have spent a long time writing a book accrue many debts and fear that memory has unduly left someone out of expressions of thanks. I hope my memory serves me well. Friends, writers, and scholars have been munificent whether by providing thoughtful and invaluable criticisms of my work and ideas (without necessarily being in agreement) or simply lending moral support (and even some dinners). Some, thankfully, simply put up with my obsessions. I am particularly grateful to friends and acquaintances in Paris, where much of this book was written, and to specialized scholars, especially musicologists, who read and criticized my work. Some of them, people I did not know and who I feared might think me a trespasser on their scholarly domains, received pleas from me to read parts of my manuscript that must have truly seemed to come out of the blue. Yet they responded with generosity and thoughtfulness.

I have dedicated this book to the memory of Irving Howe. I had the privilege of working and engaging with this exemplary intellectual for a decade, especially on *Dissent Magazine.* He wrote an invaluable book, *Politics and the Novel,* and while he would have approached my concerns in this book differently, I learned a great deal about smart writing and thinking well from him.

This book mixes primary and secondary works. With occasional exceptions, I refrain from inserting in the text itself the name of every scholar or author whose work informs my own, preferring to indicate my copious debts in endnotes. If I refer to a point made by this or that "scholar" or "historian" or "musicologist" rather than naming each, it is not to minimize my appreciation for any of them but to make these pages more accessible to nonspecialized readers crossing broad geographic and temporal grounds that are speckled by an abundance of names of composers, librettists, philosophers, political actors, thinkers, and events.

I am appreciative of many institutions that have helped me directly or indirectly: the Bibliothèque Nationale de France and especially its music division and the Bibliothèque de l'Opéra; Columbia University's Wiener Music and Arts Library and Butler Library; the New York Public Library for the Performing Arts; Stanford University's Music Library at the Braun Center and the Green Library. Special thanks to the Inter-Library loan division at Bernard Baruch College of the City University of New York.

For research funds or for invitations to present my ideas or host me, my gratitude to the PSC-CUNY Research Foundation, Stanford University and, in Paris: the École des hautes études en sciences sociales, the Institut d'études politiques (Sciences-po) and the Institut des Amériques. Special thanks to: Françoise Bagot, Steven Beller, Aviv Bergman, Michelle-Irène Brudny, Esteban Buch, Sylvie and Gil Delannoi, Donna Doyle, Benedetto Fontana, Nancy Green, Barbara Russano Hanning, Youssef Ishaghpour, Michel Kail, Richard Kramer, Mark Lilla, Corinne Mairovitz, Dominique Pignon, Benjamin Pintaux, Pierpaolo Polzonetti, Nicole Reinhardt, Setti Rezavi, Rob Riemen, Ellen Rosand, Lois Rosow, Jerrold Seigel, Charlotte Sheedy, Ellen Handler Spitz, Marcel Staroswiecki, Blake Stephens, U.D. Sunnyvale, Nadia Urbinati, Kirsten Walgren, and Steve Zipperstein. The late Renate Herpich would have been overjoyed by this book's publication. I can only hope that she knew how much she contributed to it.

At a time when books seem jeopardized, it has been a great pleasure to work with and have the support of people for whom their value is not just evident but a passion. My special gratitude to Peter Dougherty, director of Princeton University Press, to Rob Tempio, my excellent and generous editor there, as well as to Leslie Grundfest, Matt Rohal, and Ryan Mulligan for their steady help. Any flaws in this book are my own.

—MITCHELL COHEN, Paris, June 2016

PART 1: METAMORPHOSES, ANCIENT TO MODERN

Citizens . . . ! The man who holds the helm
Of State, and from the bridge pilots with sleepless eyes
His country's fortunes, must speak when the hour demands.
. . . But you too must play your part.

—ETEOCLES, in Aeschylus's *Seven Against Thebes*

Chapter 1
WHO RULES?

Were political ideas embedded in the first operas? If so, what were they and what did they imply? What does the political world in which opera was born tell us about this art form? What do operas tell us about politics? To approach these questions, we turn first not to words and music bound together for the stage, but to a wedding celebration.

The couple didn't marry for love. They wed out of political duty. It was in Florence in the autumn of 1600 that Maria de' Medici, niece of Tuscany's Grand Duke Ferdinando I, became the queen of France's King Henri IV. Their union fortified a partnership between Florence and Paris against Savoy and, in the larger picture of European politics, it strengthened them both against the Habsburg rulers of Spain (with whom Henri had recently been at war) and the Holy Roman Empire.

Spanish imperial power had grown throughout the fragmented political world of the Italian peninsula in the mid-sixteenth century. Ferdinando I had altered past Tuscan policies aiming to balance Spanish power with increased French power. In this context, he had recognized the value to Tuscany of Henri of Navarre's struggle to attain the French throne. By the time Henri, the Huguenot-turned-Catholic, married Maria, he was both King Henri IV and indebted financially and politically to her relatives. Florence's ruling clan and premier banking family supported him in French power struggles. Negotiations for a connubial alliance, with a suitably large dowry, had gone on for some eight years.

The groom didn't come to the ceremony. He was engaged elsewhere—against the troops of Savoy's Duke Carlo Emanuele I. Henri IV's love interests were elsewhere as well, with his mistress, and not with reputedly tempestuous Maria. He sent a surrogate for the nuptials in Florence's cathedral on October 5. The king missed a lavish occasion, the sort of display that princely families gave to promote their prestige at home and abroad. The banquet at Palazzo Vecchio (the old municipal citadel that had once been the seat of Florence's republic) was opulent. Each dish comprised part of an allegory extolling the illustrious couple and their kin. Icing on the cake was molded as a wintry landscape. Sugar-animals moved about on it, and changed shape.[1] Two hundred and thirty-three years later this "vast magnificence" on which "no expenses were spared" was presented as the "most distinguished occurrence" in the reign of Ferdinando I in a history written by Lorenzo L. Da Ponte, the son of Mozart's librettist, then a professor of Italian literature at a college in New York.[2]

Henri IV also missed a milestone in Western culture. A variety of public and private events celebrated the new union. The principal theme was universal peace. *The Abduction of Cephalus* by Gabriello Chiabrera with accompanying music by Giulio Caccini—most of it is lost—played at the Uffizi Theater. More important historically was *Eurydice*—*Euridice* in the original—which is often called the second opera. These works originated in efforts within Florentine circles to marry words, music, and tale in a new way. *Euridice* was performed on Friday, October 6, on the second floor of the Pitti Palace, the duke's official residence, in the rooms of a Medici family member. It recounted how mythic Orpheus, armed only with his famous voice and his lyre, braved the Underworld to retrieve his love. Poor Eurydice, the tree-nymph, had died of snakebite on their wedding day. The performance, the first that could be called public, was a present to the new queen from Jacopo Corsi, a nobleman, patron of the arts, and longtime champion of marriage between Henri and Maria. (It had probably been completed by the previous spring because there had been a performance of it in May, also in a salon at the Pitti Palace, at the request of the archduchess.)[3] The librettist, Ottavio Rinuccini, was a Florentine court poet. Jacopo Peri, a musician and singer who played a vibrant role in Florentine commercial life and served in a wide variety of Florentine governmental and legal offices, composed most of the music, although segments were by Caccini.[4] The latter, Peri's arch-competitor, was also known as "Giulio Romano" because he was born and had studied in Rome (Caccini rushed to put into print his own musical setting of the libretto within two months of the performance.)

Dafne, usually credited as the first opera, was an earlier Corsi-Rinuccini-Peri effort based on another myth. A small audience saw it in Corsi's palazzo during Carnival 1597–98. Corsi and his collaborators were men of the late Renaissance, and they aimed to create a contemporary counterpart to ancient Greek tragedy. Their experiment was also one result of several decades of discussion of music within the Florentine artistic and intellectual worlds; these, in turn, corresponded to historical and political transformations in Florence and, more broadly, Europe. While *Euridice* was published,

Figure 1.1. Jacopo Peri (1561–1633), composer of the early operas *Dafne* and *Euridice* performing in an *intermedio* at the Medici wedding celebrations in Florence in 1589. Biblioteca Nazionale, Florence. Photo: Foto Marburg/Art Resource, NY.

most of *Dafne's* music is lost. We do have descriptions of *Dafne's* first presentation. "It was performed in a small room and sung privately" with "a consort of instruments" playing, one observer recalled years later. "I was stunned at this marvel."[5] The entire work was sung through with musical accompaniment. Its novelty was a kind of musical declamation or declamatory song that later evolved into the conventions of recitative. Another witness, the composer Marco da Gagliano (he reset the libretto to his own music in 1608), commented that the experiment showed to Rinuccini "how apt song was to express all kinds of emotions," and that it could lead "to incredible delight."[6]

But it was *Euridice*, some two years later, that effectively launched the new art form.

It is improbable that *Euridice's* audience, estimated at two hundred people, mostly noble, recognized the evening's significance. Responses were mixed, and the failure of the production team to prepare the scenery fully did not help. Some in the audience found its new musical style far from pleasing. Its declamatory singing was compared to "the chanting of the

Figure 1.2. Maria de' Medici, later Marie de Médicis (1575–1642) in a seventeenth century lithograph. What is usually called the second opera, *Euridice*, was performed at the Pitti Palace in Florence as part of the festivities in 1600 for her political marriage to King Henri IV of France.

Passion."[7] Centuries later, an audience is also likely to find tedium in *Euridice*, but historical charm too. An audience won't find in it the vibrant splendor of *Orfeo*, the "myth" or "fable (*favola*) in music" written about the same mythic couple seven years later in Mantua. This collaboration by Claudio Monteverdi and Alessandro Striggio the Younger is usually considered the first "great" opera. Evidently, Monteverdi examined Peri's score in preparing his own, and scholars speculate that he may have been at the Florentine wedding. Then thirty-three years old, Monteverdi was a Mantuan court composer in his liege's entourage there. It included a young painter named Peter Paul Rubens, who may also have attended *Euridice*.[8]

II.

The story of Orpheus and Eurydice made a lasting impression on the Renaissance. Although its origins were Greek, the early makers of opera were inspired by Roman renderings of it by authors such as Virgil and Ovid. The myth tells of art, love, and the defiance of death. Orpheus had many historical trappings and a varied presence in the fifteenth and sixteenth centuries. Cultured Italians recalled how ancient Greeks such as Pythagoras and Plato had been taken by his tale. Or they may have thought of Horace's praise of the mythic singer as an "interpreter of divine will" and founder of civilized life ("While men still roamed the forests, they were restrained from bloodshed and a bestial way of life" by his song).[9]

In some ancient tellings, Orpheus is just an extraordinary vocalist and musician; in others he founds cities or a religious cult. Music could prepare your soul for contemplation and philosophy, thought Marsilio Ficino, the fifteenth-century philosopher and translator of Plato into Latin, the principal language of Renaissance learning. He founded the Platonic Academy of Florence under Medici patronage, and his intellectual sway in his native city would be lasting. Like Plato, he believed that something supernatural possessed poets. Ficino liked to sing hymns with a lyre, as Orpheus, supposedly, had done. And Ficino followed Plato's philosophical idealism, but gave it a Christian guise. Contemplation, he thought, detaches you from the material world. Your inner self is ushered into a purely spiritual and rational realm, which is also that of the cosmos. Like the ancient Pythagoreans and Plato, Ficino compared the structures of the universe to those of music. An imitation of God's mind could be heard in human music. This Neoplatonist also compared medicine and music: the former rids us of physical illnesses while the latter, both vocal and instrumental, rids us of infirmities of spirit and body.[10]

Orpheus was an obvious protagonist for a new dramatic deployment of music a century after Ficino. Orpheus demonstrated music's powers by facing the sovereign of Hades and pleading, melodiously: return my love to me. His song shook "hard hearts no human prayer can hope to soften . . .," reports Virgil, "The very halls of Death . . . were awestruck." As Orpheus sang "accompanied by plucked strings," Ovid tells us, "bloodless spirits . . . wept."[11] In the best-known versions of the myth, he persuades the Infernal Ruler, but Pluto lays down a condition if he is to permit what has been previously unthinkable. Orpheus may retrieve Eurydice, but he must not look back at her as they ascend. Alas, he does look back and she is lost.

This tale lends itself naturally to sighs, to music—and to politics in more than one way, although this may not be obvious at first. Since the Florentine *Euridice* was invented for a political-matrimonial event, the familiar end would have hardly been appropriate. How could a love story celebrate a royal wedding and end with the bride in the Underworld because the groom flouted the stipulation of a king? Spectators at the Pitti Palace learned at the beginning of the performance that the account of the myth they were to behold would not have its best-known dark climax. A figure called Tragedy first addressed them in a prologue. Usually, I make "the faces of the crowd" brim with pity. This evening, however, she sang, I "temper my song with happier notes."[12] In this version, Orpheus and Eurydice ascend safely into a happy future. French guests surely found this appealing. Their realm had been rent by bloodshed among Catholics and Protestants. Henri IV's kingship had offered deliverance. Not only had he abjured his Calvinism for the Church of Rome to secure the French throne, he then, by the Edict of Nantes of 1598, conferred various rights to his former coreligionists to attain civic peace. His marriage to Marguerite de Valois was annulled in 1599 to allow him his marriage to Maria the next year. Tragedy's prologue must have suggested to the French suite at the Pitti Palace that their land's afflictions were to be superseded by sweeter times—thanks, in part, to Florentine support for their king.

This was suggested too by Arcadian scenes that followed. Pastorals had long comprised a popular Renaissance stage genre, and they included tales of Orpheus. As early as the late fifteenth century, a *Fabula d'Orfeo* by the Tuscan humanist Angelo Poliziano was performed with music in Mantua. Often, pastorals presented a "Golden Age" which, depending on when they were written, might suggest a contrast between a happy past world and an unhappy present. Or they may have meant to hint at the good accomplished by an incumbent ruler. Ovid, who lived in the era of Pax Romana, when Rome's first emperor, Augustus, imposed peace on tumult following the collapse of the Roman republic, wrote of an early golden age when men, "though ignorant of laws" and with "no fear of any punishment" were responsible and virtuous. All peoples lived in peace and the earth itself, "untaxed" by hoes or ploughs, provided "freely" all "essentials . . . Spring was the only season . . ."[13] In *Euridice*, the set "showed the most enchanting woods, both in relief and painted," wrote Michelangelo's nephew, who was in the audience at the "premiere." The scenery was "placed in a well-composed arrangement and lit as if by daylight by means of aptly placed lights within."[14] A shepherd cheered the union of "adventurous Orpheus" and "fortunate Eurydice"; a nymph called on Phoebus ("Bright One," another name for Apollo) to double the rays shining down on them. Orpheus sang of how "courtly love" had changed his own celebrated song. No longer would it move people to sorrow. Instead, he told listeners, his voice would now praise love, "whose sweetest roses" hide among "the sharpest thorns."[15]

And then: thorns. A nymph arrives from the woods with bad news for Orpheus. A poisonous serpent bit your love. She called to you as she succumbed. Orpheus, although stunned, insists: her cry shall not be in vain. He prepares to face hell for her. Yet the shepherds and nymphs issue a warning. It begins with an observation: "A good pilot/ constant and strong/ knows how to escape the wrath of the sea."[16] No mortal is skilled enough to circumvent mortality, they point out. Orpheus will not be dissuaded, suggesting not just the strength of his love for Eurydice, but that something else is at stake. When the nymph tells him of his loss, she addresses him as the "worthy sovereign of great Phoebus and the sacred Muses."[17] Orpheus is the Sun God's son. As Phoebus-Apollo navigates through the skies in a blazing chariot, his son must now navigate through the Underworld and take up what is literally a death-defying challenge. All this implies another question: Does Orpheus also have the qualities of a prince, and thus the capacity to be a ruler?

Philosophers, beginning at least in Greek antiquity, likened political rule to captaining a ship. Educated members of *Euridice*'s audience would have detected in Rinuccini's words a debt to Plato's *Republic*. In it he told a parable about mutinous sailors struggling with a ship's master—a burly fellow who is "a little deaf and shortsighted, and no less deficient in seamanship." For Plato, who was hostile to the direct democracy that governed Athens (that is, to the majority rule of the citizens), the ship's master comprised the citizenry; the sailors were the equivalent of demagogic politicians who try to garner support for themselves and claimed that anyone can steer a vessel, whether educated and capable to do so or not. They try to divert the Master with this or that inebriation. It may be drink or an opiate, but when translated politically it means great speechifying and beautiful deceptive words. Each sailor is in fact pursuing his own interests when proposing himself at the helm and deriding anyone actually fit for this role as "a mere stargazer." And so the sailors turn a ship's journey into "a drunken carousel." They don't understand that a true navigator must be predisposed inwardly to his task and then must actually learn it.[18] Plato's point was plain. Neither politicians nor the "People" can govern. Only if you know how to rule and have the capacity for mastery can you steer properly the ship of state.

Plato's metaphors appeared persistently throughout sixteenth-century political discussions and in musical ones too. Just a decade before *Euridice*, Justus Lipsius published a text titled *Politica: Six Books of Politics or Political Instruction*. We will come across this Flemish humanist's name often as he was one of the most prominent continental political theorists of the century, along with Florentine Niccolò Machiavelli (with his "realist" view of political power), Jean Bodin (French formulator of the idea of sovereignty), and Giovanni Botero (who attempted to Christianize "reason of state"). The issues they discussed, especially what we would now call the nature of the modern state, seeped recurrently into opera. Lipsius had already edited important editions of works by two celebrated ancients, the historian Tacitus and the philosopher Seneca, both of them important for early opera. In *Politica* Lipsius defended in principle emperors, kings, and princes. They kept order in his own era of religious strife. He also compared governing a polity to piloting a ship. How difficult it is for "one head" to control "so many," he wrote. Since the "all-encompassing multitude" is "discordant" and "tumultuous," it needs to be stationed "by gentle means" under a "common yoke." Few have been able to do so, Lipsius remarked, and he observed further that inexperienced men don't see the adversities entailed in preserving "a straight course" on turbulent seas. Great virtues are needed to do so, indeed, "many-sided Prudence" must steer the ship of state "as if by a rudder."[19] The right hand must be in charge. We don't know that the first creators of opera pondered the politics of Lipsius's book, although they may well have and had certainly read Plato well and knew Lipsius's scholarship. While Lipsius's concern was not music, and while he had no role in the birth of opera, his writings and translations colored greatly the entire intellectual world of Europe. The metaphor of a good pilot appealed easily to elites who looked with fear and chagrin at shaken Europe.

III.

One can imagine that many Florentine listeners/viewers at *Euridice* nodded in approval when they heard shepherds and nymphs sing of the strength and constancy required of a good pilot. As Henri IV secured his crown and French peace, so the Medici, earlier in the sixteenth century, secured their rule by bringing some stability to Florence. They achieved this after two centuries of struggles, sometimes with rival clans, and oftentimes with republicans, that is, with advocates of some kind of popular rule. Da Ponte's son described it as "the great struggle of power and right," based on opposed principles that are the foundations of all governments. Under one set of principles—those of republicanism—Florence became, he wrote, "the Athens" of the times, a "sacred depository" of liberty under a "people's government" that rested on laws. It had been the only republic in the Middle Ages, he asserted. The other principles, however, were those of the Medici.[20] This historical description is both stirring and a simplification, since advocacy of "popular" rule could often mask the ambitions of oligarchic factions (and a republic can be run by an oligarchy rather than by a democratic citizenry).

Grand Duke Ferdinando I was the son of Cosimo I, who had pacified Tuscany and often identified himself with Apollo. Medici minions undoubtedly saw the pre-Cosimo I era as a "drunken carousel" of political events. The Medici were chased from power in 1494 and restored by Spanish arms in 1512. There were, in fact, two republican regimes between those two dates, the first characterized by religiously flavored—saturated—populism, the second dominated by aristocrats. A republic reemerged between 1527–30, only to be ousted by Habsburg soldiers. The Medicis were reinstated, but their new duke, Alessandro, was assassinated. The killer, a shady cousin, proclaimed republican sympathies: "Tyrants, in whatever way they are assassinated, should be slain."[21] (Agents of Alessandro's successor murdered him some years later.)

Following Florentine politics can seem like wandering through particularly convoluted labyrinths with too many signposts. But finally a large stake makes its mark. Alessandro's murder did not bring a republican uprising as his assassin hoped. Instead, Cosimo I came to power and brought order forcefully. He never shrank from harsh measures. Florentines who had served in republican governments were barred from holding positions as he built what one scholar called a "bureaucratic, authoritarian, centralized *Rechtsstaat,*" that is, a strong state ruled by law and (a good deal of) equality before the law. Lelio Torelli, Cosimo's legal counselor, paid special attention to ancient Roman law in the process.[22] Law in Europe was a disparate reality after the fall of the Roman Empire—recall that political states as we think of them arose with modernity—but the rediscovery of manuscripts led, beginning in the eleventh century, to a revival of interest in Roman law and the notion of uniform laws over territories (separate from those of the church). The consequences were intellectual, practical, and long-term, spreading from Italy (especially Bologna) across the continent. Under Cosimo I came a time of (relative) quiet and economic well-being. Political ideas and debate withered in a city once famous for them. Florence, after all, had been the home of Machiavelli. The Medici also attained a long-sought family goal thanks to Cosimo I. Instead of simply being its leading clan, the Medici were now recognized as hereditary rulers. Legally, however, their principality was still part of the vast and complicated patchwork of multiple jurisdictions that made up the Holy Roman Empire.

The sixteenth century was particularly knotty in the Empire's history. At its beginning, the Habsburg King of Spain, from that family's senior branch, was also Holy Roman Emperor (a role identified, since its establishment in 800 CE, as the Christian heir of the founding emperor of Rome, Augustus). In 1521 Emperor Charles V gave the Austrian Habsburg lands to his brother. When Charles V abdicated and then died (in 1556 and 1558, respectively) the Habsburg, Austrian monarch became Holy Roman Emperor. Spain maintained rule over the family's Italian lands. Cosimo I worked for Madrid's interests within the Italian peninsula, much to the anger of France. The Florentine calculation was that friendship was a way of avoiding a repeat of past Spanish intervention. In the meantime, many anti-Medici Florentines went to Paris where Cosimo's cousin, Catherine, had married into the royal family. Her father-in-law, King François I, had been unhappy with Tuscany's geopolitical orientation, and gave succor to Cosimo I's foes. Yet while Cosimo I defended the Habsburg Empire, he also used deft, deceptive, and convoluted formulas to assert Medici prerogatives—and aspirations—at home and abroad. "We are a ruler who accepts the authority of no one," he once explained, "apart from God, and, but solely on account of our gratitude for benefits received, the [Holy Roman] Emperor . . . to whom we have never paid tribute nor offered vassalage. . . ."[23] Finally, in 1569 he was recognized as "grand duke" by the Holy Roman Emperor and the papacy. Following his Medici ancestors, Cosimo I selected a laurel tree as one symbol of his rule. But it was a bent stump from which a new, fresh branch emerged. "*Lauro*" and "*restauro*" rhymed.[24] The Medici, he signaled, were renewed.

It was this successful Medici quest to reestablish, entrench, and legitimize their rule that characterized Florentine politics in the six decades before opera was born. The Medici wanted all Tuscans, as well as outside powers, to recognize their hard-won prerogatives as entitlements. Marriage into other royal families fortified their claims; it gave them an aura. So too did elaborate court spectacles. Cultural creation to political ends was a long-established feature of Europe's Renaissance courts. "Before the invention of the mechanical mass media of today," one historian notes, "the creation of monarchs as an 'image' to draw people's allegiance was the task of humanists, poets, writers, and artists. During the sixteenth and seventeenth centuries the most profound alliance therefore occurred between the new art forms . . . and the concept of the Prince."[25] Princely images aimed also to instruct future rulers. Booklets presenting virtuous, useful, and corrupt behavior by past rulers were a tradition in Renaissance political culture. One Florentine we have mentioned wrote the most famous of these Mirrors for Princes in 1513 and dedicated it to a newly reinstated Medici. Machiavelli's *The Prince* offered bracing, matter-of-fact advice about political power. It was, however, at odds with guidance proffered in *Mirrors* by earlier Christian humanists. An effective ruler, he argued, must address politics dispassionately as organized violence, not as an aspect of God's goodly scheme of things. He must know when to be cruel. Machiavelli admired ancient Roman paganism, not for any truth but because its rites, which were integrated into public life, enhanced devotion of Romans to their polity. Established Christianity simply distracted people with other-worldly concerns.

Machiavelli had a particular problem in holding up a mirror to Medici princes since he had served in high offices in the republican government that was ousted in 1512. Both *The Prince* and his overtly republican *Discourses on Livy*, an examination of the work of the ancient Roman historian, were published some four years after his death in 1527. Yet his legacy wound through the minds of Florentines long afterwards—despite the ban placed on all his works by the Inquisition at midcentury. The Medici, however, did not really need his patriotic realism. They understood power and politics, and also knew well when to be cruel. And Christian legitimacy was especially important to these great patrons of Renaissance scholars and artists who celebrated pagan Greco-Roman antiquity. The Medici made efficient use of authority together with ideology, and their clan included cardinals. One was pope when, in 1517, Martin Luther rebelled against the Roman church, initiating the Protestant Reformation.

IV.

In the latter sixteenth century, Florentine intellectuals and artists, relieved enough by relative political quiet at home and happy for ducal patronage, sought to reinforce both calm and benefaction through ideas and images presented in their art. A prince's job was to make peace, they suggested. Heaven gives to him his right to rule, and a particular power defined a sovereign: his will made temporal rules and it was his business to make sure of their fair application. The Florentine *Euridice* was not only a wedding present and a story about love and matrimony; it included a political brief for this Medici ideology. Before considering it, however, and then Monteverdi's treatment of the same myth, we need to mark out some developments within Florence's intellectual and artistic worlds.

Renaissance humanism was less a movement than an array of perspectives held by men who looked back across centuries, past medieval culture, toward Greek and Latin antiquity. Rhetoric, the art of persuasion, was a primary concern for humanists as they turned to ancients for critical lessons about style and also behavior for their own times. Petrarch, the fourteenth-century poet, is often credited as progenitor of the Renaissance, and by the fifteenth and sixteenth centuries, humanism was a major intellectual force across the continent. The term itself, one scholar notes, originated probably in a description used by university students for teachers of the humanities (*umanista*), which included history, grammar, poetry, rhetoric, and ethics.[26] Debates took place over which Latin style ought to be emulated, although by the sixteenth century the Tuscan vernacular had also emerged as a literary standard for many Italians.[27]

Musical questions were mostly latecomers to this conversation. An important figure in their development was a philologist named Girolamo Mei. Born in Florence in 1519, he was active as a young man in the city's cultural and intellectual life and became a pupil of one of the most celebrated humanist scholars of the times. Pier Vettori (who published as "Petrus Victorius") was devoted to translating, editing, and commenting on major figures of antiquity ranging from Aeschylus and Euripides to Cicero and Sallust. He paid especial attention to Aristotle. His editions of and commentaries on Aristotle's *Rhetoric*, *Poetics*, *Nicomachean Ethics*, and *Politics* were greatly admired, and the concerns (or many of the concerns) of these books can together be considered harbingers of those that would preoccupy the circles whose experiments led to opera. Florentine intellectuals were shifting some of their intellectual focus from Plato to Aristotle, whose ideas (in varied interpretations) had come to dominate European universities since his works were translated into Latin in the thirteenth century. Now, Aristotelian and Platonic ideas mixed within humanism against the background of a Christendom split between Catholicism and Protestantism. Mei focused initially on literature as a young member of a new Florentine Academy and he shared in Vettori's work on Aristotle and efforts to revive interest in Cicero's approach to rhetoric.

Mei left Florence in somewhat murky circumstances, living for a decade in France and then in Padua. He began research on ancient Greek music as early as 1551 in Lyon, and then devoted himself to it after settling in Rome in 1560. Within two years he had explored, mostly in the Vatican library, a vast array of ancient writings pertaining to music.[28] Virtually no ancient Greek music existed, so he could only read these texts with an eye toward retrieving what could not be heard. He concluded that music in his own day didn't achieve what ancient Greek music did, which was to bring about what Aristotle called "catharsis"—a purging of emotions. Central to art, for both Plato and Aristotle, was mimesis, that is, imitation or representation. Plato, however, feared unwholesome excitement by art; playing on the emotions, it could undermine rational self-control. Mei, however, followed Aristotle in finding distinct value in works of tragedy since they could arouse and purge powerful feelings such as fear and pity.

Music's particular might, Mei believed, had to be used properly, and that meant imitating and using the human voice in specific ways. He determined that a kind of song-speech gave ancient music its effect. A solo voice or choral music could declaim words in a powerfully communicative way, provided they were composed in a certain way. There had to be a single melodic line and simple accompaniment. Called "monody" in the next century, it became a key expressive aspect of early opera. On one hand, monody was mimetic; it sought a type of vocal verisimilitude. On the other hand, it aimed to enhance the presentation of feelings and ideas. It contrasted to counterpoint, the kind of polyphonic musical composition that crafted two or more overlapping melodies and musical modes for multiple voices singing varied texts. Church masses exemplified the issue. Their polyphonic textures, thought Mei, made words unintelligible and undermined religious purpose.[29]

The same could—and would—be said about polyphonic madrigals. Although they were not Mei's preoccupation, these comprised the most popular form of secular music during the Renaissance. They were well liked at the Florentine court, yet would later become a subject of contention among Florentines influenced by Mei's views. For these musical humanists, "*poesie per musica*" in madrigals appealed to listeners by means of counterpoint; it could be truly beautiful, but words were usually lost in layers of acoustical imagery made by numerous lines of multiheaded sound.[30]

V.

Here is how Mei argued in 1572. Among the ancients, he insisted, singing, with however many voices, "was in every song a single air." It was understood that nature gave man a voice with various qualities to express his diverse "inner states." Greek song had "a single end" to which the natural and "rightful means" were thereby directed. But if "several airs" mix in the same song, a listener is pulled in different directions, as if laughing and crying at once. Nothing but "supreme vanity" inspired polyphonic composers to use "many notes without natural fittingness." The result was indecipherable, "disordered perturbation," a "mangling" of words.[31] In these assertions, Mei makes an inquiry that is much like the oldest of questions in political philosophy: who rules? And to what purpose? His answer: words ruled—or should rule—music.

Music must serve what words express. Instrumental sound cannot be "the boss," for it was "invented to imitate the voice." Otherwise, our reason will be subordinate to sensation, and it is our rationality and language that distinguishes us from lower life-forms. "Nature gave the voice expressly to man," he wrote, "not so that he might with its pure sound, like animals which lack reason, express pleasure and pain, but so that, together with meaningful speech, he might suitably express the thought of his mind."[32] In short, music was not an art for its own sake; its purpose was "not to please the ear with the sweetness of consonances." Its delight arose properly when a song's "air" suited thoughts of a text, that is, when a singing voice, with its highs and lows, conveyed something to listeners "completely and with efficacy" yet differently from the "continuous" ways of "common speech."[33] Words and voice could move listeners in ways polyphony's crisscrossing lines did not.

One line, not many; one head, not many. Mei's quarrel with polyphony evokes not just Plato but an argument that took place within the Roman church. He seems to be arguing against pluralism in sound and on behalf of oneness in artistic communication just while the church was asserting—or straining to assert—its singular authority against the volatile pluralism that came of the Reformation. The consequences of polyphony in masses and motets were disputed at the Council of Trent in September 1562, the year in which Mei was hunting for manuscripts in Rome. The Christian world was then divided, the papacy's claim to unique stature wounded, and bloody conflicts consumed Europe.[34] The council was one of the church's responses. It met over decades (with interruptions) to wrestle with the impact of Protestantism, and its debate on music was a relatively minor affair, focusing on questions that had been raised previously in church circles: did polyphonic masses distract the faithful? Did their musical beauties draw believers into perilous sensual pleasure? (St. Augustine, who loved music, worried about music's effect on prayer a millennium earlier in his *Confessions*.) Perhaps monophony, that is, a single, unaccompanied melodic line, most familiar in the form of Gregorian chant, was more appropriate to devotional purposes? It was a complex discussion with much speculation about intelligibility in liturgy. A call went out to reform church music.

A legend grew from these events. Some five centuries later, it became the subject of an opera by the German composer Hans Pfitzner. His *Palestrina* was written as Europe descended into World War I, and it premiered in 1917. It presents the ordeal of Giovanni Pierluigi de Palestrina, whom Pfitzner credited with saving the church's musical heritage during the deliberations at Trent. This composer of many masses came under pressure, notably from Cardinal Carlo Borromeo, a zealous proponent of Counter-Reformation doctrines, to write a polyphonic mass characterized both by beauty and *claritas*. Pfitzner reinvented considerably what took place, and inflated the importance and novelty of the council's debate on music. He also exaggerated the impact of the mass Palestrina wrote (the "Missa Papae Marcelli"). While the Holy See did set the tone for everything, including music, throughout Catholicism, most decisions about musical matters were left usually to local church authorities.[35]

Historical distortions like those found in Pfizner's opera are not blameworthy in themselves. Theater and especially opera do not reproduce past events; they say something while representing them. Pfitzner also meant to address musical culture in his own day and in this there was a political subtext. He was a German nationalist who imagined himself as defender of a musical heritage threatened by new types of music, in particular Arnold Schönberg's "atonality." *Palestrina* was conceived as a barricade against novelties that its composer found alien and unnatural. His opera ends with an allusion linking his contemporary fears to the past. Silla, Palestrina's student has watched the composer's ordeal and decides to leave for Florence, the Tuscan city that would become known for "new music." The issues raised at Trent anticipated deliberations about (and experiments with) secular music a decade later in informal humanist circles known as the "Florentine Camerata." But the innovation was also ancient.

Chapter 2

REIGNING VOICES

Academies were essential features of Florence's intellectual and artistic worlds. Other cities had them too. Some were formal institutions, others more like salons. In the early 1540s, members of a newly founded Florentine Academy (which should not be confused with Ficino's earlier circle of the same name) sought to encourage their vernacular tongue, Tuscan, rather than Latin, as a literary language. And members pondered matters like those that later preoccupied Mei: what were proper relations among poetic texts, airs improvised for them, and those popular polyphonic madrigals? Wasn't the advancement of Tuscan better served, they wondered, by a solo song line with simple accompaniment as opposed to a mix of vocal lines that made poetry indistinct?[1] Perhaps an unintentional political suggestion—or presupposition—may be found here too: one voice should rule. It was, after all, Cosimo I's first decade.

Complex relations characterized the court, academies, informal circles, and the church. The Florentine Academy served Medici political purposes, since the ruling family wanted to stress its identification with both Tuscan well-being and history. Promotion of Tuscan cultural eminence was not, however, without problems, especially after the Inquisition established its Index of Prohibited Books. This censorship hurt Tuscany's commercial book trade as well as its intellectual life. Cosimo I's son, Francesco, became grand duke in 1574, and his thirteen-year reign corresponded not only to the many Florentine conversations that anticipated opera, but was marked by conflicts with church restrictions on literature and theater.[2]

Memberships in academies often overlapped and were mostly aristocratic. Two informal salons are of particular concern to us. They were later often blurred one into the other under the name of the Florentine Camerata (little room). Relatively recent scholarship points to the importance of distinguishing well between them. We have already met one group around Jacopo Corsi; they created *Dafne* and then *Euridice*. It was quasi-professional, and incorporated trained musicians. Corsi was a well-to-do aristocrat with assets from banking and the silk business. Earlier, in the

1570s, discussions within another circle with more erudite concerns helped open the way to experiments in monody. This Camerata met at the home of Count Giovanni de' Bardi, who was Corsi's senior by three decades (the two would be rivals in the world of Florentine cultural patronage). Mei, in Rome, served as a kind of corresponding associate of Bardi's group. Its participants looked back to Sophocles, Aeschylus, and Euripides as creators of great, indeed the greatest, tragic poetry. Music, they thought, had been intrinsic to performances of their works. Like Mei, they possessed virtually none of this music, but, following him, they believed that when these plays were performed almost two millennia earlier, they embodied the appropriate relations between words and music—among tones, emotions, and ideas.

Bardi, Count of Vernio, was born in 1534 into a banking and business family and had an illustrious personal military history. He was a Renaissance man in today's clichéd sense, with wide interests in philology, philosophy, literature, and music.[3] Like Mei, he decried counterpoint. It was "the enemy of music." When he explained, he used some sociopolitical metaphors. Imagine a palazzo in which four people move about on different stories, he wrote. The owner, *messer lo basso* (Mr. Bass) walks on the ground level "formally dressed in semibreves and minims" (whole notes and half notes). The Soprano "walks hurriedly with quick steps on the terrace, adorned with minims and semi-minims" (half notes and quarter notes). Meanwhile, Mr. Tenor and the Alto wander "the intermediate floors with still other rates of movement and dressed otherwise." In this sort of composition, the parts—notes, syllables of verse, rhythms—don't go together with purpose. The result, he asserted (invoking, of course, the authority of Plato and Aristotle) is "powerless to convert the soul" to a "moral ethos" worthy of a "free man." For that to happen, the poet leads and voice follows, adjusting "like a good cook who adds to the food that he has seasoned well a little sauce or condiment to make it pleasing to his lord." (Presumably it is a hare and not the cat prepared by Hegel's cook.) There are, then, hierarchies in the world, such as soul and body, text, and song, and, indeed, master and servant. Wouldn't it be laughable, Bardi asked, if you walked into a public square and found a servant "commanding his master, or a child giving instruction to his parent or teacher?"[4] He recalled hearing a celebrated bass sing in Rome. The man's natural talent filled Bardi with wonder, but his vocal acrobatics committed a "massacre of the unfortunate poetry."[5]

While we don't know the names of most who frequented Bardi's Camerata, we can identify Vincenzo Galilei. Born near Florence, he was a lute player, composer, and onetime silk trader. Thanks to Bardi's patronage, he had studied in Venice with Gioseffo Zarlino, then the leading theorist of music. But as he participated within the Camerata's deliberations back in Florence he came to reject Zarlino's ideas. Zarlino's influential book of 1558, *Fundamentals of Music*, held, like the Pythagoreans, Plato, and more recently Ficino, that the cosmos and music were governed by the same fixed ratios and laws; four-part harmony was deemed an unsurpassable musical form. Humans could hear it in counterpoint. A transformation in compositional techniques had been accomplished by Josquin des Prez, a virtually legendary figure of the late fifteenth and early sixteenth centuries. Before him, argued Zarlino, polyphonic composers worked from one musical line, adding voices in succession, making a compound in sound. Josquin, by contrast, positioned musical lines simultaneously, creating "texture as a whole." It displayed the laws of God's universe. It also meant the dominance of consonance (a harmonious combination of tones) over dissonance (when a musical interval or chord produces discordant sound). Consonance, wrote Zarlino, is more "agreeable" following dissonance as "the taste of sweets" is "more delicious after something bitter."[6]

Zarlino's subject was music, yet his claims suggest a view of the world with evident political implications. In it, objective laws make a whole—and because that whole overcomes dissonance, it pleases us. The many layers of the cosmos fit. One could say that in the early modern world, dissonance, in or by itself, was unsatisfying, as if individual tones don't find rightful places. Christianity, however, provided consonance. In a comparable if somewhat sweeping way, medieval Europe may be said to have had manifold domains but was bonded by the church. The Holy Roman Empire swathed a substantial part of the continent, but its borders were never delineated sharply, its languages were multiple, and its emperor's local power often partial. The church, by contrast, had a formidable coherence, both spiritual (ideological, that is) and organizational, although its authority had already corroded due to challenges, some very forceful, in the centuries prior to Martin Luther's appearance. Utopias are consonant, and so, more or less, was Christendom's self-image (despite belief in original sin), before Protestantism brought radical discord. If the sixteenth century was an age of individual and collective upheavals, a Medici principate seemed to promise new Florentine political consonance in its latter half.

Bardi had a favored place in Francesco I's court, and was charged with arranging many sumptuous entertainments for the ruler. His Camerata flourished, and Galilei wrote what became its "manifesto." The *Dialogue on Ancient and Modern Music* (published in 1580/81) elaborated on, indeed borrowed directly, Mei's ideas. In his challenge to contemporary musical authorities like Zarlino, Vincenzo—anticipating his son Galileo, in a way— also suggested alternative modes of looking at the human world and the cosmos. He challenged Zarlino's notion of oneness—"texture as a whole"— with a different oneness conceived as monody. Zarlino's oneness assumed the pluralism of the premodern world; there are layers but they are integrated by God's plan. Monody, however, subordinated sounds to a single, temporal lawmaker—a text. While they may not have imagined it this way, Mei, Bardi, and Galilei advanced a principle of oneness in song that was structured much like the oneness animating the Medici principate. Perhaps the spirit of the times was also captured by Galilei's son, for whom Archimedes was "what Virgil was to Dante."[7] The ancient mathematician and scientist from Syracuse sought a single point from which to see everything and, standing upon it, could lift the world with a lever. Here we begin to perceive counterparts in a cultural and political moment: a human voice, a single ruler and centralization of territorial power, and a man's eyes and powers.

But Renaissance humanism implied also a challenge to authority, even if many of its adherents did not intend it to be so. A striking aspect of Vincenzo's *Dialogue* is its use of political metaphors to speak of music. He inverts that practice that was common to many political philosophers since Plato—the use of musical metaphors to talk of politics. Harmony is the most obvious of them (although that word had varied meanings in different historical eras). Vincenzo often seems to assume that the structures of politics and of music are similar. His urgent question is also one we have already encountered and seems simple: Who rules—words or music? It implies other queries: Are the established laws of the day natural, and thus unmovable? Or are there other ways of perceiving and doing things? Vincenzo doesn't say or hint at it, but no query is more political than to ask about the mutability of laws.

II.

Bardi is one of two speakers in Galilei's *Dialogue*, and he presents, usually, Vincenzo's views. Another, younger member of the Camerata, Piero Strozzi, mostly poses questions. He came from an aristocratic family with a known anti-Medici history, and seems to speak also for Vincenzo when, toward the *Dialogue*'s beginning, he says that sense perception rather than "authority" ought to guide our views—or rather, hearing—of music. He asks—it is the first issue raised—about proper tuning, about adjusting properly the tone of instruments. He explains that "those who, for the sake of proving some conclusion, want us to believe simply on the basis of authority without adducing valid arguments for it are doing something laughable. . . ."[8]

Vincenzo goes on to contest Zarlino's treatment of polyphony and the objectivity of harmony. What you hear, he argues, is subjective, a matter of your sensations, and music's purpose is to move your affections. It is a means of sensuous persuasion in an individualized way; it must evoke more than joy in its sounds. He repeats the usual protest against polyphonic madrigals: they please with multiple images in sound but they obscure the texts. Instead, he thinks music ought to be regarded as a branch of the ancient art of rhetoric. Aristotle proposed to rhetoricians that their task in oratory was neither to provide scientific proof nor ornamentation, but to "detect" and bring out something persuasive in a particular subject. For Vincenzo, music brings out something being said.

Go to see a tragedy or comedy, he tells contemporary musical "practitioners." Listen to actors, and then extrapolate from what you hear in the tones you compose. When nobles speak to each other on stage, hear their "manner" and pitch along with "volume or sound, accents and gestures, speed or slowness of articulation." Notice that it is different "when one of them speaks with his servant, or a servant to another." Pay attention, of course, when you hear "a prince talking with his subjects or vassals," or when a suppliant pleads before him. Heed diverse expressions made by a "furious or excited person" or "a married woman" by comparison to "a girl, a mere tot," or "a clever harlot." Listen also to someone "speaking to his beloved when he is trying to bend her to his will." Note the differences when someone laments, or exclaims, or is shy or happy when speaking. Hear these differences "diligently"—hear how various "characteristics" sound. This is how you will learn to suit tones to ideas.[9]

Vincenzo lauds the ancient Greeks for understanding that music should be "useful to virtue," that a great "legislator" would want it to be part of the education of the foremost members of society (of the "city").[10] Vincenzo, like Bardi, believes every society, inescapably, has its elite and its untutored masses; "nobler minds" will understand his challenge to musical legislators of his day. The "common public" won't. But he does not care. He says: Let them enjoy their polyphonic madrigals! Why, commoners can even listen to trombones! They need not be concerned by what is important, which is "the imitation of the ideas that are in the words." That is what composers of polyphony cannot do.[11]

Ancient Greece was gone, and so too its musical achievements, Galilei knew. Yet he suggests its reinvention, against what "the moderns" think are "inviolable laws." Since he has proposed that the ancients did things differently, it was evident that the laws of the moderns were not eternal. Following them was actually "contrary to the good expression of the affections and ideas of any kind of poem."[12] So the argument is against the "authority" of "legislators" on behalf of what is naturally human, but he identifies what is naturally human with what the *aristoi*, that is, the best among humans, hear.

Great ancient orators and musicians had this in common for Vincenzo: they expressed "affection" (feeling or sentiment) properly—and thereby affected others. The impact of an orator provided a striking example for him, even though—he does not say this—rhetoric in Medici Florence could not play the role it did in democratic Athens or republican Rome, where it addressed citizens or courts (or also senators in Rome). What music could do, in Vincenzo's mind, was enhance meaning as it imitated literary speech intended for an elite. His goal was what became known as a "representative style," rather than one that would confuse listeners with diverse and contradictory signs.[13] "Contrapuntists," then, are like orators; they know a lot, can tell you all details of playing and composing but are "barren of invention"—the latter an important term in theories of rhetoric—and unable to do with their fingers what reason suggests.[14] Vincenzo wants "musical speech" that brings out what is inherent in poetic words.

Words, not a composer, must determine melody; music serves a speaker, individualizing his or her perspective. Vincenzo did not address theater directly in his claims, and texts he set to music were literary (for example, an excerpt from Dante's *Inferno*) or religious. He did not invent monody, but brought into focus an idea that was in the air, and it helped to open the way to what came to be called "recitative." We can draw a line from him (and the Camerata) to the first operas. "The annals of modern music," the historian of music, Charles Burney, wrote in the late eighteenth century, "have hitherto furnished no event so important to the progress of the art, as the recovery or invention of *recitative*, or dramatic melody."[15] This would require self-conscious experiment by poets and composers. The poet had to craft verse to make it susceptible to musical enhancement; but music was the word's supporting strong ally in moving emotions. "It has been the opinion of many . . ." Rinuccini, the first librettist, explained in 1600 (in another echo of Mei), "that the ancient Greeks and Romans, in representing their tragedies upon the stage, sang them throughout." It had not been attempted in his own times, he explained, because of "the imperfection of modern music." Collaboration with Peri and Corsi on *Dafne* convinced him of other possibilities in the 1590s.[16] The idea was to create a *stile rappresentativo;* a libretto would allow theatrical or dramatic monodic expression accompanied by chords.

III.

Born in 1562, Ottavio Rinuccini was of a younger generation than Bardi, but became a friend of the count. He came from an old Florentine family that had, at times, held public offices and included in its history numerous men of letters. His siblings and cousins played leading roles in various Florentine academies and some went into church service. Ottavio studied the liberal arts as a young man. His earliest passions included Ovid and Petrarch. His sonnets suggest other kinds of passions. He seems to have been an intrepid romantic adventurer, taking care, however, to disguise the various lovers he addressed in poems.[17] His great artistic talent, a later commentator remarked, was not just "at expressing in his verses all kinds of passions," but in finding "means to adopt music and singing to them so well that neither destroyed any part of the beauty of the verses, nor prevented the distinct understanding of the words, which is often hindered by an affected multiplicity of divisions."[18] Peri declared that his music for *Dafne* sought in song to imitate speech in new ways, but it is clear that his understanding of the composer's task complemented Rinuccini's view of the libretto. Both perceived analogies in aspects of music and rhetoric. "[A]ncient Greeks and Romans," Peri explained in 1601 ". . . used a harmony which, going beyond that of ordinary speech, fell so short of the melody that it assumed an intermediate form."[19] His innovative goal was midway between normal speech and the slower movements of words in song. Peri's rival in "new music," Caccini, spoke of an effort to "speak musically." He had learned from members of the Camerata how ancient philosophers perceived the proper order to be "speech, rhythm, and last, sound—not the contrary."[20]

Beyond his own Camerata, Bardi was also an eminent participant in more formal academies. One, the Accademia degli Alterati, was founded in 1569 (it continued for a half century), and its very name expressed the desire of members to alter not just themselves but aspects of intellectual and artistic life. Some among its initiators and members were from known anti-Medici families and their gatherings, it seems, incorporated some republic-like features: there were presiding secretaries but they alternated (incumbents had to be changed twice a year). Members liked dialogue. It was their habit to place writings in a vase for potential debate and then an advocate for a set of ideas would be chosen along with a foe. The debates were mainly cultural but it is easy to imagine political implications in them. The Alterati included amateur musicians, and Corsi and Rinuccini joined in 1586. Ottavio's older brother, the poet and later senator Alessandro Rinuccini, had already played a leading role for nearly a decade. Piero Vettori, whose personal history had been tinged by anti-Medici republicanism, was an inactive member and Mei, in Rome, an honorary one. Bardi joined as early as 1573 and, like his colleagues took an "academic" pseudonym: "*Il Puro*" (the Pure One).[21] Ottavio Rinuccini was "*Il Sonnacchioso*" (the Sleepy One). Young Galileo may have been a member.[22]

They debated the relative merits of great poets such as Dante, Ariosto, and Tasso. They asked: Do literary works enhance virtuous behavior or simply pleasure? How were poetry's merits to be compared to rhetoric or painting or history?[23] A February 1572 debate on the relation between "the affections" and rhetoric led to ongoing conversations on this theme that, unsurprisingly, hinged often on the worth of the ancients compared to moderns. There was no unified outlook among them, but Aristotle's *Poetics*, which Vettori had recently translated into Latin, was a compass for many deliberations. This led inevitably to a distinctive concern with that key Aristotelian idea: art as mimesis. It was a principal subject of Alterati exchanges between December 1573 and February 1574 and raised issues that pointed toward the "new music" since recitative would seek to "represent" or imitate human states and feelings through musicalized vocal expression. These themes became regular preoccupations. In summer 1584, Alterati discussed them at length after Bardi reported that Ferrara-based philosopher Francesco Patrizi was preparing a Platonic critique of Aristotle. The critique would extend to music, he explained, and would claim that instrumental compositions as well as accompanied voice could not provide meaningful human expression.[24] Reason, for a Platonist, was the means to discover timeless certainties. Art provided only pale imitations of them, since its experience is sensuous. Moreover, artistic practices could be morally hazardous because feelings can overwhelm our rational pursuits, even shepherd the young to imitate and value the wrong, temporal things.

One of the Alterati, the classicist Lorenzo Giacomini, presented opposing arguments based on Aristotle. Mimesis was a normal aspect of human life, he asserted, and could have a productive function. Great tragedies present particular characters and events in specific circumstances. We witness in them responses that are morally worthy, and since learning is agreeable, especially when by means of pleasing language—with its rhythm, melody, and own manner of music—so too is viewing tragic experience on stage. We may thus gain knowledge through viewing tragedy without actually suffering what is portrayed, but by experiencing catharsis. Giacomini, following Aristotle's *Politics*, compares this to a palliative. Catharsis lets us see the world more clearly, for clarity comes after clouds and rain.[25]

And so the integration of musical compositions can move listeners usefully in tragedy. Renaissance discussions of Aristotle linked frequently two of his most celebrated works, the *Poetics* and the *Rhetoric*. The former, as we mentioned, stressed the role of mimesis in art and human experience. The latter (also translated by Vettori) tells us that the task of eloquence is to bring out something that is intrinsic to a given subject matter. But here an interesting question arose in late sixteenth-century Florence: brought out for whom? Since the Medici governed with very firm hands there were limits on what could be imitated or said or brought into the open; persuasion and politics divorced, as one scholar puts it. This ushered in an emphasis on oratory and poetry as "sister arts," and in turn, a shift "from persuasion to style and imitation."[26] Or perhaps, it ought to be considered something else: a migration of rhetoric.

Here another element enters our story. A new interest in history arose among European humanists at this time. It was, perhaps, simply a function of all the changes and instability in the world. Many found that one ancient Roman historian, Tacitus, spoke especially to them. His vigorous style, sharp and pithy, recalled a thinker who was, at least in public, then unmentionable—Machiavelli. The thirteen-year reign of Grand Duke Francesco I coincided not only with the debates about music among Florence's humanists, but also discussions among them about Tacitus. The Rome of which he wrote was an imperial regime that had displaced a republic; sixteenth-century Florence was a principality that had banished a republic. But interest in him had important and varied implications. We need to look at some of them before turning to a celebration in 1589—an important year both for opera and political ideas.

IV.

A ruler alone—sometimes along with his closest minions—needed convincing in a principate. Humanists, preoccupied with ancient eloquence, had long taught the superiority of Cicero's combination of highly ornate rhetorical style and philosophical wisdom. But Cicero was a lawyer and senator in a collapsing republic. Late Renaissance interest in Tacitus posed challenges to Cicero's sway; it was postrepublic time.

While Tacitus had been a senator too, he held this office in imperial Rome where it was little more than a title and part of a façade behind which the emperor alone had real power. The contrast between verbally sumptuous Cicero and plainspoken Tacitus reflects, at least schematically, differing tasks of persuasion in a republic and an empire. A parallel may likewise be drawn between ornate polyphony and monody's song. The latter laid its claim as sixteenth-century princes displaced republicanism in Florence. Cicero's political thinking dwelt on what ought to be derived from an inextricable twosome: justice and reason. He inscribed them in both the cosmic and human worlds. Tacitus's ideas came from close observation of Roman court intrigue. His was a jaundiced, skeptical—some would say very realistic—view of relations among justice, power, and human behavior. He despised tyrants, yet served several in high positions, believing that "even under bad emperors, men can be great."[27] Around 1530, at the time when the Medici returned to power, Francesco Guicciardini, Florentine philosopher, statesman, and friend of Machiavelli, described Tacitus in much these same terms: a man who knew about being great in unhappy times. Yet Guicciardini also pointed out that the Roman historian provided different lessons for different audiences. He taught subjects how to live under tyrants (prudently!) and showed tyrants how to maintain power. In fact, Guicciardini's characterization of Tacitus was published in Paris and only in 1576, long after his death, thanks to a Florentine political exile with personal links to the Alterati, Jacopo Corbinelli. It was a time when many books on politics appeared in Italy—despite limits the church and rulers wanted to impose on what could be read. Intellectuals in Florence would have known it as well from an edition published in 1582 in Venice. More than one hundred authors wrote commentaries on Tacitus between 1580 and 1700.[28]

An important immediate stimulus for interest in Tacitus came from lectures by Marc-Antoine Muret in Rome beginning in the late 1560s. This French professor, who had also taught in Venice and Padua, was a forceful proponent of integrating more diverse ancient Roman authors into the curricula of universities than had then been the case. Muret was also especially interested in drama and poetry (he tried his hand at both of these). He produced an edition of Seneca in 1575, lectured in Rome on Aristotle's *Rhetoric* in 1576, and then on his *Politics*. Contemporary rulers, Muret declared in his wide-ranging lectures on Tacitus in the fall of 1580, could not be compared to the despots of Tacitus's era. Before he developed this point, however, he made a political observation of considerable importance. There were, he remarked, "few republics" in his own day. "There is scarcely a people (*gentum*) which does not depend on the will and authority of one man. . . . Therefore, from this standpoint, at least, the state of affairs which existed under the emperors came closer to being like our own times than that which existed when the People ruled. . . . The more similar to our own situation any history is, the more things . . . we [can] learn from it . . . and apply to our own way of life." Then he adds, in what may also have been some wise dissimulation on his part, "By the grace of God our age has no Tiberiuses, Caligulas, and Neros." Consequently, "it is to our advantage to know how good and wise men lived even under such as these . . ."[29]

Whether or not Muret, who was renowned as an orator, dissimulated about contemporary rulers, he had a real sense of some of the difficulties as well as the values of using an ancient language for a model in his own times. He noted that people of his own day could not deploy a language as did men "whose nurses spoke Latin." It was often impossible to know if Tacitus was actually inventing this or that phrase or formulation, because all of ancient literature was not at hand. "Take someone in our time who was born in Germany or Poland, who has never seen Italy or heard an Italian speak," he elaborated. "Assume that he has read a few books in Tuscan dialect, has understood them after a fashion, and has made a list of every little word which he has read in them." Then imagine that this stranger hears a Florentine "who is considered most eloquent among his fellow-citizens." The foreign "expert" might find all sorts of flaws because he did not recognize assorted phrases and linguistic usages he had not read in books. But it would be the "expert" who was flawed since he had relied on his own limited readings.[30] This striking observation might have also stimulated some useful considerations among the Florentine circles that were concerned to imitate or approximate ancient music; Muret's lectures were delivered not long before Galilei's book on ancient and modern music was published. His comment on language has political implications that he seems either not to have noticed or preferred to sidestep: just as the foreign "expert" might not recognize various phrases in Tuscan, so a sixteenth-century humanist might not perceive all the political resonances of an ancient author—as we, today, need to be astute to resonances in our studies of earlier historical developments.

Humanists, accustomed to taking from the past lessons for their own times, could easily understand Muret's meaning when he referred to the

Figure 2.1. The cover of Justus Lipsius's influential sixteenth-century edition of Tacitus's writings. (Bibliothèque nationale de France.)

advantages of knowing how best to live under conditions "such as these"—under problematic rulers, that is. One of Muret's students was Lipsius, that Flemish scholar and proponent of Tacitus and Seneca. Lipsius's edition of Tacitus's writings in August 1574—two years after the St. Bartholomew Massacre of Huguenots by Catholics in France raised in a very immediate way pointed questions about political order and religiously inspired violence—led to discussions about the Roman historian among intellectuals across the continent. (Muret accused Lipsius of plagiarizing his own work.) Lipsius believed that Tacitus and Seneca spoke to his own strife-filled times and his influence on their reception was wide and deep. His own writings, such as *On Constancy* (1584) and *Politica* (1589), stressed the importance of prudence and steadfastness by buffeted subjects and rulers.

V.

Tacitus admired the lost virtues of the Roman republic but he saw the future as unavoidably imperial. Unsympathetic to "the masses," he believed firmly in elite rule, all while revealing court corruption with trenchancy. In the 1570s Tacitus, and especially his style, was subject to frequent attention by Alterati.[31] In 1582, just after Galilei published his *Dialogue* and at a time when these Florentines were discussing music and monody, interest in Tacitus intensified. A striking parallel again becomes manifest. Monody's aim was simplicity and directness, and among the Alterati, Tacitus became, as one scholar writes, a "stylistic mentor." An active participant in the discussions about music was agronomist Bernardo Davanzati, who became known as the "Florentine Tacitus" as an advocate of a terse style in the Tuscan vernacular. In summer 1583, he presented to his fellow members parts of his translation of Tacitus's *Annals.* Discussion about it continued until his full text was published in 1599.[32] Davanzati was no admirer of the Medici. His father had been expelled from Florence by them, and he was a friend of anti-Medici Corbinelli, who was also a proponent of Tacitus.[33] In Florence, an eminent humanist, Lionardo Salviati, a friend and neighbor of Bardi and godfather to Peri's daughter, wrote a "*discorso*" in 1582 extolling Tacitus's style, but with manifest pro-Medici conclusions. Ancient Romans, he proposed, had different governments at different times, depending usually on what was appropriate to them.[34] His obvious suggestion was that Florence followed a similar course, and now had a government appropriate to its times—one that kept both the mob at bay along with republican advocates of popular government. Obviously, Rome needed an Augustus and Florence had needed a Cosimo I and his descendants. Scipione Ammirato, a Medici court historian and Alterati member, extolled his employers in a tract on Tacitus that he read to the Alterati June 27, 1591.[35]

Still, Tacitus could be used to more than one purpose, as Guicciardini had noted. There appears to have been a shift in how Alterati appreciated Tacitus in the early 1580s, when Francesco was still duke, to the following decade, when his brother Ferdinando reigned. This may reflect unease about Francesco's last, very troubled and tangled years, and hopes for a new era—not a republican one, but one of worthy rule. After all, Tacitus explained his approach to history as a quest for "truth" unadorned by romance and "unblemished by marvels."[36] He sensed keenly the difference between appearance and reality in the political world around him, where eloquence could have little effect and truth could not be expressed publicly.

We have seen how Galilei's *Dialogue* criticized "contrapuntalists" by comparing them to learned, uninventive orators. Such musicians could tell you in detail how to play and to compose, but, he added pithily, they cannot do with their fingers what reason proposes.[37] While the Alterati seem to have been concerned mostly with Tacitus's historical writings, Galilei's claim is reminiscent, strikingly so, of contrasts made in *Dialogue on Orators*. A work by young Tacitus, it was also a source of considerable discussion in Europe at this time. Rediscovered and published (first in Rome and then in Venice) in the fifteenth century, it appeared in Lipsius's edition (although this editor thought it was written probably by Quintilian).[38] It makes us privy to an ancient Roman conversation in the home of an aristocrat, Curiatius Maternus, and takes place in 75 AD, several decades after the Roman republic's collapse. As the aristocrat Bardi received Florentine friends for debates on ancient and modern music, so Maternus receives visitors for an exchange about "ancient" and "modern" oratory. Once an orator himself, this noble explains that he shunned "the forum" in order to write poetic tragedies on political subjects. Yet, these caused him grief when powerful people were annoyed by his sympathetic depiction of Cato, a symbol of Roman republicanism.

One caller on Maternus, the lawyer Marcus Aper, defends "modern" rhetoric and derides poetry. Poetry brings peril, he warns, adding that it affords no celebrity. Rhetoric, however, yields prestige in public and in courts. Great pleasure arises when an orator stands among silent people and moves them to take on "whatever emotion" he displays in his speech.[39] (Moreover, oratory is useful in self-defense—a point directed, obviously, to Maternus's troubles. He would one day be executed, although it is unclear if it was for political offenses.) Aper comments on recent debates about Cicero's oratory—just as there had been later among Alterati in the sixteenth century. He concurs with critics who found Cicero "swollen." Another guest, Vipstanus Messala, expresses some nostalgia for Cicero's oratory, but he still favors the sharper "modern" style of his own day. It is "much better to clothe a speech even in a rough toga than to make it stand out with the colored clothes of a courtesan."[40] Still, Messala worries that contemporary forensic orators rely on technique, and lack the culture and moral sensibility of a Cicero. This emptiness, he thinks, is due to a decline in education.

Maternus, however, argues that the real issue is not whether ancient speakers were better than moderns, but why oratory no longer has serious impact. Clearly the public performance of his own poetry, by contrast, has had an effect, or else he would not have irritated powerful men. His explanation, one that Florentines might find obvious, is that Rome was no longer a republic. Truly impressive oratory comes of liberty and public disagreements; these were gone. Where Messala pointed to schooling,

Maternus points to political change. Nothing could be accomplished without rhetoric in Cicero's day, when Rome was a republic; now nothing serious can be accomplished with it. "Great eloquence, like a flame, is fed by fuel," he says, allowing, however, that flame and fuel were out of control at the republic's end.[41] (The *Dialogue*, then, becomes a not-too-subtle discussion of free speech.)

Tacitus, one suspects, agreed on these last points, all while he accepted that the fires could not be reignited. After all, experience convinced him finally to write history rather than to continue to try to make it; and he wrote with a style that contrasted sharply to that of Cicero—his was like a "jackhammer," as one scholar puts it.[42] The impact of Tacitus's prose is dramatic, combining irony and a honed sense of how to use speeches attributed to historical figures to show the stakes in this or that political development. His written rhetoric gives readers tragedies, characters, and theatricality, seeking to evoke responses as he recounts events.[43]

Political power and rhetoric migrated in ancient Rome and in late Renaissance Florence.

VI.

Medici power had to contend with pockets of prorepublican sentiments and resistance. We can perhaps sense some of the attitudes in Alterati interest in Tacitus. Florence depended on its own links, sometimes wobbly to bigger political powers. Francesco I's reign seemed at first to have promise, but it was soon beset by problems, many of his own making. Taxation was high and the grand duke was apparently more preoccupied with chemistry and alchemy than overseeing good government. In spring 1575, young aristocrats plotted against him, only to be arrested swiftly (and some of them executed). Francesco I sent agents abroad, particularly to Paris, to murder exiled oppositionists. In the meantime, domestic matters became seamy and foreign affairs more tangled.

Since Florence owed fealty to the Holy Roman Empire, it was useful for Francesco to marry Anne of Austria, daughter of the Habsburg Emperor. This conjugal union continued his father's pattern of political alliances, and he sustained relatively good ties with the Holy See and Spain. French ire was predictable, and while Francesco was often cavalier about it, he was not entirely foolish. France was, after all, unstable. Florence had difficult relations with one of the grand duke's relatives, the powerful Catherine de' Medici. Yet within Florence, Francesco tarnished the Medici image by his offhanded treatment of his wife and then his decision, hastily upon her death, to wed Bianca Capella, his highly unpopular Venetian lover, in 1579. Then economic downturn exacerbated discontent in the 1580s.

In 1587, fortune—some think it took form as arsenic—intervened. Both Francesco and Bianca died suddenly. The duke's able brother, a cardinal in Rome since youth, succeeded him. Ferdinando de' Medici returned to Tuscany, set about restoring Medici luster, and reorienting foreign policy. Florence now tilted to France. Ferdinando consolidated his own authority by weakening a powerful group known locally as "the Florentines" (an old guard of his brother's supporters). In something of a purge, many lost positions or favored status (including Bardi) to "the Romans" (men Ferdinando knew in Rome or Florentines who had been disgruntled under Francesco and had gone abroad). However, Grand Duke Ferdinando I also faced problems that his late brother had not caused. The population of Tuscany had risen by over a third in the previous four decades, bad weather plagued the territory beginning in 1589, and crop failures due to flooding led to food shortages and rising prices. Crime rose too. Strong responses to this bevy of difficulties were needed, and this reinforced Ferdinando I's own absolutist instincts.[44]

His government, according to Robert Dallington, a visitor who surveyed Tuscany in 1596, was "despotic." This Englishman characterized the ruler physically as "of stature mean, of color of complexion brown, by age grizzled, of body corpulent."[45] Whatever his girth, the duke was effective politically, and all "matters of state" were dependent "absolutely and plenarily . . . upon his will and pleasure." Darlington did register discontent among Florentines, although they expressed it solely in private. They had "fresh in their minds their former liberties" while they bore "heavy on their backs their present yoke." Switching his physiological metaphors, the Tuscan state, wrote Dallington, was like a "stomach weakened so much by purging, as there is now nothing left but melancholy."[46] The body politic had its problems.

Ferdinando I relinquished his status as cardinal and in 1589 married Christine of Lorraine. This was a kind of nuptial balance of powers since the bride's family had ties to Spain and she was also granddaughter of (recently deceased) Catherine de' Medici in Paris. Festivities for this occasion were designed by Bardi, even though his own status was waning because of his past ties to Francesco. He shared responsibilities with Emilio de' Cavalieri, a Roman-born aristocrat who was a Ferdinando I loyalist and also a composer. He had been beckoned to Florence by the new grand duke to serve as inspector-general of arts and artists. In the next years, his service would often be political as well as artistic. He returned to Rome on numerous occasions to gather intelligence reports there, especially after several popes died in rapid succession in the early 1590s. Cavalieri was dispatched to marshal support among cardinals for pro-Tuscan—and anti-Spanish—candidates for pontiff.[47] The Holy See stabilized finally with Clement VIII's selection as pope. He came from a lesser Florentine clan, and arrived on the papal throne, in Darlington's words, "against the good will" of Ferdinando. Nonetheless, the grand duke retained influence in the papal court, especially through bribery.[48] Bardi became Clement's aide, and Caccini joined the Camerata's founder as his secretary.

When Cavalieri was in Rome in the 1590s he often lived across the street from aging Girolamo Mei, and he played his own important role in the birth of opera by composing semidramatic musical pastorals in the "representative style." After the wedding of Maria de' Medici in fall 1600, Caccini replaced Cavalieri as Ferdinando's musical director. Cavalieri was embittered, feeling he had not received sufficient recognition as originator of the "new music."

Most important among Cavalieri's musical works was *The Play of the Body and Soul (Rappresentatione di Anima, et di Corpo)*, a dramatic, sacred oratorio. Its libretto by Agostino Manni, a priest, was recited in a song-like way and in its Counter-Reformation themes and monodic style we hear distant echoes of that brief session concerned with music at Trent. It contrasted this-worldly existence, with its brevity and materialism, to God's glory and prospects of everlasting life. It was presented to acclaim, especially by Cardinals, at least twice in Rome at Carnival time in February 1600. This was, however, the same month in which the church made a somewhat different kind of statement about body and soul in Rome: the Inquisition burned philosopher Giordano Bruno alive there for heresy. It was some nine months before *Euridice* was staged in Florence and eleven years after the wedding celebrations for Ferdinando I and Christine, which included an important anticipation of opera.

VII.

The marriage took place by proxy in Blois in February 1589, and the bride then went, with great ceremony, south to her husband in Florence. Three weeks of celebration came upon her arrival. There were prayers and jousts, theater, music, and "animal baiting." A high point of these cultured occurrences, it seems, was the dismembering of a mule by a lion.[49] The principal theatrical event was a comedy about mistaken identities by the Siena humanist, Girolamo Bargagli. A reported three thousand people saw it at the Uffizi theater, which had opened three years earlier. *La Pellegrina* (The Female Pilgrim) had a tangled design. Drusilla, a virtuous woman, comes to Pisa disguised as a pilgrim. She looks for her love, Lucrezio. He had believed her dead and is now engaged unhappily to another. But his betrothed loves and is pregnant by yet someone else. The plot's coiling threads offer assorted intrigues. Finally, Drusilla casts off her cloak, reveals herself, and everyone lives happily ever after with the appropriate partner. In the original version, commissioned a decade earlier, Drusilla was Spanish. By the time it was revised for the 1589 extravaganza by the author's brother (Bargagli had died), Drusilla was French. Her native land had changed, as had Medici alliances. She remained, of course, righteous and so Christine was honored. If viewers tried also to tease a discreet message from this story, it might have been this: scrambled worlds, say, those of unstable republics or, a principate headed by an inappropriate couple (like Francesco and Bianca), can be set aright when the ruling clan's crown adorns the proper head who is in an apt union (Ferdinando and Christine).

Pellegrina is a work of modest consequence except for its place in the genesis of opera because of six *intermedi* interspersed throughout its presentation. An *intermedio* (or *intermezzo*) was a kind of interlude. It was usually comprised of drama and music presented between acts of plays at Renaissance festive events. *Intermedi* gave audiences sumptuous marvels and diverting exclamation points. They might include instrumental music, polyphonic madrigals, and inevitably had cheerful endings. They commented on the stage events as well as on the world. Not only did they become increasingly elaborate and self-standing, but often more significant and interesting than the plays they attended.

The themes of the *intermedi* of 1589 were harmony and hierarchy. They displayed the powerful ways of music—and, by allusion (sometimes much more than allusion) to the Medici. Music, they showed, was inscribed in the universe as what the ancients called "the harmony of the spheres"— spinning orbs that made up the cosmos. The harmony was also inscribed in human affairs. It is that old idea that goes back to the Pythagoreans and Plato. Boethius, the early sixth-century Christian philosopher and political figure whose writings on music were of great influence for centuries, asked, "How could it possibly be that such a swift heavenly machine should move silently in its course?" (He echoed words by Cicero.) Humans might not perceive the sounds of this *musica mundana*, but they could hear them in music in their own world.⁵⁰

Bardi and Cavalieri had several collaborators. Ottavio Rinuccini joined Bardi in writing most of the texts. Among the composers were two innovative young men whom we have encountered at the premiere of *Euridice*. One was Peri, a young noble born in 1561.⁵¹ This sometime businessman and property-owner was acclaimed for his exquisite voice (he fancied himself an "Orphic singer") and musical capabilities. The other was Caccini. Additional composers also contributed. The creators of the *intermedi* of 1589 thus included many of the same people who would craft the first operas.

We can see among them the rivalries for which opera would become notorious over centuries—jealousies among singers, composers, librettists, and impresarios. Caccini would be Peri's archrival in composing songs in the new "representational style," and later in setting *Euridice*. Of course, Cavalieri claimed his due. Another future librettist, it seems, took part in 1589 as well, but in the orchestra. This was Alessandro Striggio the Younger, who played viol. He would be Monteverdi's collaborator on *Orfeo* in Mantua a decade and a half later. (Also playing may have been his father, madrigal composer Alessandro the Elder, who divided his time between service to the Medici and his native Mantua.)

INTERMEDIO (I)

The *intermedi* of 1589 were extravagant, as befit an august matrimony that meant to make a political statement. Some sixty singers and fifty instrumentalists participated that May evening. Varied musical styles accompanied the words. The texts derived from ancient sources, and one scholar remarks that, "Count Bardi put such high demands on his audiences that . . . only classical philologists could have followed him."[1] This may be an overstatement since a sufficient number of spectators undoubtedly knew some of the myths that were used and the *intermedi* provided a kind of commentary on recent Florentine history.

Viewers could have gleaned that godlike rule brought harmony, even if equilibrium—enabled by proper hierarchy—had to be restored now and then. Interspersed though the performance, the *intermedi* comprised a coherent, albeit jumpy, political allegory; examples of a few show us how. The first and the last drew from Plato's *The Republic* and *The Laws*. Justice, for this philosopher, resided in harmony; everything and everyone, from macrocosm to microcosm, in the divine and in the human order, had to be in proper place. *The Republic*'s utopia was dedicated to this vision, positing three classes of humanity, each with inherent, different propensities corresponding to appropriate tasks. Since reason predominated in the "gold" race, its members were philosopher-kings. Courage characterized auxiliaries, and so the "silver" race defended the state. Appetite animated the "Bronze" class; its members would be productive workers. In this division of labor, the right notes struck together. The universe's harmony was displayed at the end of *The Republic* in the "Myth of Er." It told of a soldier who returns from death to describe, quite literally, a harmonic macrocosm of whirling spheres.

All of Plato's claims do not appear overtly in the opening intermedio, *named appropriately "The Harmony of the Spheres."* Er does not materialize, but Harmony herself did come forth to sing in stately, monodic coloratura that she comes from the heavens to escort the sirens. She acclaims the "noble pair" (the grand duke and new duchesse, that is). The figures of Necessity and her daughters, the Three Fates—past, present, future—emerge and planets (a choir) follow on spherical paths, a siren spinning on each, intoning a different note, creating, altogether, a totality: "We, as we sing, make the celestial spheres turn gently."[2] Here, the universe is as it should be, and what is heavenly ought to be rendered in earthly concord embodied by the new ducal couple. After all, harmony (*ΑΡΜΟΝΙΑ*) comes from *Ar* (*ΑΡ*) which means "fit."[3]

But another intermedio *tells audiences what happens when human hubris upsets equilibrium.* Rinuccini gives us a (reinvented) tale from Ovid's *Metamorphoses* in which the arrogant daughters of Pierus challenge the Muses, offspring of gods, to a song contest. These "Pierides" crow that their song cannot be equaled; they are driven by pride, a belief that their voices can defeat deities and overturn the natural order. (Ovid recounts how they deride the Muses as deceivers of the masses by means of fakery in rhyme.) Each side has a "champion," and one of the Pierides sings of primordial war between giants and gods, describing giants chasing terrified gods who take on disguises to protect themselves. The Muses are supposed to draw conclusions, but some in the audience might have noted that poets in the age of Augustus often compared these "events" to Rome's civil wars; singing of them in 1589 again identified Augustus's peacemaking with the new Medici groom. For then Calliope, Muse of Poetry, and, not incidentally, mother of Orpheus, sings on behalf of her sisters. It is easy, in the end, for the assigned judges, a chorus of Nymphs, to choose the winner. The Muses, after all, are goddesses of the arts. The Pierides, foolish in their challenge, are transformed into prattling magpies, birds that mimic. That is, they change into imitators of humans, three steps away from true art and natural beauty—and from the Muses. Is a (subtle) political message conveyed? Haughty Pierides are to Muses as republicans are to Medici. Pretenders must be punished; Muses—and also natural, godlike rulers—ought not to be challenged.

The rightful place of gods, and by extension, earthly hierarchy, is presented in the heroism of a youthful Apollo in the next intermedio. Rinuccini took this myth from Ovid too, and his "Battle between the Python and Apollo" would have an additional significance since he used it again a few years later to create *Dafne*. In the *intermedio*, the people of Delos appeal to Jove for rescue. A "cruel monster" terrorizes their lives. A golden god, Apollo, is sent and he slays the serpent. Delians gather round him, dancing and singing homage to the "invincible hand" of the "sovereign god." Animalistic irrationality is defeated by order, by light, by art—and perhaps even by an "adolescent" Orpheus, as one scholar proposes.[4] Since the Medici associated themselves with Apollo, one can read the defeat by him of a chaos-producing python as the vanquishing by the Medici of chaos-producing republicans or, indeed, of any inclination to dangerous populism and emotionalism among Florentines. Guicciardini had written that, "To speak of the people is really to speak of a mad animal gorged with a thousand and one errors and confusions . . ."[5] Rampagers must be killed or tamed. A more immediate political interpretation might be added. The growth of crime in Tuscany due to economic problems in Francesco's waning years, and his increasingly distracted governance, had to be addressed. Ferdinando did so quickly with new laws against banditry. Like Apollo, he sought order in the face of wild forces. A few people in the audience in May 1589 might well have imagined a parallel between the achievement of the golden god and the reestablishment of firm rule by the former cardinal.

If the first intermedio *envisaged perfection, like in Plato's* The Republic, *the final one was prompted by passages in his last major work,* The Laws, *in which the message changed.* The second best, rather than utopia, had now become the aspiration. In *The Republic*, Plato imagined correspondence between cosmic and human harmony in an ideal state directed by the reason of philosopher-kings. In *The Laws* he accepted instead governance by sagacious laws, and these had to shape virtuous people. While he would have banned or constrained poets in *The Republic* and was wary in it of music's impact, "The Athenian," his principle spokesman in *The Laws*, says that the gods, "in their compassion for the hardships incident to our human lot," gave to humanity festivals, the muses, rhythms, and melody. That, however, does not mean that sensuous sounds should overwhelm our reason, Plato's worry in *The Republic*. The Athenian defines rhythm as "order in movement," pitch as "order in articulation," and their combination as "choric art."[6] Order yields art; stability remains all-important. Instead of giving a lesson about the rule of law as opposed to philosopher-kings, this *intermedio* presented an assembly of gods celebrating "The Descent of Apollo and Bacchus with Rhythm and Harmony," that is, pagan deities bestowing these two gifts—art and order—on humanity. The gods and muses sing of celestial bounties brought to earth and—the motif returns—of a new golden age at hand, thanks to Ferdinando, the "great hero." He will restore "royal custom" of "benign laws."[7] Evil will be banished by a proud, "new sun."

The *intermedi* look backward and forward as a story of falls and redemption. Harmony comes to earth at the beginning and end; we see her disturbance when humans try to displace deities. We have seen a god associated with the Medici and heaven's bestowal of harmony and rhythm—a new measure—to humanity. Heaven is on Tuscany's side, at least when Tuscans embrace the right order according to the Medici ideology. The *intermedi* suggest hope for musical art as well. The more an *intermedio* takes on its own life, the more it becomes opera-like.

Chapter 3

LAWS AND LAURELS

Even though Florence's principate did not give rise to major political philosophers in the late sixteenth century, its intellectuals knew well the words "reason of state." They had been taken, somewhat imprecisely, to summarize ideas of troublesome Machiavelli and they also comprised the title of an influential book whose Piedmont-born author, Giovanni Botero, had been in contact with Scipione Ammirato, the Medici court historian. By happenstance, the dedication of Botero's book *Reason of State* was signed in Rome on May 10, 1589, the same week as the ducal wedding celebrations in Florence. In it, this Jesuit-trained advocate of the Counter-Reformation recounted how he had traveled to "the courts of kings and great princes, in Italy and beyond the Alps" and found "reason of state" to be "a constant subject of discussion."[1] It was associated with what, in Botero's view, were the disagreeable perspectives of Machiavelli and Tacitus. Ammirato, who demurred from Botero's dislike of Tacitus, wrote in 1594 that the words "reason of state" were "on our lips all day."[2] Three years later, another commentator, Apollinaire de' Calderini, declared *Reason of State* to be "the book of the day."[3]

Why? That political form—usually called the "modern European state" —had been progressing fitfully, centralizing coercive authority over territorial expanses that had been accustomed to a looser political order of local and ecclesiastical powers, and customs, kings and popes, nobles and bishops, lords and serfs (although the latter social relation was not characteristic of the city-states in which opera took shape). But did this modern state—indeed, politics itself—have its own peculiar "logic"? Now, the questions become explicit. Did this logic subordinate, inevitably, local to centralized coercion? Did it push aside ethical judgments to strengthen a *patria*? Did a statesman, to be effective, have no choice but to follow it— even though it so often seemed brutal and at odds with Christian preaching? Did politics have its own nature and rationality? If "yes," then there was foul truth in a good many of Machiavelli's ideas, most famously (or notoriously, depending on one's view) the patriotic ruthlessness prescribed in

The Prince. Reactions to, suspicions about, and threads of influence deriving from this political philosopher traversed Florence's intellectual world and beyond throughout the century. Sometimes the threads were very noticeable; oftentimes they were hidden in a society's cloth, or in between the lines of a text or by citations from Tacitus as surrogate. Florentines—especially Florentines—knew well that Machiavelli's own story was controversial. He may have written a book filled with seemingly callous counsel to a prince but his preference was really for a republic with "good laws and good arms." Perspectives like Machiavelli's vexed papal sensibilities as the Roman church struggled against Protestantism. Botero, with a faithful eye toward Catholic powers—Rome, Spain, the Holy Roman Empire—offered a reformulation of "reason of state." The Roman church's claim to represent universal morality, he argued, was not necessarily at odds with the apparently unforgiving imperatives of statecraft. Piety and politics were amenable one to the other provided that human laws were ultimately considered subordinate to divine and natural ones. This kind of "reason of state" had obvious ideological attractions for temporal rulers like the Medici. They were, after all, Counter-Reformation grand dukes, loyal to their church but unfazed by the use of vicious methods to impose their rule and to keep competing powers at bay.

Florentine political autonomy had been asserted over many centuries, and one means was legal argument (that actually reappears in *Euridice*).[4] A key idea came from the revival of interest in ancient Roman law in late medieval and early modern Europe that we mentioned earlier. Florentine lawyers fastened onto the word Roman lawyers used for emperor: *"princeps"* or "first citizen." They pointed, for one example, to an ancient jurist who proposed that the *princeps* was "not bound by the laws." A ruler could diverge from them, if he saw fit.[5] The appeal of such a formulation to princes seeking to impose centralized power is evident. *"Princeps"* could, however, harbor ambiguities. What if the political community as a whole, rather than an individual, was assigned this title? Instead of affirming a single prince, the people of a given territory could be defined as the ultimate source of political legitimacy. Consider the differences among some claims made in three successive centuries. In the thirteenth century, a Bologna-based commentator on Roman law named Accursius asserted that a *princeps* is "loosed" from—he meant not bound by—laws, whether made by himself or others. He "subjects himself" only "by his own will." In the next century, a theorist named Bartolus of Sassoferato argued that a political community (a *"civitas"*) was created by a combination of two factors: a ruler's written decrees and customary laws. The latter, strictures accepted by the people, were established over time. Extending this kind of reasoning, a prominent lawyer, Antonio Strozzi, claimed in 1517 that Florence as a whole was *"princeps,"* a collective body that recognized no superior.[6] Florentine legal theory wiggled in a republican way since, officially, there was a superior. In 1576 Vettori's Latin translation of and commentary on Aristotle's *Politics* appeared. Aristotle insisted famously that man is a political animal who cannot live outside a polity, and Vettori's explanation of one particular phrase in the text can be taken to suggest, perhaps with some ambiguity, the kind of thinking we have been tracing. It can be the case, he wrote, that "the people becomes a monarch." This means, explained the translator, that the people come together and become "one man."[7]

Whatever forms its government took, then, Florence had a right to autonomy within the Holy Roman Empire. This claim could, however, be taken further, indeed subversively. If a political community as a whole has a right to autonomy, ought not its members have a right to self-rule? Ought they not to be final authorizers of laws under which they live? A "yes" answer to these questions implies that a legitimate government must be a republic. Conflict over issues like these played out constantly in centuries of jostling over Florence's political structures. Power shifted about among executive institutions and magistracies, courts and legislative councils. Who had the right or need to consent to what? All this was backdrop to Florentine talk of law in the late sixteenth century along with the furies of the late fifteenth and early sixteenth centuries. And then came the relative stability of the Medici restoration after that three-year republic was overthrown in 1530 (thanks to outside arms—those of the emperor and pope). Even though Alessandro de' Medici's rule was cut short, he fashioned a kind of "constitutional settlement." The realm became officially a duchy. Within its borders, the urban and commercial aristocracy was, in principle, given considerable sway. But after Alessandro's assassination, the new duke proceeded to undermine patrician powers. Cosimo I, we know, was often identified in Medici propaganda with Augustus, ancient Rome's peacemaking emperor and the two rulers were comparable in another important way. The duke's secure order left Florentine elites with titles, but little more. Magistrates became increasingly toothless functionaries.[8] Order meant that a focused voice resonated within a realm; everyone and everything else had to be accompaniment.

The voice came to pronounce a particular text: law. "Who rules?" pointed eventually to another, impersonal question: "What reigns?" In the 1580s,

Botero had been in Paris during the intense religious strife there. He was impressed by a book published in 1576 by a French legal philosopher who advocated political absolutism and whose ideas became vastly influential. Jean Bodin's *Six Books of the Republic* argued that the key attribute of a state— that which gave it "sovereignty"—was an unchallengeable power to make basic laws. Otherwise, chaos and civil strife were inevitable, as had been the case in France where religious warriors had fought each other ferociously in battles that also overlapped—or underpinned—struggles over jurisdiction between the monarchy and local powers. A peaceful realm, Bodin proposed, required a single source of laws, and subjects had no right of consent. Sovereign power was indivisible. Bodin spoke of monarchy ("royal monarchy") as a "republic" (that latter word has a broad connotation, perhaps best rendered as a "commonwealth") in which a prince had absolute sovereignty.[9] If your laws required approval by anyone else, you were no sovereign.

At different points in his argument, Bodin (obviously echoing Plato) exploited musical metaphors like "consonance" and "discord" to elucidate his ideas. He even compared a musician's task to that of making a good commonwealth.[10] At first glance, Bodin's sovereign seems like the solo voice that distinguished monody. Of course it has accompaniment (the nobility or bureaucrats in the political case, instruments in the musical one). When he elaborated on what justice meant he suggested more, however, since like Plato he spoke of it as "harmony" and his language approximated a technical musical sense of the term. Again: when a student of music uses the word harmony, it describes what comes about when different tones sound simultaneously, as in a chord. If agreeable (to most ears), the combination is "consonant." If not, it is "dissonant" and the joined sounds seem off or unfinished. And a progression of chords becomes "dissonant" if it seems to call for "resolution" by means of a pleasing, completing consonant sound. Now consider Bodin's political words. "If all citizens were kings," he wrote, "there would be no king: nor harmony if the sweet intermix of diverse chords (*"les accords diverse"*), which render harmony pleasant, is reduced to the same tone."[11] A perfect government realizes "harmonic justice" by a right arrangement of "nobles and commons, rich and poor." Of course Bodin recognizes that there ought to be "some advantage" to aristocrats, but most important, he explains, is having a "rational" king (or prince) as the embodiment of unity, "exalted above all." When notes strike alone, he explained, they may have distinct charm. Yet consonance doesn't exist unless they sound together; that, in turn, means that they must be different. A sovereign reconciles subjects with each other, forestalling social dissonance.[12]

Bodin's book went through numerous printings. A Latin version spread its influence in 1586. It appeared in Italian two years later, but its impact on Italy seems to have come about more due to another now-forgotten book published in 1592 by a sometime diplomat for the church with ties to Mantua's rulers named Antonio Possevino. He was sharply critical of Bodin but this was less important than the fact that it made the French thinker's ideas known.[13]

II.

Botero seemed to echo comments by Bodin when he spoke of "Medici wisdom in matters of state" and singled out Cosimo I for praise. Perhaps knowledge of Florentine troubles of the 1580s led Botero to mention Francesco as inheritor of a title, but then to laud his brother Ferdinando as a man who was grand duke "rightly" because of his "qualities" as well as his "descent."[14] Ruler and state were still inseparable—but this identity was becoming more complex as separation of person and power-structure evolved. Botero's key question was: Can a Christian ruler be above the law? Yes, he answered, when a ruler deployed "reason of state" to sustain secure government. "Nothing," he elaborated, "is more essential to kingship than the administration of law," and the monarch alone was its maker. Only the ruler defined what was good for the kingdom. Lower officials were apt to be swept away by passions and these had to be "bound" by written pre-scriptions. "Ordinary" reason produces "ordinary law." A ruler's "reason of state," however, stood above both. Then came the important caveat (which Bodin also asserted): political reasons could not contradict divine law.[15] Ammirato argued likewise in his writings on Tacitus. The ancient Romans were devout, he insisted. The dictates of intelligent rule need not gainsay God's laws even if, as he acknowledged, a prince had to act sometimes in ways that contravened ordinary notions of justice. Of course, the prince and nobody else could determine if this needed to be done. Ammirato thus sought "reason of state" for his Medici patrons by fastening it to Counter-Reformation contentions much like those of Botero.[16]

Here we return to Lipsius, whose worldview, taken as a whole, is usually identified as "neo-Stoic," a Christianized rendition of ideas associated with ancient Hellenistic and Roman philosophical schools. He argued that the external, material matters of life were inconsequential and amidst all the historical tempests around us, we need to find what is meaningful within us, in particular our relation to God. The most valuable characteristic we can cultivate is "constancy," a word that reappeared repeatedly in operas in the ensuing centuries. Its meaning combined the qualities of steadfastness and fidelity in our lives, values, and pursuits. This perspective didn't imply that the state—an external means of imposing order—was immaterial. Its stability was urgent in bleeding times, for this allowed people to pursue the important (spiritual) things. In July 1589, less than three months after Botero's dedication of his book and the ducal wedding in Florence, Lipsius published his *Politica*, with its depiction of the masses in need of a firm pilot. This, like his book *On Constancy*, would be enormously influential, although banned by the church until 1596. Its author, based then in Leiden, was suspect in Florence because he had changed his professed religion more than once. He was accused of a great evil: Machiavellianism. Yet Lipsius also praised Cosimo I in his book, which he dedicated to keepers of order. He had differences with Bodin, but was in accord with him on a basic point: the ruler's first task is to keep domestic peace. Moreover, Lipsius, like Bodin, used a musical metaphor to make his political point. Order was comparable to musical accord; "If strings are out of tune, you don't tear them out in anger, but step by step bring them back in harmony."[17]

Political discord has multiple causes, yet one that recurs like a motif through the minds and writings of so many proponents of stable authority is the masses. The masses are compared over and over again to wild animals. Sometimes this comparison came with recognition of how painful, widespread social suffering affected the poor, but often these authors simply look askance at populist threats to the state of things. Botero called the poor prone to "violence and unruliness," yet he also was very sour when it comes to abuses by the rich. Since the masses suffered from much material want, they knew "no law."[18] Just a few years earlier, Bardi's friend Salviati compared the "multitude" to a balloon. When it inflated, it pushed everything. Better, obviously, for it to be punctured, shriveled, nonintrusive. The masses, Salviati wrote, switching metaphors, were like a "ferocious" but headless animal. They would follow any leader.[19] For Cavriana, that other Florentine commentator on Tacitus, the masses were like a multiheaded beast.[20] Implications of the various metaphors—blown-up balloon, headless animal, multiheaded beast—are shared, even if images and metaphors don't quite match. The conclusion: The People need the right head, to be directed by a single authority that lays down proper law, makes proper sense of things, and maintains tranquility. Otherwise, the People were prone to brutish, misery-causing behavior. If they are headless, a dangerous republican brain might land atop their shoulders. If they are multiheaded, they might charge in all directions, tearing the body politic apart. When in their right senses, however, they turn to those who should rule, those who slay political pythons.

We have seen how these images share lineages that go back to antiquity and reappeared often in varied ways and throughout the 1580s and 1590s. The poem (or libretto) for *Dafne* was first drafted apparently in 1594, the same year in which Ammirato declared that "reason of state" was ever present in intellectual conversation. Cavriana's work, dedicated to Duke Ferdinand, was dated 1597, the year before *Dafne*'s first performance in the Corsi Palazzo. Corsi invited a small coterie to behold terrified Delians and the feral Python. They saw the Shepherds and Nymphs implore the Gods for aid. They saw Apollo solve the problem by dispatching the serpent with his arrows. Were the Delians meant to evoke the Florentine People? Educated subjects of the Medici might easily have gleaned this, even if they never reflected on the confluence in their times of ideas, currents, and images evoked in Tacitus and Seneca, Botero, Bodin, and Lipsius, Salviati, Ammirato, and Cavriana, among others. Order and bestiality; these were the alternatives, one embodied in a prince (or a Christian grand duke), the second in republicanism or the readily agitated, easily misled masses. The first brought consonance, the other discord. The former could be discerned in Medici Florence; the latter throughout strife-torn Europe, especially France, where the issue was not only republicanism but Catholics against Protestants.

III.

Corsi and Rinuccini asked Peri to set *Dafne* to music as a monodic experiment.[21] "Ovid" himself stepped forth in a prologue to announce that "the ancient style" would be used to show how perilous it is to disparage "the power of love." After Apollo slays the python, he meets Venus and her son Cupid. The young Sun God berates the younger Love God with male bluster. You, sightless little boy, shoot arrows blindly and can attain no glories. You beget inconsequential love affairs while a Sun God sees, aims, strikes. Cupid responds spitefully, urged on by his mother, who warns Apollo that he will learn it is "risky to mock him/ even if he is only a child, nude and blind." [22] This is proven quickly. Cupid's arrow flies, strikes Apollo, and he is in love hopelessly on seeing Dafne. Things have changed. Force is not the only power. Previously, Apollo could reestablish stability for others by slaying an irrational brute; he saw and acted with purpose. Chasing a nymph, he loses his bearings. Emotional torrents drive him.

His pursuit is, of course, in vain. Dafne is a follower of Diana, the goddess of hunting. In Ovid, Cupid shoots not just a gold arrow into Apollo but a lead one into Dafne; it numbs her to the god's advances. She rejects Apollo for another important reason in the opera. A nymph is barred by inviolable law (*inviolabil legge*) from mating with a divinity.[23] These are the same terms that Galilei challenged when he argued against Zarlino and unbending musical laws. Yet in *Dafne*, the points seem different. They tell us that there are ultimate ups and downs; there are external rules that thwart feelings, even those of a god. Banned is what today might be called interracial or societal promiscuity. A god's companion must be appropriate, not just beautiful. The nymph stands by her vows; as the god bears down on her, she transforms into a laurel rather than yield. Apollo laments but a god, like a ruler, must rise finally above personal matters.

As this proto-opera concludes, he places branches from the laurel, fashioned in a circlet, on his brow. He dedicates it as a crown that symbolizes esteem for poets and "the greatest monarchs." Doleful, yes, but still a god, he stands before the audience, holding a bow and a lyre, surrounded by choruses of nymphs and shepherds. This ending pointed toward the future, but also evokes the past that gave luster to Florence's contemporary ruler. The laurel evoked for Florentines the two peacemaking principates, that of Augustus (he was, in his day, called a son of Apollo), and, of course, their own Medicis. The Medici allusion was subdivided as Cosimo had fostered a "myth of the two Cosimos." The first was the "Father of Florence" and the second himself. The laurel implied both Medici political regeneration and commitment to art. It had been a symbol of Lorenzo the Magnificent too, and for later Medici, we know, it signaled an era of well-being.[24] Moreover, *Dafne*'s pastoral setting contrasted to Europe's brutal realities, all while allowing for characters that did not seem absurdly artificial singing a mix of words and music. A Florentine protomusicologist, Giovanni Battista Doni, commented that pastoral language was melodious. Its gods, shepherds, and nymphs came from a "remote age when music was natural and speech like poetry."[25] This credibility allowed hints at a variety of things.

Political, Intellectual, and Musical Chronology

1512: Florentine Republic defeated.
1513: Machiavelli writes *The Prince*.
1527: Death of Machiavelli.

1527–30: Short-lived Florentine Republic.

1531–32: Machiavelli's *The Prince* and *Discourses on Livy* published.

1537–74: Cosimo I de' Medici rules Tuscany as duke (from 1569 as grand duke) until his death. His son Francesco I de' Medici is co-regent from 1564.

1560: Pier Vettori, an important Florentine scholar (then living in Rome), publishes his Latin translation of Aristotle's *Poetics*.

1569: The Accademia degli Alterati was founded by young patricians in Florence to discuss cultural and intellectual matters. The horizons of Academy members, it was assumed, were perfected or "altered" by its activities. Many of the experimenters in what becomes early opera will be members. Vettori is a member as well as Girolamo Mei, his student and an influential scholar of ancient music, from a distance (Rome).

1573: Meetings begin of Giovanni de' Bardi's Camerata. Participants in salons in this count's home will debate an array of subjects but there is a particular interest among members, which includes Vincenzo Galilei, in music; its discussions lead to experiments in dramatic music.

1574: Francesco I de' Medici becomes grand duke of Tuscany. Justus Lipsius publishes (in Antwerp) his widely discussed scholarly edition and commentary on Tacitus, including the particularly influential *Annals*. It also includes the "Dialogue on the Orator," which concerned change in rhetorical styles that came with ancient Rome's transformation from a republic to imperial rule.

1576: Bodin's *Six Books of the Republic* published in Paris. Vettori's translation of Aristotle's *Politics* becomes available as does *Reflections and Maxims* by Guicciardini, Machiavelli's important contemporary. His text praises Tacitus astutely but ambiguously. It is published in Paris by a Florentine exile.

1580: Marc-Antoine Muret, an eminent French humanist then in Rome, gives an influential oration on Tacitus advocating the historian's style and methods. (Lipsius had studied with him.)

1581: Vincenzo Galilei's *Dialogue on Ancient and Modern Music* appears. Lipsius publishes an additional and highly influential commentary on Tacitus. Leonardo Salviati, a leading Florentine humanist and friend of Bardi, writes a pro-Medici discourse on Tacitus.

1582: Guicciardini's *Reflections and Maxims* republished in Venice.

1583: Bernardo Davanzati presents part of his translation of Tacitus's *Annals* to the Alterati.

1584: Lipsius's *On Constancy*. Vettori's translation of Aristotle's *Nichomachean Ethics*.

1587: Ferdinando de' Medici returns to Florence from Rome to become grand duke after the death of his brother Francesco I.

1589: Florentine wedding celebrations for Ferdinando I and Christine of Lorraine in May include intermedi during the performance of a play. These are seen by scholars as important antecedents of "drama through music." Among those who contributed to them are Bardi, Rinuccini, Emilio de' Cavalieri, and Giulio Caccini. Alessandro Striggio the Younger, future librettist of Claudio Monteverdi plays strings. Giovanni Botero's *Reason of State* is finished in Rome. Lipsius's major work on politics, *Politica*, is published.

1591: Scipio Ammirato, Medici court historian, reads pro-Medici tract on Tacitus to the Alterati.

1594: Possible writing of the libretto of *Dafne* by poet Ottavio Rinuccini.

1597: Pro-Medici Florentine Filippo Cavriana publishes a book on Tacitus.

1598: The first opera, *Dafne* by Rinuccini, Jacopo Peri and Jacopo Corsi (its patron) is performed as an experiment at Carnival in Corsi's palazzo. It is a product of collaboration within this patrician's circle, one that had overlapped with but also competed with that of Bardi.

1600: Emilio de' Cavalieri's *The Play of the Body and the Soul* presented in Rome. *Euridice* with music by Peri and libretto by Rinuccini performed for the nuptials in Florence of Maria de' Medici and King Henri IV of France. Caccini, a leading figure in "new music," publishes his scoring of Rinuccini's text.

IV.

We left Rinuccini's Orpheus in our first chapter just as he learned of Eurydice's death. His loyal friend, Arcetro the shepherd, recounted at the Pitti Palace how he accompanied Orpheus to the blood-covered meadow where the minstrel-prince—he is called a "demigod" at times—fell on the grass, in tearful dirge. From Adam and Eve to Orpheus and Eurydice, serpents are a source of trouble. Orpheus's father Apollo defeated one, and now the son will seek to redeem what a snake has taken away. This time, love will lead to a path to deliverance. A "superhuman event" occurs. Venus appears in her sapphire chariot. Descend to the "dreaded city," she advises. Pray, shed tears, and sing and perhaps "the soft lament/ that moved Heaven, may yet cause Hell to submit (*pieghi l'inferno ancora*)." "*Piegare*" can mean to submit or to bend; so Orpheus descends, lyre at hand, to bend the "supreme king" of the "horrid fields," ready to pit musical plaint against the rules of Hades.[26] Which powers will prevail? Can music and the emotions it elicits overcome fixed law?

Orpheus calls on the "Shades of Hell" to weep at his loss of Eurydice. "Oh return her soul/ to my sorrowing breast," he grieves.[27] His real addressee, however, is not the shades or the "Infernal Gods." Even if they rallied to him, little would be achieved since their powers, like those of Florentine aristocrats, are minimal. His song aims to persuade Pluto, their king. Orpheus begins his appeal with a vocal bow, as a good orator would, to a sovereign. His plea reminds the sovereign of feelings for his queen. Pluto is effected as well as surprised by Orpheus's audacity. After all, the young singer has come "before his fatal day" to a kingdom that admits of no mercy. But this monarch must deliberate. His concern is law and sovereignty, not solely plaintive emotion. If laws do not apply without exception, says Pluto, they will be discredited. He sings,

> Within the Gates of Hell
> no mortal is allowed to take his stance
> and yet, hearing of your hard fate
> I do not know what new emotion
> softens my breast.
> But most rigid laws,
> laws wrought in hardest diamond
> oppose your pleas, wretched lover.[28]

The King of the Underworld wonders: can I bend my own dictates and still rule? Yes, Orpheus suggests. Real power means that you compel others to do *your* will. A supreme law says: He who is free restrains and rules others. Your will must be exercised above all existing laws.

Orpheus's oratory affects Queen Proserpina, who becomes his ally. So too Pluto's important aide, Charon, who brings new subjects to the king as ferryman of the River Styx. The queen calls on Pluto's "free and unconstrained heart" to respond to "gentle" Orpheus.[29] Hers is a claim for love, but it implies that Pluto, as sovereign, needs nobody's consent to be merciful. Charon radicalizes the case, separating it from love and making it a matter of the king's dominion. He sounds as if posing a question to Ferdinando de' Medici: why ought not Florence's grand duke to have final say in Tuscany just as he sees fit?—as do the rulers of all the contemporary powers surrounding him? A king can bend his own rules for the sake of his power. Charon tells Pluto:

> Jove commands and rules according
> to his own wishes
> Neptune commands the waves
> and creates storms and tempests as he will;
> Should you alone suffer
> to have your higher power restricted
> by a hard law
> and not be the free Lord of this vast Hell?

Charon makes his counsel plain: "O great King, make whatever laws you please."[30] We have already seen another way of making Charon's points: a ruler is "not bound by the laws." (Among Peri's civic assignments would be courts.) Pluto resists. Orpheus's passion impresses but still, how can a king "scorn the laws" of his own realm? Pluto ponders: "To break one's own laws/ is a misuse of power;/ censure and injury are often caused thus." Compassion, counters Orpheus, should move Pluto's will beyond his own laws, for "to ease the anguish of the sorrowful/ is still the noble custom of the royal heart."[31]

Orpheus's argument-in-lament seems to echo or mirror preoccupations of late-sixteenth- century political and legal theorists. Higher laws call on a ruler to temper reason of state. It was, after all, a goddess who led Orpheus to Hades's edge and pointed him on. Rulers, wrote Botero, should not pardon "capriciously," although mercy, in the end, is "the office of the prince." Judges are "bound" by law but the prince, and he alone, "can moderate its rigor and temper its severity with equity." Law must be firm; princely rule needs "regularity in behavior and habits and consistency in manner and government." These qualities are "godlike," yet Botero proposed that there may be merciful exceptions, if they are not at the expense of justice or the state.[32] Lipsius's *Politica* also stressed how laws and their administration had to be steady. Nobody, he wrote, can make laws for a prince, but ignominy results if a ruler orders what he had previously outlawed and forbids what he had commanded.[33] Nonetheless, both justice and clemency are virtues.[34] Indeed, *clementia* is "the most humane" virtue, for "she sets free the guilty, raises up the fallen, and comes to the rescue of those who ruin themselves."[35] Good judgment allows it.

In like spirit, Pluto, as if reading the Flemish neo-Stoic, decides that on this day "pity" will triumph "in the infernal fields." He commands his ministers to lead Orpheus and Eurydice up "to the serene and pure sky above." Hades's minions observe that nothing like this had happened before—pity had never revealed autonomous power in these precincts. Infernal Choruses affirm Orpheus's success. Only a great soul could "strive for such a difficult victory," they sing.[36] Besides, this was none less than the Sun God's son who had come to the dark kingdom. In the final scene, the reunited pair has journeyed out of hell, and Hades's choruses are replaced by pastoral ones. Jubilation now presents a Counter-Reformation theme in mythological setting: law there must be, but love may trump it, bringing resurrection.

And so Tragedy, who opened the opera, proves faithful. Instead of the tale's better-known calamitous denouement in which Orpheus loses Eurydice, here he saves her. The final notes allow the kind of *lieto fine* (happy ending) that was a theatrical staple of the era. Yet *Euridice* did more than entertain guests. This, the second opera, translated political questions into an artistic experiment deploying music's expressive possibilities. Its immediate appeal may have been limited, but a few years later, in another city, that young composer who might have been in the audience at the Pitti Palace returned to the same myth. Monteverdi composed his *Orfeo*.

PART 2:
MANTUA TO VENICE

---

*I am forced to wear a mask, without
which no one can survive in Italy.*

—PAOLO SARPI

Chapter 4

ORPHEUS'S WAYS

The Spirit of Music (*La Musica*) sang at Mantua's ducal palace on February 24, 1607, just before Lent. She began the prologue after a toccata and a ritornello and proceeded to recount her many powers—to comfort despair, to arouse rage, to inflame the coldest heart. Then came that story of Orpheus, whose sweet song, it was said, could "attract wild beasts."[1] This evening, however, differed from earlier experiments in what we now call opera.

The most important distinction was the musical imagination at work. Claudio Monteverdi had paid attention to "new music," including *Euridice*. However, the earlier experiments were surpassed, dramatically so, when he created his "fable in music" in collaboration with librettist Alessandro Striggio the Younger, a man versed in music as well as in politics. (Striggio and Peri were linked to both Florence and Mantua.) In *Orfeo*, we hear Monteverdi becoming an original kind of "musical orator," as one musicologist puts it.[2] Another encapsulates Monteverdi's many dimensions in a flurry of succinct phrases. For him, "words formed themselves musically." He was able "to whip the recitative line into passion" and "harried every available musical means for tension." Declamation brought "sudden halts and spurting cascades of rhythm" together with "precipitous, intense rises and falls of melodic line." Harmonic tensions came from "dissonance between the voice and the chord below." A voice could "range unencumbered above the basso continuo, which all alone provided a simple harmonic support." There was new, expressive liberty in Monteverdi's rhythms, melodies, and use of dissonance.[3]

Moreover, Monteverdi pushed beyond both monody and madrigal, using one with the other together with varied, often intentionally repetitive, musical phrases. He shaped stage events through these, elucidating characters and their actions, adding a pluralistic richness to the singularity of monody's purposes. The goal was still comprehensible stage drama, as with the Florentines, but there were novel musical and political textures. Monteverdi composed in a duchy that had no tumultuous republican history and had not undergone heady transitions between popular and princely regimes. As we look closely at *Orfeo*, we will find in it a political story for princes who would be rulers.

Carnival, rather than a political event, occasioned *Orfeo*'s premiere. Its creation was by request of Francesco Gonzaga, son of Mantua's grand duke. *Orfeo* was simply a court diversion presented in a lesser power in the northern part of the politically messy Italian peninsula. Mantua, positioned among competitive neighbors, was long concerned to enhance its cultural eminence as a means to political prestige. Art was also the great pleasure of the Gonzagas, Mantua's ruling clan for some three centuries.

Monteverdi was born a subject of the Spanish Habsburgs in 1567 in Cremona, a provincial town not far from Milan. His musical education began early and by age fifteen he published motets as well as the first of what would be eight books of madrigals. Mantua became his home at the age of twenty-three or twenty-four after its duke, Vincenzo I, hired him to play viol at court. Monteverdi spent his life in close proximity to political men, his well-being was always beholden to them, and he observed their world keenly. After Mantua, he spent the rest of his life as director of music at San Marco in Venice, an aristocratic republic. His librettists were very sophisticated. Striggio had studied law and while he remained active in court's artistic events in ensuing decades, he would serve in secretarial, political, and diplomatic posts for five dukes, eventually becoming chancellor. Striggio's text for *Orfeo* displayed an astute sense of how to provide words for a composer. A cultured Renaissance finesse and honed political intelligence are at work in it. The collaborators returned the Orpheus myth to its best-known version. Yes, Pluto bends his law, but he sets out his famous condition—don't look back—and the young singer will be unable to fulfill it. He loses her. Orpheus cannot live up to his own promise as a prince, who must look forward.

II.

After the prologue, *Orfeo* begins in rustic joy, and it is familiar. We hear that the demigod is happy with his beautiful love. But, alas! Eurydice had gone into a meadow, where a viper's fang pierced her foot. She died, her love's name on her lips.[4]

Venus does not visit the Mantuan Orpheus as she did his Florentine persona. Instead, Orpheus turns to another goddess—Hope. He goes with her to the Underworld's edge. He asks her to escort him on. She says no for—

that word reappears—stern law (*legge*) is written in stone at the entrance. They are Dante's famous words: "Leave all hope behind, ye who enter."[5] If Orpheus has courage, he must make his own way without supernatural Hope. His hopes depend on his own doing. Facing this challenge, Orpheus embodies many implications of Renaissance humanism. Monteverdi provides a fanfare to suggest his nobility and Orpheus now faces Charon, that lower-tier god who ferries the newly dead from time-bound reality to a timeless one. In *Euridice*, Charon lends his voice to Orpheus's plea, once the young singer stands before Pluto. Striggio's Charon, however, is no royal counselor; he is simply a fearsome servant of hell's sovereign. He wonders if Orpheus plots against his "master." Perhaps he has designs on Pluto's consort? Of course, Orpheus has no interest besides Eurydice.

In the end, disobedient passions undo him.

But not yet. In his first trial, Orpheus must convince Charon to let him cross over. He displays rhetorical dexterity, appealing to Charon's pride: "formidable God," it is in your power to help me. His declamatory aria, "*Possente spirto*" (O, Powerful Spirit) is one of the most celebrated musical moments of this work. Brilliant vocal and instrumental flourishes highlight his pleas while organ and *chitarrone* (a large lute) serve as continuo instruments. Orpheus insists that song alone is his weapon, a plea for compassion his sole purpose. Although all this pleases ornery Charon, he will not succumb. Compassion is for the weak.[6] Orpheus also will not yield. He sings that he is trapped between an ideal he cannot reach, that is, heavenly life with his love, and hell—into which he is refused passage in order to save her. He elaborates now, but by means of his lyre. Monteverdi gives us a *sinfonia* for this, to remarkable effect. Adamant Charon is lulled to sleep by Orpheus's music, allowing the youth to move—to slip cross the River Styx, from one jurisdiction to another. Monteverdi associates Orpheus with bowed and plucked strings (after all, he plays a lyre), but "*Possente spirto*" shifts from strings to cornets, an empowering sound for a human being, while Charon slumbers.

He sings sorrowfully on entering the other world: "Return my love to me, Gods of Hell."[7] As he descends, they respond in humanist chorus. This young man is daring, remarkably so—does he not reveal human powers? "Nothing is attempted by man in vain," is their commentary. Even nature, continue the Infernal Spirits, is defenseless as man ploughs and makes the earth fruitful. Their acclaim goes on and Monteverdi accentuates, indeed crowns it with a *sinfonia* in brass—instruments used in future opera in association with the Underworld—and in this one they bring us to the next act (by now, we are in the fourth). It is evident there that Orpheus's appeal is, in fact, ineffectual. He is, again, like a Roman in Tacitus's day, or a Florentine in that of the Medici, or a Mantuan in the Gonzaga's court. Only one will matters, that of the lawmaker. Orpheus must present his case before Lord Pluto. Here he has support from Queen Proserpina. His lament moves her. She urges compassion, calling (as she did in *Euridice*) on her husband to recall their own love.

Pluto will be responsive, but in a way that tells us about more than love's sway. Hades is still no egalitarian republic; proper hierarchy is revealed on its frontiers and within its domains. Charon is the border god who simply carries out immigration laws. Emigration is never an option for Pluto's subjects. The mere fact that Charon dozes at Orpheus's song shows that this subordinate is unsuited to a counselor's task. He does not recognize in Orpheus's voice a potential challenge by a great orator to a basic rule that secures his sovereign's (and any) realm—the determination of who is and who is not to be within its powers. The Infernal Chorus may hail Orpheus, but its members are no autonomous nobility. Their voices may at first impress an outsider—or the audience—but their ghostly breath has no authority. They are humanity's eloquent advocates in *Orfeo* and are actually powerless.

Proserpina invokes what seems to be a high ideal, compassion, for the nether kingdom. Pluto, however, is sovereign, and he understands that ruling has its own rationality. She wants something beyond reason of state to govern his decision. The terms of the argument he conducts with himself are familiar from Machiavelli, Lipsius, Bodin, and Botero. He wonders aloud: How can I be flexible? I can accept that clemency is a virtue. I will not, however, ruin my rule. I cannot simply dole out clemency, bowing to affectionate appeal. While Pluto does not use explicitly the vocabulary and ideas of all the debates on reason of state, they flavor how he formulates his decision. "Immutable Fate" (*immutabil fato*) argues against you, he tells Proserpina.[8] It is not just a matter of fate, which is linked obviously to death; it is immutable law in his kingdom. He says: I cannot dismiss it but love for you convinces me to bend it. But bend only. He can do so because he is king, because his will is law, as it was in *Euridice*. Yet here he is more circumspect politically—shrewder, perhaps—than Rinuccini's Pluto; he must defend the conditions of his power if he is to bend. He grants Eurydice leave from the abyss, but only if Orpheus does not look back at her as the couple ascends. Pluto does not say it, but this sustains his will and protects his rule. After all, consider the danger. Orpheus could lead Eurydice to the surface and suggest to everyone—using all those powers

Figure 4.1. Orpheus and Eurydice with Pluto and Proserpina painted by Peter Paul Rubens (1577–1640): Museo del Prado. Photo: Erich Lessing/Art Resource, NY.

of his voice and presenting a beautiful prize beside him as well—that hell's king capitulated.

But Pluto has not capitulated, and the Infernal Spirits now applaud their sovereign. Having previously acclaimed Orpheus's human boldness, they now hail Pluto's word as their law and salute the judgment of their "powerful king." This last phrase, *"possente re"* in Italian, contrasts to how Orpheus addressed Charon—as *"possente spirto."* Hierarchy is accented, and the Infernal Spirits declare that it is not for them to have misgivings about their lord's decision, let alone his motives.[9]

Not just hierarchy, but the notion of jurisdiction is ever present in this opera. Debates about the priority of words and music are, in basic ways, about which aspect of staged artworks is determinate. In the Florentine claims on behalf of monody, words affirmed their authority; however intelligent Striggio's text, Monteverdi asserted musical authority in the articulation of a drama. The words are not lost at all, but Orpheus's musical oratory persuades and does not solely animate his own words. While it goes virtually unnoticed in the many commentaries on *Orfeo*, jurisdiction, an essential matter for a state, was also perhaps the key political issue at the time in which this opera was written. It was, of course, hardly a new matter in Italy or Europe as a whole, with their many overlapping, contesting domains. We found this expressed already as a kind of deeper structure within Pluto's deliberations in *Euridice*. While struggles over jurisdiction were among the Gonzaga family's perpetual worries, they were not a pressing domestic concern for Mantua's duke in 1606 and 1607. His authority was well enough established; his duchy was also a fief of the Holy Roman Empire, but relations with Vienna were then amicable. Thanks to its loyalty, Mantua had considerable autonomy. Not that far away, however, a major clash was underway.

The contestants in the "Interdict Crisis" were Venice and Rome. The former was a very independent-minded republic, including in religious matters. The papacy, jealous for its due, was perennially worried about assertive Christian dominions after the Reformation. When two priests faced civil charges in Venice, Pope Paul V insisted that secular powers had no such legal prerogative. Venice demurred and in April 1606 the pope excommunicated its senate and placed the entire city-state under a religious "Interdict" (a ban). Venice responded by seizing church property and expelling various religious orders. Ousted Jesuits poured from Venice into Mantua, a hospitable environment for them (the Gonzagas had long had special bonds with their order). The crisis was resolved in February 1607— the same month as *Orfeo's* premiere (on the 24th of that month). The pope lifted his strictures, Venice maintained its laws, but turned the clergymen over to Henri IV, the Catholic King of France. In ensuing years, extensive debates within Italian universities and among intellectuals focused on who had what rights in which domains.

The fate of Orpheus in the Monteverdi-Striggio opera is, of course, not a direct reflection of these events. Neither are artistic concerns about music's relation to words. Still, the issue of jurisdiction is present persistently in all these provinces as well as within the larger picture of European politics. After all, this protagonist goes from one realm to another, seeks to persuade its authority to bend its defining law, and then, having succeeded, begins a return to the domain from which he came. If the powerless nobles—the Infernal Spirits—have no doubts about Pluto's decision and his stipulation, should Orpheus be doubted? After all, his love seems victorious. The King of Hades has made an exception. Striggio and Rinuccini depict the same conflict. The power of love and art takes one side, and law and the demands of hierarchical—or just plain political—order take the other. Pluto, in both versions, perceives the problem. Rinuccini's king, after debating the implications, frees Eurydice, allowing for a happy ending at the Pitti Palace. Striggio's monarch makes things more complex. His stipulation reasserts his own will as law. Orpheus, then, does not simply win his treasure by song. He is to be tested again; another kind of worthiness must be shown.

The singer does not recognize his disadvantage. He does not see that power does not simply tilt in his favor because of his magnetic talent. A kind of compact has been offered to him and he misperceives Pluto's flexibility. He fails to see that the compact demands the young prince's own self-mastery. This is a kind of Plutonic cunning, for Orpheus's ability to overcome his own subjective needs will make him more princelike. His ascent depends on whether or not he has an essential quality. Is not power over himself prerequisite to being a proper master of others? Orpheus's music may persuade; he has certainly been courageous. But he is impetuous. Pluto, in contrast, shows a true ruler's characteristics, a combination of will, assertion of law, and clemency. He thinks through their relations. He doesn't simply follow his inclinations or ardor. Orpheus does not grasp that a king may bend willfully but not in a way that renders his power meaningless. One Infernal Spirit makes matters plain by asking if Orpheus can avoid being conquered by his own "youthful desire" and thus be able to fulfill Pluto's decree—a decree that is effectively a command to forget that he has been to and challenged hell.[10] Can Orpheus be "constant" and put faith in the judgment of a magnanimous king?

He cannot. Orpheus's gifts have gone from his throat into his head; his head's rational part has gone wobbly. His powers are the sorts that come from and play on emotions. Yes, they make animals prance, but now they have the wrong effect on his mind. He moves forth, pouring forth spry, confident praise to the sound of his lyre and song, assuming Eurydice follows. Inconstancy does too. Doubt sets in. Is she really there? What if Pluto is besotted by beautiful Eurydice, wants her for his own, and has gone back on his word? Orpheus does not realize it, but this would require Pluto to violate his own command, just made, and we know—Pluto shows us—that a monarch cannot change rules carelessly. We, the audience, are aware of this, but Orpheus simply tells himself: Be fearless. Was he not fearless when he crossed borders into the Underworld? Now he asserts: "What Pluto forbids, Love commands."[11] Love's power—that of the god Amor (Cupid, Venus's son)—is greater than all others. Or so Orpheus fools himself.

He decides for Love's jurisdiction. He is, however, still within Pluto's dominion. A clang is heard offstage, as if to alert, warn, provoke, and try

Orpheus at once. He makes the fateful turn, looks back, and this means he must face consequences. Eurydice must do so first. She starts to fade. Since you violated your compact, an Infernal Spirit tells Orpheus, the law now condemns. You have sacrificed the possibility of clemency—you have "broken the law" (*rott'hai la legge)* and are "unworthy of pardon." As the Infernal Spirits take Eurydice away, she calls to Orpheus in plaintive question: "Is it thus, by too much love, that you lose me?"[12] The answer, of course, is yes—although he has loved his own powers and not just her. There is no returning. The king will not hear him again; to bend the law again would be to make both it and clemency meaningless. Orpheus displayed human virtues when he entered Hades, the Spirits sing further, yet virtues may be lost "in the fog of human passions." Reason struggles with these passions, yet sometimes in vain. Its light extinguished, man is led "blindfolded to the end."[13]

Striggio's point is in the manner of Plato and Stoicism. Reason distinguishes man from animal; and it makes a ruler a ruler. Pluto is constant and knows what is most important and when so. Orpheus "conquered" the Inferno only, as the Spirits observe, to be vanquished "by his passions." Glory comes only to him who "has victory over himself."[14] Another fanfare of horns concludes the scene. It is a variant of one we heard already when Hope brought Orpheus to the portal. Now the brass is somber. Orpheus succeeded as an artist but to succeed as a prince, reason of state must assert itself and feelings must adjust to it. (Perhaps Orpheus needed a Machiavellian counselor.) Monteverdi's fanfares suggest the dignity and tragedy of humanity, using them to frame a young man's encounter with the Underworld—his struggle with life and death, with love and law, with passion and reason, with ardor, art, and authority.

There are two versions of Orpheus's fate in the last (fifth) act. One is found in the librettos printed in 1607. Heartbroken, his quest defeated, he is again on the earth's surface and sings in sorrow. The countryside resonates, quite literally, with his lament. A voice—"Echo," a nymph—repeats final words of his phrases. He is grateful, he says, to hear "pity" echo;[15] in reality, the great singer, who sought to move others to compassion, now wallows in self-pity. This too is not princely behavior. Moreover, he announces his dismissal of all women. He denounces this sex as foolish and perfidious—and thereby excuses his own failure. We hear a *Sinfonia*, but then Orpheus suddenly finds himself besieged by what he calls "a hostile troop/ of women, friends of the tipsy god."[16] Striggio here follows accounts in Ovid and Virgil. These are the Bacchantes, female followers of Bacchus, god of wine and frenzy. They respond to his rejection of women by declaring him their enemy. Divine fury sets upon Orpheus in the sunlight. They sing, they laugh, and they tear his body to pieces.

The score of *Orfeo* printed in 1609 provided a very different ending, and it is based on an obscure Latin source, Hyginus. After Orpheus's denunciation of women, Apollo descends in a cloud. The Sun God offers consolation to his son and also a Christlike resurrection: blissful ascent into heavenly, eternal life and glory, leaving earthly trials (and those endured much further below) behind. The Greek deity speaks here to his son using familiar images of Counter-Reformation ideology. This-worldly desires and joys are transient, uncertain. Come, instead, with me to the heavens. You will see the form of your Eurydice there in the constellations. In other words, Orpheus will not need to look back. They rise together to the heavens as a chorus praises Orpheus for going now to a blessed pleasure, which death can never steal:

> Thus goes he who does not recoil
> at the call of an immortal God;
> Thus he obtains grace in heaven
> who down below braved the Inferno;
> And he who sows in sorrow,
> reaps the fruits of all grace.[17]

Scholars dispute the reasons for the two endings. If the first (1607) is more faithful to better-known classical sources, the other fits neatly into its own Counter-Reformation moment.[18]

If *Orfeo*'s initial impact seems to have been modest, its influence on the history of opera would eventually be enormous. *Arianna*, Monteverdi's next opera, was also based on myth, and it was a more popular success. Its first audience was much larger than that of *Orfeo*, for it was written for a public event—a political wedding, of course. The libretto by Rinuccini survives, but not Monteverdi's music, except for a lament, perhaps the most famous by this composer, sung by suffering Ariadne (*Arianna*) on her abandonment by Theseus on the island of Naxos. Before we turn to them, we need to explore the Mantuan political world in which Monteverdi composed, and how, seven years before *Orfeo*, he found himself in a spirited dispute, accused by a musical conservative of being a musical radical. The argument reenacted, in some ways, the earlier quarrel between advocates of "new music" and defenders of old, immutable laws. It is also similar to arguments about politics between advocates of change and conservative foes.

INTERMEDIO (II)

Vincenzo Gonzaga became Mantua's grand duke in 1587, just months after Ferdinando de' Medici's ascension in Florence. His father, Duke Guglielmo, had governed well and also lured to the duchy leading musicians, among them Striggio's father. The Gonzaga's domains, like those of their Tuscan counterparts, were legally fiefs—Mantua attained duchy status within the Holy Roman Empire in 1530—and, again like Florence's rulers, those in Mantua sought to bolster and sustain their autonomy. Reigning, however, was not Vincenzo's favorite pursuit. He was attracted more to travel, adventure, and romantic recreations (despite his pronounced Catholic piety). Still, he was effective politically, balancing many of the same powers with which Florence contended: Spain, the Holy Roman Empire, France, and Rome.

Geography and borders made matters messy. Mantua's dynasts ruled relatively small territories that were not all contiguous. Different family members governed different areas. Jurisdictional complications ensued inevitably from questions of inheritance and succession. Vincenzo came from the family's principal branch that, when *Orfeo* was written, reigned in the Duchy of Mantua itself and Montferrat. The latter, a valuable and populous territory, became a Gonzaga possession in the mid-sixteenth century and was a cause of perpetual disputes.[1] Between it and Mantua sat the much larger Duchy of Milan, under direct Spanish Habsburg rule. Montferrat also bordered the Duchy of Savoy (Piedmont), whose Duke Carlo Ferdinando I eyed it hungrily. He understood the variables of power and secured French backing for his ambitions, all while recognizing that France had its own interests in the Italian peninsula. (Montferrat provided a useful route south for French troops.) Savoy's duke wanted to augment and secure his realm with a league of Italian states. One means to strengthen this effort was dynastic marriages.

In short, northern Italian politics in Monteverdi's day remained a convolution of jockeying local and foreign forces. Matters were made more difficult by wars with the Ottomans. Vincenzo participated actively in them on the Empire's behalf. Wars, however, cost, as does cultural politics. Vincenzo was close to a financial sieve in his spending on the arts. One recipient of patronage, the painter Peter Paul Rubens, described the Gonzagas as "lavish spendthrifts who squandered the funds of their subjects."[2] Monteverdi's *Orfeo* was commissioned by Francesco, Vincenzo's older son and heir, for Mantua's Accademia degli Invaghiti (Academy of the Charmed). Like its Florentine counterparts, this Academy sponsored discussions, debates, and performances. It included leading officials and members of the ducal family, and seems to have also served Francesco's rivalry with his brother Ferdinando, a poet and composer with ties to Florence's cultural world.

When Claudio Monteverdi arrived in Mantua in 1590 or 1591, he found himself in a vibrant musical and commercial stronghold. In his first years there, he gained experience playing and writing music for theater events such as *intermedi*, which were popular at court. Vincenzo, whose second wife was a Medici, had been impressed by theatrical and musical innovations he had encountered in Florence and also in Ferrara, northern Italy's other important musical center.[3] Monteverdi's horizons expanded as he traveled in his liege's service. When Mantua came to the Empire's aid against the Ottomans, Monteverdi accompanied Vincenzo and his troops to Vienna as head of the musicians in the ducal escort and as leader of a martial band. They passed through the Habsburg possessions in Austria, Hungary, and Bohemia. Apparently he met Bardi, the Camerata founder, in Hungary. It is possible that they discussed Girolamo Mei's ideas. Yet Galilei's treatise seems to have had only a modest impact on Monteverdi.[4]

The appointment of a competitor to the position of Mantua's *maestro di cappella* in 1596 chagrined the young composer. He would, however, attain the post five years later and in the interim became a Mantuan subject and served in Vincenzo's escort during a mission to Flanders. He was responsible for music at various events such as banquets, and according to his brother, Giulio Cesare Monteverdi, he learned along the way about recent developments in French music and song. These shaped his emerging views about "new music," as did the experience of the wedding celebrations in Florence in 1600.[5] Monteverdi's court responsibilities led him to write many different types of music. Scholars often note his remarkable ability to assimilate the varied styles and ideas he encountered; dramatic music provides only one instance of his inventiveness.

His talent, however, was not appreciated universally, and his musical ideas, especially those found in his early madrigals, provoked a controversy in late 1600. His foe was a contemporary guardian of musical laws, and the outlines of the charge are familiar: Monteverdi had transgressed nature's immutable decrees. Giovanni Maria Artusi laid it out in a book with a long title that was published in Venice in November that year: *The Artusi, Of the Imperfections of Modern Music.* Not only did it chastise "new music" in general, but Monteverdi specifically—although unnamed, he was the obvious target. In his argument, Artus, a priest and music theorist originally from Bologna, raised matters similar to those in the debates about monody and polyphony among the Florentine Camerata, albeit from a somewhat different point of view.

"Natural laws" of sound and composition were at issue, and the quarrel focused on the disruption of "consonance" by "dissonance." We have seen how technical languages of music often echo or intrude in—or parallel—political rhetoric, and here we find this phenomenon again. Consider how the description in 1776 of these two terms—the same that Bodin used—by Charles Burney, a pioneering music historian, might also portray a political parley that attains amiable or, alternatively, unhappy results. Consonance, he explained, is a "coincidence of two or more sounds which, when heard together, by their agreement and union, afford to ears capable of judging and feeling, a delight of a most grateful kind." They yield "resolution." Absent such concord, however, there is "dissonance" due to "want of . . . agreeable union" with what comes either before or after a tone, or combination of tones. There is, Burney writes, "suspension and anticipation of some sound" in music's movement, until providing "sauce" on its "palate."[6]

Now consider Artusi's words, writing a quarter century after Bodin and long before Burney. He insists that polyphony had always to provide proper resolution. He protested that "certain" composers used sauce licentiously; "seditious" might be an equally appropriate word, given Artusi's outlook. Monteverdi imagined dissonance as a means to animate aspects of texts he set. It could bring out their content and shape in interesting or arresting ways—to express sadness, for example. Artusi charged that these were "illegal" usages. Certain composers, he scoffed, "have nothing but smoke in their heads if they are so impressed with themselves as to think they can corrupt, abolish, and ruin at will the good old rules handed down from days of old by so many theorists and excellent musicians." If your aims can be accomplished by following these established laws, why go beyond their bounds in quest of "extravagant novelties?"[7] These claims can be made otherwise: there are natural laws ordering musical practice based on immutable correlations of harmonies and proportions among tones.

It is an argument between orthodoxy and innovation. Translate Artusi's contentions from one domain into others, and the same structure of devotion to authority can often be found, for example, in conservative religious and political philosophies. The nature of things is inseparable from tradition. Defy one, you defy the other. (Later in the history of political ideas, "natural" laws and "natural" rights would be used against customs and traditions.) Monteverdi was his own Orpheus, willing to defy rules that had previously seemed staunch. Unlike Orpheus, he achieved his purpose—but that was because he was a musical reformer in a time of radical challenge to authority. He looked and listened, backward and forward. Controversy over immutable laws—including those ascribed to art—never occur in a void. Recall the historical constellation when Artusi attacked Monteverdi. Europe was transforming, modern politics was emerging; in the meanwhile, the invention of printing had altered the cultural world and literacy was growing. The year 1600 came after eight decades of murderous religious conflicts, in a "Jubilee Year" when pilgrims journeyed to Rome and other religious sites in quest of forgiveness from sin, all while Bruno was burned for heresy and Cavalieri's *Rappresentatione* was sung. *Euridice* was performed in October and Artusi's book appeared in the next month.

Monteverdi was not a polemicist, much less a politician. He wanted to compose music; that is his oratory. A response to Artusi did come, however, in the first volume of his *Scherzi musicali* (Musical Trifles) seven years later. The author was Giulio Cesare Monteverdi, the composer's brother, who also served Mantua as a composer (and organist). His "Declaration" posed the old political-cum-musical question: Who rules? In his answer, Giulio Cesare distinguished two types of "practice" when words and music meet. In the first—the *prima prattica*—harmony (meaning here music in a general sense) ruled. It "is not the servant but the mistress of the words." Claudio Monteverdi's aim, he explained, was a "Second Practice (*seconda prattica*), in which words were "mistress of the harmony." Its principal concern was "perfection of the setting" (by which he meant its melody). In it, "harmony does not rule but is ruled" by the *Padrona*. Giulio Cesare's point, then, is that the words must govern melody, although this did not necessarily mean simple monody. In short, it was evident that Claudio Monteverdi's music did indeed constitute a challenge, but his aspiration was to a "second," not an entirely "new" practice or revolutionary theory in "the process of actual composition."[8]

Just as conservatives often seek to thwart change by insisting on immutable God-given rules, so radicals often disguise their real enterprise by contentions like those advanced by Giulio Cesare. In this case, however, Claudio does not seem to have sought aural camouflage. Perhaps Striggio's libretto for *Orfeo* also appealed to him for reasons similar to those Giulio Cesare had deployed in the composer's defense. The Striggio-Monteverdi version of the Orpheus myth shows that laws of a kingdom, perhaps even of nature, cannot be discarded—but neither are they quite so incontrovertible as they seem. Now and then, in some circumstances, those rules are not all that matter; and justification by antiquity can become perpetual immobility. Yet once you take to a new, reformed path, you must indeed look forward. You ought not to deceive yourself, as Orpheus did, into believing you have simply trumped all rules on behalf of your own desires, using nothing but your personal powers. Perhaps this is what Claudio Monteverdi grasped or intuited. Perhaps it is a reason why his imagination assimilated diverse styles, creating a rich range in sound without need for either the programmatic elaborations of the Florentine Camerata or their opposite, Artusi's dogmas. Perhaps it suggests that it is also natural to individuate—which requires dissonance. Yet had Monteverdi not known the "First Practice," he could not have created his own "new music." Since Artusi could value only the old, it is difficult to envision him appreciating or even making sense musically—or politically, although that was not his aim—of *Orfeo.* In fact, Artusi, to be consistent, would have had to denounce Pluto for deciding that a savvy ruler can allow unusual dissonance. Artusi believed rigidly in a conserving discipline; Monteverdi pursued novelty, including in musical imitation, with disciplined originality, composing the unexpected. Listen, for one example, to how Eurydice's death is mourned at the end of Act 2 of *Orfeo.* After all the debates about the First Practice and Second Practice, Monteverdi gives us a chorus that sings a homophonic madrigal because it suits what needs expression.

Was Monteverdi's assimilation of varied styles an anticipation of the needs of a new era, one in which the completed cosmos imagined by the First Practice would lose coherence, its good old (eternal) rules splintering as people sought their own melodies? Consider this irony. The assertion of monody, that crucial ingredient in the first operatic experiments, paralleled, as we have seen, the development of centralizing authority in an age of rising or consolidating princedoms. Politics and music asserted a single rule (respectively). Multiplicity, rather than polyphony alone, allowed Monteverdi to create greater worlds than did his more strictly monodic predecessors in opera. He supplied narrative invention and melodic conversation. He supplied them with an engaging range lacked by the Florentine experimenters. Artusi placed "new music" under one rubric, yet like the Camerata he argued for the past's authority—albeit a different past. Monteverdi used myth and antiquity, but composed for his times and the future while learning from the past. Republicans had also looked to the past (especially Rome) and to a single authority (law), but it was not their time.

Some three decades after Artusi's attack, Monteverdi wrote in a letter that he never aimed to follow the "method" of the Greeks. Yes, he had read Vincenzo Galilei's treatise, but what he found interesting in it was its observations on "inadequate practice" in ancient music; in other words, on what Monteverdi wanted to change. Melody, Monteverdi thought, was the remedy. It could accomplish for voice and character what could not be achieved by "the principles of the First Practice, which were only harmonic."[9] He planned a treatise on *Melody, or the Second Practice*, but never wrote it. His later correspondence tells us that it would have addressed "three aspects of melody," extrapolating from passages in Plato: "word-setting" (that is, setting a text to music), "harmony," and "the rhythmic part." He wanted to reintegrate these in a new way, so that melody would animate harmony rather than demote it.[10] He wanted melody to intensify expression of the emotions and to individualize human experience. In this sense, Artusi was not wrong to perceive a threat; a truly individualized man is no longer simply one with God's firmament, whether or not the individual recognizes this.

In 1616, after Monteverdi had moved to Venice, he expressed his own distinctive humanism in what became a famous letter to Striggio in Mantua. His old friend had many political responsibilities now, and among them was deciding on entertainments for court celebrations. He had asked the composer about the possibility of setting to music a "maritime fable" titled *Le nozze di Tetide*. It was supposed to be an *intermedio*, but Monteverdi apparently thought it was to be an opera. His comments on the libretto put forth his own purposes for music in secular theater, referring back to his earlier operas, *Orfeo* and *Arianna*, and emphasizing his humanism in the ways of musical imitation:

> I have noticed that the interlocutors [in *Le nozze*] are winds, Cupids, little Zephyrs, and sirens: consequently many sopranos will be needed, and it can also be stated that the winds have to sing—that is, the Zephyrs and the Boreals. How, dear Sir, can I imitate the speech of the winds, if they do not speak? And how can I, by such means, move the passions? Ariadne [*Arianna*] moved us because she was a woman, and similarly Orpheus because he was a man, not a wind. Music can suggest, without any words, the noise of winds and the bleating of

sheep, the neighing of horses and so forth; but it cannot imitate the speech of winds because no such thing exists.

Monteverdi also found the story muddled. More important, "*Arianna* led me to a just lament and *Orfeo* to a righteous prayer, but this fable leads me I don't know to what end."[11] Musical speech had to be, for Monteverdi, the voice of an orator in sound, a voice of articulating humanity. He persuaded Striggio and the duke that setting *Le nozze*'s libretto was a hopeless enterprise.

Chapter 5

A PRINCE DECIDES ON NAXOS

Arianna, like *Euridice*, was written for a political wedding. In May 1608 Prince Francesco, the Gonzaga who had commissioned *Orfeo*, married Margherita, Infanta of Savoy. If alliance led to the Medici union of 1600, these nuptials stemmed from Gonzaga qualms about Savoyard designs on Montferrat. The celebrations in Mantua, intended to impress Savoy's rulers, did not go as well as Duke Vincenzo hoped. Restricted attendance to several events irritated a good many Mantuans, and produced some public fracas.[1] Moreover, the Duke of Savoy decided not to come, and dispatched his sons, apparently unpleasant fellows, to represent him.[2] Mantua's real interests became explicit the next year when Francesco took charge of Montferrat on behalf of his clan. Striggio became his principal advisor for this territory.

The Gonzagas wanted the gala to outdo Medici festivals. Vincenzo invited many names associated with Medici events (and from musically esteemed Ferrara) for his own, opulent display.[3] Striggio oversaw much of the planning. There would be plays with *intermedi*, ballets, including one on which Striggio collaborated with Florentine composer Marco da Gagliano, and *Arianna*. The duke himself solicited Ottavio Rinuccini's participation.

Opera's first librettist appears to have been disgruntled at this time. Florentine artistic politics had not gone well for him. After *Euridice* he received no commissions for librettos from the Medici and he was excluded from plans for festivities celebrating another princely wedding scheduled for fall 1608. A complicating factor may have been his decision to follow Maria de' Medici to Paris eight years earlier. Speculations have him in love with her, although real evidence is negligible. Music historian John Hawkins reported in the eighteenth century that Rinuccini had "a singular propensity to amorous pursuits" and "entertained a wild passion" for the queen. He was "greatly mortified by her wisdom and virtue."[4] While in Paris, Rinuccini wrote flowery verse devoted to her. This, however, was common practice among court poets, as an early biographer of Rinuccini observed, suggesting as well that the real reason for his journey there was simply a passion for novelty, pleasure, and glory.[5]

Whatever his reasons, Rinuccini had enough Medici favor to join Maria's escort to France, where she became Marie de Médicis. He also sought good-will from Henri IV with a sonnet.[6] The librettist stayed in Paris for some three years and his own account reports good treatment by the king. Rinuccini served as an intimate attendant of the royals (he was a "Gentleman of the Bed Chamber"), and this allowed him to observe the politics of a second court (after Florence) at close proximity. It seems that Rinuccini became em-broiled in some conflicts too, possibly for financial reasons.[7] The court was rife with political machinations. Often these included eminent Florentines there, like Concino Concini, a confidant of Marie who had, like Rinuccini, arrived with her and was later to be a hated minister in France's government.[8]

Rinuccini's preoccupations were not directly political, but he could not avoid notice of the intrigues faced by Henri IV in a politically and reli-giously fractious realm. The librettist's contributions to court life mostly took form as musical and dance entertainments, but he was restless and traveled frequently back to Italy as well as to England and to Flanders. His work was permeated by depictions of tension between duty and love. Love is blind in *Dafne*, and it conflicts with law. Exchange their sexes, and we can almost imagine Rinuccini and Marie in the discord. But the poet—if he was in love with her—could hardly have saved a queen who wed out of dynastic duty from the hell she thereby entered.

If by 1608 Rinuccini was marginalized in Florence (he pointed to a "cabal" against him), that year was marked by success for him in Man-tua. It began with the performance of *Dafne* at Carnival to new music by da Gagliano. *Arianna* was acclaimed in May, and Rinuccini also collabo-rated with Monteverdi on a ballet for the celebrations, which continued into June. The theme of *Il ballo delle ingrate* (Ballet of the Ingrates) may have reflected Rinuccini's own feelings about Florentine ingratitude, but it provided, first and foremost, a tutorial in proper and improper female behavior. In it, Venus is irritated by women who are impervious to Cupid's arrows and resist men. She implores Pluto to allow "ingrates"—formerly beautiful women punished with ugliness in the Underworld—to surface just briefly so they can dance a silent warning to living members of their sex.[9] Rinuccini's Ariadne needed a different kind of counsel.

II.

Sacrifice, family, and duty are at the center of *Arianna*. This Rinuccini-Monteverdi collaboration was staged on the evening of May 28, four days after the Savoyard bride arrived in Mantua, and a week before the "ingrates" danced.[10] The opera retold the story of Theseus's abandonment of Ariadne on the island of Naxos. Some four thousand people watched in a temporary theater as ingratitude was again on display, this time by the male lead. But it is justified as political duty. Theseus, unlike the protagonist of *Orfeo*, proves his princely character by recognizing that a reason of state must trump love or thankfulness.

It began, like the other early operas, with a prologue, this time sung by Apollo himself, driver of the "golden chariot." This "eternal guardian of Heaven's lyre" descended on a cloud. He explained that he had things to do on earth, that he would "imprint the lower world with the steps of a god." Should you hear a "forsaken royal bride's sighs" on a foreign shore, he told the audience—undoubtedly, he addressed the Savoyard bride in particular—then perhaps you will find much to admire in what will now transpire.[11] Then, in the opening scene, Apollo's old adversaries from *Dafne* appear. Venus explains to Cupid that they have arrived on the shores of beautiful, Arcadian Naxos with a purpose. Theseus is here, on his way home to Athens with Ariadne, his prospective bride. Venus doesn't delve into all the details from well-known mythology—that Crete's King Minos, after defeating Athens in war, extracted a terrible revenge, the annual sacrifice of young men and women; that they are delivered into a labyrinth where the infamous Minotaur prowls; that the mother of this creature is none less than the Cretan Queen herself; that she mated once with a bull, giving birth to a vicious half-bull-half-man; that Prince Theseus volunteered to join the prospective victims in order to save them; that he slays the beast, but only with aid from the Minotaur's half-sister, Ariadne, who has fallen in love with him.

This princess betrayed family and homeland by fleeing with the Athenians, and has arrived on Naxos at the opera's beginning. And now she, too, will suffer treachery. Theseus—who, it happens, was especially dedicated to Apollo—will abandon her. Cupid protests this to Venus and proposes to afflict Theseus, but the goddess says no. Let Theseus go; but help her. Bacchus, son of Jupiter and Semele, will soon come. Let Ariadne find "her bliss" with this hero.

The action shifts and we are amidst mortals. We meet Theseus's soldiers who, encouraged by him, sing of their exploits in Crete, and he rejoices with them. Honor served—for duty always comes first—they now anticipate returning home to domestic happiness with their families. They bid Theseus to slumber well with his Ariadne. But he will not, for this question torments him: What to do if duty and happiness clash? Ariadne chose to help him in fidelity to love, but he knows she is troubled by her treason. He tries to raise her morale, telling her that she will soon be queen in golden Athens, yet she sighs. Theseus understands: "No one can leave his homeland's shores/ without pain/ who does not have within his breast a heart of steel."[12]

Ariadne finally takes comfort in Theseus's "noble pledge of faith." She decides to look only to future happiness. Then Theseus observes that "the sun is in full flight"—Apollo's chariot is disappearing—and as evening comes, he suggests that they take to a shepherd's hut. Changes will take place there under night's cover. Ariadne has forsaken duty for Theseus, but political obligation will possess Theseus; he will now take charge of his priorities. Cupid works invisibly, yet the demands of politics also cannot always be evident—cannot be always articulated in daylight. As Ariadne sleeps, Theseus steps out to confer with his Consigliere (counselor).[13]

Rinuccini, the poet-courtier, fashions a remarkable scene that suggests how much attention he must have paid to arguments about reason of state. Despite his "noble pledge," Theseus thinks he must quit his love and place politics before everything. He is filled with self-reproach; the Consigliere makes things plain to him:

> Your agitated soul
> Still fights and struggles against beautiful reason.
> My lord, this, shameless passion
> assaults your loving mind
> Too strongly, an unworthy tyrant of your noble heart.[14]

Theseus truly loves Ariadne, but rulers command and love captivates. Yet he will feel disgraceful were he not to keep his pledge; his "constancy" will be stained. Again, his Consigliere warns of the consequences of losing to his passions the freedom needed to be ruler: "A soul which Love constrains/ under his harsh domain/ cannot distinguish properly and does not know the truth." Blind love is not "wise and virtuous." To change when need be is wise and virtuous—and is no crime for a prince.[15]

Follow my reasoning, urges the Consigliere, although he reveals what is already in Theseus's mind; politics, manliness, and honor are linked and ties between honor and passion must be secondary. Think, says the Consigliere, of how the heroes and generals of Athens will react if you come home to them with a foreign bride, who betrayed her own family and homeland. Think of your honor, should everyone learn that you needed her help for your glorious victory. And would you place "the daughter/ of an enemy king" on the "ancient throne" of Athens? How can Athenian mothers, whose innocent children were fed to Ariadne's half-brother, accept her? How will all this effect your ability to rule? This last question is the potent implied question. The Consigliere asks his liege,

[C]an the radiance of a delicate face
so cloud the light of your beautiful reason
that for a vain desire,
forsaking every kingly custom,
[you] should forget your kingdom and your honor?

Theseus recognizes the stakes, and resolves: passion shall not master him: "He who becomes a vile slave to his own pleasure/ is not worthy of the scepter."[16] He knows now that he and his ships must slip away under night's cover; and he must not look back. He told Ariadne not to do so for love's sake; he must look forward to be a king.

The Consigliere rejoices that "*virtù*" descends from "the eternal spheres" into the "hearts of Kings"—in this case, that of a future one, Theseus.[17] This word, *virtù*, has a famous history in political, particularly republican thought, thanks especially to Machiavelli. Its root, *vir*, means "man" in Latin, and it indicates a tough, almost swaggering civic-mindedness. A man animated by *virtù* is savvy, patriotic, ready for responsibilities and challenges. He knows what to subordinate for the public good and when. *Virtù* contrasts to "virtue" in the usual moralizing or Christian sense for, as Machiavelli said, a prince must know when to be cruel if he wants to be effective. It is not cruelty for cruelty's sake, but recognition, trained or instinctive, of the economy, dynamics, and demands of political power. It is the kind of cruelty that says: leave Ariadne behind. Sentimentalism has no place here. Feelings toss you about, rulers must be staunch. Yes, Theseus feels torment; he is human. He says that the ache of Ariadne will stay always with him. One gets over such mortal pains, remarks the Consigliere, suggesting that immortal reputation is far more important for a prince. It hardly seems honorable to quit her under cover of night and her sleep, thinks Theseus. The Consigliere, of course, sees no problem—heaven will help her, he says. We already know it will from Venus's words. Yet the irony does not escape us: Theseus's honor and prospects as ruler require dishonorable treatment of Ariadne. The Consigliere is, in the end, sinister, nefarious—but a truth teller.

If Orpheus and Theseus provide operatic counterparts to mirrors for princes, that genre found most famously in Machiavelli's *The Prince*, we find counterparts of another kind of Renaissance power in Charon in *Euridice* and in the Consigliere in *Arianna:* the counselor to or secretary of princes and nobles, who were the subject of primers. Machiavelli devoted a chapter to this kind of "minister," and then elaborated on it with an admonition against flatterers. A ruler's reputation, he explained, depends considerably on those who surround him. A secretary must be competent and faithful, always thinking of his liege's interests—and thus also those of the state—rather than his own. The prince must treat his secretary well. His advisor must feel free to speak the truth when asked and the prince must know to ask questions and to deliberate.

Machiavelli proposed that there are three kinds of mind. One understands matters directly and without aid. Another grasps things well when shown or guided by someone else (an advisor, for example). A third comprehends the world neither on his own nor with direction. The first two kinds are admirable, thinks Machiavelli. The last is worthless. Rinuccini's Theseus would seem to be of the second type, although the Consigliere appears to bring out what he already recognizes instinctively. Theseus, notably, initiates the conversation, and the conclusion reached by him and his advisor is very much like that of Machiavelli in another chapter (the eighteenth and perhaps most famous chapter of *The Prince*): a prudent ruler must know when interests require him to be fickle and to dissemble. If the reasons why he has bound himself no longer hold, he must break faith, which is what Theseus does. The Consigliere's words in the opera seem to be an allusive paraphrase of Machiavelli: You must free yourself from Amor's dominion, for this will let you see the truth properly—the truth that it is proper for a prince to change when necessary.

A good many secretarial advice booklets were written in the sixteenth century, and some were the equivalent of best sellers. Rinuccini, Monteverdi, and Striggio (who served as a Mantuan consigliere) certainly read some of them, most likely one by writer, editor, and popularizer Francesco Sansovino. His *Il Secretario* of 1564 was reprinted, translated, and imitated widely over decades. Officially, a secretary had responsibilities for letter writing. Born in Rome of Florentine origins, Sansovino adopted a republic, Venice, as his home, and his portrait of a secretary presents a figure whose responsibilities extend far beyond those of a scribe. The very word "secretary" implied secrecy, and this kind of advisor had to be utterly trustworthy. His counsel was said to reveal (presumably with heaven's aid) what was truly in the mind of the prince.[18] The arguments advanced by Rinuccini's Charon and his Consigliere would be familiar to Sansovino's "secretary." The renowned poet, Torquato Tasso, to whom the Gonzagas offered refuge in his later years, also wrote a handbook in Mantua in early 1587 titled *Il Secretario* which Striggio, Rinuccini, and Monteverdi surely knew. In it Tasso described the secretary as a man who knows power and law, but also their merciful uses; these latter are called more effective than rules deployed severely.

III.

Rinuccini's libretto gives us different roles with their varied prerogatives and demands. He structures his presentation of them by emphasizing distinctions among those who carry greater burdens—royals, in particular— and those who do not. When Theseus and his soldiers sing, not long before nightfall, of the relation between honorable duty and domestic bliss, they establish priorities. The exchange between Theseus and his Consigliere closes with a chorus of fishermen commenting on events, their voices making matters plain: be it day or night, kings and warriors cannot escape burdens. Theseus carries the greatest of them. His soldiers will soon be home with their loved ones, while his love is left behind. In contrast, fishermen, common folk on an Arcadian isle, are free of such concerns. Their lot is simple and they are content within natural, calm surroundings. They later sing, after Ariadne discovers that she is betrayed, that,

> Anxiety cannot set foot
> Within our peaceful breasts:
> No harsh severe law
> disturbs the mild delights of love;
> Love guides and governs us,
> and our only norm and law (*norma e legge)*
> is what he dictates . . .
> For us, who are willing slaves
> of noble beauty,
> a great kingdom is as nothing.[19]

Thus there are two worlds, the Arcadian one of love, and its opposite, that of politics and law. The fishermen are able only to see ambition, not political necessity in what motivates Theseus's departure. Their sympathies are with Ariadne when they sing,

Ah, if among mighty kings,
if under golden roofs,
fraud and deceit
are held to be glory and pride,
then blessed are we, whom fates assigned
to dwell on these lonely shores.[20]

In the meantime, sunlight, Apollo's "golden footprints," reveal what political logic—which worked out in the dark—brings to Ariadne. The passions (Amor—Cupid—Apollo's foe) still work invisibly, although we now hear them in the voice of devastated Ariadne.

The music of *Arianna* was extolled during Monteverdi's lifetime as the finest in his operas.[21] Its disappearance, save "Arianna's Lament," must be counted among the great losses of cultural history. We can only glean Monteverdi's accomplishment in setting Rinuccini's text. "Let me die, let me die," she sings in this masterpiece for solo female voice. "Turn, my Theseus . . ." she implores,

Turn round to look at her
who for your sake left her native land
and kingdom . . .[22]

Where is your "faithfulness?"[23] she cries. How can it be that fortune leaves me so shattered? Ariadne effectively inverts Orpheus's predicament. He turned back and lost his love, proving at that moment he does not have sufficient princely qualities; Theseus loses his love because he does not turn back and embraces political destiny. But here we must complicate the story. Accounts of its first performance report the overwhelming impact of the lament. It was so moving that "there was not a single lady in the house who failed to shed a tear."[24] The power and beauty of the lament in *Arianna* suggest that Rinuccini and Monteverdi did not want their audience to be convinced simply of reason of state. However, we can read Rinuccini's words and cannot hear what musical rhetoric Monteverdi deployed to animate strength of conviction or nuance articulated by Theseus and his Consigliere. We only know by word that Theseus's reason wins out over passion in his "agitated mind," and does so in the dark. This may be taken as a negative comment on Theseus's judgment or, more generally, on the very nature of politics, since it compels him to repudiate his oath. Yet we, the audience, have heard Venus and Cupid early on, and so know that the gods too are at work. Theseus sails to regal destiny, and cognoscenti would also be aware of what then happened, although it does not occur on stage. *Arianna* is framed by developments we do not see but would be expected to know, beginning with the story of the Minotaur. And after the opera ends, Theseus, pleased at his homecoming, forgets to change his ship's sails. This was to signal his success to his father as he arrived at Athenian shores. Believing his son dead, King Aegeus throws himself from the cliffs. Ariadne leaves her father behind in her homeland, and Theseus arrives on his own to his father's death.

We do not see that fate has not yet worked out fully for abandoned Ariadne. This will be presented on stage, for her fortunes will be the subject of the opera's second half. All of a sudden, hope arises for her on the shoreline. Boats are landing. Might it be Theseus? Has the Athenian prince changed his mind to correspond to his heart? Alas, no. But a new love comes in his stead—just as Venus ordained. Bacchus, heroic son of gods, arrives. He (like Theseus) returns from victories, having "tamed" tyrants and monsters, as a messenger reports.[25] His boats—as fate would have it—were driven off course to Naxos, where he finds the grieving woman. Your earthly lover was unworthy, he tells her. "A man rejects you," comments the chorus, "that a God may take you up."[26] Here Ficino's Neoplatonism echoes: through love you approach the divine. And politics is not divine.

Bacchus, another name for Dionysus, deity of wine and frenzy, is a god of feelings, not order or rulership. His followers, Bacchantes, destroyed Orpheus in the 1607 ending to Monteverdi's opera. *Arianna* ends on a note more like *Orfeo*'s second finale. Ariadne will join Bacchus in happy eternity, their love both flesh and divine. See what the gods bring, says Venus.

IV.

It is difficult, perhaps impossible, to specify with surety Monteverdi's political views. His letters say little about politics. Yet the political context of his life is of great consequence for his work. Politics was, in one way or another, an abiding presence in librettos he set. He wrote no operas in Mantua after *Arianna*, and left in 1612. The unpleasant circumstances of his departure were due partly to politics and partly to his own long-standing grievances. Duke Vincenzo died in June of that year and was succeeded by Francesco. The devout new ruler was less passionate about the arts (even if he had sponsored *Orfeo* five years earlier). He was more focused politically too. Duke Francesco quickly discharged a number of Mantuan officials, in part to consolidate finances but also to strengthen his rule. Musicians were soon fired, to the chagrin of his brother Ferdinando Gonzaga, then a cardinal in Rome and an advocate for Mantua's artistic world. While Francesco did want the duchy's cultural aura—it was, after all, good politics—music was a secondary priority. Yet he was dismayed as courts elsewhere wooed his musicians.

The Monteverdi brothers were already a source of irritation. Claudio had long complained of his circumstances. He knew his own musical worth, and while others in Mantua (like Striggio) did too, Monteverdi had, in his own view, been treated poorly. The Gonzaga considered him as they did all musicians; he was just another servant. The death of Monteverdi's wife in 1607 had a great impact on the composer and, overworked, he had to struggle often with the Mantuan treasury to receive his due remuneration. The achievement of *Orfeo*, the success of *Arianna*, and the majesty of his *Vespers* of 1610—he dedicated the latter to the pope and looked into the possibility of moving to Rome—did little to change his fortunes. His music brought him renown as his mood soured. He wrote a letter in late 1608—it is rather exceptional in its nerve—to Annibale Chieppio, Duke Vincenzo's counselor, in which he complained that he was ill and had labored to exhaustion. "I assure you," wrote Monteverdi, then in Cremona for a respite, "that unless I take a rest from toiling away at music for the theater, my life will indeed be a short one. . . ."[27] The composer, who frequently sought relief from official duties, asked for an "honorable dismissal."

He survived in his job another five years—until Francesco's ascension. The new duke wrote with bitterness to his brother Ferdinando in mid-July 1612 that the Monteverdi brothers were insubordinate and disrespectful. He would deal with them "when they least expect it" as "revenge for my reputation."[28] Both Monteverdis were fired two weeks later. Claudio returned to his native Cremona for a period, but then left for Venice, where he had been offered the musical directorship of San Marco. This must have afforded him special satisfaction, not only because the post was of great prestige. The previous incumbent had been Zarlino, teacher of his critic Artusi, and who, decades before, instructed and argued with Vincenzo Galilei.

Now Monteverdi would be in charge of the Venetian republic's sacred music and was free to receive commissions from aristocratic patrons there. He was treated well, but maintained ties to Mantua. Duke Francesco died of smallpox just months after Monteverdi's discharge, and Cardinal Ferdinando succeeded his brother. While Monteverdi still accepted commissions from Mantua, he resisted efforts to lure him back.

INTERMEDIO (III)

While Monteverdi made music in Venice—he composed three operas in the last three years before his death in 1643—Europeans were once again making devastating war on each other. Those famous, snarling alliances—shifting, disentangling, retangling—brought the Thirty Years War in 1618. In the meantime, Christian Europe continued its struggles with the Ottomans. Late Renaissance regimes wobbled, economic crises brought rural revolts, and Europe suffered a general economic collapse between 1619 and 1622. Then came devastating famines in 1628–29 and 1648–49, and plagues in 1630 and 1656.

The Holy Roman Empire was in constant competition with France. Branches of the Habsburgs presided in Vienna and Madrid, and these Catholics wanted a post-Reformation Christendom under their auspices while Protestants in Germany and elsewhere had their own agendas. France, while proclaiming fidelity to the Holy See, did not want Habsburg success. The French view of all the grand political maneuvering was suggested in an unsubtle "heroic comedy" by Cardinal de Richelieu, who became dominant in the Royal Council in 1624 and officially first minister five years later. In it thinly disguised figures representing European powers engage in an unseemly tangle with each other, but in the end "Europe" is saved—gallantly, of course—by "Francion."[1]

This allegory's implications for Mantua were manifold and dire, as subsequent events showed. Ferdinando had been Cardinal Protector of French interests in Rome from 1607 to 1612. After his return to Mantua, he found himself at war with Savoy over Montferrat. Soon Spain was involved, and bloodshed continued on and off for five years. During those years and after the Gonzagas would be engaged in intricate political machinations. At play would be ducal succession, foreign alliances, and domestic power. Alessandro Striggio played an increasingly important role and was involved in numerous sordid intrigues on behalf of the ruling family. He was in the center of the high drama that led finally to the War of the Mantuan Succession. Ferdinando died in late 1626. His brother, Vincenzo II, became duke, but he too was in a grave by December 1627. Neither left a male heir. Jockeying began even as Vincenzo lay dying. One claimant to the throne was Charles de Gonzague, the Duc de Nevers, a French prince who governed the frontier province of Champagne. France supported him with hesitation, and Richelieu made clear that he in fact had his own reasons for allowing Savoy dominion over Montferrat. Spain, in the meantime, promoted its own, pro-Habsburg candidate, the Duke de Guastalla, who ruled a territory south of Mantua and received support from the emperor in Vienna. De Nevers's bloc in Mantua was led by his eldest son, Charles de Rethel, and buttressed by the local anti-Habsburg, anti-Savoy faction led by Striggio. He had risen to marquis and grand chancellor.[2] When the dying duke seemed to lean toward the Habsburgs, Striggio and his associates proceeded with a series of ruthless machinations to recuperate the situation.

They succeeded. Vincenzo declared de Nevers his successor and died. The aspiring new duke arrived on January 17, 1628, enraging Savoy, Spain, de Guastella, and also the emperor, who determined that his own prerogatives had been violated. After more maneuvers by all these very interested parties, the emperor denounced de Nevers and proposed to take charge of Gonzaga lands until matters could be settled. In the meantime, de Nevers had misread his French support. Richelieu simply did not trust him, and was, in any event, preoccupied by a recent English attack on the French coast together with domestic strife with Huguenots.[3]

The emperor's troops marched into northern Italy in spring 1629, and by August some 30,000 of them stood before Mantua's capital. The siege began in December, and by May 1630, it was obvious that Mantua would fall. De Nevers surrendered. Then came the Sack. Mantua's palace, library, and virtually all domains of the duchy's life were plundered. Richelieu took a new turn at this point. De Nevers might have been inestimable, but that hardly compared to the prospect of a Habsburg victory. France primed to attack. Finally, a treaty in March 1631 returned de Nevers to devastated Mantua (and delivered part of Montferrat to Savoy).[4]

Although Monteverdi was in Venice during these evermore complicated developments, Mantua's fate affected him profoundly. It is likely that a good number of his unpublished compositions was stored there and burned in the Sack.[5] He also had personal worries. His twenty-three-year-old son was arrested by the Inquisition in Mantua in 1627, charged with possession of a scientific treatise that was forbidden by the papal Index. Monteverdi turned to someone who might be able to help—Striggio, then immersed in the Mantuan succession crisis. On January 1, 1628—a few days after Vincenzo died and two-and-a-half weeks before de Nevers's arrival—a worried father appealed to a powerful, busy man of politics. Please, try "to influence the Father Inquisitor so that he lets Massimiliano go home," the composer implored his onetime librettist. Monteverdi explained that he was trying desperately to raise bail.[6] Striggio contributed funds, Massimiliano was released, but the story did not end. Monteverdi's son entered medical school in June 1628, and shortly afterward was called again before the Inquisition. The composer sent another letter to Mantua on July 1, 1628, just as Imperial troops moved through nearby Milan. He implored Striggio for help. I thought Massimiliano was free of "his wretched plight," wrote Monteverdi, but the case of "the rogue" who had earlier given his "innocent" son a suspect book was still unresolved. He might have to return to prison and even face torture. Striggio, despite all his preoccupations, intervened again, and Massimiliano was soon on his way to Venice.[7]

The chancellor's own fate was less happy. Striggio commanded besieged Mantua on behalf of de Nevers. As the situation became desperate he traveled to Venice, now Mantua's ally against the Empire, to appeal for expanded financial and military help. Northern Italy was then wracked by plague, apparently carried by Imperial troops and spread wide by their movements and unsanitary conditions. Striggio became a victim, and may even have been responsible for bringing the plague to Venice in June 1630, just a month before Mantua was crushed.[8] He died in Venice in the middle of the month, and some 46,000 Venetians also succumbed to the contagion. Monteverdi's grief may have encouraged his decision to take minor orders in the church in 1632 (although this church standing also gave him proprietary rights in his native Cremona). It seems also to have hobbled his musical productivity for a period.

By the decade's end, something fresh was happening in the Venetian musical world, and he was stimulated by it: opera. Monteverdi had continued to experiment in dramatic music in Venice and now, the aging composer returned to opera with zest. *Arianna* had been written over three decades earlier. It was revived in Venice in 1640, and he began composing new works. Once again his librettists came from the elite, and once again they had both politics and love on their minds.

Chapter 6

THE POLITICAL SCENARIO OF MONTEVERDI'S VENICE

A curious event occurred in 1623—a decade after Claudio Monteverdi's arrival in Venice, five years after the Thirty Years War began, and a half-decade before the composer's son found trouble with the Inquisition in Mantua. A letter was sent, apparently by a singer, to the Venetian State Inquisitors, a powerful triumvirate that watched over public propriety. It charged the musical director of San Marco Chapel with treason and religious blasphemy. His loyalties, it suggested, were only a matter of appearance.

The consequences for Monteverdi were, potentially, severe. Politics and religion entwined in *La Serenissima* (the Serene Republic) and so too in his professional life. The chapel was the doge's, the ceremonial and political head of state. A number of patriotic and religious myths, not all consistent with each other, focused and fused just there, and they animated Venice's self-image.[1] One legend told how the city was founded in its lagoon on the Adriatic in 421 CE on the Feast of the Annunciation. Some five hundred years later, relics believed to be the remains of St. Mark—"San Marco"—were stolen from Alexandria and brought to the site. A magnificent cathedral complex was built to house them, and linked to the doge's palace. It became a symbol of—a visual prayer for—Venetian power, identity, and independence. Those relics allowed Venice to assert sanctified distinction from the throne of St. Peter in Rome, and also from the pope-anointed Holy Roman Empire. The beautiful, imposing facade of the cathedral sat before sprawling Piazza San Marco, the square at the center of Venetian public life. It was no place for a traitorous blasphemer to be musical director.

The accuser, identified as "N," claimed that others had heard Monteverdi's subversive remarks too. The composer, he charged, had expressed a desire to see the eagle—the imperial symbol of the Habsburgs—fly over the Piazza. Monteverdi had also asserted, or so it was contended, that the Venetian Republic should also be "subjected" to Spain's monarch for the sake of its citizens' "souls." And San Marco's musical director stood accused of deriding his Venetian employers as "fools and dotards" who didn't know his "worth." Finally, he was impeached for declaring that he detested the clergy: "to hell with them—I am Claudio."[2]

No action was pursued against him. Scholars are unsure of what to make of the undated brief—it lacked a certain political coherence—and wonder if it came from a disgruntled rival or perhaps an underling seeking for some reason to wound his superior. Monteverdi's official status may have made him an easy target. He held a visible position of high prestige but was, technically, a subject of an empire that had a long history of terse interaction with Venice, often in support of the papacy. Monteverdi's native Cremona was under Spanish dominion, and Mantua, where he had obtained citizenship (subjecthood is perhaps a better word) in 1602, was an Imperial fief, albeit Venice's ally. Monteverdi received a pension from the Gonzagas after moving to Venice, and sustained amiable contacts with and received commissions from Habsburg patrons. In short, his income came from numerous conflicting sides. This was not anomalous for artists but it is difficult to imagine that Monteverdi would have jeopardized his comfortable, eminent position in Venice, especially after the unpleasantness that accompanied his departure from Gonzaga employment. It is true, however, that he was prone to testiness. His memory of Mantua may have fostered a quiet desire to keep professional options open.

Could the accusations have had something do with the "Spanish Conspiracy"? In this seedy tangle in 1618, the Spanish resident (ambassador) was accused of plotting against the republic with the complicity of various Venetians and Frenchmen. It turned out to be more noise than anything else, but it was one of a series of affairs that nurtured an atmosphere of suspicion. Spanish agents often did bribe needy Venetian notables for information about governmental and other matters. One senator, Giambattista Bragadin, was condemned to death in 1620 for such dealings. Another, Antonio Foscarini, was tried in April 1622 for illicit ties to enemies of Venice. His throttled corpse was found hung upside down in public for all to see, provoking anxious discontent within the Venetian elite. That elite's chagrin with the State Inquisitors intensified when it was discovered that a domestic spy had testified falsely against Foscarini. Four months after the Senator's death, the informer was executed by strangulation. In the twists and turns of this affair, suspicion was cast on a visiting goddaughter of England's late Queen Elizabeth, then staying at the Palazzo Mocenigo. This linked alleged subversion to the seat of an old, eminent family (some of whose members had been ambassadors to Spain).[3]

One of Monteverdi's secular patrons was Senator Girolamo Mocenigo. Venice's upper strata had a tradition of salonlike musical evenings in their homes, and it was at one of these in 1624, in the Mocenigo residence at Carnival time, that an important experiment by Monteverdi in thespian-minded music was first sung. This was a narrated dramatic madrigal titled "The Battle between Tancredi and Clorinda"—"*Il combattimento di Tancredi e Clorinda.*" Given Mocenigo's high status and the nervousness of this period, which also entailed considerable strains between wealthier and poorer nobles, it would have been unwise to be Monteverdi's patron had the composer actually been a reckless purveyor of politically troublesome sentiments.

In *Combattimento*, Monteverdi sought to fashion in music different human "humors" (sentiments) using verses from Tasso's epic *Jerusalem Liberated*. Set during the Crusades, it expressed an overtly religious message in a story of misrecognition of enemies. Pagan Clorinda battles Tancredi, a Christian knight. She is helmeted and he doesn't recognize that she was once his love. Tancredi is victorious, and as wounded Clorinda dies, she reveals herself and asks for baptism. Appearance in this bloody fray has been different from reality—but its antagonists are united, finally, in love and the same Christian truth. "Agitation" was one "humor" that Monteverdi sought to create in sound in this work of roughly a half hour. His "*stilo concitato*" was a kind of musical rhetoric, deploying sharp, rhythmic, plucked strings and rapidly repeated notes, all like an excited, speeding heart or a clash of weapons.

Monteverdi composed *Combattimento* shortly after the Foscarini affair. In the meantime, he had continued to correspond with Striggio about musical events and personal matters. One intermediary between them was Antonio Callegari. Also known as "*il Bergamaschino*" (the little fellow from Bergamo), he often spied for Mantua. Exchanges between Callegari and Monteverdi were apparently quite innocent. Striggio sent through the former a request for the score of *Arianna*. They might, however, have easily raised some Venetian eyebrows. Callegari came in February 1623 with another request, this time for Monteverdi to accompany several musicians to Mantua. (The composer declined on grounds of illness.) The ofttime spy also kept watch on events at the Mocenigo Palazzo that spring, when Duke Ferdinando visited Venice. Both Mantua and Venice were obsessed with murky political machinations and rumors.[4] In short, treasonous accusations against Monteverdi are unsurprising given Venice's mood. The three State Inquisitors were a creation of the Council of Ten, a kind of "committee of public safety" that had been established in the fourteenth century as a temporary measure, but had remained in place.[5] Its powers were substantial; Venice may have been famous for openness, but its reality was more complex. Its patriciate kept vigilant eyes on goings-on within its jurisdiction. And its republican aristocracy was divided. A reform movement emerged in 1625 around Renier Zeno, a noble of relatively humble means. A time of troubles began.

Political reformers often appeal to their society's myths, culture, and experiences to fortify—and to legitimize—their demands. Venice's political myths, we know, were plentiful and potent; they weaved into its historical memory a number of well-imagined traditions about the city's origins and government. And they comprised a multilayered presence, especially for Monteverdi's librettists for his late operas.

II.

La Serenissima was renowned for civic patriotism and a strong sense of its specific character—of *"venezianità."* The city's patriciate projected a distinct self-image: it led a maritime republic, not a land-bound principality (although Venice did extend well into terra firma, landed terrain). It had enjoyed wealth and stability, its leaders believed, because Venice was dominated by a commercial aristocracy (comprised by them), not a feudal-style ruling class. Its political structures set Venice apart, and were unlike those under which Monteverdi lived in Mantua or that marked Florence. And the Venetian political world stressed its differences with Rome, Madrid, and Vienna. As in much mythology, there were considerable truths in these claims. Republicanism never held recent sway in any of these cities except Florence. The latter had been shaped decisively by commerce, albeit in ways that contrasted to Venice. Florentine republicans, however, were defeated decisively earlier in the sixteenth century. Machiavelli regarded Venice as flabby and spoiled by luxuries—radically dissimilar to the austere, *virtù*-imbued polity of his own ideals. Yet it was the Venetian and not the Florentine republic(s) that survived. Formidable challenges to it were overcome. Some issued from outside powers, while some sharp frictions were created at home. Centuries of relative well-being there appeared to rebut versions of republicanism that hailed "the People." Venice hailed aristocratic republican pilots. Yet here too reality was more problematic. Decline had begun set in by the seventeenth century. In fact, opera did not appear on the Venetian stage at the triumphant moment of an ascendant bourgeois class, but at a troubled one for an established commercial aristocracy.

Venetian elites insisted that their institutions were heir to the spirit of the ancient Roman republic, which they saw as the great political success of antiquity. These institutions also provided a contrast to those of the Roman Empire and those of defeated Florentine republicanism. One libretto of the 1650s, set at the historical moment when populism facilitated the replacement of Rome's ancient republic by imperial rule, was *The Unhappy Prosperity of Dictator Julius Caesar* (*La prosperà infelice di Giulio Caesare dittore*). In its epilogue, the figure of Liberty complains of maltreatment by Rome. Neptune, the Sea God, responds: Liberty's future is in a sea-girded city. The author, Gian Francesco Busenello, had collaborated over a decade earlier with Monteverdi on the first directly political and historical opera *The Coronation of Poppea* (*L'incoronazione di Poppea*); its antihero, Nero, was perhaps the most notorious example of imperial corruption. Venetian audiences were free to make associations.

La Serenissima contrasted itself to the existent Holy Roman Empire. Venetians also liked especially to point to absolutism in Habsburg Spain—but also papal Rome—as opposites of their own republic. In 1681, Cristofo Ivanovich, a Dalmation canon at San Marco (and also a librettist), wrote a *Theatrical History of Venice* in which he sought to reconstruct the early development of the city's opera. He explained that "of all the republics in the world, none was more perfect than the ancient republic of Rome; nor, indeed was there ever a better imitation of this than the republic of Venice . . . And, in fact, it was out of the ruins of the former that the latter was born succeeding no less to the heritage of a great republic than to that of the genius unfailingly present in every aspect of its magnificence." Theatrical greatness had also passed now from the Tiber to the Adriatic and "not even in this" was Venice "second to ancient Rome."[6]

An additional legend had nearby Padua and Venice founded by Trojan refugees. Led by Antenor, an elder who had warned Trojans against fighting the Greeks, this myth allowed Venice to assert for itself a status of independent venerability. It could claim that its birth preceded that of Rome by Aeneas and his famous company of Trojan exiles, as recounted in Virgil's *Aeneid*. Myths like these—Venice as heir to Troy, to Roman republicanism, to an autonomous Christianity (because of St. Mark)—overlapped in some ways, and in others were contradictory, but this hardly mattered. Venerability mattered, as it did generally for nobles lauding their family lines. Myths, like operas, don't present historical or political chronicles; they seek something beyond these, or secreted behind or within empirical events. Theater or literature or popular song can suggest hidden realities with vividness. Something is invented or communicated (or both) in them about how people have lived or are living or ought to live—or all these at once. Or about how they died. In one broad sense it does not matter if this is accomplished in mythical or historical settings. The "real story" of, say, Nero and Seneca, is not recounted but used to suggest, consciously or not, something through their staged voices. Myth, historical myth, mythological history, and history proper tethered Venice's independent spirit; unstable relations among myths, realities, and appearances would provide motifs in Venetian opera. Sometimes gods were political actors behind events depicted; sometimes myths, appearances, and supposed realities were acted out by disguised human beings in varied predicaments. Sometimes, men played women's roles and vice versa, or one sex appeared in the other's attire.

One old quarrel in Venetian politics concerned secrecy in politics. It was, notes one historian, far-reaching and difficult to sustain at once; there were many places where political conversation could take place.[7] Oddly enough, secrecy went along with Venice being an important center of publishing. Some outside observers apparently didn't see through all this. When Bodin, the French political thinker, wrote a manuscript in 1588 in which seven "wise men" of different religions and philosophies debated their views, he set it in Venice, "a port common to almost all nations or rather the whole world not only because Venetians delight in receiving strangers hospitably, but also one can live there in the greatest freedom."[8] But secrecy was assumed to be a necessary dimension of politics in the upper reaches of power, both for the sake of the regime's internal order and to secure the Republic's external interests in a precarious world. It was evident, however, that concealed authority is easily abused. Witness the State Inquisitors, their masters in the Council of Ten, and the copious examples of domestic spying and fear of plots. Venice's oligarchy never seemed to be able to define legitimate *"secretissme"* in a stable way—it was good but it was bad—which is to say that a tension between appearance and reality was a key feature of *La Serenissima*'s society and political world. It would be a key feature of its opera.

There was at least one other important myth that nurtured the city. It comprised a kind of "conservative idealism," in the apt phrase of one scholar, and its most coherent presentation was in the early- to mid-sixteenth century by a cardinal and diplomat named Gasparo Contarini. His book's imposing Latin title *De magistratibus et republica Venetorum* was translated simply as *The Commonwealth and Government of Venice*, and its argument was straightforward: this republic's success rested on a unique "mixed constitution." It sustained a balance of forces in society through various institutions, and in this resembled both the human body and, quite directly, music: "Just as a mixture dissolves if any of the elements from which the body is composed surpasses the others, so all harmony becomes dissonance if you hear one instrument or voice more strongly. In the same way, if you wish a city or a republic to last, it is above all necessary that no part should operate more powerfully than the others, but all, as far as possible, should participate in the public authority."[9]

How did a constitutional "mix" maintain a balance? The doge (duke) was designated political chief, but he was not an absolute monarch free to do as he chose. His powers had limits and he gained his lifetime tenure through a complex electoral college system, not inheritance. There was a countervailing senate of some two hundred to three hundred men that supplied the government with an "aristocratic" feature. It had been founded in the fifteenth century and contrasted to the Great Council, whose purpose was to give say to "popular" classes. However, Council membership had become hereditary and restricted over several hundred years. By the sixteenth century it had 2,500 members culled from one hundred and fifty families. These "*nobili*" are estimated to have been 4–5 percent of the population, but their numbers depended on birth.[10] The Venetian ruling class was effectively closed. The powerful Council of Ten may have been complemented by the other institutions, but its membership rotated, usually among higher patricians who served one-year terms, and it was responsible for a secret police and, generally, for guarding state security. It oversaw the State Inquisitors—the men who had to examine the accusatory letter against Monteverdi. The word "republic" means "the people's affair" or a "commonwealth," but this republican government, so lauded in its ideal image by Contarini and *La Serenissima*'s rulers, was in fact an oligarchy, dominated by the upper reaches of its society and sustained by a security apparatus. Bodin may have been in the dark about secrecy but he was right to argue, *pace* Contarini, that Venice's constitution was actually aristocratic.[11]

There were, almost inevitably, struggles each generation for reform. Some were partially successful. One took place in the late sixteenth century between "*giovani*" (the "Younger Men") and "*vecchi*" (the "Old Men") over the powers of the Senate and the Great Council relative to those of the Council of Ten. As a result, the latter was weakened.

The Council of Ten reasserted itself following a particularly tense moment in the edgy relations between Rome and Venice. The Counter-Reformation's assertiveness—its claims on behalf of the Roman church's universal and hierarchical prerogatives—challenged not only Protestants throughout Europe, but posed an increasing threat to *venezianità*. Venice insisted on its devotion to Catholicism, but also on its own independence. Jesuits were Rome's most forceful protagonists and in the 1590s, soon after opening a College in Padua, they found themselves besieged by blustery demonstrations by students from the city's university.

Many protesters were sons of the Venetian upper classes. Padua was within Venetian territory and its university, which was chartered by the republic, customarily provided higher education for the sons of its elite. It was also renowned for an open-minded faculty. The turmoil was sufficient to bring the matter before authorities at San Marco. An especially popular professor of natural philosophy, Cesar Cremonini, spoke on behalf of the students. Known for his philosophical skepticism, this friend of Galileo was disliked particularly by Jesuits for deploying Aristotle's ideas to seeming irreligious conclusions. The issue in Padua, he told Venetian authorities, went beyond rowdy students. It concerned proper jurisdiction: the Jesuit College had been authorized from afar (by Rome), not by Venice. The Senate proceeded to vote strict restraints on the college's activities.

Then came the Interdict Crisis, a more formidable challenge to the republic. It pitted a new pope, Paul V, known for his dislike of republics and for his Counter-Reformation fervor, against a new doge, Leonardo Donà, a religious patriot who had been a leader of the *giovani* and a stalwart defender of *venezianità*. After the papal excommunication decree of May 1606, the republic enlisted a Servite priest as state theologian to dispute Rome's religious justifications and to defend Venetian rights. Paolo Sarpi did so brilliantly and vigorously. He had studied in skeptical Padua (where he worked also with Galileo), and knew arguments for reason of state; he had read Tacitus and probably knew Lipsius's work. The Counter-Reformation, for Sarpi, simply swathed the quest for power by Rome, the Empire, and Spain. He insisted that a religious man served his *patria* and for Sarpi that was Venice. When the crisis finally ended and papal sanctions lifted, Venice was still left with what one scholar calls the tension between political prudence and "stern adherence to republican principle." [12] Not defeated but chastened, Venetian leaders still sought to present an image of domestic unity. Within its aristocracy, however, powerful men continued to resist reform or opening their ranks to fresh faces.

In the aftermath of the crisis, and not long before Monteverdi arrived at San Marco, an influential book of imaginary dialogues was published in Venice. Its title was *News from Parnassus* and its author, Traiano Boccalini, had studied law in Perugia and Padua. He had also developed an intense dislike of Rome while serving as a judge and administrator in the papal domains (where he was born). His sympathies were with republics, especially Venice, where he moved. He wrote a commentary on Tacitus in 1600, and although it was not published until 1678, the Roman historian also figured prominently in *Parnassus*, which appeared over several years in multiple versions. It was well known to the Accademia degli Incogniti (the Academy of the Unknowns, or Masked Ones), the circle of high-placed intellectuals and literary men from which Monteverdi's Venetian librettists would come decades later. In *Parnassus* Apollo presides over conversations, many sardonic, among celebrated "virtuosi," past and present; then he issues his conclusions about them and their propositions. In one striking passage, Tacitus finds himself in some difficulty after devising spectacles that enable its wearers to look into the minds of rulers. At another point Apollo calls a "diet of the learned" with "all the great poets, nobility, and deputies from universities" so he can propose a "candidate for eternity." In teasing tone he suggests for this distinction none less than the relentless proponent of Tacitus, Justus Lipsius, "a Fleming, whose learned lucubrations perfumed" everyone and "had sharpened the stomachs of the literati rather to devour than taste him."[13]

III.

Their city was beautiful, their city was rich, but knowing patricians would have recognized that Venice's circumstances were not Parnassus-like. Its trade and seafaring commerce had suffered due to conflicts in the Italian peninsula, compounded by clashes with the Ottomans in the Mediterranean, and the circling of the Cape of Good Hope. As a consequence, a good number of Venetian nobles had redirected their investments toward terra firma, at the expense of maritime pursuits. In 1610, the doge warned the Senate that too much capital was directed toward real estate and "amusements." Part of the nobility had become preoccupied with ostentatious display of riches, while another was increasingly impoverished. Richer and poorer nobles were in persistent conflict, and these often took form as efforts to strengthen one governmental institution (in which one fraction was stronger), as opposed to another (where other elements were advantaged). Venice's internal balance teetered. The Council of Ten's strength buoyed the wealthier patricians in an increasingly fatigued and insecure regime.

Doge Donà died in 1612—the year before Monteverdi's arrival—and Sarpi became a more isolated, though persistent champion of traditional republican sovereignty. Much of the patriciate wanted to avoid new conflicts with Rome or Spain. Then Venice had to navigate the Thirty Years War, cope with the Spanish Conspiracy, and the cases of Bragadin and Foscarini (the latter was a friend of Sarpi). Mounting economic worries led the republic, which always had a good number of foreigners either visiting or in residence, to declare itself an open port (albeit with some restrictions) in 1618. The hope was to revivify commerce. In 1645, two years after Monteverdi's death, John Evelyn, an English visitor, wrote in his diaries of his surprise at "the strange variety of several nations seen every day in the streets and piazzas; Jews, Turks, Armenians, Moors, Greeks, Sclavonians." They were "all of them in their native fashions."[14]

Commotion beset Venetian ruling circles in the mid-1620s in the form of Zeno's zealous campaign against moral decline, and on behalf of "older" republican values and *virtù*. He protested: citizens within a republic should be equal, but Venice was dominated by its affluent. He sought to reassert the power of the Great Council at the expense of the Council of Ten. It was, he proposed, a matter of constitutional principles—the need, that is, to reestablish proper jurisdictions. In effect, this would give more sway to the poorer nobility. Zeno went so far as to chastise abrasively a relatively new doge and his family for corruption. (This doge, Giovanni Conaro, had been an official at San Marco in 1613 and was among those responsible for bringing Monteverdi to Venice. The composer retained close ties to his family.) The reformer was banished and then recalled. He became a member of the Council of Ten and continued his campaigns. Turmoil intensified after an assassination attempt on him in late 1627 near the doge's palace, possibly engineered by the doge's son. Zeno's efforts were abortive in the end, and the Council of Ten sustained its preeminence. While his failure was probably due, at least in part, to his own overbearing behavior, he did draw on a broad feeling that considerable decay had set into Venice.[15] The Zeno affair and the Mantuan catastrophe culminated at virtually the same time in 1627–28. Duke Vincenzo II's death came a few days before the attempt to kill Zeno. A Venetian who had had a sense of precariousness after the Interdict Crisis would now have had an even more worried countenance. Yet again, beautiful Venice appeared a marvel while the world around it as well as its inner realm were troubled. The city's myths would not have comforted sufficiently anyone capable of distinguishing them from political realities.

A Venetian Tacitus would have been able to write well about the maneuvering within his city's elite set against the backdrop of carnival and music, canal-enhanced sheen, and architectural glories. War and plague were fresh together with anxieties roused by "the Turk." Monteverdi lived in the midst of all this.

It was in 1630 that the Accademia degli Incogniti was founded. Its aim was debate—literary, moral, and philosophical—and members published essays, literary works, and plays. Many of them had been students of Cremonini and they engaged both skeptical and neo-Stoic ideas, an uneven but hardly unusual combination in unsteady times. Philosophical skepticism challenged what we can know firmly, especially "truths" asserted by religion. Neo-Stoicism sought "constancy" in the face of what it believed transient, external disorders. And it sought "constancy" for wise men in the forms of reason or religious truths and inner equanimity. While a skeptic and a neo-Stoic might have many divergent beliefs, they might well also dissemble in a similar way—by conforming to the same customs of the "external" world. The Incogniti were reputed "libertines," that is, "free-thinking" foes of many established mores and superstitions. Since they came also from the elite, they worried about decline and the need for civic *virtù*. Such concerns may seem to wrench in different directions, but it was hardly unusual for the upper reaches of a society to pronounce one way for most of the population while assuming that they themselves could act or think otherwise. Among the Incogniti would be politicians of prominence and even some highly regarded nonpatricians.[16] The tugging perspectives and concerns would find their greatest artistic expression in Monteverdi's *Poppea*. Its librettist, Busenello, was a member. The principal organizer of the Incogniti was Giovanni Francesco Loredano, an eclectic figure who served in the Senate, wrote novel-like works and plays, and translated contemporary Spanish literature (although this latter cultural interest did not mitigate his hostility to the Habsburgs).[17]

Monteverdi's librettists would have a good deal to say about discrepancies within their lived world. Theater was one obvious means for Incogniti to do so, and especially opera. In the latter, a vital element, music, is, like them, "unseen," but ever present and sounding. Moreover, in Venice people famously wore masks at Carnival time. In a theater, or in an opera house, it was often not possible to tell who was whom in the audience and who had which responsibilities or stations in life (unless, they purchased boxes). It was possible to talk—or sing—on stage during festive times in the camouflages of myth or ancient history while addressing contemporary worries.

IV.

Although Monteverdi did not compose operas between 1608 and 1640, *Combattimento* was only one of his smaller-sized experiments in dramatic music, many of them since lost. Despite his presence there, Venice played no role in opera's earliest developments. When it did so, however, opera's character and social place changed. A court event metamorphosed into a public, marketable enterprise. Many factors were at play. One was a ruling commercial aristocracy that began to invest in theaters and productions. Moreover, Venice had a long tradition of civic pageantry and theater. Music played an important role in city life and a great choir had been fashioned at San Marco. Carnival brought huge numbers of revelers to Venice, and they were potential opera ticket-buyers. For six weeks in late winter, "the world converge[d] in pilgrimage" to *La Serenissima*.[18] Its population of some 50,000 residents virtually doubled, and with this influx came traveling theater and entertainment groups.

Foreign musicians were welcome. Monteverdi's assistant and successor at San Marco was also an outstanding figure. Francesco Cavalli was from Crema, a Venetian possession near Milan, and proved to be an exceptional opera composer too. Here, however, papal Rome adds an important dimension to the story. It too was the source of experiments in dramatic music and what became opera in the first decades of the century. These tended to emphasize Counter-Reformation themes, especially how bliss comes of heaven-granted eternal life—by contrast to either earthly misery or earthly pleasures. Emilio de' Cavalieri's earlier work helped to inaugurate these efforts, and a tradition of staged sacred music dramas flowered, drawing on an earlier tradition of plays in Jesuit schools. Saints were favored protagonists, and perhaps the most eminent example of this kind of opera was *Sant' Alessio*. Staged in 1631, its composer, Stefan Landi, then a contralto at the Sistine Chapel, had previously written music for other dramas, and it was scored for male singers and castrati (women singing on stage was impermissible in Rome) with a libretto by the future Pope Clement IX (then Giulio Rospigliosi). It was a religious, quasi-historical, and sometimes comic work that told of a fifth-century figure. Leading Roman art patrons, like the Barberini family, from which incumbent Pope Urban VIII came, were energetic supporters of these kinds of experiments. Musical education was also a priority in Rome, especially for the church, and talented musicians were attracted there. But since repertoire was restricted for religious reasons in papal territories, singers also joined traveling troupes.

One such ensemble was led by Benedetto Ferrari, a renowned theorbo player and composer, together with Francesco Manelli, also a talented musician and singer. Their five-man group brought opera to several cities, including Padua and then Venice at Carnival in 1637. There, they presented *Andromeda*. The myth of Perseus and Andromeda was recounted in a libretto by Ferrari to music by Manelli in a revamped theater owned by an aristocratic family. The response was enthusiastic. Soon itinerant performances were succeeded by commercial houses. In the ensuing four decades, some one hundred and fifty operas would appear in nine theaters. A range of conventions developed, both moneymaking and artistic, that became operatic staples.[19]

Subscribers were sought, especially aristocrats (for boxes in theaters). Visitors bought bench seats for single performances. The opening of opera houses, remarked a chronicler, was usually replete with pomp, "by no means inferior to that practiced in various places by the magnificence of princes, with the sole difference that the latter procure the enjoyment of all through their generosity, while opera in Venice is business and thus lacks that decorum with which marriages and births are frequently celebrated by princes with a view to the greater display of their magnificence and power." Yet a political dimension was also present for this author who remarked on how useful it could be for rulers to "sate" commoners with pleasures. With "nothing to gnaw," they might "turn to gnawing the reputation" of their masters.[20]

Business had consequences for the structure of the operas. If expenses were secondary matters, as they had been when spectacles were financed by Medicis, Gonzagas, or Barberinis to impress a select audience, the same could hardly be true for profitable opera. It needed paying customers; these were to be attracted by crowd-pleasing stage effects, spectacular arias, fast moving, accessible plots, and occasional comic relief. Libretti with candles were sold.[21] John Evelyn, the English visitor, described enthusiastically how he went to the opera "where comedies and other plays are represented in recitative music, by the most excellent musicians, vocal and instrumental, with a variety of scenes painted and contrived with no less art of perspective, and machines for flying in the air, and other wonderful notions; taken together, it is one of the most magnificent and expensive diversions the wit of man can invent."[22]

V.

Marketing also brought an accent on musical display and visual spectacle rather than words. This reversed, in effect, the priorities of opera's earlier pioneers in Florence and Mantua (and of religious purposes on the Tiber). Monteverdi's return to opera came at the beginning of this process and was not marred by it. He wrote music intended for artistic musical drama, not ticket-attracting boasts in sound (although he had no objection to takings). Once again his operas addressed potent themes developed by librettists of urbane sophistication and literary concerns.

After a small theater revived *Arianna* in 1640, a new Monteverdi opera was also staged, *Il ritorno d'Ulisse in patria* (*The Return of Ulysses to his Homeland*). Giacomo Badoaro's libretto was based on the last chapters of Homer's *Odyssey*. Badoaro was an eminent and politically powerful patrician as well as a habitué of intellectual and artistic circles. Soon after *Ritorno* came Monteverdi's *Le nozze d'Enea con Lavinia* (*The Marriage of Aeneas and Lavinia*) based on the latter part of Virgil's *Aeneid*. It takes place, like *Ritorno*, after the Trojan War, and its chief protagonist, like Ulysses, is a veteran who arrives on destined shores. After fighting on opposite sides, the two heroes have journeyed across the seas and lived through portentous events. Aeneas's birthplace is forever destroyed. In *Nozze* he has come to a peninsula on the north side of the Mediterranean and will found a world-historical power. The famous interlude in Carthage, where he loved and abandoned its Queen Dido, are in the past. Aeneas will marry Latium's princess Lavinia and bequeath Rome to history. In *Ritorno*, Ulysses returns home to the island of Ithaca, as fate determined. But he reestablishes an order there, rather than founding one, and after he dispatches aristocratic pretenders to his throne, he will begin life anew with his queen, and rule in his original homeland. His legendary, embattled story will be behind him.

The music for *Nozze* is lost and the libretto was long attributed to Badoaro. Recent scholarship has shown its author to be his friend, Michelangelo Torcigliani, who conceived it as a counterpart to *Ritorno*.[23] Both men were members of the Incogniti, like Busenello. The latter was a lawyer who, by his own account, had been a pupil of Sarpi and Cremonini (as had Badoaro). His family did not belong to the nobility, but to a class of "gentlemen" who were citizens able to serve in major administrative positions. A report from about 1618, apparently by a former Spanish ambassador to Venice, tells us about this part of the republic's population, and its useful but sometimes uncomfortable relations to the patriciate:

> After the nobles the citizens hold the most honourable position, so that they are accustomed to say that the nobles are princes and they themselves are gentlemen. They dress in the same fashion as the patricians. They want to be addressed as noblemen are, and they too enjoy great riches . . . Almost all of them are employed in honourable posts . . . The citizens are not well disposed towards the nobility, for many of their families think themselves just as ancient and honourable as noble houses . . .[24]

Busenello studied law at Padua, and had directed in Venice a powerful "cofraternity" (a brotherhood and mutual aid institution). His brother served as ambassador plenipotentiary in Mantua in 1628–30, was imprisoned and became ill probably from (but surviving) the same epidemic that took Striggio's life. After his return to Venice, Busenello's brother held various high administrative offices including, in the late 1630s, secretary to the Council of Ten.[25] Consequently, Gian Francesco Busenello's access to knowledge about the realities of politics was considerable, although he had little appetite for direct public involvement. Instead he preferred to display his fierce patriotism, but also his worries about the republic's future, in poetry and librettos. His first libretto, written for Cavalli, was about Apollo and Dafne; their next collaboration was *La Didone* (*Dido*), which recounted the first parts of *The Aeneid*.

Busenello's themes, like those of fellow librettists of the time, engaged and expressed Venetian politics in ways comparable to the earlier Rinuccini-Peri ventures in Florence, and to Monteverdi's Mantuan collaborations with Striggio and Rinuccini. Myths of the Ovidian kind were deployed in plenty, but so too was Homer. Their deployment often had varied contemporary political and social implications—given the backdrop of slaughter in north Europe, the Sack of Mantua, and plague in Venice. The first act of *Didone* presented Troy's cataclysmic end, and then *Ritorno* offered a hero's successful quest for postwar stability. Soon history—or a kind of history—joined myth on the operatic stage. In *Poppea*, Busenello and Monteverdi showed how the most corrupt of leaders behaved and what drove him. Not just Nero, but other distant historical figures, some admirable, and some not so, would also be heard singing in Venice's theaters in the 1640s and 1650s: Alexander the Great, Julius Caesar, and Scipio Africanus, among them.[26]

Busenello knew the available historical records well as he reinvented the story of how a tyrannical emperor cast aside his queen, replaced her with his latest female obsession, and ordered the death of his tutor and advisor, a famous Stoic philosopher, for counseling against his actions. Some history presented in the opera is true to known sources, some unrecognizable by them, but many of the political issues—and broadly human ones—raised in it are already familiar to us, although now they are in a new context: What are the proper characteristics of a ruler (or, more broadly, of leadership)? Should reason or emotion dictate decisions? What is appearance and what is reality in the political world, or more generally, in the world of elites? Or even, more expansively, what is outward show and what is certain in human existence?

Artistic form and political content intersected in these questions. One of the debates among Incogniti concerned the relevance of the "Aristotelian unities." In his *Poetics*, Aristotle argued that a successful drama needed a threefold cohesion—of action, of time, of place. This had been challenged by seventeenth-century playwrights in Spain, especially Lope de Vega, the most influential figure of its "golden age" under the Habsburgs. Political tensions between Venice and Madrid did not necessarily translate into cultural obtuseness by sophisticated Venetians, who did not dismiss artistic achievements because of their origins. At the same time, Busenello stressed repeatedly that he wrote for his own age—and that his style had to reflect this. He did not seek to recapture the spirit of antiquity like the first creators of operas. His *Didone*, he said, was "influenced by modern opinions. It is not made according to the prescriptions of the ancient rules but in accord with Spanish usage, it presents years not hours."[27] Yet while he appreciated aspects of Spain's culture, his poems were scathing in their denunciation of its social world.[28]

Badoaro was also unwilling to restrict his librettos to "classic" formulas. In a preface to one of his later operas, *Ulisse errante* (*Wandering Ulysses*), which recounted parts of *The Odyssey*'s story that preceded those in *Ritorno*, he wrote that "the ancients have prescribed rules in many things for they held it to [be] their glory that the world stopped on their precepts" and expected that "the whole world would hold" them. Perhaps, he added, this was to stymie "the faculty of invention." Whoever wishes to follow this law "in all things" is welcome to do so, said Badoaro, but he thought it was like "a reason of state besieged by interest and time. Unhappy century if the footsteps of the past should force our step onto an unalterable path." It leads to blindness, he contended—reinforcing his remarkable equation of political with artistic change. Moreover, "the precepts" of poetics are not "certain and permanent" like those of mathematics. There was no reason to fear novelty. His sole rule, he elaborated, was to satisfy his present day audience. For this, he had to take to his own course, not that of antiquity.[29]

Badoaro and Busenello may have written librettos on mythological themes—scholarship questions if there actually was a Trojan war, let alone a Ulysses—but their sense of history and change was strong. Eventually, Busenello turned directly to historical themes, but in order to exploit them. Incogniti librettos stressed often what is and is not visible in the social and political worlds, ancient settings were used to speak to their own times.[30] And contemporary Venice was also linked to places in these operas: ancient Troy, after all, was on the contemporary Ottoman mainland (even if nobody knew exactly where). Odysseus (Ulysses) and Aeneas wandered the seas—which is what Venetians and, more broadly, Europeans did, in an "age of exploration."

Chapter 7

REVEALING ULYSSES

Monteverdi's Venetian operas show how rich his imagination became over the decades. After his death they faded from public attention, but his achievement was recognized anew when scores of *Ritorno* and *Poppea* were rediscovered three centuries later. Researchers debate just how much of the music in them was actually composed by him (the existing early scores are not in his hand). Yet as we noted, one scholar rightly points out that Monteverdi reworked and reorganized his librettos to achieve music dramas; whatever doubts or questions may be raised about aspects of them, their artistic integrity—his artistic coherence—makes it legitimate to speak of them as if they are all his.[1] With artistic coherence came a certain intellectual coherence.

He was, of course, not of the same status as his librettists. Nor was he necessarily of the same mindset in every way. He was, after all, a musician at San Marco and an outsider. The Incogniti were patricians, citizens, and reputed skeptics. Still, while these intellectuals undoubtedly understood the political use of bread and circuses, they were very serious about the new art form. Certainly, they wanted it to reflect Venetian glory. And they sought to say through it something about their lives and times. They modeled their "academy" on one fashioned in Padua decades earlier by Cremonini and Galileo to discuss ethics and religion. *Ritorno* was Badoaro's first libretto, and in a letter to the composer he explained that he wrote it "to incite Your Lordship's virtues to make known to Venice that where strong emotions are concerned, there is a vast difference between a painted image of the sun and the sun itself." He hoped his "poetical perseverance" might "unleash" Monteverdi's "musical passion" which, in turn would elicit warm feelings among Venetians; Monteverdi was "the sun itself."[2] Another way of saying this might be: Monteverdi would write a real music drama, not just what seemed to be one. Perhaps this expressed a belief that the newly popular musical theater had not achieved its potentials.

Homeland, constancy, rightful rulership, and the role of elites are among *Ritorno*'s concerns; they organize and thread through the opera like motifs.

Figure 7.1. Claudio Monteverdi (1567–1643) as maestro of the ducal orchestra in Venice, as depicted by Jan van Grevenbroeck the Younger (1731–1807). Museo Correr, Venice. Photo: Alfredo Gagli Orti/Art Resource, NY.

A decade after the Zeno affair, in which Venice may be said to have struggled over what it meant to be faithful to itself, Badoaro and Monteverdi turned to a figure who wandered in quest of his *patria*. When Ulysses arrives finally there he finds his queen, Penelope, fending off the advances of "Suitors"—self-serving nobles—who seek to convince her that her husband is dead. Each wants her hand and the scepter that comes with it. Badoaro's original manuscript (or manuscripts with Monteverdi's emendations) is lost. Early printed versions begin with a prologue about the human condition, pointing implicitly toward the tests to be endured by Ulysses and Penelope. Three figures, Fate, Strength, and Prudence, convey their respective powers. The first is the most forceful among them: "if Fate dissents," then Strength is powerless and human Prudence feeble.[3] One manuscript of the score, that of a copyist, from Monteverdi's time (or apparently from close to it), makes the five acts of the libretto into three.[4] It too begins with a prologue, but the cast is different and the challenge to humanity made more blunt, taxing, and sophisticated.

The voice we hear at its outset is "Human Fragility." The worries he expresses are universal, but they might easily be interpreted as immediate warnings to Venetians. He sings of mortality, of life's inevitable perils, and of its uncertainties. The figures of "Time," "Fortune" and "Love" are with him, and they confirm his prognoses. Their boasts of their own powers, one after the other, intersperse with his plaints. Time created man, but fights him and will, eventually, undo him. Fortune, a capricious goddess, may bring him gladness, but she may bring woe. Alas, human youth is lost to the "tyranny" of Love (*Amore*—Cupid, that is). That naked little—ever reappearing—deity can even "wound Gods" and shoots his arrows blindly. "Through me, you are frail," sings Time; "Through me, wretched," intones Fortune; "Through me, troubled," brags Love.[5] Together, they offer no pity—only distress, enfeeblement, their gnawing, pricks and wounds. All of them are mezzo-sopranos—except Time, a weighty bass.

II.

"Constancy"—we return to this essential neo-Stoic word. Lipsius's mix of Hellenistic and Christian notions was well known to Incogniti and they undoubtedly recognized some of the difficulties of blending them with civic patriotism. After all, Stoicism seems to imply withdrawal from the world's tumult so that a person might fasten calmly to more important matters; this notion does not combine lackadaisically with a strong sense of public responsibilities or a Tacitean stress on political tough-mindedness. It is not, however, impossible to bring them together, which is one reason why the figure of Seneca, ancient Roman Stoic philosopher and playwright, and ambitious advisor to a corrupt emperor, was of importance in the age of early opera.

A patriotic Venetian had to be selective in his reception of neo-Stoicism, especially if he had been a student of Cremonini. Like neo-Stoics, this skeptic did believe something endured amidst the world's flux. But for him it was found in Aristotle's thought (by contrast to his colleague Galileo, who challenged the Aristotelian view of the universe). To be Aristotelian and a patriot is not problematic. This ancient philosopher believed we are "political animals," and that our humanity can only be realized as citizens within a political community. Yet a neo-Stoic cannot simply say this. If he engages the political world, he must somehow square its unrest with belief in a steady, divine, or universal rationality—and the conviction that this rationality is always paramount. One way to reconciliation was that of a curious, secretive sect called the Family of Love, and Lipsius associated with it. Its theology stressed that external matters were transient, and not of central human concern. Visible, institutionalized forms of worship counted little if a person's relation with God was aright. True beliefs could even be cloaked entirely. Lipsius changed his formal religious affiliation numerous times, depending on where he lived. If in a Protestant territory, he could be Protestant; if the realm was Catholic, the faith into which he was born, so would he be.

As a way of behaving, this is similar to Cremonini's skepticism. It seems that his favorite adage was "*Intus ut libet, foris ut moris est*"—which may be translated either as "Think what you like, but say what is expected of you" or "Inwardly according to your own mind, outwardly according to custom."[6] Cremonini, like Galileo, faced problems with the Inquisition. Unlike his colleague, however, Cremonini remained behind Venice's shield in Padua. Galileo's trial in Rome came just a few years before opera came to the Venetian Republic and showed how dangerous truth-telling could be.

For Lipsius it was constancy, not ceremony, that allowed true virtue. By this logic, he opposed patriotism; it meant devotion to something external. Ancient Stoics apparently originated the term "cosmopolitan" to indicate their bond to a rational cosmos, and thus to what was common—reason—in all men, rather than to what bound people in political allegiance. But if patriotic loyalty was belittled by Lipsius, this did not mean that politics or obedience to constituted authorities were of no consequence. He drew the opposite conclusion in *Politica*. Patriotism, in itself, might be a material, false deity but it was quite legitimate for a *patria* to impose laws and religious uniformity. This was equivalent to an endorsement of the Peace of Augsburg that, in 1555, ended the first phase of Europe's religious wars with the principle that a prince could oblige his subjects to share his religion. Today this seems illiberal. In context it was a step towards pluralism. Instead of imposing a universal Christendom by bloodshed, Catholics and Protestants accepted that neighboring kingdoms could have a different Christian faith.

Dreadful wars had demonstrated the need for peace, for only calm and order allowed men to pursue what is important. But where there was no peace or where outward conformity was compelled, dissimulation—acting—was perfectly appropriate. These kinds of ideas, given a proper remix and coloration, could attract patriots within Venice's political classes. After all, the century began for them with the Interdict Crisis—a struggle over legal prerogatives and ecclesiastical liberty. A Lipsius-like opposition to patriotism could not have appealed to devoted republican oligarchs, but "constancy" translated into Venetian *virtù* could. That *virtù*, like music sounding within a drama, wasn't visible; it was akin to the role of Incogniti, who didn't show themselves off or display their influence. A wise person, they believed, could distinguish *virtù* and true friendship from ephemeral powers and transient beauties. Such a wise person would find a parallel between civic self-mastery and that of the individual. After all, Venetians were heirs both to Troy—a city destroyed after the abduction of a beautiful woman—and the Roman republic. The heritage crystallized in an ideology, a coherent—but self-interested—worldview of an elite. Its mental structures, perspectives, hopes, and hidden fears appeared in opera. They were not always consistent or persistent, although the motifs and variants on them emerge and reemerge.

And so in Venice the choice of Ulysses's return to Ithaca must have had special resonance, particularly for Incogniti. The protagonist of *The Odyssey* is a man of cunning, but for Romans, who looked to Aeneas as their progenitor, he was a successful deceiver, responsible for that idea of a great wooden horse that concealed warriors and brought down Troy. Homer tells how Ulysses first smuggled himself into Troy to spy on the enemy city and "roamed its streets" disguised as a beggar. The hoax of the Trojan horse takes place after the events of *The Iliad*, but before those of *The Odyssey*. It is perhaps most famously described in *The Aeneid*, where Virgil has Aeneas brand Ulysses "iron-hearted" and Cassandra warns: if you know Ulysses, then you also know that any gift from Greeks—like that steed at the gates—comes of "guile."[7] Ovid also saw duplicity as Ulysses's chief characteristic. Florence looked to Aeneas as a hero and Dante placed Ulysses at hell's bottom, where he groans amidst flames because of the "ambush" of the Trojan Horse that damaged Rome's "noble seed."[8] The Monteverdi-Badoaro opera, in contrast, celebrates Ulysses's cunning, his daring, his striving to return. It is a Venetian defense of a mythological figure reviled in Rome and Florence.

III.

Some of *Ritorno*'s principal political messages and expressions, as well as its subtle commentary on rulership and hierarchy, becomes evident if we follow who is and who is not "constant"—and why—during the Ithacan king's absence. Corruption has set in while the three Suitors roam the palace. Ulysses's fate is in fact unknown. He is somewhere out in the world and has been gone already for twenty years. We first meet his Penelope singing of herself: "A queen condemned to sorrow/ I pass my days in grief . . . the years are flying."[9] She is trapped within a regal fortress; ranged against her are the forces we heard arrayed in the prologue against "Human Fragility." Walls surround her also because, for all her suffering, she accepts them. She is a queen and knows that she lives by different standards, with different dangers and demands than others.

Later, her maidservant Melanto observes how life is insecure even when it is near to a protective royal scepter; for dangerous hands grow bolder near the throne.[10] She would have Penelope assume Ulysses forever gone, would have her cast aside useless prudence, and take another's hand. But Penelope and Melanto have different characters and these correspond to different stations. The Queen believes Ulysses went to war for the right reason, to defeat impure love. She does wonder why she must suffer for this famous wrong, done by the Trojan prince Paris who abducted Helen from her husband. She scorns the Suitors, although not without slight wavering. This Queen expresses herself mostly in recitative; it is a musical means that reinforces her besieged, sorrowful, and chaste determination. For Monteverdi it is a way for us to hear her restrained self-possession by contrast to an emotional air of release that will finally come—she is, after all, human—at the finale.

As the opera progresses, Monteverdi and Badoaro present contrasts, scene after scene, to reveal what is at stake. They portray differing hierarchies, each linked internally—gods and mortals, royals, the privileged, and the commons. The relation between character and class is ever important. For example, consider the shift after Penelope's lonely lament to the voice of impassioned Melanto. The musical mood changes from solemnity to lyricism, from expressive control to exuberant, sensuous desire. Melanto and her love Eurymachus—he is apparently in the service of the Suitors—woo each other believing, as Melanto puts it, nobody loses by playing the game of love, however bruising it might be. Their voices unite to declare that inflamed love allows no restraint. Eurymachus is captivated by her. Unlike her Queen, Melanto is not chaste; she hopes Penelope will regard love as she, a servant, does.

The Queen's way in the world also contrasts to that of her Suitors. Material hunger is inseparable from love for these men. "Love once more," they implore her. Love one of them, they mean. They offer gifts; they believe that a love song is best accompanied by "the sound of gold."[11] Little wonder that for Penelope, who does not want to be hurt again, love is an idol with plumes swaying in the wind, providing momentary delight—it is a joy that turns quickly to torment. The difference between the Queen and her handmaiden is also expressed musically by different tonalities.[12]

The contrast between Penelope's constancy and the fervors of Eurymachus and Melanto reflects a lively debate that occurred among Incogniti. Does physical beauty deceive? they queried. Doesn't love befuddle men, enslaving them to passion at the expense of higher virtues like profound friendship and fraternity? The Incogniti may have had deserved reputations as "libertines" but, ironically, these questions seem to warn of dangers in sensuality. Venetian libertinage was, as one commentator remarks, not rigorous but "cultivated the paradox of producing works at once perfectly subversive . . . and sacred works that give the impression of a relative conformity to orthodoxy."[13] Loredano wrote a novelistic *L'adamo* (*Adam*), which achieved widespread popularity in 1640. It is about the first man and his fate in the Garden of Eden: "Thou, O sensual man . . . debasest thy self in adoring a face."[14] Adam, in Loredano's account, is deluded by—loses himself as a result of—the "sweet tyranny" of Eve's beauty. This despotism subjects even the "noblest minds."[15] Beware, then, of what may be solely on the surface. Unhappy he who fixates on passing externalities rather than searching for and cultivating deeper beauty within. Music, for Loredano, reveals what is within; like tears, a song expresses what is in the soul to listeners.[16] Singing in recitative, Penelope seems to ignore warnings that her attractiveness will fade as she grows older.

IV.

Unbeknownst to Penelope, Ulysses has arrived at an isolated cove of his homeland. He does not, at first, recognize where he is. He had been washed ashore before on another island, that of the Phaeacians, a seafaring people. A hapless stranger, he was welcomed by them. A crew of their mariners took him to Ithaca, leaving him asleep on the sands. Now, however, it is evident that mightier forces are at play. Neptune (Poseidon for the Greeks), who is the sea god and father of the Phaeacians, is furious. He had decreed that none may help Ulysses for the Ithacan king had, after leaving Troy, blinded Polyphemus, the wretched Cyclops who was also Neptune's son. The "insolent Phaeacians" disregarded Neptune's will, and this imperils authority, the sea god insists, in an exchange with his own sovereign, Jove, the king of the gods. Their dialogue raises our old question: what are the prerogatives and the proprieties of good rulers? What sustains their powers?

There seem to be somewhat differing humanisms animating *Orfeo* and *Ritorno*. In the former, the Infernal Spirits admire Orpheus's gumption on braving hell; they laud him as an embodiment of humanity's possibilities.

Still, Orpheus fails due to a combination of weakness and conceit. In *Ritorno*, angry Neptune complains to taciturn Jove that man's pride causes all wrongdoing. Original sin is suggested, which is, of course, not so in Homer. *Ritorno* is, in its broad strokes, close to *The Odyssey* (or to recent Italian renditions of it in Monteverdi's day).[17] Yet there is recrafting and subtle political refraction through seventeenth-century categories. Consider first how Homer presents the back-and-forth between Neptune and Jove, and then how *Ritorno* does so. Early in *The Odyssey*, Jove (Zeus for the Greeks) complains to an assembly of gods about bad behavior by the victors at Troy. Neptune is not present; he is in faraway Ethiopia and so does not hear the harangue of Olympus's King: "Ah how shameless—the way these mortals / blame the gods./ From us alone, they say, come all their miseries, yes/ but they themselves, with their own reckless ways/ compound their pains beyond their proper share."[18]

So if gods determine the fate of men, human action plays its role, accentuating the good and bad in destiny. Minerva (Athena for Homer) speaks as Ulysses's champion. His itinerant fate has been unfair, she protests. Did he not always sacrifice to the gods? Now he is trapped on Calypso's island, prisoner of this beautiful nymph's love, but he wants to go to his rightful hearth. Jove replies that it is Neptune who acts against Ulysses, forever driving his ship "off course." But the King of the Gods takes pity, and asks fellow divinities to sanction Ulysses's return to Ithaca. How to point him homeward? They deliberate. Neptune, Jove trusts, "will let his anger go/ How can he stand his ground against the will/ of all the gods at once—one god alone?"[19]

The goddess rejoices: "The exile must return."[20]

She will go to earth to guide heaven's will among humans. Jove has not responded solely to a call for compassion. He responds positively to Minerva's pleas because he knows Ulysses is wise, and not just crafty. Jove makes his determination on the basis of Ulysses's ways in the world. It is Minerva, Goddess of Wisdom, who makes her claim on the basis of compassion, and Jove understands that this must also be in the reckoning. Neptune, by contrast, is steered by fuming feelings. Constant character, wisdom, compassion, enraged emotion—Homer touches on all those themes that interested Monteverdi in his Mantuan operas.

The exile must return: *The Odyssey* tells of a man who travels the seas incognito through adventures and trials. You must always come back to your *patria*; so Homer suggests, and this is a message of *Ritorno* too. Here we must turn back to the Phaeacian sailors, for these great mariners do not return home. The Phaeacians depicted by Homer—the opera touches but briefly on them—are generous. In contrast, the one-eyed Cyclops is the thuggish head of a cannibalistic clan of giants. In Homer, this clan also differs radically in its political ways from both the gods and the Phaeacians. "They have no meeting place for council," we learn of the man-eaters, "no laws either, / no, up on the mountain peaks they live in arching caverns—each a law to himself, ruling his wives and children, / not a care in the world for any neighbor."[21] The gods do assemble and take counsel, even if Jove's word is final. Phaeacians, who had migrated to their island to be free of harassment by cyclopses, are ruled by a munificent king who confers with a council of nobles.[22]

It is after the Phaeacians leave Ulysses slumbering at Ithaca that Homer presents Neptune and Jove in conversation.[23] The sea god complains: My honor will be lost. "I decreed that Ulysses's journey would be arduous, but I never aimed to thwart the other gods. I never dreamed/ of blocking his return,/ not absolutely at least,/once you had pledged your word. . . ." Homer's Neptune accepts final authority. Jove responds with a certain irony, even contempt: why, Neptune, do you whine, with all your power? "The gods don't disrespect you," says Jove, intimating that perhaps they will if Neptune persists in protest. And men? "If any man, so lost in his strength/ and prowess, pays you no respect—just pay him back./ The power is always yours. Do what you like."[24] Neptune wants to crush the Phaeacian ship.

Jove proposes another idea. Let the "racing vessel" "metamorphose into a rock" just as it approaches Phaeacian shores. All "the ages" will see what happens when men move against a god's will. Neptune finds this appealing and does it a "stroke of his hand." Those Phaeacians who wait on their home coast for the return of their sailors are horrified when they behold their fate. And their king recalls sadly an ancient prophecy: Neptune, "vexed" by Phaeacians because they "escorted all mankind and never came to grief," would act out his wrath on one of their ships, making it "a huge mountain"—a reef—blocking their port. Phaeacians, the King announces, will have to stop helping "every castaway" who chances upon their shores. He calls for sacrifice to Neptune.[25] In the end, the Sea God maintains his authority over the seas.

It is at this moment in Homer's narrative that Ulysses awakens. In the opera, Neptune's argument has a harder, more realist edge, although driven also by anger. We gods pardon with too much ease, he tells Jove. He admonishes: "Human liberty/ dares everything." Man pits himself against fate and contends with heaven itself.[26] (Orpheus had a similar project with hell.) Homer's Jove also frowns on human assertiveness, but Neptune, in the Badoaro-Monteverdi rendering, puts much stronger stress on the utterly negative consequences of human free will. The gods will be wounded if they do not use their powers and punish as they should. Pity will become weakness.

Jove, slightly chagrined by Neptune's insistence, presents a counterargument. He speaks with a sense of balance, although with regard for the prerogatives of power. Don't be foolish, he warns. I am not necessarily averse to force, but I prefer other means. Yes, my "thunderbolt" has its sheer power, but "compassion persuades."[27] The dignity of men, Jove observes, must be sustained when they are obedient. Vendetta can undermine judgment, even if it is not necessarily to be reviled. It is not necessarily justified or wise either. "Reason," says Jove, is what gods—and the implication is, good rulers—share.[28] Yes, men who move wrongly may be halted. The implication, however, is that Ulysses moves rightly, that is, his journey can only end at his *patria*. Ulysses's violence against vicious Polyphemus is not, evidently, judged by Jove as worthy of revenge; he takes the side of Minerva—of wisdom. He has decided as Striggio's Pluto does. There can be flexibility provided order is maintained. The Phaeacians, like Orpheus, imagine that laws of the realm, whether it is the seas or Hades, can be bypassed.

Yes, Neptune may punish the sailors. But Ulysses is already on land, and thus no longer in Neptune's domain. The Phaeacian seamen are on the waves, where Neptune rules. Monteverdi and Badoaro give them a song that seems to prove Neptune's view of human insolence. We go as we please, they sing, we do as we please and the gods pay no attention. And so the mariners, like Orpheus, suffer woeful fates, much as viewers might in fact find these men attractive (certainly they are in Homer's account).

Jove, the sovereign god, has confirmed that the jurisdictional principle of the Peace of Augsburg: *Cuis regio, Eius religio*—"who rules, his religion." A ruler has authority to demand within his realm, within his jurisdiction, that subjects follow his faith. Vengeful Neptune retains his authority, no matter how kindly the Phaeacians may be; and Jove shows that kindliness must be used with discretion.

V.

When Ulysses awakens, he thinks that he has been abandoned by the Phaeacians, and by the gods too. Soon he learns that things are not as they seem. A young shepherd boy—an Arcadian figure—approaches. This turns out to be none less than Minerva in disguise. She reveals herself; she divulges that he has arrived at Ithaca and help from higher powers is at hand. Now, seeing things as they are, he swears obedience to her. "Who would have believed a goddess in human dress?" marvels Ulysses, wondering too if such masquerades also take place in heaven.[29] In your absence, she tells him, Penelope has been faithful, though pressed. I will retrieve your son, Telemachus, now in Sparta, and in the meanwhile, your appearance shall change. You will become an old beggar and be able to go to court to witness what is happening there without announcing yourself (as younger Ulysses once did in Troy). Who would believe a beggar is king? The values of guile are thus affirmed by Minerva; the presence of gods and rulers should not always be evident. "*Incognito sarai*," she says, using a word that brings immediately to mind the name of the circle to which Badoaro belonged: "You shall be incognito." Disguised, he will see the impertinence of the Suitors and the "the immutable constancy" of "chaste Penelope."[30]

Monteverdi creates relations among the characters musically. In their first scene together, Ulysses and Minerva sing in concert only when the king and the goddess, both authorities, albeit of different kinds, appear as their true selves. Their voices don't mesh when she is a shepherd and he the old beggar; then, they talk (or rather, sing in recitative). Who does and who does not sing together and how is a key feature of how hierarchical relations—proper or improper—are portrayed throughout the opera.

Minerva goes to fetch Telemachus—his role in this opera is small but his place in later opera and intellectual history will grow greatly—and sends the beggar on his way. The first person he comes across is a lowly, aged swineherd, Eumaeus, who like the Queen has been faithful to Ulysses all these years. Their meeting is framed by an idyllic reality that allows *Ritorno* to distinguish among ways of relating to material need. Just before Ulysses sees him, Eumaeus is alone in a grove, at home within greenery and amidst animals he tends. His contentment has, however, been disrupted by a disagreeable figure who is of considerable importance for the opera. Of a sudden, Eumaeus must cope with Irus, greedy sycophant of Penelope's Suitors. Here, then, are two "lowly" figures, but their relations to the world, natural and human, are opposite to one another. Irus will provide the opera's comedy—but embedded in it is sharp social commentary. Plain Eumaeus has been devoted to the memory of regal Ulysses because of his king's character; Irus's grovels before aristocratic lords because of his devotion to his ever-growling stomach. In Homer he is described as a "a public nuisance/ who used to scrounge for a living round the streets of Ithaca—notorious for his belly, a ravenous, bottomless pit. . . ."[31]

If the opera's Eumaeus, like Minerva in her first appearance before Ulysses, is a pastoral figure, Irus is a being who devours nature. Eumaeus sings of nature's joys; he provides yet another contrast to the sufferings of those who are in power—the leaders of civilization. Like the simple folk of Naxos in *Arianna*, Eumaeus's message is that the finest clothes can cover great woe while the poor and humble—like a shepherd—live more securely than do the illustrious. Woods, hills, and meadows are the domains of human happiness and it is from them that "the fruit of freedom (*di Libertade*)" buds.[32] Nature, simplicity, and freedom are identified. The use of "*di Libertade*" here is perhaps subtly but potently suggestive. The Incogniti were often accused of being "Libertines." The meaning of "Liber" is literally "free one," and Liber was a nature god identified by ancient Romans with fertility and animals. The word was, however, also a Latin name for Bacchus (Dionysus for the Greeks), the god of wine known, as his name would suggest, for bacchanalia. But this mythological figure was associated as well with plebeians and free speech. In the ancient Roman republic, Liber was hailed by "plebs" in their conflicts with patricians. When Liber arrives in Ovid's *Metamorphoses*, fields "reverberate" and people come through the city gates, "ignoring all distinctions of rank and gender."[33] This description sounds a little like Venetian Carnival. In *Ritorno*, Eumaeus is a Liber-like commoner, and he is united with his king against both the aristocrats and Irus, who can only think of material things.

Irus is also a plain figure, but in a different way. He cannot distinguish among luxury, nature, and power. He identifies nature with dinner, and liberty does not enter his mind. "I live among kings," he crows—even though the question of Ithaca's ruler is unresolved. You, Eumaeus, you live and chat with herds—which I will eat, he says. "You great glutton," responds Eumaeus, anxious to be rid of him, ". . . run, run to eat." In the libretto (but not in the score), he adds, "burst apart!"[34] Food, for the swineherd, is a natural part of life, not a reason for being. It is just after he is free of Irus that Eumaeus meets the elderly beggar. He doesn't recognize Ulysses but welcomes a destitute soul: "Mendicants are favored by Heaven as Jove's friends."[35] They will interact with warmth and decency—a concealed king and a man of paltry means. The difference between appearance and reality offers an ethos. Eumaeus doesn't yet know who this figure is. He simply extends kindness to him (and hears from him happy tidings—it has a Christian timbre—that Ulysses lives and will return).

We find here an important social and political nub of the opera. Ulysses is rightfully at the pinnacle of a hierarchy and Eumaeus is a commoner, but they are bonded. The Suitors, by contrast, are graspers, reaching for the top rung, and Irus grabs for their heels. Eumaeus will soon lead Ulysses to the palace; Irus, by the opera's end, will follow his masters to hell. But here we move too far ahead. Brief summary of the rest of it will let us tease more out of it.

VI.

Following the first exchange between Eumaeus and Ulysses, a chariot arrives with Minerva and Telemachus. Now the prince meets his father. After Ulysses's identity is revealed, Telemachus goes to the court to let Penelope know that her husband will be there soon, although without telling her that the king comes in disguise. In the meantime, at the palace, the Suitors press on. They proffer their valuable "love"; she withstands their crude enticements. And then come the new arrivals. Eumaeus escorts the old man on to the royal grounds and, of course, the aristocrats treat them with vociferous contempt. One Suitor, Antinous, snarls at Eumaeus: You have always been "villainous." Now you drag an "infested beggar" into stately surroundings. Send him to your herds, get him out of this place where "civilized nobility commands and rules." Irus, stuttering, seconds this verve. He will not stand for someone else to be on the feeding line. Eumaeus the swineherd retorts: "Refined nobility is not cruel."[36] Pigheaded Irus is happy to challenge the old vagabond to a wrestling match and is, of course, thrashed.

Penelope offers the Beggar hospitality at court. By so doing, she not only confirms humble Eumaeus's demeanor but also his impulses, for she acts as the swineherd did upon first meeting the "valiant mendicant."[37] A nature is shared, it seems, by noble souls, whatever their rank or birth. (But there is no hint that they all ought to share power.) The Queen has not recognized her husband and declares simply that poor clothes do not define the man in them. She has, of course, long seen through the glitter of the Suitors. Finally, she responds to their wearying petitions with a proposal. She will give her hand to whoever has the strength to string the bow of Ulysses and to shoot a quiver from it. The Suitors believe this is a "glorious" idea. Yet she adds as an immediate aside that her words contradict her heart.

It turns out that love—the Suitors' kind, anyway—cannot succeed. Despite Penelope's renunciations of love, she is really lovesick, as lovesick as

Ulysses has been homesick. The Suitors try, one after the other, to string the bow. One's fingers are not deft enough; the next finds the bow intractable. The third finds his own "*virtù* and valor" are to no avail and frets: perhaps even the bow awaits Ulysses. Their failures suit Penelope; titles and noble blood, she remarks, are vain. To earn the treasures of Ulysses, his merit must be equaled.

Then the Beggar steps forth. Can he join the contest?, he asks—it is for the effort's sake, he adds, not for treasures. He has thus confirmed Penelope's resolve by insisting that character, not reward, matters. Of course, he succeeds in stringing the bow. Thunder—it is Minerva—heralds triumph. The Beggar now turns his arrows on the Suitors and, to agitated music, dispatches them to Hades. (Irus soon follows.) But Penelope does not believe that the Beggar is Ulysses, despite pleas by Telemachus and Eumaeus to recognize him. Her constancy borders on obstinacy. Perhaps this is some courtier's ploy, she worries, or even a ruse by the gods. Yet all the gods are now with Ulysses. Even Neptune has finally been convinced to be merciful to Ithaca's hero, and to be placated by the fate dealt to the Phaeacians. When Ulysses describes to Penelope the silk sheet of their nuptial bed—nobody else could have seen their secret site of love—she knows her husband has returned. She can leave recitative behind, and sing that her "Phoenix/ has risen happily from Trojan ashes." *Ritorno* closes with a reunited pair singing happily together. Their final words are "*Si, si!*"—Yes, yes![38]

VII.

Going more deeply inside the opera's structure helps to gauge what has been set right and how. The story is about gods, royals, aristocrats, and men of "lower" strata. It is sung through them, and political and social implications are suggested significantly by whose voices do and do not join. There are solos; there are times when two characters sing together and three as well. At various moments a supporting cast appears. They alone gather in chorus, with no individual identities to be discerned. It is a conspicuous feature of *Ritorno*, which includes:

Nereids (Mediterranean sea nymphs) and Sirens (bird-women). Their choruses come just before the Phaeacians leave Ulysses on Ithaca (their music is missing);

The Phaeacian sailors;

Naiads (freshwater nymphs). Just after Ulysses is transformed into the Beggar, Minerva instructs them to guard Ulysses's treasures and they sing in ensemble;

Eight Moors. Their chorus and dance (specified as Greek in style) come after the Suitors call upon Penelope to love again;

Choruses from the heavens in praise of Jove and from the oceans lauding Neptune. They hail the Sovereign of Olympus for convincing the God of the Seas to yield his animosity towards Ulysses; and they salute Neptune for his concession. Not only do the two choruses overlap, but they also direct words to humanity: turn to heaven, your prayers will be answered;

A chorus of Ithacans. It provides the end of the opera according to the libretto, but is absent from the score. There, the voices of Ulysses and Penelope come together for the finale.

None of these choruses is essential to the story's progress. Voices are united only to confirm or affirm the will of the gods or, when Ulysses, marking fidelity to his people, swears before them his loyalty to Minerva and Penelope. There is, however, an exception. The doomed Phaeacians are a chorus with a complicated provenance. In some productions, their presentation is comical, but this misreads their ironic role (it is particularly evident if you have read Homer). They go under for disobeying a god, all while they carry out the will of Neptune's fellow deities by bringing Ulysses home. Their humanity is noble, but they think the gods don't pay attention to them at all.

We don't know why the Ithacan chorus disappeared from the (apparently) final version, but its absence is suggestive of political attitudes about the role of the *demos* (the People) as a collective whole in both *The Odyssey* and in Venice. An observation about *The Odyssey* by classicist M.I. Finley is equally applicable to *Ritorno*: "We are never told what the *demos* of Ithaca really thought about the whole affair. The narrative reach[es] its end without their intervention . . ."[39] Two qualifications are immediately needed. The absence of "intervention" here refers to a specific meeting of the Ithacan assembly described early in *The Odyssey*. His father long gone, Telemachus has sought support to little effect. He even remarks unhappily that the *demos* seem immobile while the wretched Suitors track his mother. An only son, Telemachus has no brothers or troops, while the Suitors are banded together in the hope of killing him, thus eliminating their competitor for the crown. These exchanges do not take place in the opera; instead there is simply affirmation of the gods and their powers, especially after Ulysses reveals himself.

Homer gives us assembly meetings in different contexts. His sympathies are antityrannical, but not democratic (to use what would have been an anachronism in Homer's day). When the gods congregate, Jove's word is final and he is firm, although he listens to and deliberates with other deities, and respects their domains. He hears Minerva plea for Ulysses with sympathy, while paying due heed to Neptune's prerogatives. Jove knows the requirements of his own authority. He tells the assembled deities, "Come, all of us here, put our heads together now, / work out this journey home so [Ulysses] can return."[40] When Neptune yields, however, it is by trade-off to protect his own sovereignty. A political logic is evident. The Phaeacian sailors travel the seas, which are under his authority; it remains his right to punish them. Jove will grant this, regardless of the lack of pity. Neptune is satisfied by the same principle in *Ritorno*, although in the opera he simply accepts Jove's "decree." Jove has been persuaded only by the entreaties of Juno (his "sister and spouse") and Minerva. Heavenly and nautical choruses salute the results, much like the Infernal Chorus of *Orfeo* hails Pluto's decision about Eurydice. But there is also the implied rebuttal of Neptune's claim that pride is the source of all sin; Jove tells the Sea God that "Destiny" writes the defense of Ulysses: "Man is not culpable if heaven thunders."[41]

Politics remains elite politics in Homer's world as much as in that of Venice. The Venetian oligarchy would have had it no other way. But if we must follow the vocal threads further throughout *Ritorno*, they tell us about different possibilities of hierarchy. One winds from Ulysses to Eumaeus. Ulysses is brave and shrewd; and by following Minerva, he shows that a wise ruler respects the gods. Goodness is both divine and natural, and thus partakes of a happy cosmic order. A boy shepherd is revealed to be a goddess, a beggar a king; when wisdom prevails, the king can retake his throne and rule, presumably well and charitably, and so his Ithacan subjects will doubtless be happy. The Goddess has guided this. Eumaeus, shepherd of animals, is happy at the prospect of Ulysses's return. The relations among Minerva, Ulysses, and Eumaeus show how reciprocity can bind governors and governed.

Ulysses never feels shame in conversing with Eumaeus. Irus, however, does not even seem to notice that his popinjay masters sing together but never entertain a word with him, the sponger. What the Suitors actually share with Irus—emptiness—would never be a subject for discussion among these hollow men in fluffy dress. Irus's begging stomach is one with his soul. When the Suitors are slain by Ulysses, Irus moans—alone—and it is a glutton's lament. If Penelope began the opera lamenting Ulysses's absence, Irus is now doleful because of his innards' prospects. Alas! he sings, he will lose the pleasures of gorging! Alas! Nobody will laugh at his ravenous exploits. The dolt seems to have enjoyed provoking hilarity from his betters who fed and clothed him. We detect here a picture of a smug, paternalistic aristocracy and a groveling lower class or even a bratty child. Irus does nothing to disprove the Suitors' contempt. Indeed, when they chortle like cruel teenagers, he craves their mockery and cannot distinguish it from approval. It is humorous all while it shows degradation. Irus yowls, beginning with an "O" that wails on for nine measures (bars) before reaching the word "*dolor*" (pain). He overflows only with a maddening despair—that is, until he concludes that his own body should "satiate the tomb" and he takes his own vacant life.[42] It is his only free act in the opera, but it is not adultlike since, by contrast to Eumaeus, he cannot stand on his own feet.

Suitors and parasite have just spoils after Ulysses's return.

When the Suitors sing together, they always express commonality of their nefarious purposes—or, when the return of Ulysses seems nigh, of concern or of fear. In one scene, however, they are in silent unison and with united direction: on their way to Hades. This scene was apparently not set by Monteverdi, who found it "too melancholic."[43] In it, we read of how the Suitors, now to be eternally silent "shades," are addressed by Mercury, Jove's son. This messenger of the gods ushers the dead downward. He tells the "once illustrious princes now dark souls" that the abyss awaits them; they are rightly to be "submerged in the kingdom of him who teaches cruelty." The Shades vanish, and Mercury then warns the audience of "eternal" punishments for the "briefest pleasures" of mortals. "Your life," he cautions, "is but a passage, / it has neither state nor firmness, / if beauty ever arises/ it fades as soon as it begins to shine forth. / Live cautiously, oh mortals, / for life marches on and time has wings/ And where hope grows greedy/ it cannot be sated. . . ."[44]

Contemptible aristocrats are fallen. But are admirable aristocrats or other elites vindicated? Certainly, the Incogniti found themselves estimable, quite so, although given their skepticism, it is not so easy to specify what Monteverdi's librettists believed goes beyond fleeting appearances. What lasts? They hoped, certainly, that Venice, to which they were devoted, would live on. Here the specific political moment raises interesting questions. The patriciate was rattled and decimated in the 1620s and 1630s. Considerable debate surfaced finally about opening ranks to worthy citizens. This would refresh the well-dressed but atrophying elite in need of competent men in power.[45]

Ritorno presented a persistently unflattering mirror to aristocrats in an aristocratic republic. The Suitors are concerned for themselves, not for Ithaca, and are not recognizable by Venetian republican ideals. Is this opera a warning from within? The word aristocracy comes from the Greek for "rule by the best" (the *aristoi*), and political philosophers have long argued that when an aristocracy is sealed off, it is likely to close in on itself. Did Badoaro and Monteverdi recognize this? Centuries after their collaboration, this problem preoccupied an antidemocratic political theorist from Sicily. Gaetano Mosca believed that every society has a "political" (or ruling) class. The very idea of rule by the People—the *demos*—was no more than a myth. Behind any order, whatever it is called—within it if not so visible—there is an unavoidable reality: one class rules others. Unlike Karl Marx, he believed this could never be supplanted.

He also argued that great troubles must ultimately befall political classes that reproduce their supremacy only by heredity and not by merit. They will finally bequeath an oligarchy convinced that privileges are due it, but who lack any sense of responsibility to their polity. Mosca concluded that only openness to new, talented men with merit could secure a healthy political class. As if anticipating this advice, the Venetian patriciate opted for some openness in the mid-1640s, but it was probably too late to forestall the republic's woes. Badoaro tried to convince his friend Busenello to take the necessary steps to rise beyond the citizen class into the patriciate. Busenello was not inclined to do so.[46]

INTERMEDIO (IV)

"Even if our *patria* is finished," Aeneas tells his son in *La Didone*, "virtue begins anew."[1] Troy is falling and response to fate's blows must be a brave heart. When Busenello wrote the libretto for this largely forgotten work, which premiered at Venice's Carnival in 1641 and was the first of many operas based on the *Aeneid*, he surely had in mind Europe's contemporary miseries. Troy's pillage, the subject of *Didone's* first part, conjures them up easily, especially the Thirty Years War and Mantua's fate. Venice had also been disconcerted by the entry into the Adriatic of North African corsairs in 1638. Quarrels the following year between the duke of Parma and Pope Urban VIII led eventually, in fall 1641, to the first War of Castro (in west-central Italy). Venice allied with the duke.

Asia's splendors lie buried beneath Troy's ruins, sings Iris, winged envoy of the gods, in the opera's prologue. That city's physical beauties and "marble images are now so much rubble. . . ."[2] Perhaps this is another admonition to Venetian elites: there are more important things than physical attractiveness, which is transient and insecure. The concerns of this opera proximate many in *Ritorno*. Some of Pietro Francesco Cavalli's music in *Didone's* even seems to echo that of Monteverdi. A battle between Pyrrhus (the son of Achilles) and Corebus (who loves Cassandra) uses fast, repeating, agitated notes that easily remind a listener of Ulysses's struggle with the Suitors (and of Tancredi's battle with Clorinda in *Combattimento*). When Sinon the Greek, who tricked the Trojans into admitting the great wooden horse within their walls, boasts of his "gusto" and "delight" in killing "accursed Trojans," he begins with a long "Ahhhh."[3] It carries on several bars and is reminiscent of "Ooooooo" in Irus's lament for the Suitors in *Ritorno*.

Sinon sings in celebration, Irus in remorse, but the prolonged vowel is a squeal of small men, who contrast to the great figures of the two operas. (Most of Cavalli's music is remarkably expressive recitative, song-speech that brings out Busenello's text.) Virgil's epic often mirrors Homer's, and these operas do likewise. They tell different stories of mettle and emotion, of *virtù* and fortune. In fact, Virgil did not present Rome's founding as the creation of a new *patria*, but as a "return," for the progenitor of Troy's ruling family, Dardanus, came originally from Rome to Troy. But if Venetians watched *virtù* renewed by Ulysses's return, *Didone* ends before Aeneas's arrival in Italy.[4]

119

There is, then, a difference in emphases in the two operas. Ulysses's return is presented as natural, god-sanctioned, and good; we see him after many of his most celebrated trials and deeds. The demands of patriotism itself have central force in Aeneas's story in *Didone*. Whatever the cause of war, its Trojans are noble characters in an opera that asks, finally, is the glory of a fallen *patria* retrievable? Aeneas prepares for a warrior's death as his wife and virtually everything he knows are consumed in a city of slaughter. Then Venus forestalls him. Troy's destruction is predestined, she tells him, but his vocation is elsewhere. Aeneas is obedient: "Patria . . . I offer you my life, my blood. . . . But religion obligates me to the Goddess."[5]

By following her, heaven and history align. His flight with a band of refugees from Troy will set things right, for it leads to Rome. Before arriving there, however, his constancy is tried in North Africa. Winds blow his ships to Carthage, to its Queen Dido.

How this happens, and especially how their love ends, suggests that destiny is no simple matter. For the gods—really, the forces they represent in human lives—can be at odds with each other. Venus has been in dispute with Juno, Zeus's queen. Their quarrel dates to events that unleashed the Trojan War, in which these goddesses took opposing sides. Now they conflict about Aeneas's future. Juno wants him to drown and enlists the winds to make this happen. Venus brings a counter-power to her cause—none less than Fortune (Fortuna). Yet Fortune is unpredictable, like the spindle of fate that she spins. She foresees problems for Aeneas in North Africa. The result of this alliance between Beauty and Fortune will then be mixed. Aeneas does not go under. His quest is saved by the intervention of another deity, the same one who sought to thwart Ulysses's journey to Ithaca. Neptune invokes the same principle he used in the earlier opera. The oceans are his realm and, angry, he asks the winds why their peace has been disrupted without his command. It is an unspeakable liberty. He calls forth nymphs to help Aeneas, and so this initial challenge to Rome's birth is overcome, although Aeneas has been driven off course.

Here, again disguise plays its telling role. Minerva appeared as a shepherd when Ulysses arrived in Ithaca; when Aeneas lands on unrecognizable shores, a nymph emerges. She turns out to be Venus. She tells Aeneas that he is at "the sublime city" where the "most beautiful queen" rules. This is the widow of "famous Sychaeus." Dido's husband, King of Tyre, was murdered, depriving her of her own rightful place. She fled and founded a new kingdom—which is akin to Aeneas's own mission.

Dido wants no suitors. Like Penelope, she is a woman of fierce constancy, yet her fidelity is to a husband who will not return. Venus, however, fears some machination by Juno may lead Dido to impair the Trojan mission. (This suggests some long-term historical anticipation; Carthage and Rome would, centuries later, beyond myth, be bloody foes in the Punic Wars.) So Venus dispatches Cupid (in disguise, of course) with his darts. If Dido falls in love with Aeneas, the queen will never act against him. All this intimates that beauty and love—Venus is, after all, goddess of both— like fortune, have complicated ways in life. Complicated, it turns out, for both gods and mortals. The little blind archer simply carries out Venus's will. Beauty alone matters to him, he says. Venus, however, has her aim—to safeguard Aeneas and his mission. And she seems not to recognize fully what her own powers can do, for Dido's loveliness incites great desire in Aeneas, and this too threatens his task. Busenello makes matters at once more multifaceted and clearer by retrieving (and expanding the role of) a third mortal player, Jarbas of Getuli, Africa's most powerful king. He loves Dido, but he also recognizes that strong feelings can threaten rule. His precaution: he disguises himself as a commoner—as a private man rather than as a monarch. His passions, he frets to the audience, are overwhelming his reason. He masks his "regal status" so that his own subjects cannot see him in such a state, madly in love. It is a state in which he is reliant on a "sweet glance" from his "idol" rather than on his own powers. His predicament tells us that reason must dominate a ruler's calculations. Getuli has become dependent on his emotions—and their object.[6]

When he approaches Dido directly, however, it is as himself. A queen, after all, is worthy only of a king. Still, the endeavor is hopeless; her feelings, she says, are with her husband in his grave. Jarbas is prepared to debase himself for Dido, but he also pleads on the bases of status—they are royals—"and reason." Together, as king and queen, they can have great passion and power. She is dismissive: "What does Cupid care of merit and reason?" Besides, Dido intends to stand on her own, which is precisely what smitten Jarbas has trouble doing because of his passion for her. When he comments that "Women always follow the worst course," her rebuke is keen: "That's quite true, for they are attracted by men."[7] Very soon, upon Aeneas's arrival, she will verify these words, although not as she had intended.

The opera tells us, effectively, that Jarbas cannot be both a king and a common man consumed by love. His status and disguise are at odds. A common man cannot rise above his emotions; a king must do so, for unable to govern himself, he is unfit to govern others. Jarbas will eventually lose his reason altogether out of love. The contrast to *Ritorno* is striking: Ulysses came to Penelope in disguise only to reveal himself as a virtuous ruler. Jarbas comes in disguise and reveals a lack of *virtù*. Ulysses transforms from beggar to king, revealing great inner resources, Jarbas hides—covers—himself as a commoner to protect his throne, and is overwhelmed from within, especially when it becomes obvious that Dido can indeed love again, but not him. Cupid's dart gives life to her deadened emotions, turning her from buried Sychaeus to breathing Aeneas. If neither Jarbas nor Dido can go beyond inner turmoil, Aeneas can. He arrives as a supplicant, hoping for safe harbor. Dido's ascetic serenity will soon dissipate due to this stranger's impact on her. Once in love, she believes her "glory" will surpass that of all queens by serving him. It is as if she has forgotten her rebuttal of Jarbas. Unfamiliar powers make her innards quake, she will sing. She is robbed of "self-control," her soul enslaved.[8]

When Aeneas first meets Dido, he tells her that his "heart honors you out of obligation."[9] Soon more than honor and obligation will engage his heart. In a remarkable scene, Dido and Aeneas seek shelter in a cave during a cloudburst. We never see or hear them inside. Instead, a chorus of hunters appears on stage. They pursue a boar; they chase, stab, and conquer it. The animal's wounds are in "a thousand places," and its "feet give way" as the tempest breaks.[10] Fulfillment, it seems, entails struggle, brutality, and is even predatory. The boar capitulates as Dido and Aeneas consummate. Then, as she sleeps, the Trojan hero recognizes that he is not sheltered; he stands on a precipice, and he must wound his love to part from it.

Mercury has appeared, sent by none less than Jupiter. "Aeneas, what are you doing?" he asks. Are you in a dream? He warns that "[a]t the table of idleness and amorous dalliance/ You have drunk a deadly beverage." Fortify your heart again, and "weigh anchor"—"Hasten to Italy, which prays for you alone/ To establish a Kingdom for your descendants."[11]

Aeneas is no Jarbas and no Irus. He resolves to quit Carthage; in this, he displays *virtù*. Dido is bereft, even suicidal. Unlike Penelope, she cannot withstand all adversity. One misfortune, the death of her royal husband, was enough. It is Dido's kind of love that the Incogniti questioned, not Penelope's, for Carthage's queen is lost when faced with Aeneas's determination to fulfill patriotic imperative, with mettle reminiscent of Theseus in *Arianna*. Dido loves too well and, like Ariadne, is left behind.

She cannot comprehend Aeneas's provenance; she cannot separate her reawakened feelings from greater matters. When Aeneas tells her "the biddings of destiny" draw him on, she calls him blind to her ruin, subversive of her person as well as her reign. She is not entirely wrong, but it is not as a queen that she beseeches him to stay, it is as a woman who is now reliant on emotions. The more love is her tyrant, the less is she royal. As Jarbas, in nonregal demeanor, threw himself at her feet, she is now prostrate before Aeneas. She is ruined—until Busenello, a proponent of a poet's right to take liberties (in this case his own with Virgil) provides an ending that varies from *The Aeneid* and serves to strengthen what we ought to learn from the opera's three principals.

Dido awakens to her circumstances, and laments, "Neither Dido nor the Queen/ Am I any longer, but rather a portent/ of desperate fate and torment." She seeks escape and calls for a "kindly blade" to send her "poor spirit to the realm of darkness." Aeneas understands, with a Machiavelli-like sense, that historical decisiveness cannot escape cruelty, although he, like Theseus, is remorseful. "My body is on board the boat," he sings, "but my soul bows to you [Dido]/ the desire you aroused in me will never die/ . . . in obeying the heavens I experience hell."[12] He left his *patria* in flames and now his love in tears. But remorse does not stop him. All readers of Virgil—including educated Venetian viewers of this opera—knew that Aeneas then crossed the Mediterranean, that the fate of both Dido and Jarbas is madness and then recovery thanks to each other. He is helped along by Mercury, who resolves that Jarbas's insanity should vanish, but not his love for Dido. As Jarbas recovers his reason, so too does he recognize that his proper clothing is regal, and not his disguise. Reason and rule are thus again aligned by Busenello. Dido does not die by her own hand as she intends, but is instead plighted to this king. These two royals, it seems, are now suited to each other. Aeneas is beyond their horizon.

The continuation of Aeneas's story would be told in Monteverdi's *Marriage of Aeneas with Lavinia*. It was offered at Carnival in 1641 with a subtitle declaring it to be a tragedy with a happy end. According to Torcigliani's scenario, it culminated in prophesy by three goddesses: while Rome has illustrious prospects, Venus, Juno, and Hymen (the Greek goddess of marriage) point to "the birth and wonders of the city of Venice."[13]

Chapter 8

SPECTACLES

The principals of *The Coronation of Poppea* play out a brutal affair of state. Ignoble Roman Emperor Nero (who reigned from 54 to 68 AD) drives away Octavia, his queen, in order to replace her with beautiful, ambitious Poppea. Seneca goes to his death calmly after arguing unsuccessfully against the emperor's ways. Reason, not momentary passions, insists this Stoic philosopher who was also a playwright, must govern a ruler if he is to rule well. Overflowing senses may lead to mindless choices.

Ancient sources about Nero are mainly historians—Tacitus, Suetonius, and Dio Cassius—but there is also a play, *Octavia* (long ascribed erroneously to Seneca). Busenello's libretto reinvents from them freely. The result is a stunning spectacle, a brilliantly promiscuous collaboration of words and music, of ideas and sounds. The opera seems to bear out Busenello's Seneca in his grand defense of reason. But Monteverdi's dramatic purpose was to depict—create—emotions musically. Complexity results.

The political implications of the opera are many, are often ambiguous, and not confined to Nero's age. *Poppea*'s setting is historical, yet it is doctored history; doctored history is always a valuable vehicle for a political opera (and usually unavoidable). Here, sung words are doing things as an opera set in antiquity evokes politics in the seventeenth century while raising some of the oldest philosophical questions about politics—questions that seem familiar in the twenty-first century too. After all, contemporary Venice had long had troubled relations with two Romes (the papacy and the Habsburg's Holy Roman Empire). In a sonnet, "To those Longing to be Prelates," Busenello expressed acerbic antipathy to the workings of the contemporary church; its corrupt, hypocritical functionaries imposed servitude on "adorned Rome."[1] The incumbent pope when Busenello wrote his libretto for *Poppea* was Jesuit-trained Urban VIII. His long reign was marked by aggressive efforts to expand papal territories (something that had to leave Venetians uneasy) along with wide-ranging nepotism, intrigue, and corruption. With some exaggeration, he might even be associated with Nero in a Venetian mind. Busenello's long acquaintance with Pietro Ottoboni likely informed his sense of internal goings-on of the papacy. This son of an important Venetian clan had, like Busenello (although after him), studied law in Padua, and served in an important political capacity in Rome under Urban VIII (until this pope died in 1644), became a cardinal, and later briefly an octogenarian pope.

II.

A letter by Busenello makes explicit links between Rome's fate(s) and Venetian interests. The *Serenissima*'s birth, he observes, came at a time when the "barbarian yoke" enfolded and enfeebled Rome.[2] His achievement despoiled, Aeneas's mantle came to rest on Venice, and in the form of a republic. One way to interpret the events of *Poppea* is as a conflict between the *virtù* of self-mastery, an idea extolled by republicans, and the uncivilized—barbaric—passions of unruly emperors. This may be perceived as admonition to republican Venetians or as celebration of their ostensible principles (by presenting their Neronian opposite). Patriotic self-mastery demands that our higher faculties dominate our lower ones to a greater good. In a "moral sonnet" on "Human Passion," Busenello suggests that passions can lacerate us from within, as if blades. They leave us torn, churning and turning without an internal compass—in contrast to gentler, reasonable guidance.[3]

It is difficult to imagine a figure more suitable than Nero to a portrayal of the abuse of power in the name of love. Cruelty, murder, depraved lust—all these are almost synonymous with his historical image. "Nero," wrote Suetonius, "practiced every kind of obscenity" and "was convinced that nobody could remain chaste or pure in any part of his body but that most people concealed their secret vices."[4] He reportedly slept with and ordered the murder of his unsavory mother, married and executed stepsisters and stepbrothers, burned Christians as torches, lived exorbitantly, and declared himself a cultural treasure. His own last words—he committed suicide on being overthrown—were, again according to Suetonius, "Dead! And so great an artist!"[5] Poppea was already dead. Three years after she became empress she died at her husband's hand, or rather by his foot. "In a chance fit of anger," Tacitus tells us, the emperor kicked his then-pregnant wife. Well, he did love her yet he lost self-control, as he often did. One emotion commanded him instead of another.[6] Many in a Venetian audience would have known these dreadful stories and also that the overthrow of his increasingly crazed reign brought the end of the imperial dynasty that had supplanted the ancient Roman republic. They would have also known that chaos came in Nero's wake. Yet the opera never proclaims a

Figure 8.1. Gian Francesco Busenello (1598–1659), the poet who wrote the libretto for Monteverdi's *L'incoronazione di Poppea* and Cavalli's *La Didone*.

simple point, moral or patriotic. Nero's own end is not a part of it. *Poppea* concludes with a couple, Nero and Poppea, cooing, remarkably like that in *Didone*. But these are different kinds of couples, and no hero goes off to pursue great deeds in *Poppea*.

Nero's era was especially interesting to Incogniti. They discussed the emperor, Poppea, and Seneca and several wrote about them. Loredano wrote a short portrait of Poppea that presented her as an Eve-like exemplar of beauty's deceptiveness—a theme of the opera. Interest in Seneca is easy to understand. His stern worldview rested on distinguishing between what is and is not important; he complimented dispassionate, discerning reason as the unifier of men with each other, and them with the cosmos. Here was something constant for a painful, turbulent century. Stoicism (more precisely, neo-Stoicism) was a philosophy for times in which old signposts seemed to fall and troubled men tried to look behind turmoil for a steadier reality, perhaps a law of nature in lawless human times. Sagacious men who found it could have judicious fortitude amidst rapacious flux. Loredano defined a "law of nature" in his novelistic treatment of the *Life of Adam* as "a sentiment born of Reason which establishes the conscience to distinguish good from evil. But in wicked minds . . . this Law is not known. . . ."[7]

Yet the matter is not so straightforward, as we have seen, if you had been nurtured, as many Incogniti were, by Cremonini, in philosophical skepticism. And politics cannot simply bypass the twists, turns, and maneuverings of the short term. Belief in a rational cosmos does not necessarily secure a *patria*'s well-being or self-mastery (or a state's secure order). Constancy can be the hallmark of patriotic *virtù*, but Busenello's Seneca fails to set Rome right. He will demonstrate how a faithful Stoic acts in the face of this-worldly failure, not how to be successful politically. Recall how Florentines in the previous century looked to Tacitus for an example of living well in unpleasant political circumstances, and the Seneca-Tacitus link becomes obvious.

Tacitus animates Monteverdi's opera even if it is only Seneca who appears in it. The opera's conflict between Nero and Seneca seems as if it were an illustration of the stakes in the differences between Machiavelli and earlier writers of Mirrors for Princes, whose ideas tended to be greatly influenced by Seneca, especially his notion of "Clemency."[8] Except, of course, that the presence of the historian Tacitus is felt instead of that of Machiavelli. And Seneca incorporates a potent dose of realism into his own arguments while Nero cannot distinguish realism in politics from his own desires. Tacitus's younger years actually coincided with the events reinvented by Busenello and Monteverdi. His writings explain them much more than do those by Seneca, especially since he provides (as Boccalini proposed) spectacles that allow us to see into realities of power, into thoughts and doings of those who hold it. *Poppea* allows something similar. Tacitus ascribed the fall of the Roman republic to the eclipse of virtues that he admired and that he associated with classical republicanism—like manly devotion to *patria* or making the good of the citizenry prior to that of an individual. He did not believe it possible to return to a republican world, but *Poppea* may be understood as a plea to Venetians not to get to that point. The spirits of Tacitus and Seneca, like skepticism and stoicism, live out tensions in *Poppea* rather than solving them, word and music cooperate in this, sometimes by being at odds with each other. Hovering over—or lurking behind—are the spirit of Cremonini and the problems of the city defended by Sarpi.

III.

If, in the twenty-first century, you attend a performance of *Poppea*, Nero and his newly crowned mistress will sing to each other at its end in perhaps its most famous moment. "Pur ti miro"—"I behold you"—is among the most ravishing settings in Western music, one of singular loveliness. Now, rejoice the regal pair, there will be no more regret or sadness (for them—so they imagine). Their voices go back and forth—the response to "Pur ti miro" is "Pur ti gado" (I relish you), then coming together, then moving apart, as if cooing into the other's void. Their voices attract each other but also at moments interrupt each other. It sounds like a happy ending, the *lieto fine*, but it is the climax of sordid events. An earlier queen loses her crown so that her imperious husband can pursue his obsession with no mind at all to any virtuous undertaking. His lover shares his interests, for she has deployed her charms to bring about her own coronation. For Poppea, as for the emperor, corrupt passion and corrupt power are married. "I leave you," she says earlier to Otto, her cuckolded, soon to be ex-husband, "to mount a throne."[9]

The opera premiered in the winter of 1642–43. Current scholarship is filled with questions because no score exists in Monteverdi's hand. At the center of much debate is the music in the concluding exchanges between Nero and Poppea. Doubts have been raised about Busenello's authorship of parts of the libretto as well. It has been suggested, for instance, that the versions known to twentieth- and twenty-first-century viewers, which usually include "Pur ti miro," follow revivals, particularly one in 1651 in Naples.[10] Regardless of these uncertainties, "Pur ti miro" still expresses the ecstasy of Nero and Poppea on achieving their aspirations. Their pursuit of each other drives the work. A delighted emperor watches exultant Poppea's coronation by Consuls and Tribunes. Officialdom declares their union to be by "universal consent" of a "happy empire."[11] Cupid, Venus, and the Graces celebrate.

Music and verse seem to engage each other with great beauty. But this beauty does not suit most of what has transpired since the opera's prologue. An intelligent viewer (or listener) will recognize—it is difficult not to notice—that by *Poppea's* end no person of redeeming quality survives in Rome. Making this denouement both beautiful and ambiguous is key to Busenello and Monteverdi's achievement. *Poppea* has its unity whether or not the closing scenes in its first performance included a joyous coronation or a love duet (or neither). "Pur ti miro" is no less beautiful when contextualized. And after all, Suetonius told us that Nero believed that people conceal their vices. In fact, any student of ancient Rome, especially of Tacitus, would have perceived vacuous symbolism here, for it was meaningless in Nero's day for Consuls and Tribunes to announce Rome's "universal consent." Their titles were charades, toothless. Unlike in the Roman republic, those who held them under Nero were at best like actors on a stage, their voices and words commanded by someone else. Aristocrats under the Medici would have recognized the circumstances, and the Infernal Chorus in *Orfeo* was in similar circumstances. The Suitors in *Ritorno* wanted, each of them, real power—along with luxury. Busenello, in a poem, displayed contempt for any preoccupation with honorific titles. They are no more than external show, he says.[12] In Nero's Rome, only the emperor's will counted, and everyone was helpless before it. The opera shows this political reality with or without the last scenes. Love and beauty appear to be victorious, with Nero and Poppea their joint protagonist. Yet theirs is a veil of happiness. Behind it are two people who live for the wrong things, for a beauty that is but on the surface, masking ugliness within. Their love for each other is venom toward others; they don't know to live well. Their victims, in contrast, reveal themselves capable of facing death or suffering well.[13] Dying properly was an important theme in Venice (and in ancient Rome) especially after the city had suffered so recently from plague. In "Moralità," a sonnet, Busenello made evident the conclusion he drew also in his libretto (and repeatedly elsewhere): the "externals" are meaningless; what matters is within us and since our time on earth is brief we must live right and be prepared for the grave, not just for changing climates and seasons.[14]

But politicians, especially leaders, must prepare for those changes too. Nero doesn't. His kind of happiness does not distinguish personal reality from political realities, and he grasps no danger if the former consumes the latter. He is an absolutist, and not a reflective one. This is evident in the opera's most potent debate. It occurs very early on and is the opera's political pivot. Nero announces to Seneca his intention to be rid of Octavia. "O Seneca, O Master," he complains, she is "frigid and infertile."[15] This is an obvious excuse. An exchange ensues between philosopher and emperor about how a ruler makes decisions. Tacitus's spectacles let us peer in on them; Monteverdi's music colors and makes brilliant what is before us, as a historical fiction becomes truthful on stage.

Seneca warns that political choices may be motivated in good or bad ways. "Passions," he admonishes, "make mischievous counselors/ for they hate law and reason they despise."[16] A ruler's unregulated will is indistinguishable from madness, he warns, pointing out that irrational commands can destroy a king's reputation and thus his power too. Though the emperor holds absolute power, Seneca suggests, it is not unconditioned. For it is still necessary to cultivate support. Offend endlessly, treat everyone, high

129

or low, with contempt, and you will undermine all obedience. Strength is in intelligent governance of the people, says Seneca, and its prerequisite—the motif returns—is good rule over oneself. It seems like the most practical advice, but Seneca places it within his larger vision: reason "governs both men and gods."[17] This is the framework within which to gauge both our immediate desires and long-term good.

That framework is what Nero lacks. The emperor thinks only of immediate fulfillment. In contrast, Busenello's Seneca has apparently read Tacitus, Machiavelli, Lipsius, Botero, and the debates about them. Perhaps he also read a Frenchman with Stoic sympathies, Pierre Charron, whose writings had continued the conversation about Machiavelli-like ideas and who was known well to Italian intellectuals. His *On Wisdom* of 1601 underlined the importance of law and prudence in politics. It cited Seneca, Tacitus, and Lipsius, and stated succinctly a theme we have come across repeatedly and that must have been struck Incogniti: "That which is done in public is but a fable, a fiction, the truth is secret and private."[18] Charron was of considerable influence on a younger "libertine"—another Frenchman—who lived for a period in the Italian peninsula, and whose work was also known there. Gabriel Naudé studied in Padua and had close friends in Venice. He befriended Cremonini and would be in constant touch with "free thinkers" even while, later, serving in Rome as secretary to a cardinal. Venetian "free thinkers" and their French counterparts had many ties.

Naudé's *Bibliografica politica*, an often reprinted handbook of political thought, was published in Venice in 1633. Politics, he proposed in it, had to be a field for dispassionate study, pushing aside past theological notions of the state or assertions of unconditional morality. Six years later, Naudé's *Political Considerations on Coups d'éstat* appeared and it became one of the most influential books on statecraft of the century. In it he surveyed contemporary Italian politics. A statesman, he asserted, had to diverge at times from ordinary justice and law—or else he would fail. His responsibilities require behavior that is different in kind from that of his subjects because his concern must be the state's well-being, not just that of any individual. Consequently, a ruler needs the right character, one that allows him to see the world plainly and to recognize when and when not to use means that are unpalatable in everyday life.[19] There was an important caveat: any reprehensible *coup* (meaning here "deed") had to be for the good of the state and in out-of-the-ordinary circumstances. Otherwise, the ruler commits offenses. It is unusual, Naudé observed, to find a single man who can keep justice, lawfulness, and prudence in equilibrium, and this experienced political secretary therefore suggested the importance to a ruler of a counselor or officer with as much of a sense of balance as possible.[20]

It often seems that Busenello's Seneca has been reading Naudé's deliberations. He recognizes that political logic sometimes demands moral transgressions, but thinks these should be solely for compelling and not personal purposes. Indeed, he says this explicitly, bordering on a claim of reason of state. Rulers, he tries to persuade Nero, "should be without guilt/ or culpable only of illustrious wrongs."[21] His example was pertinent to seafaring Venice: conquest on behalf of empire is acceptable. Wrongdoing is not tolerable if it entails no more than a pursuit of private desires. Then it is just a crime. Seneca's argument could justify easily Theseus's abandonment of Ariadne for Athens or Aeneas's desertion of Dido for Italy, but it refutes Nero's rejection of Octavia for Poppea. And when Poppea tells Otto that she leaves him for an empire, it is also evident that this is for her own sake, not for that of Rome. She suits the emperor.

Nero's responses show him to be a man of irrationality, selfishness, and sacrilege. The emperor, rebutting the philosopher, insists that heaven is Jupiter's domain, this world his own. He sounds initially as if he is defending distinctions made by Naudé. The rules are different for each realm, says Nero. But he really would render unto Caesar whatever Caesar wants—Caesar, in this case being himself, and even though Romans declared their emperors gods. "Law is for those who serve," squawks Nero. Reason's "rigorous discipline" he adds, is for those who serve too.[22] But not for him. He has no need for reason's steady direction and in this he rejects any distinct political logic—and he doesn't think of the modern state. Satisfaction of the emperor's will, not reason of state and the calculations it requires, is what matters. Those in command may do as they will, he believes, dismissing what anyone else, whether Rome's elites or the People, might think. Should someone revile him, his solution is simple: "I shall cut out his tongue."[23] His sense of efficacy extends no farther. Justice, Nero insists, "will always side with power."[24] In this, he reiterates one of the oldest contentions in the history of political thought, perhaps most famously made by Thrasymachus, foe of Socrates in Plato's *Republic*: what we call a universal or rational or god-given standard of right and wrong is nothing more than what those with might call right. Nero would have no inclination to scrutinize any implications. His brutality is not patriotic. Indeed, Seneca's warnings about Nero's own political interests—maintaining his power—seem at most to annoy this emperor.

A philosophically minded historian might point out that Nero's reign shows what happens when a ruler has no reflective curiosity about power.

Seneca, however, does not pit reason against force in a naive way. When, at the end of their exchange, Nero dismisses his "impertinent master," Seneca observes that the worst argument wins inevitably "when power contests with reason."[25] This philosopher wants power and reason together. Since it is evident that, despite his efforts as tutor, they are not so in Rome—Nero's purposes are not reasons of state, but his own whims—Seneca knows that he will soon be condemned. In this, and in ensuing events in the opera, a philosophical skepticism encroaches on stoicism. The former raises doubts about what can possibly be judged true and must raise questions about the rationality of the cosmos; the latter believed in cosmic laws that show how and why a reasonable person can bear bad times. Seneca will die imagining that he is merging with the cosmos, but happy, irrational Nero together with Poppea will carry on—at least through the end of the opera. Whose fate represents truth?

It is not the librettist alone who makes Seneca's case. Monteverdi provides the breath that brings forth the arguments in Busenello's verse—Seneca's good ones, Nero's bad ones. The philosopher's rounded voice is bass, a swell of seriousness in sound that follows lines of constant, moderate tones. He does, sometimes, verge toward irritation, needing to control his vocal temperament—he starts to get agitated—when faced with Nero's insufferable attitude. This Stoic is also human, and even Seneca can find his own self-control weakened, not least since it implies the failure of his sway with Nero. Nonetheless, he checks himself. The emperor, in contrast, is cast as a castrato (or later, a mezzo-soprano or counter-tenor). Ancient accounts tell us that his voice was otherwise. The historical Nero studied the lyre and singing. Suetonius reports that he "would lie on his back with a slab of lead on his chest, use enemas and emetics to keep down his weight, and refrain from eating apples and every other food considered deleterious to the vocal chords." Alas, his self-esteem could not make his voice more than "feeble and husky." Tacitus tells us that Seneca, whose father was a famous rhetorician, had to provide Nero with words for public oration. This was the first emperor "to need borrowed eloquence."[26] Monteverdi, however, makes the "feeble and husky" voice of the supreme power-holder into its opposite. Nero's pitch expresses itself in an increasingly strong, shrill, "agitated" style. The hint seems not so subtle, although male roles sung in female registers and males singing female parts were common enough in Monteverdi's day. In the twenty-first century the point might be deemed sexist: Nero is not man enough to rule. And as an important Monteverdi scholar summarizes deftly, Nero "may have the last word, but Seneca has the music."[27] Yet here an addendum is needed. The music contrasts frenzied Nero's emotionalism to Seneca's sobriety. Seneca's triumph is rational, while Monteverdi, ironically, creates it in sounds that aim to illustrate and contrast heightened feelings—just what Seneca argues against. A means to emotion, music helps an anti-emotional argument succeed intellectually —an argument, that is, between a ruler who had to borrow eloquence from a man he will eliminate.

Nero's last word, so far as Seneca is concerned, will be to order his counselor's suicide. This comes at Poppea's agitated urging, and was a common, dignified means of "execution" accepted by Roman elites. Tacitus writes that Seneca was forbidden by Nero to give his worldly goods to his friends. He declared to them instead, "I leave you my one remaining possession and my best: the pattern of my life."[28] Busenello and Monteverdi show the pattern of his death in order to affirm the pattern of his life (or, more accurately, of what Seneca would have wanted us to believe was his life's ideal ways). The contrast is stark, like the different voices of the philosopher and the emperor. There is Seneca's behavior as he faces his this-worldly end, then there is the elation of Nero and Poppea. We see unworthiness in the love of the emperor and his mistress for each other. And we hear and see the power of irony for at crucial moments throughout the opera, musically beautiful love veils utter baseness.

Subtle ambiguities suffuse the unfolding events in another way. When Poppea convinces Nero to eliminate the "astute philosopher," her reason appears political. This is only its outward form: Seneca, she says, wants to persuade people that he is the true power behind the throne. She knows Nero cannot tolerate this, and she simply plays on his weak character, exploiting his jealousies, fears, and insecurities. Her words echo sentiments expressed some scenes before by Octavia's page. He mocks Seneca as a pedant and purveyor of "crafty" philosophy, a man who moralizes even when he sneezes.[29] Even earlier, toward the opera's beginning, one of Nero's soldiers calls Seneca a shifty old fox. Poppea is a woman of the aristocracy, but here we find she is at one with lower orders in suggesting that Seneca's intelligence masks dubious character. Such aspersions were cast frequently upon the historical Seneca. He provoked resentment for advocating moral austerity while sitting in a powerful, enriching position next to an emperor.

Poppea is the sole detractor of Seneca for whom hypocrisy is irrelevant; it is her way of being. Yet even if Seneca were a hypocrite, his advice to Nero in the opera still makes political sense. Personal fakery, after all, doesn't preclude political or philosophical acumen. History is filled with false Senecas, perhaps including the original. Seneca's way of dying would then seem to rebut deceitful living, his own included, or make his past behavior pale beside his noble end. The triumph of corrupt love comes after his admirable death. Can these both be victories?

IV.

Mercury comes as emissary of the gods to the philosopher in his villa. You are a "true friend of heaven," he tells Seneca. You are the quintessence of "sovereign virtue" that "makes gods of men."[30] It seems that gods may have a better understanding of Seneca than those mortals who snicker at him. Mercury warns: your life will soon be over. Seneca receives this news with equanimity, and is then visited by the captain of the Praetorian Guard, whose unhappy duty is to present formally what Mercury foretold: the emperor's order for Seneca's suicide. The philosopher holds nothing against this officer, who has done no more than what he must, that is, follow a command. Seneca will do likewise. He now has a purpose that makes resistance trivial—he will be freed of earthly restraints. He accepts condemnation, as did another famous philosopher, Socrates, centuries earlier and accepts death as Cato, a republican hero, had when faced with Julius Caesar's victory. Yet Seneca observes that his own death cannot possibly satisfy a Nero. "Feeding on one vice leads to hunger for another."[31] The emperor's life will be driven by relentless, gushing desires. Seneca is ready to merge with eternity: his individual reason will join what he believes to be that of the universe, overcoming fortune, time, and his own transience. Nero will live (for a while, anyway), never at peace, even with Poppea.

So Seneca gathers his friends. They lack his steadfastness and they—an alto, a tenor, a bass—urge him to live: "[L]ife is too sweet."[32] Their voices overlap. A contrast becomes evident—between these Many, those who resist the full implication of ideals, and the One, the sage who will now follow the ideal's demand to its end. He advises his friends that death's pain is just a momentary discomfort and that it is more important to put into practice the kind of virtue he has praised. That virtue means mastery of strong passions. Here, too, the opera provides thoughtful irony in Monteverdi's engagement with Busenello's text. We see repeatedly on stage that passions must be controlled. All the same, the composer's musical imagination illustrates human "humors" by sound in order to empower what the opera, as a whole, suggests. There is another touch of ambiguity if, after Stoic Seneca joins the cosmos by exemplary death, we recall that Busenello's teacher in

Padua was Cremonini; he was accused famously of not believing in immortality of the soul.[33]

Then corrupt power, having coupled with corrupt love, bonds also with corrupted art. Nero turns cheerily to the fawning poet Lucan: "Now that Seneca's dead, let us/ sing love songs" to Poppea's beauty.[34] The merriment appeals to Lucan, and it is evident that Busenello is telling us something about artists who compliment and complement the Neros of the world. Surely, the Incogniti believed that they played just the opposite role in their *patria*, using their artistic efforts to elucidate matters rather than to display and impose their own vanities. This scene would likely have resonated in distinct ways among many educated Venetian viewers. Lucan was a poet of considerable talent but in history, as opposed to in the opera, he would one day also be forced, like Seneca (his uncle) to cut his own veins for plotting against the emperor.

Of course, we don't expect all the historical particulars since Busenello and Monteverdi were not chroniclers. They discard detailed veracity in presentation of the past in very evident ways, and it might even be said this is compelled by the genre of opera itself. After all, the historical Nero and Seneca did not converse in recitative. From Nero's female-like voice to the general role in the opera of guile, guise, and disguise, *The Coronation of Poppea* reminds us moment after moment of differences between appearances and unsure realities. We simply need to perceive in these scenes what happens at the heights of unrestrained power, especially when their depths are animated by undisciplined desire. Again, what Monteverdi and Busenello offer is akin to something Boccalini credited to Tacitus: their opera fashions glasses for us to see into and beneath the spectacle. And because it is an opera we hear this ushered in and through by sound.

V.

There are significant exemplars other than Seneca of behavior that counters that of Nero and Poppea. Otto and Drusilla provide the most important of them. He, for most of the opera, cannot let go of his love for Poppea, even when he knows his situation to be hopeless. But wounded love can take a violent turn. Murdering Poppea arises in his mind; then his nobility surfaces to thwart this thought. It is better to love without hope, he concludes. Drusilla, an aristocratic woman, loves Otto, yet has long been rebuffed by him because of his passion for Poppea. She is willing to love without hope. However, when Otto accepts finally that his pursuit of Poppea can reach no fulfillment, he yields to Drusilla's affections. She is overjoyed, although she doesn't quite understand his change. He is not entirely convincing. When alone, he sings ruefully: Drusilla's name is on his lips but Poppea is in his heart.

His lips, however, prove to be loyal, indeed righteous. Otto and Drusilla will face the possibility of death in a way that discloses their estimable characters as the opera moves toward its denouement. This comes about when yet another spurned figure, Octavia, calls Otto to her apartments. She commands him to assassinate Poppea but he shrinks before the prospect of what he had already contemplated. Octavia, however, has not yet been dethroned, and she makes plain how scorned dignity becomes ruthless. If he fails to obey her, she threatens, she will accuse him before Nero of trying to assault her, bringing inevitable execution. Otto yields again. His life has been overwhelmed by Poppea; he has acquiesced to Drusilla. Now he bows to Octavia. He also takes up the Queen's suggestion that he disguise himself in a woman's attire and prepare his act with appropriate deviousness. Of course, it will be Drusilla's clothes. She is a willing accomplice out of love (but also because Poppea slain means her competition is forever gone).

The assault fails when Cupid himself intrudes. "Amore" knocks the sword from the would-be assassin's hand just as Otto hovers over sleeping Poppea. In other words, love intervenes on behalf of Poppea's quest for power. This Love, however, is not sweet—he is angry. A rapier-wielding figure has contravened his authority. But Busenello and Monteverdi have made political morality very complex. Nero, in his debate with Seneca, insisted on the principle of jurisdiction: gods and men are in separate realms with separate rules. Yet here the emperor's new love is preserved by the intervention of a famously blind deity; and this intercession secures both the amorous bond between Nero and Poppea and also the union of Otto and Drusilla. The tie between Otto and Drusilla will be revealed to have a distinctive character, very different from that of Nero and Poppea.

Otto flees from awakening Poppea who, together with Arnalta, her nursemaid, sees a fugitive appearance. Naturally, Drusilla will be arrested. A remarkable chain of ironies links this scene to exchanges before and after it. Arnalta's role is particular: she provides punctuation points as the audience is directed toward differing stakes in events underway. She is Poppea's shrewd and self-interested counselor in the pursuit of power—but for her own sake. If you secure the crown, Arnalta says, her own help should not be forgotten. She will make clear that if she is elevated following her mistress, she will expect those of lower rank, such as was formerly her own, to bow to her. But the nursemaid is a calculator while Poppea appeals to Love to fulfill her ambitions. Before Otto's failed attack, Arnalta warns her mistress that once in power, she should never trust courtiers—although she aims to be a female one. There are, she explains, two things Jove cannot do: permit death to enter heaven's court, and secure loyalty within earthly courts. It is soon after this observation that disguised Otto enters with his sword and Cupid protects Poppea. Arnalta and Poppea both seem right—courtiers are disloyal and love (Cupid, that is) seems all-powerful. Arnalta, however, has not seen reality. It is she who accuses Drusilla: "There she is, the wretched woman . . ."[35] She has indeed changed clothes, but Otto was the assassin, Drusilla a secondary accomplice, and Octavia its mastermind. Arnalta was deceived by what she has seen, even if, in the end, all three plotters will be banished from Rome and Arnalta, presumably, will be satisfied and near the throne.

Drusilla is brought to Nero protesting innocence. The emperor condemns her to torture and death and, remarkably, she accepts painful ruin to protect Otto. A worthy lover, she proclaims, should do as she does and be a faithful friend. This kind of friendship, then, represents a profounder love than there could ever be between Nero and Poppea. After all, it is impossible to imagine Poppea sacrificing herself for Nero (or him for her). Moreover, Busenello has through her also presented to us more than one image of women. They do not all correspond to Loredano's warning about beauty-possessed creatures who deploy charms to captivate men, depriving them of the ability to perceive what is valuable in life. Poppea is certainly such a temptress, and Eden-like allusions do appear throughout the opera. (When she offers Nero her breasts, she likens them to apples.) But all Busenello's women are not Poppeas. He even suggests considerable sympathy on his part for the female plight in a male-dominated world in his counterimages to Poppea. This does not make an anachronistic feminist of him, and the fate of all the women are tied, ultimately to men in this opera.[36] (So too, however, are the men to women.) Yet it is impossible to respond numbly to Octavia's agony or Drusilla's fortitude. And Octavia's canny nurse directs us to one meaning of a world obsessed by appearances when she sings that it is at midday that the evening of a woman's life begins. Her beauties begin to pale.

Otto, it seems, has come to understand something. When Drusilla faces a death sentence, he arrives to declare his guilt. He alone should die, he now believes; it will be illustrious. In turn—and repeatedly—Drusilla and Otto insist that only one person is culpable; she points to herself, he to himself.

Figure 8.2. Cover of Busenello's libretto for Monteverdi's *L'incoronazione di Poppea* printed for the Grimano theater of Venice. (Bibliothèque nationale de France.)

They are prepared to protect each other, even by life's forfeit, and the two share nobility at this mortal moment, one already confronted virtuously by Seneca.

Deadly intrigues were familiar to Venetians, most recently an attempt on Paolo Sarpi's life, later on Renier Zeno's, and in between the Spanish Conspiracy and the Foscarini affair. A Venetian reader of Tacitus would have found Nero's day filled with very recognizable lethal schemes. One can imagine this reader thinking of Venice's distant past along with the city's more recent troubles as if perusing Machiavelli's *Discourses* on the Roman historian Livy. A chapter of it is devoted to conspiracies, yet *Poppea* seems to invert one of Machiavelli's astute observations. If a plot is discovered and only one person detained, wrote the Florentine thinker, the others may yet remain safe provided the prisoner is "a man of resolution" and has "sufficient strength of mind to be silent." The other conspirators, continues Machiavelli, must have "no less courage" and not flee, for this will give them away.[37] These points are made in a discussion of a plot to murder Nero (it was in fact as a result of its failure in 65 AD that the historical Seneca and the historical Lucan were compelled to commit suicide). In *Poppea* both Drusilla and Otto do the opposite of what Machiavelli recommends. Neither is silent; each confesses to protect the other. Otto, however, will implicate Octavia.

Even Nero appears impressed by Drusilla's "constancy"—that asset that he and Poppea so lack. Now, he decides to display "clemency," a word that was the subject of a famous essay by Seneca. A paradox should sing to us: what we have seen and heard and what is to come are all in some way deceptive. Nothing before this moment shows Nero generous; afterward there will be flattering ceremony (for Poppea's coronation). But before these final events, lenient Nero wishes Otto misery and expels him together with Drusilla to a desert, rather than execute them. (The historical Otto would participate in yet another plot—the one that succeeded—to overthrow Nero in 68 AD; and after Nero's first successor was murdered, Otto became a hapless ruler for three months, losing control and committing suicide.) By "solemn edict," *Poppea*'s Nero also banishes Octavia. She departs in moving but bitter lament—a Monteverdi musical signature—that is imbued with patriotism and personal grief: "addio Roma." Her historical person was less fortunate. Tacitus reports that Nero ordered her head "cut off" and presented to Poppea.[38]

VI.

Octavia, Otto, Drusilla—all these are defeated figures. Fortune against them, they go into exile just before Nero and Poppea swoon in "Pur ti miro" in what has been appropriately called "political eroticism."[39] And here we must go from the end of the opera back to its beginning, a prologue in which Fortune, *Virtù*, and Love debate their respective roles. Fortune dismisses *Virtù*: you are a mirage, like a fire in a painting that provides no real heat. *Virtù* retorts: I am incorruptible, a wind that steadily raises men higher, indeed to heaven—unlike the roiling vicissitudes of Fortune. Cupid then joins the exchange, acclaiming himself sovereign of all ages; he is the deity whose provenance imparts all others. His two competitors, he adds, will soon acknowledge this as they watch the world changed by Love's prowess. "Soon," here, means the opera's duration. By its end, *Virtù* will indeed be dismissed, victimized by turns of Fortune. Rome's fortunes in *Poppea* have indeed been transformed, apparently by Love and not in a lovely way. The ostensibly happy ending really joins a question: what sort of love, will, and power triumphs? If Machiavelli wrote of *Virtù* and Fortune in contest, warning rulers against seeking the love of those ruled rather than judging power properly, Busenello and Monteverdi complicated the question. Why should this have been important in Venice? It is posed, in distinct ways and moods, by *Ritorno*, *Didone*, and *Poppea*. Their creators comprised a team of overlapping collaborators: Badoaro/Monteverdi, Busenello/Cavalli, Busenello/Monteverdi. The librettists came from within a worried elite and the composers, though outsiders, were in eminent positions. The results are an optimistic scenario for leadership personified by Ulysses, anticipation for Aeneas, and in the figure of Nero, the plausibility of frightful deceit and self-deceit. Ulysses retrieves his *patria* and queen. Aeneas escapes his falling *patria*, is tested, and resumes his mission. *Poppea* closes in illusory, transitory happiness, portraying an absolutist who is the opposite of Ulysses. A sickly love is victorious, leaving a *virtù*-free *patria*.

There is, then, a coherence of concerns in these operas; it is structured first of all by antitheses, most importantly between a quest for some proper stability within a tumultuous world and a recurrent concern that a "constant" way cannot be found. Perhaps long-standing myths were being pierced by contemporary history.[40] The removal of disguise usually reveals appropriate forces, divine or human, at work. It is almost self-congratulation—or a matter, perhaps not entirely conscious, of apprehensive aspiration. By the time we move from *Ritorno* through *Didone* to *Poppea*, from Ulysses's victory over the Suitors through Aeneas's triumph over his impulses, to Nero's "success" with Poppea, we see and hear a need to fret. Monteverdi understood undoubtedly that *Poppea* required subtle volatility; his music provides and enhances this essential feature throughout the opera. Incogniti preoccupation with Nero was obviously amenable to him; Monteverdi did not select collaborators or subjects in haphazard ways. His operatic choices depended finally on a finely honed artistic sense, and not only on the fact that he owed his livelihood and comfortable status to a city that had been in conflict with Rome, the setting of his artistic finale. He began his operatic creations in Mantua with mythology's celebrated musician—who succeeds in persuasion but fails as a plausible prince. His work culminated in Venice with one of history's infamous tyrants—that emperor whose eloquence was reportedly ghost-written and who imagined he could sing well, but does so only at the end of an opera that reveals why he cannot possibly rule soundly.

PART 3:
UNDER FRENCH SUNS

The constancy of the wise is only the art of concealing agitation in their hearts.

—LA ROCHEFOUCAULD

Chapter 9
AGITATIONS AND ABSOLUTES

In September 1743, just shy of a century after Claudio Monteverdi's death, the thirty-one-year-old impecunious son of a watchmaker arrived in Venice from Paris. Touchy, jaunty, not yet famous, Jean-Jacques Rousseau was to be a secretary in the French embassy. He took this position for financial reasons but his tenure lasted less than a year. It was marked by regular quarrels with his superior, a stingy, haughty count who was ill-prepared to deal with tumultuous events around him. France had taken sides in a war over succession to Austria's throne. It spread into the Italian peninsula. France wanted to keep Venice neutral.

Working for King Louis XV's ambassador allowed Rousseau to observe at close quarters an array of political and diplomatic maneuvers. His life-long disdain for social artifice and conventions—his belief that civilization's "progress" was distinctly unattractive—surely received succor from this experience. Rousseau monitored politics within Venice's declining patrician republic, now a relatively modest power but still filled with cultural treasures and an alert secret police. His agitated imagination was stimulated undoubtedly by contrasts to Geneva, where he was born. Like Venice, Geneva was a city-state with a republican tradition. Rousseau often idealized it. But Geneva was an austere, Calvinist place. He later described in his *Dictionary of Music* how listening to a cantor in a Reform church there turned music into a wearisome experience.[1] Venice, by contrast, was like a buoyant fanfare. Yet he had to serve an inept aristocrat at the embassy, and at this time he began, it seems, to formulate ideas that appeared eventually in his most famous political essay. *The Social Contract*, published in 1762, would inspire revolutionaries with its idea of popular sovereignty.

Rousseau's great infatuation in Venice, in addition to women, was music. It had been his passion from early in life. He had come initially to Paris as a music copyist, a proponent of his own system of music notation—its chief aim was simplification of written music and it impressed but was rejected by the Academy of Sciences—as well as an aspiring composer and writer. He played several instruments. When Rousseau arrived at the lagoon on the

Adriatic, he found music everywhere. He described his enchantment: singing in opera houses, palazzos, churches, cafes, gondolas. Real singing, he claimed, had been unknown to him before Venetian barcarolles entered his ears. He bought a harpsichord and, happily for him, his responsibilities included securing embassy subscriptions to opera houses. He went often and managed also to arrange for rehearsals of parts of an opera he had begun to write.

Before Venice he had, by his own admission, shared common French biases against Italian music. By the time he left, however, "Nature" made him its partisan—a forceful and then notorious one when another kind of war broke out, this time in France's capital. It began one evening a decade later in August 1752, and lasted some eighteen months. "All Paris was divided into two camps," wrote Rousseau, who was by then a highly visible figure in the French intellectual and musical worlds. "The excitement was greater than if they had differed over politics or religion."[2] Except that the factions differed about opera, and the disagreements resonated politically in scores of pamphlets and essays. It is known as the *Querelle des Bouffons*, the "Quarrel about the Buffoons."* The Buffoons (from *buffoni*, or clowns in Italian) were players of comic opera, and a traveling troupe of them had presented in Paris a short, droll Italian work in place of the original opening of a long, more elaborate French one. That the ensuing furies had broad implications was recognized and yet another parallel between music and politics (and, more generally, French society) was made some years later, this time by Jean le Rond d'Alembert, a central figure in the Enlightenment. He expressed wonder that everyone seemed ready to write about freedom of trade, freedom of the press and of marriage, but liberty in music became a menace. It somehow implied thinking and acting; apparently the realm itself was threatened if opera changed.[3]

II.

The provocation occurred during a revival of *Acis et Galatée* at the Royal Academy of Music—the Opéra. This was the last major work by a man who had died more than six decades earlier and is usually credited as the founder of French opera. Giovanni Battista Lulli, born in Florence in 1632, became

---

*French intellectual and musical quarrels were legion. For clarity's sake, I will use the French "*Querelle*" solely for the "*Querelle des Bouffons*" and the English "Quarrel" for others.

Jean-Baptiste Lully, the leading composer in the court of Louis XIV. Royal support made him virtual lord of Paris's flamboyant musical world. Music, ballet, painting, and theater were all aspects of royal power for the "Sun King." Like the Medici, Louis XIV identified with the Sun God; Apollo was his favorite mythological figure.

It was a "grave" error to see "mere ceremony" in royal cultivation of the arts, the king remarked once. "The people over whom we rule," he explained, ". . . usually judge by what they see from outside."[4] Louis XIV was, then, astute to the political sway of his own image; spectacle was intrinsic to his "*grand siècle*." Even Lully's death in March 1687 was something of a spectacle, albeit accidental and not quite grand or political. His habit was to keep beat for musicians with a rolled-up piece of paper, but for a performance of his *Te Deum*, an immense motet with a particularly large number of performers, he used a large baton. He stabbed his own foot, gangrene set in, he refused amputation, and the end soon came. After his demise the baton became something of an object of veneration. The prince of Monaco eventually bought it as a "relic" with which he too could keep musical time.[5]

Lully fashioned the initial style and early conventions of French opera. The life of "the Florentine," as he was often known, overlapped with some of the extraordinary names of classical French theater: Corneille, Racine, Molière. He drew from them—Lully and Molière collaborated for a period—and also from a well-established tradition of court ballets to create what were known as "lyric tragedies," or "*tragédies en musique*" (although they did not all end in desolation). Most important, perhaps, was Lully's ability to craft recitative attuned to inflections and cadences of the French language. He fashioned also melodic musical suppleness in the relation between recitatives and arias. Together with poet Philippe Quinault he created a stage genre that—they hoped—would be as formidable as those written by the great tragic poets of their day. This effort was Lully's true "naturalization" into France.[6] Voltaire wrote later that compared to others before, Louis XIV's era was perhaps the most "illuminating."[7] Those who suffered its many wars might have demurred. Still, many in France believed for a long time that it was impossible to improve on Lully's accomplishments, especially those recitatives.

That conviction—and challenges to it—framed the uproar in 1752, even though *Acis* was in many ways not typical of Lully's operas. His usual partner, Quinault, did not write the libretto and it had not been commissioned, as had long been the case, by the crown. It was not the usual tragedy, but a "heroic pastoral" with a text by Jean-Galbert de Campistron, a young dramatist. Based on a tale from Ovid, it premiered in September 1686 in the Château of Anet under the patronage of its aristocratic owners, the Vendôme brothers (a duke and a prior). Its purpose was to entertain a special guest, the dauphin, the king's eldest son, who had come to join them for a hunt. The Vendômes were at the center of notorious "libertine" circles, and both the Florentine and de Campistron frequented their "debauched" extravaganzas. Lully's sexual inclinations had eventually led his longtime vital proponent, the king, to rebuff him.

Nonetheless, *Acis* could open only with a genuflecting prologue. Diana, goddess of the hunt, acclaimed "the son of the most powerful, most just of Kings."[8] Deities of Abundance and the Feast added self-referential observations. What would you do without us? So they asked the flush audience. Apollo arrived to hail royal virtues (his own, of course). Those atop the world's order provided its good things. So said divinities in praise of majestic beneficence. Then the opera itself began with a pastoral scene—but not with an idyll. *Hélas!*—Acis the shepherd loves Galatea the sea nymph, and she spurns him. *Hélas!*—Acis's friend Telemus, also a shepherd, loves Scylla, a shepherdess. She denies her wooer too. And then: danger! Polyphemos, that famous Cyclops enters to marching music. Terrified shepherds scatter before the one-eyed giant.

He is revealed quickly to be unable to distinguish brute power from love. Why do they flee? he wonders—"Do they know Polyphemus well?" He seems wounded until his demeanor changes: Don't they realize that they cannot flee "my extreme fury?" It seems they do know him. He, too, desires the sea nymph but his ugliness, he knows, does not help his suit. He tries boast instead: "Everything you see recognizes my power." He offers to make everyone pay homage to her. She isn't interested. But, to her dismay, he threatens everyone else. She feigns love to save the shepherds from this fearsome creature. Acis, of course, finds this ploy atrocious. Driven to despondency, he prepares to fight "this barbarian," knowing that he cannot survive.[9] This prospect, in turn, forces Galatea to an admission: she loves Acis after all. Only pride has restrained her affections. Sadly, for Telemus, Scylla does not requite likewise. She "despises" love's "laws."[10] Acis and Galatea prepare to marry without the other pair at Juno's Temple.

Hélas! Polyphemos arrives with his own cheering band. Galatea tries to forestall what seems will be inevitable conflict, but the Cyclops quickly

Figure 9.1. Portrait of Lully

recognizes betrayal and crushes Acis with a boulder: "Ah, What pleasure for an outraged heart/ is bloody vengeance."[11] Galatea laments and she, too, thinks of vengeance. Then she turns to the gods instead; she entreats, Orpheus-like, for restoration of her love's life. Her appeal touches Neptune, to whom she owes fealty as a sea nymph. The ruler of the waters is also Polyphemos's father; he decides to make amends for his son's deed. Acis is returned to the living and turned into a stream flowing to the sea, where he is reunited with Galatea. Water sprites celebrate:

Under its laws, Love wishes us joy,
happiness that never ends.
Tender hearts, come all
and rejoice with us.[12]

Everything seems right. Humanity and the natural order are one.

III.

The *Querelle* was not about this opera itself. By the mid-eighteenth century, it was just one grand work of Great Lully—elaborate, baroque, and delicate, filled with gods and showy decorum. It presented an allegory about the order of things, beginning with Apollo and other gods making clear who and what comprised the fount of well-being; at the opera's end, Neptune arises from the depths to right a wrong. Why, then, did the cosmos seem topsy-turvy at the revival? Because that summer evening at the Opéra the prologue, with its bows to power, was replaced by a short work titled *La serva padrona*—"The Maid-Servant as Mistress." Power was turned upside down in it. Although it did not appear between acts, *Mercure de France* referred to it as an "*intermède*"—the equivalent of an *intermedio*—about a "trifling" subject with music that was particularly praiseworthy and dialogue that was impressively natural.[13] Plots concerning a master entangled with, even dependent on, uppity or clever servants hail back to the ancients. "Mistress" in the title is the female equivalent of master, and *Serva* concerned who rules a household. Its implications, however, went further. The contrast between this cutting fifty-five-minute comedy composed originally in 1733 by Giovanni Battista Pergolesi and the dignified order of *Acis* could hardly have been more startling. The itinerant *Bouffons*, headed by Eustachio Bambini, presented it just after arriving from Strasbourg, and *Serva* would be the first of some fourteen works, mostly pastiches, they would play. Its composer, otherwise best remembered for his "Stabat Mater," was born near Naples in 1710 and died at twenty-six of tuberculosis. *Serva*'s text by Gennaro Antonio Frederico, a lawyer turned librettist, satirized social manners with themes, characters, and situations that were common stock in Neapolitan and Italian theater.[14]

The audience that in 1752 awaited a parade of deities, nymphs, shepherds, and a monster in *Acis*'s rustic world beheld first instead a contemporary setting. Viewers, accustomed to certain features in *tragédie en musique*, particularly what was called the *merveilleux* (magical and marvelous happenings on stage with the help of elaborate staging and machinery), found something very different. No god or poet praised a king or explained what would take place or suggested morals and conclusions. Instead, there was Uberto, a crotchety old bachelor, in his home. His bass tones complain: Where is my cocoa? I give orders around here! Serpina, my servant, makes me wait. Imagine!—and this even though I raised her like a father. My goodness, the maidservant is becoming the mistress. It must stop! Serpina's name—

Little Serpent—suggests temptation. (She is imagined easily as an operatic aunt of Despina, the crafty servant girl of Mozart and Da Ponte's *Così fan tutte;* both are also relatives of a stock character in Italian improvisational comedy.) Her viewpoint is quite different from that of Uberto. Just because the master is in a rush, she sings when she enters, it doesn't mean that I must be. She is ready to smack Vespone, the butler who is, notably, a mute character. Uberto is enraged at Serpina's hauteur; she, however, articulates generations of class and gender resentments and suffering:

> And so, just because I am a servant, I must be smothered?
> I must be mistreated?
> No signore! I want to be respected,
> I want to be looked up to as if I were mistress (*padrona*), the head-boss (*arcipadrona*), *padronissima*.[15]

Her nagging purpose, it becomes evident, is to change the ruling voice. Soon enough, she will.

Uberto finally orders Vespone to find a wife for him so he won't be badgered any longer by Serpina. But then we hear a joyous snicker from Little Serpent: the fool has fallen for her plan. Uberto, you will indeed marry, she tells her master—but only me. He dismisses this. However, she tells him at the close of the first act something that men famously tell women: she knows by his eyes that when he says "no" he really means "yes."[16] Serpina will finally take power—but only over her immediate world and only through marriage. Indeed, she joins the system that oppressed her as we see in her subsequent treatment of the mute butler. Her role as a female servant demanded—in principle—that she hold her tongue, but she is sassy and gives verbal thrashings to silent Vespone as well as to her master. She brought Vespone to her side by promising him that he would be her aide once she became mistress. While Serpina achieves her new position in the second act, she keeps Vespone in his old one.

How does she succeed? She disguises herself as a crazed officer in pursuit of . . . herself. Mad "Captain Tempesta" (another figure from *Commedia dell'arte*) makes Uberto jealous as well as concerned, which is just her design. After all, Serpina is his ward, and marriage to the officer will demand a suitably large dowry. And so finally Uberto thwarts the nuptials by agreeing to marry her. She then holds him to his promise even after revealing who this "captain" really is. She even compels him now to accept her imperious behavior—if, that is, she bosses him "nicely." Uberto and Serpina sing of new happiness while Vespone remains . . . silent. It appears that the world is off kilter but not quite upside down. After all, Serpina was already "bossy" before marrying Uberto, and now she has simply obtained legal status to match. Voiceless Vespone's situation is unaltered. She broke ranks with him; he will stay as he is. Serpina changes, practically speaking, as a woman. While Galatea in Lully's opera attains happiness thanks to a god, Serpina acts. She gets Uberto to bite her apple and is not just victorious but, in her own confined way, self-sufficient. Her victory would have been only within the household, not beyond its doors.

Serva's theme and melodies were different, startlingly so, from Lully's pastoral pageant. The ensuing *Querelle* involved court and high society in arguments about the respective merits of French as opposed to Italian music and opera. It gave rise to the furious pamphlet war among intellectuals. Rousseau's contribution provoked particular ire. His "Letter on French Music" determined that the acoustic effects of different languages were distinct and, consequently, some were more appropriate to opera than others. His point was not entirely original. As early as 1636, decades before there was opera in French, a theologian and musical theorist, Marin Mersenne, declared in his *Universal Harmony* that French could "caress the ear" while Italian singing "expressed passions of the soul."[17]

French was excellent for philosophical writing, but not for poetry written for music, thought Rousseau. Italian was "sweet, sonorous, harmonious and accented more than any other" language, and this was evident in *Serva*. French vowels were insufficiently vivid and French consonants too sharp. The consequence was music that had neither meter (*mesure*) nor melody. The language produced songs that were no more than "a continual barking."[18] It was perhaps typical of Rousseau that this judgment did not dissuade him from composing operas to his own French librettos. And his description of the storm unleashed by *La serva padrona* had multiple political and social echoes.

Supporters of French music, he wrote, were the "more powerful and numerous party, made up of the great, the rich, and the ladies." This was "the king's corner" in the theater, and it met behind the "king's box." But there was a cultured "little band" under the "queen's box." These were the "true music lovers, talented people, and men of genius." Naturally they, like Rousseau, were enthusiastic for the Italian alternative. And Rousseau, never temperate in his engagement with the world, felt himself besieged on account of his "Letter." The "whole nation" rose against him, he claimed. He feared arrest. Severe tension then between Louis XV and the *Parle-*

ment of Paris became a minor matter as the politics of opera trumped the politics . . . of politics. At least Rousseau saw it this way. "Whoever reads that this pamphlet probably prevented a revolution in France will think he is dreaming," he insisted, "Yet it is an actual fact." He believed that the orchestra of the Opéra had "entered into a solemn plot" to assassinate him for insulting French music. The mayor of Paris deprived him of his pass to opera performances.[19]

Serpina tells her master: "more can happen in a single/ hour than in a hundred years." *Serva* takes less than an hour to perform, but a quarter of a millennium later it is possible to see and hear in it the many historical and political rivulets, streams, even torrents that flowed into the *Querelle des Bouffons*, more than a century's worth of them. And it is also possible to see and hear what they anticipated.

IV.

Servants knew their place in the Sun King's world. Certainly, Lully did. He was brought to Paris in 1646 at age fourteen by Roger de Lorraine, the Chevalier of Guise, who apparently saw him perform in a Florence market. Lully would be a gifted dancer, acrobat, singer, and violinist—talented, one biographer remarks, in "almost everything except chastity."[20] He was also astute enough to make his way as an artist through the labyrinth of French high politics, where something fearsome could appear at each turn. Young Lully was initially a household aide, but his first responsibility concerned relations between languages—and relations between languages and aristocrats. He was to teach Italian to the chevalier's young cousin, Mademoiselle de Montpensier, whose proper name was Anne-Marie-Louise d'Orléans. Her father, Gaston d'Orléans, was uncle to young Louis XIV but in constant, often severe conflict with the crown. Lully was in her employ for six years, beginning in 1646. This enabled him to hear French music and witness a great deal of politics. "*La Grande Mademoiselle*," as she was known, was also notoriously hostile to the king's Italian-born chief minister, a man who played an important role in introducing opera to France, although it would be specifically Italian opera and its success limited and brief. Politics interfered with Cardinal Mazarin's effort.

France's long-established musical-theatrical tradition was linked closely to display of royal prowess. At its center were court ballets. These were often political allegories and kings danced frequently in them, flaunting their grace and power before nobles. The Valois monarchy, during the sixteenth century's religious civil wars, used musical extravaganza to enhance its prestige. A Medici who had married a French king figured prominently in this story. When Catherine de' Medici was France's regent, she impressed the court with elaborate *"magnificences."* Her son, King Charles IX, followed suit. Intellectual discussions and ideas comparable to those of the Florentine Camerata took place in the Academy of Poetry and Music, formed in 1570 under royal auspices. In it humanists and Neoplatonists—poets, composers, artists, actors—gathered in creative dialogue. Ficino's notions about musical antiquity had seeped into France, and even though Plato warned of music's disruptive powers, an astute ruler, it was supposed, could tame and direct them to his own purposes. Jean-Antoine de Baïf was the academy's central figure. This illegitimate son of a former French ambassador to Venice wanted to revive ancient musical ideas.[21]

The Academy did not survive, but a "national" style of music developed under its auspices. Academicians advocated *"musique mesurée"*; they stressed rhythm, believing it central to ancient music, and clarity of words in sung texts. This allowed expression of ideas and emotion in contrast to polyphony. Music, then, was not absolute; it served. These Frenchmen promoted melody with accompaniment, a "homophony" (more precisely here "homorythmic") in which voices articulated sung words simultaneously. De Baïf and his colleagues fashioned "magnificences" with many Arcadian motifs for an opulent marriage of a key financial supporter of their academy eight years before the Florentine *intermedi* of 1589. The guest of honor was the Duc de Joyeuse, and King Henri III attended. The director of these events in October 1581 was Balsassarino de Belgiojoso, a violinist from Savoy who had come to France as Catherine de' Medici's valet and became known as Baltassar de Beaujoyleaux.[22] He wrote the text for the evening's culminating event at the Louvre, *Circé*, which one scholar calls a "lyric drama" in embryo.[23] It had a story line, declamatory singing, dances, and a large chorus. "For five and a half hours," writes another scholar, "the spectators saw a succession of mortals, gods, and minor deities such as nymphs and satyrs, all entering in elaborate costume and some on richly decorated floats."[24] It told of the defeat of the disruptive evil sorceress Circé; victory went to reason and harmonious order.[25] As the Valois king vanquished enemies, it suggested, the kingdom would be well.

During the reign of Henri IV, the first Bourbon king, theatrical display continued its political role. Another Medici, Marie, was now at court and she promoted dramatic ballet and spectacles in Paris. After Henri IV was assassinated in 1610, Marie became regent, but her son, Louis XIII, finally took political control in the next decade after clashes with her. The new king usually chose subjects for the court ballets and danced in them too. The latest stage machinery was imported from Italy. The point, after all, was to impress. Performances often had very contemporary resonance. One, at the beginning of Louis XIII's reign, the *Ballet de Tancrède* of 1619, drew (as Monteverdi had) from a passage in Tasso's continuously popular *Jerusalem Delivered*. When French eyes saw Tancred and his knights fight back monsters in an enchanted forest, the allusion was obvious; the crusader was a surrogate for a young French king routing foes. Another ballet, from much later in his rule, was by Louis XIII himself. His *Ballet de la Merlaison* (The Ballet of the Hunt of the Blackbird) was performed in 1635 at Chantilly, the estate not far from Paris of the unfortunate Duke of Montmorency. He had recently been beheaded for leading a provincial revolt. Protests by courtiers were met by a simple retort by an older Louis XIII: "I would not be king if I had the feelings of private persons."[26] (Machiavelli would have smiled.)

Richelieu died in December 1642 and the monarch went to his grave five months later. Louis XIV was barely five years old and the Queen Mother, Anne of Austria, became regent. She admired Italian music and, like her royal predecessors, believed cultural eminence reinforced political power. In this she was of common mind with Mazarin, her Jesuit-educated chief minister. His ties with France were long-standing, but his knowledge of opera came principally from Rome and perhaps from Mantua too. While still Giuseppe Mazzarini, he had served as a papal diplomatic attaché, traveling to Savoy, throughout northern Italy and to Venice. He became a negotiator for Richelieu during the Mantuan War of Succession. It is possible to envisage him meeting Chancellor Alessandro Striggio in this context, exchanging views on diplomatic matters and then turning to opera.

Mazarin would one day commission a new *Orfeo* for Paris. Before his arrival there in late 1634 as Papal Nuncio Extraordinary, he had a powerful position in Rome, working for a cardinal from the Barberini family, those great proponents of early Roman opera. He had been in the clan's palazzo when Landi's sacred opera, *Sant'Alessio*, premiered in it. When choosing Orpheus as the subject for an opera in Paris, Mazarin read widely about the legend. Fortunately, he had at his disposal the library assembled by Gabriel Naudé, the "libertine" Frenchman who had studied in Padua and befriended Cremonini. Mazarin read librettos by Rinuccini and Striggio and studied Peri, Caccini, and Monteverdi.[27]

The political usefulness of opera in France was evident to Mazarin. He imagined, as one scholar notes, that "with Italian musicians, poets and machinists potentially involved in state intrigues, and the court so diverted by the spectacle . . . his own political machinations might pass unnoticed."[28] Unable to secure a permanent Italian opera company for Paris, he sought itinerant musicians and singers. They also had collateral political value. These players entertained high circles throughout Europe and could be enlisted in extra-musical roles—as spies. For one instance, Atto Melani, among the most renowned of Tuscan castrati, served as a Mazarin agent. He performed the same role for the Grand Duke of Tuscany and other rulers too.

In February 1645, Melani seems to have performed the part of "Reason" in *Caprice, or The Judgment of Reason between Beauty and Affection*. It was semistaged at the Palais Royale at Mazarin's behest.[29] It appears to have been an allegory about Europe-wide political maneuvers—Europe was still suffering from the Thirty Years War—and more specifically, about machinations by various powers to secure a Holy See attentive to their particular interests. The Barberini pope, Urban VIII, was ailing. In the succession struggle the pro-French faction in Rome lost to pro-Austrian Innocent X, and Mazarin brought defeated Barberinis and members of their entourage to Paris. Among them was the librettist of *Caprice*, Abbé Francesco Buti, who became a Mazarin adviser.[30] *Caprice* proved to be a successful first step and so in 1645 Mazarin imported a popular early Venetian opera, *La finta pazza* ("The Feigned Madwoman" with music by Francesco Sacrati and words by Giulio Strozzi). He also enlisted Giacomo Torelli, the contemporary master of stage technology and special effects. This too was well received. Young Louis XIV appreciated a spectacle with "monkeys, eunuchs, negroes, and ostriches."[31]

V.

Mazarin's enemies were many, their complaints varied and often overlapping. He had followed his predecessor's policy of centralizing state power. This came at the expense of local aristocratic autonomy and sway. Nobles were angered. Extraction of more taxes provoked restlessness. Important religious tensions emerged between Jesuits (supported by the crown) and the radical Augustinians known as Jansenists. Named after their inspirer, Cornelius Jansenius, whose major work appeared in 1640, they emerged initially in the Spanish Netherlands and became a serious force within France. Richelieu and Mazarin suspected their adherents of pro-Spanish sympathies. An additional source of alarm was Jansenist links to the legal nobility, which used courts to restrain the crown. Both church and state worked to repress this religious movement. Amidst these many pressures Mazarin faced another complaint: there was too much power in the hands of outsiders—like him and the Queen Mother (who was of Spanish descent). Cultural politics, like importing Italian opera, turned from a means of reinforcing their power into an irritant exploited by foes. When Mazarin commissioned another Italian opera for Paris, it became a surrogate target for discontent.

He selected two men to whom he was close as its principal creators. The libretto by Buti was set to music by Luigi Rossi, a Neapolitan who had been a court composer for a Barberini cardinal. Its subject, on Mazarin's command: Orpheus. The cardinal oversaw its production for Carnival 1647. The stage was filled again with spectacle. The prologue celebrated French military aptitude. "Victory" flew from the heavens in a chariot to praise young Louis XIV and his mother. French triumph was likened to Orpheus's breach of the Underworld, a display of "the power of the harmony of love and faith." The opera mostly followed the traditional rendering of the myth— Orpheus persuades Pluto and then loses Eurydice when he looks back— but it also incorporated comic figures and subplots. There were, however, some other variations that more than others distinguished this *Orfeo* from the Florentine and Mantuan versions. Proserpina still wants Orpheus to succeed but because of covetous worry that Eurydice's beauty might attract her husband. The figures of "Suspicion" and "Jealousy" urge Proserpina to convince Pluto to hear Orpheus's song. Debates on law and power of the sort found in the librettos of Rinuccini and Striggio don't enter Pluto's reasoning here. He considers Charon a "dotard," but then this boatman, sad because of his job ferrying the dead, tells of the loveliness of Orpheus's plea. And Charon adds: you may refuse Orpheus, but "the foreign musician" will return inevitably "by the power of his song." Pluto finally agrees to hear Orpheus. His justification is striking: "Sometimes/ Kings must follow the general will (*ch'al commune volere/ Servano I Regi*)"[32]

These words, *al commune volere*, are not operatic showstoppers, but they are just that in the history of political ideas. The "general will" is associated famously with Rousseau's *The Social Contract*, published more than a century later. In it Rousseau insisted that laws are legitimate only if authorized by the citizenry as a whole. Consequently, the source of law has to be the "general will" (of the citizens) to the common good; and a law has to apply to everyone. The appearance of the "general will" in *L'Orfeo* would seem bewildering or anachronistic except that this phrase had a substantial theological prehistory. It came to the fore in arguments between Jesuits and Jansenists in France just in the period in which Buti wrote his libretto for Mazarin.

The terms of debate may today seem like an obscure wrangle, but it concerned a basic theological issue then. Did God's "general will" save all human beings despite original sin? Could it be that God's grace was granted only to some while all others were destined for hell? Jansenists were accused of believing that Christ's sacrifice did not rescue humanity. Tied to this was the proposition that our behavior in this world—our merits or failures—has no impact on our salvation. Must it not be the sin of pride to presume otherwise? Would that not be an unspeakable effort to fathom God's will? It follows from these rhetorical yet deadly serious questions that earthly powers and activities were inefficacious and grace a mystery. These kinds of claim, which had considerable Protestant echoes in Catholic ears, had been asserted only a few years after the Huguenots were defeated forcibly by the French crown. Richelieu ordered anti-Jansenist preaching at Notre Dame in Paris during 1642 and 1643, and this was followed by denunciations of the movement from the Sorbonne and by Papal Bull. Jansenius's ideas were defended in 1644 by Antoine Arnauld. God's "general will" to save everyone, he argued, did not contradict the notion that only some received grace.[33] Why the saved are exceptions is beyond human grasp of God's authority and ways.

Buti and Rossi did not simply reproduce the theological exchanges, which would have been known, of course, to Mazarin. Hell was the site of much of their opera, but its action concerned a figure seeking to go there and then to leave with a beloved soul thanks to the power of love. In the midst of the myth came that famous term, the "general will," when Pluto makes a compassionate decision. There is more than one implication. A merciful king may make exceptions, even the reigning deity of a kingdom from which there is no return. An earthly realm—France—was in transition from one king to another when the libretto was written. Louis XIV was still in his minority and the chief minister and the regent had to cope with dissatisfied aristocrats. The "general will" in *L'Orfeo* seems to be comprised of the higher-ups of the lower world: Proserpina, Charon, and the characters "Suspicion" and "Jealousy." The king attends to them, that is, to something other than his own royal resolve. He finds advantage in paying mind, even allowing a kind of intelligent fealty on his part to something more than his own will at a time when kings and princes, to consolidate their states, shunned such flexibility.

The notion of a "general will" of the sovereign people in later political thought pointed to the opposite of monarchical absolutism. To suggest that it is useful for a royal sovereign to pay attention to it is a curiosity in a forgotten opera. Perhaps Buti was saying on behalf of his patrons, Mazarin and Queen Anne, that nobles would receive proper respect. It could be viewed as a cynical gesture at a tense moment. (Respect on stage can be an effective diversion from power on earth.) After all, the will here was not truly general, certainly not as Rousseau would have imagined. It doesn't originate within all the inhabitants of the realm. In the 1640s, that would have seemed as absurd, certainly among aristocrats, as the idea of all of Hades' subjects appealing to Pluto. Still, following the "general will," even if really the will of few, permits Pluto to project a sweet future for his kingdom. A ballet, that favored French form, followed.

There is no further use or elaboration of the meaning or consequences of a "general will" in the opera, except, possibly, for the fact that the action is interrupted by the announcement that Orpheus did indeed look back. The précis handed out to help viewers follow the plot simply summarized the events: Charon, without the politically and religiously suggestive phrase, and the Infernal Chorus join in the plea.[34] The result of the "general will," it seems, was misplaced confidence. By breaking his pledge, Orpheus has also taken an action more powerful than his song. He loses Eurydice, "and I my peace of mind," says distraught Proserpina. In the end, Pluto's response to the "general will" causes no problem for his authority. The opera closes with Mercury, messenger of the gods, explaining "the truth" that Orpheus's lyre is "the Royal Lily of unvanquished France." It is the source of harmony and glory everywhere; this instrument, "snatched" from hell, announces a new sun. This might be rephrased with a political accent: the transition from Louis XIII to his ten-year-old son held forth to France the promise of success.

VI.

Yet political matters became more and more complicated. There would soon be rebellion in the realm. *L'Orfeo* made a great impression on most viewers, although some felt taxed by its length (it began at 6:00 p.m. and ended at 4:00 a.m.). A story, possibly apocryphal, has teenaged Lully slip into rehearsals at the Tuileries. He knew that his lowly status precluded attendance at a performance at the Palais Royal but, exploiting his origins, he managed to meet the Florentine who sang Orpheus; "Signorina Francesca" introduced him, it seems, to Melani and to Rossi.[35]

Lully's patrons, however, were in the opposition camp, vociferous in their dislike of *L'Orfeo*. La Grande Mademoiselle found it insufferably dull and made her disapproval known. Anti-Mazarin members of the Paris Parlement complained that this opera's production wasted the realm's funds. Clergy from the Sorbonne denounced it as sinful.[36] When forces hostile to Mazarin rose up and expressed their will in a series of rebellions known as the *Fronde* (after the word for a slingshot), he had to flee Paris twice. His opera projects were collateral damage. Many Italians became scapegoats and were hounded out of the capital. Castrati were chased in the streets and Torelli was imprisoned. Melani fled with Rossi, who was trapped for a period in his living quarters and then left the country. Lully was detained briefly by soldiers who noticed his foreign accent. The man who later was renowned for linking French to music was on his way to seek Rossi's opinion on some compositions. He escaped only because those who seized him saw that he wore the insignia of the leading prorebel household—that of La Mademoiselle. However, she would have to flee Paris when the *Frondistes*, mostly aristocrats and officers, faltered and Mazarin reestablished himself. Lully went with her, but soon enough made a decision that suggests he might have perused works by a political philosopher also known as "the Florentine." Although only a teenager, Lully perceived that a new political constellation was on the horizon and like a good Machiavellian decided to place himself at the king's disposal.

He also recognized that he would have to reinvent himself. He had a substantial ally—his musical reputation—and turned to composing *intermèdes* and ballets, while participating also in a renewed effort by Mazarin to establish Italian opera in Paris. This was unsuccessful and brief, but some ballet music by Lully for use in an opera by Cavalli was well received. It was heard at festivities for the wedding of Louis XIV to the Spanish Infante, and soon Lully's court responsibilities grew. In the meantime, he distanced himself from Italian styles.[37] Lully became a French subject in 1661, the same year in which Mazarin died.

VII.

By this time, court ballets had taken on increasingly coherent form, and even what would today be called operatic shapes. This was due especially to a dramatist and poet, Isaac de Benserade, who designed scenarios that integrated episodic plots and stylish verse with dance. Louis XIV was a passionate participant, showing France—and of course its difficult nobles—that he moved always and firmly on his feet. He took part in his first ballet at age thirteen and, two years later, danced in public. He appeared as the "rising sun" in a "Ballet of the Night" in early winter 1653. Many of his subjects waited hours to see the young royal's performance in what was, in effect, a celebration of the *Fronde*'s defeat. Lully began to work with Benserade and became the preeminent figure in ballet. He helped to script the king's ballets, collaborating and dancing with Louis. Soon he became the official court composer and throughout the 1660s received one title after another.

In addition to ballets for the king, Lully wrote "comedy-ballets" with Molière, and motets. Then came operas. The emergence of "tragedy in music" in French was due to partnership with Quinault, but also jealous ambition. Lully thought at first that French was inappropriate to dramatic song. He had been unconcerned when Pierre Perrin, a poet born in Lyon, and composer Robert Cambert, formerly a musical official for the Queen Mother, collaborated on a *Pastorale d'Issy*, named for the town where this proto-opera was presented. Its success earned Perrin royal authorization for the production of opera in France. In 1671 Perrin and Cambert were acclaimed for a new work, *Pomone*, and Lully now paid attention. Here was musical terrain he did not dominate. It was inadmissible. But then scandal became his ally. Perrin involved some dubious characters in the management of *Pomone*, incurred enormous debts, and went to jail. "The Florentine" saw opportunity. He offered to rid Perrin of arrears and to provide a pension in exchange for the license (the legal monopoly) for the Royal Academy of Music. The hapless prisoner agreed.

Lully would henceforth have patents ensuring him virtually complete control over music, musical theater, and ballet. Angry protests came from musicians and from Molière as well. Nothing musical could be performed without Lully's approval, and often without payment to him. But Louis XIV wanted musical greatness to be associated with his realm, and Lully, now unquestionably loyal, was obviously the most talented musical figure in it. The monarch placed his power behind him, although this would eventually falter when both the sovereign and the church moved to tidy up "libertine" behavior of all varieties within the realm's elite. Lully's homosexuality was known, and it has been suggested that the composer's devotion to Louis XIV was more than political.[38] If there was infatuation on Lully's part, it wasn't reciprocated by the king, who became increasingly uneasy, and then intolerant of unorthodox sexual circles. Some were distinctly misogynistic. At the Duke of Grammont's parlor, which met outside Paris, members wore crosses with a depiction of a man kicking a woman. To Louis XIV's chagrin, its ranks included several royals (apparently one of his sons). It was repressed, its chief figures expelled.[39] Lully was not a member of this group but the atmosphere did not bode well for him. Campaigns were waged against "Italian morals." Louis XIV's irritation intensified on discovering that "Monsieur"—the king's brother—had been "corrupted" by a figure active in the opera world. And Lully's friend Jacques Chausson, a celebrated sponsor of "parties," was arrested in 1661 and tried for sodomy and rape of a teenaged noble.[40] After being forced to make a public apology in front of Notre Dame for "sinning against nature," he was pilloried and his tongue hacked out. His carcass was set ablaze and its smoldering vestiges thrown into the Seine. The composer was among those "noted" in the trial that preceded this gruesome drama.[41]

Lully received admonition from the king that his status was jeopardized. "The Florentine" married, had children, and took a mistress. Nonetheless, Louis distanced himself from Lully by the 1680s. The situation became even more sensitive when, in 1685, the king received a letter denouncing the composer for improper relations with a page. "Little Brunet" was sent to the priests of St. Lazare, who apparently beat him into confession. He named Lully and a number of other people, many high in the social order. Embarrassment and prudence dictated that the matter be kept quiet (even though the events were widely known), but the king was exasperated.[42]

VIII.

Lully's operatic work began and ended with pastorals. This genre was as popular in France as in Italy. The first was *The Festivals of Love and Bacchus*, a pastiche drawing from various comedy-ballets with words by several well-known hands (Benserade, Molière, Quinault). It was performed in November 1672. The last was *Acis*. In between came the tragedies-in-music that had a distinct form. They were in five acts, had no roles for castrati (French dislike for them was strong), and began with an overture and allegorical prologue extolling the king. In the prologue to their first lyric tragedy, *Cadmus and Hermione*, the "Sun"—Apollo—destroys the Python. It premiered in spring 1673 in the presence of the Sun King, who had been at war with the Dutch (a viper to be vanquished). Louis XIV's favorite opera by Lully and Quinault was drawn, like *Cadmus*, from Ovid. This was *Atys* of 1676.

In its prologue "Time" promised fame to the "Glorious Hero." Louis was again battling the Dutch and just then waiting for winter cold to dissipate so his troops could advance. The opera presents a tale of unhappy gods, vengeance, and unrequited love, as well as a chorus of "Nations" singing, "Let us celebrate immortal glory."

Quinault, a baker's son who studied law but found his vocation in poetry, was gifted in writing dramatic verse with music in mind. Lully, despite his Tuscan accent, fashioned his French recitative with a strong sense of drama. In the middle of the eighteenth century, d'Alembert would salute him as "the creator of song appropriate to our language." The composer had rendered Quinault's poems along with his own music "immortal."[43] Lully did this, as one musicologist notes, by writing music that corresponded to verbal rhythms. He enhanced clarity of poetic expression instead of "smothering" language in music. Those rhythms, and the emotions presented in the poetry, shaped "phrasing of the line, melodic curve" and "inaudible shifts in meter." Most Italian composers at this time did the contrary, "allowing the melodic curve to govern the verse" and "leaving important aspects of the rhythm to the singer. . . ." Then, instead of separating recitative and aria, the latter would emerge out of the former.[44] The *tragédies* drew from mythology or medieval epics, and while Louis XIV admired them, many contemporary literary figures, including Racine, did not. Critics determined that this new genre deformed tragic art, corrupted classicism, and—anticipating Rousseau's jeremiad—sullied the French tongue. Charles de Saint-Évremond, a celebrated literary figure, found opera an irrational art form and recitative simply a bore. This Lully was no Orpheus, he mocked, because he would have left Eurydice in hell in order to pursue young male reprobates.[45] Saint-Évremond's criticism of opera rested, however, on his belief that a singing hero or protagonist in death throes were absurdities. It made no sense to have "men deliberate in council, singing." Stage events like these would lead an audience to focus on the composer—pretentious Lully, for example—rather than on the work's subject matter. He went on to write a satire, *Les Opéra* (The Operas) in which a father tries desperately to end the appeal to his daughter of Lully's works. He judges them *"an odd medley of poetry and music, wherein the poet and the musician, equally confined one by the other, take a world of pains to compose a wretched performance."*[46]

These pronouncements derive from a rigid assertion of the tradition of French rationalism and a fierce, in this case unyielding, sense of decorum in tragic works. Saint-Évremond did not seem to recognize that similar

Figure 9.2. Lully (Lulli) and his chief librettist, Philippe Quinault
(1635–1688) in an eighteenth-century tribute.

complaints might be made against tragic poetry as well. The stage works
of Corneille and Racine achieve great beauty due to alexandrines. Might
not linguistic splendor attained by the shape of their verbal sounds—verse
meter of twelve syllables and the use of rhyming couplets—also, in their
own way, distract a viewer from the meaning of the text? Men in council
didn't deliberate in song, but neither did they in rhyme.

Most critics consider *Armide*, the final collaboration of Lully with Quinault, to be their supreme achievement. The subject, again from Tasso, was
proposed by Louis XIV, and its First Crusade theme perhaps reflected his
growing religiosity and also his recent assertions of autonomous ties between the French crown and the French clergy. Its first presentation early
in 1686 was not at court, as Lully hoped, but at the Paris Opéra (the Royal
Academy of Music) to an enthusiastic audience. Its prologue presents two
goddesses: Wisdom, who is needed in peacetime, and Glory, who is needed
during war. They are in argument: Who best loves "the august hero"? How

to share the heart of the one who (in Wisdom's words) "knows the art of putting monsters in chains," who is "absolute master of a hundred diverse peoples/ and is, moreover, master of himself?"[47]

It is an exchange of political allusions. The king had taken a momentous step the previous autumn, partly at the urging of the Jesuits and Madame de Maintenon, his stern companion (and then secret wife after the death of Queen Maria Teresa in 1683). They wanted a kingdom that was devout, with proper mores and religious unity. The king revoked the Edict of Nantes, by which his grandfather, Henri IV, had established legal tolerance of the Huguenots almost nine decades earlier. Now they were deemed monsters.[48] And, as a consequence, Louis had to worry about internal and external peace since he was regularly in conflicts with other European powers and also with the papacy. A contest for primacy pitting Wisdom and Glory—combined with the suggestion that both are in the king's heart—against Love established priorities for ruling. It was not an attack on love but asserted virtues and duties that had to come before feeling.

The story presents Armide, sorceress and niece of the king of Damascus, deploying her charms with aid from demons to capture Christian knights. Renaud (Rinaldo) frustrates her, both because he frees prisoners and because he is impervious to her entreaties. She lures him to a quiet setting for vengeance—first to make him love her and then to dispatch him. Yet Armide finds herself in love and calls out to the figure of Hate: Save me! Hate is obliging and appears with an array of appropriate accompanying passions. Still, Armide cannot muster the odium she needs. She succeeds in bringing Renaud under her charm, at least until two other crusaders make their way to her magic palace and, freed of enchantment, Renaud will leave her: duty comes first, although he will still feel pity for her. At the opera's end, however, he is wise and the sorceress furious, calling on fiends to destroy both her and love.

Armide's importance lay not only in its general artistry or its depiction of a knight set on the right path. One scene was considered to be Lully's foremost accomplishment in "ordinary recitative" (declamation in a variable meter). Armide, with Renaud before her, sings: "Finally, he is in my power." Her monologue articulates discord within: she loves but shall she kill Renaud? It became, much more than *Acis*, Rousseau's target in his "Letter" during the *Querelle*. What had been lauded as among the strongest moments of French opera was denounced by him as exemplar of its weakness.

Music, like language, must express emotions melodiously, argued Rousseau. Lully's melody, he insisted, was clumsy. He protested that Lully failed

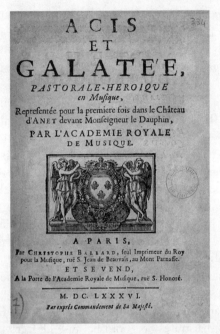

Figure 9.3. Cover of the printed libretto for the first presentation of *Acis et Galatée* (1686) with music by Jean-Baptiste Lully (1632–1687) and words by Jean Galbert de Campistron (1656–1723). (Bibliothèque nationale de France.)

to change keys as "the greatest struggle" takes place in Armide's breast.[49] If the actress is not sufficiently demonstrative, "no one would be able to endure the recitative," wrote Rousseau. The ears, he adds, need help from eyes lest the music be intolerable.[50] When Armide's heart, eyes, face, gestures—"everything"—change, "her voice" simply lowers. Underlying Rousseau's criticisms was the political-musical question: who rules? More precisely, which is prior, harmony or melody?

His answer is melody. Without it, harmony is "always cold," just chords following one another. This succession is needed, of course, but its true role is to embellish and animate melody to make it "more energetic." The "principle of harmony," this tumultuous man believed, did come from nature and is the same for all nations. However, it is also the source of "the particular character of a national music." National character depended on the "prosody" of a nation's language. If the language is not vivid in "the sound of vowels," it will "become deaf." If its consonants are rigid and frequent, any attempt at lively musical pacing will "resemble a hard, angular body rolling along cobblestones." Absent pleasing melody, "graceless" artifice must substitute, like trills (*des fredons*). If a composer makes harmony the priority, he will write bad musical parts "placed on top of one another."[51] The stakes concern how composers compose and how people hear, but might suggest much more. Readers of music see harmony as vertical forms on the page; notes that sound concurrently in a chord appear as an up-and-down alignment on a stave. Each pitch has appropriate relations to the others (intervals, in technical language). They are organized by one note; it gives the chord its identity (G major for instance). These harmonic formations move in progressions, but one follows another in a satisfying way depending on links between their vertical notes.

The suppositions in this description are those of Western tonal music, and especially ideas explicated in the eighteenth century by a great antagonist of Rousseau, the composer Jean-Philippe Rameau. These ideas imply a natural and universal order. It is erect within and not just in the way it looks on a page. Translate this into the languages of other domains, and we can arrive at ancient visions of a harmonic universe, with absolute ups and downs. Or we can also translate it into a political vision of "natural" hierarchy—with the Sun King as the political chord's defining note. Melody, by contrast, is "horizontal." It moves rhythmically in phrases or "motifs" that we hear through a succession of notes (seen as a linear movement across a page of music). The contrast between these vertical and horizontal aspects of musical texture might be, with some simplification, described this way: the "whole" of a chord is an "up and down" struck at the same time, an instance of an atemporal order; the "whole" of a melody is a line moving in time, suggesting change.

While this parallel is, admittedly, somewhat schematic (chords also follow one another in time), it is possible to suggest that the king's corner in the *Querelle* assumed that, like a chord, what is natural is vertical. A romantic individualist, however, presses his own line. Impressive harmony provided the key to—and strength of—Lully's "French" music. It was written for a king. The apparently "simple" and "Italian" melodies, textures, and phrasing of *Serva*, celebrated by Rousseau, sounded very different and carried forth a servant girl's plight and its plot. Acis and Galatea merge finally into the natural order of things; their story takes place in a mythological world, presumably universal and atemporal in its implications even if French in its statement; a patriarchal king is nature's (and God's) designee as ruler. Serpina upsets what seems to be the natural up-and-down of Uberto's household. However, the viewer—the listener—doesn't know if Vespone (which literally means big wasp) will move or speak or sting.

Unless, perhaps, it is after 1789, and the revolution Rousseau claimed to forestall with his "Letter" had begun, inspired partly by his own political ideas.

Not long after Rousseau's letter, a rebuttal of it came from the era's greatest composer and theorist of harmony. Rameau dismissed Rousseau's assertions as amateurish trivia that missed the important points, particularly Lully's subtle use of keys and musical accents. Rousseau, wrote Rameau, was so taken by Italian melodies that he could not grasp how harmony was the true basis of music's expressive powers, that it structures the movement of passions and rests on principles to which our instincts respond. This hardly meant that Rameau reduced the importance of melody; any listener to his own music hears the contrary and any careful reader of his theoretical works knows the contrary. He just did not think that music moved as Rousseau's own spirit did.[52]

Rameau's prose did not sparkle, and it was his misfortune to have as his antagonist—their animosity predated this clash—a polemicist of uncommon power and stormy political brilliance. Rousseau was also unfortunate. His antagonist had one of the foremost musical imaginations of the century. Rousseau could not compete with Rameau in composing music. We will return to this argument about natural order and natural movement.

Chapter 10

IN THE WINDS: THE
DECADES OF PERNUCIO
AND TELEMACHUS

Did states create nations, linking and identifying dissimilar populations across disparate territorial spaces, or was it the reverse? This question gripped many historians and intellectuals in the late twentieth century. Before "modernity," argued some, neither states nor nations (as we would speak of them) really existed. A king may have claimed to incarnate France, for one example, and courtiers may have vested him with mythical symbols, but it would never have occurred to most of his largely illiterate subjects, spread across the vague geographic entity that comprised his realm, that they had linguistic or cultural bonds with "compatriots" sixty kilometers from where they lived. The monarch was far away. The powers they knew on a daily basis were those of the church and local nobility. It was the assertion of a king's "national" sovereignty and its identification with a central, lawmaking order that weakened ecclesiastical and aristocratic prerogatives. Louis XIV's absolutism came in the decades after the Fronde's defeat and as Europe's state system consolidated with the Treaty of Westphalia, ending the Thirty Years War.

Other scholars propose that national characteristics and the political organization of the state had a more complicated, longer past. Certainly, they say, a vast transformation moved Europe away from its decentralized, medieval reality toward contesting states and nations. Nonetheless, states and nations need to be understood as descendants of ever-present, if transmuting, human needs for collective bonds, and not as a product of "modernity" as such. Those needs and bonds are found in various forms in the earliest of human annals.[1] Had that not been so, it would have been impossible, for one example, for someone during the Renaissance (or today for that matter), to understand why Socrates refused to flee from Athens after a jury condemned him to death—why he insisted instead on loyalty to what would later be called a *patria*. Or, for another example, it would have been and would still be impossible to study with profit Aristotle's famous taxonomy of political organization in his book *Politics*.

Reading about Socrates or understanding Aristotle also requires recognition that they and their language were of another time. This was, perhaps, not entirely or always evident to humanists who looked back to the Greeks and Romans while trying to address their own world. Yet their efforts and experiments were fruitful often enough. There is, perhaps, an ambiguous field of tensions with no permanent pointers on it, indeed, with ever shifting signposts, on which recurrent human concerns and time-bound and time-shaped engagements meet. They do so in their own ways historically, constantly and across generations. In the mid- and later seventeenth century, literary figures in France and elsewhere in Europe quarreled vociferously about "Ancients and Moderns." It was a natural extension of Renaissance debates about the value of antiquity for later eras. Now the question was: are modern times a radical break with the past? Were modern languages and styles intrinsically superior to or purer than those of antiquity? Or were claims like these just conceits—a refusal, when seen as a whole, to recognize what the true giants did long before, an inability to admit that contemporary writers were at best descendants, standing on their shoulders (as it was phrased neatly in a debate on this theme in England)? Time as well as geography had become important dimensions within art and also cultural conversation.

Surely Lully, whose fame rose at the time of this "Quarrel," found the theme familiar. Similar concerns about antiquity and modernity preceded opera's development in his native Florence a century earlier. His operas were "modern" in the novel ways they linked the French language to music, all to tell stories derived from ancient myths or medieval epics. These stories were, in turn, implicated in a heroic present by evocations of the king in prologues. François Couperin, arguably France's finest composer between Lully's death and the advent of Rameau, was very alert to exchanges about ancients and moderns; his *The Art of Playing Harpsichord* told readers that contemporary "good taste" was incomparably purer than that of antiquity.[2]

Contemporary political formations had by then appeared on stages for some time. Collective and geographic entities with distinct mores and discordant personalities could be seen in court ballets and other entertainments, and sometimes "empire" and "nation" blurred. A "Ballet of the Four Christian Monarchies" of 1635 did not rest on nationalist assumptions but it did present "Italy," "France," "Spain," and "Germany" dancing.[3] *The Bourgeois Gentleman* of 1670, a comedy-ballet by Molière and Lully, has a "Ballet of the Nations" and mocks Turks. Lully and Quinault's *Phaëton* of 1683 expanded horizons with dancing Indians, Egyptians, and Ethiopians. A somewhat narrow view of "nations" was expressed by Bishop Jacques-Bénigne Bossuet, Louis XIV's principal ideologist. He wrote a *Discourse on Universal History* in which, as Voltaire later quipped famously, the universe comprised a half-dozen nations. But more was underway. "One day, the French people, almost to a man, were thinking like Bossuet," wrote one historian about bonds between religious belief and political authority represented by the bishop, "The day after, they were thinking like Voltaire."[4] This exaggerates but still captures a truth about a large-scale intellectual transformation.

Efforts to sustain a tradition of "tragedy-in-music" after Lully were at most modestly successful. French interest in Italian music rekindled in the 1690s. It had never really disappeared. And instead of looking up and down at the order of authority and listening to its commands, eyes looked—and ears heard—horizontally, or rather they engaged what was coming from around the earth's surface. A world existed beyond France: Italy, the rest of Europe and, indeed, exotica on other continents. After all, by this time the "Age of Discovery," which began in the late fifteenth century, was closing. Everything had been "found," at least on earth. Typecast "findings" sang and danced on European stages. At the same time, however, discoverers stereotyped themselves and their European neighbors frequently. "Each nation has its character for song and for music, as in most other things, which depend on different geniuses, usages, and customs," wrote Jesuit commentator Claude-François Ménestrier in 1681.[5] The first French history of music, published in 1715, proposed in an ahistorical way that hostility between French and Italian music dated to Charlemagne. It asked, "Does an Italian behave like a Frenchman? Their tastes, clothes, manners, pleasures—are they not all different? Why should their songs and playing styles not be different also? . . . Each nation has different customs."[6]

II.

Couperin becomes emblematic in this context, even though he wrote no operas. His dramatic instincts were honed finely and theatrical references are plentiful in his works. Antoine Danchet, perhaps the most important French opera librettist at the turn of the seventeenth century, remarked in a note added to Couperin's treatise on playing harpsichord that this "Master had taken his art to the highest degree of perfection."[7] Couperin's compositional range extended far, including religious and secular vocal music. He admired greatly the composer of *Armide,* and wrote a celebratory "Apotheosis" on Lully's "ascent" to Parnassus. Yet Couperin's greatest achievements were for harpsichord (he chose to call a cluster of them an "order"). In these he was not "anti-Lully" but in a sense he was the "un-Lully." Called "le Grand" to distinguish him from others in his musically talented family, Couperin's temperament—at least as we hear it—also contrasted to the grandiosity that marked his employer, the Sun King. While Lully, the Florentine-turned-Frenchman, provided stately, royal flaunt, Couperin, a Frenchman who admired Italian music, composed extraordinary miniatures. He moved from the ornate toward the pleasing simplicity of "Galant" style. This term, fashionable in the late sixteenth and seventeenth century, indicated lightness and gracefulness in the arts, love and manners, although it could echo bravery (*gallant*), its earlier sense.[8]

Louis XIV's reign had been losing its dynamism at this time, worn by wars and the inevitable sputter that comes toward the end of a very long rule. In his life's last quarter century, the Sun King's court took a pious and severe turn. This came of his own mood but also because of prodding by Madame de Maintenon and clerics. Couperin's small, focused pieces of music were not austere; they were more like elegant, animated tableaus—sometimes tender, often spry or whimsical or wistful or teasing, or combinations of all these in carefully etched and shaped sound. Voltaire (among others) would later compare his sensibility to a contemporary artist, Antoine Watteau. Couperin's works usually bore names; but instead of actually telling listeners that his music had subjects, personal or otherwise, they usually conveyed a combination of irony and a sense of ambiguity about the world in which he lived. In 1713 he noted in his first published collection of harpsichord works that he gave to them titles to "respond to ideas" that he had. Some object or occasion served as inspiration, he elaborated, calling them "portraits" of a kind. He asked pardon for not elucidating.[9] His designations encourage mystery about the association of sounds and those ideas; they also indicate both expressive and imitative purpose in his intimate compositions-without-words, which differentiated him so much from Lully's use of music to animate libretto-based theater.

Music, Couperin also proposed, ought not to be perceived in parochial ways. He made his suggestion with a curious political tinge. He asserted in 1724 that there was a "Republic of Music" in France. This commonwealth was Italian and French at once. Was a work of music good or bad? That question could be resolved "by merit" and "without regard to composer or nation."[10] The identity of the creator or a listener, this court musician seemed to say, was irrelevant. His comment about a "republic" referred to culture and taste, but he was not living in an apolitical world, and it lends itself to speculation that his ideas may not always have been strictly musical, even when composing. This is conjecture; his correspondence and private papers do not survive and debates about French as opposed to Italian music were hardly an original concern. It is plausible, however, to listen to his compositions and to attend to a few existing hints. From these it is possible to discern imaginatively his internalization of broad currents of his times—cultural, intellectual, political—and the creation by him of a countersensibility in his artistic projects. A ruse he initiated early in his career and then exposed much later intimates this too, suggesting a wholeness to his work.

Couperin was born in 1668 and when still a young man became organist at Paris's Saint Gervais church, a family-held post. His talents garnered recognition and he eventually became an "Organist of the King." In 1692, a year before his official appointment, he announced that some remarkable trio sonatas had come into his hands. Their composer, one "Pernucio," was previously unknown and they had been sent to him by a relative in the employ of the king of Sardinia. Despite noisy anti-Italian prejudices in Paris, these musical jewels quickly became popular there. Three decades later Couperin revealed that "Pernucio" was simply an anagram of his own name. "Knowing French asperity (*l'âpreté*) towards all new things from abroad," he explained, "and not being too concerned for my own glory, I did myself a good turn by means of a small deception." He felt no need to apologize for his "Italianate mask."[11] The truth, obviously, was in the sounds. He would go so far as to refer to "*sonades*," merging French and Italian words, and pressed his point further by crediting important aspects of his own "French" style to Arcangelo Corelli, the admired Baroque composer whose influence on writing purely instrumental works was enormous. It is as if Couperin wanted to refute sentiments like those expressed by Ménestrier. It was as if he wanted to convey contempt for protonationalist pride in musical styles. When he disclosed the identity of "Pernucio" in 1726, he did so in a particular way. He admitted that he was this composer in a preface to the publication of expanded versions of the sonatas of the 1690s, renamed "Les Nations." Conjecture can make this a relatively small manifestation—even anticipation—of large historical transformations. When the eighteenth century began, absolute monarchy was the political compass; it would be challenged as "nation" and "republic" became magnets for loyalty over the ensuing nine decades. These two words together would be a symbolic diptych of the French Revolution. Scholars have called Couperin's "Les Nations" a kind of musical diptych because the composer, who also rechristened each *sonade* with a national association while making only minor changes in the original, added to each a French dance suite. The names he chose can lead to intriguing political-cultural guesswork.

The first had been called "La Pucelle"—"the Virgin Maid." In 1726 she became "La Françoise"—the French woman. "La Pucelle" brings to mind, inevitably, a French Catholic heroine Joan of Arc. Did Couperin know that "Joan la Pucelle" was an evil witch in Shakespeare's *Henry VI Part 1* of 1590? No evidence says so, even though he had been exposed to English culture. After the "Glorious Revolution" of 1688 chased King James II from London, he took harbor at the Château at Saint-Germain-en-Laye near Paris. The "Jacobite" court (after his Latin name) was composed mostly of advocates of absolute monarchy like their Gallic host at Versailles. They hoped to cross the channel again and retrieve power by force if necessary (they made an effort). Since William of Orange, a Dutch Protestant, was now enthroned in London as William III, France's very Catholic king sympathized with the deposed royal (a Catholic who had close ties to France). Moreover, the revolution established parliamentary supremacy at Westminster, an intolerable precedent for any absolutist.

However, Louis XIV had his own concerns in the web of French, British, and Dutch relations. There had been the Franco-Dutch war between 1672–1678; his revocation of the Edict of Nantes in 1685 pushed thousands of Huguenots to flee to Holland, Britain, and elsewhere. The War of Augsburg, beginning in 1688, pitted the Sun King against a "Grand Alliance" that included William III, the Holy Roman Empire, and Spain, among others. Louis was unhappy about the circumstances surrounding its end. They were not advantageous as he hoped. Among other things, the Treaty of Ryswick compelled him in 1697 to recognize Britain's new regime. Four years later yet another war brought the French, the Dutch, the Portuguese, Savoy, and the Empire into varying constellations as supporters of different contenders for Spain's throne after its last Habsburg possessor had died. At its end, the Jacobites, headed by then by James III, had to leave France. (James II died in 1701.)

Italian art and music marked strongly cultural life in James II's exiled court."[12] Evidently Couperin frequented the Château. James's religiosity, Jacobite hopes, and Franco-Dutch wars could have combined to make "La Pucelle" an appealing figure both at Saint-Germain-en-Laye and Versailles. (Some discomfort would have been entailed, however, since Jacobites wanted French help to invade England.) Couperin claimed "La Pucelle" was the first French trio sonata in the style of *sonata da chiesa* (a Baroque Italian "church sonata"). Perhaps the composer was also suggesting slyly the value of cultural interchange, since the real "Pernucio" was, after all, a Frenchman, "La Pucelle" was French, but the style of his sonata was Italian. After this virgin, who was also known for visions, came the sonata "La Visionnaire," which Couperin went on to rename "L'Espagnole." Scholars have trouble discerning the composers' allusions in both these names and identifications. Some point to a Baroque comedy by Jean Desmarets de Saint-Sorlin titled *Les Visionnaires*. Popular since 1637, it had returned to the Paris stage not long before the sonata was composed. The play is less about visions than illusions (three girls pursue love follies while their father tries to protect them from crazed male pursuers). Desmarets became devoted to "Quietism," an austere mystical Christianity that was the source of considerable contestation. It seems also to have appealed in some ways to Couperin. Consider the paradox: a man who creates sounds yet sympathizes with a doctrine animated by quiet; Couperin was a whimsical composer whose works are certainly softer than those of Lully.[13]

The Iberian association might have been due to the considerable influence in France of Spanish mysticism, beginning with Teresa of Avila in the sixteenth century. Her notion of love of God through meditative prayer was part of the spiritual background to the development of Quietism. While she was canonized, Miguel de Molinos, a seventeenth-century Spanish formulator of Quietism, found himself imprisoned in Rome for his belief in giving up the "self" to God in quest of sanctified serenity. An unhappy fate also befell this priest's French follower, Madame de Guyon, although her incarceration was in the Bastille. It was at a time when church and court argued fiercely about this mystic's advocacy of inner abandonment to God that Couperin presented "Pernucio's" sonatas (effacing his own "glory" with a pseudonym, as he put it).

Couperin was personally familiar—how much so is not clear—with a central figure in the Quietist debate, François de Fénelon, an increasingly eminent and controversial ecclesiastic who was critical of his king's wars and absolutism. Fénelon's preoccupations would have a central place in the next century's intellectual history and, along the way, in opera. Where Descartes's philosophy began with the "I" ("I think therefore I am"), Fénelon's religious and political philosophies entailed, respectively, a "disinterested" self-effacing quest for God and likewise for political rule aimed at the good of subjects, not aggrandizement of a king. He also understood something about religious tolerance and persecution, having ministered to Huguenots compelled to take the realm's Catholic faith after the revocation of the Edict of Nantes.

The third sonata was titled "L'Astrée," perhaps for literary as well as political reasons. Astraea, in Ovid's account, was a virgin goddess of justice. She lived among mortals as long as she could but fled when they become impossibly violent. Perhaps that "Iron Age" of bloodshed resembled Couperin's own and the musician longed for a new, peaceful era. Virgil's *Fourth Eclogue* tells us that her return to earth signaled a new golden age (later taken as a prophesy of Christianity). The reign of France's Henri IV, who sought to secure peace by his own conversion and the Edict of Nantes, was also often compared to Astraea's Golden Age. A long, popular work of fiction titled *L'Astrée* was written early in the early seventeenth century and dedicated to him by its author, Honoré d'Urfé. Set in Roman antiquity, one of its protagonists was often perceived as a disguised, youthful Henri. Symbolic linkage of France to Astraea was frequent in ensuing decades. It served politically to make the Bourbon kingdom legatee of true Christian empire, rather than the Holy Roman one, and suggested Gallic autonomy from the papacy. Louis XIV was hailed by admirers—or propagandists—as a Christian Mars: "Louis on the throne of Astraea," went an ode at the time.[14]

Couperin's music in "L'Astrée" does not suggest any sympathy on the composer's part for the Sun King's royal bellicosity or martial Christianity as a vehicle for peace. Why did "L'Astrée" become "La Piemontoise" in "Les Nations"? Even intelligent guesswork brings no satisfying response to this question. Three sonatas are first given women's names and then national associations, but only to close with a new piece in "Les Nations." "L'Imperiale" may have been composed in the mid-1720s, when Couperin was speaking of a republic of music. What he aimed to suggest with the title also remains mysterious, although perhaps he hoped that the changes in the last decades might still accord with Astraea's promise of a tolerant, golden age as the four parts of this work fit comfortably together.[15] But a new age of Astraea would also have to encompass a makeover of European society—including the development of nations—that was well underway in his times. He was, of course, busy writing music and not political theories. Still, "La Pucelle," changed into "La Françoise" when accompanied by a French dance; it led finally to "L'Imperiale," a much more musically mature *sonade*.

<h2 style="text-align:center">III.</h2>

Scholars express puzzlement that Couperin, though he was ennobled, honored, and played concerts for Louis XIV, never received principal musical positions at court through 1715, the year of the king's death.[16] This does not seem due to dislike of his music or ties to Jacobites. There was, however, a dimension to the composer's service that might have had political implications. Besides duties in the royal chapel, he was charged with teaching music to royal offspring. He did so for a dozen years within a formidable system of preceptors that prepared young princes and princesses for high station under the direction of a reform-minded duke, Paul de Beauvilliers. One Couperin student was the famously irascible Duke of Burgundy, the king's grandson and second in line to the throne. His primary general tutor was Fénelon. A description of princely training in 1696 speaks of its rigor and Fénelon's desire to teach "everything that is beautiful and curious and useful in all arts and sciences" but without specializations since "a definite pursuit" was "regarded as unworthy and ridiculous in a prince."[17] In a decade Fénelon went from prominence to virtual banishment in Cambrai, where he was archbishop-duke (a status which also made him a prince of the Holy Roman Empire.) He had been too sympathetic to Quietism but, more important, had been instructing the king's grandson that absolutism, pomp, and war were bad. (This would seem to concur with Couperin's tastes.) He wrote "Dialogues" between famous dead figures for the edification of his pupil and in one, Cato, that hero for republicans from Roman antiquity, denounces the "misery and infamy of tyranny."[18] Pure humanity, Fénelon sought to communicate, came before any other identity. Wars for little corners of the world were "the dishonor of the human race."[19] It would be—Fénelon doesn't say this, but it follows—like fighting over the superiority of French or Italian music.

Virtues espoused by Fénelon are usually associated by political thinkers (but not entirely) with republicanism or constitutional monarchy, particularly rule by law.[20] In an anonymous letter of considerable gumption that it seems that he wrote in late 1693, Fénelon warned the Sun King that military victories could not prevent the ground from sinking under his feet. Wars against "Hollande" by the "nation française" would only make the French hateful to their neighbors and bring rebellion at home. [21] (He referred specifically to Louis's victories at Neerwinden and Steenkerque in 1692; the latter served as the title of a Couperin sonata from this time.) He called the world a "universal republic," adding that heaven would be sickened were "each nation, that is, each family of the great commonwealth" to imagine it had "undoubted right to make good its claims upon the neighboring nations with violence."[22]

This cleric did not challenge the idea of monarchy. However, he pointed the young Duke of Burgundy to those past kings he thought had ruled well. His favored monarchs who were reform-minded and popular like Louis XII at the turn of the sixteenth century and, of course, Henri IV. The gods, Fénelon stressed in a political novel he wrote in the mid-1690s, give a king his station "not for himself . . . but for his subjects. . . ." It had not been his intention—or so he said—that this work of fiction, *Telemachus*, be read by anyone but Louis XIV's grandson, but a copyist printed it in 1699. Its framework is Homeric: it tells of Telemachus's search for his father, Ulysses. Throughout his quest the Ithacan dauphin is educated about morality, politics, and life by "Mentor," who is really Minerva, goddess of wisdom, in disguise. Their relation parallels that of Fénelon and the king's grandson. Had the Duke of Burgundy come to the throne and followed his own mentor's prescriptions, his France would have been different, radically so, from that of Louis XIV. "Those who have the laws in their hands to govern the people ought always to submit to the laws themselves," say the sages of Crete, an island that rejects "superfluities" in *Telemachus*. Their wise king, Minos, had sought to ensure that a king's "absolute power" was to do good, but at the same time "his hands are tied from doing wrong." Moreover, "he can do anything to the people; but the laws can do anything to him."[23] Since the political order was distinguishable from Minos's person—it was modern—he could not say "I am the state."

Telemachus became one of the most popular novels of the eighteenth century; many future rulers as well as philosophers read it, and operas— most famously Mozart's *Idomeneo*—drew from it. It was read to the young man who would become Friedrich the Great. Young Rousseau immersed himself in it. Gluck would write an opera, *Telemaco*, in honor of the marriage of Austria's Joseph II. When he was ten years old, Mozart visited Fénelon's tomb with his family. At age fourteen, in 1770, he was reading *Telemachus*. His *Idomeneo* used a libretto that reworked *Idoménée*, a French lyric tragedy of 1712 based on the same story (but with the end altered).

Figure 10.1. François Fénelon (1651–1715), French archbishop whose novel *The Adventures of Telemachus* (1699) was written to tutor Louis XIV's grandson. The novel became enormously influential politically and in operas throughout the eighteenth century. Young Mozart would read him. An eighteenth-century portrait. (Bibliothèque nationale de France.)

The composer of this earlier work, André Campra, once director of music at Notre Dame, seems to have shared Couperin's desire to bring together different "national" forms of music, stating once that he wanted a mélange of French delicacy and Italian "vivacity."[24] But in *Idoménée* his concern was to fashion an operatic counterpart to great works of French tragedy. Its creation was inspired by a play about Idomeneo by Prosper Jolyot de Crébillon (père) that was performed in 1705, just six years after the publication of Fénelon's novel.

The prologue of Campra's opera may have been a warning, or a suggestion, or obfuscation—or all these at once. In it, the ruler of the winds, Aeolus, is urged by Venus to hold back their currents, least they gust against a victorious soldier returning home from Troy—Idomeneo. There are, this suggests, forces greater than those at human disposal. These images might be taken as support for Louis XIV: let him withstand whatever came at him in old age and difficult times. This wish, however, might also have been no more than a useful mask to allow librettist Antoine Danchet and the composer to stage an episode in a novel that displeased their monarch—all while they point the audience toward it. The prologue could suggest that France faced gales all around and ahead of it, especially since the king, despite efforts to project him as godlike to subjects and to the world, had to succumb inevitably to the same mortal limits as everyone. Two dauphins, Louis's son and grandson, died in succession in 1711, providing a reminder of some practical realities even if absolutist ideology presumed that a monarch's spirit did not dissolve with a king's material decease.

However the prologue is perceived, its messages and those of the opera recall those of Fénelon. It can, for example, be interpreted quite obviously as a protest against war and its consequences. In the first act, before Idomeneo's arrival in Crete, his son Idamantes fosters love between his own victorious compatriots and Trojan prisoners. His own love for a captive Trojan princess suggests values more important than maintenance of a people's bloodlines. (Couperin might have asked: if a Cretan and a Trojan can find happiness together, why should French and Italian music be in opposition?) By the opera's end, however, Idomeneo, in a state of fury, will take his son's life. This killing, following on a reckless oath by him to a god, can be construed as dissent from royal responsibility, both political and religious, and the inability to make royal decisions dispassionately—all of them themes that frequent Fénelon's novel. And when Fénelon's Idomeneo goes into exile, having endangered his subjects by inciting a deity's wrath and thereby rousing frenzy against him, he goes to Salente, to found a just kingdom.

Campra also contributed music to an earlier pastiche that defined itself specifically as "modern" and was based on *Telemachus*, with a libretto mostly by Danchet. Its politics are in a lower key but its creation was obviously prompted by Fénelon, since it told of Telemachus's attraction to the nymph Eucharis on Calypso's island. While Ulysses's son and Calypso appear in literature as far back as Homer, this particular story seems to have been Fénelon's invention and could only have pointed the pastiche's viewers to his novel.[25] The same is true of a "Tragedy in Music" titled *Télémaque et Calypso* that was performed at the Opéra in November 1714, not long before the deaths of both Fénelon and Louis XIV. Dedicated to the king, its prelude included Minerva, Cupid, their suites, and Apollo. Praise for the "Hero" was effusive. Destouches, then inspector general (musical director) of the Opéra, contributed to the work. The librettist was Abbé Simon-Joseph Pellegrin. The story of Telemachus and Eucharis was central to the five-act spectacle, with scenes in Calypso's abodes, Neptune's temple, a desert, and a "Temple of Love." In addition to the well-known characters of the story, it was filled with gods, kings, a grand priestess of love, other priestesses, shepherds, symphonic interludes, extensive dancing and choruses.[26] Fénelon's novel was only at the beginning of Telemachus's wide-reaching stage journey.

IV.

Fénelon's views infuriated both the king and Bossuet. The bishop of Meaux was a stern proponent of absolutism and Gallicanism (that is, limits on the papacy's powers in France). Once an advocate for the younger Fénelon, he was a foe of Quietism. The title of Bossuet's principal political work, published posthumously, encapsulated his worldview: *Politics Drawn from the Very Words of Holy Scripture.* "Royal authority is absolute," he insisted, yet this did not mean arbitrary. The king was subject to the laws of religion and his kingdom—but "by the rightness of his will." In other words, his rightful will ruled. Beyond this he "need not account to anyone for what he ordains" and there could be no "co-active"—countervailing, that is—forces that constrained legitimately his exercise of power.[27] Bossuet was no less blunt about his own prerogatives when he explained why he could persecute all kinds of foes. It was simple: he was right, they were wrong. Fénelon's temperament was different, dramatically so. Political redemption and high office became possible only after the deaths of Bossuet and (later) this religio-political ideologue's pupil, the dauphin. The Duke of Burgundy then became heir to the throne and Fénelon, who retained good ties to his former student and was the most formidable figure in his reformist circle, drew up plans for regime amendment. A stronger role was to be given to the aristocracy and the advisory role of the General Estates (assemblies of legal social strata) was to be strengthened. Moves like these were conceived as restraints on centralized royal sway.[28] It was a program that would have tilted absolute towards constitutional monarchy but it came to nothing when the duke also died. Fénelon went to his own grave less than three years later.

Fénelon's Quietest leanings were expressed in a belief in "disinterested" and "pure love" of God. However, when the church condemned Madame de Guyon's doctrines and his own expressed views, he, a loyal prelate, bowed to its judgment. Still, Quietism's flavor—which seems to have neo-Stoic seasoning—suffused, strongly so, his ideas in all realms. A monarch ruled for his people; a free man was "detached" and has "tranquility of mind";

similarly, a good sovereign rejects luxury and "expensive show."[29] "Perfect virtue," says Socrates in a dialogue by Fénelon, "detaches man from himself. . . ."[30]

What of the arts? They are a sensuous matter and ought to have been something of a problem from Fénelon's "disinterested" perspective; his disdain for display could easily have been translated into hostility to Lully's aesthetic. The arts were not Fénelon's chief preoccupation, although he sided with ancients against moderns and the high literary quality of so many of his works makes evident his concern with rhetorical style, form, and communication. His "Dialogue on Eloquence," whose focus was on preaching, echoed Cicero's assertion that a speaker needed to be well-versed in philosophy and virtue. Poetry and painting were, for Fénelon, interchangeable except that one was for the ears and the other the eyes. Yet in another dialogue, this one between Demosthenes and Cicero, he favors the Greek rhetorician for simplicity in presentation, in contrast to the Roman's more flamboyant speech.

Fénelon had a robust, if conflicted, mistrust of artists. Music, however, is present in *Telemachus* as well as in his other writings. While it is never a principal concern, he makes striking, if allusive, comparisons of it with morals and politics. Music is presumed by him to be a necessary feature of education, albeit with many of Plato's caveats. Since the wrong music corrupts youth and may lead to chaos, Mentor proscribes bacchanalia. Proper music is best found in temples and at special celebrations; it should never be ostentatious. (This recalls differences between Lully's grand "spectacles" and Couperin's chamber miniatures.) Still, Orpheus's talents are described and praised. Mentor plays lyre and sings with great artistry and this disguised goddess thinks governing is like the arts. She embraces balance in decision-making and rejects artifice in virtually all domains of life. A good ruler, says Mentor, is like a musician who invents "melodious sounds" and places them in sequence and within proper order. An architect does likewise, situating details within a bigger picture. "Do not doubt," Telemachus is told, ". . . that the government of a kingdom requires a certain harmony, like music, and proportions as exact as those of architecture."[31] Composition requires proper laws. Composers and rulers worry about similar things, like the good of the whole and how its parts fit together.

Was there an affinity—elective or due to a spirit of the times—between Couperin's music and Fénelon's leanings toward Quietism? There seems to be, and at least one mid-twentieth-century student of this composer proposed it.[32] Couperin's music, like Fénelon's spiritual outlook and politics, breathe in their historical moment and exhale an alternative to it in artistic ways, taking to one side of what Couperin called mysterious barricades (or perhaps seeing through them) by rejecting superfluities and luxury, all while creating petite wholes. "Pernucio" was invented as a disinterested advocate of music. And the light, often subtle joy in many of his works contradicted the severity of the latter years of Louis XIV.

V.

The year 1697 was not a good year for Louis XIV nor for Fénelon. The latter would be fixed in Cambrai, and a good deal of bloodshed took place in his territories due to his king's wars. The king's nine-year battle with a coalition that composed the League of Augsburg ended. He had hoped to take advantage of worries then unsettling the Holy Roman Empire, particularly the Ottoman threat. But Emperor Leopold came to a temporary accord with the Turks, and France had to yield Lorraine. Direct conflict dissipated in stages as Charles II of Spain reached an understanding with Louis in August, as did William of Orange. Leopold followed suit in November. It was a dramatic dance of European powers, each circling around, sometimes fighting, sometimes allying with or balancing off one another.

The Parisian theater world also suffered an upheaval. The Italian Comedy was ousted that year—its exile would last two decades—after it played a satire titled *The False Prude*. It infuriated Madame de Maintenon, who believed herself its target (not without reason), but the public popularity of the company, which now used French in productions, had also unsettled the Comédie-Française. The government went so far as to tell the police shortly after the expulsion "to efface the inscription" on its theater.[33] Watteau painted a sympathetic depiction of the departure of the Italian "*comédiens.*"[34] However, a transitional operatic form had a considerable success in 1697. "Opera-ballet" seemed to offer other possibilities. The text for Campra's *L'Europe galante* was by Antoine Houdar de la Motte and it was commissioned by the Duc de Sully as a home entertainment.[35] De la Motte, a law student turned dramatist, was a friend and great admirer of Fénelon—so great that he declared a preference for *Telemachus* to Homer's epics. His libretto, written before the novel was published, began in a mythological world and proceeded to evoke contemporary politics in many ways.

Opera-ballet did not use plot to unify stage events. There would be an overture followed by a prologue, and usually four (sometimes three) self-contained "*Entrées*" (acts). Each had its own story, and librettos were short because the spectacle was filled with dances, songs, and *divertissements*. What made them whole was a common theme threading through them. Louis de Cahusac, who would be a librettist for Rameau, later characterized them as something "entirely new." *L'Europe galante* compared to pretty Watteaus. Quinault, he explained, imagined for Lully "large action worked through five acts," comparable to paintings by Raphaël and Michelangelo. La Motte, by contrast, provided Campra "piquant miniatures," demanding "precision of design, graceful brushstrokes."[36] Another important feature distinguished *L'Europe galante* from Lully's operas. Mythological figures, whether ancient or chivalric, played roles only in the prologue and at the end. They set forth the theme—a struggle between principles, those of love and conflict—that moves through the *Entrées*. Moderns then follow ancients; these figures are replaced by contemporary characters. These tend to be stereotypes. Each *Entrée* gives recognizably human characteristics to those somewhat indistinct entities that had danced through the seventeenth century—nations. One act after another is named for a nation, takes place in a different venue, yet rebuts the principle of strife. The brief stories reveal, finally, love's animating power, despite human variety, despite customs, dress, and roles. Each part contains or ends with a dance or musical interlude, anticipating the diptychs of sonatas and suites in Couperin's "Les Nations" and, later, the structure of Rameau's *Les Indes galantes* of 1735. (The latter would have a broader geographic scope.) "We chose the nations of Europe whose characters contrasted most and which promised to play best in the theater: France, Spain, Italy, and Turkey," explained de la Motte. "We pursued the ordinary ideas of what composes the spirit (*genie*) of their peoples. The Frenchman is portrayed as flighty, indiscreet, coquettish; the Spaniard is faithful and romantic; the Italian is jealous, proud, and violent; and finally we have expressed, as much as the theater permits, the haughtiness and sovereign dominance of the Sultan and the passion of the Sultana."[37] And it is a case of stage events suggesting correspondences to those of the times.

After an overture, Venus appears with friends and allies making love-arrows, only to be told blithely by "Discord" that it is hopeless to imagine Europe obeying her laws. But the Goddess of Love will not yield. The exchange, placed on stage at a time when France and its adversaries were making peace, asks: Which force will triumph ultimately? Will Love or Discord preoccupy Louis XIV? This opening suggests the danger of renewed wars (they would arrive soon enough) in an unhappy military and political year for the French crown. To choose France, Spain, Italy, and

Turkey while leaving out the empire—the foremost representative of Discord for the French—suggests ongoing worry. One way to interpret each *Entrée* is in light of contemporary events.

The first, "France," presents Silvandre, a shepherd in pursuit of Céphise who, knowing his flirtatious character, rebuffs him. Trust and alliance are complicated matters. She sings of her passion for "peaceful places" but also of her disinclination to find a "thousand shepherds" at her knees.[38] This might imply an irritating question for Louis XIV: Is not concord at home preferable to homage by vast numbers of foreign subjects? After light dances, the opera-ballet moves to Spain where, in an *Entrée* sung in French and Spanish, Don Pedro and Don Carlos, cavaliers, sing of their constancy and the women they love.[39] Lucile and Leonore are unresponsive, but a "Spanish girl" sings of perseverance before the act ends with a rondeau. Love is as important to the Spanish as to the French, but in addition to peace and trust another value has been suggested for frustrating times: resolve. A viewer at the time might note that Spain had been in an alliance against Louis XIV, but its aged ruler, cousin to the Habsburg emperor in Vienna, had made his own peace with Louis in August 1697. It was evident that succession was soon to come, and Bourbons and Habsburgs laid claim to the Spanish throne.

The third act is in fragmented Italy where Octavio, Venetian aristocrat and chronic complainer, worries that Olympia, his love, is to go to a masked ball with another. Threats and fears finally resolve into an appeal for forgiveness. This scene's characters sang of love and jealousy, of fickleness and loyalty just as Louis XIV's relations with Rome improved. He had acted to papal satisfaction against the Jansenists and lured Piedmont-Savoy into switching sides. A lively dance from northeastern Italy takes place before the opera-ballet moves to Turkish domains which, it seems, are also part of Gallant Europe. There, in a harem, two Sultanas vie for their sovereign's affections. One, Roxanne, seeks victory over her rival by an equivalent to war. She tries to stab Zayde, and her warlike act turns Sultan Zuliman from her. Happy Zayde, though she had come to his hands as a captive, now explains how a tender heart dwells beneath his famously fearsome appearance. A chorus praises his laws.[40] This is another way of saying that Europeans have had the wrong image of Turkey. The story is flimsy but its politics justify France's past alliances with the Muslim Ottomans against the Catholic Habsburgs. "Zuliman" is a name that conjures up Suleiman the Magnificent, the Sultan who besieged Vienna in 1683. As it happens, in 1697 the Ottomans temporarily sued for peace with the Habsburgs. In effect, Zayde recognizes expressly that the Sultan has weaknesses all while foreseeing good prospects for the French and the Ottomans, which allows for Venus's triumphant return. Campra also unites beginning and end with a musical motif. Heard initially in Discord's words, it sounds again as this force of strife heads toward hell.[41]

Taken as a whole, the different parts of *L'Europe galante* comprise an allegory about France and her neighbors and rivals engaging and allying, stepping toward and then back from each other. It was presented in an operatic form in which old and new shapes mingled, along with ancient (mythic) and modern characters; it may not have been entirely novel, but something old-new. The mix, sometimes uneven, of structures drew from the century before and pointed to the next. This is also a way in which, broadly speaking, the politics of the day, including Fénelon's place in them, can be perceived. It was an age of transition. Embedded in *L'Europe galante* as in Europe itself were images of "nations." If they are "modern," then modernity came upon stages more fully when the centrality of mythological and pastoral figures of Lully and Quinault were displaced by dancing nations in Campra and de la Motte. Nonetheless their opera-ballet suggests—hopes, is perhaps a better word—that nations need not be in perpetual battle since love is common to them all. This proposes, then, an alternative emerging within. Europe's ensuing decades, indeed centuries, brought another, contrary mix: vast wars and upheavals along with achievements. Due to specific historical constellations, they would result, just after the turn of the twentieth century, in the forceful reemergence of an old idea: humanity's impulse to aggression and violence is as basic as the instinct to love or harmony.

VI.

French intellectual arguments about opera continued apace through the era of Couperin and Campra and then proceeded into that of Rameau. Should not serious poetry remain in its own formidable domain, empowered by its own tones, rhythms, shapes, and senses rather than those of music? Ought music to inhabit its own sphere, perhaps adding some pleasant touches to verse but no more? Doesn't a synthesis of the arts undo each individual art? Social, political, and religious implications often mixed with these kinds of critical observations. Bossuet had in 1694 worried that music led listeners astray from what was important. The Word, after all, does one thing, sensuous sound another, and if these contraries blend confusion results inevitably. It brings social and political havoc.[42] Nothing and no one would be in place. (Might not demands for restraints on absolute rulers come next?) Eight years later a proponent of Italian music, the Abbé François Raguenet, took the same kind of claim to a different conclusion. On returning to Paris from Rome, he wrote a comparison of music and opera in France and Italy. He conceded Lully's genius but protested that after him French music had become tedious and too preoccupied with conventions. Composers failed to recognize when there were good reasons to break them. Certainly, there had to be firm order, but in music, he explained, Italians seemed to be absolutists who know to be lithe. Raguenet's points about musical composition are reminiscent of claims made by Pluto on behalf of flexible absolutism in the Florentine *Euridice* and the Mantuan *Orfeo*. The "despotic sovereigns and masters" in contemporary Italy knew when "to follow laws" of music and when to venture beyond and break them.[43]

A reply to Raguenet came from Jean-Laurent Le Cerf de la Viéville, a champion of Lully and Quinault. He returned the debate to one about the contrasting sounds of the two languages in a dialogue in which a *Chevalier* chastises sounds in Italian for "excessive sweetness" and "effeminate puerility." After all, "its frequent *z*, its perpetual endings in *e*, in *i*, in *o*, etc. divest it of gravity, noble vivacity, and spiritual expressions." French, so different, was "prudent, unified, and natural and only tolerates extraordinary harmonies and very unusual ornaments."[44] Music's evocation of and impact on emotions could also, he worried, endanger proper ways of thinking about the world. It could bring out what ought better to be hidden or quiet or dominated by our more rational capacities, including in art. A different suggestion came from a professor of Latin and Greek at the Collège Royal. Politics, wrote Abbé Jean Terrasson in 1715, that year of change, aimed to secure a stable realm. Virtuous behavior by subjects was, consequently, a high priority for rulers and *pace* Le Cerf, opera and music could encourage appropriate sentiments. A tranquil shepherd or a hero on stage could suggest, respectively, calm and loyalty in viewers.[45] Moreover, Terrasson thought opera was an artwork for his times. It was specifically modern since it used music not only to decorate but to express inner life. This distinguished it and its role from ancient tragedy, and this meant that opera ought to be judged by another standard.[46]

Imitation and expression are different things. The impact of *mimesis* is among the oldest and most important ideas debated about the relations among politics, morality, and art. The questions it raises return again and again. What constitutes successful and appropriate imitation in the arts and with what effects? Plato's worries were like those of Le Cerf but Aristotle, disagreeing with or modifying the ideas of his teacher in this as in many things, argued that arts differ according to what they imitate and how. As the French debates continued, Abbé Jean-Baptiste Du Bos argued in 1719 that music effects emotions directly and powerfully and, consequently, opera works in ways that a text alone cannot. "As the painter imitates the traits and colors of nature," he wrote, "so the musician imitates the tones, accents, sighs and inflexions of the voice . . . He imitates all the sounds that nature herself uses to express the feelings and passions." Song may originate as a "pleasure of the ear" but it "becomes the pleasure of the heart." Its truth lay "in the imitation of tones, accents, sights and sounds that naturally relate to the sentiment contained in the words." He found the same verity "in harmony and in the rhythm of the entire musical composition."[47]

Another writer, Charles Batteux, complicated further the notion of imitation some decades later. The principal idea of his book of 1746 is announced by its title: *The Fine Arts Reduced to a Single Principle*. He spoke of imitation, however, as emulation and as expression. "To imitate is to copy a model," he wrote.[48] Nature provides the model, but just as "a letter or syllable in speech" is only a beginning, so too imitation can take to varied directions. Music's main "function" is to imitate feelings; it compared to portrait painting. It could, however, also create sounds comparable to "nonpassionate" nature (trees on a countryside, for instance).[49] Batteux also makes an analogy with oratory: "Music and dance can well shape the accents and gestures of the orator on his rostrum and the way in which the citizen recounts a story in the course of conversation."[50] Feelings have corresponding sounds as ideas have corresponding words, he proposed, citing Cicero.[51] Art ought to unify music, poetry, and dance since "Measures, movement, melody, and harmony can equally well govern words, sounds, and gestures."[52]

Five years after Batteux's contentions were published, the first volume of the *Encyclopedia* appeared under the editorship of Dénis Diderot and d'Alembert. It initiated the most representative project of what was later called the Enlightenment and some fifty *philosophes*, many of them quite different philosophically from each other, contributed to the first volume. The Enlightenment was a much more diverse phenomenon than its adherents and foes often make of it, but there were unifying and interlinking elements. A *philosophe*, said Diderot, was both a rationalist and an observer of facts in the world. He did not assume that everything could be explained. Still, reason displaced Christian grace as life's essential mediator. And the *philosophe* was a man of the world, engaging it—truth was not found by neo-

Stoic contemplation and distance. D'Alembert explained that the *Encyclopedia* aimed "to set forth as well as possible the order and connection of the parts of human knowledge" and to present "general principles" that form the basis of each science and each art . . . and the most essential facts that make up the body and substance of each."[53] He remarked that music, of all the fine arts, had made the greatest progress in the previous fifteen years: "The French at last appear to be persuaded that Lully left much to be done."[54] Something had been achieved by a theorist and composer of music, particularly opera. At one point in 1748–49 six of his operas could be seen on stage in Paris. Yet he declined an invitation to write for the *Encyclopedia*. And Rameau was contemptuous of the man who did write many articles for it on music—Rousseau.

UN COURT INTERMÈDE

In 1748, a time of political unease in Paris, an anonymous novel mixing politics and sex was published and then impounded by the police. Four years before the *Querelle des Bouffons*, *The Indiscreet Jewels* told of another fracas among musicians—in "Banza," the capital of the Congo, which is recognizable as France.

It was the first novel by Dénis Diderot, then emerging as a central figure in the Enlightenment. Like many of its other protagonists, he sought to hold up a mirror to his own society, sometimes by disguising it—barely—in fiction set in an exotic locale. The French monarch, who projected himself as *le bien-aimé* (the Beloved One), was at this time very sensitive to what was being said about him, especially concerning his copious exploits with women (he was indeed well loved, as it were). Poems with a political edge pointing to him became popular songs, leading to arrests of students and priests among others in spring 1749. (Diderot was arrested that summer because of another book.) The brother of a higher-up assigned to investigate rumors and critics and to spy on malcontents wrote that Louis XV craved to know "everything people say, everything they do."[1] The *Encyclopedia*, a more straightforward matter, began appearing in 1751. Its first volumes were suppressed within months.

Geography, human and terrestrial, is multidirectional in *The Indiscreet Jewels*. The Congo's ruler has a title that is neither French nor African, but Ottoman-like. Sultan Mangogul was born at a time of turmoil, when people in his part of the world "had tired of obeying imbecilic idiot sovereigns, and had cast off the yoke of their posterity. . . ."[2] In fact, the Sultan is discernible easily as Louis XV. His Congolese predecessor, the late King Kanoglou, who presided over a golden age in which people "sang of victories and died of hunger," resembles Louis XIV. We are told that Kanoglou had been a believer in uniformity, so much so that he decided that everyone would be happy in the realm if they looked like him: "blue eyes, snubbed nose, and red moustache." He expelled millions of Congolese—on another continent they might have been called Huguenots—who wouldn't "counterfeit" his appearance.[3]

The Duke of Orléans took charge when Louis XIV died. His regency didn't aim to challenge monarchy or abolish its royal bureaucracy but it did strengthen countervailing forces. The decades after the Sun King's death were, in varied ways, a reaction to his absolutism. Many questions were raised. Had absolutism shown that France would be best served by social and institutional restraints on centralized power? Perhaps by means of the aristocracy or judiciary? Fénelon had suggested this during Louis XIV's lifetime, and now the Baron de Montesquieu took a comparable view. Others, however, found little commendable in the unmerited privileges and influence of nobles in France or in the formidable sway of an entrenched, dogmatic church hierarchy. Might it not be better to have a vigorous king who, allied with commercial and middle classes, would liberalize the regime, to the detriment of aristocrats and priests? Voltaire thought so.

The regency period was unsteady, relaxed, and became renowned for overindulgence. Louis XV attained his majority at age thirteen in 1723. As he grew older he was often much more interested in the pomp of monarchy, in hunting, and in his mistresses than in serving as an effective anchor of a political system. Yet he would also have his absolutist moments. His education was extensive, like all royal progeny, and he had learned history, literature, and the sort of subjects Fénelon had once taught to another royal youth. And more. By age twenty, as Diderot's sly narrator observes, "Mangogul" knew "to eat, drink and sleep as perfectly as any other potentate of his age."[4] He would indeed have some accomplishments—military victories, domestic reforms, and cultural endeavors too (even "without knowing a single word of Latin . . ."). Mangogul's court favorite, Mirzoza, is modeled on Madame de Pompadour, confident and chief mistress of the philandering king; jewels and other gifts he gave her (and other women) were one source of quiet public displeasure with the king.[5] (Louis XV had lost interest in his Queen Marie Leszczynska, daughter of an ousted Polish monarch.)

Mangogul's attention span is short, but he is "no less amiable in his seraglio than he is great on his throne." He never thinks "to regulate his conduct according to the ridiculous practices of his country" and rids the harem of gates, entrusting "his" women to their honor: "What a good sultan he was! There wasn't his like, except in some French novels."[6] Music is quite present at his court. Like Louis XV, Mangogul feigns comprehension of it. Sophisticated Mirzoza, however, knows it and like Madame de Pompadour, is a friend of the *philosophes*.

Banza is especially fortunate to have famous French singers perform regularly at its opera house. One evening, the sultan arrives for a performance wearing a special magic ring. He obtained it from a genie with the aim of "some pleasure at the expense of the ladies." Turned toward them, it makes their "jewels" sing or talk "indiscreetly." They "recount their intrigues" clearly and loudly "from the most frank part of them."[7] When the mischievous band is turned differently on his own pinkie, nobody can see him—a useful capacity for a monarch or anyone with an ulterior purpose. Invisibility is better than a disguise. Diderot alludes to a fable in Plato's *Republic* about Gyges, a shepherd who possesses a ring that has this same power. Thanks to it he can seduce the queen, murder her husband, and take his place. Such is human behavior absent all fetters. (Louis XV, who indeed had few fetters, did not arrive on the throne in a Gyges-like manner and simply got there by the magic of birth.)

Mangogul deploys his round object for the sake of hilarity. Indeed, it proves more entertaining than the opera on stage. Many things can happen if a sultan can hear what is not normally said aloud—or simply cannot be—and can view what is usually hidden from him. It is in fact a contentious moment in the Congolese opera world. A public fray—it is partly generational—is underway between advocates of two composers. One of them is "Old Utmiutsol." His odd name is contrived of notes of a C-major chord. The "ignorant and the graybeards" were his enthusiasts, we learn. His music "is simple, natural, integrated (*uni*)"—sometimes too much so. But nobody could compose recitative "like the Old Man," observes the narrator. Only he "understood dialogue." And he is obviously created in Lully's image.[8]

The youth and the virtuosi, however, applaud a "young" composer. He is Uremifasolasiututut—recognizable as Jean-Philippe Rameau with a proxy moniker fashioned out of the notes of a musical scale. The name suggests the expansiveness of his music. Uremifasolasiututut, Diderot's narrator tells us, was "distinctive, brilliant, composed, learned, too learned at times. . . ." Moreover, "study and experience" led him "to discover . . . the sources of harmony." Nobody before "had ever distinguished the delicate nuances that separate the tender from the voluptuous, the voluptuous from the passionate, the passionate from the lascivious."[9]

II.

Discord between acolytes of Utmiusol and devotees of Uremifasolasiututut was real before Rameau and Rousseau had their noisy squabbles. "*Lullistes*" denounced Rameau vigorously for his musical novelties—"witchery" in sound. His first opera, a "tragedy in music," was *Hippolyte et Aricie*, a

Madame de Pompadour plays Galatea in *Acis et Galatée* by Lully at Versailles
before King Louis XV in 1748. Lithograph following Charles Nicholas Cochin
the Younger. Chateaux of Versailles and Trianon. Photo: Gerard Blot.
© RMN Grand-Palais/Art Resource, NY.

reworking of Racine's version of a myth that had been dramatized long before by Euripides: Phaedra falls in love with her stepson Hippolytus during
the absence of her husband, King Theseus, with ensuing complications.
After it played to great success at the Opéra, it stimulated the clash spoofed
in *The Indiscreet Jewels*—although the reader is told little by Diderot about
the opera by Uremifasolasiututut.

In the historical debate, traditionalists found in Rameau a threat to their
classical tastes. He seemed to them to push music beyond its natural, appropriate borders. Instead of serving a tragic text, his music claimed its own
autonomous beauties as a system of sound, as if to give music and words
equal claims. He proposed in theoretical writings that music had its own
laws, founded on those of harmony and not dependent on spoken verse.[10]
He certainly employed music to inflect verse and drama, as had Lully, but
he endowed it differently when he represented its natural structure as that
of the universe. Although accused of being "anti-Lully," Rameau never saw
himself that way (and, as we have seen, Rameau defended the founder of
French opera against Rousseau's criticisms). Still, *Lullistes*, punning on
French for "chimneysweep," denounced *Ramoneurs* for brushing out past
glory.

This was hardly why Diderot suggests Uremifasolasiututut was perhaps
too learned. Rameau's *Treatise on Harmony* remains through today one of
the most important texts on the theory of music. Diderot admired it as
much as Rameau's music and later helped the composer, not a nimble prose
writer, to defend his ideas in article form. Why was Rameau's book so influential? He wrote a letter in 1727 to Houdar de la Motte that a musician

had to study nature "before painting her."[11] Since harmony was inscribed in the cosmos and our musical instinct is receptive to it, their constitution was common. Rameau "never evinced any sophisticated understanding of subjects outside music," writes one of his biographers.[12] There are, however, political implications, even if unintended, in his claims about the structure of the cosmos. Most important, perhaps, is that the old Aristotelian political question is posed again about music—the question raised in disputes between Galilei and Zarlino, the Monteverdi brothers, and Artusi: What (or who) rules? Rameau made counterparts of music and spoken language, by insisting on equality—by asserting that the former had its own laws.[13] In opera, it seemed, there was a balance of entwined powers. And there was another implication: to subsume music under the idea of mimesis—of imitation of humans—reduced it. Harmony had to have a foundation, a center—an anchor. Rameau would call it the "fundamental bass" and he cited approvingly Zarlino's comment that "just as the earth is the foundation of the other elements, so does the bass have the property of sustaining, establishing, and strengthening the other parts." Zarlino imagined that as "all the beautiful order of nature would fall into ruin" without the earth, so "if the bass were to disappear, all the beautiful order of nature would be filled with dissonance and confusion . . ."[14]

Rameau also viewed the world in terms of order, although he had his own style and, living in another time, different priorities. He nonetheless affirmed unequivocally that music in itself depended always on hierarchy and that reason alone allows us to understand its properties. Beyond Rameau's music, it is this contention that made him so appealing to the *philosophes*. It is "the light of reason," he wrote, that dispels "doubts into which experience can plunge us at any moment." Experience does enlighten, but "it alone cannot lead us to discover the principles" underlying music.[15] But analyzing music was one thing and responding to it another. "We may judge music only through our hearing, and reason has no authority unless it is in agreement with the ear," wrote Rameau, "yet nothing should be more convincing to us than the union of both in our judgments. We are naturally satisfied by our ear, while the mind is satisfied by reason. Let us judge nothing, then, except by their mutual agreement."[16] He never seems to explain mutuality fully, but he has in fact bound reason, sensibility, and experience, like many *philosophes*.

He did insist that analysis required a systematic approach. And this, in turn, required an unquestionable starting point. This was what he called the "sounding body" (the *corps sonore*), a kind of natural, material, and vibrating, core. We can understand his claim if we compare—as he did—his quest to find "the sounding body" to Descartes's search for certainty over a century earlier. This philosopher thought that if he could find one unquestionable truth, then anything deduced properly from it would likewise be valid. To show this, he proposed first to doubt everything. If he could clear his mind of all biases, any preconceptions, every past notion, and all the world's clutter, there still had to be one indubitable reality: a thinking something had to exist in order to do this clearing and decluttering. A famous dictum resulted: "I think therefore I am." All rational assertions presumed this "thinking I."

What the "thinking I" was to Descartes can be compared to the "sounding body" for Rameau. Its vibration became the natural and prime mover of what we hear; it is the ear's pilot. Similarly, what love was to the different nations of Campra's *L'Europe galante*—and would later be in Rameau's *Les Indes galantes*—the sounding body was to music. In Rameau's compositions, he was a master of baroque style using, as one musicologist notes, an "advanced harmonic language" in his compositions and sophisticated polyphonic forms. His music had many layers, but he understood that an acoustic base—or bass—permeated the auditory superstructure.[17] The "fundamental bass" generates chords and harmonic series, Rameau explained. (This tonal center was later known as a chord's "root.") A simple chord—a "triad"—is comprised of it and two other tones. But the fundamental bass organizes them. Imagine a single tone made by a voice or a string or a bell or a tuning fork. The specific sound of this resonating object is due to its pitch—a frequency of vibrations, movements of stimulated air. The C note, for example, organizes and is the tonal center of a C-major chord and "intervals" set it apart from the other notes—E and G—that make the chord. Each has a different frequency of vibration and might be called the necessary auxiliaries in the chord. When the three strike at once, their combined pitches are agreeable; they harmonize, as if comprising a moment in a utopian sound realm.

A "perfect chord," wrote Rameau is "made up of the harmony of the sounding body."[18] Not only does a "progression" of chords, one following another, satisfy a listener depending on how their notes link one to the next, but different chords "excite different passions." Some are sad, others tender; some are pleasant, others surprising. The same was so for the progressions themselves. And these depended, finally, on relations among the notes to a fundamental bass.[19] (There were basic rules for these relations—Rameau numbered them ten—that allowed one chord to follow another and make musical sense.) Melody "emanates" and "draws its strength" from harmony, proposed Rameau, while he admitted that melody doesn't follow rules in the same way as harmony.[20] Here again was what separated him, so famously in the argument about *Armide*, from Rousseau's insistence that melody was prior to harmony.

Rameau explained at the time of the *Querelle* that he had concluded that harmony is "natural to us" as a result of a personal experience. It seems that he heard nature itself expressed in human form. Once, four decades earlier, he had been in the pit of an opera house and heard remarkable singing in the empty hall. Rameau discovered a seventy-year-old artisan in the parterre. He was untutored in music and his daily work was "hard and coarse." Yet "fortune had favored him a little," and so he had begun to come to the opera. Rameau had heard his voice singing, unaccompanied but heartily, "the fundamental bass of a song."[21] The composer was amazed as he heard tones emerge from it.

III.

One evening in not-so-distant Banza, Mangogul, wearing his ring, and Mirzoza went to see an "excellent work" by Uremifasolasiututut. A renowned soprano captivated the audience. But, alas, operas can be too long. By Act 4 the sultan became restless and mischievous. (Louis XV was accused of like behavior when it came to governing.) So he turned his ring toward thirty girls singing in chorus. "Never had a more unusual and comical sight been seen on the stage." Suddenly, they all became mute, but with mouths open. Gestures came to a standstill. Then sounds emerged. Their "jewels" began to sing, mostly bawdy songs. Their tone was "high," it was "baroque"—it was "mad." A natural, sounding body can, it seems, create unexpected words and tones, not necessarily bass. "What? Twelve times?" sings a jewel. "Who will do (*baise*) me?" asks another. The orchestra played on as laughter and cacophony spread through the hall. Some of the actresses, fearful that their own jewels might hum, ran off stage. Then Mangogul turned his ring again. The strange *intermède* quelled and Uremifasolasiututut's opera continued. When the curtain fell, king and escort left and "the jewels of our actresses" went elsewhere—"to be busy with something other than singing."[22] These lyric gems caused a considerable stir in Banza. Men were jocular about them, women worried.

Diderot has used the "jewels" to link—sometimes obviously, sometimes allusively—music to natural sensuality and the cosmos in the midst of a "learned" composer's opera and all this with a political subtext. That is not all. He also deploys them to sting pedantry. It seems that a leading member of Banza's "Academy of Sciences" was especially satisfied by the events at the opera house, for the indiscreet jewels confirmed his theories. French readers of the time would have identified Diderot's "Doctor Orctomus" with Antoine Ferrein, a professor at the Collège Royal. He had invented the term "vocal cords" and proposed that they were comparable to the strings of a violin. Doctor Orctomus has a somewhat expansive, "learned" view. "I have seen jewels in paroxysm," he harangues, "and . . . I have been persuaded that what in Greece is called the *delphus*"—the womb—"has all the properties of the trachea." Half the human race, consequently, "can speak as well with the jewel as with the mouth." Doctor Orctomus explains that the *delphus* "is a string and wind instrument, but more string than wind." He compares it to vocal cords that "quiver" due to the "soft collision" of air with their fibers. Different sounds result from faster or slower vibrations; they can be modified "at discretion." These vibrations, he elucidates, correspond to distention and contraction of the *delphus*, which can therefore "render sounds more less keen" together with "all the inflections of the voice and all the tones of song." This academic "anatomist" even believes he can make the *delphus* and the jewel reason.[23] (Everything seems to connect in his theory.)

It is as if Diderot, for all his esteem for Rameau's artistry, was making a surreptitious, ironic comment about him through this portrait of Doctor Orctomus: Rameau the theorist insisted that reason allows our understanding of sound while Rameau the composer knew that listeners respond, finally, to music through experience—to harmony's sensuousness, not an analysis of its rational structure. It is also as if Diderot was wary not only of systems but of radical oppositions—reason versus sensuousness—in art or judgment of art. After he describes the sides supporting, respectively, Utmiusol and Uremifasolasiututut, he says, in almost a quiet afterthought, that those among Banza's young and old with "taste" admired both composers.[24]

Diderot has presented an unlikely but telling picture of what is seen and unseen and heard; and he links it to women and to political power. When the sultan becomes a voyeur, he turns his ring and desires emerge—aurally. Does this imply that a less repressed world unleashes a natural but otherwise uncontrollable female sexuality, and that it relieves the boredom of men? It is a relatively enlightened but not a protofeminist vision; the king, after all, releases and then quiets as he pleases. A quarter-century after his novel—he had by then disowned it as a youthful indiscretion—Diderot wrote an essay, "On Women," which chastised their confined status. Yet he also characterized their senses as more primal than those of men, which could be taken to mean more responsive to music too. When, in another late work, he examined relations between men and women in Tahiti—a popular subject due to the writings of French travelers—he clearly approved of the more "natural" and uninhibited life there. Like the ring's effect on the chorus girls, he suggests that behind roles and role-play and decorum, of both women and men, is a noisier, natural reality.

Diderot's messages are often hazy, perhaps intentionally so. *The Indiscreet Jewels* compares to Rameau's own words in a startling, amusing way. His singing artisan is a gruff man whose bass was naturally in tune; Diderot's unfettered chorus of women are naturally out of control. And then there is this subtle political message from the Banza Opéra—and from a *philosophe* who would suffer censorship: a monarch who allows for more relaxed expression will, inevitably, hear of previously repressed forces. They may serve for unexpected pleasure or embarrassment at the opera, but if this ruler finds that he cannot twist his ring back, freed expression may pose various problems for him. Diderot does not suggest this latter possibility patently; he was not a political revolutionary. He seems to allow here that political authority can and perhaps ought to be able to reassert itself by sleight twist. At Banza, the old order is interrupted by laughter at the expense of women, and then recommences with an opera by a fictional Rameau.

Chapter 11

VERTICAL, HORIZONTAL

Rameau's *Treatise on Harmony* was published when he moved to Paris in 1722. He had not yet written operas, but his book earned him considerable renown. Born in Dijon in 1683, he was the son of an organist and educated by Jesuits. He studied in Italy for a period and had been working out his book's theses for some time while serving as a provincial church musician and harpsichord composer. Soon after arriving in Paris he had had a valuable benefactor.

Tax farmers—administrators with royal deeds to "harvest" from subjects —played important roles as patrons of culture in Paris. The composer became a principal in the salons of one, Alexandre le Riche de la Poupelinière. Rameau also became his wife's music tutor and had his patron's private orchestra placed at his disposal. "Rameau was the sun and the stars" of de la Poupelinière's circle, wrote a rueful Rousseau later.[1] In it Rameau was introduced to an array of intellectual figures, musicians, and future librettists. These included Voltaire, a man not known for a relaxed temperament and with whom Rameau, a prickly man, had a difficult relationship, punctuated by tempestuous efforts at collaboration. At de la Poupelinière's home Rameau met Abbé Simon-Joseph Pellegrin, who had written the libretto for Destouches's opera about Telemachus. In 1733 he would write the text for *Hippolyte et Aricie*, the work that brought Rameau to the attention of the theater world and so irritated partisans of Lully. Another person Rameau met there was young Rousseau. Their problems began promptly. Two years after *Hippolyte et Aricie*, Rameau's opera-ballet *Les Indes galantes* premiered and a decade later, in 1745, Rousseau's *Les Muses galantes* was presented to de la Poupelinière's circle. Indebted greatly to Rameau, Rousseau's opera extolled love by a combination of song, dance, and instrumental music. Disdainful Rameau thought its most competent elements imitated Italian composers and the rest typified the worst in French music. Obviously not his own; most of Rousseau's music for this opera is not extant and so no comparisons are possible.

Rousseau, for Rameau, was simply an amateur. There were also philosophical differences and they are illustrated poignantly by Rameau's censure of Rousseau's earlier attempt to invent a new musical notation system. Its principle aim was simplification of scores. Rousseau's scheme, observed Rameau, might make it easier for singers to follow their lines but members of an orchestra had to be able to perceive the music as a whole, to view the bigger musical picture from top to bottom as well as across a page. The orchestra would be at a loss using Rousseau's methods. Rousseau, to be fair, came to recognize validity in Rameau's censure as well as with the older composer's criticisms of *Les Muses galantes*.[2] Yet here in embryonic form was also the argument over the primacy of harmony and melody, about a world with a natural, vertical order as opposed to one in which individuals moved naturally, horizontally, following their own line.

Had all music by these men vanished, it might be possible to imagine Rousseau, despite his many concessions to (and corrections by) Rameau, as victor in their arguments. In written combat Rousseau's gifts were hard to rival. Still, Rameau countered him effectively with a flourish, joining music to politics and to cosmic mockery: a "faulty ear is a great obstacle for any-one who pretends to make himself a Legislator in music."[3] For Rameau, nature, not Rousseau, was music's lawmaker.

II.

Rousseau proposed in his *Essay on the Origin of Languages*, written not long after the *Querelle*, that human speech emerges from inarticulate song. His claim came of a larger project whose most famous result was his *Discourse on the Origins of Inequality among Men*. He imagined in it a "state of na-ture," but not with unalterable cosmic harmony. Instead, he portrayed in-dividuals wandering, alone in the forests, able to fulfill basic needs, taking nourishment from trees, land, and streams and desiring little more. Then came a tale of physical and emotional enfeeblement—a fall of humanity—corresponding to the rise of civilization, hierarchy, and property. Rousseau admitted readily that there had never been a state of nature (however much he liked to walk in the woods). Its explanatory powers excited him. A roam-ing imagination gave him his political theory and a vision of the birth of melody that contrasted to Rameau's analyses of objective intervals among tones in harmony and harmony as melody's grid.

Rousseau described accidents in his *Discourse*. At some point people, free and unrestrained in those woods, cross paths. From chance encounters, webs of relations begin. They create signs and link them. Languages form, facil-itating more complex communication. Comparisons of things and people become possible, marking off differences. But then come assertions of "mine and thine"—the rise of private property, bringing in turn societies and rules. People lose, increasingly so, natural self-sufficiency. The more civilized, the more they need rules to manage life with others. Rousseau's essay on language (published after his death) moves similarly. He envisions a fortuitous meeting of a young man and a young woman at a well. Passionate, melodious vocal sounds emerge and simple, emotional bonds. Rousseau went so far as to propose that laws too were sung at first and so understood easily, for instance, in an ancient public square. Yet once this initial musicality is lost, he says, laws are no longer grasped so readily by assembled people. Their community comes to depend on external constraints. (A free society, Rousseau determined, did not entail a return to nature, which he deemed impossible, but rule by laws willed by the People as a collective citizenry.)

These entwined stories of nature and society, of language and music, linked also to climate. Rousseau thought that in gentle, southern European environments, like Italy, nature was like a primary caregiver; consequently, pure sounds of love were sustained naturally. In the colder, abrasive north, however, language intellectualized. Vocalized emotion became complex grammar, allowing communication to address new, more elaborate needs. But as passion became articulation, laws became monotones. Melody and gesture became increasingly distinct from each other and together they receded from rational pronouncement. Separation of melody from language, thought Rousseau, gave rise to the need for harmony. Chords made lines engaging that might otherwise drone. These claims lay behind his assertion of the advantages of southern over northern languages for music. They are why he insisted harmony was subordinate to melody. For Rameau, music came of a perfect, unchanging natural and rational system; social and cultural questions had nothing to do with it. For Rousseau, civilization is a journey, increasingly unfortunate, away from our natural state. While Rameau heard a structured cosmos in music, Rousseau asserted not just horizontal movements but bonds among people, brought together by hearing each other with the simplest vocal melody. Rameau's system made music its own sovereign. Its signifying role was secondary, although for him harmonic procedures did indicate that a shift in a sharp or flat direction could suggest, respectively, sorrow or delight. For Rousseau, music was a moral and sentimental matter. (This strong emphasis on sentiment as opposed to reason distinguished him sharply from most thinkers of the Enlightenment.)[4]

III.

Despite his highly sophisticated theory, despite his systematic analyses of music, Rameau did not compose operas deductively. Despite an aesthetic of musical autonomy, mimesis found its way in. After all, characters on the operatic stage are men and women, even if they are sometimes stick figures or stereotypes. He understood that reason and passion had to be married. "A good musician should surrender himself to all the characters he wishes to portray," he wrote. Like a dexterous actor, the composer "should take the place of the speaker, believe himself to be at the locations where the different events he wishes to depict occur, and participate in these events as do those most involved in them. He must declaim the text well, at least to himself, and must feel when and to what degree the voice should rise or fall, so that he may shape his melody, harmony, modulation, and movement accordingly."[5]

Part of Rameau's achievement came from his ability to write remarkable music for librettos that were often enough interesting but poetically unimposing. He had no Busenello or Quinault. Striking dance music was, however, intrinsic to the spectacle and did not need words. *Les Indes galantes*, arguably his finest stage work, illustrates why. It was called an "Heroic Ballet" and it represented a partial return to the style of court ballet. Dance and musical interludes comprise a good deal of it. *Les Indes galantes*'s librettist was Louis Fuzelier, a man in his sixties who had lived on two sides of French society—that of its elite and that of its popular culture. He wrote some two hundred and forty texts for stage ranging from librettos and cantatas for Campra to vaudevilles for fairs and marionette shows. He would serve twice as coeditor of the monthly *Mercure de France*. Founded in 1672 (as *Le Mercure gallant*), it was the most influential cultural journal of the era and Rameau chose several librettists from among its editorial personnel. Like many of his contemporaries, Fuzelier was intrigued by exotica and the world beyond Europe. In particular, he found China, Turkey, and Persia alluring. *One Thousand and One Nights* had been translated into French in the first decade of the eighteenth century and widely read. Montesquieu's *Persian Letters* of 1721 described impressions by traveling Persians—but in order to dissect the French. *Les Indes galantes* was part of this same trend, which took audiences and readers not just across Europe but to lands that were at least as far from France as was Diderot's Congo.

Travel, real and imaginary, became a way for Europeans to look at themselves as they looked at others. Frequently, they portrayed those others as more natural (or naturally wholesome) than themselves and often as more admirable, with a greatness of spirit lacking on their own continent. Antiquity had once played this mirrorlike role for Europeans, even while they also saw themselves as heirs to distant Greek and Roman myths, culture, and history. Now the world stirred and time whorled; and perceptions changed. Four years after *Persian Letters* Fuzelier collaborated on an opera titled *Queen of Fairies* with composer Jacques Aubert. Fairies, commented Fuzelier, always do good, are of both sexes and are celebrated by Romans, Turks, and Persians. In a forward to this "Comédie Persanne," the librettist proposed that "*le système fabuleux*" of the "*orientes*" was as deserving as Greek or Roman mythologies of a place on "our" stage.[6]

Fuzelier did not look to myths of the orient in *Les Indes galantes*. Instead, he began with Greek antiquity and then showed that love should rule all lands and peoples—and in all times. His effort was a descendant of *L'Europe galante* but with horizons beyond his continent. The four *Entrées* recount separate tales, each slightly flimsy but creating together a more telling whole. Despite its title, they are not properly about the Indies—a locale with a somewhat slippery definition for Europeans—but places inhabited by Turks, Incas, Persians, and (North American) Indians. This geography is not as unusual as twenty-first-century minds might find it. When the French West Indies Company was created in 1663, its preserve included the Caribbean and on up to Newfoundland. The Spanish West Indies were territories in the Pacific and Asia.

The opera's premiere in 1735 included only a prologue and the stories of the Incas and the Turks. The Persians were added at the third performance and then the North American *Entrée* a year later. Fuzelier explained in a forward that he would present "the most distant climes" to satisfy his audience's endless taste for novelty. (Several arts would come together to show how love—Cupid's domain—is all-encompassing and expressed in different languages. Even if lovers have different characters—or national characteristics—"the universe is his [Love's] *patrie*," he declared. So he would present "necessary" variety on stage within a framework of "simple" and "natural" commonality.[7] Whatever limits to Fuzelier's poetic skills, the libretto did fashion a remarkable interplay between universalism and particularism, humane instincts and contemporary prejudices (not all of them negative) when it comes to distant peoples. Fuzelier and Rameau must have imagined that they were using theater to comment on all times while engaging their own. Consider the prologue at Paphos, mythical birthplace of Venus. It is about ubiquitous human phenomena: war, peace, and love.

Europe (prepares for War)
Prologue
Paphos (Cyprus, birthplace of Venus)
Hebe challenged by Bellona.
***French, Spanish, Italian, and Polish youth dance.* Cupids fly away from Europe to:**

Turkish island
(Indian Ocean)
Entrée 1: The Generous Turk
Sultan Osmin is generous to the Christian lovers
Emilie and Valère. Love reigns. Slaves load boat
with presents.

Peruvian Desert
(Spanish Conquest)
Entrée 2: The Incas of Peru
Christian love reigns for Pizarro's officer Don Carlos and
Incan Princess Phani. Pagan priest Huascar destroyed.
Festival of the Sun

Persia
(In a harem and
amidst flower festival)
Entrée 3: The Flowers
Love reigns for Tacmas and Zäire
and for Ali and Fatima. No Europeans.
Dancing and singing musicians and
slaves. Ballet of the Flowers

North American Forest
(Canada/New France)
Entrée 4: The Savages
The "savages" (and pagans) Zima and Adario fulfill their love;
Civilized (Christian) Spanish and French suitors, Don Alvar and
Damon, rejected even though on the victorious side in war.
Dance of the Great Peace Pipe

Figure 11.1. *Les Indes galantes.*

Figure 11.2. Portrait of Jean-Philippe Rameau (1683–1764).

Here mythological figures appear, but they mix with eighteenth-century Europeans. Eternal forces represented by deities are amidst humans.

The scene is also set for meeting up with the rest of the world, since Paphos is not in the center of Europe, but on the coast of Cyprus. We are first in the palace of Hebe, goddess of youth, cupbearer to divinities. She calls on those who follow her "laws" to gather at dawn.[8] Youth from French, Spanish, Italian, and Polish "nations" dance "gracefully" as she urges them to follow their "ardor." Ballet and song will, however, be interrupted by drums and trumpets. Enter Bellona, war goddess, followed by banner-waving fighters. She recruits: "Glory calls you; hear the trumpets! Hate! Arm yourselves! . . . Quit these peaceful retreats . . ."[9]

A real war was underway offstage, in part another consequence of perennial French-Habsburg rivalry. The prize was Poland's throne, a matter for French attention because Louis XV's Queen Marie was Polish, her father once its occupant. The War of the Polish Succession began in 1734 and by the following year France, Spain, and Piedmont had dealt severe blows to the Habsburgs. Rameau's opera was written and performed in the midst of it. Negotiations throughout 1735 brought a fleeting peace but fighting renewed. France had pro- and anti-war blocs within its elite, and the prologue suggests that Fuzelier sympathized with those who wanted resolution. (Combat would not end until the Treaty of Vienna of 1738. It left Maria's father as Duke of Lorraine; a competitor became Poland's monarch.) The opera obviously doesn't represent this history directly, but comes of the mood in which it took place.

Bellona's martial lure is considerable and Hebe appeals to heaven for help as if, without saying so, she hopes to secure an end to the offstage war. Much of its bloodshed did not take place in Poland itself and Polish references are at most allusions in the opera; two Poles dance a slow air at one point in the prologue and in the third act (in Persia) a character is disguised as a Polish slave. Aid to Hebe takes visible form as Cupid appears, bearing love arrows and accompanied by a flag-waving suite of little cupids. The kinds of conflict that so often mark opera plots materialize again here: between love and glory, between love and war. Hebe calls on Cupid "to replace the hearts wrested (*ravit*) from you by Bellona." Yet Europe seems to deflect his arrows. She urges their conveyance, together with their pleasures, to "distant climes." Cupid and Hebe together command the little cupids to take flight over "vast seas."[10] They head to "India (*l'Inde*)"—so say the stage directions—which becomes today's Caribbean and some Latin American coasts. What might, out of context, be seen as a call to Christian and European imperialism is actually the result of a sense of hopelessness about Europe. "Indians" as well as Europeans will be portrayed in both stereotypical and surprising ways.

The first "Indian" locale is . . . Turkish. The *Entrée*, "The Generous Turk," is an operatic foreign policy brief. French-Ottoman strategic ties, the first between a Christian and a non-Christian domain, began early in the sixteenth century. *Les Indes galantes* was anticipated already in *L'Europe galante* when Zayde declared the Sultan's outward fierceness ought not to be misunderstood. A wave of "*Turquerie*" swept France at the turn of the eighteenth century and fascination for Turkish exotica included "Turkish music." And Ottomans were interested in France; two powers gazed at each other. French-Ottoman relations were good when Rameau arrived to Paris. In 1720–21, the sultan sent a delegation to Versailles, ostensibly to announce that France would be permitted to repair the Church of the Holy Sepulcher in Jerusalem. However, the Ottomans really wanted their emissaries to see what might be learned from their frequent ally against the Habsburgs. The delegation's leader became the first Ottoman ambassador stationed abroad and, in addition to diplomatic activities, he attended the opera. Mehmed Effendi saw revivals of works by Lully and Quinault, Destouches and Houdar la Motte, and Campra and Danchet.[11]

Turkish themes had a long, cultural trajectory in France that preceded *Turquerie*. They could, however, become complicated in the context of both international and dynastic politics. Molière's lampoon of Turks reflected twists and turns of Turkish-French-Habsburg relations. Racine's *Bajazet* of 1672 treats of a grand vizier, Ottoman palace politics, and the inevitable harem. After a discussion of Racine's tragedy decades later in *Le Mercure galant*, there followed a curious letter about an Ottoman grand vizier and a French adventurer in Istanbul. It addressed "Turkish gallantry," a regular interest of the journal, and it distinguished between Islam, which was still criticized, and Turkish "character," toward which it was respectful.[12] Fuzelier explained that the "Generous Turk" in his libretto for Rameau was based on a real Turk.

Topal Osman was born in Mora on the Greek peninsula. He may have been a convert to Islam and seems to have been a Janissary, a member of that special military service for the sultan whose recruits were often young boys drawn from minorities in the empire. He served in various capacities and locales before becoming the grand vizier in September 1731. Almost immediately, he called on the aide of a quirky friend named Ahmet Pasha, who was well known to French elites as Count Claude-Alexandre de Bonneval. This French noble from Limousin—he was Fénelon's cousin—lived a swashbuckling life after leaving his homeland (an act of prudence after insulting Madame de Maintenon). At one time or another he fought for France, the Habsburgs against the Ottomans, and managed to provoke a duel with none less than Prince Eugène of Savoy, the famous military strategist.

After fleeing the Holy Roman Empire, Bonneval had made his way to Bosnia. There he met Topal, then serving as its bey, and placed himself at the sultan's disposal.[13] Conversion to Islam thwarted extradition demands from Vienna. Claude-Alexandre became Ahmet, and Vizier Topal assigned to him military tasks that came eventually with political sway. Topal lost his own position in March 1732 but this loyal subject went on to lead the sultan's armies to victories in Persia, where he died in battle in late 1735. Bonneval, who was with him, continued to serve the Sublime Porte. Topal's replacement as grand vizier found him useful during the maneuvers that accompanied the struggle over Poland's crown. Fuzelier described Topal as a "virtuous pasha." When he loved, wrote Rameau's librettist, he was "susceptible to a most noble tenderness, more delicate than that of Orientals. His heart is capable of the most magnanimous efforts."[14] The letter in *Mercure*, dated January 18, recounted how, decades earlier, a certain Vincent Arniaud of Marseilles ransomed the future grand vizier from slavery

Figure 11.3. Eighteenth-century print-sketch of a production of "The Generous Turk," the first *Entrée* of Rameau's *Les Indes galantes*, libretto by Louis Fuzelier (1672?–1752). Sketch by Canaletto (Giovanni Antonio Canal) (Bibliothèque-Musée de l'Opéra/Bibliothèque nationale de France.)

in Malta. Arniaud and his son came to visit the now-powerful man in 1732 and Topal not only thanked him again but extended his gratitude from his "old liberator" to "the whole French nation." He praised Arniaud's selflessness, for the Frenchman could have known nothing about the captive or his future. "Where is there anyone, even a Muslim, capable of a similar act of generosity?" asked Topal.[15]

The combination of preparations for the Polish war and this story of a Francophile Turk (with a Frenchman-turned-Turk advisor) provide the immediate matrix from which came the prologue and the first *Entrée* of *Les Indes galantes*. The intrigue of "The Generous Turk"—it anticipates Mozart's later *The Abduction from the Seraglio* and echoes *L'Europe galante*—focuses on Emilie, a "young Provençale" who is prisoner of Osman the Turk, "Pasha of a Turkish Island in the Indian Ocean (*la mer des Indes*)." She resists his advances and tells him that in her birthplace, France, she had already wed a man "worthy of my constancy."[16] But brigands had seized her and now she is Osman's slave. He, however, truly loves her and pleads: "Forget your troubles on this happy shore." She rejects his offers and frustrated Osman exits with the observation that "Love must take flight when it sees hope depart. . . ."[17]

This, of course, is why the little cupids flew from Hebe's province on Europe's edge. Now, however, new prisoners arrive on the Turk's island from a shipwreck and it turns out that one shares Emilie's *"patrie"*—indeed it is her love Valère, who has been searching for her. She rejoices but warns "my tyrant loves me."[18] Her fears seem confirmed when Osman reappears, warning that he can do what he pleases to Valère. Emilie brands him "barbarian."[19] Her judgment, however, is wrong. Osman, it turns out, was once a slave and his master was none less than Valère, who freed him. The good deed is reciprocated and a liberated couple is sent off into freedom on a ship filled with gifts from the Osman. "Was there ever a more generous heart?" sings Valère. "Reign love!" sings Emilie.[20] These messages, presumably, will carry back to France and Europe. The Turk, though sad, is virtuous, munificent, and no tyrant. He loves as Europeans do, contrary to any image of lusting "Orientals." (Nothing is sung of African slaves who carry Osman's offerings aboard Valère's vessel. They seem to be just part of the landscape. Slavery, common in the Muslim world then, became a subject of debate among some intellectuals in France in the 1730s, but this is not reflected in the opera.)

The second *Entrée* takes its audience across another sea. Its story is painful. "The Incas of Peru" does not present the factual tragedy of the Spanish conquest of 1531. Francisco Pizarro's armies, taking advantage of a civil war within the native population, brought wanton destruction two centuries before *Les Indes galantes* was written. Now, in 1735, Bourbon Spain was Bourbon France's ally in the Polish war. Much of it was fought outside Poland, although not at all on the other side of the Atlantic. Madrid's gains would be considerable. Perhaps Fuzelier turned to Peru for his second act in response to Spanish ire at French attempts to negotiate an end to hostilities. (Spain also had factions opposing each other about the conflict.) Spain's king was also monarch of the "Spanish Indies" and his eldest son, then Duke of Parma, was conqueror of southern Italy in 1734 and 1735. Don Carlos's relations with the papacy were terse. Before his crowning in Naples in July 1735, he told his new subjects that the Inquisition would be restrained.

The first voice heard in "The Incas of Peru" is also named Don Carlos. He is one of Pizarro's officers. On a stage designed as a Peruvian desert with a volcano, he pleads with his love, Phani, who comes from Incan royalty. Why has she not "banished from her soul" the "criminal error that seduces the Incas?" he asks.[21] She tells him that he simply doesn't understand "the bonds of blood and laws."[22] She fears the violence that may come from her "proud Incas," who are to assemble for their Festival of the Sun and watch her.[23] This princess expresses contempt for her own people's "barbaric, implacable" ways, and wants her love, the "conqueror," to spirit her away.[24] Don Carlos and Phani may have been inspired by Fuzelier's reading of Garcilaso de la Vega's influential commentary on Peru's conquest. Son of a Spanish officer who wed an Incan princess, his writings are recommended specifically to "the curious" in Fuzelier's preface. They instruct "on everything" concerning Incas.[25]

We discover quickly that that Don Carlos has a challenger for Phani's love. This is Huascar, the Peruvian high priest. He not only wants her hand, but he aims to salvage the battered Incan people and religion—and to enhance his own power while doing so. Thus a conquering officer is pitted against a religious-ethnic "native" leader. The officer, however, is an apostle of true love (which means, presumably, Christianity) and Huascar might be taken for an inquisitorial papal fanatic of the kind disliked by the other Don Carlos in Naples. When Huascar tells Phani that he speaks with God's voice, she responds pointedly that impostors often claim to speak for heaven. Huascar understands that Phani loves Don Carlos but warns that the Spaniards, those "barbarians," those "tyrants," want only gold—that is their true god, noting too that it is only an ornament for Incan altars.[26] (Spanish behavior in Peru makes it hard to disagree.) While Huascar is malignant, Fuzelier puts truthful words in his mouth. Things are not so simple.

When the Incas gather for their mass devotion, Huascar provokes an earthquake. It terrifies everyone and he hopes Phani will be frightened into seeing that the deity—the Sun—disapproves of her intentions. As the volcano erupts, she does fear he is right. Don Carlos emerges to save her. The flames, he charges, are really the Sun's anger at Huascar. As Huascar rages, molten rocks flow, apparently to confirm that he is the "criminal" (as the stage instructions call him).[27] He calls on "vomiting" lava to consume him, which it does. Since Pizzaro's troops, not little cupids, shattered Incan life and since the atrocities visited on the Incas are barely suggested apart from Huascar's accusations of Spanish cupidity, the conclusion of this *Entrée* presents a picture of European relations with non-Europeans that is quite different from the "Generous Turk." Christian love triumphs between Don Carlos and Phani and over paganism. Incan protonationalism is destroyed in an event that can be discerned as either natural or heaven-sent. And yet there is real ambiguity if this scene is taken not as a commentary on events in Peru but on Europe. With just some imagination the victory of Don Carlos and Phani can be taken as that of Prince Don Carlos (and a true concept of love) in Naples over the papacy and inquisition.

IV.

The little cupids have now visited two parts of the world. Threatened lovers have been united in both, even though forces arrayed against them, non-European and non-Christian, one admirable and the other fanatical, seem formidable. A French couple sails homeward hailing a Muslim; the second couple must produce inevitably mestizo progeny (of Christian faith, of course). The cupids flew no further than Peru in the original production. Soon a new version was on stage and it included travel to another locale in another *Entrée*. This addition takes place in the land where Topal died in battle late in the same year as the premiere of *Les Indes galantes*.

In "Les Fleurs," the "Indies" are Persia and it was perhaps appropriate that this *Entrée* begins with a ruler in disguise. It continues on through a particularly convoluted plot. Four people pursue secret loves and when the truth of mixed-up identities—of Tacmas the Persian prince (also described as "King in the Indies"), his noble friend Ali, and two female slaves—are revealed, all join happily to adoring partners. Tacmas dresses as a female merchant in the seraglio. He loves young Zaïre, who belongs to Ali and the prince is so smitten by her that he calls her his "sovereign."[28] This is convenient for Ali, who says in an aside to the audience that he "burns" for Fatima, who is Tacmas's property (she is a slave from Georgia). Yet when the two men meet, Ali asks his prince: Why the disguise? Tacmas explains that he wants to look into Zaïre's heart before "her beautiful eyes read the tender sentiments of my ardor."[29] When Tacmas meets Zaïre, she is singing of love's miseries and is beset by jealousy, imagining her affections are already taken. Concealment, however, has more to reveal. After she flees the stage, another disguised figure appears. This is Fatima who, dressed as a male Polish slave, announces that she is in quest of her own love. Tacmas concludes erroneously that this must be the man Zaïre loves. He also supposes that the "Pole" fears that Zaïre loves Ali. This twist would mean, in turn, that the veiled prince was betrayed by his noble friend. After more confusion and drawn daggers, matters get sorted out. Zaïre, we learn, is of royal blood (the published libretto makes her a Circassian princess.[30] But Tacmas declares that this doesn't matter to him.

They are happily united, as are Ali and Fatima, and they rejoice at the great "Festival of Flowers," amidst extensive dancing and singing musicians and slaves. "Pretty odalisques of the diverse nations of Asia" wear flowers in their hair and on their gowns, say the stage instructions.[31] Fuzelier's contorted plot, reworked frequently for future productions, is finally saved by Rameau's music and the dancing.[32] One aspect does not change: this is the sole *Entrée* in *Les Indes galantes* with no Europeans. It may be presumed that Tacmas has European slaves since Fatima disguises herself as a Pole. (Slavery, again, is unquestioned, and a woman's sole path out of it is marriage.) The act ends with happiness for all; however, the instructions for "The Ballet of the Flowers" that concluded it in 1735 presented a kind of dance parable about conflict and Persian resilience. Flowers were long an important aspect of Persia's visual culture as well as its terrain; writings by visiting foreigners often remarked on them. This ballet, reads the libretto, "represents in a picturesque way the fate of flowers in a garden."

But what is happening in this garden? The "gallant tableau" comes alive as the flowers, played by "amiable" male and female slaves, arise in the breeze. Their queen, the Rose, dances alone and they form a parterre that changes shape. However, a storm, brought by Boraeus, the strong north wind, disrupts the festival. The Rose resists this persecuting enemy. Her steps suggest both sweetness and fear in the face of Boreaus's movements. But Zephir, the west wind, arrives to reanimate the battered flowers, enabling them to face the tempest, which dissipates. They can now pay homage to their queen.[33] The ballet transforms what seemed to be oriental bliss into a representation of troubled contemporary realities. This bliss, then, is like an imaginary tableau of Persia before its ruling dynasty was overthrown in 1721, coupled to the hope that with friendly assistance it might return. Harsh winds—invasions—came after the Safavid rulers fell and Persia suffered Afghan and Turkish troops battling across it for many years. What began as convoluted love stories becomes representation of the times in ballet.

The third version of *Les Indes galantes* was soon superseded by yet another with the addition of "The Savages," a fourth *Entrée*—this one set in North America. It premiered in March 1736. "Savage" has a generally pejorative if not vicious connotation in English, but "*sauvage*" in French can sometimes imply a broader, not necessarily negative meaning as well, suggesting naturalness. Rousseau, for instance, was sometimes mocked for wanting to be a "noble savage" because of his professed devotion to simple life, closer to nature, distant from the "civilized" world. "The Savages" in *Les Indes galantes* presented European conquerors and conquered Indians, but the events are dissimilar to and with implications different from those of "The Incas of Peru." In a grove between Spanish and French colonies a "Great Peace Pipe" ritual will occur to signal the end of conflicts—but also European victory. Adario, commander of the "Savages," is no fanatic, no Huascar. Content with the end of the war, he has assembled his troops to celebrate peace. He is, however, unhappy, because his love, Zima, the daughter of the chief of the Indian "Nation," is pursued by two colonial officers. "Rivals in daring feats, rivals in love," sings Adario, "Alas! Must I always cede victory to you? Do you appear in our forests only to triumph over both my love and my glory?"[34] Fuzelier smuggles protest into these words, and while the military tide has gone against the "Savages," the same cannot be said of the opera's moral flow. "Civilized" Europeans in it are hardly commendable.

Adario hides himself so as to overhear conversation between a Spaniard, Don Alvar, and a Frenchman, Damon. The former insists that love rewards faithfulness, the latter demurs. Alvar has a clichéd view of the Indians. For him, they know only to frolic and need to be saved from this behavior, so contrary to his own traditions. Damon is happy to be in haunts where hearts don't follow "tyrannical constancy."[35] They even recall his native land. When Zima arrives, these men implore her affections, but her perspective is very different from theirs: "We follow innocent nature," she sings, explaining that love in these domains is simple, without pretense. She tells the two suitors that they have not understood what inconstancy means among the "Savages." They find it suitable until marriage brings happiness.[36] Her words provoke quarrel between the Europeans. Wedlock never restrains those who live by the Seine, charges the Spaniard; suspicious Spanish husbands yoke their wives and make them miserable, says the Frenchman. This debate about love and constancy, whether or not intended quite this way by Fuzelier, captured a question facing imperial policy: should colonists merge with conquered populations all while remaining faithful to their metropolis in Europe? The issue was already raised by Don Carlos and Phani in the second act. Spain wanted a uniform, global Christian empire under its king. Colbert described Iroquois as inhuman "savages" whom the French needed to civilize. He advocated miscegenation with Indians to this end. When the French West Indies Company was founded, it gave "civilized" children from such unions the same rights as native French without need of legal naturalization.[37]

Zima rejects both French and Spanish suitors. She doesn't want a jealous or a fickle husband. Not this Spaniard—he "loves too much." Not the Frenchman—he does "not love enough." When vivacious Adario appears, she takes his hand. She delights in his simple sincerity, to the regret of her other wooers, who now clash between themselves. Alvar mutters that he should slay their Indian competitor—for all his talk of faithfulness in love, violence is still an easy option for him—but Damon restrains him. Your perseverance, says the Frenchman to the Spaniard, inspires "unjust rage." The Spaniard's urge lends irony to this *Entrée*'s title. In the end, the two Europeans are resigned and a little ashamed as "savage" Zima has chosen a native over them. And then it is time for the peace ceremony, heralded by a fanfare of trumpets.

The stage fills with "French maidens in Amazon dress, French and Indian soldiers, Indian women, and shepherds from the colony." Adario tells his fellow Indians to rejoice in the peace created by their conquerors and to share the resulting pleasures. Love must reign. The ensuing "Dance of the Great Peace Pipe" became for audiences the opera's most popular event. Zima and Adario join their fellow "savages" in singing praise of calm forests and love. The entire company, soldiers and Indians, dance minuets (it seems that American savages learned some civilized European steps in addition to the value of being invaded) and Zima calls on nature to be their guide.

Fuzelier read various first-person accounts of North America when preparing this concluding *Entrée*. It proposes, effectively, peace between amiable natural savages and European conquerors. The former are happy to yield, yet the "civilized" behavior of the latter is questioned humorously but forthrightly. The former triumph in love while the latter, apostles of a religion of love, have done so in battle. (It implies a view of conquest at odds with that of "The Incas of Peru.") Viewers who had been attentive to and recalled the prologue might be able to draw very divergent conclusions: either that in distant climes, except perhaps Peru, things can be otherwise, indeed better than in their own war filled-Europe, or that colonialism is a good thing.

Still, Turks, Persians, Incas (at least one of their princesses), and Indians are treated with sympathy. The exception is Huascar, whose model may have been Incan but who could also have been a surreptitious European target. The Europeans, themselves often stereotyped, may be victors in Peru and North America, but they are not gallant in everything they do or bring to the "Indies." Each *Entrée* has its story, yet finally couples are linked by Cupid's arrows:

Emilie and Valère, but allowed by Osman's dignified generosity;

Don Carlos and Phani, upon Huascar's defeat (and, presumably, that of paganism);

Tacmas and Zaïre as well as Ali and Fatima, with disguises shed and the truth with their hearts visible (and the truth is no different from that of Europeans);

Zima and Adario, with embarrassed Don Alvar and Damon, constant and inconstant, losing their quests for nature and its beauty. Why "savages" should be content with military defeat is not evident beyond Adario's somewhat ironic laudation of good things Europeans bring to Indians.

A knowing listener to Rameau's music will recognize in *Les Indes galantes* a harpsichord *rondeau* that he wrote a decade earlier and that was also called *Les Sauvages*. In 1725 two American Indians were brought to Paris from French colonial Louisiana to dance before fascinated French eyes at a fair. Rameau's music was, just afterward, a result. It is easy to imagine, however, that this musical form was auspicious. A *rondeau* begins with and is structured by a basic motif. Call it theme "A." As the piece progresses, "A" alternates with contrasting themes—call them "B" and "C." "A" is, in a way, like its sounding bass, in that it orients the musical whole. The result is A-B-A-C-A, through to a conclusion (the return to A). While Rameau could not have had this in mind when he wrote his original rondeau, his later opera can be interpreted as having the same kind of structure. The themes—peace, war, love—presented in the prologue, weave their ways through four locales around the world. The first *Entrée* provided is a kind of drama, then comes a tragedy, afterwards a comedy of identities, and finally a sort of pastoral in which "natural" and "civilized" people meet and peace is hailed.

The North American Indians in *Les Indes galantes* were not modeled on Native Americans from Louisiana but on Hurons in Canada and Fuzelier's source, like the *Entrée* itself, also does not quite fit into the caricature assumed by many critics of Western perceptions of non-Europeans. In this case, the librettist almost certainly took the figure of Adario from a book by a French aristocrat, Louis-Armand, Baron de Lahonton who traveled to "New France" (Canada) with the French military at the end of seventeenth century. He spent a decade there and wrote extensively about his experiences, and particularly about the Indians. Some of them he found despicable, especially in war, but some he found admirable. His fictional *Dialogues between Baron de Lahonton and a Savage in America* even begins by referring to the peoples that "we"—the Europeans, that is—"have given the name savage."[38] The dialogue is between himself and one Adario, a Huron chief who has even traveled to France. This allows the interlocutors to compare the mores of two parts of the world, and the Huron comes across often as much superior to the Europeans in religion, law, and marriage. He even advises Lahonton to turn Huron. Adario is a communal being, a member of his tribe, and thus not the kind of "natural man"—who begins by wandering alone in the forests—described famously by Rousseau later in the century. It cannot be doubted that Rousseau read Lahonton with attention. Both Fuzelier and Rousseau display a dislike for European avariciousness and one can imagine them being struck when Adario tells his interlocutor that "despite their poverty" the "savages" are "richer" than people—Europeans, that is—who are obsessed with what is "mine and thine"; this possessiveness leads them "to commit all sorts of crimes."[39] Rousseau used just these words, "mine and thine"—the establishment of private property—to designate the point at which the human race declined sharply from its more natural well-being into unhappy civilization.

Les Indes galantes contains multitudes of European prejudices, but they emerge while it questions hypocrisies of the Europe that produced them. Only a blind ideologue could fail to perceive that this opera presents at least two sides. Its prologue suggests that its aim is to speak to Europeans, even to shame them slyly, rather than to provide operatic discourse about exotic places (even if the French were then attracted to these). Still, both Campra's Europe, earlier in *L'Europe galante*, and Rameau's Indies are gallant for the same reason: the triumph of love. There must be, then, something alike about all lovers. The dates of *Les Indes galantes*'s creation—1735–36—coincided with the beginning of decades of strong criticisms of colonialism by some of France's leading intellectual figures. These were often contradictory criticisms, yet like Fuzelier and Rameau's opera they questioned what Europeans did abroad and how they understood themselves. Montesquieu was then working on his influential *The Spirit of the Laws*, whose harsh words about the despotism of a non-European power, China, aimed among other things to show the French what had been wrong with their own regime under King Louis XIV. Voltaire soon wrote his *Essay on the Morals and Spirit of Nations*, which praises the Ottomans at the expense of Europeans and chastises the latter's overseas conquests and meanness. Later in the century came the Abbé Guillaume Raynel's *Philosophical and Political History of the Settlements and Commerce of Europeans in the Two Indies.* It would be translated into many languages, becoming the equivalent of a best seller. A reader would have to conclude from it that Europeans were the barbarians. "[W]e are too dangerous as guests," wrote Diderot, who skewered colonialism and slavery in various writings, and collaborated with Raynal.[40] *Les Indes galantes*, for all of its stereotypes, was an early staging of questions later posed by these writers.

Chapter 12

NATURE AND ITS DISCONTENTS

Nature or civilization? This question, so central to Rameau's opera, has been linked as few others to Rousseau's name. Few have had their views more caricatured than Rousseau. Did he not want humanity to return to a state of noble savagery? Voltaire, on reading Rousseau's *Discourse on Inequality*, declared himself inspired to walk on all fours. Rousseau extolled nature and envisioned civilization as a persistent process of decline, yet no careful reader of him can conclude that he believed men and women could find their way back to a primitive reality.

In the preface to a play of his youth, Rousseau warned: once people are corrupted, there is no return to innocence. Although we don't begin as original sinners, once we have left the garden—nature, that is—we always need rules. When Rousseau wrote in *The Social Contract* that "Man is born free, yet everywhere he is in chains," he did not intend that life be manacle-free. Those chains were laws, but only laws endorsed by the political community as a whole, by its "general will," were legitimate. The People were the sovereign, not a king, with or without a ring. And the People had to be wary of corruptions and luxuries, like those found in Paris—where often-contradictory Rousseau lived. His preference was for a plain, self-sufficient life. He lived it much like he wrote opera in French after declaring this impossible. Nothing demonstrated his partiality more than *Le Devin du Village* ("The Village Soothsayer"). His opera's popularity in the second half of the eighteenth century was enormous. Although Pergolesi is clearly a great inspiration, Rousseau wrote it before the outbreak of the *Querelle* and it premiered after the fray began. He called his short work an *intermède*. Much to his satisfaction—and despite his politics—its first performance in October 1752 was at the royal château at Fontainebleau before the king with one of the foremost tenors of the day, Pierre Jélyotte, who had played leading roles for Rameau, singing. Rousseau's own description of the event suggests the politics within *Le Devin*. He came in his "usual careless style, with a rough beard and an ill-combed wig." He sat in a box and was visible to the king and Madame de Pompadour when the lights went up. He wondered if he was "in the right place." Was he properly "attired" amidst "an overdressed crowd?" He decided that indeed he was. He had been invited to see his own work performed. Who other than Rousseau had a "right" to enjoy the result of Rousseau's talents?

He went on to say to himself (or so he wrote): "I am dressed in my ordinary way, neither better nor worse. If I begin to pander to public opinion over one matter, I shall pretty soon be doing so over everything. To be consistent with myself, I must not blush, wherever I may be, at being dressed according to the position in life I have chosen." If this offended anyone, so it had to be, thought the future advocate of popular sovereignty. "I must know how to bear ridicule and censure," he added, "provided they are undeserved." He expressed great joy at his opera's enthusiastic reception. Murmurs gathered, there was "mounting excitement" and then delight in the audience. "I surrendered myself, completely and unreservedly, to the pleasure of savoring my glory." Indeed, he wept. Even though applause was proscribed in the monarch's presence, this ban had an advantage, he observed. Every note could be heard.[1] *Le Devin* was also presented in Paris the following March. In the meantime, pamphlet after pamphlet appeared in the *Querelle*.

Le Devin is not set in a state of nature but nearby, in a hamlet among trees and fountains, by the home of a Soothsayer (a *Devin*, or Diviner). The music is simple and melodious, more like Pergolesi than Lully or Rameau. Rousseau's style, then, is one with his *intermède*'s plot and—if it can be called this—its message. After a spritely overture, slow rhythmic music brings forth Colette, a shepherdess. "I've lost all my happiness," she laments. Colin the shepherd, her love, roves. He is infatuated by a city lady, a lady of luxury. The shepherdess counts out a meager sum she will offer the Devin for help (Rousseau's libretto tell us that many villagers confer with him bearing "country products" as gifts). The Devin tells her that Colin, although unfaithful, still loves her. She can, he advises, regain him by coquetry: "Love grows if it is upset."[2]

The clever counselor advises the audience that he knows well the problems that afflict the pair and this becomes evident amply when, with Collette's departure, another advisee appears: Colin, also troubled. He does love Colette and fears he has lost her. The Devin tells him that indeed he has and not just to another shepherd but to "a handsome Monsieur from the city." When jealous Colin asks what to do, the Devin asks to be left to himself. In a musical interlude, he "consults" a "conjuring book," waves a wand—young peasants, who awaited also his guidance, are scared away—

Figure 12.1. Jean-Jacques Rousseau (1712–1778),
political philosopher and opera composer.

and then he casts his spell: the couple will be together again. The spell is simply jealousy that he nurtures in both their hearts. There is no magic in his soothsaying, just a grasp of human motivations. And like *Serva* there is no stage spectacle, just a melodious acting-out of human behavior.

When Colin, alone, pines for his shepherdess, he sings a Rousseauist message. His competitor for Colette must be rich and powerful, one of the "great lords," yet all their advantages don't bring happiness. Colin declares that he needs no more than a shepherd's meager goods if he has Colette, his "jewel."[3] The prospects, however, do not seem so fortunate when the two meet. She follows the Devin's advice, even when Colin supplicates himself and blames his inconstancy on possession by an "evil spirit." Colette responds that she no longer cares for him and points out that Colin sports in his hat an ornate ribbon, a gift from his fancy city lady. When he makes a simple act—he tears it off and throws it to the ground in disdain—she yields, finally, to her true feelings. She gives him a simple ribbon, which he dons as they sing rapturously of their reconciliation. The Devin is happy to take credit for the turn of events, yet when offered a present in thanks, he declines. Their happiness, he says, suffices for him, and he calls on the young shepherds and shepherdesses to celebrate—which, of course, they do in dance and song that also praise the "brilliant power" of the Devin. Colin sings of how he and his beloved will live together happily in a cottage. At this point Rousseau provides a pantomime with accompanying music that illustrates his vision further. A Village Girl dances to sedate music while an aristocrat watches. The music speeds up, suggesting that something is ado. He offers her a purse; she refuses. He offers a sumptuous necklace and she tries it on just as a Village Boy appears to rhythmic sounds. The necklace pleases the Girl but she rejects it on seeing his distress. The Boy is now threatened, however, by violence from the frustrated noble. The Girl tries to placate the noble, perhaps reminding some viewers of a scene with two lovers and a monster in Lully's *Acis*. Finally, the Girl and Boy throw themselves at the noble's feet. He is touched and relents—this a change of heart that hardly corresponds to Rousseau's political views—and accepts their love for each other. All then delight, "the Villagers for their union, and the noble for his good deed."[4] Within their merriment comes a "vaudeville" that directs the *intermède* to its finale as the Devin retrieves a sheet from his pocket. On it are words about art and love and he sings them. They highlight the difference between town and country, and, interspersed among them, comes a repeated declaration of love's changeable, childlike character ("*C'est un enfant! C'est un enfant!*"). The younger and more innocent humanity, the better it loves. Love, sings the Devin, may be "most considerate" in the city but "one knows best how to love in the village." Colette takes the sheet and sings a verse about natural naïveté that Rameau's Zima would have appreciated. Colin chimes in with a passage about innocent hearts and the villagers dance and sing. Artificiality—let it stay in the city.

Neither *Les Indes galantes* nor *Le Devin du Village* had outstanding librettos. Yet seen in each other's light, a matrix of their times emerges. *Les Indes* sends a valued emotion out into the world: to an Ottoman island; to a South American desert; to a Persian harem; to a North American grove. Love, having become an airborne fundamental bass, triumphs in all of them. While the first *Entrée* of *Les Indes galantes* resolves with two Europeans reunited, it is due to the "Other." His nobility is displayed when he yields the "mixed" marriage he so wants. The opera concludes with the two North American "natives" together while European suitors lose their opportunity for mixed marriage and look doltish. The middle two *Entrées* raise like matters. A racially "mixed couple" loves, while artifice and power fail in Peru and Christianity triumphs over paganism (or is it over the papacy?) The Persian episode pivots on the prospect of socially mixed marriages. A king and nobles trade and marry slaves. Zäire does announce her royal blood but this means, presumably, that she ought not to have been in a harem in the first place. Still, dependence of the plot on disguises and mistaken identities, a theatrical commonplace, suggests ambiguity in how we perceive things. The place of women is subordinate in all four scenarios, although in the end they are freed from some form of captivity and are destined apparently for happier futures as wives. The men, however, always possess the rings. While slavery isn't questioned in any of the *Entrées*, happiness for their protagonists requires its transcendence.

Those little cupids bring to foreign lands (on a stage) what they are unable perform in Europe. What colonialism brought to indigenous populations was usually something else: Bellona and brutality. In a sense, the first staged version of *Les Indes* reflected realities more accurately than the revisions since it ended with irruption and destruction of an indigenous world. Still, the final act in the four-part version also offers lessons in each exotic locale (except perhaps Peru). By contrast, Rousseau's Colin and Colette learn from each other, with some guidance from the Devin. The one-act setting of *Le Devin* contrasts dramatically to the multiple *Entrées* of *Les Indes*. And a good deal is at stake in placing events in a hamlet. It is half in nature and half outside of it; it contrasts town to countryside, sumptuous to simple existence. In his *Discourse on Inequality*, Rousseau imagined that humanity was probably "meant" to live just beyond a state of nature, but not too far from it, in a world that existed (in his mind) before the arrival of base opulence, money, and private property. The hamlet of *Le Devin* seems such a place. The peasants offer the Devin goods, products of their labor, not cash for wisdom. In his *Discourse*, Rousseau first imagined solitary self-sufficient individuals wandering through nature; then they run into one another much like the boy and girl at the well in his description of the origins of language and music. People are already living together in the hamlet at the beginning of *Le Devin* and they have a problem—loving relations are disrupted—when they run into a well-to-do someone from the city. The moral is tangible. Colette's simple ribbon ought to be in Colin's hat. It is difficult to imagine either of these country-folk at Versailles or Fontainebleau—except on stage, while their inventor and composer, bedraggled, sits in the audience. The same cannot be said of characters in *Les Indes*. They can all, eventually, be imagined in luxurious surroundings, except for two "savages." Zima's embrace of Adario may take place deeper in nature than the return of Colin to Colette, but both unions issue a common opposition to the same attractions. The two operas, for all their differences, share certain sentiments about what ought to animate human

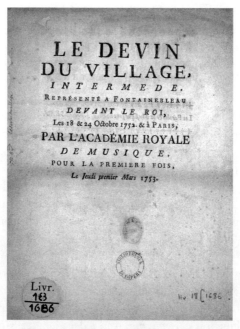

LE DEVIN
DU VILLAGE,
I N T E R M E D E.
REPRÉSENTÉ A FONTAINEBLEAU
DEVANT LE ROI,
Les 18 & 24 Octobre 1752. & à PARIS,
PAR L'ACADÉMIE ROYALE
DE MUSIQUE,
POUR LA PREMIERE FOIS,
Le Jeudi premier Mars 1753.

Livr.
1̶6̶3̶
1̶6̶8̶6̶

Figure 12.2. Cover of the printed libretto for the first production of Jean-Jacques Rousseau's *Le Devin du Village* at the royal palace at Fontainebleau and in Paris. (Bibliothèque nationale de France.)

values. Both begin with conflict only to end with pastoral embrace. When their political and social content is considered, harmony and melody bring both to a similar provence.

Apparently, Louis XV so liked *Le Devin du Village* that he suggested an allowance for Rousseau. (It was declined by the philosopher-composer.) If we take seriously Diderot's portrait of the Congo's ruler, the real monarch and the fictional one display a paradoxical consistency in musical taste. It is when he is bored by an opera by Uremifasolasiututut that Mongogul turns his attention to the jewels. Their voices disrupt a work by a man—Rameau, in Diderot's imaginary reality—who believed in order, who was concerned throughout his life only with music, which he believed embodied order, and who ridiculed Rousseau. But Rousseau, whose most popular opera premiered before royalty, would soon articulate incendiary political ideas that inspired many of the revolutionaries who overthrew and executed this same monarch's successor in the name of the People. *Le Devin* played more than five hundred times in the seven decades after its premiere. Yet it became, eventually, an historical oddity, a theatrical illustration of Rousseau's own concerns more than anything else. His worldview was structured by an intriguing, persistent refusal to accept what most thinkers and the public took to be irreconcilable opposites. Take, for example, law and individual liberty. The first coerces, the second implies freedom to do as one pleases. But *The Social Contract* argued that law and liberty in society actually implied each other, lest life be made of capricious dangers. Rousseau had some difficulty claiming for harmony and melody what he proposed for law and liberty; and while Rameau was lauded by the *philosophes*, his musical views, translated into politics, implied strict hierarchy.

Not long after its first performances *Le Devin* was parodied by the (now reestablished) Comédie-Italienne in Paris. Colin and Colette became Bastien and Bastienne. The Devin was renamed Colas. This lampoon traveled on to Vienna in 1755. Giacomo Durazzo, the emperor's director of theater there, paid considerable attention to the French cultural world. He had a German translation prepared and scored. Readapted, it was set by a twelve-year old from Salzburg in 1768 and it was performed in Vienna. It was two years after he composed *Bastien and Bastienne* that this unusual talent read at least part of Fénelon's *Telemachus*. And a decade later Mozart composed his first mature opera. *Idomeneo* had a distinct structure, making it an "opera seria"—serious, as opposed to humorous, opera. It would be superior to most earlier efforts in this genre.

PART 4:
ANCIENTS IN MODERNITY

I am more grateful for the offensive truth than for the pleasing lie.

—EMPEROR TITUS in *The Clemency of Tito*

A man who wishes to make a profession of goodness in everything must necessarily come to grief among so many who are not good.

—MACHIAVELLI, *The Prince*

Chapter 13

FROM ELYSIUM TO UTICA

Scipio Aemilianus, a renowned figure from a Roman clan known for its culture and military prowess, had a dream in the second century BCE. Young Mozart set it—or rather a short text based on it—sometime in spring and summer 1771. Its key theme is the maturation of a young man who learns his worldly responsibilities. We don't know that the historical Scipio actually experienced this reverie; it was recalled over centuries by an imaginative chapter of Cicero's *On the Republic*. It echoed that final book of Plato's *Republic* in which the slain hero Er ascends into the whirling firmament and hears the "harmony of the spheres." Cicero's sleeping protagonist also goes to sonorous heavens and to famous Elysium, where heroes and other greats reside in a blessed afterlife. He has a conversation there about a cherished Ciceronian ideal.

Cicero obsessed about "civic virtue." Once, he believed, intelligent patriotic devotion informed the Roman republic, giving it tether and greatness. But this ideal, he feared, was being overwhelmed in his day by what he saw as populist demagogy in the politics and person of Julius Caesar. In fact, the Republic's defeat was also Cicero's doing because this senator and philosopher, while rich in thought, was inflexible in public life. He could not grasp that as his beloved republic had become an empire, political change was needed. You cannot manage one as the other. Both Cicero and Caesar would finally be murdered but Augustus, Caesar's adopted son, would provide a successful substitute: an imperial system that maintained powerful republican myths with powerless republican institutions.

Emperor Augustus could not assure, however, that those who followed him would have his political acuity. Western literature and early opera are filled with depictions of the travails caused by his successors. Lessons of various kinds were sought as we saw in Monteverdi and Busenello's portrayal of the ruinous conflict between Nero and Seneca. A century and a half after their *Poppea* came Mozart's *La clemenza di Tito* (*The Clemency of Titus*). Seen first in Prague in early September 1791—*The Magic Flute*, not yet quite finished, would premiere a few weeks later in Vienna—*Tito* presented in an entirely positive light an emperor who reigned from 79–81 AD.* Its staging was part of festivities accompanying the crowning of Leopold II of the Habsburgs as King of Bohemia (which was also part of the Holy Roman Empire) and it was commissioned by the Bohemian estates. Titus in Mozart's opera is a largely fictionalized representation of a historical figure but the audience—again like that of *Poppea*—would have been familiar with ancient Rome's fortunes and would easily have found them comparable to problems faced by Leopold II. His predecessor and brother, Joseph II, was a famously "Enlightened" absolutist who pursued extensive reforms across his vast territories only to step back as they seemed to unleash unexpectedly disruptive forces. From his capital in Vienna, Joseph II sought to centralize and to rationalize governance of a sprawling realm. Much of the aristocracy, the church, and local powers resented these efforts, as did non-Austrian peoples and minorities, particularly as he sought to impose a common language of administration, German, on his multilingual lands. An intelligible order required increased political monody for Joseph II.

Scipio's Dream (*Il sogno di Scipione*)† was composed by Mozart two decades before his *Tito* during a period of change in his native Salzburg. In this conservative although musically illustrious city a rancorous power struggle had taken place recently after the death of its prince-archbishop, an employer and supporter of the Mozart family. His successor, Hieronymus Colloredo, was liked politically by the imperial court in Vienna, then jointly under Empress Maria Theresa and her son Joseph II. Despite an intolerant personality he wanted liberalizing reforms for Salzburg like those initiated for the empire by Joseph II. When Mozart composed *Scipione* at age fifteen, he did not yet know that he would seek freedom from Salzburg, which was then relatively independent of the empire, in order to pursue the life of an independent musician in Vienna. And *Scipione* distilled at least two, linked imperatives for a new ruler—any ruler. One was the need for steadfastness—constancy—in the face of adversity. The other was to maintain focus on what is important. Both implied something unpolitical: continued support for the Mozart family in Salzburg. To its chagrin, Colloredo eventually cut the musical budget.[1]

---

*For simplicity's sake I will refer to the opera as a whole as *Tito* and the character in it as Titus.
† I will refer to Mozart's work as *Scipione* and to the character as Scipio.

II.

The contrast between city and country in *Bastien and Bastienne* becomes in *Scipione* that between earth and Elysium. Scipio dreams while he is on his way to a military campaign. Rome faced challenges in Spain and turmoil in Carthage. The historical man was a successful warrior in both places, but utterly brutal. This latter record is not suggested in the opera, in which those two goddesses whom we met before representing opposite ways in the world, Constancy and Fortune, vie to attract him. Valor for one means recognition of persistence in the order of things; for the other it requires recognition of perpetual flux.

Listen to the harmony of the spheres, says Constancy. Their unequal sizes and differing movements come together in a fitting way. That is why the sound they create is beautiful. Their dissimilarities assemble properly, and so the link between proportion and order is the key to the cosmos, even if unheard on earth. Indeed, proportion and order are keys to each other. When all is steady, all is well, all in place (even if spinning). This is what a hero must perceive. Constancy argues for steadfastness on earth, for limits and laws. Fortune, however, proposes that it is impossible to be a hero without seeing the unstable nature of reality. Better to recognize chance—Fortune's dominion—in the world and, indeed, in the cosmos. Round images circle each other in these arguments. If Constancy points to harmonious, ordered spheres, Fortune is a Roman goddess whose whirling spindle has unpredictable results. For the first, spheres turn immutably; for the second a spindle moves constantly but you cannot know where it arrives. By the opera's end Fortune will argue: worship me as the real arbiter of good and bad on earth. I destroy empires, I renew them; I change hovels into thrones. All good things come from me.

But so too must, fatefully, all bad things.

Scipio has questions. However, in the midst of posing them his dream draws him to his ancestors in the Elysian fields. They make claims about the cosmos as well; they can perceive its bigger reality and also those on the little "speck," earth, with all these rival kingdoms on it, as Emilio, Scipio's father, puts it. Up and down are there by nature. Up is always harmonious. Down is often tumultuous and the duty of patriots is to put things right, to steady the relation between up and down as much as possible. Scipio also meets the man who led Rome to victory in the second Punic war, defeating Hannibal and Carthage in 202 BCE. This is his partial namesake and, through adoption, his grandfather. "Publius"—better known as Scipio

Africanus Maior—explains in recitative that only his body died. His spirit is happy in Elysium among others who loved their *patria*, who devoted themselves to public well-being. Anyone who lives for himself alone, he sings—but now in an aria—does not merit birth in the first place. The recitative presents the issues; the aria professes his point.

While he would prefer to stay in his Elysian reverie, Scipio decides he must do otherwise. Between the goddesses, he chooses "lovely Constancy" while Fortune rages against his presumption and threatens storms. He judges Fortune unjust. His duties, he determines, are in contemporary Rome, his *patria*, and so he awakes to them. He feels constancy within himself; civic virtue girds him. Scipio learns mettle that Orpheus lacked; immediate desires must be subordinated and one must be steeled facing hardship. Scipio and Orpheus return to the earth's surface, one from above, the other from below. One heads for glory, the other (in some tellings, as we know) is lost in his failure. The historical Scipio did not, however, come to a splendid end. As Fortune would have it, his life and career went into decline after his many military and political triumphs. His death in 129 BCE may have been due to murder; possibly it was suicide.[2]

III.

The libretto of *Scipione* was written initially in 1735, long before Mozart's birth, by Pietro Metastasio, the "Poet Caesara"—"Caesarian" or Imperial Poet—of the Holy Roman Empire. A year before he wrote the libretto that became later the basis of Mozart's *Tito*. The Habsburg empress commissioned both for occasions honoring Charles VI, her long-reigning husband. Music had been an important part of his life and court. In *Scipione* a young man yields a dream on behalf of political responsibilities; in *Tito* the protagonist is already in power and shows himself to be self-sacrificing and benevolent. Both figures illustrated Metastasio's lifelong derision of "self-love." It limited horizons to a "single individuality," as he wrote to his close friend Carlo Broschi, famous to opera history as the castrato Farinelli.[3] "Self-love" thwarted greatness. Titus wears antiquity's garb but he is obviously meant to be an eighteenth century Holy Roman ideal. It is an ideological portrait on behalf of Metastasio's patron, claimant to the ancient Roman heritage but Christianized, ruler of an empire whose ill-defined borders were rearranged over centuries, but eventually covered most of central Europe. Officially it was the empire "of the German Nation" by the fifteenth century, although it was linguistically and ethnically diverse.

There was nothing unusual about its Caesarean Poet writing in Italian. There were few opera librettos in other languages. The realm was amorphously federal (and included Italian lands). Local ruler-vassals ("electors") selected and paid obeisance to the emperor while presiding in their own territories. By Mozart's day, the crown had, save a brief interlude, been long in Vienna on the brow of a Habsburg, family heir to Austrian lands.

Metastasio's many librettos were reset by a good many composers over decades. When Leopold Mozart sought to demonstrate to the Viennese that his son was a genius he declared (or so he reports in a letter): Give Wolfgang any text by Metastasio and he will set the first aria he sees.[4] The music for the first *Tito* was by Antonio Caldara, then the Habsburg court composer, and some forty more versions followed with the libretto often revised. *Tito* does not seem to have made a strong impression on fourteen-year-old Mozart when he saw it in Cremona with music by the now obscure Michelangelo Valentini. Forgotten as well is the original composer of *Scipione*, Luca Antonio Predieri, and Mozart's musical account of it was apparently never heard in public in his lifetime.

Yet the politics of both *Scipione* and *Tito* reflect essential aspects of opera's evolution in the eighteenth century and of Mozart personally. Among the texts by Metastasio that he set was a cantata, *Betulia Liberated* (*La Betulia liberatà*, 1771). It was derived from the story in the Apocrypha of Judith, the Hebrew heroine who slew the murderous Assyrian general Holofernes in order to free her town of the tyrant. One of Mozart's earliest opera settings was *Il re pastore* (*The Shepherd King*, 1775) whose "chief incident," as Metastasio put it, was "the restitution" of a kingdom to its "lawful heir."[5] Proper bequeathal was a frequent motif in works by Mozart and Metastasio and also a principal concern of ruling and elite families. Preoccupation with kin, political inheritance, and attendant duties was characteristic of ancient Rome, where numerous Metastasio operas take place. Scipio takes up his legacy after speaking to his ancestors and Titus will be portrayed as the legitimate inheritor of his imperial title. By Metastasio's time, the Habsburg family believed itself entitled to the empire's throne and the century was filled with one "War of Succession" after another (across Europe, in fact). Charles VI lacked sons and in 1713 had instituted the "Pragmatic Sanction," an effort to circumvent legal norms that barred his daughter, Maria Theresa, from the throne.

Politics alone does not capture these (or any) operas. Mozart's life was entwined with an overbearing father who was a musician. Psychological readings of his works suggest easily that he had a natural, if very thorny, affinity to the theme of inheritance. Of course, composers at this time, young or old, did not often choose topics for commissioned operas. Nor did court librettists. Nonetheless, subjects like inheritance—but also the burdens of civic duty and the nature of proper, rightful rule—reappear in Mozart's works, from his early efforts to his *Tito*, performed just months before his death. And in the nine years between the Caesarean Poet's death and Mozart's own in December 1791, the maturing composer from Salzburg would take these subjects to his own places in collaboration with other librettists. But we are ahead of ourselves.

IV.

Born in 1698 in Rome, Metastasio came to his post by Charles VI's invitation in 1729. He succeeded Apostolo Zeno, also a noted librettist and an initiator of "opera seria." This term, "serious opera," came into use only later in the century. It indicated, among other things, dissimilarities between a musical drama with weighty themes and a distinct structure and lighter, works with middle and lower class figures at their center; it alternated recitative and arias, castratos were especially prominent in it, and it contrasted to forms of comic opera, especially "opera buffa" that were also developing.[6] Metastasio would standardize the form of opera seria taking Pierre Corneille's playwriting as particular inspiration, and his Habsburg patron took the genre very seriously. The emperor was a religious, fastidious man whose "character and court" inspired Metastasio's "muse" to make "a virtuous prince" the protagonist of most of his operas, commented Charles Burney, who edited Metastasio's letters in English. Nonetheless, the Caesarean Poet insisted that he never addressed in his works the many "important events" he witnessed at court. This is true only if political allegory, which had a long tradition on the Viennese stage, is disregarded.[7] Habsburg sustenance of artists aimed to enhance the ruling family's prestige in (among other things) a display of inheritance of the prestige of culturally rich Roman antiquity. Anyone on the Habsburg cultural payroll knew this, including those writing librettos for Viennese opera in literary Italian.

Tito and *Scipione* were written at a trying time. Between May and September 1734 the empire suffered setbacks in Italy and was humiliated by France and Spain in the same War of the Polish Succession that occasioned *Les Indes galantes* in Paris. When Don Carlos took Naples, Charles VI lost the largest city on the peninsula. The empire's losses had, however, some collateral cultural benefits. The new Spanish Bourbon ruler in Naples was ambitious and wanted the luster provided by culture and impressive buildings. San Carlo, subsequently among the most renowned opera houses, was built. Metastasio's chagrin at his Viennese benefactor's defeats evidently spurred creativity. His oratorio about Judith is easily interpreted as a protest against the illegitimate seizure of lands. *Scipione* lauds fidelity to Roman duty; Scipio dreams before he moves against Spain. *Tito* shows an emperor overcoming adversity by greatness of spirit. His realm is besieged from within by fecklessness, even though Rome is depicted as the world's ruler. A universe outside Rome hardly exists in the libretto except for Titus's love for a foreign princess, whom he has sent away before the opera's events begin.

Scipio's choice of goddess conformed to Metastasio's view that "fortune" was his own "enemy." This poet, as he explained it, was faithful to the empire he served because it stood for "charity, justice, and good faith, the necessary bonds of society."[8] Metastasio had no sympathy for republicanism, least of all Machiavelli's version. He deemed it anti-Christian. The "Florentine secretary," he wrote, often "elevated vice into a science," deploying "false reasoning" in which "utility always takes [the] place of honesty." But utility and honesty were inseparable, insisted the Caesarean Poet. He believed firmly in paternal authority although at least once he granted that someone "*wholly* initiated" into politics might think otherwise. [9] Metastasio sought to skirt the political limelight beyond the stage as best he could. He had no particular fondness for courtiers, he said—although he certainly played the role himself. Perhaps his humble origins had something to do with this. "You know my dear Gemello," he wrote late in life, perhaps in self-service, to Farinelli, "that I am a kind of a duck that remains in the water without being wet. During an almost thirty-six years residence in Court, I have never been able to acquire either the mysterious air or pompous exterior that generally reigns there, or that learned discussion that borders on fraud."[10]

"Metastasio" means "mutation" or "transition," and it was an apt name for his century even if his own instincts, like the changes he pursued in opera, can be called conservative. It was a Greek version of his name at birth, Trapassi. Two eminent men took a special interest in him when he was simply a boy from a poor grocer's family. The first was his godfather, a cardinal, Pietro Ottoboni, who also wrote librettos and was a patron of the arts. Although young Trapassi would take minor orders in the church and become an "*abate*" (an abbot) at age sixteen, his true passions were Homer,

Ariosto, and theater. These were due especially to an eminent lawyer and man of letters who noticed the youngster improvising verse in the street, recognized unusual talent, and decided to take responsibility for his education. Gian Vincenzo Gravina, Metastasio recounted, was "no less a father than a master to me."[11] Gravina thought the youth might go into law, a field that would allow him to display oratorical skills, and Pietro did practice law in Naples for a brief time after Gravina's death in 1718. He was more interested, however, in poetry and he wrote plays and verse for aristocrats there, also becoming involved in tumultuous personal ties with the leading soprano of the times, Maria Anna Berti. Known as "la Romanina," she introduced him to an array of important cultural figures. His accomplishments were also noticed by the Habsburgs, then still ruling Naples.

Earlier, however, Gravina had sent Pietro to the Calabrian town of Scalèa to study Descartes's philosophy. His teacher, Gregorio Caloprese, Gravina's cousin, was its foremost exponent in Italy. Trapassi may have been renamed "Metastasio" because Gravina was the central figure in the Arcadian Academy and introduced him to it. Members of this cultural and intellectual association followed the tradition of similar Italian circles by taking pseudonyms. Founded in Rome in 1690, it was the descendant of a group of literary figures who had begun to meet decades earlier under the auspices of Christina, the abdicated Queen of Sweden and a convert to Catholicism. A leading Arcadian, Ludovico Antonio Muratori, wrote that his colleagues aimed to bring together "the most remarkable" men of culture on behalf of reform of the arts and sciences "for the good of the Catholic religion, for the glory of Italy, for public and private benefit."[12] Arcadian groups proliferated throughout the peninsula and sought to "purify" morals and literature. This did not lack in broader political context, one that made French philosophy and theater attractive. The late-seventeenth-century empire under Leopold I had grown in strength and its assertiveness in parts of Italy worried the Holy See. While the papacy had its problems with Louis XIV, this Bourbon king was a useful counterbalance to the Habsburgs. With this political backdrop, Cartesian rationalism appealed to Arcadians. Debates among them about Italian literature and literary language were an almost inevitable consequence. Arguments about opera were much like those that took place in France. They agreed that poetry was the pinnacle of artistic creation but uniting it to music, which had such a strong impact on human feelings, was a contentious matter. Did it not subvert intellectual seriousness? Descartes did not write, "I emote, therefore I am." Opera originated in efforts to make texts intelligible and expansive through music—would not words, ideas and, inevitably, poetry became secondary to composers, prima donnas, spectacle, and theater machinery?

The development of comic opera provoked fussy frowns on these serious literary men; artistic matters of consequence were not for laughing. Similarly, Metastasio would be contemptuous of appeals to lower pleasures rather than to "understanding."[13] His interest was to fashion formidable figures in great predicaments. The issue was posed succinctly when Muratori asked in 1706 a question that had by then taken many forms in debates about opera in more than one land: "Now when are men ever singing in the midst of . . . serious matters?"[14] Muratori determined that musical theater was becoming "effeminate." Skilled singers were inspiring "a certain softness" that "secretly" turned "common people . . . to lowly vices, as they drink in the affected languor . . . and savor the vilest passions, seasoned with unwholesome melodies." Who knew what they might do under this influence? And "What would the divine Plato say . . . ?" Harm comes inevitably to "public mores" if everything is not in its right place and if poetry becomes music's "auxiliary." Theater like this was not "socially useful."[15] Audiences would guffaw were "matters of state" presented through song. Besides, operas were "just too long."[16]

In *Passions of the Soul* (1649), Descartes argued that a man is virtuous and free to the extent that his rational will is decisive and not buffeted by passions. Arcadians believed poetry appealed first to the intellect and Gravina feared that musical sensuality would dissolve imitation of great behavior on stage; pleasure would supplant edification. He recognized—or believed— that ancient Greek tragedy brought texts and music together without succumbing to such hazards.[17] He seems to anticipate Rousseau in claiming that "[t]he early creators of civil society" sought "to instruct the people" by using "the very same poetic forms that the people had contrived for their own pleasure." Song could "enrapture" the heart, and by it "the measured discourse of the laws was conveyed more readily through the ears to the soul." Since "salutary precepts" could be expressed by making a couple out of poetic and "vocal harmony," Gravina suggested an accord had existed in antiquity among the efforts of philosophers, musicians, and poets. Somewhat like Rousseau, he presented this as a story akin to the biblical fall of man. With antiquity's end, the three kinds of talent took separate paths and were no longer united "for the utility of all." The philosopher went off into an intellectual world, the musician into one where voice became "pure" but "contentless" and the poets vanished into their own domain of words. Now, by Gravina's own day, words and emotions had been established as supporters of music "when it should be the reverse." The ear might be "appeased" but the soul was harmed.[18] Should poetry be the "mistress" or the "maid?" another Arcadian asked rhetorically, protesting that verse was being "humiliated" in opera.[19]

Metastasio's librettos sought redress. They posed in their own way— but provided a different answer to—the metaphorical question in Giulio Cesare Monteverdi's defense of his brother Claudio's music more than a century earlier. What—or who—governs the work? A rationalist literary aesthetic provided Metastasio's answer. Failure to think properly of the words, he warned, will gain praise for a composer only from "those who judge with the ear and not the understanding." He pursued a program of rectification on behalf of reason. It was opera seria. And he fought for it when challenged, indeed besieged, by what would be called Gluck's opera "reform," but which might better be classified a counterreformation. (We will turn soon to Gluck's desire for direct dramatic expression.) When music "rebelled against poetry," thought Metastasio, ostentation in sound resulted inevitably. Musical thrall subverted "true expression" and drama. "Pleasures which are unable to gratify the mind, or touch the heart, are of short duration," he determined, "for though men corporally suffer themselves to be easily captivated by unexpected mechanical sensations, they do not forever renounce their reasoning facilities." Music could with poetry "illustrate and enforce every emotion of the human heart," but when music "aspires at preeminence" it confounded drama.[20]

Metastasio's solution to an aesthetic question—that of how tragedy could be linked to music—was structured like the ideology of the empire he served (and all hierarchies). Everything and everyone had to have proper places. Tragic characters on stage had to be "persons of high rank"—never to be satirized, especially when they wrestled with a daunting fate.[21] Common people had no (or at best a subsidiary) place. He contrasted the requirements of a closed theater in his own day to rhetoric in an ancient forum before a general public. Someone who "sings in the open air or to a whole people" must deploy "his utmost force to make himself heard." Since "the art of sound" depends on the regulation of air, he explained, "it is necessary, when a great body is to be moved, that it should be done by means infinitely different from those employed for one that is circumscribed." The "vocal tricks" required of a "more subdued voice" are for a more en-

Figure 13.1. Pietro Metastasio (1698–1782), Imperial Poet of the
Holy Roman Empire, early nineteenth-century engraving by Paolo Caronni.
Philadelphia Museum of Art, The Muriel and Philip Berman Gift, acquired
from the John S. Phillips bequest of 1876 to the Pennsylvania Academy of
Fine Arts with Funds contributed by Muriel and Philip Berman, gifts (by
exchange) of Lisa Norris Elkins, Bryant W. Langston, Samuel S. White 3rd
and Vera White, with additional funds contributed by John Howard
McFadden Jr., Thomas Skelton Harrison, and the Philip and
A.S.W. Rosenbach Foundation, 1985.

closed area.[22] Booming oratorical simplicity persuades in the Roman Forum; subtle simplicity evokes understanding in the theater.

A theater allows music to display its "enchantments" and had to give it
its "rights," but this also gives rise to danger. It may mean that "the reigning
taste of the people is propagated." Contemporary singers aren't trained in
oratory as were the ancients. Metastasio, moreover, claimed to be writing
librettos with elites in his mind and not trying to sway masses.[23] Alternation was his structural prescription: recitative, then aria, recitative, then
aria. Characters of high station articulated ideals and their own circumstances in song-speech in Metastasio's librettos; then emotion poured forth

in song. This allowed for poetic-dramatic seriousness and emotional expression. Opera seria and politics did, finally, share a negative commonality for Metastasio: neither ought to be what Cicero called a commonwealth, *res publica*—the People's affair. This he believed in an eighteenth century suffused by conflicts among rulers and ruled.

V.

Metastasio provided an exposition of the link between his political and aesthetic attitudes, perhaps inadvertently, in a remarkable letter in early 1766. He wrote it in response to the ideas of François-Jean de Beauvoir, the Chevalier de Chastellux. This colorful French officer and noble with republican sympathies had written an essay contending that recitative hindered the dramatic potentials of music. The Caesarean Poet of modest origins explained to this aristocrat that he dissented from the belief that "as there is a *republic of letters*, there should be a *republic of arts*." He went on to assert, "I am no republican. *I cannot give this form of government* . . . preference because it boasts of having virtue [alone] for its support." In other words, patriotic devotion is insufficient to sustain a decent polity. That is why, he elaborated, "I am seduced by the venerable example of supreme paternal authority." (Surely his sinecure enhanced the seduction.)

He granted that all forms of government had "infirmities," but history showed the durability of "the most simple and uncompounded machines." Indeed, "the most jealous of all *republicans*, the Romans" found it useful to elect dictators. They were "persuaded of the advantages of authority united in one person during times of difficulty." States risked ruin by the mistaken "expedient" of dividing authority. These comments by Metastasio suggest some naiveté, if not confusion of his ideals (or the ideology of the regime he served) with reality; or perhaps it was obfuscation. Republicanism had usually aimed for a certain simplicity by means of uniform laws throughout a territory, claiming the citizenry to be sovereign (at least officially). Dictatorship was envisaged as no more than a temporary expedient in republican Rome, whose political system was a compound of Consuls, Tribunes, a Senate, and Assemblies. But Metastasio's own Holy Roman Empire was hardly an uncompounded machine; it was a complex, many layered, and amorphous entity whose paternalistic emperor owed his position to electors. It was only as monarch of Austria—one part of the empire—that a Habsburg was absolute (or tried to be so). Moreover, the fall of the Roman republic was due to social and factional conflicts within upper classes. Stubborn elites used the Senate on their behalf, *Populares* the assemblies all within an insufficiently flexible framework. Its myths removed, the Holy Roman Empire had structures that twisted and turned through multiple spheres of power. It would try but fail to adapt to changing realities by streamlining power and law in the second half of the eighteenth century.

After articulating his somewhat wobbly objections to republican principles, Metastasio proceeded to link disparate domains by using similar terminology to characterize both. He remarks on the difficulty of creating a drama in which "all the five acts concur." To do so it was necessary to "elect a dictator." Yet troubles would come should music win this role. How could music "take upon herself the choice of the subject, the conduct of the fable"? Emotion, which Metastasio identifies fairly persistently with music, cannot design the requisite understanding any more than—he does not make this point directly—the People could design principles by which they would be governed. Music should confess that she cannot "command" and ought to "obey." Obey whom? The librettist. Were poetry to be even an "occasional servant," he thought, she would "inevitably become a rebellious *republican*." She would demand rights—those of the ruler.[24]

VI.

In January 1728 Metastasio presented the death throes of the Roman republic to an audience in Rome's Teatro delle Dame. Four years earlier in Naples he had recounted Dido's desertion by Aeneas, set to music by Domenica Sarro, a popular local composer. Now the scene went from myth to history, to Utica, a North African city not far from Dido's Carthage. It was the last redoubt of republicans who fled Julius Caesar's army and they prepared their stand there in 46 BCE. The principal protagonists of *Cato in Utica** are Cato the Younger, the unbowed republican, and the dictator himself. Face-to-face exchanges between them provide the opera's political core. Metastasio makes a case for admiring something in both men, although he sides finally with Caesar. Neapolitan Leonardo Vinci wrote the music for the first production of *Catone*, but a long list of leading composers reset it throughout the century. The libretto drew significantly from a popular English play by Joseph Addison.[25]

Cato's suicide at age forty-eight provided yet another example from antiquity of heroism unto death. Like Socrates (and Seneca), Cato can flee

---

*I will refer to the opera as *Catone* and the character in it as Cato.

but does not: he dies in the name of Roman republicanism. This, at least, is how historical myth portrays him. Modern historians complicate matters when they contextualize the opposed ideological assertions of Cato and Caesar. Cato's purpose, noted one, was to save a teetering republic from tyranny represented by Caesar yet Caesar claimed to be liberating the same republic from an oligarchy (which had in fact included both these men as well as Cato's ally Cicero).[26] Plutarch's portrait of Cato, filtered through Addison and recent French tragedies, perhaps best revealed the man Metastasio put on stage.

Cato was a man "unmoved by any passion," wrote Plutarch. He was a Stoic devoted to "steady and inflexible justice which is not to be wrought upon by favor or compassion."[27] This senator was "as constant to his public duty as the bee to the honey comb."[28] For one famous example, when the Senate debated penalties for insurgents, Cato demanded capital punishment lest the republic be ruined by "soft words and popular speeches." Julius Caesar, however, called for mercy. (The executions took place.) Bitterness between the two men was not only political. Caesar had "corrupted" Cato's sister and there was no corruption, personal or political, that Cato would stand.[29] Machiavelli would have told him that such principled fortitude is not always wise. When Pompey sought a marriage alliance, proposing to wed Cato's niece, the response was scorn. The character of Plutarch's Cato shows how overly stern moral fiber can asphyxiate political judgment. Pompey married Caesar's daughter instead and promptly joined the advocate of "dividing the lands among the poor people." Aristocratic republicans like Cato and Cicero who stood against Caesar and Pompey would soon be on the defensive. By the time Pompey saw the problem incurred by his own choices—the problem was Caesar's ambitions—it was too late. Caesar would defeat his troops and Pompey fled to Egypt where he would be murdered.

If you are ready to fight the advancing dictator on behalf of liberty, Cato bravely told the republic's remnants in Utica, I will lead you. But Cato subverted his own military position too. He rebuffed a proposal backed by the majority in a council meeting to free slaves willing to join their struggle. Twenty-first-century observers might note (and frown about) how slavery and liberty didn't contradict each other in this ancient republican worldview. Plutarch aimed to show the outcome of unmovable devotion to the republic's laws. Cato did not object to this or that individual freeing slaves. He did insist that more than that was illegal and unjust (obviously, to the slave owner). This provoked questions among those gathered: why die here in futility? While Cato's virtue was blind, he could still see that the situation was hopeless. He brought close friends together for a final dinner. There was wine and discussion of Stoic doctrines. If you are good, he declared, you will always be free—if bad, a slave. He then retired and prepared to raise sharp steel against himself. Afterward, says Plutarch, the victor showed mercy to the suicide's son.

VII.

In a plot summary, Metastasio noted that even Caesar mourned Cato's end, leaving posterity to wonder who, finally, was more admirable. Was it the republican, who could survive only with "his *patria*'s liberty"? Or generous Dictator Caesar?[30] Metastasio's Senator Cato stands on stage like a living statue from antiquity, masterful in form, unable to bend. He cracks inevitably while Caesar, a flexible and clement fighter, remains firmly on his feet.

Political conflicts are presented adroitly amidst tousling, complicated personal relations. Affinities of character to politics are revealed. Passions undergird, or come to undergird, them all. Even Cato is, finally, not impervious to their swells as he tries to respond to contradictory demands. Unbeknownst to him, his daughter Marcia is Caesar's lover. Make peace, she implores her father. Arbace, a Numidian prince, loves her too and exhorts Cato to battle, offering support. To Marcia's chagrin, Cato will offer him her hand, a kind of pragmatic sanction as Metastasio's Cato, for all his severity, seems to have learned perhaps something from Pompey's refusal by Plutarch's Cato. Resolute yet vain, Cato defends his republic's values in an aria, identifying them with himself.

Still another affair of the heart weaves through the unfolding events. Caesar first comes to Utica unarmed in hope of persuading his adversary to yield. He is seconded by Fulvio, a trusty legate dispatched from Rome to the same purpose. Caesar has barely proffered peace without retribution when the story becomes more complicated: angry Emilia, widow of Pompey and hater of the dictator, arrives to denounce any negotiation as treason. Retribution, not patriotism, drives her. When she is alone with Fulvio it becomes evident that he is devoted to her and that she aims to exploit him to murder Caesar. Yet when the two men are alone, torn Fulvio discloses his predicament: love for her, fidelity to him. Caesar is understanding. Step by step he reveals himself as a man of compassion, and Fulvio will stay loyally by his side.

Within this mesh are opposed notions of rule. Cato rebuffs a letter from the Senate, now subordinate to Caesar, calling on him to submit not to the dictator but to the Roman public. It wants peace. These senators are Caesar's slaves, Cato retorts. True Rome, he declares, resides where the republican spirit of glory and liberty prevails—which means within him and his followers, not within a physical place. Metastasio wrote his libretto for an audience in Rome, the papacy's city, but with a curiously mixed message. It blurs patriotism (or perhaps protonationalism) into Christianity (and Christianity's Stoic antecedents—or perhaps more recent neo-Stoicism). A constant hero, faithful to old laws, Cato insists that the Roman polity exists in spirit and not within a material reality. However, his contentions are made with overwhelming pride, by tradition an unchristian disposition. He dismisses popular opinion in principle. In contrast, Metastasio's Caesar is lithe and loves a person, not just an ideal. He swears to Marcia that he will find a peaceful resolution for her sake. This Caesar is an ideological creation. Based on a historical pagan (although known for generosity), he appears like a magnanimous Christian ruler.

When Caesar comes to Cato's house, stage directions instruct each man to sit and stand as they converse. They alternate and reverse their positions. Sometimes they are eye to eye, seated, or on their feet. It is effective without affect and the exchange is animated also by their differing voices. In Vivaldi's version, Cato is a tenor and Caesar a soprano. Since both sing in higher registers, there is not the same kind of radical vocal juxtaposition as between Monteverdi's Seneca and Nero. But then little is admirable in Nero; opposed voices in *Poppea* are dramatically illustrative in a distinct way while closer sounds in *Catone* suggest a certain acknowledgment, albeit differing, of value in both antagonists. Caesar tells his foe to choose terms of peace. He will accept them as if vanquished, says the man with much stronger forces at his disposal. Cato takes this as mendacity. Surrender, he tells Caesar, and I will serve as your lawyer when the republic tries you. Here again, comparison to *Poppea* sets matters into relief. As Caesar fails to persuade a Stoic republican, Seneca the Stoic failed to persuade an emotion-drenched emperor. Rational constancy animates Cato's obstinacy; Caesar's constancy is expressed in his generosity. Contrasting kinds of wisdom fail to temper in both operas, but emotion does play its role—intrudes—in Cato's case. Hate will worm into gravitas, upsetting from within implacable, rational equilibrium. When you ask surrender, Caesar tells Cato, you are telling me no less than to yield my life. You know your demand means judgment is already rendered. (Caesar undoubtedly remembers their disagreement in the Senate over the death penalty.) You love your life more than your *Romanitas*, retorts Cato. They cannot find common terms. Caesar proposes that they share the empire but for Cato this means participating in Caesar's crime. Love, Caesar proposes, is the alternative. He offers to marry Marcia to seal peace; this Cato cannot endure. It would mean an entwined end to all he holds dear—family and patriotism.

And so he refuses to live with what he cannot change. War, war—that is what I want, he announces. But his breaking point is reached when, soon after, Marcia tells him that she actually loves the man he hates most. Cato tries to strike her; austerity again turns fanatic. He knows he cannot win and that a union of his daughter with Caesar would bring peace to Rome, but not his Rome. Despite everything Caesar remains a man of humane perspicacity. He sings that his power is wretched; he may be supreme but he is disarmed by his love's agony. The opera draws to its conclusion after Emilia's plot against him fails and his troops take Utica. In victory Caesar tells his soldiers that fortune, not bravery alone, brings triumph. A conqueror, he explains, must know when to be judicious. Roman *virtù* for him includes forgiveness, not just military prowess. He remains willing to pardon Cato and Emilia. Cato, however, is adamant, unwilling to forgive Caesar or Marcia; and Emilia still swears revenge. As a final chorus celebrates love and peace, Cato raises his blade against himself. *Catone* presents clashing political principles and asks what happens if clemency and constancy don't fit each other. A viewer who knows history (or popular versions) might find in Cato the sole figure without illusion; true, he will not yield his ideals yet he recognizes that they, indistinguishable from his person, are to disappear. Fortune's spindle, after all, turned its points against Caesar only two years after Cato's death and just after he became "Dictator in Perpetuity." And while the Caesarean Poet could not have known it, Metastasio's Holy Roman Empire had only eight decades to live.

VIII.

The opera caused troubles for Metastasio. These may have been due mainly to contemporary taste or to politics or to both. Happy endings were then the standard, and suicide and death on stage unacceptable, especially in Rome. A notable French observer of Italy, the magistrate Charles de Brosses, spoke later of a stage rule never "to make things bloody."[31] The opera premiered at the beginning of a particularly tense year in relations between the papacy and the empire (and the Austrian head of the latter). Pope Benedict XIII, who was not known for perspicacious political judgment, announced plans to celebrate in 1728 the legacy of Pope Gregory VII, an eleventh-century predecessor. This prospect left Emperor Charles VI unhappy because Gregory VII, known as a zealous reformer, excommunicated and humiliated a Holy Roman Emperor, Henry (Heinrich) IV, in a famous dispute over papal prerogatives. An operatic clash between a zealous republican and a generous Caesar might easily have seemed too contemporary when Metastasio's work was first staged. Yet varied political morals might be discerned in it. Did Metastasio suggest in 1728 that the incumbent Holy Roman Emperor ought to overlook a political affront by the incumbent pope? Or simply that Caesar and Charles VI, despite tensions between them, had comparable, laudatory characters?

Burney reported that the librettist chose his subject "to please the Romans, supposing that he should gain applause and gratitude by displaying the virtue of one of their heroes." Presumably this meant viewers in Rome rather than the ruler of the Holy Roman Empire. Nonetheless, the production of *Catone* was suspended quickly and attacked as frivolous. Those who thought otherwise were "a few learned men, less invidious than the rest, who if they knew of no modern Cato, had read at least about the ancient" one.[32] Did they take Cato for a hero? It might be that Metastasio understood the political issues raised by the confrontation between Caesar and Cato better than he understood the politics of his own time in Rome (or later in Vienna). Someone in Metastasio's audience might easily have imagined a scene in which Cato and Caesar stand, sit, and face each other as an allusion to a pope and an emperor.

Perhaps Metastasio revealed his own conflicts when he included differing versions of the opera in his published collected works. In 1728 he certainly understood professional imperatives, and it was soon after *Catone* that he became Caesarean Poet. In the meantime, he rewrote the third act so that Cato's death was announced but not staged. In Vivaldi's version, composed almost a decade later for Verona, which was in Venetian territory, the plot altered again. Cato was pardoned. If a positive and victorious Caesar might have been a problem in papal Rome in 1728, the suicide of an unbending aristocratic senator could well have disturbed an elite in Venice's moldering republic. (Its Council of Ten barred the original *Catone*.) Metastasio was a "virtuoso of submissiveness."[33]

Among those who came to see Vivaldi's version in spring 1737 was the Imperial Elector of Bavaria, Charles Albert of the Wittelsbach dynasty. Five years later, after miniwars over succession following Charles VI's death, he became Charles VII, the first non-Habsburg emperor since the fifteenth century. This was possible principally because of setbacks suffered by his predecessor in various continental conflicts. Charles VII's ascension came with miniwars among German powers that changed the political constellation. The Habsburgs reasserted their hold on the title on his death in 1745. Francis Stephen, Duke of Lorraine and husband of Maria Theresa, became Emperor Francis I, remaining on the throne until his death two decades later. But it was his wife who had effective power. By this time, however, the rise of Prussia threatened Austria and there was a *"renversement"* of alliances. Paris, the old rival of the Habsburgs, became their ally. These political fortunes would affect Metastasio and opera in Vienna.

ZWISCHENSPIEL (I)

We have seen often how a number of political philosophers deployed metaphors associated with music, such as harmony or dissonance, to articulate or illustrate their ideas. Burney, the pioneer music historian (and professional musician), sometimes used political terms to elucidate musical ones. He spoke, for instance, of opera's founders such as Monteverdi or Lully as its "Legislators."[1] He referred disparagingly to the fugue as a republican-like musical form, undoubtedly because one "voice" isn't sovereign in it; it presents a theme that is then repeated by another or several "voices" at various pitches together with responding counter-themes. Burney does not call this a counterpart to an argument in a public square—or the equivalent of talking back to an authority—but it can, with a little pliability, be taken this way.

Burney was on amicable terms with an array of important political and literary figures in England ranging from King George III to Samuel Johnson. An intense observer of London's musical world, he also traveled extensively to report and conduct research on music and opera. He visited Metastasio in Vienna and became acquainted personally or as a correspondent with an array of composers including Handel, Haydn, and Mozart. Burney met Voltaire and Diderot in Paris as well as "a little figure, with a very intelligent and animated countenance, with black eyebrows and small piercing black eyes." This was Rousseau. Burney shared Rousseau's enthusiasm for Italian music and praised the controversial "Letter on French Music." The French, thought Burney, needed to be "weaned from Lully and Rameau."[2] He translated *Le Devin du Village* for staging in London. Yet Burney's esteem for Rousseau was limited to music. Otherwise he found him a man of "eccentricities" and was averse to his "principles" and "paradoxes."[3]

Burney was friendly with another political thinker—Edmund Burke, acclaimed later as the father of conservatism because of his vigorous critique of the French revolution. Though Rousseau died before the upheaval, his writings were an inspiration for many French republican revolutionaries. Unlike Rousseau, with his enormous ambitions as composer and critic, Burke wrote little on music. His early but influential *A Philosophical Enquiry into the Origins of our Ideas of the Sublime and Beautiful* of 1757 devoted only a few pages to a field in which the author acknowledged no "great skill."[4]

However, a look at Burke and Rousseau in light of Burney's political-musical vocabulary suggests some elucidating parallels and disjunctions among political ideas on one hand, and musical and operatic history on the other. Burke, Burney, and Rousseau provide cross-lighting on their age.

For Burke, a political society was not comprised of individuals who simply pursue self-interest; it was a multilayered whole contrived by men to cope with the needs of living together. It possessed of a collective wisdom —or what he imagined was collective—nurtured over long periods of time by tradition, custom, and convention. It could not, as many eighteenth century radicals claimed, be a product of rational beings deliberating to reach an agreement with each other on how to secure their natural rights. Passions or feelings—"prejudices"—dominate people, he thought, rather than their rationality, and he considered their rationality relatively frail. Burke, like Rameau, believed in a grand hierarchy that preceded any individual. Unlike Rameau, he did not believe reason was the key to its provenance. Rousseau, like Burke, rejected any belief in the omnipotence of reason but unlike Burke or Rameau he rebelled against hierarchy. In Burke's view any attempted remake of society and politics in reason's name or in any way other than slow amendment would bring grief. Consequently, he favored government by prudent elites, the opposite of Rousseau's advocacy of popular sovereignty. Rousseau posited—he did not hide that this was imaginary—that men were first of all self-sufficient individuals who stumbled into each other, eventually fashioning society. After all, expressive melody was "prior" to acoustical harmony in Rousseau's theories of music. Yet again musical constructs suggest (imprecise) parallels in human relations. And Rousseau did not see harmony in the civilized world, which was corrupt, unjust, fragmented. While Burke aimed to conserve a complex social and political whole, in which one might say that (irrational) harmony was prior to any melody, Rousseau sought a new, simpler one in which melody was buoyed by harmony.

Burke's claims did not derive from musical metaphors, but his *Philosophical Enquiry* proposed that beauty in sound was comparable to beauty in other arts. He believed also, as he wrote shortly after his *Enquiry*, that there is an "art of government," not a science of politics.[5] The exploration of correspondences among the arts was then a prominent consideration of aesthetic conversation. Burke approached it in a revealing passage conveying his appreciation of John Milton's expression of "the affections of one sense by metaphors taken by another." He pointed to a poem of Milton's youth about *L'Allegro* ("The Merry Man") who spends the day happily in a pastoral setting and then a jovial evening in town. "Lydian airs"—the softer of antiquity's musical modes—are presented as an antidote to worry as their "melting voice" runs through mazes, "untwisting all the chains that tie/ the hidden soul of harmony." Milton more than intimates an underlying cosmic music. Following from the poem, Burke suggests that the varied perceptions of beauty by our different senses can "help to throw lights" on each and helps to elucidate "the idea of the whole. . . ."[6] Beauty was a matter of the senses and diverse qualitative parts had to melt "into each other."[7] This stress on wholeness and dislike of individualism also characterized Burke's social and political views; and there was, for him, always a bigger reality that had to inform, indeed limit, singular judgments.

When he addressed music, he was especially concerned with how it evokes "passions." Loud, shrill, or deep sounds were inevitably ugly, and so too their effects, he thought. Moreover, "great variety and quick transitions from one measure or tone to another are contrary to the genius of the beautiful in music." They can "excite" what Burke calls "sudden and tumultuous passions," while beauty should evoke something more like "melancholy" (by which he meant serenity and reflection). This, however, comes better to a "good head and skillful ear." He complained of "the immense crowd of different, and sometimes contradictory ideas that rank vulgarly under the standard of beauty."[8] Although Burke's claims comprise an aesthetic argument, they also anticipate everything he would fear in noisy revolutionary turmoil—excited, mass agitation pursuing rapid transitions. If correspondences could be found among the arts, it would seem that the art of politics could be compared to them as well.

Burney wrote just after Burke's death in 1797 that while he "did not subscribe" to all of his friend's political "passions and prejudices," he still considered him "the best orator and statesman of modern times."[9] He certainly appreciated Burke's views on the French Revolution. "I own myself," asserted Burney in an earlier letter, "a determined rebel to all *tyrants*." The greatest tyrant, he determined, was a "monster" called "*the majesty of the people*."[10] It had, he believed, bad political taste. Consider also the words Burney chose as he pondered the to-and-fro of different elements in operatic history:

> As the British government consists of three estates: King, Lords, and Commons, so an opera in its first institution consists of *Poetry*, *Music*, and *Machinery:* but as politicians have observed, that the balance of power is frequently disturbed by some one of the three estates

encroaching upon the other two, so one of these three constituent parts of a musical drama generally preponderates at the expense of the other two. In the first operas POETRY seems to have been the most important personage; but in the middle of the last century, MACHINERY and DECORATION seemed to take the lead, and poetry and music became of less consequence. . . .

A fourth estate, dance, impinged as well when "instead of being a dependent or auxiliary" it aimed "not only at independence but tyranny." Burney warned that "for the common interest," none of the "constituent parts . . . should arrogate to itself more than its due share of notice." Should poetry and music become "humble" wards, drama need be no more than a pantomime.[11] Likewise, while Burney valued monarchy, he worried at a time of political upheaval and a fierce election campaign in Britain that the public did not understand that the House of Commons was the "sole barrier between them and tyranny."[12]

It is not difficult to read Burkean sentiments about a properly ordered whole into Burney's imagery (although some phrasing sounds a little like an English rendition of Muratori). Two revolutions that preoccupied Burke were the political clef and coda of Burney's four-volume work (and of all Europe's late eighteenth century): the opening tome appeared as Americans declared independence, the concluding two in the year of the French Revolution. However, Burke's duly constituted authority was not embraced by Metastasio in Vienna. As a Whig, Burke was a proponent of the settlement secured by the Revolution of 1688, which he interpreted as a balance (in principle) among the monarch and the lower and upper houses of Parliament. King George III's assertiveness at home and in North America threatened it. Constitutional monarchy stood "on a nice equipoise" but there were "steep precipices, and deep waters upon all sides" and a dangerous tilt in one direction risked "oversetting" in the other for the sake of balance.[13] A similar principle brought his censure in 1790 of foes of a king, now Louis XVI. He thought French revolutionaries exalted reason— although Rousseau never did—and disregarded the equipoise of reason, customs, and "prejudices" that allowed people to live together.

Even a cursory glance at opera history reveals the perennial reappearance in it of issues of balance and "oversetting," together with what Burney called the search for a "common interest." Like matters worried the Arcadians, although they sought rebalance in reason's name—which, translated into politics, would have been rejected by both Burke and Rousseau. In Metastasio's ideology of hierarchy, the emperor ensured the common interest as reason's primacy enabled an operatic work to succeed—a "dictator" who induces "all of the fine arts" to "concur." It may be, however, that this kind of oversetting—imbalance favoring one element—went too far. Certainly Burke, had he discussed music with political metaphors, would have been averse to any dictator as well as radical resetting. For Rousseau, by contrast, melody directed a drama to its whole; likewise, the "general will" of the citizens had to be the animating melody of their political society.

If Metastasio, Zeno, and the Arcadians sought purification and simplicity, the great challenge to opera seria came in C. W. Gluck's "reform." This composer credited it, however, to Ranieri de' Calzabigi.[14] Scholars believe this librettist wrote Gluck's programmatic statements. In fact, the two reformers accepted many Arcadian premises while taking them to different aesthetic consequences. In a way their differences with Metastasio were like those between Catholicism and Protestantism at the time of the Reformation. They all claimed Christianity but they diverged in their views of a church. Metastasio would have concurred with Gluck's proposition that music's "true function" in opera is "to enhance poetry in terms of expression and the situations it relates." However, Gluck also protested "interrupting the action or numbing it with useless and superfluous ornaments." The target was not seriousness but excess in opera seria. A singer, he explained in the preface to his opera *Alceste* of 1767, ought not to be halted "in mid-word on a favorable vowel . . . to display the agility of his beautiful voice in a long melisma." There should be "no sharp break in the dialogue between aria and recitative."[15] Due seriousness, then, was not dependent on the dualism that—as if two social strata—characterized the very structure of Metastasio's operas. Gluck and Calzabigi required a robust continuity to create a musical-dramatic whole and had their own ideas of dramatic simplicity.

After Burney visited Vienna, he described its opera world as if it were a battle between conservatives and reformers—indeed like political parties or factions. This observation is striking given the influence of Rousseau's musical theories on him and that of Burke's political thought. Rousseau was antagonistic to political parties; he believed that they produced factionalism and never led to the common good. In Burney's Britain, however, political fissures would in 1784 lead to the first truly competitive elections since early in the century. Burke would be one of the first proponents of the idea of competition among political parties espousing contrary principles to enhance the general good. Burney reads almost as if he were applying Burke's definition. He observed that "party runs . . . high among poets, musicians and their adherents" in the Habsburg capital. Metastasio, whom he met then, and composer Johann Adolf Hasse, who set several of Metastasio's librettos, were at "the head of one of the principal sects." These traditionalists regarded "all innovations as quackery" and sustained "the ancient form of musical drama, in which the poet and the musician claim equal attention from an audience. . . ."[16] (This was imprecise given Metastasio's advocacy of poetic dominance.) It was an argument about change—much as had been the case between Artusi and Monteverdi (and scores of political thinkers).

Calzabigi and Gluck led the "quack" party, and it is easy to imagine that the epithet "quack" may have had something to do with the librettist's curious life—one that might well be the subject of a comic opera. Born in Leghorn in 1714, Calzabigi began his literary career in Naples emulating Metastasio. He had to flee, however, under extenuating circumstances: murder charges. He went to Paris, where, oddly enough, he was secretary to the Neapolitan ambassador. Calzabigi published an edition of Metastasio's works with an introduction lauding the poet and a dedication to Madame de Pompadour, but his French sojourn also ended in flight due, it seems, to involvement in a seamy business scheme with a Venetian-born wanderer named Giacomo Casanova. Calzabigi went to Vienna where he then managed to be appointed privy counselor at the treasury. This was under the administration of Prince Wenzel Anton Kaunitz, formerly imperial ambassador in France and, after his return to Vienna in 1753, a principal architect of the Austrian-French foreign policy *renversement*. Michael Kelly, the Irish tenor later recruited to the Viennese opera world, described Calzabigi as "a most eccentric personage" who was said to be especially proud of arranging the marriage between Joseph II's sister, "the unfortunate Marie Antoinette," with the future king of France.[17]

Kaunitz became state chancellor and was a vigorous proponent of French culture, theater, and opera in Vienna. He introduced Calzabigi, who had supported Rousseau in the *Querelle*, into the capital's theater world, presenting him to the musical director of the French theater there, a composer who had previously set librettos by Metastasio.[18] This was Gluck, the polyglot son of a Bohemian farming family who had been hired by yet another outsider to Vienna. Count Giacomo Durazzo had arrived there in 1749 as ambassador from Genoa and managed to become superintendent of theater. Also a proponent of French music, he wanted nonetheless "reconciliation" between it and Italian opera (his preferences were Italian comic opera and lighter French works rather than lyric tragedy). This odd constellation marked out the court culture in which the parties of Metastasio and Gluck struggled.

The *Querelle des Bouffons* was raging during Calzabigi's Paris stay and had an important effect on his view of musical theater and subsequent abandonment of the Metastasian model. He admired Lully and Rameau, yet was impressed by Rousseau's arguments for melody as a driving force and unifier, and the need for simplicity. Metastasio avowed that his goal was simplicity in language and drama but this was often combined with considerable complexity in plot—sometimes too much complexity—together with alternation of recitative and ornate arias. Calzabigi aimed for something different and his libretto for Gluck's *Orpheus and Eurydice* of 1762 focused on one character (Orpheus). Moreover, as he wrote to Kaunitz in March 1767, dramatic purpose required a change in the relation between words and music. It was, for instance, "ridiculous to prolong the sentence 'I love you' . . . with a hundred notes."[19] Gluck concurred and would praise Rousseau's claims as well. But while Rousseau sought to link specific languages to kinds of music, Gluck, harking to classical yet also modern cosmopolitan ideals, aimed for a "musical language for all nations." He found the notion of "national styles of music" to be "ridiculous."[20] The program of the Gluck-Calzabigi party, summarized Burney, was opera based "on theatrical effects, propriety of character, simplicity of diction, and of musical execution."[21] However, what they wanted above anything else was thoroughly musicalized and unified drama. Their concerns recall those raised in Florence and Mantua at the turn of the seventeenth century, and they displayed their purpose in *Orpheus and Eurydice*. And in its denouement, like that of the Florentine *Euridice*, the two lovers ascend successfully from the Infernal Fields. They are happily united even though Orpheus looks back and fails the test.

A prince, it seems, remains a prince. After all, Gluck and Calzabigi were writing for royalty. So too had Rousseau, of course. Still, there is something arresting to be perceived about the age in the disparate worlds portrayed by Metastasio, Gluck, and Rousseau. The first was perhaps best known for his historical themes, which nonetheless mythologized (and reinvented) figures like Cato, Caesar, and Titus. Gluck and Calzabigi returned to myths, while *Le Devin* presented common folk in a pastoral world. A reflective viewer who went in turn to historical, mythical, and pastoral operas sometime between the 1750 and 1770s might have imagined himself on a tour of and through all the tensions and desires of a tumultuous, many-faceted Europe, yearning for some calm. Of course when the viewer left the theater, he or she would, like Scipio waking up, be in the world of historical burdens and realities, of relentless tension between fortune and constancy. The same might be said of Metastasio's fate, since Maria Theresa's priorities in European power politics had unavoidable economic and cultural implications. The new alliance with France also took the usual political-familial form with the marriage of Louis XV's grandson (and Gluck's voice student, Marie Antoinette). (Louis XV's son died before ascending to the throne.) If Gluck's opera reform aimed to simplify, so too did political changes initiated in Vienna where rulers pushed toward establishing a single locus of power (themselves). All this had to have an effect on opera, which was, after all, a court concern. Maria Theresa took control of French and German theater in the capital, the Italian opera was closed for a period, and the Caesarean Poet could be found complaining (in private) during the Prusso-Austrian war that "Mars" rather than "Minerva" was being sustained in a "ruinous military system."[22]

When Maria Theresa died in 1780 her adult son had been sharing the Austrian throne with her (a woman could not be Holy Roman Emperor). A remarkable if increasing unstable time ensued, marked by accelerated political and cultural innovations and then retreat from them. "Such a rapid change in the general attitude," commented Tobias Philip von Gebler, a baron, member of the state council, and sometime playwright (for whom the young Mozart once wrote incidental music), "—even among common people who put many obscurantist members of higher classes to shame—is, so far as I know, unexampled."[23] Joseph II believed in the importance of theater for general enlightenment. Opera seria, which he disliked, was in eclipse in Vienna, and soon French theater was as well. Italian comic opera was hampered, its regular opera buffa troupe dismissed and then reestablished. Other stage forms came to the fore. The Burgtheater, established in 1741, became the German "National" Theater. "Singspiel," a "song-play" in German (a genre that seems to have had its beginnings in Leipzig) took on—temporarily—new importance with its combination of spoken dialogue and song (it would come to be regarded as a genre of opera). For a half decade beginning in 1778, it was the sole kind of musical theater played in the National Theater. In the meantime, Metastasio died in 1782 and Mozart had moved to Vienna, where he was one of many composers seeking to make a living by their talents. His next decade brought one remarkable opera after another. On its cusp his *Idomeneo*, an opera seria in Italian set in Crete, premiered in 1781 in Munich. In 1791, just months before his death, he would return to a Roman theme for an opera seria based on a Metastasio libretto. It premiered in Prague.

Chapter 14
FROM CRETE TO ROME

Mozart composed ten operas before *Idomeneo* was commissioned for Carnival in Munich by Karl Theodor, a prince-elector of the empire.* Scion of the Wittelsbach house, he moved for political reasons to Bavaria's capital in 1778 from Mannheim (where Mozart had visited) and his court was known for its musical richness and cosmopolitan orientation. With this came the influence of French styles.

Mozart paid considerable attention to France's musical world and spent half a year in Paris in 1778. It was a traumatic time for him—he suffered the death of his mother—but it was enriching in part because of ties to Baron Melchior Grimm. This eclectic German writer and music critic, a friend of Diderot and foe of Rousseau, played a vigorous role among enlightened French intellectuals and had been a figure in the *Querelle*. While Mozart was in Paris yet another musical ruckus broke out, this time between adherents of Gluck and those of Niccolò Piccini, the latter composer best known for his Neapolitan opera buffa. It seemed to be about who—one identified as cosmopolitan and the other Italian—could best set French texts. But as one scholar observes, it also seemed to be a controversy "without any underlying general theme." There was a lot of fury about sound but without much of a point. A student of Mozart recounted, however, that his teacher studied French operas for their "musical effects" rather than their melodies.[1] Mozart knew well the works of Gluck and appreciated syntheses of French and Italian styles.

Idomeneo did not derive from a Metastasio libretto but marked, as we know, a return once again of the influence of Fénelon's novel. Its themes had never really left the stage. Not too long before Mozart's opera Gluck had composed one (in 1765) about Telemachus and we have already mentioned that the Mozarts, traveling in France the following year, stopped at

---

*I refer to the opera itself by its Italian name, *Idomeneo*, which is how it is best known. I will refer to its title character as Idomeneus.

Fénelon's tomb in Cambrai. In late summer 1770 Wolfgang reported to his sister that he had reached the second part of *Telemachus*.[2] Munich's Carnival had featured *Telemaco*, an opera by Franz Paul Grua, the year before Mozart composed *Idomeneo*. A commission was offered to Mozart in summer 1780 and the libretto prepared by Giambattista Varesca, a Salzburg court cleric. It was based considerably on Danchet and Campra's *Idoménée*, although with some changes. Mozart incorporated lessons he had learned from Gluck, insisting on thinning out and simplifying the text for dramatic purposes; and music had to drive the drama. *Idomeneo* is more focused, straightforward, and flowing in its development than most opera seria.

Its concern, however, is the typical conflict between love and duty in a royal setting. The heir to Crete's throne, Prince Idamantes, waits anxiously for his father's return from Troy. He holds many enemy prisoners, among them Ilia, daughter of Troy's fallen King Priam. Much to her distress, she loves the prince and wonders: How can I feel this way about a Greek, this "barbarous enemy"? Does this not mean abandoning country, kin, and especially their call from the grave for vengeance?, she asks in an aria. Circumstances are complicated because she has a Greek competitor for Idamantes, none less than Electra of Argos, now also a refugee in the aftermath of the murder of her father, King Agamemnon. And Electra is furious at Idamantes—not only for "protecting the enemy" during King Idomeneus's absence but for deciding to set at liberty all the captives as a gesture of princely clemency and as an expression of his own feelings for Ilia. Only one prisoner is left, Idamantes tells Ilia, and that is the man enchained to her by her beauty—himself. Idamantes insists on rising above victory. The world will now see "our two glorious peoples bound by the ties of true friendship. Helen brought Asia and Greece to war, and now a new heroine . . . brings peace to Asia and Greece, together again."[3] Fénelon, amidst Louis XIV's wars, would have approved these sentiments and so would Metastasio's Caesar at Utica. Viewers in Munich in 1781 would likely have shared the approbation since bloody battles were fresh to them too. Yet another war of succession, a Bavarian one, had taken place in 1778–79 between the Habsburgs and a Prusso-Saxon coalition.

Fortune seems to spin rapidly in *Idomeneo*. First, news arrives that Crete's monarch drowned in a Mediterranean tempest. Then a pantomime shows this is not so. Idomeneus has been saved because he begged Neptune for deliverance and swore unwisely that his thanks to the Sea God would be to sacrifice the first person he encountered ashore. The myth takes its first decisive turn when it is his son whom he meets. Dismayed, he seeks a way out of his commitment and resolves to unite his son with Electra and send them to safety in Argos. But he discovers a terrible truth. He has always been a laudable king but no matter how goodly his reign, he too cannot defy hierarchy—here embodied in a deity. In a remarkable scene, Idomeneus announces to his people his intent to send his son abroad. "If you would learn how to rule," he tells Idamantes, "begin . . . by making yourself the champion of the downtrodden." As Idamantes, who accepts this as his duty, and Electra prepare to board the ship, the seas turn violent and a great monster emerges: "What anger and what hatred/ Neptune shows us!" sing the terrified Cretans. What have they done?[4] Idomeneus now sets a kingly example. He declares his culpability and calls to the god: Kill me, not an innocent. Yet this makes the situation more complex, for it implies Neptune is unjust. Idomeneus is now also a blasphemer. Torrents rage.

Must piety, allegiances, duties, and desires war among themselves? Idamantes provides an answer by demonstrating his mettle all while fright turns the Cretans toward rebellion. He announces that he will go off to slay the beast on behalf of his people—or die trying. The opera's last scenes take place in public space. Idomeneus's subjects will be present all around, as if offering a picture of the whole society in a great square before Neptune's statue. The Sea God's Priest insists with a New Testament echo that everything now depends on the king: "Render to Neptune what is his . . ." Idomeneus tells his people that he must slaughter his son, and they are duly horrified. But the Priest also protests, this time almost as if questioning the New Testament: "Heaven most clement!/ The son is innocent/the vow inhuman/ Stay the hand/ of a father so pious."[5]

Yet Fortune turns again, for Idamantes has killed the beast. He reenters, robed in white, ready now to be sacrificed. Everything in the opera shows how this young man rises to regal stature. He is clement; he is brave; he is pious and prepared to forfeit himself for the greater good. When Idomeneus falters, Idamantes urges him to strike. "Remember your duty. Though you lose a son, you gain a thousand gods as friends. Your people are now your sons."[6] He calls upon his father to regard Ilia, the foreign princess, as his own daughter.

It is Ilia's turn to show nobility. She demands to be the sacrifice since Idamantes is "the hope of the kingdom." She protests that the gods cannot be such "tyrants." To think so must be to misinterpret divine will. While she may now be Greece's friend, she goes on, she is "by nature" its foe since she is still Priam's daughter.[7] The deity proves just in Mozart and Varesco's ending. Neptune's statue quakes and a deep voice announces: "Idomeneus shall no longer be king. Idamantes shall reign and Ilia be his bride."[8] With this, the divinity will be appeased but Electra is bitter; she, unlike Ilia, is unable to rise above herself. Her side conquered at war yet she cannot accept love between a Trojan and a Greek and prefers to go "into the deep abyss."[9] For everyone else fortune and fortitude mesh. Idomeneus commands— these are his last as Cretan king—fidelity to the gods, obedience to his son as the new sovereign, and peace.

II.

Joseph II died in winter 1790. His successor, Leopold II, who had been an astute reformer as Grand Duke of Tuscany, moved quickly to calm commotions left by his brother. Sympathetic to French Enlighteners, interested considerably by the American revolution, he promoted a liberal legal code for Tuscany and he spoke once of enacting a constitution with representative government. (Joseph II blocked this.) Now he announced publicly to rebels against the Habsburgs in the Netherlands that "a hereditary sovereign is only a delegate and employee of the people . . ." The sovereign and the People, he explained, had to have a "fundamental law or contract" that limited the rulers' powers. A ruler's abuse of power meant that "the people are no longer obliged to obey him." Moreover, the Estates had to endorse the sovereign's laws.[10] These sentiments were closer to those of Fénelon than to Joseph II's absolutism. Nonetheless, Leopold II revoked some of his brother's strictures in order to stabilize the realm and brought closure to a war with the Ottomans. His clemency toward the "rebellious Netherlands" earned him the title of "the German Titus."[11] In Tuscany Leopold had already been associated with this Roman emperor whose short reign was identified with building projects, magnanimity, and peacefulness. Titus's image did not correspond entirely to the historical record. Before becoming Rome's emperor he had been responsible for completing the brutal repression begun by Vespasion, his father, of revolt in Judea against Rome. His political controls in Rome included a practice well known to the Habsburgs—extensive networks of informers.

Leopold II sought to enhance his rule's beginnings with opulent coronations. He overturned many of his brother's musical policies, restoring eminence to both church music and opera seria. And so when it came to his crowning in September 1791 as King of Bohemia, the local estates decided that opera seria would be among the entertainments. Metastasio's *Tito* was still well known and a prominent playwright, Giovanni de Gamera, had recently written an essay acclaiming it as the kind of work that made theater "a means" by which a sovereign could "inculcate in his subjects the most useful and important beliefs."[12] A decision was taken to ask a "celebrated master" to create new work or to reset *Tito*.

After an unsuccessful approach to Antonio Salieri, Vienna's imperial *Kapellmeister* (court musical director), the commission was given to Mozart. He wrote his music rapidly in summer 1791; scholars believe that some of the recitative may be by his student, Franz Xaver Süssmayr.[13] The original 1734 setting by Caldara had hewed faithfully to Metastasio's words but the libretto was often altered for (its many) later renditions set by other composers. Caterino Mazzolà, briefly Vienna's court poet and formerly the same in Dresden, was given responsibility for revising the text for Mozart. The composer pressed him for a work that was leaner than the original. Mozart had not composed opera seria since *Idomeneo* eleven years earlier and his dramatic sense, which had become more and more sure, played an essential role as Metastasio's three acts became two and arias were removed. There were few ensembles in Metastasio's original but Mozart added "action ensembles" that advanced stage events. By contrast, the few ensembles in *Idomeneo*, however potent, mostly commented on or conveyed events.[14] *Idomeneo* was conventional enough as opera seria, alternating recitatives and arias. Yet a notable aspect of its arias was their kinship to a particular structure of instrumental music for which Mozart is given particular credit: organizing arias in sonata form.[15] In simplified outline—and in terminology that was not deployed until later—it may be compared to an argument in music: an "exposition" presents musical ideas that then "develop" and are finally "recapitulated."

Tito, which reinterprets history liberally, was written at a time when ensembles of people, often masses of them, had taken historical action, often in the streets and particularly in Paris. Europe seemed consumed by social and political argument. The eminent audience that saw *Tito* in Prague was not enthralled by it but not for political reasons. One viewer, Count Johann Zinzendorf, a high Viennese official, found it "most boring." He reported hearing the empress say that "almost all of us went to sleep." Leopold II did not like it either. *Tito* did, however, garner increasing esteem as its performances continued into the next month.[16] Stendhal, in mischievous praise, years later called *Idomeneo* and *Tito* the first great opera seria. [17] (In fact, the genre's era was almost over.)

<h1 style="text-align:center">III.</h1>

What marks out a good ruler? What ought he to learn on the throne? We have encountered these questions posed over and again in opera history, sometimes in thought-provoking ways, often in the form of propaganda. Scipio met his ancestors and decided to take up his this-worldly duties. Idamantes demonstrated kingly qualities and supplanted his father. *Tito* presents a ruler whose capacity to judge grows all while his disposition is constant. When he first appears in front of the Capitol it is to decline tributes to him. He prefers that gold booty due to adorn a sanctuary honoring him be used instead to relieve poverty-stricken survivors of the eruption of Mount Vesuvius.

His character is much like Metastasio's Julius Caesar. He does not identify the public good with his desires and, however tested by betrayal, he rises above whatever menaces him. And as Caesar was threatened in *Catone* by Emilia's plan, Titus faces attempted assassination instigated by Vitellia, daughter of an emperor ousted by Titus's father. She rages: my rights are usurped. Moreover, Berenice, a "barbarian" princess from Judea, had displaced her in Titus's heart. Personal and political are intertwined in Vitellia. And so she plots to exploit for murderous aims the infatuations of Sextus, a young patrician and friend of Titus, who loves her. But Sextus, unlike Fulvio, grows only after he is discovered and arrested. Early on, when Vitellia confronts him with the classic choice between passion and duty, he tells her, despite a bad conscience, to command him as she pleases. Still the two sing of a "thousand emotions" fighting within them.[18]

Titus is Sextus's opposite. He "commands the world and himself," says Annius, a close companion of Sextus.[19] The "hero"—in fact the head of state—in Titus, he asserts, conquered "the lover" in Titus when he sent away Berenice. A Roman emperor must have a Roman wife. Even though we never see Berenice, we learn that she understood political reality and accepted her fate. She is *Tito*'s Ilia; Vitellia is its Electra when it comes to an inability to accept a good greater than herself. And Vitellia contrasts to Servillia, Sextus's sister. Titus now chooses her to be his empress and Servillia, faced with that wrenching operatic dilemma—her love for Annius versus her duty to her emperor—restrains her passions and acts with integrity. She tells Titus that she will marry him since he is her sovereign but confesses that her heart belongs to another. Titus discovers greatness in this admission; she, like him, is willing to subordinate personal happiness to duty. Were all Romans like her, he sings, ruling would be no burden. Only ignoble sentiments could lead him to force marriage upon her. His empress, he decides, will be Vitellia.

Vitellia, not knowing of this turn, has already set her deadly intrigue in motion. The finale of Act 1, one of Mozart's greatest theatrical accomplishments, brings entwined characters, events, and stakes into keen focus. "Nowhere in eighteenth century music," comments one scholar, "has political turmoil been more vividly evoked. . . ."[20] It is anticipated, however, in *Idomeneo*'s conclusion when Cretans erupt in confusion in the face of a storm only to find resolution in divine clemency and a sovereign's surrender of his crown. In *Tito*, the people celebrate their godly emperor only to turn turbulent when the attempt is made on his life and the Capitol set afire. An ensemble knits everything together. It evolves as a quintet interacting with a chorus. First, self-accusing Sextus sings of his grief, culpability, and inner conflict. Then Annius enters to query his friend and hears Sextus announce his own doom. Servillia arrives to make it known that a suspicious fire has led to uproar at the Capitol. In the distance—offstage—the Roman People is heard in choral—collective—cries. Their "*Ah*'s" punctuate the scene in growing crescendo. Publius, head of the Praetorian Guard, comes now to alert all that a malignant conspiracy in action. "*Ah!*," calls the chorus. Servilia, Annius, and Publius sing of their horror. ("*Ah!*") Vitellia appears, first desperate because she has learned of Titus's choice, then shocked to discover that the attack she initiated was carried out. The five sing of screams they hear; their voices intersperse, backed by the chorus, which seems more and more present.

Believing Titus dead, the five mourn, but each with distinct motivation—even though the entire company joins them finally in unison: "Black betrayal/ Oh day of sorrow."[21] Grief advances *andante* and builds as a sense of political commotion intensifies. It is generated musically by combinations and exchanges among single voices, the chorus, and the orchestra; these are colored by syncopation, tonal variations, and shifting musical dynamics.[22] Political reality is shown musically, as Monteverdi did in *Ulysses* when voices of his characters come together or overlap, depending on their roles in unfolding conflicts and how they signify different social orders. In *Tito*, figures sing together and then come apart depending on their nobility of character and where they stand in the events. Sevillia, Annius, and Publius sing together at first, sounding a link of perceptions and places. They don't know the traitor's identity and are simply horrified. When Vitellia's voice enters, it is also in horror but for selfish reasons. When Sextus arrives to tell her that the deed is done, they exchange words in recitative; song-speech distinguishes them from the others. She will urge flight. Annius urges him to yield himself to Titus's mercy. Sextus will be seized for trial.

This portrays crisis in Rome's ruling class (and among its minions). The collective People, however, never responds with any revolutionary fervor or aspiration. Of course, this would be out of place at an opera presented to an emperor—especially since there was uproar in French streets just that summer. But while the People is not at stage center of *Tito*, it is always there. If bad monarchs may one day bring furor forth, it will not be here, not at this time in the age of Titus. But is it his age? Or is it the age of Leopold II? Or of his sister, Marie Antoinette and her husband? Perhaps *Tito* provides a warning, intended or not, in "*Ahs!*" by observers—but not hushed ones—of power. These "*Ahs!*" stress bonds between a good monarch and his People—bonds every ruler would insist exist (and would certainly like all subjects to deem are there). The People had lost confidence in Louis XVI by the time of *Tito's* premiere. Only part of the aristocracy loses control of itself for ignoble purposes in the opera. And as character after character comes on stage, moving the first act to its conclusion, the chorus reacts over and over with its "*Ah*"s. Though not at all the voice of plebeians rising in insurrection, their sound intensifies in impact. And they cheer when they learn in the second act that the assassin struck the wrong man. It is relief for the opera's cast but hardly for history. Metastasio placed little emphasis on the chorus in his operas; in Mozart's *Tito* of 1791 it cannot be missed.

IV.

A ruler has been presented, his character depicted. His aching understanding of power's burdens is articulated together with his devotion to Rome's welfare. Yet the immediate consequences are an attempt on his life and all those exclamations. So in the second act it is his judgment under duress that must be shown. What Metastasio, Mozart, and Mazzolà give us is actually the model of an anti-Machiavellian emperor. In fact, it is difficult to imagine the Titus of this opera surviving long in the Italian or European worlds of the sixteenth, seventeenth and eighteenth centuries—in a modern state, that is. He is shocked at Sextus's guilt, confounded by the contradiction between the appearance of deep friendship and fickle behavior in reality. Pub-

Some Time Markers: Roman History and Opera

ROMAN HISTORICAL FIGURE	WORK
Scipio Aemilianus (185–129 BCE), general and politician	*Il sogno di Scipione* (Scipio's Dream) 1735: Mestastasio libretto 1772: Mozart's version
Cato (95–46 BCE), republican senator defeated with remnants of the Roman Republic by Julius Caesar, 46 BCE	1728: *Catone in Utica* (Cato in Utica) Libretto: Metastasio Music: Leonardo Vinci
Nero (37–68 CE), emperor, 54–68 CE, last of the Julio-Claudian dynasty (founded by Augustus)	1643: *L'incoronazione di Poppea* (The Coronation of Poppea) Libretto: Gian Francesco Busenello Music: Claudio Monteverdi
Titus (39–81 CE), emperor, 79–81 CE	*La clemenza di Tito* 1734: Metastasio libretto 1791: Mozart's version

lius acts the emperor's counselor—the Machiavellian kind—and summarizes his sovereign's circumstances when he tells him, "My lord, not everyone has the heart of a Titus."[23] After all, a man who has never been treacherous expects everyone to be faithful. Still, all that Publius perceives to be power's imperatives weighs heavily on Titus. Later, agonizing about the prospect of Sextus's execution, Titus says words in accompanied recitative that are again like those of Metastasio's Caesar, words that Rousseau might have commended and which we have also heard expressed in Monteverdi's *Arianna* and *Ritorno:*

How unhappy is the lot of those who rule! We are denied what is given to the lowly. In the midst of the forest any poor peasant, his scabby body clad in coarse wool, his squalid hut a shaky shelter from the ravages of the heavens, sleeps soundly and peacefully, and passes his days without fear. He has few desires, knows who loves and who hates him. In company or alone, he walks in safety to his forest or his mountain, and sees each man's heart mirrored in his face. We, amid all this splendor, live in uncertainty. In our presence, hope or fear changes a man's face.[24]

Titus decides that Sextus's judge will be his "prince not his friend."[25] It is not a decision that Nero could imagine, but then he could not imagine reason of state or reasons of friendship.

An exchange ensues between Titus and Sextus that is as compelling as that between Caesar and Cato and that between Seneca and Nero. It was left by Mazzolà as Metastasio wrote it, but its motif is found throughout Mozart's stage works: the value of friendship and the conflicts that arise from it. Here it is a conflict between friendship and rulership. Titus asks: How did your prince offend you that you would seek his death? Sextus, consumed by guilt (but protecting Vitellia) abases himself and asks stubbornly only for his own end. Titus does not allow this, at least not at first. He changes roles. "We are alone. Your sovereign is not present. Open your heart . . . confide in your friend. I promise you the Emperor will not know of it . . . Let us, together, find a way to pardon you."[26]

Titus sounds as if he is wrestling with principles found in Cicero's celebrated dialogue on the nature of friendship, which stresses that true friendship must be among good and virtuous people. At one point in it, Cicero's chief interlocutor, Laelius, declares that one law of friendship is never to ask of a friend to do ill to the republic.[27] Of course, Titus is head of an empire, but the point is the same. And we also read in Cicero that "Those of higher rank who are bound by friendship . . . should make themselves equal to their inferiors. . . ."[28] The problem is evident; it emerges with acuity once Titus tries to separate his public from his private person in hope of saving his friend, who has become a man of constancy. Finally, rising above his past self, he has become faithful to a feckless love and also to his status as treacherous villain who betrayed both his friend and his sovereign. However tormented, he accepts execution as his due and has become virtuous in his own way—a way different from the virtue of clemency. Titus perceives Sextus's agony but also that he as emperor must now reappear as sovereign. Titus as friend has been—and is—frustrated. Seeing no other possibility, he must return to his political role. The emperor orders the prisoner to the Coliseum where wild animals wait to rip at him. Titus, like Seneca and Caesar before him, has failed to persuade—a curiously repetitive feature in the politics of a stage genre so preoccupied by Orpheus and influenced by ideas of rhetoric. He prepares to follow harsher, if inevitable, obligations. Yet once Sextus has been taken away, and before the emperor fixes his name to the condemnation, he debates with himself. He considers how desire for vengeance welled up in him—the personal intruded on the political—when Sextus rejected his outstretched hand. Metastasio's voice comes through an argument—in recitative, of course, since it is a serious matter—in Titus's mind about Machiavellian principles:

This vengeance—why, it is always a base sentiment, Titus thinks at first. He resolves to let his onetime friend live.

But no: blood was shed and the law, of which an emperor is custodian, was broken. The libretto thus assumes that the state is an entity distinct from its ruler (a sign of modernity). He must sign the sentence.

Then he wonders: what will posterity say? That some rulers weary of cruelty but Titus wearied of clemency? He resolves that his clemency will be constant and tears up the execution order. "If the world wishes to accuse me of mistakes, let it accuse me of mercy not severity."[29] The emperor, believing compassion is a key characteristic for a ruler, has now tilted away from the claim put in Laelius's words by the republican Cicero. But at the same time, like Cicero, Titus wants justice to be aligned with the law.[30]

Yet when Publius—a bass to Titus's tenor—comes to query of Sextus's fate, he is told that the man will go to the arena. Publius takes this to mean Sextus will die and he sighs, "Oh, poor soul!"[31] It is a remarkable exclamation because it is ambiguous: is this "poor soul" Sextus, soon to be mangled? Or is it Titus, the poor soul who has had to choose between killing a friend-turned-traitor and granting leniency to his would-be assassin—which means endangering his own rule by the appearance of weakness? Titus sings to the gods: if such a severe heart is needed to rule, take the kingdom from me. Or give to me another heart. He does not want to stand above cowering people.

The final scene takes place in the famed open amphitheater that Titus himself built. Here Romans await those who will die. A symmetry in staging characterizes the two acts of this opera. Both begin in private quarters and end in public spaces. The first begins in Vitellia's apartments where she conspires with Sextus. The second begins at an imperial retreat where, again, two people confer—Annius and Sextus, but after the plot's failure. Act I's culmination is before the Capitol, with the quintet and the invisible People in chorus. Rome's fate is a question mark. Act II closes at the Coliseum. The People and all the characters are there as all questions resolve.

Openings present issues, circumstances, predicaments; finales provide emotional, focused, and searing responses to them. There is an important difference between the ends of Act I and II: the closing ensemble in the latter becomes a sextet instead of a quintet because an additional—essential—person, Titus, is now part of it. The chorus is there but of course the emperor's voice issues the last word. Before then, however, events take one last twist. Vitellia is moved finally by Sextus's devotion to her—that is, she is moved by something other than her own furies—and she finally rises above herself. She throws herself at Titus's feet and admits her "evil" ways.

"What kind of day is this?" the emperor asks, "At the very moment I pardon one criminal, I discover another. When, just gods, shall I find a loyal soul?"[32] In fact, he has found one already in Servilla. And two other souls, Vitellia and Sextus, have now become newly loyal before his eyes. They are not like Drusilla and Otto who, in *Poppea*, try to safeguard one another by declaring personal culpability. It is true that they even manage to move Nero. His clemency, however, is more limited. He still serves his own purposes, which always confound personal with political aims, when ordering banishment instead of execution. Drusilla and Otto's willingness to sacrifice themselves is, in any event, not for Nero's sake (and he is, after all, a man incapable of friendship). Unlike the animating cynicism of *Poppea*, with its culmination in loving voices of emperor and new empress while everyone else is in ruin, the title character of *Tito* elevates himself again and again through to the finale. He articulates the inner turmoils of a ruler. He decides that his mercy will trump Fortune, which always seems to conspire against him. His spirit seems to conjure advice that might be found in *The Prince*, and then he rebels against it. Machiavelli proposed that a prince needs to know when to be and when not to be cruel, when to lie and when to be truthful, when to be faithful and when to break faith. Like Machiavelli, Titus imagines that Fortune battles Virtù, but this (pagan) emperor's virtue is Christianized by the eighteenth century and he struggles between patriotic constancy (like Scipio) and constant clemency. It is almost as if the historical Titus had read his own historical contemporary, Tacitus, and sought by his behavior to refute him. *Tito*, in this sense, rebuts *Poppea* by its model of a Holy—Christian—Roman Empire.

Titus ends the opera by hailing repentance over loyalty to self. He pardons all. Tacitus could have written the finale of *Tito* only through ironic spectacles and probably with a smirk. While the quintet and chorus praise Titus, the emperor sings, "Eternal Gods, think to cut short,/ Cut short my life and all my efforts/ On that day the good of Rome/ Is not my duty, strong and steadfast."[33] Now it is a sextet; he stands above and within it, incarnating the ideology—and illusions—of an old regime.

Contests between history and constancy, like between change and stability, are unpredictable. The Titus of history was dead after two years as emperor. Leopold II would be dead within two years of Mozart's opera about Titus. The emperor's brother-in-law and sister, France's royals, were guillotined the following year by revolutionaries who identified with the ancient Roman republic. Napoleon Bonaparte brought the French republic to an end when he became France's emperor and in 1806 his armies put the finish to that vestige of feudalism, the Holy Roman Empire.

And Mozart was dead within three months of the premiere of *Tito*. Overlapping his work on it would be the composition of *The Magic Flute*, which hailed a realm of Enlightenment in opposition to forces of darkness. In the meanwhile, French turmoil continued. And between those two kings, *Idomeneo* and *Tito*, Mozart composed works that showed, expressed and questioned realities and values that both sustained and rattled an old world's pillars.

PART 5:
". . . AND ALTHOUGH I AM
NO COUNT . . ."

---

*Generally speaking . . . the "impossible" has to be
justified on grounds either of poetic effect, or of
an attempt to improve on reality, or of accepted
tradition. As far as poetic effect is concerned, a
convincing impossibility is preferable to an
unconvincing possibility.*

—ARISTOTLE

Chapter 15

MASTERS AND SERVANTS

In March 1781, soon after Idamantes came to power in Mozart's Crete, the twenty-five-year-old composer went to Vienna, then a city of approximately 200,000. He was called there by his principal employer, Salzburg's prince-archbishop, and a famous clash soon took place between Mozart and Colloredo's chamberlain, Graf Joseph Arco. Its immediate cause was Mozart's desire to quit his past responsibilities and devote himself to a musical career in the imperial capital. There was a convergence between developments in Mozart's life and changes in the political world around him.

Mozart had difficulties with authority. Biographers and analysts recount the complicated nature of his familial relations, especially with his father. Leopold Mozart had come to Salzburg as a young man thirteen years before Wolfgang's birth. He was supposed to study theology but focused his attention on jurisprudence and logic before deciding to devote himself to music. This strong-headed man recognized his son's uncommon talents and sought to define every facet of young Wolfgang's life and that of his sister Nannerl. Their home, remarks an influential biographer, was like "a miniature authoritarian society whose benevolent leader made every decision, organized all enterprises, and took complete responsibility."[1] This despotism was not simple or narrow-minded. Leopold Mozart harbored Enlightenment sympathies that would also appeal to his son. Clerics left Leopold Mozart sour, even though he was attached to the church. A disdainful view of aristocrats can be teased out of allusions and a mix of metaphors in his *Treatise on the Violin*. A polished appearance can be deceptive, Leopold Mozart warned in it. No shimmer could define an instrument or its player; to think otherwise is to be taken in by the "universal deception" of "external show," akin to valuing "a bird for its feathers." An attractive "lion's head" on the instrument's scroll improved its tone "as little as a fancy curled wig can improve the intelligence of its living wig stand."[2]

Emperor Joseph II would have concurred in his own context. There were, he thought, an overabundance of curled wigs on living stands in his realm. Many Mozart scholars note that when Wolfgang determined to leave Salzburg for Vienna, he was in effect exchanging the household of one enlightened despot for the capital of another. An imperial metropolis, however, probably seemed to him the less constricting of the two. Joseph II shared power with his once reform-minded but increasingly reactionary mother, Maria Theresa, for fifteen years. Her death in late 1780 allowed him to be a "Philosopher on the Throne," as he was later often called (even though he was hardly a philosopher).

The initiation of Josephine reforms piqued many social elites, but was surely appreciated by young Mozart. He was confident of his talents and would always be filled with resentments at his treatment by Salzburg's prince-archbishop and his minions. These did not translate into hostility toward rulers in principle and especially not toward Joseph II. They did become a robust, often-expressed aversion to unmerited privilege. "It is the heart that ennobles a man," he wrote to his father in June 1781, "and though I am no count, yet I have probably more honor in me than many a count." Alas, everyone seemed to recognize his accomplishments except his own superiors. He was treated poorly in Salzburg, he thought, and paid badly. He was like a servant there. In fact, his circumstances were not very different from those of most court musicians but he, after all, had been a renowned child prodigy and had traveled across Europe to perform for and receive laudations from royalty and dignitaries. Colloredo's concerns were not those of a musician; Mozart's were not those of a governor. Salzburg's finances were strained and the prince-archbishop wanted to revamp them along with the city's educational system. Budgetary considerations meant reductions in cultural expenditures. For Mozart these were simply acts against music. He expressed unhappiness incautiously and was cavalier about his responsibilities. He gave the impression—an accurate one—that Salzburg was not a priority.[3] The absence of a theater there and his ambition to compose operas added to his chagrin.

Vexation translated into animosity toward what he perceived to be arbitrary power. His letters complain constantly of Colloredo's "injustice" and he finally asserted his "undeniable right" to quit. Mozart's letters leave the impression of an innocent artist mistreated by an *ancien régime*. While Europe's old regimes were indeed abusive, the young genius was also bullheaded. Colloredo kept busts of Voltaire and Rousseau in his chambers, and was reform-minded, albeit often obtuse. Mozart, for his part, seems to have been proud of his own insolence. He recounted how Colloredo once berated him, declaring he would no longer have anything to do with the impertinent musician. Replied Mozart: "Nor I with you."[4]

This was not long before his famous confrontation with Arco. Mozart's description of it is not entirely fair, as numerous scholars note. The Graf had actually had sympathy for the Mozarts and cautioned Wolfgang that popularity in Vienna might be fleeting. Yet Arco finally ran out of patience with the quarrelsome composer and evicted him from his rooms with what Mozart described as "a kick on the arse."[5] On learning of the incident, worried Leopold dissuaded his son from rushing to return the humiliation. Wolfgang took no physical action but his contempt remained. "I care very little for Salzburg and not at all for the Archbishop," he wrote later, adding, "I shit on both of them."[6] Instead of a vulgar act, his disrespect for counts would resound in *The Marriage of Figaro*. In it a master—a count—will end up dancing to the tune of servants.

It was not only a matter of a personal incident. Mozart had gained a certain social acuity. The summer after suffering Arco's boot, he recounted in a letter a "shocking" story circulating in Vienna. One Herr von Wiedmer, a noble whom Mozart knew, had gone to Innsbruck with the theater company he had founded. On a Sunday stroll he found himself followed by some disagreeable gentlemen uttering epithets. A "Baron Buffa"—the name seems contrived—blustered out loud that von Wiedmer was an "idiot" who "ought to teach his dancer to walk before he lets her go on stage." When von Wiedmer looked back at the bully, "Buffa" demanded to know why he was being scrutinized. Von Wiedmer responded in good spirit, "Why, you are looking at me as well. The street is free, *anyone can look around if he pleases.*" This led to more taunts and a "box on the ear." The injured party struck back, going promptly to see the local governor, also a count, at his home, in order to complain. He was, however, arrested promptly by soldiers. Twenty-five lashes followed "on his behind." Wounded von Wiedmer protested: "I am a nobleman and I will not submit to be beaten when I am innocent. I would rather enlist as a soldier in order to have my revenge."

Mozart's commentary on these events is evocative. In Innsbruck, he observed, there is a "stupid Tyrolese custom . . . that no one may hit a nobleman, no matter what right he may have to do so." His point was not simply that it ought to have been possible strike someone of high rank. Even if von Wiedmer, who was a noble like his abuser, was wronged, his protest was not quite right. Why should an innocent noble be untouchable but not an innocent valet? The mistreatment is arbitrary whether of a man of rank, a soldier, a valet, or a dancer. Or a musician. While Mozart wanted to return Count Arco's kick, the implication is that a wrong ought to be righted properly, not vengefully or according to rank. It seems that after von Wiedmer's humiliations, he was taken to jail and, still affirming innocence, given fifty more strokes by a sneering corporal.

The angry victim planned to complain to the emperor himself but news of his calvary reached Vienna before he did. Instructions were sent by Joseph II to Innsbruck that nobody of any rank could be punished without his own approval. This impressed Mozart, although he did wonder if von Wiedmer ought to be compensated. And perhaps that rotten local governor should receive fifty lashes. Perhaps von Wiedmer should run a sword "through his heart." Wolfgang noted that the victim had refused an offer of money to keep quiet about the incident. Indeed, von Wiedmer became something of a hero as "the people of Innsbruck" began to call him the man "who was scourged for us and who will redeem us." In fact, the abusive troops were guarding the Innsbruck governor's house because this Herod-like figure—Mozart probably associated him with Colloredo—was widely disliked by those whom he ruled. It was von Wiedmer's misfortune to come upon his armed pack expecting fair treatment.[7] In the imperial capital, however, the emperor understood injustice.

Mozart's letter paints a whole society and makes connections about the workings of the reality in which he lives. There is an arrogant nobility, filled with socially advantaged scoundrels. There are smug, local potentates of no merit but sustained by force. There are common people who, in their helplessness, hope an innocent's suffering might save them, even if von Wiedmer was hardly a Christ. There was, finally, the high authority who knew to administer justice fairly. Suggested too, perhaps intentionally, is that there ought to be a free public domain, "the street" to which von Wiedmer referred.

But enlightened absolutism and freedom in the streets are not the same thing. "The emperor has been seen as a revolutionary," writes his foremost biographer, but "from above." He never intended to give the People "a role in politics."[8] Mozart, though viewing himself as a kind of spiritual aristocrat and quite fixated on respect for his own honor, identified with the emperor's disdain for wealthy wastrels with titles. The contrast between a judicious ruler—or a ruler who becomes sagacious—and self-absorbed nobles recurs in one form or another in his operas. Mozart's disdain also suited well Joseph II's goal: a more rational regime. It would have to be achieved at the expense of and with resistance by entrenched strata.

II.

A perspicacious *Sketch of Vienna* was written in 1786. It was overwhelmingly admiring, although with some hints of worry, since by this time an uneasy Joseph II had begun to step back from his own liberalism. Many of his sympathizers hoped that retreat was only temporary. In his tableau, Johann Pezzl, a member of the Free Mason Lodge that Mozart joined, remarked that "anyone who wants to enlighten a whole nation or a wide public must take two major steps: the first is to rid oneself of old, unworthy and damaging prejudices; the other is to accept truths and principles which are new and beneficial to him and which encourage his spirit to self-understanding and reflection and which accustom him to distinguishing appearance from reality, nonessentials from essentials." He left out an inevitable, complicating factor. A liberalizing absolutist must almost by definition unleash paradoxical and unexpected forces. Joseph II encouraged the development of commerce, reformed education and law. He built hospitals, and abolished the death penalty, all while administrative centralization and Germanification provoked resentment among non-German subjects. At the same time the emperor opposed narrow-mindedness in religious matters—confession had been compulsory while Maria Theresa lived—and in public conversation. Toleration Edicts in 1781 and 1782 relieved Protestants and Greek Orthodox of legal restrictions and eased the circumstances of Masons and Jews. The reforms rested, wrote Pezzl, on a laudable principle: good citizenship (or subjecthood) ought not to depend on adherence to this or that rite. It was "wrong to try to impose ideas on someone who cannot be convinced of their correctness."[9]

Relaxed censorship brought forth an energetic press and foreign newspapers were readily available as well. Mozart had already encountered and found congenial enlightened ideas, in both French and German variants. His life was contemporaneous with what was arguably their brightest moment. In Vienna, *Aufklärung* (Enlightenment) brought openness. Anyone could arrive in the brimming cosmopolitan hub, wrote Pezzl, and assimilate into it, whether a soldier, a businessman, a philosopher, a churchman, or an artist seeking "to lead an independent life." The variety of dress in the streets—German, Hungarian, Armenian, Polish, Jewish, Moldavian, Muslim, Greek—came with an "endless Babel of tongues." Due to this mix, "pure native blood" was rare. The population divided between those who lived within the walls of the old town (about 52,000 people) and those in suburbs. Hospitality was, however, taxed by "some malicious foreigners" who came to take advantage of economic opportunities. Differences of class and status also produced tensions.[10]

The church and the established aristocracy, each for its own reasons, felt threatened by Josephine reforms. The former's privileges were limited by them and restrictions on church music came as well. Nonetheless, tolerance was hardly complete. Non-Catholics still had to tip their hats at Catholic processions. Rome, however, was irritated persistently by Joseph II, and not least because of his use of Masons to counterbalance clerics and more reactionary aristocrats. He also took actions against monasteries and their possessions. The emperor's strongest supporters comprised a small, prominent group of "the Enlightened"—*"Aufklärer"*—who shared his reason-oriented outlook.[11] These included high figures in the administration but also active secretive societies such as the Free Masons, which had originated as a fraternal "craft" (as they styled themselves) among medieval and early modern stonemasons, particularly in England. Their associations aimed to further members' interests and cultural needs but in the eighteenth century had expanded ranks beyond men in building trades, metamorphosing into fraternities imbued with a virtually mystical rationalism. Among the "Enlightened" in Vienna were also more radical and strongly anticlerical freethinkers called the Illuminati ("Enlightened Ones"), who had first emerged in Bavaria. Masons insisted that their members— "brothers"—had to believe that the cosmos had a supreme "architect" and be "free born." Women, bonded servants, and slaves were long excluded from their ranks (although the place of women was an issue in Mozart's day). While their lodges maintained a hierarchy within, they insisted that all were equals, regardless of social status, origins, or religious affiliation. Austria's leading *Aufklärer*, Joseph von Sonnenfels was a principal figure in "True Harmony," the most influential, secular, and radical Masonic lodge in Vienna. This proponent of the arts—but forceful advocate of their educational and utilitarianism purposes—came from a family of converts to Catholicism. His grandfather had been chief rabbi of Brandenburg. Mozart joined the "Beneficence" lodge in late 1784 but already had personal ties to Masons and to Illuminati when he was in Munich and earlier.[12]

Pezzl's acerbic treatment of the older aristocracy accorded to both Mozart's and the emperor's sentiments. These counts and barons, many in financial straits, showed themselves off at important events while doing little of consequence. The founts of their honors and privileges were "old parchments and new clothes."[13] Joseph II encouraged social fluidity and the development of a well-to-do bureaucracy along with a professional stratum which bought titles. This newer "second rank," wrote Pezzl, embraced "many different classes of the public and [was] pluralistic in outlook." It was even open "to honorable but non-titled sons of the earth."[14] Distinct middle strata emerged—they nestled advocates of *Aufklärung*, and Masonry—and Mozart found in them proponents and friends. He attained the highest grade in his lodge and composed music for it. He may have been a member of the Illuminati.

Social change also brought a new focus on lower strata. High-ranking women, Pezzl observed, often confided secrets of "fashionable" Vienna to their female servants, providing the latter extensive knowledge of its workings. Many of these servants were also exposed to Enlightenment ideas, making them unlikely sympathizers without too much deference. Chambermaids in the "Great Houses" had a reputation for flirtatiousness and Viennese, over all, were "very sensual."[15] Uppity servants getting the better of their "betters" could hardly be protagonists for opera seria. Metastasio's reign was, however, already a thing of the past and the mounting popularity of works like Pergolesi's *La serva padrona* made them acceptable as *intermezzi*. Humorous stage works, both plays and operas, were well established in Italy by the mid-eighteenth century. While opera buffa's principal progenitors (like those of opera seria) came from south of the empire, especially from Naples, its orientation was obviously different. It became what a scholar calls a "counter-genre" to opera seria in Italy and in Vienna too, where it was part of theatrical life by the 1770s and also contrasted to Gluck's reform operas.[16]

A theatrical reform had taken place in Italy with important implications for opera. Carlo Goldoni, a Venetian playwright and librettist, onetime lawyer and ofttimes adventurer, had challenged *Commedia dell'arte*, the peninsula's foremost comic medium. This improvisational theater of gags had stock characters in masks—a pompous doctor, a clever, old merchant and servants, one usually buoyant and the other shrewd and opportunist. Actors worked with little more than a scenario depicting common travails of (unmasked) lovers who overcame obstacles to their passion. Goldoni, by contrast, wrote comic plays. The dialogue was set down on paper and consequently the story presented and its pace crafted and more controlled. Everyday Venetian types appeared in place of masked figures and humorous character development displaced stylized ad lib. Goldoni would write buffa librettos as well as plays and opera seria librettos. He often satirized middle-class aspirants to aristocratic lifestyles but didn't target directly the upper strata because, he noted dryly, "the noble and the wealthy are

entitled by their rank and fortunes to outdo the others."[17] Goldoni's comedies didn't look at the world from the top down and were often populated
by young common women beset by older men or maidservants tussling
with desire-filled masters. Opera buffa stirred with everyday life, passions
and foibles, licit and illicit, acted out by the kind of figures most viewers
might encounter off stage. It entertained the Viennese but also provided
a theatrical gloss on society and could suggest social and political change
and conflict. Maria Theresa had urged her police to pay special attention
to violations of the Sixth Commandment, but adultery and love were topics
of public discussion during Joseph II's reign and featured prominently in
press debates about chambermaids in 1781.[18] Pezzl claimed that romantic love and marriage retained popularity mostly in the lower and middle
classes and among servants.[19] This atmosphere is discernable in the three
operas Mozart composed to Lorenzo Da Ponte librettos: in *The Marriage
of Figaro* an abusive count asserts a feudal "right" to have his way with a
female servant on the eve of her matrimony; in *Don Giovanni*, a swaggering
aristocrat preys on women of all classes, carefree about consequences; and
in *Così fan tutte*, two sets of lovers find that their affections are not as absolute as they imagined (a learning process mediated by a philosopher and
clever servant girl).

A key feature of these works was again the elusive relation between appearance and reality. Absolutism, however, was not only a matter of appearance, even if Joseph II was committed genuinely to enlightened ideas. His
regime had a whiff of what the twentieth century would call totalitarianism. At court the emperor was "the soul of all his departments; he wants to
hear and see everything personally," commented Pezzl. He was, however,
"available to anyone, regardless of rank or name, nearly every day."[20] While
tolerance and liberality were real, they existed at his discretion. While society became more relaxed in many ways, real politics took place behind
closed doors. While his Enlightening eyes scanned all strata, focus was
sharpened by a formidable network of police informers. (Joseph did not
invent it in Vienna, but he re-organized it; such spying was a commonplace of many European regimes.) There was no escape from this "swarm,"
reported Pezzl. It flitted from gambling tables and balls to theaters, cafes,
beer halls, and brothels—"all-knowing, all registering, all hearing." His
next comment revealed, perhaps unintentionally, enlightened absolutism's
essential incongruity: this spying was in a city that seemed to have unhindered free expression.[21] It was unhindered until the emperor decided oth-

erwise, which he did toward the end of his reign. Aging and ill, he found his domain and Europe as a whole testier and testing. The French Revolution, initially celebrated by Austrian Enlighteners but worrisome to their ruler, strained matters, as did a costly war. Conflict between Russia and the Ottomans brought Joseph II to the aid of Catherine the Great in 1787 because of treaty obligations. The fight was popular until financial stress mounted and led many Austrian subjects to resent involvement. "The Turks are in no sense an enemy to be despised," Pezzl remarked even before the war began.[22] Paying for military actions led to state budget retrenchments, and musicians like Mozart, who had obtained a court post and composed patriotic music saluting Habsburg victories, had to cope with a decline in private subscription concerts.

III.

Ottomans and Austrians came to terms in late summer 1791 just as *Tito* was readied for Prague. A decade earlier, however, Mozart had prepared a stage work on a Turkish theme that he hoped would establish him in Vienna. *The Abduction from the Seraglio* was intended for a political event: festivities for Russia's Grand Duke Paul on the signing of the very accord that eventually brought Joseph II into war. The retinue on behalf of Catherine the Great was due in September and Chancellor Kaunitz aimed to make a very strong impression on it. Among the planned events was an opera and Joseph II decided it should be a Singspiel.[23] Mozart's opera wasn't ready for the visitors, who saw works by Gluck instead. It premiered in July of the following year.

Exotic settings were popular on the Viennese stage. Gluck had composed numerous "oriental" operas and *The Unforeseen Meeting or the Pilgrims of Mecca* of 1763, based on an older French play that Haydn also set in an Italian version, exemplified what would be known as "rescue" operas. A princess flees Persia to avoid a forced marriage and is captured by pirates. She arrives a slave in Cairo where the Sultan has designs on her. Yet her true love is there too and in the guise of pilgrims they try to flee, only to be exposed by a dervish. When the Sultan appraises the circumstances he decides to free them and to impale their ransom-seeking betrayer. The lovers appeal for clemency for the dervish enemy, it is granted, and all praise love and a fair ruler.[24] Here are separated lovers, prisoners, and harems, unforeseen encounters, an insidious figure—and all these come with a sovereign who displays nobility after having been resisted by a female captive with whom he is enamored. It is reminiscent of "The Generous Turk" in *Les Indes galantes*, except that the prisoners are not Europeans. The Muslim ruler is not an apostate from Christianity, as was frequently the case in operas and plays. Captured Europeans were a particular preoccupation of this era because of a rash of piracy in the Mediterranean. At the same time a long list of converts to Islam played major roles in the Ottoman Empire, ranging from de Bonneval to Koca Yusuf Pasha, the former Georgian who governed the Peloponnese for the Sublime Porte and would serve as grand vizier during the Russian-Austrian-Ottoman conflict of the later 1780s. The characters in Mozart's principal contribution to the genre included Europeans held on a forgiving Sultan's summer estate, and he is an apostate.

An earlier "Turkish" effort by Mozart had been discarded. It had a similar scenario and cast and most of the libretto by Johann Andreas Schachtner is lost. Parts set by Mozart were found long after his death and given the title *Zaide*. Its plot is immediately familiar. Captives of a Sultan fall in love and seek to escape. Aid comes from the Sultan's favorite slave, who turns out to be their father. The Singspiel's portrayal of the Sultan is not hostile. He loves Zaide and, distressed by her flight, brands himself a slave—to love. That love is a nobler custody is evident by its contrast to lust, embodied in Osmin, another slave (an Osmin will appear in *Seraglio* and shares features with him). *Zaide* presents, then, slaves of different kinds: the Sultan to love (he finds nothing amiss with any other bondage), Osmin to lust and his master's power, and all the prisoners to the Sultan's brute force.

The fugitives are, of course, captured. In incomplete *Zaide* they face a death sentence. At this point, matters become interestingly allusive. The libretto was derived from an earlier, now long-forgotten, North German Singspiel of 1777 titled *The Seraglio or the Unexpected Encounter in Slavery between a Father, a Daughter, and a Son*. In it the Sultan pardons and frees them. It is possible that a finished Mozart version would have concluded likewise. Moreover, what is extant includes a striking plea for compassion. "You powerful ones look down/ indifferently at your slaves;" says the Sultan's favorite slave, "and because you have fortune and authority, you don't recognize your brothers."[25] These words, which have Masonic resonance, call for equality in the voice of the oppressed—whether slaves, servants, or women. Moreover, the man who speaks them turns out to be a European in oriental costume and the "Oriental" potentate responds with clemency

Figure 15.1. Wolfgang Amadeus Mozart (1756–1791).
(Bibliothèque nationale de France.)

and a grant of liberty. *Zaide* is filled with stereotypes yet also suggests a challenge on behalf of those below in life's scales—on behalf of a common humanity among Europeans and Turks (a fraternity proclaimed among Cretans and Trojans in *Idomeneo*).

One biographer insisted that the composer was "not a political animal," noting that he rarely discussed political events. It is true that Mozart's letters don't address the French Revolution and, so far as we know, he never spoke openly of political ideas such as freedom, equality, or natural rights.[26] Yet this represents a limited truth. Certainly, Mozart did not go to Vienna to evaluate its political order. His operas were political even if he was not directly so. A libretto, notes one scholar more recently, was at this time the sole part of an opera "that could be carefully checked by authorities." Composers were more at liberty to suggest ideas in music.[27] Moreover, the political issues of Mozart's times arise repeatedly, often subtly, in the librettos of the operas he set. His own moral concerns and sympathies are persistent in them and he reshaped actively the words he set.

Social and political motifs can be engaged on the operatic stage in more than one way. An artist can show, stage, suggest, and make us hear them. They can also be presented as if a tract. Mozart did not write pamphlet-operas.

To hear Mozart's constancy, consider music for the slave's chorus toward the beginning of *Zaide*. It echoes sorrow expressed by the character Gomatz combined with the assertion of the need to bear fate bravely: "The world and misery are here to stay." Mozart composed for these words a passage of repeated fourths that, as one scholar observes, reappears in various ways in other operas. They are there at the beginning of *Don Giovanni* when Leporello, the Don's servant, objects to his fate. They sound near the end of *The Magic Flute* when the Queen of the Night and her entourage wander beneath Sarastro's Temple, in lack of what is needed to raise themselves up.[28] The Queen is a sympathetic figure in the first act but by this point her evil has been revealed. Mozart suggests that she is at home below in the dark, while nobler, enlightened figures live in the sun's rays. A politics of up and down seems represented in a short motif that, in a way, unites earlier and later works. Escaping fate—or living with it—is a metaphysical motif that threads through Mozart's operas too; it is visible in the pyramid of power displayed in his *Seraglio*.

IV.

Not long before he was offered the commission for what became *The Abduction from the Seraglio*, Mozart wrote to his father that there ought to be "as little frivolity" in an opera seria as "seriousness" in an opera buffa. The former required weightiness and "solidity," the latter "gaiety." People like some "comic music in an opera seria," he admitted, but added that he could not "help" that.[29] Mozart sounds as if he is unwilling to make concessions. Yet the achievement of *Abduction* as well as most of his future operas lay often in comic representation of serious matters.

His librettist, Gottlieb Stephanie the Younger, was prominent in Vienna's theatrical life. Born in Breslau, he was a man of many roles: actor, author, director, and reviser of librettos for Joseph II's *National-Singspiel*. Once a law student, he had been a Prussian hussar before being taken prisoner by the Austrians, becoming their soldier, and proceeding to rise in the Viennese cultural world. The text he provided Mozart was "freely adapted" (as he put it) from yet a third person's work. Christoph Friedrich Bretzner, a popular German librettist and Leipzig businessman, wrote *Belmonte and Konstanze or the Abduction from the Seraglio* in 1780 and would be irate on learning about the Mozart-Stephanie rendition. For Mozart *Abduction* represented a professional and personal turning point. He was abducting himself from Salzburg's authority and not only by settling in Vienna. He married in August 1782, to his father's annoyance. His wife's name was the same as that of the female principal in his opera.

Konstanze (Constance) has been kidnapped by pirates and sold into Pasha Selim's harem. He loves and pursues but won't force himself on this Spanish noblewoman. She, like her name, is steadfast, for she tells the Pasha that she loves another. Blonde, her maidservant, has been given to Osmin, overseer of Selim's estate. He is a brute (like his namesake in *Zaide*) and she loves Pedrillo, another European slave, whose gardening talents have secured for him a good position. It turns out that Pedrillo was manservant to Konstanze's love, Belmonte. And, of course, this young Spanish noble arrives in search of her. Attempted escape will inevitably be stymied; denouement will again depend on a ruler's clemency. The scenario is predictable and can be perceived readily as prejudices on parade. But if probed in multidimensional ways, something more interesting emerges. Consider four sets of relations in this opera and how they interact. A kind of crosslighting on the world comes from them:

First: a series of pairs. In these pairs one person's role ties to that of another either by differing status (such as master and servant) or by love. Each person links to additional figures as well. And so we have the Pasha and Konstanze, Konstanze and Belmonte, Belmonte and Pedrillo, Konstanze and Blonde, Blonde and Pedrillo, Blonde and Osmin, Pedrillo and Osmin, Osmin and a black slave—he will inform on the Europeans when they flee—and finally Osmin and the Pasha. (I leave aside a minor figure who helps in the attempted escape.) The Janissary Guards, representatives of direct force, are persistently in the background.

Second, the principal characters divide between "Orientals" and Europeans.

A third array contrasts or opposes men and women.

Finally, relations among all of them constitute a pyramid. Three servants are toward its base (but not at the very bottom): Blonde, Pedrillo, Osmin. Two of them, those who love, are allied. Osmin, a bass, is simply the thuggish hand of a higher power. At the next level is a noble and loving couple, Belmonte and Konstanze. The Pasha is at the summit. His voice, the ruler's, is distinct: he speaks but never sings. His radical opposite, however, also does not speak. He is a mute black slave under Osmin's command. The pyramid looks like this:

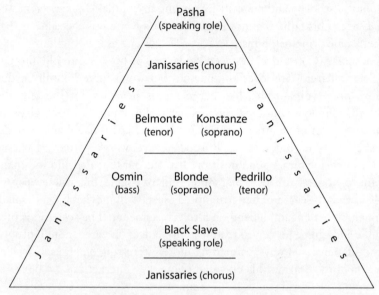

Figure 15.2. Pyramid of *The Abduction from the Seraglio.*

When we first meet Blonde she is struggling with Osmin, obviously, not for the first time. Her name alone suggests fair hair and skin and tells us that she is not of the Orient. Moreover, she refuses acquiescence to her fate. Her words (following cliché) distinguish Eastern from Western women. "Do you think . . . that you have a Turkish slave girl at your feet, who trembles at your commands? You are very much mistaken! European girls cannot be treated this way." They need tenderness and flattery, she explains. "We're in Turkey here," admonishes Osmin, "and another tune orders things. I'm your master and you're my slave."[30] As he is subservient to the Pasha, so must Blonde be to him. Blonde's riposte is straightforward: "Pasha this, Pasha that . . . I'm an Englishwoman, to freedom born."[31] Her salutary feistiness identifies England with liberty and may reflect a Viennese rage at the time for things English. It might suggest also Masonry, which was easily identified with England on account of its origins. Stephanie was a Mason and while Mozart was not yet one, he did call himself "an out and out Englishman" in a letter in October 1782 (just after a British naval victory).[32] Pashas represent authority in this opera, Blonde a spirit of liberty, and its conclusion will be an embrace of humanity. Her circumstances may constrain her, but Blonde insists her heart cannot be enslaved. Not only does she laugh when Osmin orders her to love him, she declares, despite her position of disadvantage, that women are really in charge. (After all, when it comes to relations between the sexes, men are chained to their desire for them.) Blonde insists also that she is "to joy born."[33] Her words suggest a notion of natural rights: subjugation is imposed, a matter of convention. This claim can, however, take different political forms. Servants and women often did not factor into assertions of the "rights of man" in the eighteenth century. Had it been available to her, Blonde, although English, might have appreciated a recent Declaration of Independence that asserted natural rights to life, liberty, and the pursuit of happiness.

Even though Blonde seems to assert at first what today would be called identity politics, she shifts in a striking way. She responds to Osmin's warning about where they are with words that reverberate with her earlier disdain of authority: "Turkey this, Turkey that! A woman is a woman wherever she is! If your women are foolish enough to let themselves be under your thumbs, so much the worse for them. In Europe we understand these things better."[34] This forcefulness can be taken in more than one way. A sly protest might be discerned, since European women were themselves born into a distinct and subordinate status in their societies, even if it was not equivalent to that of a concubine. But does she suggest that Europe also fails to understand things well enough? It is possible to extend this query into a commentary on Masonry, which played such a vigorous "Enlightening" role in Vienna, which insisted that its members be "free born," which excluded servants, and which had once strictly barred women from membership. Yet Blonde, an English maidservant in Ottoman captivity, insists she is born free; perhaps there was something for the Masons to reconsider as they determined that all are brothers and social equals in the outside world whatever their origins. Blonde's words propose that Ottoman women can understand their reality and that she could help to change them, given the opportunity. This captive seems to suggest a white sister's burden. However, the power of her assertions is in her insistence that the position of Turkish women is no natural, much less racial, matter. Knowledge is a first step toward remedy and freedom, it is accessible to all; her contention is "Enlightened."

Konstanze makes Blonde's same point when Selim tells her that she "must" love him. "Do you really believe that our women are less happy than those in your lands?" he asks. "They don't know any better," she replies.[35]

Mistress and maid assert a universal principle; freedom for them as women implies freedom for all. This is incomprehensible to ornery, stereotypical Osmin. (It is not evident, however, that Belmonte or Pedrillo would grasp the point either.) Osmin is a creature of crude desires. He reflects on little, hankers for a European female, and Englishmen are, in his view, buffoons for letting women be willful. Entrusted with the virtue of his Pasha's women, he believes in lock and key.

Selim obviously has great faith in Osmin, even though harem-keepers usually posed no risk to concubines. They tended to be eunuchs, although it seems that Osmin is not one, at the least given his pursuit of Blonde and his voice—he is a bass. Perhaps the Pasha gave Blonde to him to direct his cravings. Still, Selim's confidence rests explicitly on Osmin's religiosity, and Osmin insists on his own faithfulness. The Pasha believes Islam nurtures fidelity, and it is indistinguishable from obedience. This Singspiel displays multiple kinds of steadfastness. Osmin never wavers unless plied with wine. Suspicions and resentments well up in him and translate quickly into wrath as he wields clumsy authority in his limited realm within a realm. In a famous aria he tells of brutalities he would inflict gleefully and exhibits his unpleasant, dutiful, if bellowing, makeup. Mozart sought to convey "Osmin's anger" through what, in a letter of September 1781, he called "Turkish music."[36] Tempi are swift and keys change. At various points throughout *Abduction*, beginning just bars into the spirited overture, Mozart uses configurations, instruments, and sounds that he and other European composers associated with the Ottomans, particularly band music of the Janissaries. Deploying this music to color character and events, Mozart aims for a kind of authenticity. There was a vogue in Vienna for what was taken to be Janissary music, regardless of the conflicted realities of contemporary international politics. A band precedes Selim's entrance, and Mozart explained with a touch of contempt that the Janissary chorus had "all that can be desired": it was "short, lively and written to please the Viennese."[37] In the next century Hector Berlioz, who had little fondness for *Abduction*, wrote of the "priceless naiveté" provided by the combination of a "tall bass drum," cymbals, a triangle, and piccolo.[38]

Mozart credited himself specifically for the idea of Osmin's aria. It was neither in Bretzner's original nor in Stephanie's adaptation. A letter demonstrates his concern to turn wrath into musical art. "For just as a man in such a towering rage oversteps all the bounds of order, moderation, and propriety and completely forgets himself," he writes, "so must the music too forget itself. But since passions, violent or not, must never be expressed

282

to the point of exciting disgust and as music even in the most terrible situations, must never offend the ear but must please the listener . . ."Mozart wants a ruffian's sounds to provoke laughter.[39] We hear "Turkish music" at various points of the opera, such as the drinking song sung when Pedrillo distracts Osmin to facilitate escape by the Europeans and again when Osmin rejoices at the tortures they face once recaptured. But while his music thumps, it is more blustery than ominous. Osmin's joy also had a contemporary rebuke: torture had been abolished in the Habsburg empire in 1776 thanks especially to the efforts of Sonnenfels.

V.

Perhaps the encounter between East and West in this opera provides brighter cross-lighting than is assumed usually. Consider the first meeting between Pedrillo and Osmin, just after the latter has a grumpy exchange with Belmonte. A suggestive, even subversive acuity is discernable in it. Osmin denounces Pedrillo in terms that Westerners use commonly to describe "Orientals": he is a shirker, lazy, duplicitous. He is always trying to go where he ought not to be—among the Pasha's women. Osmin cannot imagine genuine affections between Pedrillo and Blonde because he cannot imagine affection at all. Pedrillo asks amiably why Osmin is so hostile and proposes peace between them. "Peace with you?" comes the rejoinder, "With a sniveling, wicked little creep who is always looking for ways to make a fool of me? I would rather strangle you."[40] Champions of Austrian-Russian alliance might cheer the point: Turks don't want peace. After this pronouncement Osmin proceeds to his aria gushing malice towards scheming dandies, by which he means European men. Though they may think him a dunderhead, he warns that he knows their "conniving ways" and watches them day and night. Mozart has Osmin sing numerous times that he "knows" all the tricks, as if to say he won't be taken for a fool. "*Ich hab auch Verstand*"—"I have understanding too"—recurs to the same rhythmic and melodic pattern.[41]

Does he merely want to understand, or is there something that he has actually grasped? Osmin may be cartoonish, yet he makes a valid point from a Turkish perspective. There was no especially good reason for Turks to trust outsiders—Russians and Austrians, for example—against whom they had warred and whom they believed mocked them. Perhaps it was fortuitous that Osmin did not sing that he would not be duped before the representatives of Catherine the Great. The Russians might have chortled at first: yes, you will be. Then we see almost immediately after Osmin sings that his suspicions are founded. Pedrillo, knowing the Pasha's obsession with grand edifices, smuggles Belmonte into the Pasha's household under false pretenses (as a celebrated architect trained in Italy). The Turk's palace will be vulnerable—if not to Russia and Turkey then to Pedrillo, working its grounds, and then to Belmonte who will be within its walls. Pedrillo will later hoodwink Osmin again when he gives him potion-laden wine. Osmin hesitates because of Muslim laws against alcohol but Pedrillo convinces him that Muhammad is asleep and, anyway, has other concerns. Then something telling happens.

Osmin drinks, becomes tipsy, and joins merrily in a song with Pedrillo: "Viva Bacchus!" He calls the European a "brother." Solidarity among European and Turkish servants appears to require boozy devotions to the same alien deity. But solidarity dissipates quickly. Osmin, unused to spirits, goes into a slumber and Pedrillo then expresses contempt for their fraternity. Pedrillo himself is, as he says later, a descendant of "good, old Christian stock" in Spain. He may have asked Osmin for peace earlier, but by now he denies they are of the same brood.[42] In fact, the word used for "stock"—*Geschlecht*—can have a racial ring in German (and also can suggest noble descent).

Osmin, then, was sober to sing *"Ich hab auch Verstand."* He warned Pedrillo that he is on watch and from his standpoint (really that of his master), he is shown right to do so. His words might also be taken in yet another way. Pedrillo calls Osmin an "old snoop" who would "poison" with his "eyes." While Mozart's music makes this overseer barbaric and humorous, the libretto makes a curious point in a Vienna of copious informers. Such spies are poisonous, thuggish fellows. Presumably that is true anywhere.

VI.

What then of the European noble couple, on the pyramid's next level? Konstanze harbors within herself that prized Stoic virtue: self-mastery. Her spoken words to Selim contrast poignantly to her own sadly lyrical arias and to Blonde's cheeky buoyancy. When she tells the Pasha that her affections are elsewhere, she says she will respect him, but no more. When she expresses steadfastness in song, it becomes a defiant coloratura aria, "Tortures of Every Kind" ("Martern aller Arten"). She is ready to suffer these rather than yield. Selim's frustration—he reminds her where she is— hints strongly that the Pasha and Osmin share at least something: both wield power bluntly. However, she also tells Selim that she is able to be truthful because she perceives generosity in him. Selim seems not to understand at first but he will go through a learning process kindled by her rebuff. Osmin, also rebuffed, is unable to learn, but he does understand ploys and their dangers, even if he is still deceived. And so by the Singspiel's end, Selim will be sad and Osmin frustrated. Konstanze's aria is in C major as is Belmonte's first aria—the same key as the opera's overture and finale. Mozart's use of it suggests unity of concerns.

Konstanze and Blonde, who want to be free to love, are constant in virtues and affections even though Belmonte and Pedrillo don't perceive this entirely. On the verge of escape, the two men, Orpheus-like, have qualms. They don't doubt that their beloveds will follow, but wonder about their past fidelity. The women, who have more tether, are annoyed. In their displeasure at the assumptions of the opposite sex, this mistress and her maid form a sisterly unity beyond their social differences; in their lack of confidence, master and manservant likewise comprise each other's complement. But gender solidarity is only one aspect of what the Singspiel shows. There are also social resentments. Blonde and Pedrillo are indentured in multiple ways. Blonde pities Konstanze and finds her too "delicate"—too prone to pining. The manservant is annoyed by an offhanded comment made by a rather oblivious Belmonte to him: "Ah Pedrillo, if you only knew what love is." Pedrillo, who is just then helping Belmonte at his own life's risk (but also for Blonde's sake) responds, "Hm, as if for people like me there were no such thing!"[43] Both gender and class get their due in these interactions. Yet Blonde, Pedrillo, and Osmin never say that they ought not to be servants of Konstanze, Belmonte, and Selim. And the conflict that frames the opera remains that of Turks and Europeans. It is captured when Blonde speaks in an unassuming way of returning with Konstanze to their common "homeland"—"*Heimat*"—even though the former is English and the latter Spanish.[44]

Belmonte and Selim are *Abduction*'s tree males, although the former will eventually be seized by the latter and the latter is prisoner emotionally to Konstanze. Their characters are nonetheless different. The Spaniard is hardly more than a stereotypical hero. He has the daring to infiltrate foreign shores for love's sake but there is little interesting about him. Even his bravery is not very impressive. When he and Konstanze are seized, she declares her willingness to die to save her lover. Belmonte, agonizing about a horrible death, prostrates himself and begs for mercy. On what basis? His noble lineage. Then comes a crucial twist. He announces his name,

Lostados, and swears that his family will pay any ransom. He simply assumes that this will bring a positive outcome but at this point there is a significant departure from Bretzner's original plot. Bretzner allowed for a happy ending—is it silly or easy?—in which Belmonte is revealed to be Selim's long lost son. By contrast, Belmonte's declaration only endangers him more in *Abduction*. His name identifies him as the son of Selim's greatest enemy, the commandant of Oran. This town, today in western Algeria, was contested between Ottomans and the West and served as a place of settlement for Spanish Muslims fleeing compulsory conversion to Christianity. Seized by the Spanish in 1509, then by the Ottomans in 1708, it was a base for Mediterranean pirates (who provided plots for operas by taking scores of Europeans into captivity). Spain reconquered it in 1732.

The Pasha, it turns out, is a convert to Islam. There has already been an indication that his captives know this, or at least Pedrillo. In a worried moment he calls Selim *"ein Renegat"* who is nonetheless "fully a Turk" when it comes to vengeful beheadings.[45] But Selim's conversion was a consequence of the behavior of an ignoble Christian grandee. Belmonte's pitiless father was (in the Pasha's words) the "barbarian" who forced him to flee his homeland years before. "His greed tore from me my beloved . . . He stripped me of my honors, my wealth, everything." Now, remarkably, the persecutor's son is in the hands of his father's victim. The Pasha asks Belmonte what his father would do in this situation. The response is frank: "My fate would be dire." Selim agrees and orders tortures to be prepared.[46]

Yet the Pasha reverses himself and affords a lesson. You and your brood, he tells Belmonte, take wrongdoing for granted. You expect me to mete out woe. That is why you expect me to act as the Commandant of Oran would. The Pasha, however, has decided to rise above the past and not to visit a father's sins on the son. He releases the prisoners. "Tell your father that you were in my power [and] that I freed you." It is better "to repay a grave injustice with kindness."[47] Osmin is, of course, now chagrined. It is easy to discern an "orientalist" construction of the "eternal Turk" in Osmin's inability to understand the clemency of Selim. Such an interpretation is useful, however, only in a very limited sense because it occludes half the story. It doesn't account for Belmonte's father—the Christian who is absent from all the stage events but whose mercilessness generated them; and so he is always present.

Selim appreciates constancy but has learned to reject rigidity. Does he expect Belmonte's father to change on hearing of what has happened? This question is left open. Perhaps the power-wielding Spanish grandee will learn something from the once Christian but now Muslim Pasha. Or perhaps the grandee will remain the Christian equivalent of peace-refusing Osmin. At no point does the renegade Selim indicate regret at being a Muslim or any inclination to reconvert. He simply breaks the pattern of injustice. In this he confirms a principle dear to Mozart: status, inherited or not, doesn't identify character. After all, Selim's origins did not prevent him from becoming Pasha, and Mozart believed that Europe's titled aristocracy blocked true nobility and talent—like his own. Mozart and Stephanie's Singspiel shows that cruelty is not only an "oriental" or Eastern trait and that clemency is not solely a Western or Christian virtue. Bretzner's Selim, by contrast, saves his own by his grant of clemency. His Europeans are united properly thanks to common blood, their forgiveness is easy and natural, and slavish Osmin remains his brutish self. In the Mozart/Stephanie denouement Osmin rages for vengeance to "Turkish music," the four Europeans praise "a great soul" who shuns revenge, and the Janissaries, who were in fact converts and descendants of converts and who are ever-present supports of the Pasha's power, hail Selim to "Turkish music"—which is now their own music. Clemency is a human virtue, not Christian, not Muslim. It is only if origins and religion are all determinant that this Singspiel, indeed the genre of "Turkish operas" as a whole, can be classified as "orientalist," that is, largely a product of prejudiced, imperial mindsets of Europe. [48] Otherwise, a more complicated and contradictory understanding of the dynamic that unfolds within them is warranted, whatever stereotypes may be present. Stories of hijacking, rescue, and magnanimity in the Mediterranean long predate the modern period. They are already found in antiquity, many centuries before there were any such things as Christian-Muslim clashes or before *Turquerie* excited Europeans periodically beginning in the fifteenth century. Power, sexuality, tensions between realities and appearances, and characters who appear in one guise—a slave, for instance, who is revealed to be of noble lineage—were regular aspects of such tales. Europeans certainly typecast non-Europeans but they did the same to their immediate European neighbors.

And Muslims did likewise. One important example is *One Thousand and One Nights*. The translation of this classic compilation of tales from the Islamic golden age, with origins in Persian, Arabic, and Indian folk cultures, had an enormous impact on how cultured Europeans perceived "the Orient."[49] It is framed famously by a story of a king who discovers his queen in lusty entwine with a black slave. His brother, also a ruler, finds his own spouse in a similar incline. The king decides all women are untrue and resolves to bed all the virgins in the realm before executing each the next morning. His hand is stayed only when his vizier's daughter, the famous Scheherazade, begins to recount marvelous fables. She ends each by introducing another to maintain his curiosity, saving her life as he waits to hear the next tale. The stories tell of power, travels to distant lands, and sexual conquests and engagements. Fate and determination, cruelty and compassion loom large in them. Behavior that twentieth- and twenty-first-century readers would judge to be deeply prejudiced is presented as normal. Isn't it only natural that royal siblings dispatch unfaithful women and their rude ravishers?

Consider the tale of Sinbad the Sailor, possibly a later addition to the collection. He travels constantly from Baghdad out into the world, often making his way to the sea where he suffers shipwrecks and meets up with all manner of monsters and strange figures. These depictions of alien dangers abroad can be imagined easily as encounters with "Others." They are not appreciably different from Western representations of "the Orient." The same might be said of domestic dynamics if the role of black slavery in *One Thousand and One Nights* is compared to *The Abduction from the Seraglio*. In Mozart's opera the escaping Europeans are captured thanks to a black mute—the lowliest figure in the hierarchy—who betrays them to Osmin. While the opera ends on a humanist note, and while slavery was a source of considerable contention in Europe at this time due especially to criticism of it by figures identified with the Enlightenment, this mute makes only a brief appearance—as if his condition were as natural as that of many black slaves found throughout *One Thousand and One Nights*.[50]

Yet there are generous, just rulers in *One Thousand and One Nights* as well as plentiful assertions of common humanity and the value of clemency along with display of prejudices. Moreover, Westerners, as we have seen, do not come across uniformly well in European operatic encounters with non-Europeans and non-Europeans are not all portrayed as foul foes. *Les Indes galantes* was not an isolated case. "Not only in Europe, but also Asia can produce virtuous souls," says the Sultan in *The Seraglio*, that Singspiel of 1777 that served as the basis of *Zaide*. In *Adelheit von Veltheim*, a "play with songs" staged in Frankfurt in 1780, a Pasha asks captured Europeans who conspired against him—but who receive clemency—to "sometimes remember that you found a human being in the so-called barbarian world." He adds that "I did not learn to act this way from the history of your conquests of foreign continents."[51]

VII.

Mozart's use of C major makes it the opera's human key. It provides coherence and a framework for differentiation as the events and their music proceed. It appears and reappears. It returns at times as if it were the premise of an argument that has been worked out in deliberation, rearticulated in the conclusion. Musician and critic Charles Rosen pointed out that *Abduction* initiated a regular feature of Mozart operas: they would begin and end in the same key. Musical organization around a particular tone, he wrote, was essential to the emergence of the "classical style," of which Mozart was the greatest representative in the eighteenth century.[52] The C major takes us into *Abduction*'s drama, beginning with the overture's back-and-forth between swift rustling strings and bouncy "Turkish music." The former seems to move until it comes up against the latter as if it were a barrier to be overcome. It then reasserts itself. Konstanze's aria of defiance—here a human emotion of resistance to domination—is in C major, as is the finale's praise of Selim's justice by Janissaries.

Another dimension of classical style is important here: sonata form. Although its purposes were musical, its shape, heard in a particular way, can conjure up the idea of political rhetoric. Its sounds advance like an effort to combine consideration and persuasion, rather than simply insisting on ideas or commanding a response. The word "sonata" initially indicated simply instrumental as opposed to vocal music but "sonata form" came to designate patterns of first movements of larger works like symphonies.[53] As we have mentioned earlier and in simplified (if slightly technical) outline, an "exposition" presents musical ideas that then "develop" and are finally "recapitulated." More specifically, a theme emerges at first in the work's "tonic" (a home key that organizes it). Then a modulation (or "bridge") brings differentiation, leading toward new thematic terrain, now usually in the "dominant" key (organized, that is, by the note that is five scale degrees from the tonic). Potentials and contrasts of the themes are explored by various means such as key changes and the incorporation of new configurations. After the development, the tonic key finally returns, bringing "resolution" through restatement ("recapitulation") of themes and ideas. The whole and the parts, writes Rosen, "mirror each other," although "imply" might be a better word.[54] Drama comes of flow, direction, and complexity rather than by ornamentation of an original theme. Something "different from the exposition" arises and works out in it. In this, the form lends itself deftly to opera.[55] Music doesn't serve as background to prettify stage events but provides an "equivalent" in sound to the action.[56] This, Rosen proposed, explains something essential in Mozart's accomplishment: a fusion that makes stage intrigue and music indissoluble. And words are not simply servants of music, even if Mozart once put it that way, but integrated parts of a theatrical whole.[57]

Two years after *Abduction* premiered, an early musicologist compared explicitly the conventions of oratory to sonata form. Johann Nikolaus Forkel wrote that "one of the foremost principles of musical rhetoric and aesthetics is careful ordering of musical figures and the progression of the ideas to be expressed through them so that these ideas are coherently set forth as in an oration, according to logical principles—still preserved by skilled orators—that is, *exordium, propositio, refutatio, confirmatio,* etc."[58] These Latin terms, drawn from ancient canons of rhetoric, mean, in turn, an introduction (in which the purpose is laid out), assertion, rebuttal, and proof. Forkel is describing a formal structure; achieved properly, it ought to work with any type of argument by logic, its extrapolations and developed recapitulation. The way in which *Abduction's* content is worked through is also like a well-made political argument—roughly in sonata form. A key idea is presented. There is an exposition. Belmonte meets Osmin and the issue of liberty versus servitude is posed. The idea is entwined with issues of East versus West. It bridges into another theme, love, which is explored through the interactions of different characters and through raising questions of constancy and reciprocity. These developments lead to a differentiated whole. In it Selim recognizes that love must be mutual and so he resolves to act justly and refuses to behave as Belmonte's father did.

While working on *Abduction* Mozart wrote words to his father that subsequently became famous: "In an opera, poetry must be altogether the obedient daughter of the music."[59] After all, feeble verse might survive on stage if "music reigns supreme" and "all else is forgotten." Words had to be written "solely for the music and not shoved in here and there to suit some miserable rhyme."[60] These contentions, often cited as a summary of Mozart's operatic aesthetic, are easily misinterpreted to mean that librettos are, more or less, props. When he wrote them, however, he was working on a Singspiel. Its structure demanded a mix of spoken text and song. Mozart, notes one scholar, was addressing poetry for song.[61] In *Abduction* he achieved a balance of song and spoken dialogue for a relatively sophisticated libretto.

Many years later, in 1819, Mozart's finest librettist, Lorenzo Da Ponte, wrote as if he wanted to refute Mozart's claim (or perhaps Da Ponte simply shared its misinterpretation). "If the words of a dramatic poet are nothing *but a vehicle*," he complained, the composer might just as well use "a doctor's recipes, a bookseller's catalogue or even a spelling book." Mozart "knew very well" that the poet determined an opera's success. A composer is to a drama "what a painter is in regard to the colors." The poet opens "the door" to music's beauties.[62] This may be often so but Da Ponte's claims cannot explain why his many works without Mozart, often very witty, well-constructed, and entertaining, never secured long-standing approbation. Doors open and close. Yet while they shared a space, Da Ponte wrote for Mozart three of the most important librettos in the history of opera. Ideas, criticism of ideas, and censure of convention weave nimbly through them. Yet Da Ponte misconstrued, at least in significant part, his own achievement: he knew how to write for this composer—this great composer.

When specifically political or philosophical ideas come to a musical stage, matters become particularly complex. Bad and even criminal notions, political or moral, can, we know, be well-argued. They can be expressed beautifully and successfully. Socrates made the point at his trial. Accusers could defeat him with rhetoric—piercing his own strong point, which was understanding that there was so much that he did not know. His student Plato was chary both of rhetoric and music because of their impact on reasoning. Adept lawyers—and many, many librettists, from Busenello to Metastasio to Goldoni, were trained in law, not just in classical culture and rhetoric—can argue the same case from contending viewpoints. (A number of librettists—but also some composers—had been on trial or in trouble with the law for one reason or another.) Music can alternate as accomplice for either side; it can subvert by suggesting something wrong with what words say or actions do. An old query returns inevitably both for rhetoric and opera—if their content is intended seriously. We are back with Hegel's hare-pie set before us. And again: Who rules? Bad librettos with good music can be interesting, even enjoyable, but only as expressions of their times. Music from a Mozart opera (and those of many other composers) can be woven into engaging, even extraordinary concert or just musical versions. Their original role in an opera then becomes relatively meaningless except as a source of inspiration. For Mozart, however, "the best thing of all is when a good composer who understands the stage and is talented enough to make sound suggestions meets an able poet."[63]

ZWISCHENSPIEL (II)

Like Mozart, Lorenzo Da Ponte had a problem with authority. His impish pen and mutinous lifestyle led inevitably to troubles for this perennial outsider. Da Ponte would kneel often enough in Vienna, yet he would rise inevitably and turn things over, not always recognizing that they might land on him too. He was a curious figure even in a Viennese theatrical world rampant with rambunctious, unusual personalities—men who had, often more than once, changed names or converted identities or loyalties or public costumes.

Salzburg, Venice, Vienna—the Mozart-Da Ponte collaboration could be told as a tale of three cities perched on a historical brink as the French revolution rushed up from below on them. Mozart was "kicked in the arse" by a Salzburg count because he was determined to be in the Habsburg capital; Da Ponte came there after fleeing legal proceedings against him in *La Serenissima*. In the last years of the Josephine era they created operas together in Italian that teased out and teased directly Europe's social order; embedded in them were smiling, very sharp barbs that had been chiseled out of a combination of lucid wit and luminous sounds. And all the political, social, and economic orders they knew were soon enough besieged. Within two decades the prince-archbishop would be chased from Salzburg by Napoleon's troops—which would also end Venetian independence and the Holy Roman Empire (although Austria would avenge itself later against France).

After arriving in Joseph II's capital, Da Ponte wrote librettos for its most eminent composer and head of the Italian opera there. Known to posterity as Mozart's great rival, Antonio Salieri had helped Da Ponte become a Habsburg court librettist. Although Metastasio's works had lost their allure by this time, Da Ponte admired his poetry and managed to be invited to the home of the old Caesarean Poet to read some of his own verse. His host, who died several days later, expressed appreciation and Da Ponte's reputation soon spread. Mozart took notice. "Our poet here is a certain Abate Da Ponte," he wrote to his father in May 1783. After *Abduction*'s success Mozart had been scouring librettos—over a hundred by his count—and was unable to find one to his liking. Da Ponte promised something but Mozart was skeptical. "As you are aware," he continued in the same letter, "these

Italian gentlemen are very civil to your face. Enough, we know them! If he is in league with Salieri, I shall never get anything out of him. But indeed, I should dearly love to show what I can do in Italian opera."[1]

Mozart first met Da Ponte in the home of Baron Raimund Wetzlar von Plankenstern, the composer's benefactor and landlord, and godfather of his newly born son. There was a certain commonality among the three men. Da Ponte was a Jewish convert to Catholicism and the Baron was too. (Mozart refers to him in a letter as "the rich converted Jew Wetzlar.")[2] Mozart, a commoner born Catholic in a town ruled by a churchman he disliked, would become a Mason (although he maintained his Catholicism and belonged to a lodge with a Catholic orientation). They all had reason to prefer tolerance to inflexible conventions. While Mozart's conflicts with authority in Salzburg were different from Da Ponte's with Venice's elites, they shared umbrage at unearned privilege.

II.

Da Ponte's experiences in Venice shaped his ways of looking at the world. *La Serenissima* was rife with conflicts within its republican aristocracy, and some of the tensions recall Monteverdi's age. Problems were often solved only in appearance. A foreigner in Da Ponte's day would have come to a city of some 160,000 inhabitants with theaters, seven opera houses, brothels, gambling dens, and Carnival. The vibrant mix of culture and libertinage was due partly to rules of social hierarchy. Some two-thirds of male aristocrats were unmarried due to regulations designed to uphold family lines and wealth. Courtesans were, consequently, plentiful. Many girls without marriage prospects found themselves in orphanages and convents (some with decidedly unchaste reputations). The circumstances of single females had a collateral cultural benefit. Orphanages, especially their choirs, became important mainstays for the city's musical world. They were subsidized by the state and eminent composers were frequently attached to them. Even gambling houses hosted musical entertainments.[3]

The titled elite divided between richer and poorer elements—again, it recalls Monteverdi's age—and they vied with each other through competing state institutions. The well-to-do (basically forty-two families) sought to fend off reform through control of the Council of Ten, the executive power. It was, not surprisingly, a major target for the discontented. So too were the still busy Inquisitors of State. Public behavior was observed closely by these three feared men as it was by an extensive secret police. Less prosperous aristocrats mobilized through the Great Council, with its larger membership. They became increasingly susceptible to radical, populist republican and enlightened ideas, especially those coming from France. In the early 1760s, brawls over institutional prerogatives were fueled especially by poorer nobles concentrated in the parish of S. Barnabà. Aristocratic status kept them from modest money-making pursuits (like artisanal work) and many lived in special lodgings that were effectively poor houses. The Inquisitors kept vigilant watch over "*Barnabotti*," who were unable to gain any significant state posts and were accused by foes of a wide variety of social and economic vices. They were "a sort of proletariat within the patriciate."[4]

Memoirs composed decades later by Irish tenor Michael Kelly described Venice as magnetic and perilous. He arrived in 1783, at age twenty-one, and would in due course move on to Vienna, where he sang in the first productions of *Figaro*. (He was coaxed there by Count Durazzo, that odd Genoan who promoted Gluck and had now become Vienna's ambassador to *La Serenissima*.) With more than a touch of exaggeration, Kelly called "[d]ear beautiful Venice" a site of "harmony and love." Like Rousseau four decades before, he heard gondoliers singing barcarolles and verses from Tasso and Ariosto. Like observers early in the preceding century, he beheld "merchants of all countries" at the Rialto Bridge, a constant "bustle" of Christians, Armenians, Turks, and Jews. The latter population, he reported, was "obliged to wear a piece of red cloth in the hat" and were restricted to living in "a particular quarter."[5] As in Monteverdi's day and in Rousseau's, appearance and reality did not always correspond.

Kelly became friendly with Michael de l'Agato, manager of the St. Benetto Opera house, then the city's center for opera seria. One night de l'Agato cautioned him:

> In this city you will find innumerable pleasures; your youth and good spirits will lay you open to many temptations; but against one thing I warn you:—never utter a word against the laws or customs of Venice . . . You never know to whom you speak; in every corner spies are lurking, numbers of whom are employed at a high price to ensnare the unwary, and report the language of strangers, but with no other protection than a *silent tongue*, you can do whatever you like.

One of your countrymen, de l'Agato went on, visited Venice with his Swiss valet. His lodgings were robbed and, frustrated, he denounced the hotelier and his staff as "Venetian thieves." He cursed a city where belongings were so insecure. Sometime later, the visitor was "roused out of his sleep" and conveyed hurriedly to a room "hung with black." He found himself face-to-face with the city's terrifying Inquisitors. Reprimanded severely by them for slander, he was ordered to depart Venice quickly. He agreed ("trembling") but then, as he prepared his exit, he was surprised to be presented with his stolen money, now found. And behind a curtain was the body of the thief—his own valet, now strangled. "I confess," commented Kelly, "this instance of the summary mode of administering justice in Venice made a deeper impression upon me than all the good Signor's advice."[6]

Kelly's visit was four years after Da Ponte's flight. This poet-abbot would never quite learn how a "silent tongue" could bestow protections. Pietro Antonio Zaguri, a Venetian aristocrat who knew him, later wrote a letter to a Da Ponte friend—Giacomo Casanova—describing the *abate* as a "strange man, known to be a rascal of moderate talent, with great aptitude for becoming a man of letters" and attracting women.[7] Da Ponte reportedly played violin dressed in clerical gowns in a brothel, which (if it happened) certainly did not endear him to authorities.[8] His later reputation in Vienna was not bland either. Kelly recalled how once, when acting the role of "an amorous eccentric poet" in an opera by Da Ponte and composer Vicenzo Righini, he began to mimic the librettist. His "friend" Da Ponte "had a remarkable awkward gait, a habit of throwing himself (as he thought) into a graceful attitude, by putting his stick behind his back and leaning on it; he also had a very peculiar, rather dandyish, way of dressing; for in sooth, the [abate] stood mighty well with himself and had the character of a consummate coxcomb; he had also a strong lisp and broad Venetian dialect." Da Ponte was sitting in the boxes during the performance "more conspicuously than was absolutely necessary." The tenor's impersonation provoked laughter from Joseph II, who was present; Da Ponte was (apparently) not offended.[9] He liked attention.

III.

Emanuele Conegliano was born in 1749 in the Jewish ghetto of Ceneda, sixty kilometers from Venice but within the republic's territory. He took the name "Lorenzo Da Ponte" from the bishop who baptized him and his brothers. His father, a tanner, had converted to marry a Catholic woman (his first wife died in 1754).[10] Apparently Lorenzo became a reader and a thief of sorts at a young age, stealing leather—he was caught—from his father's stocks in order to make a trade with the town's bookseller. He took minor orders in a local seminary in 1765 and then went with his brothers to another in Portoguaro. There he grappled with demands that were normal enough for a religious establishment but that did not appeal to him. He would complain that he had to wear black; worse, dancing was prohibited. Nonetheless, he rose to vice rector. Eventually, Da Ponte determined that he needed a change. He was engaged more by poetry than by worship by the time he went to Venice. He frequented literary cafes there, befriending well-known writers, including the celebrated Gozzi brothers, Gasparo and Carlo. He began a tumultuous relationship with a young woman from a Barnabotti family. Her unsavory brother, an obsessive gambler, sought retribution against him for his inability to provide alchemical secrets for making gold or formulas for winning in gaming houses. Another change was in order. Da Ponte took refuge at the Treviso seminary where he spent two years in a relatively liberal atmosphere with a literary community. Placed in charge of the library, he also taught rhetoric and music, and this suited him since he was also composing more and more verse. Soon he was in trouble again. In 1776 he was assigned to write poetry for pupils to read at the closing ceremony of the academic year. An illustrious and powerful crowd would attend. He provided fifteen poems addressing this question: "Are men happier or less so due to laws and their place in civil society, or was humanity more content in its earlier state?"[11]

This query and the responses provided by Da Ponte make it appear as if he were reimagining the world poetically on the basis of Rousseau's *Discourse on the Origins of Inequality* (although not with great accuracy). If Rousseau imagined free, instinctive individuals descending from nature into misery with the development of laws, private property—in short, "civilization"—Da Ponte's verse criticized rules and celebrated pursuit of natural happiness. It was a rash theme for the location and occasion. The recitation took place on August 1, barely a month after the American Declaration of Independence denounced violation of "unalienable" rights by earthly rulers. It was too soon for news of it to have arrived, but shooting had begun outside Boston a year earlier, American grievances were known and European philosophers had long debated government abuse of the "natural rights of man."[12] Da Ponte admitted later that his theme "and especially the manner in which I treated it . . . appeared—or at least was made to appear—scandalous, unwise, and contrary to the good order and peace of society."[13]

The poems began in a theologically acceptable way by declaring the impossibility of perfect happiness in this life. Certainly, he said, laws secure order and prosperity by threatening punishment for bad behavior. But Da Ponte becomes particularly persuasive when his voice does something different: he raises doubts about external restraints on humans. How, he asks, can a constricted world be better than the golden age of which many poets—especially ancient ones—sang? In that world love was humanity's sole law. It is as if Da Ponte wanted fallen man to pick himself up, break free of chains, and find a lost, true, natural happiness. (Rousseau, by contrast, believe it impossible to return to a state of nature.)

In "The American in Europe"—the title is arresting since Da Ponte would spend his last decades in the United States—the poet-abbot elaborates on these themes and suggests that laws prevent men from following their hearts, creating fear and sorrow. He supposes natural equality when he declares—he sounds not only like Rousseau but also Mozart—false the claim that nature gives the fortunate their privileges. Poverty prevents talented men from attaining education and achievement. Even if humans are flawed and need them, laws encourage rather than deter vice. In one poem he imagines himself transformed by a nymph into "a different man from the/ one I am." He would be an "absolute monarch" who abolishes laws that did not enhance the "the well-being of suffering citizens." It is easy to imagine discomfort among listeners when Da Ponte announced that "Nature, inside my breast/ Gave me the only law:/ Not to do in action or in word/ That which I do not like . . ."[14]

Publication of his words brought denunciation, including by a Venetian Inquisitor, to a patrician committee charged with overseeing education in the republic. Da Ponte later described its members puckishly as men in need of "being reformed."[15] His case went to the Venetian Senate. This poet's sentiments, the Inquisitor complained, could come only from a Jew or an atheist. Da Ponte returned to Venice to prepare a defense and to garner supporters. Among them were eminent figures: Zaguri, Bernardo Memmo (an ex-senator from an old noble family and a friend of Goldoni) and Gasparo Gozzi. Da Ponte did not actually attend the trial and so did not watch as senators became incensed when his poems were read aloud. Gozzi's support miscarried when he insisted on the poet's talent. Senators concluded that this made Da Ponte more dangerous. The guilty verdict came with a relatively light sentence. He lost his post, his poems were confiscated, and while allowed to remain within the republic, he was barred from teaching. He took all this flippantly—he was now a celebrity and liked it—but the affair had political consequences beyond him, most notably repressive investigations by the government of radical tendencies in educational institutions.

Lorenzo Da Ponte (1749–1838), a nineteenth-century portrait of
Mozart's librettist for *The Marriage of Figaro*, *Don Giovanni*, and *Cosí fan tutte*.
HIP/Art Resource, NY.

Da Ponte became Memmo's houseguest and mingled again in intellectual circles. He met Casanova in these circles and while Da Ponte's personal reputation did not quite match his, he was at the least a competitor. An
amorous intrigue with his host's mistress soon compelled him to leave Memmo's home, despite protests of innocence. After a sojourn to Padua—his
absence intended apparently to calm matters—he returned to the city of
canals, this time to Zaguri's home.[16] Then Da Ponte was accused of helping
a woman (pregnant by him) to give birth in the street. It was Zaguri's turn
to oust him. It was almost impossible to believe anything Da Ponte said,
Zaguri wrote later to Casanova. The man was "insane in every sense."[17] In
1792 Zaguri echoed legendary words attributed (questionably) to Joseph
II's reaction to a Mozart opera—"Too many notes, my dear Mozart, too
many notes." He told Da Ponte, *"Troppi casi, Ab, troppi casi."* ("Too many
incidents, Abate, too many incidents.")[18]

Other incidents finally put Da Ponte's Venetian years to a close. After Zaguri evicted him, he managed to obtain a position that placed him

at the center of opposition politics in increasingly fraught times. He was engaged to tutor privately the children of Giorgio Pisani. This eminent lawyer, a leader of the Barnabotti and radical republicans, was campaigning against what Da Ponte called "the party of the powerful and the wealthy."[19] Da Ponte's tongue—or rather his words—went to work on behalf of this "Gracchus" of Venice. The poet-abbot infuriated conservatives, this time with a poem extolling Pisani as a reforming foe of despotism and corruption. He chastised senators in a biting tone and insisted that protest was a right in a republic.[20] The targets of protest, however, were not accommodating, especially since his poem was in Venetian dialectic, making it broadly accessible. Da Ponte bragged that his poem became rapidly "the talk of cafés, assemblies, and dinner tables." Apparently it was very important to Da Ponte that "the ladies who liked Pisani and me learned my lines by heart, despite the togas, wigs, and the aristocratic poses of their husbands."[21]

Pisani's struggle against the Council of Ten and the Inquisitors reached its apex in 1779–80. The doge died in December 1778 and his successor, chosen by corrupt election, was an old reformer. He immediately switched sides, recognizing that his new title did not make him the principal power. The real power was "the Boss," a fierce advocate of Venice's "old values." He was Andrea Tron, who believed that the republic was in danger of being taken over by "foreigners." His dislike of Jews, which presumably included converted Jews, was intense. Tron was, as one historian writes, "virtual dictator" of the city for a generation "by virtue not of any offices . . . but by his character and personality alone."[22] Pisani and his allies came close to defeating him, securing a majority on the Great Council in favor of constitutional amendment and redistribution of wealth. However, adept Tron reversed the opposition's tide by spring 1780.

The Inquisitors sent Pisani to prison.[23] Da Ponte fled just before Tron's triumph, and it may be that accusations against him were also part of efforts against Pisani. What better exemplified the threat to traditional standards than a dissolute cleric of Jewish origins who had been barred previously from teaching but now was educating the children of the leader of the opposition? Besides, Da Ponte's poem mocked Tron personally and called for Pisani's appointment to the magistracy so that "arrogance" might be fought. And his words seemed again Rousseauesque—this time, however, with a claim for the advantages of popular sovereignty. In one of his numerous paradoxical formulations in *The Social Contract*, Rousseau proposed that when the People was sovereign, individuals were protected as members of the collective citizen body: each person, he contended, would give himself to all and therefore to none. Da Ponte urged readers to, "Keep in mind/ That this is a people's Republic/ Which belongs to everyone and to no one."[24] Sentiments like these could not comfort leaders of what was still in fact an aristocratic republic, and very much not one of "the People."

Allegations against Da Ponte were placed in the mouth of a lion's head —another symbol of Venice—that jutted from San Moisè's church. Claudio Monteverdi was accused of treason a century and a half earlier by a note placed in this same customary repository for anonymous charges. Unlike Monteverdi, however, the threat to Da Ponte was not suppressed. The denunciations were many: adultery, rape, public concubinage, forgery, insulting patricians, eating ham on Fridays, and disgracing Christianity in general. Da Ponte realized that he had no more options. "I abandoned my ungrateful country."[25] The fact is that he was facing arrest. He fled in late August, was tried in absentia, and condemned in December 1779 to seven years in prison. A stipulation was added: if not apprehended, he was banished for fifteen years.

He made his way to Habsburg territory. He went first to Gorizia, a town north of Trieste where Venetian political dissenters often harbored. There he began to write plays and ingratiated himself with a powerful local figure. Count Guidobaldo von Cobenzl led the local Arcadian society, which Da Ponte joined. He recommended Da Ponte to his son, who was Kaunitz's vice chancellor and in coming years also a supporter of Mozart. (He too seems to have been a Mason.) Da Ponte went first through Vienna just after Maria Theresa's death. It was not then his destination. Dresden was, in the belief that a position awaited him in the Saxon capital. He had been misled about this prospect, but while there he translated *Atys*, the libretto Philippe Quinault wrote for Lully. His friend Caterino Mazzolà, another Venetian and later reviser of Metastasio's *La clemenza di Tito* for Mozart, read it and suggested that Da Ponte had found the appropriate literary form for his talents. Da Ponte returned now to the imperial capital with a letter from Mazzolà recommending him to Salieri who, born near Verona, grew up as a Venetian citizen before becoming eminent in Vienna.[26] Lorenzo Da Ponte, fellow traveler of radical Venetian republicans, would now write librettos in a world of enlightened despotism.

Chapter 16

GAITS OF HISTORY

Speedy currents carry us into the opera, as if effervescing nature rustles into our human condition. They become slower (but not slow) in a passage of notes that meets up brusquely with amplitudes of sound. They seem to comprise a hurdle to be overcome. Then the initial streams return and press on. Back and forth go dynamics in an overture that tells us that much will happen in coming hours—motion, obstacles, and commotion.

Then we find a steward in a half-furnished room in the castle of Count Almaviva and his Countess Rosina near Seville. The opera is named for the steward: *The Marriage of Figaro.*

The aristocrats are not present at this moment and the setting tells us that things are unfinished. Figaro paces. He assesses floor space for a bed he is to share with Susanna, his betrothed. Then she is there sizing up a wedding hat before a mirror and asks him to look at her. *The Marriage of Figaro* tells its viewers to see, to hear, to reflect, to take measure. The behavior of an absent Spanish grandee unleashed the intrigue of *The Abduction from the Seraglio;* here assertion of lordly license by a Grand Seigneur, also Spanish, generates events. But *Figaro* had a considerable prehistory in a controversial play filled with humorous barbs directed at Mozart's favorite target: unmerited privilege. In *The Barber of Seville* French playwright Pierre-Augustin Caron de Beaumarchais introduced a wily but younger Figaro helping a younger Almaviva woo young Rosina. She is ward of older, obtuse Doctor Bartolo, who wants her for himself. Conceived originally by Beaumarchais as a comic opera, his play became the basis of famous ones composed by Giovanni Paisiello—it was enormously popular in Vienna in 1783—and later by Gioacchino Rossini. Acclaim greeted Beaumarchais's play in Paris in 1775, but also furies. Da Ponte must have appreciated Beaumarchais's penchant for bringing himself fame and grief at once by ridiculing or clashing personally with powerful people.

The principals of *The Barber of Seville* reappeared in Beaumarchais's *The Mad Day or the Marriage of Figaro,* the basis of the Da Ponte-Mozart opera. By now the Count is bored both with his Countess Rosina and other women he chases on his estates. He wants to exercise his *"Droit du Seigneur,"* a noble's feudal "right" to bed a servant who is a virgin just before she weds. Almaviva, who imagined himself forward-looking, has abolished just this privilege of "the first night" (as it became known) yet still wants inequality before the law when it pleases him. *Droit* translates into his desire. The opera shows how his pursuit of Susanna is thwarted. One scene dances into the next with an interplay of varied tempi designed by the surest of musical and theatrical imaginations. Ingenious assimilation of buffa and Goldoni by Mozart and Da Ponte combined with a sense of movement in time that was also Beaumarchais's offspring.

Before achieving notoriety, his craft provided valuable training for anyone in theater. Beaumarchais was a master clockmaker (as was his father). He became the "King's *Horologer*," and went on to obtain a quasi-feudal position at court, "Keeper of the Royal Warren." Because he had to cope with various legal tasks in this capacity, he became familiar with France's judicial world. These would be useful in his escapade-filled life. Beaumarchais made and lost substantial wealth. He traveled through Spain to solve a family marriage issue but also to engage in murky business matters that included munitions sales. His time there, described in memoirs, colored his plays. He also ran arms to American revolutionaries on behalf of the French crown. He was a man of music, theater, and polemics (in which corruption of justice, particularly as applied to himself, was a favorite theme). He clashed with this and that *Seigneur*, was in court numerous times, suffered censorship, lost his civil status, and was condemned by the Parlement of Paris, the bastion of the legal nobility that was also in regular conflict with the monarch. Louis XVI, it might be supposed, would enjoy Beaumarchais's disrespect of aristocrats. (Marie Antoinette did.) However, he had his own reasons to be infuriated by *Figaro*. "The Bastille," the king judged, "would have to be destroyed in order that the performance of this play not be dangerously irresponsible." Goethe, who wrote a play about him, remarked that "Beaumarchais was a mad fellow . . . Lawsuits were his element. . . ."[1] Even if the aristocracy was Beaumarchais's obvious target, kings also placed themselves above all law, save heaven's (most of the time). Almaviva could be taken easily for a little sovereign, presiding clumsily over a little domain.

Production of Beaumarchais's play about Figaro was blocked for some six years. Even a very liberal-minded Majesty would have been unsettled when, in its last act, its protagonist imagines that he is addressing Count Almaviva within these notorious words:

Because you are a great noble you believe you are a great genius . . . Nobility, fortune, rank, positions! . . . What have *you* done to deserve all these goods? You went to the trouble of being born—nothing more! For the rest, an ordinary enough man. Whereas I, the devil take it, lost in the obscure crowd, have had to show more knowledge, more cunning, just to survive than it has taken to govern all Spain for a century.[2]

Few lines of social denunciation in literature rival these. They finally reached the Parisian stage in 1784. Placing events near Seville hardly provided enough distance to obscure Beaumarchais's offenses; only a change in letters distinguishes a *Signor* (in Italian; *Señor* in Spanish) from a French *Seigneur*.

The Barber enjoyed success in German in Vienna, where Joseph II permitted potentially controversial works on stage often. These included a version of *La serva padrona* with music by Paisiello, and while the emperor initially forbade translation of Beaumarchais's *Figaro*, he reversed himself. Da Ponte recounted in his often unreliable memoirs that only days after the ban Mozart asked him "whether I could easily make an opera from a comedy by Beaumarchais." The librettist claimed that it took six weeks to prepare it in later 1785—"as fast as I wrote the words, Mozart set them to music"—and that it was done in secret.[3] Da Ponte took credit for convincing Joseph II that *Figaro* could be an opera in "good taste."[4] It premiered in May 1786 with particularly incendiary passages expunged. Figaro no longer told the Count that birth was his sole merit. Joseph II was contemptuous of hypocritical aristocrats but he also understood that royals, whatever their own family mythologies, also owed their own eminence to random natal occurrence. Nonetheless, one scholar goes so far as to say that Joseph II was actually "in on the 'secret'"—the writing of the opera— "from the beginning."[5]

The tendency among some late twentieth- and early twenty-first-century critics to suppose that the opera was emptied of most of the play's politics is plausible only with an exceedingly narrow definition of politics and ignores variety in the forms—as well as disguises—of power. Matters that permeated Beaumarchais's times in France and those of Mozart and Da Ponte in Vienna get excluded. The most obvious one is the issue of law. If law—the rules by which people live—is irrelevant to politics, then *The Marriage of Figaro* is indeed apolitical. If it is relevant, then politics is central to it. And while this opera ends cheerily with understanding and happiness, this happens only after a society is revealed, its authoritative ways made evident, its abuses and tensions between classes and between sexes exhibited. Despite their self-censorship, Da Ponte and Mozart's "comedy through music," as it was characterized, reinserted politics in subtleties in the revised libretto, in music, and in dances that speckle it. At one illuminating point, for example, Figaro will insist that he was kidnapped as a child and was really of "illustrious" birth. His teasing proof is his birthmark, as if a physical characteristic that entered the world with him signified his special value. (He could not have chosen to have it any more than royals, nobles, or any others choose their parents.) More important, consider how Figaro presents the stakes once, in the first act, Susanna presses him to recognize Almaviva's designs. He sings a famous cavatina—"Se vuol ballare"—to words not in Beaumarchais's play (but echoing its spirit). Angry Figaro repeats his opening line for emphasis:

> If you wish to dance, my little count (*Se vuol ballare, signor contino*)
> If you wish to dance, my little count
> I'll play for you my little guitar
>
> If he wants to come to my school
> I will teach him the capriole.[6]

The music in the repetition sung by Figaro suggests a minuet, that is, a graceful but aristocratic dance.[7] If Almaviva is taught the capriole, however, he will move less gracefully in a bounding theatrical dance motion. Capriole—the word indicates a goat's jump—can also mean a leap with a backwards kick by a boar or trained horse or someone tumbling, perhaps from power.[8] Figaro's singing goes on to alternate between and to mix both stateliness and defiance. Near the end of the same act he arranges for a chorus of peasants to shower Almaviva with flowers in gratitude for abolishing the right the Count is just then trying to exercise. "Here we are in the dance," says Figaro aside. Almaviva has no choice but to accept— or appear to accept—the laudations because he is in public. After all, he admits to cheers, it was an "unjust right." He was simply yielding to nature. "Such *virtù*!," Susanna acclaims. "Such justice!," adds Figaro.[9] These masters and servants, men and women, all in close proximity in a Spanish count's domains, seem a good deal like Vienna as described by Pezzl. Who will dance to whose tune? The opera is organized around this question. Linked to it are two other queries. What are the relations among legal restraints, human nature, and happiness? How is human nobility defined? Mozart, we know, saw it as a quality of soul, not as a matter of birth. In fact, the very term *"nobilitas"* originally meant an esteemed moral feature that some people had and others did not; but it was also used to separate or to distinguish social strata.[10] Sometimes it indicated both feature and rank but sometimes there were people deemed to have noble qualities who did not have noble status. Sometimes people had noble status but ignoble qualities. What—who —is noble and who—what—is not?

The tale presented by Beaumarchais, and by Mozart and Da Ponte, takes place in a single day, culminating after dusk falls on its characters but also on social and social tensions that they embody. As the sun sets on this Count's world, is endless night enveloping these characters? Or will another, more Enlightened world come on the next dawn's horizon? Torches are needed in the final scene to allow the characters, some disguised in the clothes of others (masters in those of servants and vice versa, a young man driven by rampant hormones dressed as a girl). Nobility, status, human qualities, and human desires will all be revealed finally in a pastoral setting, a forest clearing, as masks peel off those dancing out of an Old Regime in a great ball. Natural truths, it seems, emerge where laws and conventions no longer impose themselves.

II.

Law dances across public and private domains in this opera; both are within Almaviva's prerogatives. As a result, there is conflict between rules and what is presented as the highest, natural feelings of human beings. Although debated by jurists in the sixteenth and seventeenth centuries, (and references to it in criticisms of lords may be found in earlier village documents), some scholars today doubt that the *Droit du Seigneur* was more than a mythological custom.[11] It did, however, became a fecund symbol for a world of different rules for different people. It was discussed in Diderot's *Encyclopedia*, and Voltaire wrote a play titled *Le droit du seigneur* a decade and a half before Beaumarchais wrote *Figaro*. As the ways Europe was ruled changed over several centuries, dramatic shifts took place in the roles of customary and written laws. France and Austria provide good (if different enough) examples of these complex, uneven processes. One aspect was codification of local or regional customs. Another was translation of codes into a state (or what would be called an emerging national) legal system. The latter reinforced centralizing power, subordinating outdated privileges and customs. A sovereign, as Bodin asserted two centuries before Beaumarchais, is the final legal authority. Tensions arose inevitably between the crown and local legal nobles who had initially helped the king but wanted to sustain their own powers, particularly in the French *parlements*.

In the eighteenth century, intellectuals and jurists continued to deliberate about what it meant to have a rational and modernized civil code for an entire country. Important rights for individuals were at stake. Civil law entails the most basic matters: rights of contract, property, and inheritance. Debate about civil codes was, in simplest terms, about universalism (or the pretense to universalism) and particularity in rules. Should law be defined as the manifestation of humanity's common reason? Did ancient Roman law provide a guide to it, as many jurists thought? Or ought law to be better regarded as an expression of local customs and cultures seeking to resolve conflicts in specific societies? If the answer to the first question was positive, codification had a powerful support. If it was yes to the latter, it could be argued that generalized legal principles might not be appropriately or well applied locally. And the answers also served or masked different interests. For our purposes, they are important background. But in the quarter century before Beaumarchais wrote his plays, Robert Joseph Pothier, a law professor, distilled customs along with principles of Roman law into a proposed civil code for France. His work was known and translated widely.

The Austrian story was comparable if distinct and suggests why a *Figaro* was, in some ways, so suited to Austria's world. Maria Theresa was a firm believer in hierarchy. "There is no country where there is no distinction between overlords and subjects," she declared, "To free the peasant from his obligations to his overlord would make the first irresponsible, the second dissatisfied. From every angle it would collide with justice."[12] Nonetheless, she wanted a modern state and ordered codification of private law. Defining a sovereign was, however, a tender matter in the Holy Roman Empire, since its constituents sought to guard their powers. Bodin's idea of sovereignty, which served centralized power, had been the source of argument early on, and schools of public law had developed in the early seventeenth century.[13] The situation was complicated by the very fact of empire: there were imperial laws of the Holy Roman Empire, local laws in the many territories within it, and laws of hereditary Austrian lands. Allowing for the survival of local laws did not rest easy with efforts at unified political administration of the empire. While local customs were to be taken into account, the purpose of the code first proposed under Maria Theresa was to supplant past social privileges that had legal sanction with a general, rational system of law.[14] A draft representing a middle ground using local and Roman law became the *Codex Theresianus* of 1766. It distinguished among persons, things, and personal relations. This knotty endeavor tried to establish a realm-wide new system of law that would function along with provincial customary laws. Among other things it gave equal legal status to individuals, a novelty in the empire.

The *Codex* did not fit its many-leveled world well. Those who benefited by local laws and privileges wanted to sustain them. There was an obvious tension between the idea of "natural" (meaning rational here) laws covering an entire realm, and maintaining a local order in which the lower classes remained . . . lower, in all matters. At the same time, the *Codex* was to be written in the vernacular and not Latin; this made it accessible to subjects who were not lawyers. (Laws in German were, however, a political problem for another reason: the non-German populations in the empire dissented.) This is the legal nub—the multidimensional legal environment—in which Figaro and Susanna find themselves in both the play and the opera. The *Codex*'s treatment of "master-servant relations within a household" provided, notes one scholar, "a curious mixture of feudal and legal thinking." On one hand, the relation was considered contractual; and this was in an era in which capitalist relations and liberal ideas, for which market and social contracts are central, expanded. On the other hand, a peasant was the master's "subject." Consequently, the master continued to rule his household in a feudal way and could deploy "moderate compulsion" to maintain order and loyalty within it.[15]

Both conservatives and reformers were unhappy at the prospects of legal change; the former protested that proper privileges were being taken away and the latter believed codification had to go much further. Among the most important advocates of "modern law" in Austria was Karl Anton von Martini. He published a book in 1783—two years before Mozart and Da Ponte began work on *Figaro*—that stressed how law had to be based on reason. This was the way "to distinguish necessary from arbitrary laws." But adjustment and review of the *Codex* continued for another two decades in consultation with localities and amidst constant disputes over the monarch's precise status. Yes, the ruler was above conventional law, but he was restrained by "natural law"—rules inherent in nature and that all men, inasmuch as they were rational, could perceive. Martini, born in Revò (today in northern Italy) and then professor of law at the University of Vienna, wrote a massive work in Latin that became the legal touchstone of Josephinism: he wanted rational laws to encompass all domains and to be known in public.[16] While at the university, he made a strong impression on Joseph Eybel. The two had been in classes taught by an eminent proponent of natural law, Paul Joseph von Riegger—an advocate of radical Catholic reform on the basis of theories of natural law (that is, law based on rational precepts at a time of tensions between secular and church powers) and tolerance. A devoted advocate of Joseph II's policies and strongly anti-Jesuit, Eybal's criticisms of the pope in pamphlets, especially at the time of a papal visit to Vienna in spring 1782, made him especially visible, and his writings were placed on the Index. In fact, his efforts reinforced Joseph II's goal of subordinating church interests to those of the state. One law that was reformed in January 1783 gave the monarch rather than the pope ultimate authority over marriage. Its passage was prepared in part by an Eybel pamphlet claiming that the church's authority over marriage in the past had been only a temporary "delegation."[17] There is no direct link between his argument about appropriate authority over marriage and *The Marriage of Figaro*'s Vienna success, but the issue of reform was certainly known to Mozart—who was Eybel's friend and would be a member of the same Masonic lodge—and Da Ponte. Certainly, the pope was not comparable to Almaviva, but the allegation against the church was intrusion on natural love and marriage.

Martini's best-known student, and a man who took Eybel's ideas very seriously, was Sonnenfels. He was also an advocate of a constitution based on principles of natural law and the author of numerous political science textbooks. While his influence in Vienna was greatest under Maria Theresa, he remained a relentless advocate of legal reforms and a foe of feudal exploitation and serfdom, which he branded legal authorization of despotism. His argument made points that will seem very familiar to a viewer of *The Marriage of Figaro*. In particular, he chastised the "right of the lord" to make people "endowed with equal rights of body and soul" into the equivalent of personal property.[18] A public—constitutional—code of law was also needed, in his view, alongside codified civil law.

Sonnenfels's works were in Mozart's personal library. Martini, Sonnenfels, and Baron Gottfried von Swieten, who served as imperial librarian and censor and who was a strong supporter of Mozart, were leading figures of the "party" of Enlightenment in Vienna. A Mozart letter reports that the latter two were at a performance of *Idomeneo*. Mozart was very active in the relatively small social world of cultured Vienna and he went regularly to von Swieten's Sunday salons. [19] He met Sonnenfels there and it is conceivable that at them he became acquainted with Martini, whose name is on the subscribers' list to his concerts in March 1784.[20] Given these ties and interests, it can be assumed that Mozart had a familiarity with legal issues in Austria. They rise implicitly or explicitly in *Figaro*.

Without the questions of law and justice, authority and hierarchy, *The Marriage of Figaro* would be a droll but not especially consequential comedy of the sexes and about marriage that hinges on a callous quirk of supposed custom. Except, of course, for music that is astonishing for its many beauties in an array of forms. These animate and dramatize deftly the stage events: arias and dues, trios and a sextet, recitative and accompanied recitative, dances and choruses. *Figaro* sings from, of, and to a whole world in transition. It is not reducible to a "political opera," but no great opera is solely anything. However, laws, rules, rights, customs, and privileges concern how societies seek—and either fail or succeed—to solve conflicts, keep order, and reproduce it. No questions are, finally, as political as these. The opera does not sloganeer about these matters; it is not a broadsheet. Instead, political pulsations are sung through characters in predicaments within the framework of theater, in a sly, humorous, and musical unfolding of a story.

The Count's *Droit* to Susanna's body is feudal; it presumes different rules for different kinds of human beings. Soon after its claim is raised, another kind of law, one that had emerged over centuries, appears, and it is used to lay claim on Figaro. Marcellina, the Countess's old governess, tries to compel Figaro to wed her on the strength of the law of contract, here based partly on cash. He had once borrowed money from her, and his bond was consent to marriage should he fail at repayment. It is an agreed-on exchange by contrast to a feudal obligation. Here, then, are contesting and puzzle-making principles concerning civil society, household, and status that animated arguments and confusion in Vienna over legal codification. But *Figaro* takes issue with both these forms of regulation. By the first, an older Count uses "right" to seek sexual advantage with a younger servant; by the second, an older woman wants to ensnare by contract a younger man. Different rules, in both cases, work against what is natural—love. Doctor Bartolo speaks as if he were Marcellina's lawyer—her "*avvocato*," he says.[21] The Doctor even has a "witness," Don Basilio, an indiscreet music master. The opera's treatment of law is much briefer than in Beaumarchais's play but both revel in exposing brute coercion masquerading as justice.

Almaviva calls for adjudication. He is, after all, the Signor, and therefore the repository of justice. And so adjudication of a contract will be as impartial as the *Droit du Seigneur*. It is not, however, for justice's sake that he delights in the prospect of Figaro married to Marcellina. It is to remove an obstacle. So the contract will be read, declares the count, and then proper procedures followed.[22] Almaviva believes the contract is his surreptitious ally in asserting the feudal *Droit* he renounced. He doesn't quite understand the historical picture—that a world modeled on capitalist-like contracts is at odds with one of feudal authority, privileges, and obligations. Moreover, there is a slip in reasoning that seems to have escaped Almaviva and the creators of *Figaro*. If Figaro must marry Marcellina, the Count ought thereby to lose his *Droit*, since it is to a virgin servant's "first night" before marriage. Obviously the Count doesn't want to sleep with Marcellina, who is, in any case, neither his servant nor a virgin. Yet if Susanna does not wed, the Count can only take her by direct force and not by justification of *Droit*.

The rules, then, go to work from different directions on behalf of established power, old and new. And yet more is at play. While customary rights and cash-based exchange embody differing principles, both now appear as artificial rules that function on behalf of lower, aggressive human impulses. By exercise of his *Droit*, Almaviva hurts his Countess, whom he once loved and who still loves him. He hurts Susanna and, of course, Figaro, who as the barber of Seville once helped him win the Countess (from Bartolo). And while legal contract entails reciprocity in appearance, it serves Marcellina's baser quest together with Bartolo's grudge against Figaro for his past help to the Count. Bartolo insists on rules but his aria tells us that it is not legal rationality that shapes his role. Something else churns in his guts: "Vendetta," he sings, accompanied by drums and trumpets. Vengeance, for him, is "how a thinking man" gains redress. Only the lowborn forget insults, and he wants to deploy any and all codes together with all his learning against "the scoundrel Figaro."[23] With bass voice and accented forceful tune, his aria is Osmin-like in sound and brutal aspiration. The difference, of course, is that Osmin has no recourse to—or thoughts of—legal contracts. But they contrast both to Figaro's angry desire to change the dance and to the constancy of the Countess, who sings powerfully of self-mastery as Konstanze did before her.

The underlying point of both the *Droit* and the contract is much like that asserted in Da Ponte's Rousseau-like poems: laws and conventions repress natural desires. Consider Susanna's words after she allows Almaviva to "convince" her to meet for an assignation. (She is really conspiring with the Countess to expose the Count; they share a common interest in the failure of his expedition.) No lawyer, she says, will be needed to win the case. In other words, the *Signor*'s human foibles will undo him; argument on behalf of stale rules will not govern the outcome. When Almaviva guesses that there is a plot underway, he has the same emotions as Bartolo—fury and vengefulness. Naturally, he looks to law on his own behalf (again, like Bartolo). In the next scene, Don Curzio, a judge and the Count's lawyer, announces that Figaro must fulfill the contract. A ridiculous twist then makes the law an ass. It turns out that Figaro was kidnapped in his youth, and that Marcellina and Bartolo were his parents as proved by that birthmark. Figaro cannot marry his mother; nature here trumps contracts. And so in an opera filled with characters who don disguises and unveil themselves or find themselves unveiled, a meaningless nexus exposes customary rights and contracts; it reveals them to be masks covering the realities of power in human relations. Da Ponte apparently inserted some personal camouflage into the opera. In Beaumarchais's play Figaro's birth name is "Emmanuel," the same as Da Ponte's own name at birth. In the opera it becomes "Raphael." Cut from the opera was a brilliant and hilarious trial scene in which Beaumarchais further derided the legal world. Da Ponte and Mozart leave mockery of how law functions mostly to the imagination of an attentive audience (that would surely have known that legal reform was a principal issue of the day).

Sometimes, however, dress also reveals truth instead of being a disguise. At one point we meet Almaviva in his hunting outfit. He has been out in nature on a chase—using naked force for his pleasure. The choice of prey is his, of course, since the territory is too. When it comes to Susanna, he simply extends his license from one breathing quarry to another with *Droit* still his cover. Mozart and Da Ponte rearticulate through music, dance, and a sly scenario what they extract from Beaumarchais's play for the sake of political propriety. Figaro's "Se vuol ballare"—its music is like a quick minuet, a dance more associated with the upper classes than his own—marks out the moves. In fact, a ban on dance on stage had been instituted in Vienna. Da Ponte, who had once been so disgruntled by the same prohibition in his seminary, claimed that he persuaded the emperor to lift it for *Figaro*.[24] Whether this is true or not, the mere appearance of dance in the opera raised a question about rules. Dance or dancelike episodes and movements punctuate or speckle the entire opera. They are an important component of its specifically political accomplishment. We have mentioned some examples. Consider a few others:

- When rivals Susanna and Marcellina face each other in a duet of mutual hostility, their animosity is not expressed directly by words but more in a virtual dance around each other, their exchange begging for expression in body movement. False gentility masks repartees. Marcellina praises Susanna as "the Count's favorite." Susanna compliments Marcellina's age. In many stagings they finally curtsy to one another, true feelings seeping into subtle, antagonistic body movements, especially when they try to exit the same door. "I know what is due," they sing concurrently, each insisting the other take leave first.[25]

- Figaro will again sing "Se vuol ballare" after he, Susanna, and the Countess work out the many steps of a scheme. This is when Almaviva thinks he has persuaded—at last!—Susanna to come to a rendezvous. His challengers, however, will dispatch an anonymous letter to rouse his jealousy by indicating that his wife has also agreed to meet a lover—indeed that very evening in the castle garden during a masked ball. In Susanna's place the young page, Cherubino, will be sent dressed as a girl. The Countess will thus be able to catch the Count with "her." As it happens, Cherubino has been officially dispatched to the army by the Count for doing what the Count does: pursue females (although Cherubino does so more innocently and he swoons for the Countess).

- The second act culminates in a famous, long ensemble in which the characters move about in a hide-and-seek of intentions in a succession of baffling events. Susanna, for instance, will emerge from a dressing closet to the surprise of the Count and Countess. He expects to find his Countess's lover there and she, in turn, anticipates Cherubino, who was secreted within. But Susanna, understanding the mix of things, has taken Cherubino's place. She saves her mistress and mystifies her master. Her appearance comes with minuet-style music, and so to the sounds of courtly dance the servant trips up the Count's latest move. When Figaro appears and exchanges words with Almaviva about a certain anonymous letter, the music becomes gavotte-like—and a gavotte is a dance for aristocrats. It turns into a musette (a leisurely pastoral dance, that is, one with rustic associations) when Figaro, having apparently manipulated Almaviva with success, projects a happy wedding.[26] But when matters become complex again and the Count perceives deception, he declares, "Let's finish this dance."

- In the opera's finale, the Count will come to a pastoral setting expecting to fulfill his desire. By the end, however, he will indeed dance to a tune that is not his own as he is exposed by his Countess and by Susanna—who are disguised as each other. Movements of master and servant will, in a way, tangle in the Count's own body when he dances—or is led to dance—what is in effect an aristocratic gavotte; afterward he will have to step in another way, in what is in effect a peasant contredanse (a seventeenth-century English country dance adopted in France). His fury seems unbounded when it becomes clear that he has been made the fool by those beneath him, including by his feet and those of his servants.

Call it the politics of gait. Mozart did not use contredanse by happenstance. Consider how one scholar, Wye Jamison Allanbrook, brings out a strikingly political and social dimension to contredanse due to its lack of a fixed rhythm by the late eighteenth century. Because its meter altered, she proposes that its role in reinforcing social hierarchy did too. It had become extraordinarily popular in dance halls that had emerged in major European cities. Court dancing had used predetermined meters, and an aristocratic dancer's ability to follow them precisely was considered to be a revelation or expression of his (or her) character and thus confirmation of an appropriate place in the social hierarchy. Indeed, proficiency distinguished the noble dancer from common people (amateurs, that is). But the appearance of contredanse without the same regulation in music halls reflected a change in "the relation between meter and expression." In Louis XIV's court spectators "watched individual performers, each straining to the utmost to perform the correct expressive gestures of their dance." However, the following century's dance hall did not have an audience comprised, in the main, of observers. They were, instead, "participants restively waiting their turn." Instead of watching "a mass of gay but obedient dancers following the leader about the room" as if "points in an abstract geometry," the audience now participated in what was effectively a "danceless dance," since everything was not fixed.[27]

The contredanse plays an essential, symbolic role when it—or hints of it—reappears at telling points in *Figaro*. Take, for instance, the *duettino* toward the beginning of the first act, before Figaro has understood why Almaviva wants him and his bride to move into an easily accessible room. Figaro still thinks it is simply a comfortable spot that will allow him and Susanna to serve their masters better and more quickly when they are called by a bell, as was the custom. He sings to his bride-to-be that "If Madam/ should call you in the night/ 'Ding-ding'/ in two steps you can be there/ And then, if the Count should want me,/ 'Dong-dong'/ in three bounds I can be there to serve him." The varied paces by which they will reach their superiors are simple if, of course, obligatory. Then Susanna intimates to him what Almaviva really has in mind. If the Count sends Figaro on an errand, the lascivious "devil" can "in three bounds" be in the room with her. Anticipated here are all the coming movements of masters and servants, as if the opera were a dance of classes. Figaro's first words in the *duettino* are, Allanbrook points out, in a characteristic contredanse figure (four measured phrases recur three times without variation).[28]

Contredanse reappears throughout the opera as if a case is being made; it is a key element in its artistic rhetoric. Once Figaro grasps the Count's purpose, the dance becomes for the clever but annoyed servant a means—in sound and body movement—"to forward the attack" with "simple, rhythms, strong downbeat and rapid steps." As he sings those famous words, "If you wish to dance, little count," as he thinks of Almaviva's deceit and prepares his repartee, his tempo will alter momentarily toward one typical of a contredanse.[29] The rest of the opera may be considered this repartee, for Figaro's aim is for his master to dance to the servant's tune. What we behold, writes Allanbrook, is "the dancing master"—but he is Figaro the servant— "dragging his recalcitrant student"—that is, the aristocrat—"through the paces of social dance" that would "naturally end with a contradance, the dance which regularly followed the minuet in the middle class society of the danse halls." However, in the salons of the Old Regime, "the minuet stood alone, a dignified couple-dance performed by practiced dancers." It is improbable that a Count would become a member of "the throng dancing the relatively rowdy contredanse." But the member of the throng envisages the member of the nobility "transported . . . into an alien social setting, with rules of behavior appropriate to the more 'democratised' city life Figaro must have led before coming to the aristocratic seclusion of Count Almaviva's castle; he has lured his victim onto his own turf."[30] The turf is music and dance. And on it people—like music in everyone's ears—become equal; the same rules apply to everyone. It is less an assertion of democracy per se than of equality before the law—a reality in dance halls where classes intermingled, as opposed to their fixed places on estates with castles. Thus the essential political issue of the century is transposed into art.

And perhaps the opera pushes a little further. After all, the confounded Count is unforgiving of his anxious servants at the end, though they entreat of him on bent knees. Yet when his intent to betray his Countess is revealed in front of everyone he must, humiliated, beg forgiveness and so he must assume their position.

Masters and servants; men and women; rules and human relations (especially love), rational and customary—these distinct themes overlap, cross paths, interlace, and interface. Their development constitutes the body and soul of the opera—its plots and subplots, the comings, goings, guises, and disguises of its characters. These characters dance or sing to rhythms that are sometimes appropriate and sometimes inappropriate to their stations and to convention. By the end, the aristocrat cannot continue as he pleases —as he thought he always could. Instead, all those who people the opera become, increasingly, simply people, including him. Revealed beneath mistaken or disguised identities and beyond pretensions of rank, sex, and *Droit* is common humanity, with its errant and erring ways as well as its dignity. A call for equality is implied, if never quite made. Instead there is a call to see nobility in something other than artifice. It is not, however, a call for revolution. All the characters reconcile at the end. The precondition, however, is Signor Contino's patellae to the ground. And natural love is victorious.

III.

Many of *Figaro*'s themes wind again brightly and darkly throughout *Don Giovanni*. Sinister filaments—murder, hellfire—are anticipated in the overture. It begins, unlike *Figaro*, with formidable blocks of sound, chords played one after the other by the entire orchestra. Matters of great moral scale are to emerge, they tell us, although lighter music soon alternates with them. (Those strong chords return at the opera's end to confirm and to frame the message musically.) The overtures of *Figaro* and *Don Giovanni* share the key of D major and the stage events in both open with a servant in a predicament. But the differences in titles tell us something too: Figaro's amiable guile moves one opera, the Don's sinister guile drives the other. Leporello, Don Giovanni's manservant, never calls the tune, but orchestrates a ball on his master's behalf. Figaro is mutinous once he comprehends what Count Almaviva seeks; Leporello says often that he wants to quit his position but just cannot do so since he is as drawn to Don Giovanni's behavior as he is appalled by it. The premiere of *Don Giovanni* in Prague in October 1787 and its later Viennese debut featured bass Francesco Bernucci as Leporello. He had sung the first Figaro. Unfortunately, there is no account of Mozart or Da Ponte instructing him on differences in playing two subordinates who engage the world in such dramatically different spirits.

Don Giovanni's theatrical lineage extended back at least a century and a half before the second Da Ponte-Mozart collaboration. Its origins were probably in Counter-Reformation stories cautioning against amoralism. A political tint came early in a Jesuit-influenced tale about one Count Leonzio. His ideas, it turns out, are inspired by a political theorist notorious for his views on religion: Machiavelli. Leonzio's story anticipates Don Giovanni's last supper. In *Don Giovanni*, the antihero invites a Stone Statue—actually the ghost of the Commendatore, whom the dissolute Don slew after pursuing his daughter—to a feast, only to be sent to hell by him. Leonzio is an equally unscrupulous fellow and derisive of religion. He invites a skeleton to dinner to converse about the relation between body and soul only to have the boney figure haul his living flesh to just deserts with Satan.[31] A character named Don Giovanni was also popular in plays in Spain and Italy by the 1630s. Many accounts of him—in plays, ballets, operas—were to come by some of the major cultural figures of the seventeenth and eighteenth centuries, including Molière, Goldoni, and Gluck. One version, set by Veronese composer Giuseppe Gazzaniga, was staged in Venice in February 1787. Da Ponte would borrow liberally from its libretto by Giovanni Bertati, who was, notably, from Treviso.

Don Giovanni is the aristocracy's unrepressed id siphoned through egotism. His libidinal quests generalize the *Droit du Seigneur*, since his realm is the world. Every female body is his project, and his justification is little more than a declaration that women should feel ennobled by being his object. He contrasts to Count Almaviva, whose appetite has scope enough but who deploys a "right" within his private domains and, finally, has a particular woman in mind. We meet Figaro measuring space for a bed. We find Leporello, who was pacing at the beginning of *Don Giovanni* (waiting for his master) pacing again a few scenes into the first act. He is singing with due musical pace—in the key of D, suggesting the opera's subject by its home key—the data of his master's prowess: 1,003 women in Spain, 640 in Italy, 231 in German lands, 100 in France, 91 in Turkey. The Don, though a Spanish noble like Almaviva, is more cosmopolitan and more on the move, not only among countries but social strata and ages. Virgins may be his favorite, but variety satisfies him most in the larger scheme: chambermaids, city girls, and aristocratic women, young and old, beautiful or ugly.

Don Giovanni thinks nothing of the unhappiness he causes and has no concerns about complicating niceties like a wife's honor. He is (of course) unmarried, and so the latter matter doesn't figure in, although it is difficult to imagine that it would even if he were married. Almaviva, by contrast, becomes contrite, and restrained. He also survives his own antics in *Figaro* to appear in *The Guilty Mother*, a later play by Beaumarchais about the same principal characters. It was written after the French Revolution and takes place in Paris where he is no longer "*Signor Contino*," although Figaro still works in his household. The Don, of course, does not survive his own opera. Indeed, he pays no heed to the consequences for himself of his own behavior. He is blunt: he despises repentance. He is defiant even as the Commendatore's icy handclasp signals that he will no longer be a law unto himself. He had always been able to circumvent this-worldly rules and customs until then. The opera points us to something more consequential than those rules and customs but also to the formation of an alliance of those he has injured. They close in, accompanied by ministers of earthly justice, although he descends into the flames before their arrival. By then, it is evident to all (except him) that he has lost his touch.

And the audience has also watched his final ventures fail, one after another. Donna Anna wants revenge twice over, first for his lascivious behavior toward her and then for his killing of the Commendatore. (Leporello, as if anticipating Freud, comments wryly, "Bravo!/ Two impressive acts!/ Rape the daughter and kill the father.")[32] We learn in an epilogue following Don Giovanni's downfall that she will marry Don Ottavio after some time for mourning. Donna Elvira initially loves Don Giovanni, despite his typically uncaring seduction of her. She ventures to save him but also to protect his other targets until it is clear that the cause is hopeless. She turns against the rake and will announce her intention to retreat to a monastery. Zerlina, the young peasant girl whom Don Giovanni lures with his status and whom he almost despoils, will go off to dinner with Masetto, her original intended, and rustic friends. A simple marriage will, presumably, provide her happiness (in this she is like Rousseau's Colette).

And here we return to Leporello. If a noble's name gives the opera its title, the frustrated, nervous manservant is a pillar of its substructure. Leporello's first words flow right out of the overture, anticipated as the last bars in D major that change into another key, F major, for him. Mozart—one suspects—aims to suggest comparison by musical means since Figaro's "Se vuol ballare" is in F major (and *Figaro* has a D-major overture). Leporello grumbles about his status while the Don is nearby—offstage—trying to have his way with Donna Anna. He knows what this is about while Figaro, who believes initially that he is to be well treated by his master, finds his head turned around by deceit.

In short, both operas begin with servants in quandaries, even if their characters are different enough. Leporello lives in perpetual cognitive dissonance; it renders him humorous. Knowing his master, he wiggles around

317

him as much as he wiggles on his behalf. The Don's tie to Leporello is simple and limited; a servant is useful. Leporello's bond with the Don is complicated; it goes beyond obligations and not only because of his desires. The servant has an ideal of nobility and of the nobility. As long as his ideal survives, he cannot imagine a world without masters and servants. Yet his ideal is challenged continuously before his eyes—and he helps the Don while disdaining what his master does. He sees the unsavory benefits of rank but is drawn to them. "I want to be a gentleman/ I don't want to serve anymore," he sings in the opening scene.[33] There is something tragic in this conflicted buffa figure. He always finds excuses to stay with the Don and is dependent on him—emotionally, certainly financially. Despite Leporello's desire to be a gentleman, his mindset is service.

Even the Don's end doesn't lead Leporello to think of liberty but of finding a new, better master. It does not occur to him that perhaps there ought not to be masters and servants. The opera does not propose this radical idea either, harboring only conflicted protest against hierarchy and ignoble nobles. It doesn't suggest that all those of lower status come together naturally in opposition to an oppressive man of rank. Zerlina recognizes that shared subordination doesn't necessarily make for a coalition between a servant and a peasant (and the other peasants think like her). This is explicit and not only personal in scenes that Mozart and Da Ponte added to the second act for the Viennese staging of 1788 but are shed nowadays from most performances.[34] By this point Leporello is trapped by the growing anti-Don alliance. Servant and master switch cloaks to mischievous purposes and the former thinks his interests are those of the latter. The Don's aim is to pursue a girl of lower status and Leporello intends to play at being of higher station in the hope of seducing a female of rank.

While the Don has gone off Leporello is mistaken for him, cornered, and then exposed. He is menaced by knife-wielding Zerlina, whom Leporello has just recently sought to ensnare for his master's pleasure. A brief effort by him at persuasion through seduction is to no avail; the cloak never made him the Don. Endangered, he calls out to peasants for help; they do not hear him. The Don's death scene is actually prefigured here in Leporello's circumstances, but it is a character both comical and sad who is on display, not a swaggering, if doomed one. (The Don's behavior can sometimes seem comical but his character always reveals the fraud of nobility.) Zerlina demands to take Leporello's hand and he resists at first. Fearful for his life, he finally yields—unlike the fearless Don who will soon clasp the damning Statue. With a peasant's help, Zerlina grabs and binds Leporello to a chair that, in turn, is secured to a window frame. He is trussed to an exit he cannot take.

Leporello feels as if he is losing his breath, as if he is unable to tell day from night, as if the earth is shaking—as if he is to be pulled into darkness. Zerlina exits and he appeals to a peasant for help, calling him *"Amico"* ("Friend").[35] The peasant just leaves. Peasants in *Don Giovanni* are mostly deferential toward "superiors," but here one of them shows he has no use for a noble's servant. It is as if he were to say silently: We may bend a knee out of fear, but you are an accomplice in the order of things. We are not friends. Alone and writhing, Leporello will even appeal aloud to Satan to free him. It is to no avail but he will eventually yank the chair from the window's fastening and drag himself away. Leporello becomes a kind of hobbled evil sprite who frees himself in a way, staggering off since he is still bound and unable to stand up, let alone go through the window. Leporello's master will, of course, go to the devil, the earth opening up, after insisting—*Viva la libertà!*—on his own liberty. Closures and openings are ambiguous.

From that first appearance bemoaning his status to the announcement in the epilogue that he will seek a new master, Leporello raises issues concerning authority, human ties, and the human psyche. The peasant's non-response to his call of *"Amico"* points to an important motif, an essential one of the opera, even if this scene was an addition and often dropped. Repeatedly, in telling ways, the nature of friendship is interrogated in this opera. It was also central in all major Mozart operas, as we have seen, as well as among the Masons. It is, in *Don Giovanni*, more poignant in ways than the obvious and simple conclusion that punishment comes for bad behavior. (Indeed, all the characters might have done well to consider Aristotle's comment that "[c]hoosing a friend should not be like choosing a cloak.")[36] Don Ottavio wonders aloud how Don Giovanni can behave as he does under "the sacred cloak of friendship."[37] Questions raised by friendship run throughout all other themes of this opera—master/servant, men/women, rules/society—and knit them together while exposing them individually. Unsettling implications, many of them political, are suggested thereby for the world in which the opera takes place, for the world in which it was initially staged—and that in which it is still staged, our own. They may be derived, in a way, from the fact that Leporello and Don Giovanni are both friendless.

Early in Act 1, Leporello asks if he can speak freely—with "complete liberty" —to the Don. Can he address his master without fear? The Don answers yes, swearing on his honor. How could a nobleman respond otherwise?—and that

319

alone should have told Leporello not to trust him. Then the servant speaks truth to his honored master: you live as a rogue. We find immediately that truth to this Don is as *Droit* to Almaviva: a matter of convenience. Habitually suave and usually cool (even in female pursuit), anger wells up and he reverses himself. How dare Leporello? Don Giovanni even denies that he has just sworn to hear out his servant without retribution. Such liberty is his province and no servant's prerogative. The honor of his word hardly matters. Meek Leporello backs off. His feelings will have to be cloaked since frank talk can obviously be only between equals—or perhaps with a superior who at least sometimes recognizes the worth of heeding more than his own promptings or of hearing unpleasant truths. No underling may hold up a mirror to Don Giovanni. After establishing that truth cannot define relations between master and servant, Don Giovanni allows, "Thus we'll be friends."

Like the Don's truth, however, such friendship cannot have substance. Indeed, friendship hardly makes sense between a man of privilege who hurls onwards like a force of nature, groin first, and an underling running by his side, trying to catch his breath, unable to engage in anything that might be called an amicable exchange. For the dutiful attendant who wishes to be a gentleman, nobility entails truth-telling but this is not so for the *Signor*, an extreme egotist for whom a servant, like women, exists only for the using. But after his banter with Leporello, Don Giovanni's passions refocus—or rather his will directs him to the next female prospect, Zerlina, on her wedding day. He tells her that he will "protect" her and Masetto. They will be "friends." Yet true friendship requires trust, faith in behavior that goes beyond the short-term. This is precisely what cannot be expected of him. At another moment Donna Anna asks Don Giovanni for his "friendship" in her pursuit of the man who attacked her, unaware that she speaks to the evildoer himself. The noble proffers it immediately. Leporello has a "friend" on whom he is dependent but on whom he certainly cannot depend. Don Giovanni wants to ennoble his female "friends," Donna Anna and Zerlina. And he turns his back on Donna Elvira's hand, stretched out to him repeatedly. Don Giovanni's view of friendship is not at all relativistic; the very word "relativism" is as meaningless to him as friendship is empty.

Even if the Don incarnates self-serving aristocratic power, Mozart and Da Ponte don't portray all nobles this way. In one sense it would have been unwise and impractical to do so since they needed patrons and audiences (and Joseph II had support from reform-minded aristocrats against reactionary ones). The opera's other aristocrats don't see themselves in the

Don and they don't recognize any truth about the social order that sustains them (and him) in his behavior. It is when Don Ottavio, the (apparent) love of Donna Anna, recognizes the guilt of Don Giovanni, his "friend," that he is taken aback at what is behind this particular noble's "sacred cloak." He doesn't ask if there is something wrong with birth into higher social status (let alone birth into a privileged sex). He feels torn between his duty to "a friend" and to Donna Anna. "Friends" in woe—that is what Donna Elvira calls those now allying with her. They are united against the professor of duplicitous amity and, perhaps not so ironically, they are so beneath masks. Friendship—in contrast to love of Don Ottavio for Donna Anna or Masetto for Zerlina—would seem at first approach to have only a negative reality in this opera. Bonds among characters are created only in opposition to the malefactor.

"True friends do not wrong one another," wrote Aristotle, adding that "people will not act wrongly if they are just." He used for "friendship" the Greek word *philia*, which can also mean love. He also made a threefold distinction that is helpful when looking at the place of friendship in *Don Giovanni* and that presses us to look beyond a simple moral (that bad men will suffer). In friendship based on utility, according to Aristotle, people use each other without real regard or sense of mutuality. "Pleasurable" amity, however, is something else—a matter of ephemeral feelings. We can discern the first type in the relation between master and servant in *Don Giovanni*, certainly from the Don's perspective. The second overlaps with it in his relations with women, who discover that what for them was comity to be shared and lasting is for him momentary gratification. Friendship based on pleasures may not necessarily be between good people. "Bad men may be pleasant to each other not because they are bad," comments Aristotle, but because they have something in common. "They are both, say, musical," he writes. So one is a musician and the other harbors great passion for music. (A composer reading these words might imagine assigning a common key to the two.) The same may be so of a good and a bad man. Yet a third "primary" form of friendship—at one point Aristotle calls it the "pure" form—comes of virtue; it can be only among good people, and makes them happy.[38]

In fact, this third kind of friendship projects both an alternative beyond Don Giovanni's personal horizons and provides a regulative idea for understanding the politics of the opera (even if its creators did not imagine themselves to be translating these Aristotelian moral notions into a stage work). The philosopher believed that men are "political animals" who can only realize themselves through a polity. Friendship, moreover, "implies likeness and equality"; it is, he insisted, the "special task of political skill" to further friendship.[39] Perfect friendship, argued Aristotle, entails enduring reciprocity. It demands a virtuous constancy for the good among people who regard each other as equals, and as of value for their own sakes.

A communal vista opens from this kind of friendship; it implies attachments that cannot be reduced to the evident usefulness of living with others or to brief pleasures they may afford. It implies a world in which a Don Giovanni could not survive. But the other characters cannot create it either. Once he is gone, they part, some in couples, to their different ranks and ways. They do have a certain limited goodness about them, but it never translates into something more. Constant Don Ottavio will wait for Donna Anna's hand; Donna Elvira will go to an ascetic life that, presumably, allows escape from quotidian unhappiness. Zerlina and Masetto—the only figures who attain at the end what they wanted initially—return to their rustic community and Leporello looks for a master. Struggle against Don Giovanni does not bring them all into a new, equality-friendly human community. Aristotle, however, would not have disapproved of this ending, since he believed that people were naturally masters or slaves and that women ought to be restricted to the household. True friends are equals, for him. (We, today, would extend far this equality and thus the possibilities of friendship.)

Aristotle's third kind of friendship can also be formulated and extended to subvert both the *Droit du Seigneur* and Don Giovanni's generalization of it. The celebratory reconciliation that concludes *Figaro* intimates that there might be an alternative to the social and political relations of the old regime but doesn't articulate or demand it. The order of things, while exposed, survives amidst the rejoicing. There is relief but no general reconciliation at the conclusion of *Don Giovanni*; what brought everyone together is gone. Perhaps the historical moment is captured in these different ends. When Mozart and Da Ponte worked on *Figaro* in late 1785, Joseph II was already worried about what his reforms had unleashed. A reversal of many of his more enlightened policies was on Vienna's horizon. This included new regulation of the Masons, who so stressed friendship and "brotherhood." Reconciliation was plausible then but *Don Giovanni*, two years later, begins to suggest otherwise.

IV.

Leporello's relation to Don Giovanni displays the consequences of inequality for utilitarian friendship. This constant servant lives in hope to the point of breaking. When the Don exchanges cloaks with him, Leporello's own seduction is evident, and instead of a woman, it brings jeopardy. Appearance doesn't bring success in the Don's practices. Yet while the noble does not succeed anymore either and is doomed to eternity's bowels, the servant is not quite enlightened. Leporello sees an individual aristocrat's bad conduct but doesn't perceive the social order in it. The Don's behavior does, however, trigger a rebellion of lower strata in Act 2. Masetto and armed peasants search for him but, secreted under Leporello's cloak, Don Giovanni misleads them. They divide at his urging and go off in different directions, never recognizing that their true enemy is in front of them. Poor Masetto, who has always been suspicious of Don Giovanni, is held aside by him and beaten by the false Leporello. Thus the servant will be blamed for attacking the peasant.

He has acted "for us all." These are Zerlina's words in praise of Don Ottavio after he brings earthly ministers of justice at the very end (in a scene added for 1788).[40] But another force, through the Stone Statue, has already acted, telling us that Don Giovanni's behavior is unnatural and has no place among fellow humans. *Philia*, especially what Aristotle called its primary kind, has no need of external enforcement. The Don's end ought to leave an audience wondering if his fate incarnates a truth about the society in which the characters on stage live. But the characters that survive do not perceive this; for them Don Giovanni is an episode. Lessons learned, the regime can carry on. *Don Giovanni*, like *Figaro*, reveals to its audience what its characters don't perceive. Masters and servants have again danced around each other, taking steps that would not be their own by the dictates and structures of the whole social order.

Earlier, we know, the Don orders Leporello to coax Zerlina, Masetto, and their rustic companions to a ball in his villa for "entertainment." With masks and three orchestras, the stage will be set quite literally to pose Figaro's question: who dances to whose tune? There will be three different dances, entwined with the separate orchestras playing. All are at cross-purposes but Mozart's music links them, even if none are bound to the others. The whole society and its contradictions are in movement. Each couple has different motivations. And so Don Ottavio and Donna Anna, both aristocrats, step to an elegant, slow French courtly dance of small steps and bows. This minuet is in G major, in 3/4 time, and the orchestra is composed of strings, oboes, and horns. Don Giovanni, however, takes Zerlina into a spry country "contredanse," in 2/4 time, accompanied by a second orchestra of violins and bass. Perhaps the Don wants to make her at ease with movements more familiar to her—all the better to mislead her to private quarters. But the fact is that they dance together, two figures from different classes. Mozart, writes Allanbrook, saw the contredanse as "generally appropriate to the Don" because "just as it cuts across the established orders of danse gestures, so does the Don cut across the world of Donna Anna and the other characters, threatening to subvert it."[41]

If we follow this claim and compare it to the role of the same dance in *Figaro*, we find that it indicates that a world is being pulled apart from more than one direction; rules are failing to hold. Don Giovanni moves to his own beat and contredanse suggests that he ignores the old norms and what is considered to be aristocratic respectability. In his famous "Champagne Aria" in the first act, he tells Leporello that he wants a big party in his own palazzo and that all the peasants should come. Bring as many young girls as possible, he urges, and let wine flow so copiously that everyone becomes tipsy and he, in the meantime, can flirt behind the scenes. Allanbrook compares this aria, with its plain rhythms, downbeats, and swift movements, to the contredanse moment of Figaro's declaration that he will make Almaviva dance to his tune.[42] In the first case, then, the aristocrat, Don Giovanni, seems inebriated in his reckless pursuit of whatever he wants, and in the second, the servant Figaro seems similarly driven to undo his master's pretensions. In his aria, Don Giovanni declares that everyone can do whatever dance pleases in his palazzo—in other words, the peasants may do aristocratic dances, if they would like to do so. Let them do the minuet, for all he cares. He is not concerned about their status as they move; he cares about how he makes his moves in his next seduction. And the association of Figaro with contredanse also serves to cross class lines, although not to the same end. While the Don's behavior shows the rules crumbling from above, Figaro is acting from below. These are operas about their own characters but also about the decade in which they were written, the 1780s. They suggest different possible conclusions about where their era may end.

Masetto refuses to dance at first but Leporello will finally coax the peasant into a *Deutscher*, a fast waltz (also known as an Allemande) in 3/8 time, also to strings and bass and played by another orchestra. Mozart, as one scholar notes, synchronizes music for the orchestras, one leading into the next, and remarkably brings them together with three dances in different rhythms.[43] As aristocratic movements finish, the next orchestra is tuning for the contredanse, and finally there comes the fast waltz in which two men are dancing together, suggesting that something is perhaps not quite right. Notably, Leporello is trying to deceive someone who is, like him, of subordinate status.[44]

It was Don Giovanni who had invited Donna Anna, Donna Elvira, and Don Ottavio to this dance (through Leporello, of course) and these aristocrats are masked too. The Don perceives no danger in what is underfoot, and welcomes everyone with a famous declaration: "*Viva la libertà.*" Masked balls seem to suggest that liberty needs anonymity in this society. In any event, the Don fears little when his id surges; in any event, he has his cloak. Yet freedom for him becomes always self-deception on behalf of his appetites—these, too, make him friendless—and that is why freedom for him has no relation to fear. It has no relation to responsibility and thus always seems safe—as long as it is liberty for him. This is not a condemnation by Mozart and Da Ponte of desires or sensuality in themselves but of friendless desire and of friendless sensuality. The three disguised aristocrats join the Don and Leporello in repeating "*Viva la libertà!*" but this sounds ironic since what four of them want is to be free of Giovanni.

Contrary but (as yet ordered) gaits of a whole social world have been presented in changing sounds and moving bodies. The Don will finally face moving stone, an implacable father who does not dance and embodies hard prescriptions against his cavalier liberties. He met the Statue that harbors the ghost of Donna Anna's father in a cemetery after yet another escape from pursuers, and he invited him to dinner. In the denouement, the Don gratifies himself with a hearty meal. It is hardly surprising that he doesn't wait for his invitee to arrive before he satiates himself. He repeats, again without sensing danger at hand, his own cheer. He specifies further his vision of the world, while also showing its limits: "Long live women, Long live good wine, the sustenance and glory of humanity."[45] In the end, the opera shows, however, that freedom must be social and not a matter of egotistical craving; eros is an insufficient bond without friendship. Still, the Don's utter fearlessness is remarkable, although it comprises no less his blindness to any law but his own. After rebuffing more pleas to mend his ways by Donna Elvira, he dismisses the Commendatore's command to repent. Both in the cemetery and now he ignores terrified entreaties by Leporello. When the Statue invites him to dine, suggesting repayment, the Don takes the outstretched stone hand—in D major again as Mozart continues to link events and themes by keys. Recall that the overture was in D major, as was Leporello's enumeration of the Don's exploits; soon the finale will be in D minor, before the epilogue in D major.

Clasped hands often symbolize camaraderie and not just an accord. In *Don Giovanni* they are ironic and, most importantly, hands in it often touch without reciprocity. Hands come together and move apart in the various dances. Zerlina takes Leporello's hand only to tie him up. When the Don takes the statue's hand, he is really being gripped by a larger reality. And still he refuses to become a penitent. "Ah your time is up!" the statue then says. The Don's strut can now go nowhere and as he sinks he waves his hands with what Leporello calls "gestures of the damned."[46] Nobody else grasps his hands—at least nobody else with warm blood. He lived freely, without limit in the short-term, only to bring to himself long-term catastrophe. In fact, he recognizes his impending lot as chill travels from the statue into him, but like France's Old Regime two years later, it is too late. The rhythms have chilled. Does the opera truly offer an alternative dance to that of the old regime? There are several possible answers and all feature ambiguities. One might be found in friendship conceived as mutuality. But we know that those who survive Don Giovanni no longer have bonds among them. Authority and hierarchy seem intact.

Don Giovanni suggests many things about human behavior and often slyly, which is hardly surprising given the librettist's personal history. Da Ponte's adventurous life had continued in Vienna and would do so as well after he left the Habsburg capital. (His friend Casanova may have helped him write some parts of *Don Giovanni.*) But the opera's target isn't simply an overly libidinous male, but an egotistical one shielded by his class. Almaviva is tamed, Don Giovanni must be destroyed. His fate is complicated, however, by that call of "*Viva la libertà*" and its repetition by "*Tutti*" (Everyone.) It is one thing when an individual who follows his own law hails freedom on his own behalf; it is another when everyone does so, but for one and all. A proposition of Rousseau's *Social Contract* (later echoed by Karl Marx) was that the conditions permitting the liberty of one person ought to be those enabling the liberty of all.

"Long live liberty!" had multiple meanings in 1787, not least concerning the retreat from reform in Vienna. The Don first sings it to great musical emphasis—which means Mozart found particular meaning in it—when he welcomes Donna Anna, Donna Elvira, and Don Ottavio in their masks to the ball. There is freedom of the dance when nobody can see who is who or detect anyone's motivations, desires, and intentions. As one scholar points out, "*la libertà*" may mean either liberty or license.[47] The opera is poised between these two possible meanings; sometimes they part ranks and sometimes they join together.

Those three words and Mozart's setting of them have been the source of considerable attention. Charles Rosen, while arguing that "extramusical" effects arise from "the music alone" in the "classical style" tradition of the late eighteenth century, points to "*Viva la libertà!*" as an example of how "politics can enter into music." A straightforward call for political freedoms would have been impossible. A musical call for "freedom from convention," however, is something else—indirect but also evident. Mozart does this by making an unexpected key change between the Don's declaration that "everyone is welcome" and the salute to liberty, and he supplements this with orchestral emphasis. "Starting with a surprising C major (the last chord was E-flat major) Mozart brings out the full orchestra with trumpets and drums *maestoso* (that is, with decorum or dignity) in an exhilarating passage full of martial rhythm." While Mozart's C major comes from how he conceived the musical logic of the finale in an opera's act—he returns to restate the tonality in which it began—Rosen notes that it is unlikely that listeners in a tumultuous era would have missed "a subversive meaning," especially given the dozen musically potent repetitions of *"Viva la libertà!"* In Vienna, another scholar points out, authorities changed *"libertà"* into *"società."*[48] The meaning was thereby reversed.

"Viva la libertà!" raised the same subject that we found in Da Ponte's Treviso poetry: conflict between the natural expressions of human desires and external constraints on them. The opera does not protest these desires in themselves, but only when they become privileged extremism. The Don's behavior may be insupportable, but the same cannot be said of a call to freedom by everyone else on stage. At minimum they will be free of him at the end. Yet when they sing that the evildoer has gone where he belongs, they cite an authority: "the oldest of proverbs."[49]

Proverbs, of course, articulate moral conventions, but Don Giovanni's fate is conventional only in the sense that a father—a traditional authority figure—comes from beyond the grave for him, as if an avenging superego more than a supernatural hand. The conventional authorities arrive when it is too late and the Don, by refusing to repent, has taken full responsibility for his free acts and thus has a truly admirable—even noble—dimension despite himself, despite what constitutes his self. In this sharp sense, he is a mixed character; we laugh sometimes at his cavalier brutality and are supposed to find him humorous (sometimes). What is jest at convention and rules and what is serious about breaking them is not entirely distinct.

V.

Convention is at the center of *Così fan tutte*. It is questioned in *Figaro's* presentation of upper and lower strata and the *Droit du Seigneur*. Don Giovanni defies conventions, and his "nobility" allows rampaging individuality. Dance, in which nobody stays in place, tells us to see through what is firm and visible. *Così fan tutte* was the final Mozart-Da Ponte collaboration. Even though the librettist initially offered to write it with Salieri (who apparently made a start and then put it aside), it comprises part of a whole with Da Ponte's earlier collaborations with Mozart. Conventions are again scrutinized. They are revealed to be not products of nature but social norms, masked as natural and accepted. This time a philosopher—he is obviously an enlightener—and a servant will focus the interrogation. Together they provide cross-lighting—and cross-enlightening. The constellation of protagonists will be different, at least in part, from the earlier Mozart-Da Ponte operas. Two young soldiers will go through a learning process about appearance and reality. *Così's* subtitle (and Da Ponte's original title) is "The School for Lovers," but it anticipates education on a higher as well as more political level that comes in *The Magic Flute*, Mozart's next opera. Among the questions posed to the characters (and implicitly to the audiences) by all these operas are: What shall be learned about the authority of ruling conventions—and how?

"Così fan tutte" may be translated simply as "That's what they all do." These same words had already appeared in *Figaro* when Don Basilio explained female passions and wiles. They come with a brief trilling passage that sounds again in *Così's* overture. *Così* takes place in eighteenth-century Naples and its plot is simple. Ferrando and Guglielmo are engaged to two sisters, Fiordiligi and Dorabella. These men, both soldiers, hold romantic, conventional beliefs in fidelity. The women, they exclaim, are as beautiful as they are faithful. Challenge comes from a graying skeptic. Don Alfonso proposes that faith in faithfulness is unsustainable. In other words, if you hold a light up to the beliefs that hold society steady, you find other things— including change. Ferrando and Guglielmo, as military men, are pillars of order and expect things to be in form. They are ready to duel with Don Alfonso because of his words but he is a clever philosopher and so he proposes a civilized wager of wits instead of the usual swords or pistols: smarts versus arms. They accept, and inform their betrothed that they have been called to battle, and weep farewell.

All the while, Don Alfonso laughs. The terms of the wager require the two men to return in pursuit of the sisters disguised as lovesick Albanian nobles. When they do, Fiordiligi and Dorabella resist their entreaties. But the "Albanians" maneuver until constancy waivers. The men pretend to take poison for love's sake—"Arsenic frees me," they sing, "from all this cruelty"[50]—and Don Alfonso urges pity to the sisters. They prove as gullible as the soldiers are deceptive, will eventually sign a marriage contract, and then will be mortified when their old sweethearts return from "battle." Contract, once again, appears to trump love. Naturally, Fiordiligi and Dorabella are furious at Don Alfonso when they learn that they have been tricked. Yet they have indeed been fickle and they will see, as do Ferrando and Guglielmo, that Don Alfonso's reason, working through human disguises, has demonstrated a truth about human behavior that must, however, be excused. Don Alfonso explains that his scheme only aimed to "undeceive" the officer. These lovers ought to have been unforgiving of Fiordiligi and Dorabella and angry about losing their wager, but they recognize that experience has enlightened them. Don Alfonso instructs the young men to repeat his words, "*così fan tutte*"—and they do. The couples reconcile and the opera concludes with everyone praising the philosopher. Happy is he, they sing, who lets "reason" guide him through life's adversities.[51]

But the philosopher has not succeeded on his own. There is an alliance between his reason and a rightfully resentful servant's shrewdness. His collaborator is the maid of the two sisters; she knows her mistresses and always expects them to succumb. Despina joins Don Alfonso in writing the tune to which conventional young men and women will dance. It is not that the philosopher and the maid perceive the world in the same way. When we first meet Despina she has just made breakfast for her mistresses—hot chocolate for her superiors, as Serpina prepared for Uberto in *La serva padrona*. She repeats complaints we have heard from Figaro and Leporello, but with more ire. Her recitative echoes (rather obviously) those indelicate sentiments in Beaumarchais's *Figaro* that Da Ponte excised for political reasons. Says Despina,

> . . . I labor and get nothing for myself!
> The chocolate has been ready for half an hour,
> Am I not as good as they are?
> and I must stand here and smell it, mouthwatering,
> O gracious mistresses,
> who apportioned to you the substance and me the aroma?[52]

She then takes an illicit sip. Despina, like any human being, wants to taste the good life. Alas, she must then run to wait on the two ladies.

Don Alfonso must bribe Despina to aid his plot; this suggests things are complicated. He is trying to prove a point to which she doesn't object, but clearly she has her own interests. After all, the philosopher can have chocolate whenever he wants it. A servant must calculate. Leporello doesn't betray his "better," but Despina does, and she is right to do so. She needs her mistresses for material, but not emotional, reasons. At first she resists Don Alfonso's scheme, suspecting that this older man wants to take advantage of her. Indeed, just before he approaches her for help in introducing the "Albanians" (whom she also doesn't recognize initially), she lectures her mistresses about male behavior. They are unfaithful, inconstant. Why should women behave differently? (Or servants, for that matter, but she does not add this directly.) In other words, as Don Alfonso describes females—*così fan tutte*—so she depicts males. Despina's irritation at men is no less than her irritation at being a servant. Why—but she does not say this to her mistresses—should servants not betray too? "Donna Arroganza" is how she speaks in private of Fiordiligi. Two central motifs of *Figaro* and *Don Giovanni* reemerge, then, in *Così fan tutte:* the relations of men and women, and the relations of masters and servants. Their exposition comes about through ploys and antics within the opera. And again the use of disguise leads finally to a recapitulation of the point that Don Alfonso made at the beginning: the man of reason understood human relations.

The role of disguise here, as in the earlier Mozart-Da Ponte operas, is essential. Only as "foreigners" can the officers know the women they love. And the "Albanians" teach their lovers about themselves. Despina also takes on disguises, as if to say her own position is just a matter of role-playing—rather than her humanity—because of her own circumstances. At one point she is disguised as a doctor, and another point as a notary. While these moments are parts of Don Alfonso's scheme to press the four young lovers to see the world more clearly, Despina is also busy exposing pompous, professional authorities in society. Mozart and Da Ponte, inspired by Beaumarchais, launched earlier barbs at doctors and lawyers in *Figaro*. The "doctor" in *Così* is the butt of satire in an additional way. "He" follows popular fashion by "curing" the "Albanians" with a magnet, a "Mesmer stone." Named for a charlatan whom the Mozart family knew in Salzburg, Franz Anton Mesmer's "discoveries" had become a pan-European rage. His pseudoscience continued to "mesmerize" even after a French Royal Commission exposed it as a fraud in 1784.

Mozart and Da Ponte signal something important to their audience when they present a servant disguised as a doctor who uses Mesmerism to cure a sham poisoning. Counterfeit solutions ought not to be sought to false problems. Fakery is chastised once more when Despina, again in mufti, plays the role of a legal notary who confirms contracts. If in *Figaro* a real contract in the hands of a real lawyer threatens true love, in *Così fan tutte* the same point is made by the bogus legal official who signs up the sisters and the "Albanians" in marriage: love is not a formal legal tie. Reality and appearance, whether it is a matter of scientific or social authority, are exposed by the tools used by Despina when she is a "professional."

Despina's mistresses can't see through her disguises any more than they perceive her *ressentiments*. When the "lawyer-notary" is revealed to be their servant, Fiordiligi and Dorabella sing: "It's Despina! It's Despina!/ I don't understand what's happening."[53] That is just the point. Don Alfonso reveals what is conventional (fashionable views of love) and what is natural. He says frankly that it is "philosophy" that leads to the conclusion. "Nature can't make exceptions," he observes, adding in an aria, "that's what women do."[54] The opera is obviously sexist, to use an anachronistic label, but it would be wrong to see Despina simply as a collaborator in Don Alfonso's demonstration of the order of things. Her immediate source of discontent is her status; her mistresses have their own unquestioned assumptions about subordination. This is what we must see and hear when Despina and Don Alfonso together sing, "*Bravi, Bravi, in verità!*"[55] Don Alfonso may say that all women behave in a certain way and Despina has said just the same for men. But Despina's mistresses are inconstant when it comes to men, although quite constant when it comes to their servants. Don Alfonso and Despina collaborate, but not as Don Giovanni and Leporello do because she is acting against her superiors and helping to reveal them. Indeed, she is wise in the ways of the world, having seen it from below while observing those above and she has done this before; she joins Don Alfonso's designs. She comes with schooling acquired by being a servant. Only her wiles in cahoots with Don Alfonso's reason shows things for what they are. Neither reason nor wiles stand alone.

Little is known about the collaborative process that produced *Così*, and scholars debate its sources, pointing to various Greek myths and Italian classics. It had no principal model as did *Figaro* and *Don Giovanni*. Da Ponte's enemies in Vienna—they were copious—accused him of plagiarism.[56] An unsigned, blistering pamphlet titled *Anti-Da Ponte* was published in 1791. *Così* was written probably in 1789 and premiered on January 26, 1790. These dates can perhaps tell us something about its ambiguities. A revolution had begun in France; its apostles championed reason against supposed verities. What had long been declared the natural order of things proved to be a fake, and reason was declared the key to nature. A caveat is, however, needed. Rousseau was also hailed, despite his belief in sentiment as key to natural human behavior, as opposed to the primacy of reason. The world was becoming intricate.

The two couples in *Così* had agreed on love only to find themselves in a warren of deception and self-deceptions. Add in a fake lawyer and a fake doctor, and little truthful is left about this world besides a philosopher and a maid. Reason is steady in this opera, not sentiments, and challenges to sentiment by reason provide illumination. What they show, however, is that things can finally never change radically because of human nature: *Così fan tutte*. And yet there is a moment that subverts this very point. Even though Da Ponte's libretto is suffused with eighteenth-century stereotypes about women (and his life leaves little doubt that he believed in them), he destabilizes them just after Don Alfonso gets Ferrando and Guglielmo to repeat those very words, "*Così fan tutte*." Fiordiligi and Dorabella ought then to have entered to prove his point, but it is Despina who appears, as if to rebut what has just been said by the three men. The whole opera has shown that she is not like her mistresses.

Nonetheless the opera is not revolutionary even if it presents a new alignment of forces—intellectuals and lower classes. Expressed instead is the hope that once rid of deception, all may live happily. Enlightenment philosophers were not revolutionaries even if, in France, their progeny were. If Mozart and Da Ponte had French events on their minds, then their opera can be perceived as a warning: don't mistake social and political appearances for realities, take counsel about quackery, take real account of the complaints of exploited servants. It is finally a brief for reasonable reconciliation based on what an Enlightened person would think. Perhaps, then, things could turn out well in uncertain times.

Still, Don Alfonso asserts that things—human beings—will always be "that way," just when historical developments showed this was not so. What can reason accomplish? The opera seems to say that it can reveal and illuminate, but this will lead those tutored by it to accept that some things don't change. There is, in short, a startling ambiguity in this opera's salute to reason. On one hand it rids us of delusions, on the other hand, this elucidation is not supposed to be a threat to society. *Così*, so lighthearted and charming, is very serious. The emperor was ill when the opera was being written and he died in February 1790, just weeks after its premiere. Mozart and Da Ponte had thrived under his rule. They hoped that what they believed best in it would be sustained. Thus they saluted reason amidst tempests. Everyone is happy at *Così*'s end. But their happiness is theatrical appearance, while edginess constituted historical reality.

The librettist wasn't to be happy. His status became shaky as soon as Joseph II's brother ascended the Habsburg throne. It was the old pattern: Da Ponte landed in trouble because of another poem. There were assorted plots against him, he claimed, and he addressed a letter to the new emperor in blank verse. He asked Leopold II to be just—not merciful, he specified—to him. The tone of his language, however, was Despina-like. He adored his new ruler without fear, he declared, but then added that his fate was ultimately not in Leopold's hands. Indeed, "all your power/ and all the power of possible kings/ Have no rights over my soul."[57] He cautioned presumptuously that "sycophants" surrounded the new emperor. It turned out that one of Da Ponte's personal "friends" was a police agent who arranged for the letter-poem to be leaked in more than one version. It was reproduced in *Anti-Da Ponte* and the target, reckless as ever, wrote and disseminated a satire of Leopold.

He always found a way to destroy himself, observed his Venetian friend Zaguri.[58] Da Ponte was soon informed that the emperor "had no further need" of his services. He had almost no money—due to "my excessive liberality," he later explained—and thought to return to Venice, even though the ban against him was still in effect. He also thought to go to Paris but went finally to Trieste, where he was living in poverty when Mozart died. Da Ponte finally made his way to London, where he worked again as a librettist.[59] London was then also a center of French exiles, and they clearly had an effect on him. He was shocked at the fate of the French royal couple. "Poor King, Poor family!," he exclaimed in a letter to his friend Casanova, "I hope that England breaks this Gordian knot." He published a small volume in tribute to Marie Antoinette and the king: "Poems by Lorenzo Da Ponte, Poet for Six Years for Emperor Joseph II." He dedicated it to a supporter of Louis XVI. Still unable to restrain his words, his poem "Confession of a Jacobin" mocked his principle rival in the London Italian opera world, Carlo Francesco Badini, as a radical. Da Ponte was again repaid: Badini let everyone he could know of Da Ponte's past misadventures, undermining his London career.[60] He finally made his way to the United States, dying there an old man after colorful years as a grocer, as a promoter of Italian opera, and as the first official professor of Italian at Columbia University.

Between March 1791, when Da Ponte fled Vienna, and Mozart's death the following December, the composer wrote *The Magic Flute, La clemenza di*

Tito, his clarinet concerto, and a requiem mass, among other works. Those months must be counted among the most astonishing episodes of creativity by a single human being. At the center of those two operas were royal figures—the kind of characters that had disappeared from Mozart's works with Da Ponte. The last came with an appeal for wisdom and compassion, exemplified in the character of Titus. Enlightenment rationalism would be found elsewhere, in another realm, where it was reinvented in a high priest named Sarastro.

Chapter 17

LOOKING FOR ENLIGHTENMENT

Uncertainties marked 1791. Political turns in France encouraged the new Habsburg emperor, despite his liberal proclivities, to sustain his predecessor's retreat from activist reformism. A rein was needed on some of the unwieldy impulses that had been unleashed. Censorship had been reintroduced in the previous year, in fact just at the time when *Così* premiered. A memorandum by the new minister of police, Count Johann Anton von Pergen, summarized the mood of authorities. Secret societies have become a European "mania," he worried. They threatened Austrian order and undermined "the reputation and power of the monarch. . . ." Emissaries from these societies had been sent around Europe to stimulate sedition.[1] Pergen's fright was not entirely irrational, since the Enlightenment had given rise to a new domain—a "public sphere," as it came to be known—next to (or within) regimes in France and the German-speaking lands (and elsewhere). Reading and discussion groups and a variety of clubs emerged, meeting in homes and cafes. (*Così* begins with a philosopher issuing his challenge to the young soldiers in a Neapolitan tavern.) Their activities were encouraged and supplemented by a vast expansion in publishing of both journals and newspapers. Literacy had grown extensively in previous centuries along with expansion of middle and capitalist classes. All this began to reshuffle the social and political constellation.

And all this brought a swell of dangerous ideas. Free Masons, to Pergen's mind, were key purveyors of them, along with the radical Illuminati. He saw conspiracies everywhere. The "defection of the English colonies in America," was "the first operation" of a "secret ruling elite," he determined. Undoubtedly, "the overthrow of the French monarch" was due to a clandestine sect. In fact, Louis XVI still reigned when Pergen wrote these words, but the Bourbon king's once-absolutist powers had been restricted after the Bastille's fall. The difference between "overthrow" and limitations probably counted little in Pergen's policing mind. He reported also on a letter that originated in the Masonic Lodge of Bordeaux that linked Masonry to a dangerous notion: liberty. It asserted, he wrote, that "every good French citizen in the future is worthy of being a Mason because he is free." He ascribed political changes to malevolent "Masonic" concepts like "freedom, equality, justice, tolerance, [and] philosophy."[2] Similar qualms led to repressive measures, especially against Illuminati, in several Catholic kingdoms in winter 1791.

Masons, of course, had a different perspective on events. They did, in fact, conduct rituals covertly, but they were not necessarily foes of the established social order (at least not in public). They worked closely with it at times, especially in Vienna. Masonic political currents had, however, moved in diverse ways in previous decades. In Paris, one leading member, the "Chevalier" Andrew Michael Ramsay (a Scotsman by origin), declared in 1737 that their aim was to craft "an entire spiritual nation." His speech was spread across Europe. French lodges influenced considerably German counterparts. Ramsay, a convert to Catholicism and a Jacobite, was a devoted pupil and translator of Fénelon, and had been taken greatly by Quietism, serving as secretary to the elderly Madame de Guyon. Following Fénelon's words closely, Ramsay spoke of the world as a great republic made up of families (nations) and children (individuals), all of whom ought to live in fraternal friendship. In an earlier discourse, he proposed that "the principle doctrines of revealed religion" could be discerned in the mythology of all nations, including among the ancients.[3]

Masons proposed that they could be loyal to political authorities all while sustaining a cosmopolitan outlook and chastising war. They opposed social distinctions (at least in principle), insisted on equality among men (at least in principle), and castigated religious intolerance. Although Ramsay's sympathies were for a kind of constitutional monarchy, lodges later in the century had structures that might be taken for little republics. (In this they were like some of the Italian academies in the sixteenth century.) One historian compares lodges in Vienna to a state in which members, like citizens, had participatory rights. This is perhaps an overstatement, but the Grand Lodge of Paris did gather together a kind of assembly to which "brothers" came from around the realm like deputies, each with a right to vote.[4] The Grand Lodge of Austria in the 1780s declared, "every lodge is a democracy."[5] In fact, the Masons had their own system of ranks and lent strong support to Enlightened sovereigns like Friedrich the Great (who was a member) and Joseph II, but who were in no way democrats.

This world was, in the Masonic view, a kind of "experimental stage" on which "brothers" performed virtuous deeds, exemplifying a combination of moral self-mastery and fraternity. One day, they supposed—but never said

Figure 17.1. A meeting of the Freemasons in Vienna, possibly the "True Concord" (*Zur wahren Eintracht*) lodge circa 1785. Artist unknown. Mozart and Schikenader appear to be in the bottom right corner, although this identification is disputed. (Copyright Wien Museum, Vienna.)

loudly—these principles would render obsolete both politics and the state as these had been previously known. Human beings did not exist for the state's sake; the state exists to serve human happiness, says Falk, a character in a dialogue about Masons by Gotthold Ephraim Lessing, the preeminent figure of the German Enlightenment. (He became a Mason but was disenchanted by the fraternity's failure to live up to its egalitarian professions.) "[G]ood deeds" comprised the Masonic "secret," Falk goes on. They teach the young by example. Eventually such deeds might, Masons hoped, be rendered "superfluous" as the good behavior of all rendered external restraints unnecessary. It is as if the order of things was to wither away the more fraternity spread. In the meantime, the "wise man" always knew "what is better left unsaid."[6]

A discerning viewer of and listener to *The Magic Flute* will find in it an array of precepts, hints, and messages similar to these, and their political implications are many. Monarchy, for instance, is never opposed, but the

Queen of the Night's realm, imbued by her emotionalism, represents ill will and deception; it contrasts to the enlightened fraternal community of Sarastro that stands on its own, based in truth and reason. Anyone who would join the brotherhood's egalitarian kingdom, including young royals in the opera, must pass initiation trials leading toward its wisdom. (Learning to hold one's tongue when appropriate is the first of them.) When the high priest Sarastro is asked if Prince Tamino can endure these tests, he not only answers affirmatively but explains why: Tamino is more than a prince, "he is a man." To be human, then, is not an artificial status. The libretto's German—"*Noch mehr—Er ist Mensch*"—resonates more than English renditions. "*Mensch*" is not gendered; hence the absence here of an article.[7] It suggests humanity writ large, beyond this one person, beyond status, and in contrast to the animal world. Sound may suggest human equality too. It has been proposed that Mozart's use of counterpoint in *The Magic Flute* can be taken to suggest fraternity and egalitarianism "rather than subservience to one melody." It thus promotes the Masonic idea of brotherhood.[8]

All this is embedded within what seems to be a fairy tale. Outlining it will allow us to probe more deeply into *The Magic Flute*'s features and mysteries and more directly into its ambiguous politics.

After the overture, Prince Tamino is pursued by a vicious serpent and runs into the Queen's realm. He collapses, unconscious, but is saved when the beast is slain by her Three Ladies, each veiled and each quite taken by his youthful good looks. They depart and on awakening Tamino meets an odd, jovial figure covered in feathers. This is Papageno, the kingdom's Bird-Catcher. He lives for humanity's lower pleasures, especially food (but he is a good-natured creature, unlike Irus in *Ritorno*). He will soon be seconded to the prince, for the Ladies recruit Tamino to a noble task: the rescue of Pamina, their sovereign's kidnapped daughter. They simply show him her picture and he is in love. The young princess, they tell him, is in the clutches of "a powerful evil demon" in a neighboring kingdom.[9] Here, again, their German words are important to the opera's sense—or rather to its uncertainties: "*ein mächtiger, böser Dämon.*" These can be taken as a playful hint that things are not what they seem, for it is a description of an evil *Dämon* (demon) who, as the story develops, turns out to be good and no demon. The three *Damen* (Ladies), it turns out, serve evil. Tamino is given a magic flute whose sounds have special power: they change the way people feel (like music itself, more generally, can do). It is supposed to help his quest on the Queen's behalf, but its notes will affect him too. He finds eventually that he has been misled, although not by the image of Pamina.

The accused demon turns out to be a wise man, Sarastro, who will explain that Pamina was always intended for the prince by the gods, and not for a life in her mother's darkness. Tamino will then undergo the trials—both to win her and to become an initiate of Sarastro's enlightened band. Joined—indeed led—by Pamina in the final tests, the couple unites with each other and the community while the Queen is revealed to be a hate-blinded being.

II.

After *The Magic Flute* came Mozart's reinvention of *La clemenza di Tito* (the composer still had some additions to make to *The Magic Flute* after *Tito* premiered). *Tito* fetes a reasonable and clement emperor with qualities much like those of Sarastro. The politics of the two works are compatible in many ways (but not all). Neither expresses or promotes republican or democratic sympathies. Viewed side-by-side, they suggest Europe's complicated and varied realities. Both the modern state and absolutism arose between the fifteenth and seventeenth centuries to secure public peace, especially amidst virulent religious wars and a host of other problems. But then both this state and absolutism would find their own order-imposing solutions under siege in the eighteenth century. The difficulties of enlightened absolutism expressed, indeed incarnated, these developments. Questions posed by Enlighteners inevitably led to intellectual interrogation of justice and injustice in the existing order. It was not, however, a uniform matter; neither the political conditions nor their critics were the same everywhere. After all, the zigzags of Joseph II's tenure presented a different story from France if only because Louis XVI was a more limited man.

The overlap among Viennese Enlighteners and Masons is an essential backdrop to *The Magic Flute.* Once the coregency of Maria Theresa—who was hostile to the Masonic "Craft," as it was known—and Joseph II was over, the Brothers found themselves at first in happy, liberal circumstances. These altered in the mid-1780s when Joseph II ordered a reorganization of lodges; eight in Vienna were collapsed into three and these were watched by police. In a Freemason journal published in 1784, Ignaz von Born, the "Grand Master" of Austria's lodges, explained that "We . . . make it clear to the initiate, as soon as he has seen the light" that the aim of the Masons was not a "hidden society." However, he elaborated, secrecy might well be necessary among them if they were faced by "tyranny and vice." In the meantime, he wanted to address "everything that may have a relevance to our honorable order." Born extrapolated usefully on its attitudes when he spoke to the relation

Figure 17.2. Emperor Joseph II is welcomed by the people in Vienna at the opera house. From a copperplate engraving. Artist and date unknown. (Copyright Wien Museum, Vienna.)

between "the mysteries of olden times"—which included rituals of ancient Egypt, especially the cults of Isis and Osiris—and Masonic ceremonies. All good things were not European in the mysterious Masonic imagination.

This syncretism, like that promoted by Ramsay, would reappear in *The Magic Flute's* evocations of Egypt. Mozart had close ties to "Master" Born, who was also a member of the Illuminati. It was under Born's tutelage that Mozart became a Mason. Born subscribed to his concerts, and Mozart composed a Masonic cantata to celebrate the "Master's" ennoblement for scientific achievements. (These latter were mainly in mineralogy.) Born's Masonic activities seem to have ended in 1786, not long before the emperor took measures against lodges in the Austrian Netherlands (Belgium today), leading to considerable turmoil. It appears, however, that Emmanuel Schikaneder, Mozart's longtime acquaintance and the librettist for *The Magic Flute* and a onetime Mason, consulted Born's essay while he wrote. Born died in 1791, at the time when *The Magic Flute* was being finished. The opera echoed his writings and is filled with Masonic symbols and imagery, especially in its emphasis on the struggle between good and evil—between Enlightenment and Darkness. This struggle also echoed Zoroastrianism, which resonated within Masonry. (The name Sarastro may derive from Zoroaster.) During Carnival in February 1786, Mozart disguised himself as an oriental philosopher and circulated a pamphlet of sayings and riddles preoccupied with virtue and vice and other moral themes. It was titled "Excerpts from the Fragments of Zoroaster" although he wrote it himself. These "Fragments" consisted of well-known formulations, and reflect social sensitivities. "If you are poor but clever, arm yourself with patience: work," reads one. "If you don't get rich," it goes on, "you will at least remain a clever man—If you are an ass but rich, then use your prerogatives: be lazy. If you don't become poor, you will at least remain an ass."[10]

Thanks to Mozart's music, *The Magic Flute* has been aptly called the "supreme product" of eighteenth-century popular theater in Vienna.[11] Specialists disagree about the literary founts of its libretto. There are several, however, to which they point invariably, and together they suggest a mélange of images, sentiments and ideas, especially Masonic ones.[12] One source, the twelfth-century romance *Yvain, the Knight of the Lion* by Chrétien de Troyes, is the story of a knight who aims through heroic deeds to win back his true love. It includes a distant anticipation of the story of Tamino and Papageno: a lion is saved from a serpent by Yvain and becomes his traveling comrade. An interesting, perhaps Zoroastrian, link to *The Magic Flute* was through *Dschinnistan*, a collection of what appeared to be oriental tales. Christoph Martin Wieland, a leading figure in the German Enlightenment, published them in the late 1780s. The title means "the Land of the Jinn" (or Genie) and while Wieland presented himself as its editor, scholars agree that he wrote most of them himself (he was an eager reader of a recent German rendering of Galland's French translation of the *One Thousand and One Nights*). One story in *Dschinnistan* was "Lulu or the Magic Flute" and was written apparently by August Jacob Liebeskind. It told of Fairy Queen Perifirime, living in an abandoned castle near the capital of Khorassan. The name of this ancient Persian and central Asian territory derives from Middle Persian for "the Sun" (*Khor*) and "the coming or rising of" (*assan*). The castle is said to have been built by Jamshid, a legendary king who presided over a golden age and seems to have had a physical shine about him in myths. But when he became smug about his own powers, he was overcome by demons.

"The people call her the radiant fairy," we read, since a blaze literally surrounds her and blinds, at least temporarily, all who see her. Perifirme is a source of great fear, yet she takes to Lulu after he gets lost hunting in her forest. Invited into her castle, Lulu is convinced to accept a task that requires "wisdom" rather than strength.[13] Sidi, Perifirime's daughter, has been seized together with a jewel encrusted, incandescent talisman of forged steel that once made all "spirits" of the world obey Perifirme—it made her all-powerful. The villain is Dilsenghuin, a cunning sorcerer.[14] He lives on the other side of the mountains in a castle perched on a high cliff and has many attendants managed by a fat, clever, nasty dwarf. Perifirime gives to Lulu a magic flute to aide him in his undertaking: rescue Sidi. Its sounds—like those of the flute given later to Tamino—change the temperament of whoever hears it. She also gives him a ring that allows its wearer to change shape by turning a diamond on it; and if the ring is thrown away, it will signal his need for help. The tale progresses through many twists. The brutal magician, we learn, wants Sidi to love him and after Lulu arrives, hopes to exploit the flautist to beguile her. If only the flute's notes would change her feelings toward him! But Lulu has a musical heart; he insists that his flute's notes should sound only for their own sake. By the story's conclusion, the talisman will be back in the Fairy Queen's hands, and Sidi will be liberated, along with a bevy of virgins who attend her and have been forced to work with no respite at spinning wheels, overseen by the dwarf. Along the way, Sidi displays her own character by telling Dilsenghuin that she is ready to yield to him if they are freed. And the Fairy Queen's light will finally turn the untoward magician into a blind owl, able only to bang about in his darkness; his castle tower collapses. Lulu and Sidi will wed in the land where the sun rises.

The extent to which this story and its motifs are reinvented in *The Magic Flute* is palpable. Mozart and Schikaneder would make some changes and role reversals but along with Liebeskind they tell of the victory of good over bad, of liberating light and sound over blindness toward and deafness to unhappiness and suffering. Opposed kingdoms provide the backdrop of both works and both works urge us to see the truth, albeit with somewhat divergent use of symbols and characters. Liebeskind's Fairy protagonist, with piercing light emanating from her, seems at first to be terrifying, yet turns out to be acting for the good while the "Star-blazing Queen of the Night" in Mozart and Schikaneder's opera appears to be a victim at first and is later revealed to be evil. While the Fairy had been given the powerful talisman by King Jamshid's tribe (Lulu's own clan) and it was stolen and misused by the evil Magician, Sarastro wears a "Sacred Band" of the "Sun's Seven-fold circle," a kind of breast shield or cloth that was given to him by the Queen of the Night's husband before his death because he did not trust her with its powers. Liebeskind seems comfortable with a powerful Queen. At first, it seems that Mozart and Schikaneder are not, but as we will see they may have been more conflicted because of a debate among the Masons.

Nonetheless, the opera, like Liebeskind's story, is a call to keep power in the hands of Enlightened people. The opera, like the story, assumes that Enlightenment comes of a learning process; both pit cleverness or cunning (the Magician and the Queen of the Night are plotters) against understanding (which has music as its ally). Lulu, like Tamino, undergoes trials and learns that what appears one way can have another reality.

III.

A novel published in 1731, a half century before "Lulu," by Abbé Jean Terrasson, a professor of Greek at the Royal College in Paris, is also widely acknowledged as an important source for the opera (and Born pointed to it in his essay). This is the same Terrasson whom we have already met as a defender of opera as a modern art against its critics. Scenes in his novel correspond closely to *The Magic Flute*. It again points to one of its—and Fénelon's—preoccupations: the education and testing of a young prince.

Terrasson pretended to be only the translator from Greek of an anonymous work from antiquity called *Séthos: The Story of a Life Taken from Monuments and Anecdotes from Ancient Egypt*. Its princely protagonist goes through initiation rites of the Egyptian mysteries, taking Osiris as his inspiration. In fact, Séthos's name is found in historical records at least as far back as Herodotus and appeared in *Thamos, King of Egypt*, the play by Baron von Gebler, a leading Mason, for which Mozart composed incidental music at age seventeen. Terrasson's Séthos is a deposed Pharaoh. Disguised as a (Sarastro-like) High Priest of the Sun, he saves virtuous young prince Thamos from a plot against him, and the finale anticipates that of *The Magic Flute*. Set in the Temple of the Sun, obedience to the gods is hailed, evil's downfall is celebrated, and a chorus calls to the divine to protect the crown.

These depictions of a highborn youth who overcomes obstacles and challenges as he matures point to yet another possible source of *The Magic Flute*. It is an indirect one to which scholars generally don't point but which has important political implications: Fénelon's *Telemachus*, the novel Mozart read, which partly inspired *Idomeneo* and aimed to educate a future

French king through tales of Ulysses's son and his tutoring by the Goddess of Wisdom in disguise. We don't know that Mozart actually returned to this enormously influential text at the time of *The Magic Flute* or that Schikaneder was then looking at it, but a reading of parts of *Telemachus* suggest strongly that they might have done so. The inventory of books in Mozart's personal library at the time of his death contained more than one edition of *Telemachus*.[15] We have pointed to the broad impact of this book on the writings of Rousseau and in opera. Karl Philipp Moritz, an almost exact contemporary of Mozart, wrote an autobiographical novel, *Anton Reiser*, that featured *Telemachus* prominently in it. Although not in the inventory of Mozart's library, Moritz's book was exceptionally well-known in Vienna, and in the year after the composer's death Schikaneder wrote a libretto for a "heroic-comic opera" based on the Telemachus theme. Titled *The King's Son from Ithaca*, it focused on a Fénelon addition to past tellings of the Telemachus story: the youth's relation with Calypso and her chagrin when another nymph becomes his love interest.[16]

The sojourn in Egypt of Fénelon's protagonist is of most interest to considerations of *The Magic Flute*. Telemachus is captured at sea and taken there.[17] Its king, Sesostris, is described by Mentor as a wise man who cares for the poor, and promotes education and religious devotion in a bountiful land of stately obelisks, temples, and flute-playing shepherds. The unfortunate prisoner sees these glories but briefly before he is sent to a miserable life in a desert oasis as a slave shepherd. One day, Telemachus, by now worn out and utterly despondent, lies down by a cavern and everything around him abruptly quakes. A voice declares that the son of Ulysses and future governor of Ithaca must overcome adversity. The captive prince feels enlightened by this message but his testing is not over. He decides that he needs books to help him endure and to his surprise he meets an old, bald and bearded man who supplies them. He is jovial Termosiris, the priest who presides at the temple of Apollo. His name is an interesting construction because "*thermos*" in Greek means hot—as the sun is—and Osiris was the compassionate Egyptian God of the Underworld and considered the founder of Egyptian civilization. He was also linked to regeneration and cycles of nature and has been identified with Dionysius. "*Termosiris*" would seem to be an amalgamation of opposites that comes of a syncretism of Egyptian and Greek mythology; and he appears as the means of Telemachus's rebirth.[18]

Fénelon compares the priest to Orpheus; he recites poems and accompanies himself on an ivory lyre. His sounds attract animals, and satyrs dance around him as he sings of the gods and the virtues of heroes. He tells Telemachus that the Sun God was once compelled to descend to earth and also lived as a shepherd. On earth Apollo, who is also the god of music, played a flute whose tones attracted all the shepherds, who have lived as savages but now became civilized by the arts. Soon they all had flutes and, says Termosiris, became more content than kings. Telemachus is told: You, today, are like Apollo once was. You can make the desert burgeon with greenery and teach swains the loveliness of harmony; you can civilize them. Termosiris gives him a flute whose mellow sounds echo everywhere, attracting all the swains. They listen to Telemachus sing a "divine melody" in tribute to nature, making him feel almost "supernatural." Like Orpheus's lyre and like Lulu's flute—and later like Tamino's—the sounds of a musical instrument are transformative.

It is, however, a nonmusical deed that brings fame to Telemachus: his bravery in a struggle with a ravenous lion. When King Sesostris hears of this and of Telemachus's accomplishments among the shepherds, he calls him to his capital. But, alas, he dies before the youth arrives. Prince Bocchori comes to the throne and is the opposite of Ulysses's son, whom he sequesters in a tower. This new king rules arbitrarily, spawns revolt, and finally defeat. Yet despite his past bad behavior he proves courageous in the battle in which he is killed. Telemachus reaches an interesting conclusion: this was an able fellow who became king without first having to overcome hardship, to repair errors—to learn to reverse himself when need be. He never learned to be a ruler.

Consider some parallels between *Telemachus* and *The Magic Flute*. In both,

- a prince learns wisdom in an Egyptian setting;
- important roles are played by wise old rulers and priests;
- there are contrasting domains and the prince's education entails going from one to the other;
- there are encounters in nature (and thunder at choice moments);
- there are father figures who teach young men and bring them into temples of the Sun;
- magic flutes civilize feelings through their music; the beneficiaries create or live in a kind of utopia symbolized by the Sun;
- a young hero endures hardship and tests and grasps that both reason and compassion ought to dominate a man.

A path, often winding, sometimes more direct, can be detected from Telemachus to Tamino.

And there are other mediating figures—predecessors in Mozart's own operas. One is Idamantes, who overcame adversity with a spirit imbued by compassion and a steeled will. The protagonist of *Telemachus* travels to Crete just after Idomeneus's ouster as king, although in the novel, as in ancient accounts (but unlike the opera), Idomeneus has killed his son. The Cretans are in the midst of choosing a new monarch with special attention to sustaining their laws. They are cosmopolitan: one need not be Cretan to compete in physical tests and games that make a candidate eligible, and Telemachus is a success in them. Prowess of mind must be shown, and this happens in a secret wood before old judges. They are devoted to a venerable ancient book of laws. Its animating principle: rule by law, rather than men.

Questions—three groupings of them—are posed to Telemachus and his responses show that he is able:

- Who is the freest of men? they ask. An absolute ruler? Is it someone who can gratify all his passions? Or is it someone who travels endlessly but breaks laws where he goes, never marries, and takes on no responsibilities? Is the freest man perhaps a "savage" who is self-sufficient and needs no government?
- Who, they query, is the most miserable of men—someone sick, someone poor, someone without titles, or someone who is friendless?
- Finally, they ask if it is better for a king to be skilled at war or at ruling in peacetime?

Telemachus, by now, has learned much. He replies that a man, even a slave (as he was) is free if he fears none but the gods and follows reason. The most miserable man is a king who is "a slave to his passions" and thinks himself happy, all while making everyone else wretched. And a king needs to know the arts of war and peace. If he does not know both, he must be wise enough to rule well at home—which means legally and without extravagance or "effeminacy"—and to have good generals in case of war. But he ought to avoid wars and ought not to seek to dominate other lands. Idamantes, presumably, ruled Crete like this after the end of *Idomeneo*. His father, in *Telemachus*, goes on to rule well in a new city. The novel also portrays another good realm, Baetia (*Bétique*), which incarnates a golden age. It is a land of peace and needs no judges because its citizens—here again is an anticipation of *The Magic Flute*—comprise a fraternity in need only of conscience.[19] Fénelon certainly hoped his young charge would absorb these ideas; it is easy to imagine that Mozart and Schikaneder would have been happy had Joseph II fulfilled them, and they hoped Leopold II would live up to his liberal reputation.

Telemachus is wise enough to decline the Cretan crown when it is offered. He is as yet too young, he senses, and besides he had responsibilities in his own *patria*. The lessons he absorbed received an additional formulation in yet another novel about a young man gaining knowledge of the world. Fénelon's pupil Ramsay, who became tutor in Rome of Prince Charles Edward of the exiled Stuarts, carried on the tradition in *The Travels of Cyrus*, published in 1727 in both French and English. It described educative adventures throughout Asia and the Mediterranean of an heir to the ancient Persian crown. These included meetings with Zoroastrians and a visit to Egypt. This Egypt is different, for its King Sesostris is a militaristic despot who brought "calamities" by his efforts at world conquest. The realm's religion has harsh rites including human sacrifice (done to "delicious music"). His reign contrasted to those of ancient Egyptian kings who would begin the day with prayers beseeching Osiris to give them "royal virtues" such as piety, justice, generosity, and mastery of passions. And there is worship at the Temple of Isis, built as an oval—"the egg of the world." Tolerance and Natural Man are lauded. By the time of Cyrus's visit, however, most of Egypt's ancient laws had lost vitality. One, however, maintained its force: the king, though hereditary, was "subject to the laws."[20]

Séthos appeared four years after *Cyrus*, and both Mozart and Schikaneder knew it. A German version appeared in 1777–78 and was popular in the Habsburg capital.[21] Like *Cyrus*, it appears to link Masonic and ancient Egyptian rites. It identified Osiris as the model for its protagonist. In a preface, Terrasson explained that a good work of fiction had to "combine and melt several great men in history and to unite the events of many ages" in the story of one figure, "a single hero," who would be worthy of "admiration and imitation." He pointed to *Telemachus* and to *Cyrus*. In each, as he saw it, the protagonist searches for "instructions from all the wise men of his times in order to introduce into his own dominions whatever he found good and profitable in the different customs of the most celebrated kingdoms and commonwealths." Fénelon's novel, Terrasson observed, had great success in "reforming our judgments and softening our manners." Séthos was virtuous because his "motives" derived "from durable and enlightened principles."[22] Can we find something similar culled in *The Magic Flute*—in the stories of Tamino and Sarastro? Not simply as a series of one-to-one correspondences but in anticipations of Mozart and Schikaneder's Sing-spiel, Séthos must cope with an evil Queen and will undergo three tests. *The Magic Flute* can be seen and heard as a descendant of these works and as a child of their preoccupations.

In Mozart's day there was a king who was introduced to *Telemachus*, in particular its passages on well and badly run kingdoms, at age eleven and a half. This was Louis XVI, brother-in-law of Mozart's ruler. And so Mozart and Louis XVI read this same book, or parts of it. The first imagined him-self a spiritual noble and took from it means to creative ends. The future king studied intensely the responsibilities of a ruler, believing that "I owe it to God for having chosen me to reign." [23] He seems to have ingested little from *Telemachus;* it is doubtful that *Cyrus* or *Séthos* would have helped either.

IV.

Mozart began detailed work on *The Magic Flute* with Schikaneder, an im-presario, actor, and family friend, in spring—probably March—1791 (just at the time when the pope censured the ideas of the French Revolution). Schikaneder's sentiments seem to have been like those of Mozart, Da Ponte, and Beaumarchais when it came to authority. Music for the opera was mostly completed by mid-summer. By then Mozart had also returned to composing works with a Masonic orientation after a hiatus that cor-responded roughly to Joseph II's restrictions on the "Craft." Now, he set a cantata using a text by an educational reformer with Rousseauist sym-pathies, Franz Heinrich Ziegenhagen, which called on all good men to embrace anyone who honored the universe's creator, regardless of the rit-uals or sect they followed. There was a single humanity; it ought to "love order, proportion, and harmony!" Its members ought to seek truth through friendship and wisdom, spurning "delusion's bonds" and war. [24]

Sentiments akin to these appear in many texts Mozart set. It is as if the currents and turbulence of his times take form and substance within his works. The changing world around him was not in an appeasing mood and events in Paris—Mozart certainly knew of them—sang other, troubled songs. Nothing in his correspondence suggests that these events preoc-cupied him as he worked on *The Magic Flute*, at least not in June 1791, a time when France's tensions intensified and in which Mozart could write simply in a letter that, "From sheer boredom I composed today an aria for my opera." [25] No bright beam directs us from Europe's political atmosphere to Mozart's creativity, but history quickened in the last months of his life, just as his remarkable talents turned extraordinarily productive after a relatively fallow period.

As Mozart and Schikaneder crafted *The Magic Flute*, pressures mounted on Louis XVI. Social discontents had not been relieved by post-1789 restrictions on the crown's powers and the breaking of feudal legal bonds. The wobbly new order was challenged especially by hungry Parisian commoners urged on in early 1791 by populist clubs, associations, and fraternities. The "Rights of Man" had not found a way into the bellies of the poor. It is as if a collective, urban Papageno was turning sour. Food and drink also preoccupy the self-declared Natural Man, whom Tamino meets early in *The Magic Flute*. He is a gentle caricature of Rousseau's "natural man"— human beings as Rousseau imagined they might have been before the development of too much rationality and "civilization." He is also a kind of "naturalized" descendant of "Hanswurst" (Hans-Sausage), a comic character concerned especially with his bodily well-being who was familiar in German language, especially Viennese improvisational theater.

Mozart and Schikaneder give us an amusing Papageno, but we laugh at his behavior all while the opera uses him to say serious things. And while Papageno is ravenous, he is also always passive and fearful, unlike the restive and assertive commoners in Paris. Perhaps he would have been different had he found himself accompanied by famished Pedrillos, Blondes, Figaros, Susannas, Leporellos, Masettos, Zerlinas, and Despinas. At just this time, conservative forces within France as well as émigrés were increasingly apprehensive, and Louis XVI, chafing at limits imposed on him, finally attempted to reverse the run of events. On June 21, 1791, he fled with his queen in secret, hoping to reach proroyalist forces and Austrian protectors. Their seizure in the town of Varennes was speedy and in circumstances that might have made for a play by Beaumarchais or an opera by Mozart and Da Ponte. The Bourbon king and Marie Antoinette fled in disguise as commoners but were recognized along the way.[26]

As it happens, one of the original Viennese cast of *The Marriage of Figaro* was then in Paris. Michael Kelly, the Irish tenor whose memoirs portrayed so vividly the police-state atmosphere of Venice and who had created the roles of Don Curzio and Don Basilio, recounted later how he visited the Café de Foix in the Palais Royal, where he heard loud denunciations of the French royals. He found himself at a table with a famous man articulating strong views—"the notorious republican Tom Paine." Popular insurrection against abusive government had been defended vigorously in Paine's recent book

The Rights of Man. Perhaps because of the tenor's positive experiences in Vienna or possibly due to family ties with Edmund Burke's friend, Charles Burney, Kelly's "blood boiled" as he listened to Paine's "infernal doctrines." And the tenor was in the crowd watching the captured king and queen arrive at the Tuilleries on June 25—"a heart breaking sight," he recalled.[27] Perhaps he thought of the throngs around him as a collective serpent about to engorge a royal. Paine, by contrast, undoubtedly thought that a successful escape would augur the return of darkness.

In mid-July crowds gathered in Paris to demand the king's ouster, only to face bullets from the National Guard. By then Mozart was turning to work on *Tito* for presentation at the Prague coronation of a more secure crown, that of Marie Antoinette's brother. Leopold II was much more perceptive than the French king and had little enthusiasm for intervention on his behalf. For some time he had advised Louis XVI to accept a restrained, constitutional status. Nonetheless, continuous French upheaval led Leopold II to fret, and French émigrés increasingly had his ear. The idea of the "Rights of Man" and natural law, promoted by Sonnenfels, were one casualty, although Leopold II did not turn into a simple reactionary. In early August he told Sonnenfels, then charged with compiling a code of political laws, to eliminate any mention of human rights and to include only *Recht der Bürger* (civil rights).[28] By the end of the month the Habsburg emperor issued a joint declaration with Prussia's monarch threatening action on behalf of the Bourbon monarch. A new, written constitution was forced on Louis XVI on September 3 (three days before *Tito's* premiere). France's sovereign, it asserted, was the People; a legislative assembly was its lawmaker and although the king would retain executive powers, they were weakened. Leopold II urged Louis XVI to yield and with little other choice he did so. Marie Antoinette groused of betrayal.

The Magic Flute premiered on September 30 at Schikaneder's Theater auf der Wieden in a Viennese suburb. Although Mozart had thought before to compose for popular audiences—all his previous operas were court commissioned—this was his first completed opera for a theater for the broader public. The National-Singspiel, founded by Joseph II in 1778 in part for reasons of cultural nationalism, had closed in 1783, although the genre continued to be staged in the suburbs. Another Court Singspiel was established in 1785 only to close three years later, again leaving this kind of stage to theaters on the capital's periphery. And so Mozart's last two operas provide a juxtaposition that illustrates both socially and politically the rattling Habsburg—indeed, European—world. One was in German for a theater linked to this language and on the edge of the empire's capital (although this did not dissuade attendance by Viennese high society). In *The Magic Flute*, plot developed through Singspiel means: spoken dialogue and song. The other was an opera seria in Italian commissioned for a crowning ceremony of the ruler of a supposedly cosmopolitan empire in one of his domains (Bohemia). Thus it was not presented in the imperial capital. In it recitative and aria alternated.

Here some recapitulation is useful. We have discerned sets of political and artistic events with some curious, close symmetries. Although they took place physically far enough away from each other, they seem often to entwine. Roughly from March to September 1791:

— a rigid, weakened French crown faced an edgy population; the king and queen fled but were detained; protests called for his removal; a new constitution was authorized, stressing rule by law and diluting his powers. (Fénelon would have surely approved.) Louis XVI's wary brother-in-law's coronation took place in Prague.

— Mozart and Schikaneder began work on *The Magic Flute*, which opens with a prince chased by a serpentine ogre. He will meet up with Natural Man and then be deceived by a "Queen of the Night" into doing her bidding. By the opera's end, however, he will be a changed young man—as Telemachus, Cyrus, Séthos, Scipio, Titus, Ferrando, and Guglielmo were at the end of their stories—and he is initiated into a brotherhood based on Enlightenment and tolerance. Mozart's effort on this Singspiel of much humor and many serious ideas was interrupted to compose *Tito*, an opera seria that extols clement rule and forward-thinking authority. He completed the last numbers for *The Magic Flute* just before its premiere at the end of a turbulent month for Louis XVI's power, and several weeks after *Tito* was first presented.

If Mozart followed his usual procedures, he contributed substantially to the libretto's character. Intense collaboration between the composer and librettist of *The Magic Flute* started just before much of the year's French tumult, although advocates of Enlightenment and Masons in Vienna already felt besieged. We have seen that some literary sources drawn on by Mozart and Schikaneder predated their efforts by many years. Yet the temporal proximity of their efforts to significant historical unrest is close enough to postulate that they distill, consciously or not, the conflicted spirits of the political era in their musical pseudo-oriental fairytale.

We can find the epochal questions posed in 1791 in *The Magic Flute* and they are in apparently timeless guises; they follow on those posed in the Mozart/Da Ponte operas. It is in this train of interconnected questions rather than in any simple or simplistic correspondences to political events that the continuity between *Figaro*, *Don Giovanni*, *Così*, and *The Magic Flute* can be discerned, despite a change in librettists. *Figaro* asks: Who will dance to whose tune? *Don Giovanni* asks viewers to consider an unachieved ideal of friendship as the opposite of unrepentant individual privilege. *Così* asks if a philosopher and a servant can be guides to self-knowledge of rather thoughtless people. The beginning of *The Magic Flute* inquires of its times: who is being pursued by whom? Why? To where? Was Europe's elite running from people gone mad? Was it fleeing from that monster—"the People"—portrayed as far back as Plato? From foul, reckless revolution? This was certainly Marie Antoinette's view of things. She told a Spanish ambassador in January 1791 that "Louis will fail in his obligations to himself, to his subjects and to all of Europe, if he does not cast out the evil that besets us, no matter what the price."[29]

Or was it flight from the disasters created by the old regimes?

Or is humanity chasing something in itself in *The Magic Flute*—something that must be banished before it goes on to better domains? If so, it is not really a serpent chasing a prince at the opera's beginning, but one aspect of one human nature chasing another, suggesting that a human being needs to find the right way to its own realm of self-mastery—to self-mastery of its multiple dimensions. Entering the Queen's kingdom is then a detour, perhaps an unavoidable one—a temporary delusion on the way to Enlightenment.

There are no firm answers to these questions, for *The Magic Flute* is no exercise in realism of historical or philosophical or political argument. Yet if politics is not announced in it, politics is in the fabric of its notes and words.

Chapter 18

TAMINO'S WONDER

It is at the beginning of *The Magic Flute* that the definition of humanity is first posed. "Who are you?" wonders Tamino, when confronted by a strange feathered figure. It is after Tamino has been pursued by the viper, after his collapse into unconsciousness, and after he reawakes to meet downy Papageno—the name comes from parrot in German—with a bird-cage on his back and a panpipe at his mouth.

"Who am I?" asks Papageno in response. That's a "dumb question," he tells himself, but he answers the stranger, "A human being (*Ein Mensch*) like you. What if I asked who you are?"[1] It is almost as if a colonial conqueror had landed on distant shores and a "savage" told him that they were alike. But not quite. Tamino wears oriental—not European—hunting garb and has a bow with no quivers. He announces proudly that he is of royal blood. It seems as if a youthful but not very knowing member of a civilization's elite has just met up with two very different aspects of nature: one is a threat (the viper), the other simply bizarre or goofy. Tamino is defenseless before them both, although in different ways. Arrows would be needed against a beast, but he has none. His own naiveté constitutes his frailty on meeting Papageno—who is also an innocent creature and finds Tamino no less odd. But Tamino is also a civilized youth waking up to nature in the person of Papageno. The Prince is curious about him, and while this Bird-Catcher fibs to the escapee, it is not with malice. Like Adam and Eve before they meet the biblical serpent and eye the apple, this Natural Man has no knowledge of the difference between good and evil.

Papageno, played at the premiere by Schikaneder (while Mozart directed the music), has no understanding of the world around him. He just lives day to day in it. He doesn't know what royalty means. "My father," Tamino boasts, "is a sovereign who rules over many lands and peoples. That is why I am called Prince." This confuses Papageno: "Lands? Peoples? Prince?" He had no idea of "more lands and people beyond the mountains."[2] While his livelihood depends on bartering his captured birds, it never occurred to him that there might be anything beyond the horizon. He has never before speculated that there might be anyone in distant places who wants his winged captives—or that the birds may have come his way from elsewhere. Commerce is unknown to him; there is no coin of the queen's realm. He only catches pheasants and other birds and wishes a wife might come into one of his nets too, attracted perhaps by his panpipe. His song is simple and tuneful, perhaps identifiable—although with a touch of burlesque—with Rousseau's melodic musical ideal. Asked by Tamino how he lives, Papageno describes natural functions: "By eating and drinking." Asked about the region (*Gegend*) they are in, Papageno can describe only physical features. It is "between valleys and mountains." When asked his home region's name and "who rules you?" he has no idea. "I know the answer . . . as little as I know how I came into the world," says Papageno. Is nature his ruler? Yes and no, it seems. After all, he eats and drinks and human rulers can be distant from natural men. This Natural Man does have a this-worldly sovereign but he isn't really aware of it. He is only aware that an old man brought him up and that his mother was a servant in the temple of the "Star-blazing Queen of the Night." He has never seen her.[3]

Is this Bird-Catcher fully human? Civilized Tamino must wonder. After all, Papageno doesn't know his origins or where he lives or who rules him. Much of the *The Magic Flute* develops Tamino's wonder. But the wonder reaches far and it is not only about Papageno, whom he nonetheless calls his "jolly friend"—and we can sense here that the theme of "friend" is to play a central role in this as in earlier Mozart operas. Mozart and Schikaneder ask: What is a man? What is best for man? Where does he come from? Where should he go? Are there different kinds of man? What does friendship among men look like? The questions suggest responses that comprise an overlap of Masonic and Enlightenment notions. Tamino, accompanied by a magic flute, will eventually learn self-mastery and to distinguish appearance from reality. His triumph will be animated by something greater than reason or nature by themselves but in need of them both: wisdom as a harmonizing principle of the universe and of human society. The prince who was pursued into a zone of darkness will mature in a sunlit kingdom as a familiar operatic and philosophical theme increasingly mediates his experience: the tension between emotion and reason. *The Magic Flute* does not submit, however, that our emotions are bad. Love and friendship are indeed all important in it. But the opera also proposes that humanity must master its darker emotional dimensions, notably our urge to vengeance.

This Singspiel may tell us over and again to distinguish appearance from reality, but it often blurs them. Discerning one from the other is, of course,

Figure 18.1. From Mozart's autograph score for *The Magic Flute* (1791). Papageno's entrance in *The Magic Flute* (KV 620). Mendelsohnn-Archiv, Staatsbibliothek zu Berlin, Stiftung Preussischer Kulturbesitz, Berlin; bpk Bildagentur, Art Resource, NY.

essential for someone engaged successfully in politics. It is not always a virtue for a stage work, especially one raising awkward questions in an unsure time. Myths and fairy tales allow for ambiguities that are fruitful (and are often a safer means of expression than versions of realism). Mystery was important for mystical rationalism of the Masons, whose belief in moral brotherhood could, alternatively, appeal to political powers or make them nervous by suggesting that fraternity might make political order unnecessary. A state with a healthy constitution, says Falk in Lessing's dialogue, permits Freemasonry "to flourish alongside it." However, "a weak and apprehensive state" will repress the Brotherhood—even though Masonic ideas will nonetheless continue "covertly." Freemasonry "depends basically not on *external associations*, which can so easily degenerate into *civil regulations*, but on the shared sentiments of kindred spirits."[4] Juxtapose how the Queen rules her domain to life in Sarastro's community and the point is illustrated.

It is often difficult to distinguish what represents certainty, what is facade, and what is suggestion in *The Magic Flute*. Surely this was intended. It is simple and reasonable to suppose that the serpent chasing Tamino is the People, or revolutionaries, yet there is no reason to think that this prince is culpable or capable of wrongdoing. At most he esteems his own noble descent; and this is not at all what leads him into (temporary) alliance with Darkness. Innocence and love do. Perhaps, then, he is pursued by the unpleasant demands of modern politics itself. Mozart and Schikaneder might then be suggesting that by later crossing the border into enlightenment, he reveals that virtuous order that needs no political regime. When Tamino first runs on stage he appeals to heaven before collapsing in front of a temple. He does not know that the three veiled Ladies of the Queen, not the gods, have emerged from it to slay the beast. When he meets Papageno just afterward, he doesn't know that the Bird-Catcher is taking credit falsely for saving him. (Natural Man, it seems, ought not to be taken quite at face value.)

We, the audience, a kind of collective third person viewing and hearing events, can see that nature may be false salvation even if Papageno's character is innocent. He is a being of drives, he does not reflect on himself or anything else. He talks and talks as naturally as he fibs and fibs. The Ladies, on returning, fasten his lips with a golden lock and later an adage is sung when the bond is released: "If all the liars/ were given a lock like this on their mouths/ then love, brotherhood would replace hate, slurs/ and black gall."[5] The Ladies explain that babble is not so much the problem as falsehoods. Yet, they seem to accept that nature cannot control itself. Papageno gabs as birds twitter, and his name tells us that he parrots.

Something seems missing. Wouldn't relentless lying also be natural in the absence of self-mastery? If Rousseau depicted "natural man" as a being who doesn't know right from wrong and can only have compassion for others, Schikaneder and Mozart suggest that understanding right and wrong comes from being civilized. Rousseau proposed that misery increases with civilizing, not least because we become more dependent on others. Civilizing deprives us of the kind of autonomy possessed, apparently, by a man alone in—and deeply in—nature. But Mozart and Schikaneder interrogate such a worldview. Natural Man is never really alone, not even Papageno. In fact, he barters his birds to the Ladies in return for food and drink. He is a precapitalist being, since cash has no role in his economic behavior, which aims only to satisfy his needs—by trading away something that satisfies the needs of others. Nonetheless, the realm's powers also expect control of his voice in exchange for his sustenance; the Ladies are his police in this, although he seems to require no other regulation. For Mozart and Schikaneder, civilization brings wisdom; it is cultivated. Did precocious Mozart know this when he composed his satire of Rousseau's *Le Devin du Village*? Perhaps it helped to teach him that wisdom is higher than nature and reason. Wisdom requires both of these in *The Magic Flute* just as it calls for voice and silence at the appropriate times. Tamino, in contrast to Papageno, is civilized enough to know that there is right and wrong, but before his initiation into the brotherhood he does not yet how to distinguish them fully.

All this won't be clarified before Tamino, like Telemachus, undergoes his learning process. Through this experience he finds out that the Ladies don't serve truth. They serve the Queen, and having told Papageno not to deceive, they do just that to solicit Tamino. The Prince however, does know some things if not others. He knows that he comes from somewhere; he does not know in the beginning where he is going. It will become evident as well that he has special qualities and these will allow him to ascend to a higher but still human incarnation (far beyond Papageno's capacities; people are not equal in this opera, as much as Mozart disliked unmerited honor). The "star-blazing" Queen's cause, her appeal to free Pamina from malevolence, appears—sounds—to be what it is not. After all, blazing stars tend to be distant, and while they may shine through the night, their illuminating powers are limited and their glow often flickers or dissolves before human eyes. The Queen's coloratura begins plaintively and gains intensity, pointing to a much later moment in the opera when, in her most famous aria, one obsessed by vengeance, she will call on her daughter to murder Sarastro. The very range and power of her voice will betray fierce determination, as if to right a wrong. But the issue of vocal control, required of an aria that leaps up and down octaves, has also been raised in a different way by Papageno's chatter. As Tamino goes through initiation it is evident that he can control his sounds in an entirely different way—by remaining silent. Natural Man, in his innocence, and the Queen, in her evil, cannot do so. Ironically, the soprano singing the Queen must have masterly voice control to convey a woman whose flaws are indicated by apparently uncontrollable vocal torrents.

Righting wrong did not persuade Tamino to help the Queen—Pamina's picture did. She will be as beautiful and good as her image makes her out to be, yet the opera reveals that she has been kidnapped in order to save both her and Tamino from bondage to the past. Sarastro's realm is that of the Sun. Were Tamino to return Pamina to the Queen, it would be akin to retreat from Enlightenment, a danger that Mozart and Schikaneder perceived, undoubtedly, was present across Europe. The interplay among wisdom, reason, and nature along with darkness, light, and an actual historical moment is elusive and allusive and profound in this portentous fairy tale.

II.

"Who are you?" leads to another question: What can you be? Papageno will prove that Natural Man cannot be more than a goodly servant, not alert to the larger purposes of mistresses or masters. While Tamino, at first, can be led astray, he moves differently as he sees more—as he takes step after step in Sarastro's sunlit realm. His education has aspects of destiny, perhaps determinism, in it, since the Queen and her Ladies give him the magic flute, Pamina's picture, and other incentives and aids. These are to shield him while they spur him on to the Queen's purposes but they end up inevitably doing the opposite; they spur him toward truth. The flute, which was made by the Queen's late husband, once head of Sarastro's Brotherhood, is given to Tamino just after Papageno's mouth is unlocked and lying is denounced. It leads Tamino to the Brotherhood, as his feelings and mind change. He had believed, as the Queen wanted, that Sarastro is "inhuman, a tyrant," only to discover in him his own enlightener—and that enlightenment is not tyranny.[6]

The "sacred" band of the "sun's seven-fold circle," given to the Brotherhood by the Queen's late husband, also yields knowledge of nature's secrets. The implication: if the Queen possessed the sacred band, what would not be out of control? It also makes Sarastro the Guardian of the Sun's power. The number seven is just one example of the numerical mysticism that permeates *The Magic Flute* and was favored by Masons. It derives from a long tradition. Ancient Pythagoreans believed the number seven represented light and energy since it corresponded to what they believed to be the number of celestial orbits. In "Scipio's Dream," by Cicero, seven is the key to the universe and harmony. Seven rings also correspond to the seven notes on a diatonic scale. It seems that the Queen's King handed the Circle Band over to Sarastro to secure enlightenment, while the Queen gives the flute to Tamino in hope of retrieving the Band and its powers—but also of retrieving Pamina. The Prince becomes her foe. Papageno is also given musical fortification in the form of bells in a frame, a kind of glockenspiel used by military bands. This is, perhaps, appropriate as he joins Tamino in penetrating Sarastro's territory. But his first appearance is with panpipes, which are open while the glockenspiel is encased. Natural Man's tunes, this seems to hint, really do need a framework. Tamino's flute, by contrast, points toward individual growth and transformation. Both are finally instruments for the good; the bells provoke laughter and dance, the flute love, joyousness, and wisdom. And then Three Boys on a flying machine—the Ladies call them "young" but "wise"—who are appointed to guide Tamino and Papageno once they have passed into Sarastro's realm, are airborne, like a flute's (indeed all musical) sound is. They are not grounded in the Queen's domain. These Boys finally point Tamino and Pamina to where the Bird-Catcher cannot go. Earlier, when he first crosses into Sarastro's realm, Tamino will stand before three temples—one of Nature, the next of Reason, the third of Wisdom. The Three Boys sing counsel that would have served Orpheus well:

> This path leads you to your goal,
> But you, youth, must win it in manly fashion . . .
> Be steadfast, tolerant, and discreet.[7]

Tamino says this advice will be engraved in his heart.

III.

A vast literature speculates about the Queen's transformation from ostensible victim into malevolent force. Some judge her change incoherent, others mystifying. The opera's meanings are at stake in the disagreements about her, even if they allow for no final or comprehensive characterization. The reason is simple and applies to so many other aspects of *The Magic Flute*: it is so intelligently allusive, and its allusiveness shrewd. Still, this can be said with some surety: while Tamino is coaxed to Sarastro's realm for nefarious purposes, he and Pamina will come to see the world anew and be united happily in an embrace of each other that is inseparable from their embrace of Sarastro's moral ideals. And these ideals are fraternity, friendship, and love, all within a framework that is natural and reasonable to wise initiates. The Queen of the Night is, in the end, like Mephistopheles in Goethe's *Faust:* she does good while intending the opposite and while never becoming good. Goethe's Gretchen mounts the scaffold because of Faust, Pamina will lead Tamino through final trials of fire and water.

Mozart and Schikaneder made many things plain in the penultimate scene. The Queen and her Ladies, to whom Tamino and Pamina are now lost, make a final cross-border assault. They collude with brutish Monostatos, a Moor who is slave to Sarastro and who hankers for Pamina. Ever-manipulative, the Queen promises her daughter as reward to him—as she once offered her to Tamino. Revenge and power, not Pamina's welfare, is the Queen's abiding concern. Her ally's motives are no better. Monostatos rebels out of resentment of Sarastro who has thwarted and punished his lust for Pamina. Ideology and self-interest blur in this new coalition of women and a Moor. The Queen and the Ladies sing of wiping out all "*Die Frömmler*" in order to appeal to Monostatos. This word can perhaps be rendered best here as "the sanctimonious bigots."[8] By contrast, Sarastro has told his priests that the Queen "thinks herself great [while she] hopes through deception and superstition to fool the people. . . ."[9]

Biases and conflicts of Mozart's day are stark here. Yet if we look closely they are also, at least in part, exposed as prejudice, as if the opera were at times casting a disinfecting light upon them. The opera contrasts the Queen's emotive female cunning—treacherous and spiteful—to Sarastro's rational and male moral intelligence, presenting stereotypes as well as Masonic attitudes. Women were long viewed by Masons as naturally indiscreet and incapable of true enlightenment. They needed "guidance" and could not be lodge members, at least until this proscription was challenged in some places in the mid-eighteenth century. The negative judgments are voiced repeatedly and in different ways in *The Magic Flute*. We learn that the Queen cannot rule on her own and lost powers after her husband's death. Sarastro tells Pamina that without a man "every woman/ steps beyond her proper domain."[10] When Tamino first encounters the priest at the Temple of Wisdom, he is warned that he has arrived due to (the Queen's) guile and "the tongue's game."[11] Tamino and Papageno are told to maintain silence in their trials and are counseled that the loose lips of women distract from wisdom. Sagacity requires discipline, quiet, and not fearing death. Papageno, the frightened Natural Man, says he would prefer to be a girl.

There are five female characters in *The Magic Flute*. The Three Ladies are no more than extensions of the Queen. She is comparable to Vitellia, daughter of a deposed emperor, who plots murder to claim power in *Tito*. Titus turns out to be the opposite of what she says he is, much as Sarastro is not what the Queen claims he is. And Titus, like Tamino, emerges as a man in command of himself. Vitellia loses control of her situation, is humbled and accepts her place; the Queen is defeated. Yet Pamina contrasts to the Queen and Vitellia. She shows courage and a strong sense of dignity. While she wanted at first to return to her mother, we also see her prefer death to losing her virtue with Monostatos; and then she will not follow her mother's command to kill Sarastro. When Tamino's silence, required by his testing, leads her to think she has lost him, she takes the dagger her mother provided, declares it her "bridegroom" and prepares to kill herself. (Her hand is stayed only by the reappearance of the Three Boys.) She has come to see also that Sarastro is and her own late father was virtuous. And the audience, by now, should see that she is clearly a superior being to chattering Papageno. Tamino and Pamina emerge triumphant, looking forward, ascending together. Sarastro, of course, abets them.

It is assumed often by critics and viewers that the conclusion is as anomalous or contradictory as the Queen's role. Pamina gains admittance to the fraternity despite all of the opera's admonitions about women. Historical research, however, allows for some conjectures that may make this less perplexing. As early as the 1740s Masons in the Hague proposed that women be able to join their ranks. It was impossible, some members argued, to believe in equality and do otherwise. "The Lodge of the Just," formed in 1751, admitted both sexes. Some lodges in France "adopted" female members. Considerable controversy came when women's lodges formed. A "Queen of the Amazons" presided over ceremonies in some of them. Male "tyranny" was denounced and calls issued for equality between "Amazons" and "Patriarchs." When a leader of the Paris Grand Orient Lodge responded to remonstrations against its decision to allow in women, he reminded his associates of Isis and Osiris.

The full impact of these debates on Viennese Masons is unclear, but Masonic fraternities across Europe had close links with each other, often discussed the same matters, and knew each other's concerns. A historian points out that an acting ensemble of men and women that included members of "The Lodge of the Just" came to the Habsburg capital in 1752. Ongoing links were established between them and important Viennese Freemasons, some well placed in the government.[12] Born's lodge, which had counted Sonnenfels and Joseph Haydn as members and Mozart as a regular visitor, included women.[13] There was a parallel debate within Masonry about lifting its ban on Jewish membership. One result was the formation in Vienna of the "Order of the Asiatic Brethren" in 1780–81. It included leading nobles, and in a parallel to the "Amazon" lodges formed "Melchizedek" lodges (named for the biblical figure whose name meant "My Just King"). Its membership was in principle open to Christians and Jews, but also to Turks, Armenians, Persians, and Copts. Like the more mainstream Masons, its belief system—if it can be properly called that— embraced rationalism and Christian notions, but unlike them there were also aspects of kabbalistic mysticism derived from Sabbatianism, a Jewish heresy of the preceding century. After Joseph II's decree reorganizing the Masons, the Asiatic Brethren moved their hub to northern Germany.[14]

Issues of tolerance and equality were thus very present among the Masons and within the Viennese intellectual world during Mozart's time. No empirical evidence links directly the roles of women in *The Magic Flute* to internal Masonic arguments. Still, if we imagine, as we have throughout this book, that works of art can distill, among other things, key aspects of their times and represent them anew through imagination—sometimes by subtle suggestion and sometimes in contradictory or revelatory ways—then it can be well supposed that conflicts about the place of women within Freemasonry appear in costume and voice and orchestra in *The Magic Flute*. The Queen's character might present more than a stereotype and hint at a threat perceived by those Masons who did not want females in lodges. The Queen of the Night was their Queen of the Amazons denouncing tyrants, reproving the position articulated by the priests and Patriarch Sarastro himself—those who insist on male supervision of women.

The Magic Flute tells us that Queens of the Night ought to be rebuffed, restricted, and also that their progeny ought to escape them. Yet the Queen is not all women in this opera. While Pamina accepts Sarastro's authority and while the magic flute itself was made by her father, she does undergo transformation; she and her status are not unchangeable by nature. At one point, Sarastro addresses the priests of the Temple of Wisdom as fellow "servants of Isis and Osiris."[15] The Temple, then, has both female and male deities. Isis and Osiris, besides being siblings and marrying, were both great-grandchildren of the Sun God. Osiris, who cannot do without Isis, came to symbolize reason for Enlighteners, and Isis symbolized nature. Since Tamino is rebuffed when he tries separately to enter the Temple of Reason as well as that of Nature, *The Magic Flute* would seem to imply that sagacity—the Temple of Wisdom—requires and synthesizes the other two.

IV.

And Monostatos? When the Queen, Monostatos, and the Ladies are vanquished together, Enlightenment defeats both a social alliance and darkness. Partnerships, often coercive, among varied "lower class" and "upper class" figures were steady features of operas Mozart set by different librettists: Konstanze and Blonde, Belmonte and Pedrillo, Susanna and the Countess, Leporello and Don Giovanni, Despina and Don Alfonso. Sometimes the alliance is for better, other times for ill. Both Papageno and Monostatos align with "higher" figures and both change allegiances. Papageno begins as the Queen's subject and then, at her charge, becomes Tamino's helper. He finally goes over to Sarastro because Tamino does. Monostatos begins as Sarastro's groveling slave but ends up as the Queen's point man. Yet neither Papageno nor Monostatos rises above himself, however different their selves.

Viewers might well be reminded of Osmin in *Abduction* when they behold Sarastro's slave (Mozart's use of a "Turkish" piccolo in some of Monostatos's music may help their recall). That he is a Moor, that he aligns with "Darkness" in pursuit of white Pamina—he is night, she is day—injects stark racial categories. Yet the categories are not injected in entirely simple or consistent ways. Pamina, after all, descends from a Queen of Darkness who is obviously fair-skinned; presumably, Pamina's late father, Sarastro's companion, was too. Pamina is often portrayed on stage as a Germanic blonde. However, when Papageno first meets her and compares her to her portrait, he says that her eyes and hair are black. (Some early editions of the libretto specify her as fair-haired.)[16] In either event, the opera ascribes the Queen's "darkness" to the absence of male guidance, not to any racial quality.

But if Pamina's status changes, Monostatos remains like his name (even when he changes masters). Sarastro tells him "your soul is as black as your face."[17] Still, a certain pathos emerges in the opera that perhaps can also be taken as a subtle criticism of its own prejudices. When Papageno and Monostatos first meet, these two "lower" human beings terrify each other. Each imagines that he encounters a devil. Papageno, however, asks aloud: if there are black birds in the world, why not black men too? Variety is human and natural. The two figures also have different voices—Mozart makes Monostatos a tenor and Papageno a baritone—as variants of a similar, limited species. And don't all creatures of nature respond to music? When Monostatos and slaves under his command seek at one point to capture Pamina and Papageno, the Natural Man's defense is his glockenspiel. Its sounds captivate and animate—immediately and quite literally—the assailants, who dance and sing, dissipating their threat. Orpheus's lyre inspired creatures of nature to dance but his music was also deployed to persuade a sovereign to liberate Eurydice. Tamino never uses the flute to convince Sarastro of anything. Instead, its sound changes the Prince himself and will help him through his trials—but with his voice quieted on his own accord (Papageno cannot but babble). Threefold chords strike as Tamino succeeds.

Sarastro is not alone in frowning on Monostatos. He is despised by the other slaves. They call him "our tormenter, the ever-spying Moor," suggesting not only malice based on race but that life for slaves is like life in a police state (perhaps another hint about a less attractive feature of Vienna).[18] They rejoice that Pamina might escape his clutches. Monostatos again evokes Osmin. Both accept an inferior position as their due but also that those beneath them ought to receive their due too. There is psychological insight into hierarchy here: acceptance of their own lowliness makes it important for Osmin and Monostatos to beat down others. The two cope by this means with aggravations they don't really understand. Osmin is goaded by the Pasha's clemency; vengeful Monostatos faces reprimand for bad conduct for which he expected reward (when he captures Pamina trying to escape). Even though he benefits from his master's clemency, he doesn't understand the basis of Sarastro's rule. He cannot grasp that force is not its secret. And still, an ambiguous, even humanist protest emerges again. It is almost as if Mozart and Schikaneder also tell us that Monostatos's circumstances are not fair. At one point, Monostatos asks openly: just what is my offence? Why am I to be punished for falling in love with this foreign flower, Pamina? Could any man—the word "*Mensch*" is used here—have resisted? Recall how Tamino came as a foreigner to the Queen's world and fell in love with a picture. Moreover, it is possible to detect echoes of Shylock's celebrated challenge to Christian anti-Jewish prejudice when Monostatos wonders if he is to be deprived just because "a black man is considered ugly." He asks, "Didn't I receive a heart as well? Am I not flesh and blood?" I love, he sings, "because I am alive."[19] His aria goes from frenzy to *piano*—sleeping Pamina is nearby—and expresses gentleness despite what might be taken for his natural meanness. Cruelty reemerges, however, as the inability to realize desire turns his mood; he then seeks to convey it by force. His love, then, is an imposed physical drive, not reciprocal and transformative.

Neither Monostatos nor Papageno is suited to Sarastro's world. But while the former's fate is joined to the Queen's, Papageno will have a loving Papagena to join him in happiness—though not in wisdom. He accepts his lower place in Sarastro's domains, never really thinking to have things otherwise and so is without resentment. He can live happily beside (really below) Sarastro and Tamino. If Monostatos reveals unhappy aspects of humanity, guileless Papageno displays a more amiable dimension. Together, they refute the idea that original sin is constitutive of human nature. They offer instead a more multifaceted notion—there is good and there is bad—which is shown, even on its lower levels. Resentment underlies Monostatos's inability to control his worst impulses; this leads to hurt. And this is something different from Papageno's natural lack of self-control. Wisdom and reason can govern neither of them from within; and neither can, finally, do without a ruler. While the audience is expected to react with disdain to conniving Monostatos, Papageno has a dithering charm and will be merrily subservient to what is better and higher in human nature. Papageno doesn't think twice about it—or in the first place.

He is at home in a premoral, instinctive realm, outside the Brotherhood's wisdom. After Tamino declares that he seeks friendship and love and explains that wisdom is his goal and Pamina will be his prize, Papageno is asked by a priest if he will endure trials to become wise. The reply: "Struggle is not my thing." When told that there are higher and lower pleasures, he opts for the latter. Lots of people are like him, he points out: "I am a man of nature (*Ich bin ein Naturmensch*) who is satisfied with sleep, food and drink." He needs only "a beautiful little wife" for happiness.[20] Yet because he is easily panicked, he is willing to remain single rather than endure great challenges. Sarastro, however, determines that there is no need for this poorer human creature to suffer. He provides Papageno with Papagena. She materializes first as an ugly old hag, ruffling the Bird-Catcher's feathers, but the clemency of Sarastro trumps appearances. She turns out to be beautiful and an ideal mate—she too is covered by feathers. Mozart and Schikaneder seem again to make gentle fun of Rousseau in the joyous meeting of Papageno and Papagena. As Rousseau explained how musical sounds turned into the first articulate speech when a boy and a girl chanced to meet and began to emote, Papageno and Papagena do likewise, singing "Pa-Pa-Pa-Pa-Pa-Pa" to each other before pronouncing the beloved's name.

V.

By contrast to the gentle flute—or to the chimes of Papageno's glockenspiel, which delight and protect—it is a forceful bellow of strings, winds, and brass that sounds when the Queen's forces are repelled in their final attempt against Sarastro's Temple. "Smashed, annihilated is our power," they sing, "we all plunge into eternal night."[21] They arrive in C minor, a key which Mozart used to suggest death as well as dark powers. Then the Singspiel shifts to E-flat major, the key in which its overture began with three chords. It signals alteration on stage, suggesting the triumph of Sarastro's values and establishment of wholeness. The audience sees a great sun shining on Sarastro, Tamino, Pamina, the Boys, and the Priests.

Masons had a mystical attachment to E-flat. They considered it their tonic—their "home key." Mozart links it to love, an animating principle of fraternity. It returns at telling moments throughout the opera. We hear it, for examples, when Tamino first looks at Pamina's "divine image" and when Sarastro enters. Keys (and interaction among them) provide one means by which Mozart speaks musically and constructs a meaningful totality: F appears with the Priests, G major with comic figures, G minor with suffering. At important points the principal antagonists move into sharper key: Sarastro into E major and the Queen into D minor.[22] The number three, which had mystical potency for Masons (as for Christians), is also evident throughout *The Magic Flute*. It is often pointed out that there are three temples, three Ladies, three Boys, three slaves (apart from Monostatos), and three trials that Tamino undergoes. The key of E-flat major has three flats—B-flat, E-flat, A-flat—and a chord in B-flat strikes in the opera at three key moments.[23]

It announces when Tamino and Papageno face their tests, suggesting the powers of music in a scene in which Mozart and Schikaneder again allude, unabashedly if with some gentle humor, to Orpheus. Tamino has been ready to proceed while Papageno is preoccupied with victuals provided by the Three Boys. Natural Man insists aloud (of course!) that he won't be parted from his food even if threatened by lions. Of course, the lions appear to his terror and the sounds of Tamino's flute charm them into an exit. Papageno is now ready to join Tamino when the chord sounds again (twice). Papageno asks nervously (in a passage that is sometimes cut): What will happen now? Tamino points upward. Only the gods know. The chord chimes again, linking music to heaven. B-flat has a particularly important structural relation to the opera's tonic. In technical terms, it is the "dominant" of E-flat, that is, five degrees from it. There is a necessary movement back and forth between a tonic, which establishes a framework of sound, and the dominant, which contrasts to it, allowing elaborations of both melody and harmony as the music goes forth.

Tamino's readiness for his trials is signaled by the flute's sounds and these in turn indicate his change—his recognition of the rightness of Sarastro's kingdom. The tests, we know, require silence, no matter how difficult.* He must remain mute even if it causes Pamina agony. Unlike Orpheus, Tamino

---

*Seventeenth- and eighteenth-century Quietists and their sympathizers from Madame de Guyon to Fénelon and Ramsay might have appreciated this requirement, although quiet in this opera is integrated as one dimension of what wisdom requires, and Quietism's austere notion of self-obliteration of the individual in prayer is obviously at odds with *The Magic Flute's* vision of this-worldly, sensuous spirituality, which is expressed especially by its music and humor.

demonstrates steadfastness by always looking forward. He attains values that he lacked when just an innocent if proud prince. The pain Pamina suffers at his silence and, more broadly, her own ordeal—her refusal to murder Sarastro—bring her to a new human level as well; suffering enables her to join the Brotherhood.

Sarastro tells Tamino that passing the tests will allow him one day to "reign as a wise prince."[24] This is equivalent to saying that he will learn essential political requirements. Remarkably, Sarastro has no royal or political title. The priests acclaim his rule by referring to him as their "Idol";[25] by contrast Monostatos calls him "Lord" (*Herr*),[26] which is how any slave or feudal underling would address a master. It is, however, always wisdom, something he can share among his brethren (but not with his lessers), that secures his authority. He "rules in Wisdom's Temple, "says a priest to Tamino, who thinks initially that Sarastro is a "tyrant" because the Queen told him so.[27] There are variations on the German words *Herr* (Master or Lord) and *Macht* (power) in *The Magic Flute*. *Er herrscht* comes from the verb *herrschen* (to rule). Hence Monostatos addresses Sarastro as his *Herr*. There is a kind of natural relation between what Hegel later called *Herr und Knecht*, Master and Servant (or Slave), but it differs from the natural hierarchy of the Queen and Papageno, who does not grasp his subordination.

Indeed, Sarastro's world integrates nature into it. By contrast, the opera begins with Tamino chased within nature, into the Queen's realm, by a monster that the Ladies kill while singing "Die . . . by our power" (*unsere Macht*). But then they say Tamino is free, suggesting freedom is from brute nature.[28] When Tamino hears of the Queen from Papageno for the first time he wonders if this is the "powerful ruler" (*mächtige Herrscherin*) of the Night of whom his father once spoke. On deciding it is, the Prince says it is outside his power (*ausser meiner Macht*) to grasp how or why he arrived in her realm.[29] (Obviously he knows that the serpent chased him there but the implication is that this beast was not alone responsible.) Tamino will discover, however, that the power of the Queen is duplicitous, in direct contrast to that of Sarastro. His themes are fraternity, clemency, tolerance, and discretion. Self-discipline is necessary for them all and demands a sense of limits—just the quality lacking in Orpheus as well as Don Giovanni and Almaviva (although the latter, perhaps, learns it somewhat).

Tamino's initiation proves that he can be a wise ruler, and *The Magic Flute* thereby returns to the principal subject of *Telemachus*, *Cyrus*, and *Séthos*. It is a staple of Mozart's operas from his earliest efforts. Young Scipio was not a prince, but his dream teaches him patriotic responsibilities. Idamantes displays his ability to be Crete's king, and Titus Rome's emperor. Sarastro could undoubtedly applaud Tamino's predecessors.

VI.

The Magic Flute's implications, as well as its political suggestions, are much greater than its fairy tale. Some three decades after its first production Hegel made powerful claims for the opera's quality, including its libretto, which by then was a target of considerable derision. Mozart's music was exquisite—few would deny that—but critics complained that Schikaneder's words served up something flighty. Great artworks, thought Hegel, captured the historical journey of the human spirit. They disclosed its "higher interests," its "will," and "the true depths of the heart." These "glean through external appearances," through any "transient" material in them that is "purely historical." Consider, he asks, what is "present for us" when we read in the Bible of the "grief of the prophets." Is it "Babylon and Zion" or is it celebration of God's goodness and the "wrath of his omnipotence"? Likewise, when Sarastro sings his "moral theme," presenting his fraternity's ideals against a backdrop of obelisks and temples, all viewers, Egyptian or not, are pleased "because of the inner kernel and spirit of its melodies."[30] Ridicule of Schikaneder was no more than "chatter," wrote Hegel, by critics who failed to perceive that the libretto was exceptional precisely because it was not protean. Instead of presenting a detailed map to the composer, its "intermediate kind of poetry" provided a foundation allowing Mozart to "erect his building on the lines of his own invention, exhausting every motive and moving in a living way in every direction." A "unity of effect" came about as words and music came together. In *The Magic Flute*, "the realm of the night, the queen, the realm of the sun, the mysteries, initiations, wisdom, love, tests, and along with these a sort of common place morality excellent in its general principles" combined with "the depth, the bewildering loveliness and soul of the music [which] broadens and fills the imagination and warms the heart."[31]

In the twentieth century, an eminent political thinker, Isaiah Berlin, judged highly problematic just what Hegel applauded. The opera's "commonplace morality" masked something insidious, Berlin proposed: it finally makes freedom meaningless because it allows but one choice—that of the Brotherhood—to be moral. A telos governs human options, which is to say that they are not truly elective but a one-way route determined by "reason." If Hegel's view of the opera was right, Tamino takes no real moral decisions in his journey—and does not create himself—because all of right and wrong exist in advance. Sarastro's "moral theme" presupposes that humanity is free only by accepting and then finding its way into a preestablished, rational design. "When ends are agreed," Berlin writes, "the only questions left are those of means." These means are at best no more than technical matters, and so ethical or political choices by the individual vanished into belief in some "immense, world transforming phenomenon, like the final triumph of reason." (Later this takes other forms such as proletarian revolution, says Berlin, providing a clue to his own thinking.) Consequently, a necessary logic works itself out and can reach only one conclusion, regardless of the vicissitudes of human life and history. When self-mastery and this kind of "liberation by reason" coincide, they both become equally hollow; instead there must be rules for every aspect of life for such "freedom," least we fall "prey to . . . irrational desire." This ill-conceived notion of liberty is lodged in Sarastro's temple. In it, rational self-determination of an individual's life becomes identical with integration into a rationally planned world—which is no freedom at all.[32]

Tamino's maturation becomes what Hegel called—and Berlin protests—recognition of necessity. Sarastro becomes the high priest of despotism by "the best or the wisest." Were he to remake the world, Tamino and Pamina would be "wholly law-abiding and wholly free" at once. But whatever is defined as not strictly—some would say simplistically—rational can only be a source of conflict and tragedy.[33] Berlin's objection to Sarastro is a traditional one made against Hegel. Because this German philosopher insisted that history is a process by which the human spirit becomes increasingly more rational—an arguable proposition—Berlin thinks it makes inevitably for tyranny. Since reason always abstracts, the specifics of human lives and history dissipate by its conceptualizing force. Emotions ranging from fear to love are suffocated and with them real individuality and experience. The Genevan literary critic Jean Starobinski made a similar claim about the "vocabulary" of the Enlightenment and the French Revolution. While there was considerable variation in the use of words like "humanity, liberty, the homeland, the Supreme Being," he wrote, the result was nonetheless a "new authority" and "always a particular subjection."[34] Lurking within *The Magic Flute*'s Enlightenment, then, is a blinding totalitarian light; it shines the way back into darkness. The Singspiel's many meaningful charms harbor a false, dangerous promise of freedom as the replacement for an Old Regime's oppressions.

Totalitarianism is, however, a twentieth-century notion. Does it truly apply in this eighteenth-century context? Or is its use an anachronistic imposition? The teleology—the notion that the goal is implicit in the beginning—to which Berlin objects can also be ascribed to Christianity and most religions as well as to a variety of political idealisms. Contextualization of Berlin's argument brings us from *The Magic Flute* to perpetual, weighty contentions among students of political thought about how to place words and ideas in history. It is partly a consequence of the great political upheaval of Mozart's day and how it is—or ought or ought not to be—linked to the catastrophes of the twentieth century. Here is one twentieth-century way to put it: did Stalin's regime of mass murder in the 1930s find its formative moment in the French Revolution, particularly the Terror of 1793? After all, the Soviet regime often drew on the French vocabulary. However, here it is useful to return to Skinner's argument that questions must be posed not only about what someone said (or wrote or composed) but also about what he or she was doing when saying (or by extension writing or composing) something.[35] Deep contextualization rather than judgment by our own lights alone is required if our interest is the politics of *The Magic Flute* rather than finding in it only our own concerns. We cannot simply escape our own concerns; but we need to be enlightened about them when we look back at art and politics.

The opera's bigger ideas, however elusive, allusive, and ambiguous, need to be discerned first of all in 1791's temporal surroundings. Complete domination by Reason was not then the foremost issue in Paris. The issue was, instead, securing constitutional monarchy in the face of a recalcitrant monarch who hewed to the irrational belief that birth, status, and God placed him above any earthly law and above all men and women. In Vienna the issue was an apprehensive regime at an uncertain juncture—a regime whose past, enlightened policies wobbled all while a firm step was needed. But the terrain was not steady. And after all, the new Habsburg ruler believed (more or less) in the kind of regime that Louis XVI rejected. It is decontextualization that allows for Berlin and Starobinski's assertions about *The Magic Flute*.[36] Berlin's argument ignores the opera's targets: the powers of unreason in the eighteenth century, particularly unenlightened political regimes and obscurantism in the church.

The Queen of the Night does not desire a pluralistic world with free choice by contrast to Sarastro's totalitarianism. She is single-minded and disingenuous but not yet a supreme despot; she wants full power beyond her own borders together with domination over everyone and everything on behalf of her own irrationalism. She tricks Tamino into the first choice he makes in the opera, and has control—when she chooses to exercise it—of all matters within her realm. Recall that Sarastro says that her aim is to pilot the people by "deceit and superstition" all while he (and the opera) identifies wisdom continually with tolerance. Mastery of "our difficult art," says Sarastro, will lead to the end of "evil prejudice."[37] He presses this openly and forcefully when he insists to skeptical priests that Tamino should be allowed to undergo initiation. As much as Sarastro's wisdom is hailed throughout *The Magic Flute*, his need to persuade his presumably enlightened brothers implies that disagreement is legitimate in his community, that he might be wrong, and that he is not a dictator of Reason. A successful initiate does indeed attain self-mastery; it implies what Louis XVI lacked—balanced intelligence. This king's failure, his recalcitrance, and that of Europe's old regimes had more to do with unleashing the terror that marred the French revolution than did a teleological view of reason's role in history described later by Hegel in philosophical texts. Moreover, when Sarastro proposes Tamino as a member of the Brotherhood—he pronounces it, we recall, the most important decision it will make—three Priests wonder if the young man can be virtuous, quiet, and charitable. These are not characteristics that come to most people's minds, philosophers included, when they think of twentieth-century tyrannies and political terror.

Mozart and Schikaneder undoubtedly hoped balance would characterize their own new emperor. At issue for them in 1791 was no contest between totalitarianism and free individuality but between a world dominated by unenlightened political and religious authority and enlightened friendship. Tamino and Pamina don't seek to rid themselves of fear or love and their self-mastery does not dissolve into a mystical rationality. Their love precedes their initiation. Reason undoes superstitions, certainly, but it is an enlightened wisdom that will triumph in "the noble pair." Their mature union makes their love more profound. Moreover, the rules of Sarastro's realm are always tempered by clemency and generosity. Vengefulness is a sin in his realm, a negative emotion. Sarastro shows clemency even to Monostatos. The invading Queen of the Night is repelled, but she does not end at the stake. Successful initiates are bound by friendship, which is not structured like a syllogism, leading somehow and inexorably to terror. Sarastro is not a liberal democrat, but were he Robespierre or Andrei Vynshinsky, Papageno would have been guillotined for his inability to be wise.

Any interpretation of *The Magic Flute* must account for the distinction in it between reason and wisdom. Recall: three temples stand in Sarastro's realm and that of wisdom is in the center between reason and nature. When Tamino first approaches the temples that flank the Temple of Wisdom, a voice calls: "Stay back!" He cannot simply enter Reason or Nature. When he knocks on Wisdom's door, a priest tells him that a quest for virtue and love cannot be animated by vengeance—the Queen's motive. (Tamino says his hostility aims only at an evil man; he has not yet learned the truth.) Things will only be clear, the priest tells Tamino, if friendship leads him into the "eternal band." And Sarastro tells the priests that should prejudice dwell within a potential initiate, then "wisdom and reason" will pluck it apart as if it were "a spider web."[38]

Wisdom does not reside in prejudice; it encompasses all human dimensions together with knowledge of what should be subordinate to the others and when. This is the most important lesson Tamino learns by his journey—where his wonder takes him.

SARASTRO'S SABBATICAL: THIS IS NOT A FINALE

When the final chorus of *The Magic Flute* sang for the union of wisdom and beauty in late September 1791, it suggested also the hope that a wise and tolerant community might with art sound triumphant together. No form of government was recommended, only broad principles for a virtuous life. Sarastro had towering authority as articulator, persuader, and especially as exemplar. The Queen of the Night's minions were vanquished. Even if Mozart and Schikaneder inclined to a republican allusion—and there is no indication that they did—it would have been impossible in imperial Vienna, especially when the emperor's sister, the Queen of France, was in difficulty. Tolerant, virtuous Titus in *Tito* shows us the alternative—how admirable an emperor can be. Younger and of Metastasian descent, he is an imperial counterpart to nonroyal Sarastro.

In the ensuing decade political realities strained severely even the most optimistic of imaginations. Multiple, rapid historical turns came. Sometimes they arrived as speedily as the Queen of the Night's change from victim of Sarastro into enemy of enlightenment. Sometimes they veered as rapidly as it takes to perceive that the future as projected in *The Magic Flute* really depends on the kidnapping and liberation of Pamina.

Our exploration of politics in opera began some two centuries before *The Magic Flute*, when those Florentine experimenters, and after them Monteverdi, fashioned stage works set in (mostly) mythical settings. Orpheus's story has been reinvented many times since then in opera and in virtually every art form, often with political as well as artistic ramifications. Monteverdi's Orpheus fails at self-mastery and can neither bend nor escape laws of earth, hell, and heaven. In one of the two endings of his Mantuan opera, the defeated protagonist becomes part of a celestial constellation. His salvation comes through integration into the upper reaches of a cosmos he could not alter, with its permanent up and down, with its bright points and dark stretches.

Tamino, by contrast, integrates into an apparently novel order in an unknown if very Egyptian-looking locale on earth. Osiris and Isis are hailed, but they—as opposed to the mystical number three—do not appear. This

Singspiel is finally about ideals for life in this world. Tamino, an Orpheus-like figure with a flute whose sounds transform a listener's feelings to the good but that was given to him by an evil ruler, also made return appearances in opera, although not as often (or as successfully) as did Orpheus. We will soon close by looking at two of them, but first, consider the historical distance from Orpheus at the turn of the seventeenth century to Tamino at the end of the eighteenth. Turmoil is found at both ends and in very many intervening decades. Extended calm was only occasional, but longing for it was persistent. Change and constancy contested through myriad political forms: principality and empire, absolute rule and constitutional monarchy, kings and republicans. In the intellectual background, tussles between "ancients" and "moderns" carried on. While both the idea of the modern state and opera were born of the same era, there were variations on kinds of "state" as there were of types of "opera" between Monteverdi's and Mozart's worlds; now, in Mozart's age, the idea of nation-state took sharper shape. Yet while Mozart was a proponent of opera in German, it was without nationalist impulse, let alone rancor.

Orpheus: it is as if there is an eternal return, albeit through varying riffs, in Western culture to this figure who fails when he looks back. He is especially apposite because he also brings us back to Ovid, that vital source for so many operas. I am hardly the first to recognize their importance, one a mythological musician and prince who crosses borders, the other a storytelling poet of change who was exiled by his ruler. My reasons for emphasizing them were political and historical in broad senses, and not only musical or literary. Orpheus tries by art to persuade the Underworld's absolute monarch to be flexible. Splendid temerity seems to succeed before hubris brings his fall. Similar quests for alternative futures have often gone wrong throughout history, all while they nonetheless foment new political realities that can be good. Sometimes art suggests what Irving Howe called, in a different (political) context, "a margin of hope," an image of promise.

Juxtapositions abound in *Metamorphoses;* they can be perceived or interpreted musically, like a change in keys or dynamics or colors or among motifs—or in the mood and speed from one movement of a symphony to another. Ovid's juxtapositions, like those in operas, often raise unsettling questions: about relations between divine and human worlds and within human domains; about humanity and nature; between past and the future. This Roman using Greeks allows many things to be said on multiple levels, some evident and some less so; so too would opera, a millennium and a half later. As Ovid sang to change, he dreamed of a golden age; he did so all while extolling at his poem's end the great political authority of his present, Emperor Augustus, who banished him to Rome's frontiers (not, apparently, for political reasons), and who replaced a crumbling republic with an empire disguised in republican garb. Appearances and power always mix in the theater of politics, as both Tacitus and Machiavelli knew, and as Monteverdi and Busenello showed as well when they took opera from myth into history (or a kind of mythologized history) by presenting Nero and Seneca to Venetians.

Mozart, who transformed musical forms, died amidst political metamorphoses; *The Magic Flute* often slides from one part of its story to another to suggest things on multiple levels about contemporary Europe. Consider an assertion by Hegel in an essay of 1795, unpublished during this philosopher's lifetime. "Great revolutions," he proposed, are not simply a matter of a single historical blow or event, even if one of these seems often to make hazy matters evident as a historical pattern. Instead, he proposed, revolutions are heralded by a "secret" transformation "in the spirit of an age." Its realities may be imperceptible to contemporaries, he explained. Hard to discern or depict, it is only "lack of acquaintance with this spiritual revolution which makes the resulting changes astonishing."[1] The era's great blow was, of course, the French Revolution. Nowadays, however, we tend to more modesty in grasping what happened and may even speak of multiple transforming spirits and circumstances that emerged before and in and after a clarifying event and an age. We find complexity and contingencies rather than obvious, sturdy signposts pointing to a conclusion that was foreseeable in hindsight. Yet something is also lost if we sweep aside Hegel's too-broad brush. Looking back, it is indeed possible to perceive connections and patterns of far-reaching significance that those in their midst usually didn't detect. And we can see that some artists perceive them sometimes—perhaps without intent, perhaps by ingesting the spirits of their times in nonconscious ways—and make art of them.

We can discover coherence within sensuous and intellectual distillations or representations of currents and causes and human dilemmas over a time. Coherence does not mean absolute consistency; each detail or part does not have to fit all others in a perfect pattern or in a treatise-like way. And if both politics and art are our concern, as they must be when it comes to a political opera, then stage events cannot be judged only by their aesthetic powers or, by contrast, by reduction to entertainment (or, indeed, to any one thing, including politics). However, if we make interpretive claims about politics in opera, these must come with a checking and testing of ourselves against the politics of an age and not just by explication let alone by imposition of our own theories; we cannot make a political opera our own without taking into account distorting blurs brought about by our own interpretative conceits or visions or just the distance of time. We need political history in the face of these of blurs.

I have tried to avoid or correct my own interpretative conceits through-out this book by means of a constantly changing methodological medley —by applying different means of criticism or analysis or raising alternative questions when they seemed appropriate. Most important among these means has perhaps been an effort to contextualize rather than to apply a scheme formulated fully in advance of any explorations. Interpretive conceits are never entirely avoidable; an author does not always recognize them. It is too easy, however, to say simply that everything is a matter of interpre-tation even if, on one basic level, it is true; better to be explicit about the bases of one's own interpretations. Better to recognize one's own specta-cles. In "Backstage," this book's appendix, I try to be plain about some of my own interpretations. In a sense, this book represents more of what its author learned while writing it than what he theorized in advance. I did assume, however, that understanding politics in operas requires a grasp, broad if unavoidably imperfect, of the worlds in which operas were shaped by librettists and composers (and directors). This, in turn, meant trying to understand, to the extent possible, those worlds and times on their own terms.

Mozart operas, we know, had origins in earlier stories or myths or plays (and operas). His mature operas come one after another over an eleven-year period that was portentous, both in his own life and in that of Europe. Political and social landscapes come together in cultural form as themes in these operas. One after another—but they are linked—they present his age to us through artistic imagination. That imagination lets us reflect intelli-gently on the epoch in which they were fashioned, but on our own too if, at the start, we look at probable or at least plausible meanings in context. Yet we easily see that in these operas those on top and bottom have varied fates. There are humbled kings and aristocrats (Idomeneo, Almaviva, Vi-tellia); a defeated Queen; a self-destroyed noble (Don Giovanni). There are slaves and servants who are in the end either miserable (Osmin, Mon-ostatos) or entering a suitable, limited, but happy life (Papageno). Those of lower rank but without noble spirit are usually where they should be in Mozart's worldview.

His operas sing, sometimes loudly and sometimes softly, on behalf of freedom and equality. But, speaking politically, his tones go only so far. A masterless world is not proposed even while masters and their unmerited privileges are exposed. Conflicted Leporello captures this in a particular way, aspiring to be like the Don, fretting over what Giovanni does and despairing of his own complicity—and finally, when freed of this aristocrat, seeking a new master. There are many metamorphoses in Mozart's operas and the ends of both *Tito* and *The Magic Flute* would seem to proclaim resolution, or at least the hope for resolutions. History tells us that there were none. And for Mozart, Osmin, Leporello, Papageno, and Monostatos do not change.

Without proceeding by medley it would be impossible to say much about the politics of *The Magic Flute*. It would be a fairy-tale-like work with re-markable music telling of good defeating bad, and love triumphing thanks to a wise man. Someone may protest: isn't love the key Mozartian theme? Certainly it permeates his operas, but there is more to them, just as love, for all its importance, is not the sole dimension of human life or human hearts. Mozart's operas suppose that there is a human condition and that it is multidimensional. One important aspect is politics. Here, in recapitula-tion, are some principal themes and situations we found:

• *Idomeneo:* A ruler faces the consequences of rash judgment—it has hap-pened to many in his place—and is humbled. We are shown that authority does not always issue wisely. Yet Idomeneo's son, with courage and noble ideals, comes to the throne, and it is obvious that youth brings change. This is intimated early when Idamantes, still a prince, repudiates hostility among peoples—Cretans and Trojans. Past shibboleths are cast off.

• *The Abduction from the Seraglio:* After several centuries of European en-gagements, many (but not all) bloody, with non-European worlds, Mozart's Singspiel presented to its audience relations and prejudices among Euro-peans and what would later be called "Others." This theme—Europe and the world—is flushed out and made many-sided by portraying both rela-tions among masters and servants and those among men and women. The opera suggested, strongly so, that conflicts of religion or race or gender are not interminable—Idamantes would have agreed—but that they are complicated. Moreover, Osmin may be brutal but Selim is not and unlike Idomeneo, he is not rash.

• *The Marriage of Figaro:* Class and gender conflicts are exposed and ob-jectionable advantages of unmerited privilege spotlighted by libretto, music, and dance. Mozart's first collaboration with Da Ponte points constantly to how laws and customs sustain hierarchy. It tells of love and desire among its principals too, but not only these; it ends with the lord of the domain in which the opera takes place on his knees. It is possible to pretend that *Figaro's* world has nothing to do with power, order, and authority—that is, with politics. But then you must also forget that Mozart had no need of a libretto or of the idea of opera to write profound music.

• In *Don Giovanni* another aristocrat prowls and is undone. Costs are revealed of his exploitative behavior to those below him—women, generally, but also to all those born his social inferiors—and then the consequences to himself. He does not end up merely a humiliated "nobleman." The story was not new but *Don Giovanni* was staged shortly before many European aristocrats took comparable plunges, often heads first. A complex nexus among friendship and alliances and authority, already at the center of *Figaro*, is explored and the music is multicolored. It laughs, it dances, and it provides shades of warning, anger, worry, and utter darkness. Although evil is dispatched, *Don Giovanni* has no really happy ending, unlike any other mature Mozart opera. The Don asserts unrepentant, self-absorbed individuality, becoming frightened only in his last instant. Before then, he has needed no friends but only to gratify his needs; is it surprising that no warm hand stretches to him when an icy one clasps his? Like many in Europe's old order, this Don never sees what is coming. Indeed, he invites it and he grabs it—the statue's hand—as if the world, high and low, near and far, must always be subject to his whims. Servants, well, they exist to clean up afterwards. But are all those aligned against him enlightened? They—or most of them—came together only as the Don's foe, not as friends of each other in Mozart's last opera before the Revolution.

• *Così fan tutte* reveals the breadth of late eighteenth-century illusion. Don Giovanni skimmed the world's surface before being pulled under; in *Così* a philosopher's reason collaborates with a servant girl's wiles to show how façade—customs and dress—can be taken too easily for reality. The opera's title tells us that things are always that way but there is a pregnant moment when the gray-haired Philosopher instructs the opera's two young men to repeat after him the truth about women: *Così fan tutte*. Yet just as these words are sung, Despina enters. She is not at all like her mistresses—she is shrewder—and we already know that she would like to have and not just to serve chocolate. Her appearance when the title words are sung challenges those very words. In the meantime, she is in league with Alfonso—but for her own reasons.

• *Tito* presented, two years after the Bastille was stormed, a ruler struggling with the differences between appearance and reality. We found this in *Così*, except that the political problems are now evident directly. This emperor must also face dilemmas forced upon him by betrayal and discord. Everything he faces is complicated by conflicting demands of compassion, friendship, and political power.

• As the French Revolution headed toward furious territories, *The Magic Flute* presented the world as a struggle between wisdom's light and dark obsessions. Filled with ambiguities and hints, it presented to its audiences a community, Sarastro's, of reason, tolerance, and friendship—but not democracy. And it is besieged by a competing realm of deception. The latter's defeat recapitulates Mozart's hopes.

Then there was Part II of The Magic Flute.

II.

Part II of *The Magic Flute?* Actually, two sequels were written in the seven charged years after Mozart's death. The story is not over, they tell us. In both, the forces of evil recuperate and attack again, as if the sequels were commentaries on what was happening offstage in Europe. Sarastro's personal leadership does not determine the outcome in either case, although his presence—or absence—is very much felt. In one he plans to step aside from past duties and in the other he goes, effectively, on a community-mandated sabbatical. He has not fashioned a community of wisdom and defeated the Queen to create a cult of himself. He feels great responsibility to his fellow members—yes, because of his stature but also simply because he is part of the community. He also has no desire to preside for life. Tamino will, in both cases, fight resurging dark powers, but he does not have an easy time.

Malevolence will again be defeated, but its reappearance tells us that the librettists knew that history had not ended by fairy-tale means with *The Magic Flute's* last chorus. In one sequel, the Enlightenment's powers will lose purity; in the other they are not entirely efficacious, will be subject to some profound questions and also to teasing. In these plays of light and dark, it is useful to recall the questions that presented themselves in the first moments of *The Magic Flute*: Who or what is that serpent chasing a young prince? Unbridled, all-consuming nature? Old Regimes pursuing their own, as yet unwitting, children? Angry, hungry masses? Perhaps that serpent is something within humanity pursuing humanity itself. Or perhaps it is something within royalty that creates a monstrous situation.

The librettists of the sequels, both Masons, were not revolutionaries. Neither, however, sympathized with obscurantism or political evil. It is best to look at the later sequel, from 1798, first for its librettist was Schikenader. The other, although written three years earlier, points beyond his horizons. Schikenader's follow-up was staged in the same Theater auf der Wieden on Vienna's outskirts where *The Magic Flute* premiered. The librettist played Papageno again; the Queen of the Night is now named Luna. The music mixed echoes of Mozart with the new composer's hope, at best modestly achieved, to make the work somewhat his own. Paul Winter, now forgotten, was then a popular musician. This "Part Two," a Singspiel like the first, was written with moneymaking in mind. Mozart's *Magic Flute* was so successful that its librettist thought that much could be gained with the same characters. The new effort attracted enthusiastic viewers for a time. Yet its inferiority to the Mozart-Schikenader work is obvious and not only a matter of Winter's music. It becomes easy to suppose that Mozart's contribution to the original libretto—he did meddle extensively, and fortunately, with the work of his collaborators—may have given or at least helped significantly to fashion *The Magic Flute*'s allusive genius. This claim is largely speculation, but Hegel's defense of Schikenader's libretto for Mozart may, unknown to the philosopher, also be a defense of Mozart.

Schikenader called his sequel *The Labyrinth*, subtitled "The Struggle with the Elements"—earth, fire, air, and water. At the time of its writing, political principles and contesting kingdoms were again pursuing one another in what must have seemed to be a dangerous European labyrinth for the Habsburgs. The year before its staging was difficult for Austria, which moved into a reconfigured anti-French coalition (involving Russia for the first time). The overly complex plot begins where *The Magic Flute* ended, but the characters are often strikingly different. Tamino and Pamina are relatively weak figures who don't seem to have gained much virtuous stamina from previous travails. Sarastro assigns one more test: to overcome two elements, earth and air (fire and water were surmounted earlier). Princely couples must go through a dark labyrinth to do so, each starting from a different point, and search for the other. Why Tamino and Pamina need to find each other once more is not evident. Tamino is given the flute again and tells frightened Pamina that she will hear it when he is near. The flute, then, is now merely instrumental; its sounds don't transform. Yet if Tamino and Pamina are successful he will be given that "powerful" talisman, the Circle of the Sun, and Sarastro will step aside.[2]

Brothers protest that Sarastro should stay as king, but he seems to recognize the need for change. He tells them: You must protect what he now called the throne together with the temple and the "fatherland."[3] Luna has a new alliance involving another power, Tipheus, King of Paphos, who has been promised the hand of—who else?—Pamina for victory over Sarastro. When Pamina is abducted, Papageno is assigned to rescue her but he is still not the man for such an undertaking. When he protests that he wants to be a father and live normally, he is told that Tamino must be "father" to many peoples (like a Habsburg emperor, one supposes) and cannot risk his life.[4] That is, Papageno is expendable. And yet, *The Magic Flute*'s Tamino would never have allowed another, let alone his old companion, to take such mortal chances on behalf of his own love.

In the meantime, Monostatos, again in league with the Queen, is now in pursuit of Papagena. *The Labyrinth* lacks any edge in presenting his character. If *The Magic Flute* provided a moment of consideration for Monostatos when he asked why he too was not permitted to love, here he appears true to the most bigoted of stereotypes—a lusty, cruel black man who says he wants to wash his hands until they are white.[5] His Moor henchmen and the Three Ladies, who go disguised into the maze in sexually suggestive disguises, combine to assault the enlightened realm from within as Tipheus does so from outside. By the time that the opera heads to its denouement— with kidnappings and rescues—Sarastro, initially a generous figure, calls for revenge, mobilizing his Brothers, who sing, Victory! Victory! Pamina or death![6] It seems that the 1790s have taken these stage characters far from their Mozartian incarnations.

When neither side proves able to defeat the other, Sarastro proposes man-to-man combat between Tamino and Tipheus. Of course Tamino wins, although with difficulty. Taken as a reflection of 1798—even if set in a timeless, placeless, although Egypt-looking world—this Singspiel captures Europe at war, driven by anger and emotion. Still, one side is victorious and the Queen, Tipheus, and their allies go to eternal punishment. The opera ends in a joyous chorus of Brothers, together with Papageno's clan (the subject of a subplot). This happiness on earth is presumably also eternal, but we thought that as well at the end of *The Magic Flute*. And there is little telling or interesting about the contesting realms of *The Labyrinth* that wasn't in the Mozart-Schikenader collaboration.

III.

The other sequel was by Goethe, who was not only the greatest German language poet of the age but served as a high official in the ducal government—an absolutist one—of Saxe-Weimar-Eisenach. Unlike the many German intellectuals who greeted the French Revolution enthusiastically only to be disillusioned, he was never keen about it. Goethe did think France's elite had helped mightily to bring ruin upon itself but he was always loyal to his own liege and when it came to change, he preferred—perhaps because of his studies in botany—greening, development, or evolution, to radical cutting. This was not without self-interest; Duke Karl August supported him well. It also reflected Goethe's sensibility. He was an elitist, a believer in enlightened authority. His greatest work was not about a Papageno; *Faust's* concern was engagement with ominous powers on behalf of a very human quest to know and experience all.

Goethe participated in two campaigns against the French (as an observer in his duke's suite). In September 1792, he declared—or later said he declared—that "a new era in the history of the world had begun."[7] It was with this victory, one year after *Tito* and *The Magic Flute* were first staged, that France abolished its monarchy. Goethe wrote several works addressing the political events of the time, and his "Second Part" of *The Magic Flute* dates to 1795. It remained an unfinished fragment, which is perhaps appropriate since it concerned the birth of a new era. Hegel's essay discussing the spirit of revolutionary times—Goethe could not have read it as it was left unpublished then—was written in the same year as the sequel to *The Magic Flute*. The year 1795, coming after the Terror, after a king's beheading, after a French republic's proclamation, and amidst continual war, was fertile for formidable minds. In that year Immanuel Kant published "Perpetual Peace," arguing that war could be restrained by a cosmopolitan league of republics.

The principality's duke was nineteen years old when he invited Goethe, twenty-six, to serve him. Perhaps Goethe thought of him as a Telemachus in need of a Mentor. Goethe became director of the Court Theater in the year Mozart died, and no opera appeared more frequently on its stage than *The Magic Flute*. He hoped that a popular Viennese composer, who contacted him initially for a libretto, would set his "Second Part." Paul Wranitsky declined. It is difficult to imagine anyone plucky enough artistically to be a Mozart to a Goethe.

Neither sequel to *The Magic Flute* was a "great work." Both are interesting in light of the opera they "continue" and in the conflicted moods and judgments embedded in them.[8] Goethe's Sarastro still epitomizes wisdom. The enlightened community he fashioned and serves has, however, a somewhat different character from the one in *The Magic Flute*. In the latter, a foreign prince becomes a Brother upon proving that he can attain the community's standards. Glad prospects then appear in the offing, although they don't propose that wisdom's world is forever static. If it were, we would have to assume that Tamino, who had to become wise, would have no further use for wisdom. Then we would have to assume that his wisdom would not change once deployed. Mozart's finale celebrates Tamino and Pamina and the victory of goodness. Yet it doesn't propose an end to fairy tales.

Goethe's Tamino is not especially impressive. More important, Goethe's "Second Part" tells us that the community's reasonableness is not self-sufficient; it doesn't glow in a container and ought not be closed in on itself. It must engage what is beyond its precincts. One member takes an annual leave to explore the "raw world." The sabbatical is not for personal enhancement but to attain enlightenment through experience that can, upon his return, enrich his Brethren. This solo Wanderer-Explorer is no imperial conqueror since his aim is not to stay abroad but only to bring back wisdom. He must, moreover, be granted permission to reenter by proving himself unblemished by his experiences. He carries a stone throughout his travels; if it is still bright and clear on his return, he can bring into the community what he has learned. The Wanderer, then, engages the world, learns from it, yet must remain pure. Goethe does not seem to have pondered how this purity itself might have had to change by worldly encounters.[9] Nonetheless, this Wanderer's task suggests that the future is never determined entirely from within, even for the wise. Sarastro explains that "only the Wanderer who has roamed over the fields of the earth can learn to recognize the sublime language of nature and the sounds of humankind in need."[10] Sarastro's realm, as Goethe saw it, could not flourish unless its reason goes out to learn more of nature and of the rest of humanity; this is prerequisite for knowing more of itself. Rather than simply suggesting the Enlightenment's limits, he seems to propose how human reason can become wiser, more sensible. Perhaps Goethe was also saying that a tolerant, humane community cannot close its eyes and ears to events beyond its borders, however much he was inclined to flee from the world's turmoil into poetry. He may have meant those cries of need to be calls for the natural rights of man—sounds he thought misleading; perhaps he hints too that French armies ought to think of whether or not they can return home in purity with their revolutionary ideals.

Still, Goethe has made a claim against enclosure and tells us that wisdom and life cannot be still: they must move. It is a striking claim in an age of change, invasion, and imperialism.

Who wanders each year? Here Goethe mixes a kind of egalitarianism with authority. Members don't select a Wanderer by vote but by lottery.

Anyone can be chosen. (A comparable system informed ancient Athenian democracy. A lottery there allowed all citizens, at least in principle, to obtain office, forestalling undue political reach thanks to wealth or influence.)[11] This year, Sarastro himself wins the lottery and he is obedient. "I do not hesitate for a moment to submit to [the lottery's] command," he declares.[12] Indeed, he supposes his choice to be that of the gods so that his community may be tested.

For while he is outside, external evil will seek to make its way within. "I leave, a pilgrim outward bound," says Sarastro, and he calls on the Brotherhood to guard wisdom and thereby itself. He is indeed worried that the Brothers might stumble without him, but this does not dissuade him. The Brothers worry aloud about his loss, suggesting a lack of self-confidence. By Sarastro's sabbatical, Goethe poses an old question, found in many forms in political and religious literature: Can a community constituted or swayed initially by a singular lawmaker (in this case, a wisdom-maker) survive his absence? This uncertainty was raised in Jewish and Christian texts by the figures of Moses and Jesus; and it was raised by Rousseau, who imagined a legislator issuing grand principles for a community and then withdrawing, leaving the future to the "general will" of citizens. Sociologist Max Weber later wrote of the singularity of "charismatic authority" and how it becomes "routinized" when its embodiment is gone.

Goethe leaves matters more open: we do not know what fertilizing knowledge Sarastro will bring back with him. Nor do we know its effect, since the libretto does not culminate in his return. Sarastro's sabbatical only shows that he is committed to serving his community and its needs and that he ought not to be an indispensable leader. Tamino, now beloved by all, will be placed at its head in Sarastro's absence. The battle for the future resolves by transcending the worlds of the original *Magic Flute*. But Tamino and Pamina will, as in *The Labyrinth*, have great difficulties when the Queen, her Ladies, and her self-declared "disciple" Monostatos return. The latter mobilizes Moor minions who kidnap the son of Tamino and Pamina.

This newborn is encased in a golden sarcophagus and placed under the Queen's seal. A double curse is pronounced by her: should the child's parents see one another, they will go mad; should they see their son, he will die. Gleeful Monostatos believes that he will finally be able first to deliver Pamina to the Queen of the Night and then receive her as reward. That, of course, would mean that the future is "dark," given the racial allusions. Delight turns to frustration when Monostatos and his men find that they are unable to lift the sarcophagus. He blames Sarastro's magic. Can it be that

Sarastro left behind enough wisdom to thwart evil's reassertion? Perhaps Monostatos has it wrong. Perhaps Goethe wants to say what Monostatos cannot perceive: even a gilded case cannot restrain the future forever. That is a warning to Old Regimes.

Breaking the gilded encasement is also beyond the powers of Sarastro's followers. Although the priests of his realm recuperate it—they bring it to Tamino's palace for care by its ladies—they cannot open it.[13] They cannot free the boy, that is, reach the future themselves. Yet he is in constant motion within it. The Queen, whose strength seems to have been enhanced since Sarastro's journey abroad, does not retreat in frustration but makes the casket sink into the ground. She surrounds it with lions, soldiers, fire, and water. The question becomes: Will a kingdom ruled by Tamino with Pamina be able to resist evil's reassertion and its efforts at blackmail? The opposing sides, good and evil, are both wanting and neither is able to assert itself in a struggle over unseen prospects, here the child conceived by the union of Tamino and Pamina with Sarastro's blessing. Neither can control the sarcophagus and the movements within it. (Like in Schikaneder's sequel, and European armies then opposed, forces seem stalemated.)

Music will not provide salvation or transformation. Goethe is consciously writing a libretto for not-yet-written music and emphasizes where a composer must shape its events. And Tamino's famous flute has even been given to Papageno and Papagena as a wedding gift. Living a rustic life, they use it along with their glockenspiel to attract animals—not to get them to dance as Orpheus did but for capture for their dinner. Sarastro, on his pilgrim's way, will meet this pastoral couple and find them sorrowful because they have had no children. The wise man provides them with eggs; bird children will come from them, ensuring the future of a simple life. In the meantime, two other realms—those in which Papageno and Papagena do not live—struggle over their futures.

Sarastro tells Papageno of Tamino and Pamina's woes and sends him to them with the magic flute, hoping its sounds will provide some relief. It does but no more than that; the music is only a temporary balm. Goethe seems to suggest despite himself—a poet, music and opera lover—that art can be only one dimension of well-being. The flute's music is not transformative and does not lead to the child's liberation. Instead, his parents will make their way through fire and water—tests again!—to him, and the child is finally empowered when he hears their voices. The power of sound is ever important. The child's restlessness and consciousness merge unseen in the sarcophagus and, finally, he breaks out. Identified as "Genius," he soars up, beyond contesting realms, as if the human spirit itself, surging by its own force toward a future, a dying domain left behind. His parents' voices may have helped to galvanize him, but he breaks the constraints himself. Guards and lions move toward him but they cannot capture this *Geist*, who declares himself his parents' heir and then flies out of their reach—as well as that of everyone. His movement, enabled by the past, turns into his own power.

Not the Queen's minions, not the Priests and the Brotherhood, and not a gold-laden box can restrict him. The past, good and bad, cannot hold him. After all, a golden sarcophagus is still a sarcophagus.

He takes wing, but where will he land? Or will he continue to soar, without rest, as Goethe's Faust wants to do? Since the libretto was not finished, Goethe provides no answer. We also don't know if this *Geist* is meant to be artistic genius, or more. The "Era of Genius" was often used to describe the "Storm and Stress" and romantic periods of German literature, in which Goethe loomed so large. That was mostly before the French Revolution and his libretto, written after it, looks to the future. Is the Genius—the *Geist*—supposed to be humanity writ large, as Hegel would have it? Or is it individualized? Is it, though free and no longer confined, doomed finally, along with contemporary dogmas? If we look to *Faust* for answers, we find like—although not identical—images; they do not permit a clear or necessarily optimistic finale. Euphorion, the son of Faust and Helen of Troy, tries to fly upward but plunges to death. Homunculus, an artificial man, is forged in a furnace by Faust's aide, Wagner. Ever needing activity, sparkling in the dark, he is a man-made imitation of a man but with no natural, material body. He briefly hovers over sleeping Faust, "shedding light on him"; he will lead Faust to illusion. Homunculus desperately wants a "real existence," a material body to replace the vial that encases his flaming, rational spirit. But it will hurtle into the sea. His surrogate body smashes at the feet of Galatea (Venus's successor) in a kind of union of elements, with sea and shore in "burning embrace."

Or would this *Geist* become Faust, a being who embodied all the conflicts of modernity's human experience and then, finally, loses his wager with the devil but is saved despite himself?

IV.

Mozart could have set *Faust* to music, thought Goethe late in life. What he heard in Mozart was surely the ability to capture in music struggles that preoccupied him—between good and evil, light and dark. It is imaginable that the young *Geist* of Goethe's sequel to *The Magic Flute* was conceived with Mozart at least partly in his mind. Goethe would recall "perfectly" a concert he heard when he was fourteen in Frankfurt (in 1763). A "little man, with his friseur and sword" played—it was Mozart, aged seven.[14] He also observed that "genius" and "productiveness" lived in propinquity. "For what is genius," he asked, "but the productive power by which deeds arise that can display themselves before God and Nature?" The example was Mozart, "all" of whose works, he judged, were "of this kind." In them lay "a productive power which operates upon generation after generation and still is not wasted or consumed."[15]

Today it is easy to suppose that Beethoven would have been obvious as a possible composer for Goethe, but not because they shared political sentiments. If we are to believe the account, illlustrative but suspected to be anecdotal, of their meeting in the Bohemian Spa of Templitz in 1812 (while Napoleon's troops were in Russia), their temperaments as well as politics were at radical odds. On a walk, they crossed paths with the Habsburg empress. The composer simply ambled on, the poet bowed. Beethoven found Goethe servile, Goethe found Beethoven wayward. The poet was properly reverential toward authority, the disheveled composer often contemptuous of it. One had held political power, one had as an early teacher a leader of the Illuminati. Beethoven had admired of Napoleon—Goethe met the French conqueror and compared great political leaders to great artists— and had thought to dedicate to him his third symphony, but apparently changed his mind when Napoleon declared himself emperor. Perhaps such factors precluded partnership between Goethe and Beethoven. Yet contrasting tempers, artistic or political, are not necessarily bars to collaboration; after all, words and music in opera begin their collaboration disposed differently.

Beethoven composed only one opera, *Fidelio*. It was a decade after Goethe's sequel to *The Magic Flute*, and its themes, drawn from a French libretto, were obviously political: love and the liberation of a prisoner jailed illegitimately by abusive authority. The familiar motifs flow through this "rescue opera": good versus evil, light versus darkness, freedom and captivity. The prisoner, an aristocrat, does not burst out like Goethe's child in the golden sarcophagus; instead, his disguised wife steals into a dungeon to free him. The opera's most forceful political moments occur when prisoners step momentarily into the sunlight and sing in chorus: "Freedom!" Freedom and light were the great demands of the age, but the opera doesn't quite permit too simple a view of them, however rebellious Beethoven was. It is a mistreated aristocrat, not an oppressed commoner or confined genius whose freedom is secured and affirmed, finally, by properly reconstituted authority in the person of the king's minister. The first staging was in Schikenader's theater during the French occupation of Vienna and it would, of course, have been impossible to present a democratic republican as the victim then—or under Habsburg rule. Still, *Fidelio*'s politics may be said to go beyond its plot, since in it rescuing an aristocrat allows for united voices calling for freedom. Beethoven's "absolute" music—his symphonies, sonatas, concertos, quartets—signaled dramatic transformations in sound at a time of dramatic political transformations across the continent. Toward the end of his life he united voices in chorus in his Ninth Symphony, calling for friendship and human solidarity using Friedrich Schiller's words: "*Alle Menschen werden Brüder.*" This "Ode to Joy" was originally called "Ode to Freedom."

An appeal for solidarity of all humanity suggested uniting the voices of many on opera's stage, but also a powerful force that was emerging in the nineteenth century and that we have seen anticipated in the seventeenth and eighteenth centuries: nationalism. It brought together cultural and political identities, the latter usually in terms of popular sovereignty. The modern state—or many modern states—was taking another guise in reimagined territory, the nation-state. Beethoven, like Mozart, was no nationalist. But a collective cry for "*Freiheit!*" lends itself easily to the demand for national freedom. A nation's voice, the voice of its People—or the voice of an imagined nation-in-the-making—can be heard in different and powerful ways in famous works by leading composers and in lesser works too in the century after the French Revolution. Did its surge displace Goethe's "genius"? Sometimes that voice can draw sympathy across borders, while at other times nationalist appeal may repel. Gioachino Rossini's opera *Guillaume Tell*, based on Schiller's play *Wilhelm Tell*, premiered in Paris in 1829 and extols what would be called national liberation. It culminates in a Swiss chorus hailing nature and freedom. Ironically—or perhaps obliviously—when French troops invaded Algiers the next year, a band accompanied them playing this opera's overture. In 1841, Verdi's *Nabucco* presented exiled Hebrew slaves in Babylon singing a now famous chorale—"Va, Pensiero" (Fly, Thought)—which became an Italian nationalist anthem. Hector Berlioz returned to Virgil, Dido, and Aeneas; *Les Troyens* (1856–58) announces the imperatives of founding or reconstructing a national home (or, perhaps, a renewed empire). Before Germany united under Bismarck's lead, anarchist-cum-nationalist Richard Wagner's *Die Meistersinger von Nürnberg* mythologized a sixteenth-century artisan-poet-singer who warns townsmen of insidious forces threatening newly found cultural and communal unity. They hail him in unified voice.

Europe and its operas, especially those interpreted politically, entered a new world as the eighteenth century turned into the nineteenth century. The emergence of mass movements of varied stripe—nationalist, democratic, socialist, mixes of these, and antecedents of fascism—would find operatic counterparts in choral protagonists. Statements were also made on behalf of tolerance or against mass hysteria in less-remembered works. Frommental Halévy's *La Juive* of 1835, set at the time of the Council of Constance in the fifteenth century, protested prejudice. Giacomo Meyerbeer's *Les Huguenots* of 1836 illustrated the murderous consequences of fanaticism. It was set during the French religious wars of the sixteenth century, in the era of opera's birth and then that of a modern French state—a monodic, absolutist one. In 1854 a comic opera composed by a German Jew in Paris satirized the political world of France under Napoleon III along with much of the history of opera. Jacques Offenbach returned to Orpheus. He and his librettists made alterations, as had so many of their predecessors in treating the tale. Their Orpheus is in a bad marriage with Eurydice; she is having an affair with Thebes's beekeeper, who is really Pluto. Shortly after she goes to Hades, the gods—the aristocrats—will land there too; bored to hell by ambrosia and Olympus, they prefer the can-can and wine in the Underworld. *Orpheus in Hell* retrieved a feature from early opera, but with a twist. Instead of a prologue with a god or "Tragedy" or "Music" or Ovid setting out themes, a figure named "Public Opinion" appears, its voice neither liberal nor democratic; it narrates on behalf of stodgy morality, accompanying Orpheus wherever he goes, urging appropriate behavior.[16] Europe had changed since Peri and Rinuccini, and Monteverdi and Busenello and Cavalli.

The metamorphoses of political opera in the nineteenth and also the twentieth centuries, from unifying the voice of the People to the birth of atonal music (a revolution in music on the eve of a world blowing apart), comprise other stories, other librettos, and other sounds.

APPENDIX: "BACKSTAGE"

The book you have just read is made up of a series of interlinked explorations. Readers uninterested in methodological matters—how one goes about exploring and linking—can stop here and avoid some thorny academic-sounding discussion.

I sought throughout this book to minimize or to avoid the sort of labored "discourse" that tries the patience of many people these days. Sometimes the impatience is justified, especially when authors seem interested in a theory of their subject but not the subject. Why, after all, engage an opera or a novel when you are only interested in a theory of it? I am, however, also impatient with people who dismiss discussions about how what they hear or read or see was constructed. The way out of both kinds of impatience is to grasp philosophical languages without getting too lost in philosophizing. Consequently, I offer brief ruminations about what went on backstage (in my mind) as this book was written. Some motifs were there at the beginning of my effort and changed as I moved along; others emerged only through research and writing; some came when the manuscript was more or less finished, reread and/or found in need of rethinking or amendment or refinement or rectification. I did not make a detailed scenario for every movement. Rather, I tried to take ideas from different thinkers, using them (I hope) constructively to correct one, the other, or others (and to correct my own predispositions).

This book is nonetheless synthetic in an important sense: its explorations are based, in varied proportions, on research by the author but also substantially on scholarship by many others. Its more or less chronological movement interacts with a methodological medley. Here I return again to (and slightly abuse) Hegel's metaphor: in order to swim, I jumped into the water, into human developments and creations. I did not believe that my own ideas about culture and politics would remain immobile and simply applicable as I moved. There are many notions, even deeply contradictory ones, embedded in these pages and that is because the materials I explore don't fit into a single model and are not seamless. By a medley I simply mean that I apply varied intellectual tools—or ideas or concepts and sometimes intuitions—to matters that seem in each case most appropriate to them. Others ideas or concepts or intuitions are deployed for other matters or aspects of the same material when it seemed proper and useful. This procedure is not arbitrary because it requires constant testing through writing about specific matters; it refuses to apply one standard or paradigm to explain everything at all times. I hope that I have been unfaithful to all my own ideas (or at least that I reshape them in using them) when it proved intelligent to be so. The French word *recherche* has a special appeal because of its suggestive duality, signifying a study (in the more traditional sense of research) or a quest. The quest is not an all-explanatory effort, monistic in outlook, but a succession of historically grounded engagements. It does not reach an end that explains all that went before, as it did not start with one.

If I have tried to avoid the kind of entrapment by intellectual detail that can ruin not just books but philosophies and theories, my debts are still considerable. Since they are not always manifest, I hope the following unavoidably partial sketch of some of what went on "backstage" gives due credit to thinkers, philosophers, and arguments:

From Hegel: I exploit, rather liberally and I hope very flexibly, a general emphasis on the need to engage art from a historical and not solely from an aesthetic perspective (or more properly not from an isolated or narrowly conceived or conceited aesthetic perspective). Politics found in operas are always discernable in other, nonartistic domains of life. Political ideas, and those represented or expressed in art, are not worked out in private even if they are achievements of minds we might call remarkably singular. In saying this I leave aside—because I was long ago disabused of it—Hegel's grand scheme in which Reason works itself out in history goes through various adventures, and gets inevitably and supremely embodied in a highest end (which Hegel believed visible in his own times and especially in his own philosophy). I am an un-Hegelian Hegelian, or at the least a very, very soft one. Worse, I accept what he branded "bad infinity" and think history is open-ended, shaped by a medley of structural and contingent interacting factors, not a teleological journey. Historical or logical necessity did not make Monteverdi's Orpheus into Mozart's Tamino. Some structural factors are very deeply rooted. If we want to find political criticism or political statements or descriptions or suggestions of political possibilities—or utopian projections—in operas, we must see how and in what ways the history of this art form entwines with or has affinities to and has been informed by the politics of an age. Music and musical forms certainly attract us to operas in the first place, but examining them in isolation cannot explain the politics in them (although it is valuable in other senses).

From debates among musicologists: I do not try to be a musicologist for the sensible reason that I am not one. Instead, I lean on musicians and musicologists, even if their questions are distinct or distant from or with accents other than mine. However, the questions and accents are not always utterly different. Think of the frequent use of political metaphors we have found throughout this book by students of music and the use of musical metaphors by political thinkers. More important, perhaps: some students of political thought contend that ideas cannot be considered properly or grasped meaningfully apart from their historical context. Obviously I lean decidedly towards this perspective, but without bowing to it. Others insist that certain basic human problems are rarely, or in an extreme version, ever altered. Key ideas, they think, are debated over and again, even if in different guises, whether by Plato in ancient Greece or Thomas Hobbes in seventeenth-century England or by us today. These two contrasting approaches parallel, in a broad way, certain arguments among philosophers and scholars of music, some of whom emphasize that broad historical developments and ideas are internalized or embedded in music while others stress that music should be understood solely in terms of its own autonomous structures (of sound)—apart from anything outside music itself.

In recent decades, a "new musicology" has been informed greatly by political, social, and historical issues. It has been shaped especially by "postmodern theory," that popular late twentieth-century academic perspective (actually perspectives) that is antagonistic to "grand narratives," to "foundations," and to older humanistic approaches, whether of the left or the right, to culture.[1] While my medley owes much to humanism, I have profited from the work of "new musicologists." I must admit, however, that I have perhaps gained—learned—more from reading "old-fashioned" humanists. The latter scholars or philosophers or critics protest with considerable force those approaches taken by new musicologists and postmodern theories but would also dissent from some of my ways of going about things. I don't approach musical material only on its own terms; it is impossible to do so in the specific case of my subject, political opera, and not because of disinterest in how, say, musical analysts explore harmonic relations in operatic music. I could contribute little to such an assessment. Still, those musicologists who, in their most acute formulations, protest any focus on ideological premises expressed in artistic forms are comparable to students of political thought who engage in philosophical decontextualization. Approaches of both new and older musicologists are invaluable counterballasts to my own nonmusicological thinking (and to each other). As in the study of political arguments, contextualization and decontextualization can serve as useful regulative ideas in both fields as specific materials—musical, political, philosophical—are examined.

One of the most influential twentieth-century philosophical musicologists, Theodor W. Adorno, made fertile although not always defensible claims, especially when it concerns opera. He insisted that social and historical categories are congealed in and shape artistic creations; deposits of the human spirit are found in music, not just varied sound-making vibrations of air. He discerned pointers toward human emancipation in challenging musical innovations and in novelties drawn from or worked out through artistic materials. Art is never "reality," and these pointers hardly make art less of an illusion. They do suggest to Adorno that intimations of "redemption"—one of his favorite words—can be perceived in art, especially in the struggle of artworks to appear autonomous in the constricted, unemancipated (or unredeemed) realities of the surrounding world.

The whole of society, thought Adorno, can be found in a detail of "good serious music."[2] By contrast, mass culture, like popular music, helps an existing order reproduce itself through numbing, repetitive, and manipulative effects. Compelling though this claim is, and not without truth, it is lacking notably if, for example, we think of political and cultural rebelliousness that came—I am not the first to note this—with a good deal of rock 'n' roll in the 1960s. Combine that with Adorno's dramatic inability to appreciate what was important in jazz: its innovative mix of pattern and improvisation. I bracket what an emancipated world might look like and how redeemed music in it might sound. I am not sure it would be like Adorno's most famous example of musical "progress," which was the early twentieth-century's "new music." Introduced by Arnold Schönberg, its essential technical move was to remove the traditional keynote that organized composing. The resulting "atonality" (a disputed term) produced novel relations of sounds; listeners were pressed to hear differently. Sometimes, this results in powerful experiences, yet at other time, it must be admitted, it becomes the aural equivalent of cramps. Adorno, rightly, reacted against cruder notions of "realism" (especially "socialist realism") that made artworks simple reflections of society. He considered "immanent critique" to be the basis of his own approach: a critic ought to evaluate a work of philosophy or of art or, indeed, a society, by taking hold of its constituent elements or techniques or presuppositions, and by revealing their intrinsic character and how they can be made to "turn back on themselves."[3]

One problem with Adorno's approach is a tendency, as Richard Taruskin puts it neatly, to reduce art (more specifically music) to a historical "battleground of heroic resistors" fighting a "homogenizing commercial jugger-naut."[4] It may be added that for all of Adorno's emphasis on the political-aesthetic importance of novelty in twentieth-century musical modernism, he seems to have lost his way when he spoke of opera's birth. Like the "modern" music of the twentieth century, opera was an avant-garde phe-nomenon in its (sixteenth and seventeenth century) context. Adorno reduces it to a "specifically bourgeois genre." It may be argued that—as he pre-sents it—opera tried in important ways "to preserve the magical element of art" at a time when the world was becoming "bereft of magic." [5] Yet this hardly justifies his initial generalization about its "bourgeois" character and erases the desire of opera's inventors to bring out human feelings and ideas through monody. Opera's founders were enchanted by antiquity and their efforts were not simply a consequence of the role of commerce in Florence or Venice. How is polyphony with incomprehensible texts less enchanting than monody bringing out the meanings of texts?

Monody was no juggernaut, and it was only with the sense of pluralistic artistic reformism in Monteverdi's operas that this genre's greatest possibil-ities begin to be evident. It was not the triumph of market relations or re-sistance to them, either in music or libretto, that accomplished this. When Adorno, relying apparently on the scholarship of others, insisted that the Florentine "connoisseurs" invented a "rudimentary madrigal-opera," he obscures how monody was perceived to be in opposition to the madrigal and as a means to meaning. In the twentieth century, linguistic philosophers, fol-lowing J.L. Austin, argued that language is not simply a matter of presenting truths but "speech acts"—words do things. Without stretching this claim too far, it can be said that deploying monody was a sound-act. But because of how monody was linked to words and a story in opera it aimed to bring out truths—feelings, ideas—ascribed to its players. At the same time, it is useful to note that the overlap of musical lines in madrigals, while they tend to make meanings of words obscure, has its own magic. It is curious that Adorno, within pages of making his claims about the "connoisseurs," speaks of monody as an effort to surmount the "contradiction" between the speech of "real people" in drama and singing.[6] It certainly does try to bridge speech and singing, but as we noted earlier in this book, the same charge of contradiction can be made when it comes to poetry in drama. Political leaders (as well as common people) don't speak to problems in alexandrines. And Adorno somehow manages to declare within pages of his statements about monody both that Monteverdi's *Orfeo* was the first "au-thentic" opera and that opera "first blossomed in the republic of Venice."

Orfeo, however, came out of Mantua, as did the lost *Arianna*. *Orfeo's* pre-occupations, as well as the conditions in which it was produced and the worldviews that percolated within its composer and librettist, can hardly be captured or summarized by "bourgeois." Moreover, to say that Venetian opera emerged "under the social conditions of an evolved bourgeoisie," as Adorno does, is problematic. It is true that Venice's commercial republicans had been a famous success story. However, they were in long-term decline when Monteverdi wrote his Venetian operas. The values in them have more Venetian than simply bourgeois specificity; and the pursuit of luxury was not invented with capitalism. This does not mean that the role of social class should be absented in them, only that it does not provide the whole story and itself needs contextualizing and to be treated flexibly and perceived expansively. The fate of the Suitors in *Ritorno* is better understood as worry about the circulation of elites than a comment on the circulation of capital. Aeneas's quest in Cavalli and Busenello's *La Didone* is for *patria*, not profits. He wants to refound a homeland, not bring riches back to an old one (that has been destroyed in any case). The music does not congeal something else, even though the crises of Venetian overseas trade (a threatening loss of markets) and that of the Venetian state (the contrast between appearance and reality in its constitutional order, which seemed to many unsustainable) are indeed keys to the context. *Poppea* warned of enfeeblement, but not in terms reducible to bourgeois or commercial aristocracy.

Venice's physical attractiveness, its wealth and onetime power, may indeed be ascribed to the assertive pursuits of markets by commercial aristocrats, and the beginnings of commercial opera did correspond to the birth of Venetian opera, but that does not mean that the musical or social or political spirit of Monteverdi's operas (and that of his collaborators) can be subsumed usefully or sensibly under one category—a practice Adorno often protested but in which he engaged too. Even though he writes that "disillusionment" is the "overall aesthetic tendency of the bourgeois era"—a grand, if challengeable generalization—it is hard to describe disillusion in *Poppea* as simply a bourgeois characteristic, not least since Venice's downturn corresponded at least temporally to the continued rise of what is often called the bourgeois era elsewhere in Europe. Because the opera speaks poignantly and anxiously to the tensions between appearances and realities, and because this preoccupation is hardly the private property of bourgeois times, it is better understood by medley. A methodological medley, rather than imposition of a singular characterization, tells us that the opera has a great deal to do with a troubled polity whose sustaining myths were menaced together with a troubled ruling strata threatened, among other things, by changes in markets at a time when Europe was shaken by religious wars and the emergence of new political forms.[7] The same may be said about the motif of redemption—the opposite of disillusion. Only one of the two endings of the Mantuan *Orfeo* suggests redemption (and that is for Orpheus but not for Eurydice); there is no redemption in *Poppea* except for the (short-lived) love of its two least attractive, and politically most powerful characters. When Nero exchanges Octavia for Poppea, it is not for the sake of realizing more profit or power. Moreover, his egoism is presented in ancient accounts of him.

In short, a good deal of provocative value can be gleaned from Adorno's ideas, especially when they press on us the importance of social or political material congealed in art, but he sometimes stumbles badly when his deploy of them lacks adequate perspective. The problem goes further, in fact, since it is possible to detect in him a contempt for the pluralistic frame of mind required of methodological medley. Consider a letter he wrote to his friend Walter Benjamin in which he vented fury against Siegfried Kracauer's study of Jacques Offenbach. Kracauer drew a broad, textured historical picture of an artist in nineteenth-century Paris. He described his goal as a biography of both Offenbach "and a society," focusing on the composer's "social role," and compared Offenbach to a mockingbird whose sardonic song demystified pomposity and "empty authority."[8] This is a way of valuing and understanding Offenbach as a critical figure in time and place (France's Second Empire). This also means, however, that he ought not to be judged by the identical standards that might, rightly or wrongly, be applied to Schoenberg in Vienna on the eve of World War I. When Adorno judged Kracauer's effort shallow because it did not work by means of "immanent critique," it revealed Adorno's inability to imagine that two different approaches—his own and that of Kracauer in this book—might yield complementary insights or provide crosslighting (to borrow a term from Marc Bloch, the French historian). It is a failure of imagination.

The critical became the personal for Adorno too often. He thought to sever all ties to Kracauer, who had in many ways been his mentor. "I am myself considering whether or not I should break off relations with him," he wrote to Benjamin. Kracauer's treatment of Offenbach was "so irremediably bad," determined Adorno, "that it could easily become a best seller."[9] This deeply antidemocratic sneer assumes that any positive response to a book by a broad audience must be due to wrong-headedness and manipulation. It would seem that only by means of engaging "atonal" music or an "atonal" philosophy or an "atonal" book can masses of people break from the culture industry and grasp the premises of their own society. But that is in fact to say that they cannot and will not do it at all. In the meantime, the less the sales, the better the book, since its value—and by extension the same can be said of a painting or opera—is interchangeable with commerce. Adorno would have been the first to point to the reduction of quality to quantity as one of the most untoward characteristics of modernity (or capitalist societies). Yet this leads me to a different conclusion from him: it is necessary to understand a work (or an artist) both from within and—adequately—from an internalized context. A frame of interpretive mind must also suit the inevitable tensions among plural approaches to make effective use of them.

One of Adorno's most redoubtable and penetrating adversaries was musicologist Carl Dahlhaus. Yet they shared, at least in part, some judgments. Dahlhaus determined that the survival of the early Florentine operas was due not to "their own aesthetic merit" but because of "their consequences," principally their impact on Monteverdi. This observation has much merit: Monteverdi composed in part with the much lesser works by Peri in mind and he invents in response to them rather than solely by engaging earlier "great" composers or music. Dahlhaus thought also that beyond the consequences, the Florentines did not stand out "from the general run of antiquarian endeavors" among Renaissance humanists. While it is true that Peri and Rinuccini survive mostly as a subject for study and their works are rarely performed, this claim enfeebles the role and claims of innovation, which is just what can lead to greater artistic works. Dahlhaus also speaks with contempt of "the literary intelligentsia" that joined with "harmless lovers of popular music" to struggle against the "self-styled 'serious' concert public" in order to "create a place in the pantheon" for someone like Offenbach. [10] The Florentine works (and those of Offenbach) lacked what Dahlhaus called "aesthetic presence." More simply and less definitively, this could be called significantly superior, lasting musical quality.

After all, few people would contend that Peri's music was better than Monteverdi's or Offenbach's than, say, Berlioz's compositions. Still, that is too easy. For Dahlhaus, "internal, aesthetic observations and external documentary ones" must always be sharply distinguished; it is a matter of choosing what is relevant to your concerns. Music history, as he saw it, concerns "significant works of music" that "have outlived the musical culture of their age." In this effectively romantic formulation, it is the "aesthetic presence" of individual works throughout history that matters; how they internalized historical changes of the era of their genesis is an entirely subordinate issue just as knowing the origins of something does not explain its "essence."[11] But is it possible to discern this in the first place without addressing intentions and the temporal meanings of the terms in which they are expressed? Adorno, Dahlhaus argued, may have insisted that any historical approach to artworks requires judgment of particularity without the use of external criteria, but this inevitably dissolves in practice. Certainly Dahlhaus makes a strong point here. When Adorno articulated his philosophy of modern music, he could not avoid abstractions—for example, notions like a chord or dissonance—that must always go beyond specific cases or become meaningless. No chord sounds just once and is named a chord. For Dahlhaus this means that a score should be approached in terms of musical aesthetics, not of embedded politics or political possibility. Yet again, how can this be claimed without adequate treatment of politics? Is it possible to say that something is not "there" in an important way without first treating that something sufficiently? My suggestion is that "medley" is more useful here than "presence," which can too easily make aesthetic categories religious.

Dahlhaus runs into trouble—interesting trouble—when he articulates why he thinks musical and political history are radically and fundamentally different. An "aesthetic presence," he writes, can be "recaptured in later performances" even if responses—our own, for instance—are always historically conditioned. By contrast, a political event "belongs once and for all to the past and only extends to the present by virtue of reports or remnants of it." The political past survives and can be reconstructed "merely on the basis of its implications."[12] This contention again downplays the importance of novelty on behalf of a tradition comprised of "aesthetic presences." Consequently, Dahlhaus chastised critics who approach culture by thinking that "the only alternative to overt bias is covert bias."[13] He targeted not only Adorno, whose ideas grew out of yet broke in basic ways from Marxism, but also East German Marxists like George Knepler— Dahlhaus was a West Berliner during the Cold War—who remained faithful to ideological dogma. [14] However, Dahlhaus's approach also allows a history of German cultural "presences" to be separate from German political history.

It can be argued that Dahlhaus simply inverts the error he sought to counter. He even seems to have been alert to the possibility of this allegation when he admitted readily (in a robust echo of the methodological writings of Max Weber and R.W. Collingwood) that to determine an artwork's "historical significance," it is necessary to know what problems a historian—in this case one of music—seeks to solve. It is not intrinsically wrong, he explains, for a historian of opera to choose certain works in order to disclose underlying "formal principles" of "music drama." The problem, he explains rightly, is when such an effort supposes that it can reveal "the single most important aspect" or the whole of opera's history. For instance, "music drama" is a nineteenth-century term associated with Richard Wagner's worldview—one that saw this composer's own work as the culmination of operatic history. Wagnerians contrasted "music drama" to traditional opera (as if the latter were not plural). While Dahlhaus remarks that "one sidedness is not irreconcilable with objectivity," he warns that taking "critical bearings" from Wagner alone risks silence about Rossini, for example, that becomes "unwarranted disparagement."[15] (Wagner despised Rossini.)

In short, there is much to be said for Dahlhaus's argument about how historical significance is determined, especially in arguments about aesthetic reductionism. Yet it leads inevitably to the conclusion, which seems to me unwarranted, that exploring overt or covert biases in art is uninteresting or unimportant or at most very secondary. He actually makes "aesthetic presence" an absolute alternative to exploring embedded ideology, as if the two were wholly separable one from the other—just as music and political history are detachable, radically so, for him. But the impact of patterns of thought, mindsets, and political categories—political culture, the state, citizenship, or sovereignty, for examples—that animated events centuries ago may or may not have embedded presences in contemporary political life. It is not simply a matter of "implications." Does not the notion of "the state" still exist, in various forms, in institutions, and shape them? Moreover, there are weighty and trivial implications. Asserting that the development of the state in early modernity is only "present" by "implication" centuries later depends on knowing and interpreting its earlier meanings and impacts. To say that a seventeenth-century opera or musical work has a timeless, aesthetic presence must, in some sense, depend on what it sounded like initially, which we cannot reproduce with absolute surety if, say, pitch and voices were different then from today. Otherwise, "presence" becomes so indeterminate that it risks being a mystification.

Is the same presence always with us? How do we establish that? If, in the case of political opera, there are words linked to sounds and a plot, we need to know as best we can what those words implied then, and why this or that sound is tied to this or that political sentiment or idea. Reducing this to a documentary matter risks trivializing meanings. It is impossible, observed

400

R.W. Collingwood, "to find out what a man means simply by studying his spoken or written statements even though he has spoken or written with perfect command of language and perfectly truthful intention." To discern meaning, he went on, "you must also know what the question was . . . to which the thing he has said or written was meant to be an answer."[16] This goes not only for philosophical tracts, but also for politics in librettos. Must one not also ask about the music to which a composer responds? It is impossible to say that there is only an "aesthetic presence" that transcends its time, say in Monteverdi's operas, when they are treated politically. That is, without knowing the political history that this presence purports to transcend.

From Lucien Goldmann, an unjustly forgotten humanist of the mid-twentieth-century left—an unorthodox Marxist who also called himself a "genetic structuralist"—I take, with some caution, the notion of a "trans-individual subject of cultural creation." This somewhat loaded term was meant to indicate that artistic accomplishments don't simply spring out of the inventive spirit of isolated geniuses. Goldmann's ideas drew on a synthesis of the "genetic epistemology" of psychologist Jean Piaget and the early writings of Marxist Georg Lukács to propose that artists of any kind (indeed, all people) have within them changing "mental structures" that mediate our relations with the world, inform, and structure and enable our ways of understanding it. These are products of learning and are often nonconscious: mental forms that allow us to assimilate aspects of, to accommodate to, or try to challenge the world into which we are born and live. That world is social and historical and not reducible simplistically to this or that individual. Yet it is individuals that transform into art what they take from the world around them. Sometimes they do so coherently and purposefully and sometimes less so; sometimes they do so self-consciously and sometimes not. What they internalize may form into perceptions, or into what is taken as knowledge or as wisdom about life's limits or joys, its troubles or emotions or foolishness or despair or hope for upheaval and changes. These comprise a nexus of historical, social, and individual domains (hence, "transindividual"), but each person (or, in this case an artist) has his or her own makeup that needs to be explored along with the world around him or her. Only a critic's interpretive hubris ordains such explorations entirely unnecessary, situating the interpreter in a godlike stance.

Goldmann's theory was at its most effective in his study of seventeenth-century France, and aspects of it are usefully mentioned here. He tried to demonstrate that there was a common "tragic worldview" expressed in the philosophy of Blaise Pascal and in the plays of Jean Racine. This worldview, he argued, crystallized and expressed in theoretical and artistic form mental structures that developed in common particularly among individuals of a social stratum that shared a common plight. The *noblesse de robe* (the legal nobility) had been thrown into crisis as the modern French state took firmer form. Many of its members, finding their lives and vocation dislodged by this process, embraced a severe form of Augustinian theology, Jansenism. Goldmann's claim, in schematic form, was that the French monarchy, seeking to consolidate and centralize its authority, had faced resistance from local aristocracies and fostered the *noblesse de robe* as a counterpower to them beholden to the crown. However, the more this succeeded, the more the crown—actually, France governed by Cardinal Richelieu—preferred, in turn, to augment powers of royal provincial governors at the expense of the *noblesse de robe*. These latter were thus enmeshed within but also pushed aside by an increasingly strong state.

This situation, and the resulting perplexity and sense of loss, made Jansenism appealing as it spread in France in the later 1630s. This religious movement emphasized the vanity of this-worldly existence; it considered heaven's ways in the world along with human salvation to be unfathomable. God seemed to be hidden, sureties in the world intangible. In its most acute form it rested on what Goldmann called the "tragic paradox" of saying "yes and no" to the world at the same time and received its most compelling cultural elaboration in a "tragic vision" in two different cultural media. Pascal's fragmentary *Penseés* and Racine's tragic theater articulated the "tendency common to the sentiments, aspirations and thoughts" of an ensemble of individuals whose lives were mediated by a common social (and existential) predicament.[17]

The Venetian Incogniti were unlike the *noblesse de robe* in fundamental ways. The Incogniti were powerful figures in a wealthy if troubled republic, rooted in the legacies of a city-state with which they identified; the *noblesse de robe* had at best secondary powers within a rising absolutist state in a much bigger realm with a feudal heritage. The former were at once anonymous and public in Venice, where they were perceived often as "libertine." Public life had no comparable domain in France of the 1630s and the austere Jansenists, who faced persecution by both state and church and who were anything but free thinkers (in any usual sense), became advocates of retreat from the world. Still, despite these and other contrasts, the two social groupings shared a parallel in existential disquiet about decline. Worry was generated at a time of general transition and shakiness. I have tried to interpret *Ritorno*, *Didone*, and *Poppea* in light of such transition, the first two suggesting hope but recognizing menace; the latter warning of tragic possibility or simply representing despair, although ironically by a happy ending. Badoaro, from the viewpoint of a member of the aristocracy and Busenello, a man from the upper-middle stratum of his society, can be seen as patriotic coherent articulators of elite unease. The former does so through his treatment of Ulysses's search for home and by suggesting (in the aristocratic Suitors) a need for a circulation of elites. Busenello's unease is presented through his contrasts in *Poppea* between appearance and reality, corrupt rule and virtuous constancy, and juxtapositions among rationality, skepticism, unmastered emotionalism, and self-deception. A dialectic of "Yes and No" plays out persistently in *Poppea*.

In short, differing disquiets in France and Venice in the fourth decade of the seventeenth century led to parallel cultural expressions. Venice's decline would continue for more than another century and a half. During this period, however, the *noblesse de robe* would play roles of great and mounting political consequence, especially in growing challenges by *Parlements* [courts] in which they were powerful to the crown.

From Jean-Paul Sartre: Although I find Goldmann's case for seeing in artworks the coherent elaboration of the worldview of "transindividual subjects" both powerful and fertile, and while his notion of "transindividual" does not, in my view, lose sight of the individual per se, a kind of counterbalance is still needed. It is provided, I think, succinctly by Jean-Paul Sartre's protest against turning too much of an artist's work into sociological queries. His dissent may also be seen as a forceful one against the "antihumanism" of postmodernism, although preceding it (it is a dissent with which Goldmann would have agreed).

Sartre did not deny the important insights derived from the sociology of culture, but he made of poet Paul Valèry an example with which to warn against some of its tendencies, especially found in those critics (often but not only orthodox Marxists) for whom social and political factors constituted the sole domain of worthy exploration. "Valèry is a petty bourgeois intellectual, that is without doubt," remarked Sartre, "But every petty bourgeois intellectual is not Valèry."[18] It is with this in mind that I have found value in addressing, within some limits, the lives of the composers, librettists, and essayists whose works and politics I consider; and I look for commonalties among the structures of those works and political developments.

Yet Sartre's point, when standing alone, is also insufficient; it needs to be joined by arguments made by Adorno, Dahlhaus, and Goldmann in medley, both to look within and allow for cross-lighting of never fully definitive subjects and objects and their links—artists and artworks, human beings and the worlds around them, political and musical history. The medley seeks to bring out the interaction among their shifting subjective and objective structures and dimensions, its elements functioning as counterpoints or antitheses depending on what is most useful. No unwavering rule can establish these applications, only immersion in the material that they would elucidate; that, hopefully, enables a sense of usefulness of them in various combinations by a critic or scholar or philosopher. The premium is on corrections and self-corrections rather than theoretical imposition.

From debates on the history of political thought: I have already mentioned a major divide among students of political ideas that parallels some arguments among musicologists about context and aesthetics. To repeat, in simple terms, it is a debate between those who insist on the need to place historically political ideas and their languages in order to perceive their meanings, and those who propose instead that there has been a continuous argument about the same or very similar notions since the beginnings of (recorded) political philosophy. Quentin Skinner's "Cambridge School" may be taken to represent the first position and Leo Strauss as an exemplar of the opposite approach (although the latter's is an extreme formulation that drives thinking into a closed circuit).

Both are concerned particularly with the emergence and consequences of modern political thought. While I believe that Skinner's methods in his influential study of *The Foundations of Modern Political Thought* lead us to a greater understanding of its subject—say, of Machiavelli's political thought—it too needs qualifications.[19] To be more explicit: contextual and historical methods help me understand texts better than the supposition that political philosophers approach important questions by standing—thinking—out of time and place. The same may be said if we want to grasp politics in opera. It is nonetheless true that some comparable political ideas and problems reemerge in different ways and guises throughout what we know of human history; at the least, it must be said that political thinkers in one period often take political thinkers in earlier periods to be making claims that also address poignantly their own times. I find it fruitful to inhabit the tension between those who think constantly of historical context and those who insist on perpetual problems; the same tense space is valuable when talking about contemporary politics as well as in research and when engaging a political opera on a stage. Going back and forth, to and fro, enhances our own perspectives, interpretations, and engagements. There is perhaps much, or enough, that is compelling in a sixteenth-century text that a twenty-first-century reader can recognize in a distinct enough way, and the same may be said of a seventeenth-century opera (as well as in Plato or Aristotle's discussions of "justice," for that matter). Out of context doesn't necessarily mean no understanding. As context is not everything in art, the same is so in political argument. Yet context is essential to a fuller understanding and appreciation of both. My emphasis on contextualization owes a great deal to Skinner's historical understanding of the development of the modern concept and reality of the state. Drawing productively on Collingwood and also Austin's notion that words do things, Skinner stresses the importance of asking the right questions. This means, first of all, looking to the arguments to which this or that political thinker responded. A great work of political ideas is often in conversation with lesser works of the same era rather than responding to great works of another era. Consequently, the lesser works—part of the context— must be examined. I have tried to suggest that it is reasonable to assume the same for music history (knowing Peri yields a fuller grasp of Monteverdi's achievement) and certainly it is the case of operas with librettos that have political implications. Why does Pluto wrestle with the meaning of law and authority in Rinuccini and Peri's *Euridice* (a lesser work) and also Striggio and Monteverdi's *Orfeo* (a greater one)? It is not enough to read Ovid and the librettos of these operas in order to reply. It is also essential to look to the emergence of the modern state together with the politics of Florence and Mantua. It is insufficient to read Tacitus and Seneca to discern the politics of Busenello and Monteverdi's *Poppea*; it is also essential to know about Venetian (more generally, European) politics and political language in the first half of the seventeenth century along with—especially—debates on rhetoric. Without these, it is impossible to perceive the translation of politics into artworks or musical languages.

Again: none of these observations makes Peri a better composer than Monteverdi. It makes the politics of the time a key to understanding essential dimensions—not all— of *Orfeo* or *Poppea*. Dahlhaus, thinking surely of German history and not solely the Napoleonic era, wrote that "to claim that 'greatness' in music is as insidious and ambivalent as its political counterpart, being a greatness for which other historical agents had to pay the price, is to miss the point. No-one had a burden to bear because Beethoven wielded authority in music."[20] This, surely, constructs a straw man and misses the point—unless *Fidelio* is entirely comprehensible and should be engaged with no sense of the transformation of Europe in the eighteenth and nineteenth centuries.

NOTES

Note to the Reader: Orthographic irregularities or differences from contemporary usages in names or titles are due to those in original sources.

Prologue

1. Paul Robinson, *Opera and Ideas from Mozart to Strauss* (Ithaca, New York: Cornell University Press, 1984), pp. 2–3.
2. Lewis Namier, *Personalities and Powers* (London: Hamish Hamilton, 1955), pp. 4–5.
3. G.W.F. Hegel, *Aesthetics*, Vol. II (Oxford: Clarendon Press, 1998), p. 945.
4. Hegel, *Aesthetics*, Vol. 1 (Oxford: Clarendon Press, 1998), p. 392.
5. Hegel, *Aesthetics*, Vol. 2, p. 946.
6. *Dialogo di Vincenzo Galaliei nobile fiorentino della musica antica et della moderna* (Florence: Giorgio Marescotti, 1581). In English: *Dialogue on Ancient and Modern Music*, trans. Claude V. Palisco (New Haven and London: Yale University Press, 2003).
7. Niccolò Machiavelli, *The Discourses* (London and New York: Penguin Books, 1970), pp. 398–99.
8. Quentin Skinner, "The Idea of a Cultural Lexicon," in *Visions of Politics, Vol. 1: Regarding Method* (Cambridge: Cambridge University Press, 2002), p. 160, and his "What Should You Learn from Machiavelli," *New York Review of Books*, June 5, 2014, p. 51. My description of the emergence of "modern" politics and Machiavelli's place in its conceptualization is indebted to his various works, especially *The Foundations of Modern Political Thought, Vol. 1: The Renaissance* (Cambridge: Cambridge University Press, 1978). Also see his *Machiavelli* (Oxford: Oxford University Press, 1991) and, for a contrast, see Isaiah Berlin, "The Originality of Machiavelli," in *Against the Current* (New York: Viking Press, 1979), pp. 25–79.
9. On the itinerary of the word "opera" see Donald Jay Grout with Hermine Weigel Williams, *A Short History of Opera*, 3rd ed. (New York: Columbia University Press, 1988), pp. 2–3 and Carolyn Abbate and Roger Parker, *A History of Opera* (New York and London: W.W. Norton and Company, 2012), pp. 38–41. On the German itinerary, see Gloria Flaherty, *Opera in the Development of German Critical Thought* (Princeton: Princeton University Press, 1978), pp. 18, 25, 73. The German commentators were, in turn, Daniel Georg Morhof, Heinrich Elmenhorst, and Johann Huebner.
10. R.W. Collingwood, *An Autobiography* (Oxford: Clarendon Press, 1991[1939]), p. 2. The notion of a "work" is contested through today for reasons like his. Operas were (and are) often changed or modified for production. Consequently, words, music, and staging cannot be regarded as historically immutable, even if autograph copies of a libretto, score, or stage directions exist. Yet it is obvious that Claudio Monteverdi's "work" *Orfeo* can never be so modified that it becomes

Mozart's *The Magic Flute*. I will sidestep this debate since my attention on political ideas in operas entails finding meaningful content that may transcend different staged versions or written texts in the first place and can be—indeed must be—also discerned in the world outside opera. As such I am less concerned with detailed production history (an important subject in its own right) and speak of a "work" in its more commonplace usage.

11. Quoted by Christopher B. Krebs in *A Most Dangerous Book: Tacitus's Germania from the Roman Empire to the Third Reich* (New York and London: W.W. Norton, 2011), pp. 247–8.
12. Joseph Kerman, *Opera and Drama* (Berkeley and Los Angeles: University of California Press, 1988), pp. 4, 9.
13. Cited in M.H. Abrams, *The Mirror and the Lamp* (Oxford: Oxford University Press, 1953), p. 15.

Chapter 1: Who Rules?

1. Alois M. Nagler, *Theatre Festivals of the Medici, 1539–1637* (New Haven and London: Yale University Press, 1964), p. 93.
2. Lorenzo L. Da Ponte, *A History of the Florentine Republic and of the Age and Rule of the Medici*, Vol. 2 (New York: Collins and Hanny, 1833), p. 287. Da Ponte drew from the *Universal History*, a multiauthor, multivolume eighteenth-century English work.
3. Tim Carter and Richard Goldthwaite, *Orpheus in the Market Place: Jacopo Peri and the Economy of Late Renaissance Florence* [Hereafter: Carter and Goldthwaite] (Cambridge: Harvard University Press, 2013), pp. 112–13.
4. On the many dimensions of Peri's life, see Carter and Goldthwaite.
5. "Pietro de' Bardi on the Birth of Opera," in Piero Weiss, ed., *Opera: A History in Documents* (New York and Oxford: Oxford University Press, 2002), p. 10.
6. Da Gagliano's words in the preface to his resetting of *La Dafne*. Cited in Tim Carter, *Monteverdi's Musical Theater* (New Haven and London: Yale University Press, 2002), p. 17.
7. Quoted in Carter, *Monteverdi's Musical Theater*, p. 45.
8. See Simon Towneley, "Early Italian Opera," in Gerald Abraham, ed. *The New Oxford History of Music, Vol. IV: The Age of Humanism, 1540–1630* (Oxford: Oxford University Press, 1968), p. 826.
9. Horace, "On the Art of Poetry," in Aristotle, Horace, Longinus, *Classical Literary Criticism* (London: Penguin, 1965), p. 92.
10. Paul Oskar Kristeller, "Music and Learning," in *Renaissance Thought and the Arts* (Princeton: Princeton University Press, 1990), pp. 157–9.
11. Virgil, *The Georgics* (London and New York: Penguin Books, 1982), p. 140. Ovid, *Metamorphoses* (New York and London: Norton, 2005), p. 342.
12. Ottavio Rinuccini, "Prologue" to *Euridice*, in Jacopo Peri and Ottavio Rinuccini, *Euridice: An Opera in One Act, Five Scenes* [Hereafter: *Euridice*] Howard Mayer Brown, ed. (Madison: A-R Editions, Inc., 1981), p. xvi.
13. *Metamorphoses*, pp. 18–19.

14. Michelangelo Buonarroti the Younger, "L'Euridice, the Second Opera," in Weiss, ed. *Opera*, p. 12.
15. *Euridice*, p. xvii–xx.
16. *Euridice*, p. xxv.
17. *Euridice*, p. xxi.
18. Plato, *The Republic* (Oxford: Oxford University Press, 1974), pp. 195–6.
19. Justus Lipsius, *Politica: Six Books of Politics or Political Instruction*, trans. Jan Waszink (Assen, the Netherlands: Royal Van Gorcum, 2004), p. 227.
20. Da Ponte, *A History of the Florentine Republic*, Vol. 2, p. 69 and the "Preface," p. x.
21. For his defense of the assassination, see Lorenzino de' Medici, *Apology for a Murder* (London: Hesperus Press, 2004), p. 11.
22. Eric Cochrane, "The Failure of Political Philosophy in Seventeenth Century Florence: Lorenzo Magalotti's 'Condordia della Religione e del Principato,'" in Anthony Molho and John A. Tedeschi, *Renaissance Studies in Honor of Hans Baron* (DeKalb, Ill.: Northern Illinois University Press, 1971), pp. 559–60.
23. Quoted in J.R. Hale, *Florence and the Medici* (London: Phoenix Press, 2001), p. 129.
24. Janet Cox-Rearick, *Destiny and Dynasty in Medici Art* (Princeton: Princeton University Press, 1984), p. 238; Hale, *Florence and the Medici*, p. 97.
25. Roy Strong, *Splendor at Court: Renaissance Spectacle and the Theater of Power* (Boston: Houghton Mifflin Co., 1973), p. 19.
26. See Paul Oskar Kristeller, "The Moral Thought of Renaissance Humanism," in his *Renaissance Thought and the Arts* (Princeton: Princeton University Press, 1990).
27. See Kristeller, "The Origin and Development of the Language of Italian Prose," in his *Renaissance Thought and the Arts*.
28. I have taken numerous specifics from various scholarly works but especially those by Claude V. Palisca. See his "Girolamo Mei, Mentor to the Florentine Camerata," *The Musical Quarterly* Vol. 40, No. 1, January 1954, pp. 1–20 and his *Humanism in Italian Renaissance Musical Thought* (New Haven and London: Yale University Press, 1985). Also see Dunatella Restani, "Girolamo Mei et l'héritage de la dramaturgie antique dans la culture musicale de second moitié du XVe siècle," *La Naissance de l'Opéra: Euridice 1600–2000* sous la direction de Fr. Decroisette, F. Graziani, J. Heuillon (Paris: L'Harmattan, CollectionArts, 8, 2001), pp. 57–94.
29. Palisca, "Girolamo Mei," p. 16.
30. Lorenzo Bianconi, *Music in the Seventeenth Century* (Cambridge: Cambridge University Press, 1987), pp. 11–12, 18.
31. "Letter (to Vincenzo Galilei) of 8 May 1572 from Girolamo Mei," in Charles V. Palisca, *The Florentine Camerata: Documentary Studies and Translations* [Hereafter: *FC*] (New Haven and London: Yale University Press, 1989), pp. 57–9, 61–3.
32. "Letter (to Vincenzo Galilei) of 8 May 1572 from Girolamo Mei," in *FC*, p. 72.
33. "Letter (to Vincenzo Galilei) of 8 May 1572 from Girolamo Mei," in *FC*, pp. 73–4.
34. Some recent historiography contests notions like "Counter-Reformation." For an overview of scholarly discussions see, William V. Hudson, "Religion and Society in Early Modern Italy—Old Questions, New Insights," *The American Historical Review*, Vol. 101, No. 3, June 1996, pp. 783–804.

35. For an overview see Craig A. Monson, "The Council of Trent Revisited," *Journal of Musicological Society* Vol. 55, No. 1, Spring 2002, pp. 1–37. On local control see p. 26.

Chapter 2: Reigning Voices

1. See Robert Nosow, "The Debate on Song in the Accademia Fiorentina," *Early Music History*, Vol. 21, 2002, pp. 175–221.
2. Michel Plaisance, "Littérature et censure à Florence à la fin du XVIe Siècle: Le retour du censuré," in *Le Pouvoir et la Plume: incitation, contrôle et repression dans l'Italie du XVI siècle: Actes du Colloque international* 1982, pp. 233–4.
3. Nino Pirrotta, "Temperaments and Tendencies in the Florentine Camerata" in Pirrotta, *Music and Culture in Italy from the Middle Ages to the Baroque* (Harvard: Harvard University Press, 1984), p. 218.
4. Giovanni de' Bardi, "Discourse Addressed to Giulio Caccini, called the Roman, on Ancient Music and Good Singing," in Palisca, *FC*, pp. 111, 113, 115.
5. De' Bardi, "Discourse Addressed to Giulio Caccini," p. 123.
6. See "High Renaissance Style," in Piero Weiss and Richard Taruskin, *Music in the Western World: A History in Documents* [Hereafter: *WT*]) (New York: Schirmer, 1984), pp. 111–113.
7. J.L. Heilbron, *Galileo* (Oxford: Oxford University Press, 2010), p. 5.
8. Galilei, *Dialogue on Ancient and Modern Music*, p. 6. My discussion has been informed by and draws material from Palisco's introduction to this volume.
9. Galilei, *Dialogue*, pp. 224–5.
10. Galilei, *Dialogue*, p. 6.
11. Galilei, *Dialogue*, pp. 261–3.
12. Galilei, *Dialogue*, p. 196.
13. Galilei, *Dialogue*, p. 263.
14. Galilei, *Dialogue*, p. 361.
15. Charles Burney, *A General History of Music from the Earliest Ages to the Present Period*, Vol. 4 (London: Becket, Robson and Robinson, 1789), p. 13. Orthography updated.
16. Ottavio Rinuccini, "Dedication of Euridice" (1600), in Oliver Strunk, ed., *Source Readings in Music History* (New York: W.W. Norton, 1950), pp. 367–8.
17. Francesco Raccamadoro-Ramelli, *Ottavio Rinuccini* (Fabriano: Stab. Tip. Gentile: 1900), pp. 35, 37–8.
18. Claude-François Ménestrier, quoted in John Hawkins, *A General History of the Science and Practice of Music*, Vol. 2 (London: Novello, 1853 [1776]), p. 524.
19. Jacopo Peri, "Preface to *The Music for* Euridice (1601)" in Strunk, ed., pp. 659–60.
20. Giulio Caccini, *"Nuove musiche"* (1601) in *WT*, p. 170.
21. Claude V. Palisca, "The Alterati of Florence: Pioneers in the Theory of Dramatic Music," in *New Looks at Italian Opera: Essays in Honor of Donald J. Grout*, William Austin, ed (Westport: Greenwood Publishers, 1968), p. 15.
22. Heilbron, *Galileo*, pp. 11–12.

23. See Bernard Weinberg, "The Accademia degli Alterati and Literary Taste from 1570 to 1600," *Italica*, Vol. 31, No. 4, December 1954, p. 208 and Palisca, "The Alterati of Florence: Pioneers in the Theory of Dramatic Music," p. 23. Here and throughout, I take again many details from Palisca's accounts.

24. Palisca, *Humanism in Italian Renaissance Musical Thought*, pp. 404–5.

25. Baxter Hathaway, *The Age of Criticism: The Late Renaissance in Italy* (Ithaca, NY: Cornell University Press, 1972), p. 254.

26. Paul Oskar Kristeller, *Renaissance Thought and its Sources* (New York: Columbia University Press, 1979), p. 251.

27. Tacitus, "Agricola," in *The Agricola and the Germania* (London and New York: Penguin, 1970), p. 95.

28. See Francesco Guicciardini, *Maxims and Reflections (Ricordi)*, (Philadelphia: University of Pennsylvania Press, 1992), p. 45 and the translator's preface by Mario Domandi, p. 37. Also see Robert Bireley, *The Counter-Reformation Prince* (Chapel Hill and London: University of North Carolina Press, 1990), p. 49 and Burke, "Tacitism, skepticism, and reasons of state," in J.H. Burns, ed. With the assistance of Mark Goldie, *The Cambridge History of Political Thought, 1450–1700* (Cambridge: Cambridge University Press, 1991, p. 484–7.

29. Marc-Antoine Muret, "The Defense of Tacitus, November 4, 1580," in Joseph Francis Desmond, *Muret's Defense of Tacitus* (Tufts University, Doctoral diss., 1966), p. 73. Translation amended. Desmond translates the complete Muret lectures with the original Latin en face. Where he translates "nation" I change it to "people" since the Latin word is *gentum* and "nation" has a different resonance. See pp. 72–3. Desmond provides a very useful introduction and annotations from which I take some details. Also see p. 2 on Montaigne in Muret's play.

30. Muret, "The Defense of Tacitus, November 4, 1580," p. 97.

31. See Michel Plaisance, "L'Académie des Alterati au travail," in *La transmission des savoirs au Moyen Age et à la Renaissance*, Vol. 2, 2005, pp. 211–25.

32. See Kenneth C. Schellhase, *Tacitus in Renaissance Political Thought* (Chicago and London: University of Chicago Press, 1976), p. 141.

33. Richard Tuck, *Philosophy and Government: 1572–1651* (Cambridge: Cambridge University Press, 1993), pp. 40–1.

34. My sources for Salviati are Samuel Berner, "Florentine Political Thought in the Late Cinquecento," *Il Pensiero Politico*, Vol. 3 No. 2, August 1970, pp. 182–3, 192, 196, Peter Brown, "Lionardo Salviati and the 'Discorso sopra le Prime Parole di Cornelio Tacito," *Italian Studies*, Vol. 15, 1960, pp. 55–7 and more generally Brown's *Lionardo Salviati* (Oxford: Oxford University Press, 1974).

35. Eric Cochrane, *Florence in the Forgotten Centuries: 1527–1806* (Chicago: University of Chicago Press, 1973), pp. 118, 119 ("stylistic mentor"), and Berner, "Florentine Political Thought" p. 95. The "Diario" of the Alterati was published in part by Bernard Weinberg as "Argomenti di Discussione Letteraria Nell'Accademia degli Alterati (1570–1600)," in *Giornale storico della lettaratura italiana*, Vol. 131, 1954, pp. 175–94.

36. Tacitus, *The Annals of Imperial Rome* (London and New York: Penguin Books, 1996), p. 163.

37. Galilei, *Dialogue*, p. 361.
38. Marc Fumaroli, *L'Âge de l'Éloquence* (Geneva: Librarie Droz, 2009[1980]), p. 63. For a bibliography of Tacitus publications see pp. 735–6.
39. Tacitus, "Dialogue on Orators," in *Agricola, Germania, Dialogue on Orators* (Indianapolis: Bobbs-Merrill, 1967), p. 70.
40. Tacitus, "Dialogue," p. 90.
41. Tacitus, "Dialogue," pp. 100–101.
42. Ronald Mellors, *Tacitus* (New York and London: Routledge, 1993), p. 27.
43. On Tacitus's "Dialogue" and style, see especially Mellors, *Tacitus*, pp. 16–19 and 113–36, and Ronald Syme, *Tacitus*, Vol. 1 (Oxford: Oxford University Press, 1958), pp. 100–120. My discussion is indebted to both these authors.
44. For these details see N.S. Davidson, "Northern Italy in the 1590s," in Peter Clark, ed, *The European Crisis of the 1590s* (London: George Allen and Unwin, 1985), pp. 157–76.
45. Robert Dallington, *A Survey of the Great Dukes State of Tuscany* (London: Eduard Blount, 1605), p. 39. Orthography updated.
46. Dallington, *Survey*, pp. 56, 69.
47. See Claude V. Palisca, "Musical Asides in the Diplomatic Correspondence of Emilio de' Cavalieri," *The Musical Quarterly*, Vol. 49, No. 3, July 1963, pp. 339–55.
48. Dallington, *Survey*, p. 55.
49. Nagler, *Theatre Festivals of the Medici*, pp. 70–1. I have also drawn details about the 1589 events from James M. Saslow, *The Medici Wedding of 1589* (New Haven and London: Yale University Press, 1996).
50. See D.P. Walker, ed. *Les Fêtes du Marriage de Ferdinand de Médicis et de Christine de Lorraine, Florence 1589: Musique des Intermèdes de 'la Pellegrina'* (Paris: Éditions du Centre National de la Recherche Scientifique, 1963), p. xv. For Boethius's question, see Weiss and Taruskin, eds, *Music in the Western World*, p. 32.
51. For details on his life, see Tim Carter, "Jacopo Peri (1563–1633): Aspects of His Life and Works," *Proceedings of the Royal Musical Association*, Vol. 105 (1978/79), pp. 50–62.

Intermedio (I)

1. Nagler, *Theatre Festivals of the Medici*, p. 75. For a recent study see Nina Treadwell, *Music and Wonder at the Medici Court: The 1589 Interludes for La pellegrina* (Bloomington and Indianapolis: Indiana University Press, 2008).
2. Palisca, *Humanism in Italian Renaissance Musical Thought*, p. 188.
3. On different meanings for musical vocabulary that derive from Greek, see Thomas J. Mathiesen, "Problems of Terminology of Ancient Greek Theory: 'APMONÍA," in *Festive Essays for Pauline Alderman; A Musicological Tribute* (Provo, Utah: Brigham Young University, 1976), pp. 3–17.
4. Barbara Russano Hanning, *Of Poetry and Music's Power: Humanism and the Creation of Opera* (Ann Arbor: UMI Research Press, 1980), p. 11.
5. Guicciardini, p. 76.

6. Plato, *The Laws*, (2:653), in Edith Hamilton and Huntington Cairns eds., *The Collected Dialogues of Plato*, (Princeton: Princeton University Press, 1961), pp. 1250–1, 1261.
7. See Treadwell, *Music and Wonder at the Medici Court*, p. 169.

Chapter 3: Laws and Laurels

1. Giovanni Botero, *The Reason of State* (London: Routledge and Kegan Paul, 1956), p. xiii.
2. Burke, pp. 480–1.
3. Quoted in Robert Bireley, *The Counter-Reformation Prince* (Chapel Hill and London: University of North Carolina Press, 1990), p. 45.
4. On the history of Florentine legal claims I rely on materials in and draw from Lauro Martines, *Lawyers and Statecraft in Renaissance Italy* (Princeton: Princeton University Press, 1968), and R. Burr Litchfield, *Emergence of a Bureaucracy: The Florentine Patricians, 1530–1790* (Princeton: Princeton University Press, 1986).
5. Hans Julius Wolff, *Roman Law* (Norman, Oklahoma: University of Oklahoma Press, 1976), p. 87. The citation for the assertion that "*princeps* was not bound by the laws" by Ulpanius is *Dig.*, 1.3.31.
6. See Brian Tierney, "'The Prince is not Bound by the Laws': Accursius and the Origins of the Modern State," in *Comparative Studies in Society and History*, Vol. Vol. 5, No. 4, July 1965. pp. 378–387. Also Martines pp. 412–14, 419. Strozzi is quoted on p. 438.
7. The Latin is "*princeps enim fit.*" Quentin Skinner, "Surveying *The Foundations*: A Retrospect and a Reassessment," in Annabel Brett and James Tully, eds., with Holly Hamilton-Bleakley, *Rethinking The Foundations of Modern Political Thought* (Cambridge: Cambridge University Press, 2006), pp. 251–2.
8. Litchfield, p. 65.
9. Jean Bodin, *Les Six Livres de la république* (Paris: Librairie Iuré Samaritain, 1577), p. 331. For his theory of sovereignty see especially Book 1, chapter 8.
10. Bodin, *Livres*, p. 1099.
11. Bodin, *Livres*, p. 15.
12. Bodin, *Livres*, pp. 1096–1102.
13. See Albert Cremer, "Les théoriciens de la raison d'état, juges de Jean Bodin," *Revue d'histoire diplomatique* Vol. 89, 1975, pp. 249–61.
14. Botero, *The Reason of State*, p. 61.
15. Botero, *The Reason of State*, pp. 16, 25, 3.
16. Burke, "Tacitism, skepticism, and reasons of state," pp. 479–81.
17. Justus Lipsius, *Politica*, pp. 227, 397. For Bodin's use of a musician and his violin as a metaphor see Bodin, *Livres*, p. 740.
18. Botero, p. 82.
19. Brown, "Lionardo Salviati and the 'Discorso sopra le Prime Parole di Cornelio Tacito," pp. 177–8.
20. Berner, "Florentine Political Thought," p. 196.

21. See, Jacopo Peri, "To My Readers," *Euridice*, p. xlii.
22. See Ottavio Rinuccini, *La Favola di Dafne* [Hereafter: *FD*] in *Drammi per musica dal Rinuccini allo Zeno* [Hereafter: *DM*)], Vol. 1, ed. Andrea Della Corte (Turin: Unione Tipografico-Editrice Torinese, 1958/1978), pp. 49–50. Also see the transcription of the 1598 Italian libretto in Appendix A of Hanning, *Of Poetry and Music's Power*, pp. 245–67.
23. Rinuccini, *FD*, p. 66.
24. See Cox-Rearick, *Dynasty and Destiny in Medici Art*, pp. 15, 18, 201 and chapter 6 (pp. 233–250).
25. Cited by David Kimball, "Opera," Peter Brand and Lino Pertile, eds., in *The Cambridge History of Italian Literature*, (Cambridge: Cambridge University Press, 1999), p. 337.
26. *Euridice*, p. xxviii.
27. *Euridice*, pp. xxviii-xxix.
28. *Euridice*, p. xxix.
29. *Euridice*, p. xxx.
30. *Euridice*, p. xxxi.
31. *Euridice*, p. xxxi.
32. Botero, *The Reason of State*, p. 56. See Fn 28, which points out that Botero's use of "equity" is in the classical sense, *aequitas*, implying "a merciful exception" to a general rule because of particular circumstances.
33. See Lipsius, *Politica*, pp. 429–35.
34. Lipsius, *Politica*, pp. 317–21.
35. Lipsius, *Politica*, pp. 323–27.
36. *Euridice*, pp. xxi-xxxii.

Chapter 4: Orpheus's Ways

1. I use the English translation in Claudio Monteverdi, *Orfeo: Nouvelle Edition et Restitution Edward H. Tarr* [Hereafter: *Orfeo*] (Paris: Editions Costallat, 1974). It has Striggio's original en face along with French and German translations. (For "attracted wild beasts" see "Prologue," p. xi). I have also made use of Lionel Salter's translation in the John Eliot Gardiner Edition of Claudio Monteverdi, *L'Orfeo* (London: J. & W. Chester/William Hansen, 1985; Arkhiv Production/ Polydor, 1987) with occasional modifications done in consultation with the singing version by Anne Ridler in *The Operas of Monteverdi* (London: Calder, 1992).
2. Gary Tomlinson, *Monteverdi and the End of the Renaissance* (Berkeley and Los Angeles, California: University of California Press, 1990), p. 33.
3. Kerman, *Opera and Drama*, pp. 19, 22.
4. *Orfeo*, "Demigod," p. xi; the snake, p. xvii.
5. *Orfeo*, p. xxi.
6. *Orfeo*, p. xxiii.
7. *Orfeo*, p. xxiii. Translation modified.
8. *Orfeo*, p. xxiii.

9. *Orfeo*, p. xxv.
10. *Orfeo*, p. xxv.
11. *Orfeo*, p. xxv.
12. *Orfeo*, p. xxvii.
13. *Orfeo*, p. xxvii.
14. This passage does not appear in the 1607 version of the score. See the Ridler translation, p. 53 (which I modify).
15. *Orfeo*, p. xxix.
16. *Orfeo*, p. xxix.
17. See Salter's translation p. 121 and Ridler's, "The Original Ending of Act Five," p. 57.
18. One scholar argues by stylistic comparisons of both endings that that the second may well be a reworking by Ottavio Rinuccini. See Barbara Russano Hanning, "The Ending of *L'Orfeo*: Father, Son, and Rinuccini," *Journal of Seventeenth Century Music* Vol. 9, No. 1, 2003, http://sscm-jscm.press.uiuc.edu/v9/no1/hanning.html. Also see her "Apologia pro Ottavio Rinuccini," *Journal of the American Musicological Society*, Vol. 26, No. 2, Summer 1973.

Intermedio (II)

1. Here and in my general discussion of Mantuan politics I draw material and details from David Parrott, "The Mantuan Succession, 1627–31," Vol. 112, No. 445, 1997a, A Sovereignty Dispute," *English Historical Review* [Hereafter EHR], pp. 20–65.
2. Quoted in Susan Helen Parisi, *Ducal Patronage of Music in Mantua, 1587–1627: An Archival Study* (University of Illinois, Urbana-Champaign, Doctoral Diss., 1989), p. 117. My discussion of Mantua relies often on and borrows from this study and also John Whenham, "'Orfeo': A Masterpiece for a Court" in *The Operas of Monteverdi* (Paris, London and New York: Calder and Riverrun Press/ English National Opera Guide 45, 1992), p. 20.
3. I draw here from Iain Fenlon, "Music and Spectacle at the Gonzaga Court, c. 1580–1600," *Proceedings of the Royal Music Association*, Vol. 103, 1976/77.
4. Tim Carter, *Monteverdi's Musical Theatre*, p.186.
5. Silke Leopold, *Monteverdi: Music in Transition* (Cambridge: Cambridge University Press, 1991), pp. 1–6.
6. See Charles Burney, *A General History of Music*, Vol. 1 (London: Becket, Robson and Robinson, 1776).
7. Giovanni Maria Artusi, "L'Artusi," in *WT*, p. 172.
8. Giulio Cesare Monteverdi, "Declaration," in *WT*, p. 173. For a somewhat different translation of passages see Strunk (revised edition Treitler), pp. 596–7.
9. Monteverdi to Giovanni Battista Doni, February 2, 1634, in Denis Stevens, ed. *The Letters of Claudio Monteverdi* [Hereafter: *LCM*] Revised edition (Oxford: Oxford University Press, 1995), pp. 423–7.
10. Monteverdi to Doni, October 22, 1633 in *LCM*, pp. 420–1. See Plato's *Republic* 1, 10.
11. Monteverdi to Alessandro Striggio, December 9, 1616, in *LCM*, p. 110.

Chapter 5: A Prince Decides on Naxos

1. Nagler, Appendix, p. 178.
2. See Prunières, *Monteverdi*, p. 74; Hanning, "Glorious Apollo," p. 507 and 509 fn. 62, and Silke Leopoldo, *Monteverdi: Music in Transition* (Oxford: Clarendon Press, 1991), pp. 184–5.
3. See Ian Fenlon, "Music and Spectacle at the Gonzaga Court," p. 101.
4. See John Hawkins, quoted in *Memoirs of Alessandro Tassoni* (London and Dublin: C.P. Aiclor, 1815) p. 230, and John Hawkins, *A General History of the Science and Practice of Music*, Vol. 2 (London: Novello, 1853[1776]), p. 524 (note).
5. Raccamadoro-Ramelli, pp. 47–53. See Warren Kirkendale, *The Court Musicians of Florence during the Principate of the Medici* (Florence: Olschki Editori, 1993), p. 148–9. The rumor of Rinuccini's love for Maria de' Medici is also reported in Prunières, *Monteverdi*, p. 74. Raccamadoro-Ramelli, pp. 41–2.
6. Raccamadoro-Ramelli, *Ottavio Rinuccini*, pp. 41–2.
7. Raccamadoro-Ramelli, pp. 44–6.
8. Raccamadoro-Ramelli, pp. 47–53.
9. For feminist-oriented examinations see Suzanne Cusick, "'There was not One Lady who Failed to Shed a Tear': Arianna's Lament and Construction of Modern Womanhood," *Early Music* Vol. 22/1, February 1994, pp. 21–45, and Bonnie Gordon, "Talking Back: The Female Voice in *Il Ballo delle ingrate*," *Cambridge Opera Journal*, Vol. 11, No. 1, 1999, pp. 1–30. On the event itself see Denis Arnold, *Monteverdi* (Oxford: Oxford University Press, 1990), p. 106.
10. Nagler, Appendix, p. 178. For a discussion of *Arianna*'s first performance, see especially Bojan Bujic, "Runiccini the Craftsman: A View of *L'Arianna*," *Early Modern Music*, Vol. 18, 1999.
11. *L'Arianna. Tragedia del Sig. Ottavio Rinuccini* [Hereafter: *Arianna* (Florence: Stamperia de'Giunti, 1608), p. 7. Translation by Patrick Boyle, for Alexander Goehr, *Arianna: Tragedy in a Prologue and Eight Scenes (lost opera by Claudio Monteverdi)* [Hereafter: Boyle](London: NMC Recordings, 1998), p. 8.
12. *Arianna*, p. 17; Boyle, p. 15. With occasional modification I use Boyle's translation.
13. *Arianna*, pp. 17–18; Boyle, pp. 15–16. The Florentine text uses "*Consigliero di Teseo*," which I modernize as "*Consigliere*."
14. *Arianna*, p. 21; Boyle, p. 19.
15. *Arianna*, pp. 21–23; Boyle, pp. 21–2.
16. *Arianna*, pp. 21–23; Boyle, pp. 21–2.
17. *Arianna*, p. 24; Boyle, p. 23.
18. My thanks to Nicole Reinhardt for pointing me to Sansovino and allowing me to read her unpublished lecture, "The Knowledge of Friendship in Early Modern Secretarial Handbooks." On Sansovino and Tasso, also see Douglas Blow, *Doctors, Ambassadors, Secretaries: Humanism and Professions in Renaissance Italy* (Chicago and London: University of Chicago Press, 2002).
19. *Arianna*, p. 33; Boyle, p. 31.
20. *Arianna*, pp. 38–9; Boyle, p. 36.
21. F. W. Sternfeld, *The Birth of Opera* (Oxford: Oxford University Press, 1995), p. 34.

22. *Arianna*, pp. 39–40; Boyle, pp. 38–9.
23. *Arianna*, p. 40; Boyle, p. 39.
24. Nagler, Appendix, p. 179.
25. *Arianna*, p. 46; Boyle, p. 45.
26. *Arianna*, p. 49; Boyle, p. 48.
27. Monteverdi to Annibale Chieppo, December 2, 1608, see *LCM*, pp. 8, 61.
28. Quoted in Anthony Pryer, "Approaching Monteverdi: His Cultures and Ours," in John Whenham and Richard Wistreich, eds, *The Cambridge Companion to Monteverdi*, (Cambridge: Cambridge University Press, 2007), p. 11.

Intermedio (III)

1. R.A. Stradling, "Mantua Preserv'd or the Tragicall Historie of Count Olivarez, Great Favorite of Spayne," *The Seventeenth Century*, Vol. 4, No. 2, Autumn 1989, p. 97.
2. On Striggio's relation to de Nevers see Émile Baudson, *Charles de Gonzague, Duc de Nevers, de Rethel, et de Mantoue, 1580–1637* (Paris: Librairie Académique Perrin, 1947), p. 258.
3. See R.A. Stradling, "Prelude to Disaster: the Precipitation of the War of the Mantuan Succession, 1627–1629," *The Historical Journal*, Vol. 33, No. 4, December 1990, pp. 778–9.
4. Again I rely on Parrott, but also David Maland, *Europe in the Seventeenth Century* (London: MacMillan, 1977), pp. 126–9, 174–5.
5. Leopold, *Monteverdi: Music in Transition*, p. 6.
6. Monteverdi to Striggio, January 1, 1628, *LCM*, p. 391.
7. Monteverdi to Striggio, January, 1, 1628, *LCM* pp. 400–401. Also see the editor's notes on these pages.
8. Paolo Fabbri, *Monteverdi* (Cambridge: Cambridge University Press, 1994), p. 223.

Chapter 6: The Political Scenario of Monteverdi's Venice

1. On their presentation in the visual arts, see especially David Rosand, *Myths of Venice: Figuration of a State* (Chapel Hill and London: University of North Carolina Press, 2001).
2. I summarize extensively and take most points from Jonathan Glixon's introduction to his annotated translation of the document, from which I also take the quotes, in *Music and Letters*, Vol. 72, No. 3, August 1991, pp. 404–6.
3. On the details of politics in Venice at this time I draw from Horatio F. Brown, *Venice: An Historical Sketch of the Republic* (London: Rivington, Perival and Co., 1895), pp. 405–7; John Julius Norwich, *A History of Venice* (New York: Vintage Books, 1989), pp. 525–9.
4. See Monteverdi's letters to Striggio, March 17, 1620, March 21, 1620, and February 10, 1623, together with the Denis Steven's introductions in *LCM*, pp. 195–7, 198–9, 267–69.

5. Brown, *Venice*, pp. 398–9.
6. Cristofo Ivanovich, *Memorie teatrali di Venezia* in "Source Readings," Bianconi, *17th Century*, pp. 303–4.
7. Filippo de Vivo, *Information and Communication in Venice: Rethinking Early Modern Politics* (Oxford: Oxford University Press, 2007), pp. 46, 13.
8. Jean Bodin, *Colloquium of the Seven Concerning Secrets of the Sublime* (Princeton: Princeton University Press, 1975), p. 3.
9. Quoted in William J. Bouwsma, *Venice and the Defense of Republican Liberty* (Berkeley, Los Angeles, London: University of California Press, 1984), p. 149. "[C]onservative idealism" is Bouwsma's phrase, p. 145.
10. See Bouwsma, *Venice and the Defense*, p. 60.
11. He makes the argument in Book 2, Chapter 1 of *Les Six Livres de la république*.
12. Bouwsma, p. 438, 411–12. Sarpi was influenced by Pierre Charron's *De la Sagesse*, which was in turn indebted to Lipsius. See Wooten, *Paolo Sarpi*, p. 70.
13. Traiano Boccalini, *Advices (News) from Parnassus* (London: L. Stokoe, 1727), p. 49. Also see the discussion in Burke, "Tacitus, Sceptism, and Reason of State."
14. *The Diary of John Evelyn*, Entry in Venice, 1645 (London: MacMillan & Co., 1908 [1818]), p. 122.
15. On the Zen affair, see Norwich, pp. 530–8; Brown, pp. 410–13. P.N. Miller, "Friendship and Conversation in Seventeenth Century Venice," *Journal of Modern History*, Vol 73, No. 1, March 2001, pp. 1–31, C.J. Rose, "Marc Antonio Vernier, Renier Zeno and the Myth of Venice," *The Historian*, Vol. 3, No. 36, May 1974, pp. 479–97.
16. My account is indebted significantly to Ellen Rosand, *Opera in Seventeenth Century Venice*, especially pp. 37–42, and Iain Fenlon and Peter N. Miller, *The Song of the Soul: Understanding Poppea* (London: Royal Musicological Association Monograph 5, 1992).
17. Carter, *Monteverdi's Musical Theatre*, pp. 271–2.
18. Ivanovich, "Memorie teatrali" pp. 303–4.
19. Again, for detailed discussion of these matters and of what follows see Rosand, *Opera in Seventeenth Century Venice*, especially pp. 2–3, 14–15.
20. Ivanovich, p. 304.
21. Rosand, *Opera in Seventeenth Century Venice*, pp. 2, 7, 8, 13.
22. *The Diary of John Evelyn*, Entry in Venice, 1645, p. 122.
23. See the discussion in Ellen Rosand, *Monteverdi's Last Operas: A Venetian Trilogy* (Berkeley, Los Angeles, London: University of California Press, 2007), pp. 8–9.
24. "Nobles, Citizens, and People in Venice, c. 1618," in David Chambers and Brian Pullan, eds. with Jennifer Fletcher, *Venice: A Documentary History, 1450–1630* (Oxford: Blackwell, 1992), p. 259.
25. Arthur Livingston, *La vita Venetiana nelle opere di Gian Francesco Busenello* (Venice: V. Callegap, 1913), pp. 2–23.
26. See Leopold, p. 198 and Bianconi and Walker, "Production, Consumption, and Political Function in Seventeenth Century Italian Opera," *Early Music History*, Vol. 4, 1984, p. 248.

27. Quoted in Michael Collins, "Dramatic Theory and the Italian Baroque Libretto," Collins and Ellen K. Kirk, eds. *Opera and Vivaldi* (Austin: University of Texas Press, 1994), p. 25.

28. See "Madrid: Palinoda" and "Descritione di Madrid," in Gian Francesco Busenello, *Sonetti morali ed amorisi di Gian Francesco Busenello: testo critico per cura di Arthur Livingston* (Venice: Prem. Stab. Grafico Fabbris, 1911), p. 112.

29. Giacomo Badoaro, "Letter of L'assicurato [The Assured One], Member of the Accademia degli Incogniti written on his *Ulisse Errante* to Signor Michel'Angelo Torcigliani" in Tim Carter, trans., *Composing Opera from Dafne to Ulisse Errante, Pratica Musica 2* (Crakow: Musica Iagellonica and Katedra Historii I Teorii Muzyki UJ, 1994), pp. 83–5, 189, 189–97.

30. See especially Ellen Rosand, "Seneca and the Interpretation of *L'incoronazione di Poppea*," *Journal of the American Musicological Society*, Vol. 38, No. 1, Spring 1985, p. 37 and her discussion in *Opera in Seventeenth Century Venice*.

Chapter 7: Revealing Ulysses

1. See Rosand, *Monteverdi's Last Operas*, especially her persuasive discussion on pp. xvi-xvii of why these works should be regarded as if they are all by Monteverdi, even while recognizing that some parts may have been by other hands.

2. "Open Letter from Giacomo Badoaro to Claudio Monteverdi," Claudio Monteverdi, *Il ritorno d'Ulisse in patria* [Hereafter: *Ritorno*] libretto by Giacomo Badoaro, edited by Alan Curtis (London: Novello, 2002), p. xxi. Rosand makes this point in *Monteverdi's Last Operas*, pp. 3–4.

3. Rosand, *Monteverdi's Last Operas*, p. 138.

4. On these manuscript matters see Ellen Rosand, "Iro and the Interpretation of *Il Ritorno d'Ulisse in Patria*," *The Journal of Musicology*, Vol. 7, No. 2, Spring 1989, p. 142, fn 3; Rosand, *Monteverdi's Last Operas*, pp. 52–5, 69–88, and Carter, *Monteverdi's Musical Theater*, pp. 246–7.

5. Monteverdi, *Ritorno*, p. 9. Given the particular difficulties—or impossibility—of establishing the text as performed in Monteverdi and Badoaro's day, I have simply followed Anne Ridler's English singing version in Curtis's edition, however with a certain number of alterations and amendments based on the corresponding Italian text and additional materials accompanying her translation in *The Operas of Monteverdi: Orfeo/ Il ritorno d'Ulisse in patria/L'incoronzione di Poppea* [Hereafter: *Operas of Monteverdi*), p. 103.

6. Edward Muir, *The Culture Wars of the Late Renaissance* (Cambridge and London: Harvard University Press, 2007), p. 56. Translation modified.

7. Virgil, *The Aeneid*, trans. Robert Fagles, (London and New York: Penguin Books, 2006), pp. 75–7; and 44–63.

8. Dante, *The Divine Comedy: 1. Inferno* (New York: Oxford University Press, 1981/82), p. 323.

9. *Ritorno*, pp. 12–13.

10. *Ritorno*, p. 195.

11. *Ritorno*, p. 146.
12. Rosand, *Monteverdi's Last Operas*, p. 271–2.
13. Jean-François Lattarico, *Venise Incognita* (Paris: Honoré Champion Editeur, 2010), pp. 430–1.
14. *The Life of Adam written in Italian by Giovanni Francesco Loredano, A Venetian Noble-Man, and rendered into English by J.S.* (London: Humphrey Mosley, 1659/ Facsimile by Gainesville: Facsimile and Reprints, 1967), p. 1.
15. Loredano, *The Life of Adam*, p. 32.
16. This theme is central to the important account of the collaboration of Busenello and Monteverdi in Fenlon and Miller, *Song of the Soul*, especially pp. 36–40.
17. See Rosand, *Monteverdi's Late Operas* on sources.
18. Homer, *The Odyssey*, Robert Fagles, trans. (New York: Penguin, 1996), p. 78.
19. *Odyssey*, p. 80.
20. *Odyssey*, p. 80.
21. *Odyssey*, p. 215.
22. *Odyssey*, pp. 168, 170.
23. *Odyssey*, p. 290–2.
24. *Odyssey*, p. 291.
25. *Odyssey*, pp. 291–2.
26. *Ritorno*, p. 39.
27. *Ritorno*, p. 42.
28. *Ritorno*, p. 44.
29. *Ritorno*, p. 64.
30. *Ritorno*, p. 65–6.
31. *Odyssey*, p. 375.
32. *Ritorno*, p. 86–7.
33. *Metamorphoses*, p. 111.
34. *Ritorno*, p. 88–90. For "burst apart," see *Operas of Monteverdi*, p.103.
35. *Ritorno*, pp. 92–3.
36. *Ritorno*, p. 161.
37. *Ritorno*, p. 166.
38. *Ritorno*, pp. 234–5, 237.
39. M.I. Finley, *The World of Odysseus* (New York: New York Review of Books, 2002), p. 93.
40. *Odyssey*, p. 80.
41. *Ritorno*, p. 211.
42. *Ritorno*, pp. 187, 193.
43. Quoted in Rosand, "Iro . . . ," p. 160.
44. Rosand's translations in "Iro . . . ," pp. 160–1.
45. See James Cushman Davis, *The Decline of the Venetian Nobility as a Ruling Class* (Baltimore: Johns Hopkins University Studies in Historical and Political Science, Series 80, No. 2, 1962), pp. 55–7, 102.
46. Arthur Livingston, editor of the English edition of Mosca's most important book, *The Ruling Class*, wrote the first biography of Busenello and edited a volume of his poetry.

Intermedio (IV)

1. Gio: Francesco Busenello, *La Didone: Opera Rappresentata in Musica nel Teatro di San Casciano* [Hereafter: *Didone*] (Venice: Giulini, 1641), p. 10. Citations refer first to the original printed libretto of 1641 but I have also made considerable use of Clive Williams's translation in Pietro Francesco Cavalli, *La Didone* (Deutsche Harmonia Mundi/BMG Classics, 1998) with some alterations and additions. I indicate these as e.g., Williams, p. 32.
2. *Didone*, p. 6; Williams, p. 28.
3. *Didone*, p. 25; Williams, 49–50.
4. Busenello provided several librettos for Cavalli. On Cavalli see, Henry Prunières, *Cavalli et l'Opéra vénitien au XVIIe siècle* (Paris: Les Éditions Rieder, 1931) and Jane Glover, *Cavalli* (London: B.T. Batsford, 1978).
5. *Didone*, p. 19; Williams, p. 40.
6. *Didone*, p. 30–31; Williams, pp. 60–1.
7. *Didone*, pp. 32–3; Williams, pp. 64–6.
8. *Didone*, p. 54; Williams, p. 86.
9. *Didone*, p. 50; Williams, p. 80.
10. *Didone*, p. 60–1; Williams, p. 96–8.
11. *Didone*, p. 63–4; Williams, p. 100.
12. *Didone*, pp. 64–5, 68–9, 75–6; Williams, pp. 102, 106, 116–18.
13. "Argomento et scenario delle nozze d'Enea con Lavinia" (1640), in Rosand, *Opera in Seventeenth Century Venice*, Appendix 1, p. 411 and Rosand's own text, p. 133.

Chapter 8: Spectacles

1. Busenello, "Ai bramosi di prelature" (To those Longing to be Prelates), *Sonetti morali ed amorosi*, p. 89. Special thanks to Nadia Urbinati for helping me examine these poems.
2. Anon., "Lettera dell' autoroe ad alcuni suoi amici," Rosand, *Opera in Seventeenth Century Venice*, Appendix I, p. 411. Also see Bianconi, *Music in the Seventeenth Century*, p. 256–7.
3. Busenello, "Le Passioni humane," *Sonetti morali ed amorosi*, p. 86.
4. Suetonius, "Nero," in *The Twelve Caesars* (London and New York: Penguin Books, 1989), p. 228.
5. Suetonius, "Nero," p. 243. For the history of the Seneca-Nero relationship, see James Romm, *Dying Every Day: Seneca at the Court of Nero* (New York: Vintage Books, 2014).
6. Tacitus, *The Annals of Imperial Rome* (London: Penguin Books, 1997), p. 306.
7. Loredano, *The Life of Adam*, 75.
8. Christopher Brooke, *Philosophic Pride: Stoicism and Political Thought from Lipsius to Rousseau* (Princeton: Princeton University Press, 2012), p. 21.
9. Gio: Francesco Busenello, *L'incoronazione di Poppea: Opera Musicale Rapressentata nel Teatro Grimano l'anno 1642* [Hereafter: *Poppea*] (Venice: Andrea Giulini, 1656), p. 27. The printed dating of this published libretto is anomalous. The

opera was first performed in 1643. The Grimano Theater, named for the family owners, was also known as the Teatro SS Giovanni e Paolo.

10. On these debates see Bianconi, *Music in the Seventeenth Century*, pp. 194–5. Alan Curtis, "La Poppea, Impasticciaa or, Who wrote the Music to *L'Incoronazione* (1643)?," *Journal of the American Musicological Society*, Vol. 42, No. 1, Spring 1989, pp. 23–54. "Pur ti miro" is missing in the Venetian libretto cited above (8-YTH-52351 at the National Library of France). It closes with celebratory exchange between Venus and Amore and then declares "The end of the Opera."

11. *Poppea*, p. 60.

12. Busenello, "La vanità," *Sonetti morali ed amorosi*, p. 71.

13. On the illusory triumph of love and the misunderstandings of the end of the opera, see especially *Song of the Soul*, Fenlon and Miller, pp. 92–3.

14. Busenello, "Moralità," in *Sonetti morali ed amorosi*, p. 72.

15. *Poppea*, p. 22.

16. *Poppea*, p. 22.

17. *Poppea*, p. 22.

18. Pierre Charron, *De la sagesse*, quoted in Burke, "Tacitism, Scepticism, and Reason of State," p. 496.

19. The original title was *Considérations politiques sur les coups d'estat*.

20. For a short, useful study of Naudé, from which I take several details, see Jack A. Clarke, *Gabriel Naudé: 1600–1653* (Hamden, Conn.: Archon Books, 1970), pp. 13–15, 47–57. Also see Burke, "Tacitism, Skepticism, and Reason of State."

21. *Poppea*, p. 23.

22. *Poppea*, p. 22.

23. *Poppea*, p. 22.

24. In other circumstances, and years after writing *Poppea*, Busenello made a plainer statement about defamatory tongues. His concern here was not Nero and his point is made only in passing. However, it captures effectively the emperor's brutality in a way that went beyond politics all while illustrating how this poet distinguished civilized from barbaric behavior. Busenello writes that "a good conscience is calm and knows/ No storms, nor vexes at the wind that blows/ Let envious tongues my name with slander tear/ I am at peace within, and do not hear." See Francesco Busenello, *A Perspective of the Naval Triumph of the Venetians over the Turk*, trans. Thomas Higgons (London: Henry Harringman, 1658), p. D 8 (Pagination unclear in the original; orthography updated).

25. *Poppea*, p. 23.

26. Suetonius, "Nero," p. 222; Tacitus, *Annals*, pp. 363, 285.

27. Ellen Rosand, "Seneca and the Interpretation of *L'incoronazione di Poppea*," p. 11.

28. Tacitus, *Annals*, pp. 375–6.

29. *Poppea*, p. 20.

30. *Poppea*, p. 30.

31. *Poppea*, p. 32.

32. *Poppea*, pp. 33–4.

33. Pierre Bayle, "Crémonin (Cesar)," in *Dictionnaire historique et critique*, 5th ed., Vol. 1 (Amsterdam: P. Bunel, 1740), p. 224.

34. *Poppea*, p. 37.
35. *Poppea*, p. 52.
36. Recall Dido's retort when Jarbas asserts that women follow the wrong path; she says she agrees because they follow men.
37. Niccolò Machiavelli, *The Discourses* (Harmondsworth and Baltimore: Penguin Books, 1970), pp. 406–7.
38. Tacitus, *Annals*, p. 343.
39. Jean-François Lattarico, *Venise incognita*, p. 41.
40. The cultural role of the Incogniti can be compared usefully to a very different social group in crisis in the same era but in France. Lucien Goldmann sought to trace to the *noblesse de robe* (nobles of the robe, a legal aristocracy) a "tragic vision of the world" that found expression in Blaise Pascal's philosophy and Jean Racine's theater. See the Appendix to this book, "Backstage" and Lucien Goldmann, *Le Dieu caché* (Paris: Gallimard, 1955), p. 27.

Chapter 9: Agitations and Absolutes

1. Jean-Jacques Rousseau, "Chantre," in *Dictionnaire de Musique*, in Rousseau, *Oeuvres complètes* Vol. 5, *Écrits sur la musique, la langue et le théâtre* [Hereafter: Rousseau, *Oc, V*] (Paris: Gallimard: 1995), pp. 697–8.
2. Jean-Jacques Rousseau, *The Confessions* (Harmondsworth: Penguin, 1953), p. 358.
3. Jean Rond d'Alembert, "De la liberté de la musique," in Denise Launay, ed., *La Querelle des Bouffons: Texte des pamphlets*, Vol. 3 (Geneva: Minkoff, 1973), p. 2199.
4. Quoted in James B. Collins, *The State in Modern France* (Cambridge: Cambridge University Press, 1999), p. 121.
5. Jérôme de La Gôrce, *Jean-Baptiste Lully* (Paris: Fayard, 2002), p. 345.
6. I owe this formulation of Lully's musical "naturalization" to musicologist Catherine Kintzler.
7. Voltaire, *Le Siècle de Louis XIV* (Paris: Le Livre de Poche, 2002), p. 121.
8. *Acis et Galatée: Pastorale Heroïque en Musique Réprésentée pour la premiere fois dans le Château d'Anet devant Monsieur le Dauphin. Par l'Academie Roiale de Musique* (Paris, 1690), p. 3.
9. *Acis et Galatée*, pp. 14–16.
10. *Acis et Galatée*, p. 19.
11. *Acis et Galatée*, p. 28.
12. *Acis et Galatée*, pp. 32–3.
13. *Mercure de France*, September 1752, pp. 166–7.
14. For the background see Bernard Toscani, "*La Serva Padrona*: Variations on a Theme," in F. Degrada, ed., *Studia Pergolesiani*, 2 (NP: La Nuova Italia Editrice, 1988), pp. 185–93. Also see Patrick Barbier, *Jean-Baptiste Pergolèse* (Paris: Fayard/Mirare, 2003), ch. 3.
15. Gennaro Antonio Federico, *La serva padrona* [Hereafter: *Serva*] in Giovanna Gronda and Paolo Fabbri, eds., *Libretti d'opera italiani dal seicento al novecento* (Milan: Arnoldo Mondadori, 2007), p. 604.

16. *Serva*, p. 609.

17. See David Maland, *Culture and Society in Seventeenth Century France* (New York: Scribner, 1970), p. 83.

18. Jean-Jacques Rousseau, "Lettre sur la Musique françoise," in Rousseau, p. 328.

19. Rousseau, *Confessions*, pp. 358–9.

20. R.H.F. Scott, *Jean-Baptiste Lully* (London: Peter Owen, 1973), p. 12.

21. Here and in my general account of the late sixteenth century I cull from Robert M. Isherwood, *Music in the Service of the King: France in the 17th Century* (Ithaca and London: Cornell University Press, 1973), especially pp. 59–68.

22. See Isherwood, *Music in the Service of the King*, pp. 72–81.

23. See James R. Anthony, *French Baroque Music* (London: B.T. Batsford Ltd.), pp. 27–8.

24. Lois Rosow, "Power and Display: Music in Court Theater," in T. Carter and J. Butt, eds., *The Cambridge History of Seventeenth Century Music* (Cambridge: Cambridge University Press, 2005), p. 200.

25. Anthony, *French Baroque Music*, pp. 27–8.

26. A. Lloyd Moote, *Louis XIII: The Just* (Berkeley, Los Angeles and London: University of California Press, 1989), pp. 267–8, 226. For various ballets on political themes see Isherwood, p. 107 and Moote, pp. 267–8. The full title of *Ballet de Tancrède* was "The Ballet of Tancredi's Adventure in the Enchanted Forest" ("Ballet de l'aventure de *Tancrède* en la forêt enchantée").

27. See Christian Dupavillon, *Naissance de l'opéra en France, Orfeo, 2 Mars 1647* (Paris: Fayard, 2010), p. 39.

28. Anthony, *French Baroque Music*, p. 46.

29. I cull extensively from the account of Neal Zaslaw, "The First Opera in Paris: A Study in the Politics of Art," in J.H. Heyer, ed., *Jean-Baptiste Lully and the Music of the French Baroque: Essays in Honor of James R. Anthony* (Cambridge: Cambridge University Press, 1984). Also see de La Gorce, pp. 77–8.

30. Zaslaw, "The First Opera in Paris," pp. 16, 20. There are disputes about the production of this work. See the discussion in Roger Freitas, *Portrait of a Castrato: Politics, Patronage and Music in the Life of Atto Melani* (Cambridge: Cambridge University Press, 2009), p. 48.

31. Anthony, *French Baroque Music*, p. 47.

32. This is in Act 3 of the original 1647 manuscript from Rome (including libretto and score) copied by Roman Rolland, at the Bibliothèque nationale de France, Department of Music, Res. 1785.

33. See Patrick Riley, *The General Will before Rousseau: The Transformation of the Divine into the Civic* (Princeton: Princeton University Press, 1986), pp. ix–xiii, 4–14.

34. "Histoire d'Orphée," reproduced in Luigi Rossi and Francesco Buti, *Orfeo* (Montpellier: Opéra de Montpellier, 1990), p. 21.

35. Scott, *Lully*, p. 15; also see de La Gôrce, p. 45.

36. Isherwood, *Music in the Service of the King*, p. 124; Anthony, *French Baroque Music*, p. 47.

37. James R. Anthony, "Jean-Baptiste Lully," in *French Baroque Masters* (New York and London: W.W. Norton, 1986), pp. 18–19.

38. For one instance, see the film *Le Roi danse*, made in 2000 and directed by André Corbiau.

39. Scott, p. 100.
40. Scott, *Lully*, pp. 64, 67.
41. De la Gôrce, p. 120.
42. See Scott, pp. 100–105 and de la Gôrce, pp. 306–13.
43. Jean d'Alembert, *Preliminary Discourse to the Encyclopedia of Diderot* (Chicago: University of Chicago Press, 1995), p. 68.
44. Isherwood, *Music in the Service of the King*, p. 213.
45. Philippe Beaussant, *Lully ou le musicien du soleil* (Paris: Gallimard, 1992), p. 800.
46. See Weiss and Taruskin, p. 202, and also "Saint-Évremond's Views on Opera," in Pietro Weiss, ed., *Opera: A History in Documents* (New York and Oxford: Oxford University Press, 2002), p. 56.
47. Philippe Quinault, "Livret" in Jean-Baptiste Lully, *Armide*, édition de Lois Rosow in *Oeuvres complètes*, Série III, Vol. 14 (Hildesheim, Zurich, New York: Georg Olms Verlag, 2003), p. 9.
48. For background see the "Introduction" in Lully, *Armide*, Rosow edition.
49. Rousseau, "Lettre," pp. 325–6.
50. Rousseau, "Lettre," p. 328.
51. Rousseau, "Lettre," pp. 304–5, 292–3.
52. For valuable commentary on the Rameau-Rousseau debate on *Armide* see Charles Dill, *Monstrous Opera: Rameau and the Tragic Tradition* (Princeton: Princeton University Press, 1998), pp. 65–7.

Chapter 10: In the Winds: The Decades of Pernucio and Telemachus

1. For examples of opposed views see Anthony D. Smith, *The Ethnic Origins of Nations* (Oxford: Blackwell, 1987) and Benedict Anderson, *Imagined Communities: Reflections on the Origins and Spread of Nationalism* (London: Verso, 2006). I sidestep important but more elaborate discussions of words like nation, nationalism, patriotism, and polity.
2. "*Enfin former son jeu sur le bon goût d'aujourd'hui qui est sans comparaison plus pur que l'Ancien.*" François Couperin, *L'Art de Toucher le Clavecin,*" in *Oeuvres complètes de François Couperin*, 1, *Oeuvres didactiques* (Paris: Éditions de L'Oiseau-Lyre, 1933), p. 58.
3. Anthony, *French Baroque Music*, p. 34.
4. Paul Hazard, *The Crisis of the European Mind, 1680–1715* (New York: New York Review of Books, 2013), pp. xiii, xviii.
5. Claude-François Ménestrier, *Des représentations en musique anciennes et modernes* (Paris: 1681), p. 107.
6. Jacques Bonnet, "From *History of Music . . .*" in Enrico Fubini, "Introduction" to *Music and Culture in 18th Century Europe: A Source Book* (Henceforth: *Fubini*) (Chicago and London: University of Chicago Press, 1994), p. 160. This book was written partly from research and notes taken in previous decades by other members of the author's family.
7. Antoine Danchet, "Approbation," in François Couperin, *L'Art de Toucher le Clavecin, Oeuvres complètes de François Couperin*, 1, *Oeuvres didactiques* (Paris: Éditions de L'Oiseau-Lyre, 1933), p. 72, It is dated March 1716.

8. See Daniel Heartz and Bruce Alan Brown, "Galant," in *The New Grove Dictionary of Music and Musicians*, 2nd ed., Vol. 9 (London: MacMillan, 2001), pp. 430–2.

9. François Couperin, "Préface" to "Premier Livre," *Oeuvres complètes de François Couperin, II, 1; Pièces de Clavecin* (Monaco: Éditions de L'Oiseau-Lyre, 1980), p. 10.

10. François Couperin, "Préface" to "Les Goûts-réunis" (1724), *Oeuvres complètes de François Couperin, IV, 2; Musique de Chambre* (Monaco: Éditions de L'Oiseau-Lyre, 1988), p. 13.

11. François Couperin, "Les Nations," *Oeuvres complètes de François Couperin, IV, 3; Musique de Chambre* (Monaco: Éditions de L'Oiseau-Lyre, 1987), pp. 6, 14. Also see Philippe Beaussant, *François Couperin* (Paris: Fayard, 1980), p. 68.

12. My discussion here rests on and draws many details from Edward T. Corp, "The Exiled Court of James II and James III: A Centre of Italian Music in France, 1689–1712," *Journal of the Royal Musical Association*, Vol. 12, No. 2 (1995), pp. 216–31; Corp, "Melfort: A Jacobite Connoisseur," *History Today*, Vol. 45, No. 10; Corp, "The Musical Manuscripts of 'Copyist Z': David Nairne, "François Couperin, and the Stuart Court at Saint-German-en-Laye," *Revue de Musicologie*, Vol. 84, No. 1, 1998, and Corp and Eveline Crutsckshanks, eds., *The Stuart Court in Exile and the Jacobites* (London: Hambledon Press, 1995).

13. David Fuller, "Of Portraits, 'Sappho,' and Couperin: Titles and Characters in French Instrumental Music of the High Baroque," *Music and Letters* Vol. 78, No. 2, May 1997, p. 165.

14. I draw from Frances A. Yates, *Aristaea: The Imperial Theme in The Sixteenth Century* (London and Boston: Routledge and Kegan Paul, 1975) and Corrado Vivanti, "Henri IV, the Gallic Hercules," *Journal of the Warburg and Couthauld Institutes*, 333 (1967). See Thomas A. Downing, *Aesthetics of Opera in the Ancien Régime, 1647–1785* (Cambridge: Cambridge University Press, 2002), p. 88.

15. On imperial self-justifications, see Anthony Pagden, *Lords of the World: Ideologies of Empire in Spain, Britain and France c. 1500-c.1800* ((New Haven and London: Yale University Press, 1995).

16. Thomas Higginbottom, "François Couperin," *New Grove*, Vol. 4, p. 861.

17. Comte de Louville quoted in E.K. Sanders, *Fénelon: His Friends and Foes* (London: Longmans, Green, and Co., 1901), p. 46.

18. François de Fénelon, "César et Caton," in *Dialogues des morts composés pour l'education d'un prince*, in *Oeuvres* 1 (Paris: Gallimard,/Pléiade, 1983), p. 406.

19. Fénelon, "Socrate et Alcibiade" in *Dialogues des morts*, p. 508.

20. On Fénelon's political views as well as his influence on Rousseau, see especially Patrick Riley, "Rousseau, Fénelon, and the Quarrel between the Ancients and Moderns," in Patrick Riley, ed., *The Cambridge Companion to Rousseau* (Cambridge: Cambridge University Press, 2001), pp. 93.

21. Fénelon, "Lettre à Louis XIV," in *Oeuvres* 1, p. 544. This edition dates the letter as "Dec. 1693?"

22. François de Fénelon, *Telemachus, Son of Ulysses*, Patrick Riley trans. (Cambridge: Cambridge University Press, 1994), p. 307.

23. Fénelon, *Telemachus*, pp. 61, 67, 60.

24. "Avertissement" to *Cantates françoises, mêlées de symphonies par Monsiuer Campra, Livre premier, Nouvelle Edition* (Paris: Ballard, 1721), p. 3. Facsimile in André Campra, *Cantates*, Vol. 2 (New York and London: Garland Publishing, 1990).

25. The unsigned libretto acknowledges the contributions of others. See *Télemaque: Tragédie, Fragmens des Modernes, Représentée pour la première fois par l'Academie de Musique, L'Onzième jour de Novembre 1704* (Amsterdam: Henri Schelte, n.d./ Recueil des Opera, Vol. 10, 1708).

26. See *Télémaque et Calypso: Tragédie en Musique* par Monsieur Destouches, Inspecteur Général de l'Académie Royale de Musique (Paris: Ballard, 1714), at the Bibliotèque de l'Opéra, Paris, A. 90.a.

27. Jacques-Bénigne Bossuet, *Politique tirée des propres paroles de l'Écriture sainte* (Geneva: Librairie-Droz, 1967), pp. 92, 96–7, 94.

28. See Nannerl O. Keohane, *Philosophy and the State in France* (Princeton: Princeton University Press, 1980), pp. 322–43.

29. Fénelon, *Telemachus*, pp. 66–7, 298.

30. Fénelon, "Socrate, Alcibade et Timon" in *Dialogues des morts*, p. 338.

31. Fénelon, *Telemachus*, pp. 300–301.

32. Wilifred Mellers, *François Couperin* (London: Dobson, 1950), pp. 168–9.

33. Jeffrey S. Ravel, *The Contested Parterre: Public Theater and French Political Culture, 1680–1791* (Ithaca and London: Cornell University Press, 1999), p. 110.

34. Georgia J. Cowart, *The Triumph of Pleasure* (Chicago: University of Chicago Press, 2008), p. 223.

35. It included several airs by his friend André Cardinal Destouches (both men preferred at first to remain anonymous). See Andrew Stiller, "L'Europe galante," Vol. 12 of Grove.

36. Quoted in James R. Anthony, "The French-Ballet Opera in the Early 18th Century: Problems of Definition and Classification," *Journal of the American Musicological Society*, Vol. 18 No. 2 (Summer 1965), pp. 202, 197–98. (My translation).

37. Houdar de la Motte, "Avis," *L'Europe galante: Balet en musique* in *Oeuvres de Monsieur Houdar de la Motte*, Vol. 6 (Paris: Prault, 1754), p. 10. I have quoted from different early printed librettos because of additions and changes made in early performances. The same quote is found in the "Avis" between the Prologue and the beginning of the *Entrées* in *L'Europe galante, Balet, Remis au théâtre par l'Académie Royale de Musique* (Paris: Ribous, 1724), p. xvi. It played also on August 20, 1715 and June 20, 1724. Citations from *Entrées* come from the latter text.

38. *L'Europe Galante, Balet*, p. 4.

39. *L'Europe Galante, Balet*, p. 11.

40. *L'Europe Galante, Balet*, p. 37.

41. This is pointed out by Anthony, p. 139.

42. See Jacques Bénigne Bossuet, *Maximes et réflexions sur la comedie* (Paris: Annison, 1694), especially part 3.

43. François Raguenet, *Paralele des Italiens et des François ce qui regarde la Musique et Les Opéra* (Paris: Moreau, 1702) [Geneva: Minkoff reprint, 1976], pp. 36–7. My discussion is informed by Fubini's introduction to these debates in his anthology.

44. Jean-Laurent Le Cerf de la Viéville, "Comparison of French and Italian Music," in *Fubini*, pp. 74–5.
45. Jean Terrasson, *Dissertation critique sur l'Iliade d'Homer* (Paris: F, Fiunier and FA. U.- Coustelier, 1715) quoted in Isherwood, *Music in the Service of the King*, p. 44.
46. See Downing, *Aesthetics*, p. 48.
47. Jean-Baptiste Du Bos, "*Réflexions critiques sur la poésie et sur la peinture*" in Peter le Huray and James Day, eds., *Music and Aesthetics in the Eighteenth and Early Nineteenth Centuries* [Hereafter: *L H/D*] Cambridge and New York: Cambridge University Press, 1988), p. 19; Trans. modified. See Jean-Baptiste Du Bos, *Réflexions critiques sur la poesie et sur la peinture* Vol. 1. (Paris: P-J Mariette, 1733), pp. 444–6.
48. Charles Batteux, "Les Beaux-arts réduit à un même principe" in *LH/D*, p. 36. While I use this translation I have made occasional modifications on the basis of the published version of this essay in Charles Batteux, *Principes de littérature* Nouvelle édition, Vol. 1. (Gottigue and Leide: Elie Luzar Fils, 1755), p. 6 and p. 8.
49. Batteux, in *LH/D*, p. 38.
50. Batteux, in *LH/D*, p. 37 (*Principes*, p. 10).
51. Batteux, in *LH/D*, p. 41.
52. Batteux, in *LH/D*, pp. 43, 45.
53. D'Alembert, *Preliminary Discourse*, p. 4.
54. D'Alembert, *Preliminary Discourse*, p. 100.

Un court intermède

1. See Robert Darnton, *Poetry and the Police: Communication Networks in Eighteenth Century France* (Cambridge Mass. and London: Harvard University Press, 2010), pp. 7–11, 41–2.
2. Dénis Diderot, *Les Bijoux indiscrets* (Paris: Gallimard, 1981), p. 39.
3. Diderot, *Bijoux*, p. 288.
4. Diderot, *Bijoux*, p. 42.
5. Darnton, *Poetry and the Police*, p. 43.
6. Diderot, *Bijoux*, p. 43.
7. Diderot, *Bijoux*, pp. 46–7.
8. Diderot, *Bijoux*, p. 77.
9. Diderot, *Bijoux*, p. 77.
10. Catherine Kintzler, *Jean-Philippe Rameau: Splendour et naufrage du plaisir de l'esthétique à l'Âge Classique* (Paris: Le Sycamore, 1983), p. 133. My understanding of Rameau's musical thinking is indebted to her study and to Thomas Christensen's *Rameau and the Musical Thought of the Enlightenment* (Cambridge: Cambridge University Press, 1995).
11. Quoted in Cuthbert Girdlestone, *Jean Phillippe Rameau, His Life and Work* (New York: Dover Publications), p. 7. The letter was dated October 25, 1727.
12. Girdlestone, pp. 21–2.
13. Kintzler, *Rameau*, p. 133.

14. Jean-Philippe Rameau, *Treatise on Harmony* (New York: Dover Publications, 1971), p. 59.
15. Rameau, *Treatise*, pp. xxxiii-xxxv.
16. Rameau, *Treatise*, p. 139.
17. Maynard Solomon describes the "the superstructure of Baroque style" in comparison to classicism. See his *Beethoven* (New York: Schirmer Books, 1979), p. 295.
18. Rameau, "Observations on our Instinct for Music and its Principle," trans. in Jean-Jacques Rousseau, *Essay on the Origins of Language and Writings Related to Music* (Hanover and London: University Press of New England, 1998), p. 178. The fundamental bass is indeterminate in twentieth-century atonal music.
19. Rameau, *Treatise*, 154–5.
20. Rameau, "Observations . . .", p. 175.
21. Rameau, "Réflexions de M. Rameau," *Mercure de France*, October 1752, pp. 91–2.
22. *Bijoux*, pp. 78–9
23. *Bijoux*, p. 96.
24. *Bijoux*, p. 77.

Chapter 11: Vertical, Horizontal

1. Rousseau, *Confessions*, p. 312.
2. Cranston, *Jean-Jacques: The Early Life and Work of Jean-Jacques Rousseau, 1712–1754* (Chicago and London: University of Chicago Press, 1982), p. 158.
3. Rameau, "Erreurs sur la Musique dans l'Encylopédie," (Paris: Sebastien Jorry, 1755), p. 13, reproduced in facsimile in Rameau, *Complete Theoretical Writings*, Vol. 5, Edwin R. Jacobi ed. (N.P.: American Institute of Musicology, 1969), p. 203.
4. See Kintzler, *Rameau*, p. 133. My thanks to Lois Rosow for clarifications of Rameau's claims about harmonic procedures.
5. Rameau, *Treatise*, p. 156.
6. Louis Fuzelier, "Avertissement," *La Reine des Péris, Comédie persane, répresenté par l'Académie Royale de Musique L'an 1725* (Paris; Ribous, 1725), p. 2.
7. Louis Fuzelier, "Avertissement," to *Les Indes Galantes: Ballet Héroique Représenté pour la première fois par l'Academie Royale de Musique Le Mardy Vingt-troisème d'aoust 1735* (Paris: Ballard, 1735), p. iii.
8. *Indes*, p. 6.
9. *Indes*, p. 6.
10. *Indes*, pp. 8–9.
11. Fatma Murge Goçek, *East Encounters West: France and the Ottoman Empire in the 18th Century* (New York: Oxford University Press, 1987), pp. 2, 47, 154 fn 99; and *Mercure*, March 1721. Mehmet Effendi saw *Thesée* by Lully and Quinault, *Omphale* by Destouches and Houdar la Motte, and *Les Fêtes Venitiennes* by Campra and Danchet.
12. On these developments see Orhan Kologlu, *Le Turc dans la presse française des débuts jusqu'a 1815* (Beyrouth: Maison d'Editions al-Hayat, 1971), pp. 149 and 181.
13. See, Le Vte de Jonquière, *Histoire de l'empire ottoman*, Vol. 1 (Paris: La Hachette, 1914), pp. 292–3. Peter Wilding also devotes a chapter to Bonneval in his *Adventurers in the Eighteenth Century* (New York: G.P. Putnam's Sons, 1950).

14. Fuzelier, "Avertissement" to *Les Indes galantes,* p. iii.

15. "M. D.L.C. to M. D.L.R." *Mercure de France,* January, 1734, pp. 74, 79, 87–8. It is likely that the author of the letter, "M. D.L.C.," was explorer-scientist Charles-Marie de la Condamine. "M. D.L.R." was probably Antoine de la Roque. The letter is dated January 18, 1734. He was Fuzelier's colleague at this publication and had been a friend also of Watteau. On de la Roque, see Georgia J. Cowart, *The Triumph of Pleasure* (Chicago: University of Chicago Press, 2008), p. 223.

16. *Indes,* p. 14.

17. *Indes,* p. 4.

18. *Indes,* p. 19.

19. *Indes,* p. 21.

20. *Indes,* pp. 23–4.

21. *Indes,* p. 29.

22. *Indes,* p. 30.

23. *Indes,* p. 30.

24. *Indes* , p. 31.

25. Fuzelier, "Avertissement," *Indes,* p. iv.

26. *Indes,* p. 34.

27. *Indes,* p. 42.

28. *Indes,* p. 46.

29. *Indes,* pp. 46–7.

30. *Indes,* p. 44.

31. *Indes,* p. 55.

32. This *Entrée* was redone a number of times because its weakness was so evident. In its first revision Fatima is Sultana and disguises herself as a slave to find out if Tacmas, her husband, is unfaithful. (He isn't.) My discussion is based on the first published libretto, cited above, that included this act along with first two *Entrées.*

33. *Indes,* pp. 57–8.

34. For "Sauvages": *Les Indes Galantes: Ballet-Héroïque représenté par l'Académie Royale de Musique par le premier fois, le Mardy 23. Aoust 1735, Remis avec la Nouvelle Entrée, Les Sauvages, le Samedy dixiéme Mars 1736* (Paris: Ballard, 1736), p. 4.

35. "Sauvages," p. 5.

36. "Sauvages," pp. 6–7.

37. On the Pizzaros and on Colbert's miscegenation policy see Pagden, *Lords of the World,* pp. 149–50.

38. Louis-Armand, Baron de Lahontan, *Dialogues de Monsieur le Baron Lahontan et d'un Sauvage dans l'Amérique* (Amsterdam: Chez le Veuve de Boeteman, 1704), n.p.

39. Lahontan, *Dialogues,* p. 23.

40. Dénis Diderot, "Extracts from *Histoire des Deux Indes,*" in *Political Writings* (Cambridge and New York: Cambridge University Press, 1992), p. 175.

Chapter 12: Nature and Its Discontents

1. Rousseau, *Confessions*, pp. 352–3.
2. Jean-Jacques Rousseau, "Le Devin du Village," in *Oc.* Vol. 3. (Paris: Gallimard, 1964), nf, a, p. p. 1886 (stage direction) and p. 1102 for the text. It is easy, nonetheless, to imagine that Rousseau enjoyed the fact that the original published text of the libretto declared that it was first presented before the king. See *Le Devin du Village, Intermède, Représentée à Fontainbleau avant le Roy les 18 & 24 Octobre 1752 & à Paris par l'Académie Royale de Musique, Le Jeudy premier Mars 1753* (Paris: V. Delformel & Fils, 1753).
3. Rousseau, "*Le Devin*," in *Oc*, p. 1105.
4. See fn "a" in *Oc*, providing the directions to "*Le Devin*," pp. 1887–8.

Chapter 13: From Elysium to Utica

1. See Cliff Eisen, "Salzburg under Church Rule," in Neal Zaslaw, ed., *The Classical Era* (Englewood Cliffs, New Jersey: Prentice Hall, 1989), pp. 166–77.
2. Josef-Horst Lederer, "Scipio as a Historical Figure," in booklet accompanying Mozart, *Il Sogno di Scipio, Complete Mozart Edition* (Philips: London, 1979), p. 28.
3. Metastasio to Farinelli, December 12, 1765, in Charles Burney, *Memoirs of the Life and Writings of the Abate Metastasio in which are Incorporated Translations of his Principal Letters*, Vol. 2 [of three volumes. Hereafter: Burney/Metastasio] (London: Robinson, 1796), p. 363.
4. Leopold Mozart to Lorenz Hagenauer, July 30, 1768 in Emily Anderson, ed., *The Letters of Mozart and his Family*, [Hereafter: *LMF*] Vol. 1 (London: Macmillan, 1938), pp. 130–1.
5. Metastasio to Sig. Filipponi, June 10, 1751, in Burney/Metastasio, Vol. 2, p. 7.
6. See Isabelle Moindrot, *L'opéra seria ou la règne des castrats* (Paris: Fayard, 1993), pp. 20–2. The history of comic opera is also more wide-ranging than implied by the use of the term "opera buffa." Published libretti usually did not employ these terms. I will nonetheless use them for the sake of simplicity.
7. Burney on Metastasio's "Muse" in Burney/Metastasio, Vol. 1, p. 158; for Metastasio's disclaimer, see Metastasio to the Count of Udine, February 13, 1760, Burney/Metastasio, Vol. 2, p. 227. For a source on the general background, from which I have taken many details, see Jacques Joly, *Les Fêtes théâtrales de Métastase à la cour de Vienne (1731–1767)* (Clermont-Ferrand: Université de Clermont-Ferrand II: Faculté des Lettres et Sciences Humaines, 1978), especially pp. 17–18. Also see the special issue on Metastasio of *Early Music*, November 1998.
8. "Fortune" in Metastasio to Farinelli, August 26, 1747, in Burney/Metastasio, Vol. 1, p. 202; "On the Empire," in Metastasio to Carlo Cavalli of Ravenna, cited in Burney/Metastasio, Vol. 2, p. 179.
9. Metastasio to "A Gentleman of Modena," in Burney/Metastasio, Vol. 2, pp. 42–4.
10. Metastasio to Farinelli, July 18, 1765, in Burney/Metastasio, Vol. 2, p. 252.
11. Metastasio to Nicola Jomelli, May 29, 1769, in Burney/Metastasio, Vol. 2, p. 387.

12. Moindrot, *L'opéra seria*, pp. 32–3.

13. Metastasio to Chevalier de Chastelleux, July 15, 1765, Burney/Metastasio, Vol. 2, p. 320.

14. Ludovico Antonio Muratori, *Della perfetta poesia italiana (On Perfecting Italian Poetry)*, quoted in *Fubini*, pp. 19–20.

15. Muratori, *Della perfetta*, pp. 39–42.

16. Muratori, *Della perfetta*, pp. 45–7.

17. See Fubini, "Introduction," p. 20, Don Neville, "Moral Philosophy in Metatatasian Drama, in *Studies in Music from the University of Western Ontario*, Vol. 12, 1982, pp. 28–46 and his "Metastasio" in *The New Grove Dictionary of Opera*, Vol. 3 (London: Macmillan, 1982), pp. 351–61.

18. Gian Vincenzo Gravina, "On Tragedy," in Fubini, pp. 36–7.

19. Quoted by Nino Pirrotta, "Metastasio and the Demands of his Literary Environment," *Studies in Music from the University of Western Ontario*, Vol. 71, 1982, pp. 15–16.

20. Metastasio to Farinelli, December 27, 1749, Burney/Metastasio, Vol. 1, p. 297; Metastasio to the Chevalier de Castellux, July 15, 1765, Burney/Metastasio, Vol. 2, pp. 318–20; Metastasio to the Chevalier de Castellux, January 14, 1766, Burney/Metastasio, Vol. 2, p. 322.

21. Metastasio to Tommaso Filipponi, October 14, 1762, Burney/Metastasio, Vol. 2, p. 262.

22. Metastasio to Saverio Mattei, July 9, 1770, Burney/Metastasio, Vol. 2, p. 412.

23. Metastasio to Saverio Mattei, April 25, 1770 and July 9, 1770, Burney/Metastasio, Vol. 2, pp. 404–5 and Metastasio to Chevalier de Chastellux, January 14, 1766, Burney/Metastasio, Vol. 2, p. 326.

24. Metastasio to Chevalier de Chastellex, January 14, 1766, Burney/Metastasio, Vol. 2, pp. 324–6. I have on occasion modified the translation. De Chastellux's book, published in 1765, was titled *Essai sur l'union de la poésie et de la musique*.

25. For the play's history see Stephen Miller, "Why Cato Had to Die," *Times Literary Supplement*, October 1, 1999, p. 14. I also draw upon the "Note" to *Catone in Utica* in *Tutte le opere di Pietro Metastasio* a cura di Bruno Brunelli, Vol. 1 (NP: Arnoldo Mondadori Editore, 1953), n.p. Also see Ernest Warburton, "Introduction," *Catone in Utica: Opera Seria in Three Acts. Libretto after Metastasio, The Collected Works of Johann Christian Bach, 1735–1782* Vol. 2 (New York and London: Garland Publishing Inc., 1987), p. viii.

26. Lily Ross Taylor, *Party Politics in the Age of Caesar* (Berkeley, Los Angeles, and London: University of California Press, 1971), p. 163.

27. Plutarch, "Cato the Younger," *The Lives of the Noble Grecians and Romans*, Vol. 2, John Dryden trans. (New York: Modern Library, 1992), pp. 270–2.

28. Plutarch, "Cato," p. 281.

29. Plutarch, "Cato," pp. 284–5.

30. "Argomento" of *Catone in Utica* in *Tutte le opere di Pietro Metastasio*, Vol. 1, n.p.

31. Charles de Brosses, *Lettres familières sur l'Italie*, Vol. 2 (Paris: Firmin-Didot, 1931 [1753]), p. 354.

32. Burney in Burney/Metastasio, Vol. 1, pp. 40–1.

33. Ivan Nagel, *Autonomy and Mercy* (Cambridge and London: Harvard University Press, 1991).

Zwischenspiel (I)

1. Charles Burney, *A General History of Music*, Vol. 4 (London: Payne and Co., 1789), p. 27.
2. Charles Burney, *An Eighteenth Century Musical Tour in France and Italy* (Oxford: Oxford University Press, 1959[1773]), p. 314 and Burney, *The Present State of Music in France and Italy* [2nd edition] (London: Becket, Robson, Robinson, 1773), pp. 47, 27.
3. Burney to Frances Burney, October 12, 1806, in "Some Burney Letters," Percy A. Scholes, *The Great Burney*, Vol. 2 (London, New York, Toronto: Oxford University Press, 1948), p. 310.
4. Edmund Burke, "A Philosophical Inquiry into the Sublime and Beautiful" [Hereafter: *Philosophical Inquiry* for this essay] in Burke, *A Philosophical Inquiry into the Sublime and Beautiful and Other Pre-Revolutionary Writings* [Hereafter: *PI* for this volume] (London / New York: Pengiun, 1998), p. 156. Throughout this discussion I update spellings.
5. Edmund Burke, "Thoughts on the Cause of the Present Discontents" in Burke, *PI*, p. 232.
6. Burke, *Philosophical Inquiry*, pp. 155–6.
7. Burke, *Philosophical Inquiry*, pp. 151.
8. Burke, *Philosophical Inquiry*, pp. 156.
9. These comments were made just after Burke's death. Burney to Fanny Burney, July 20, 1797. *The Letters of Dr. Charles Burney*, Vol. 2 (Oxford: Clarendon Press, 1991), p. 410. See Scholes especially on the relation between Burke and Burney.
10. Burney to Mrs. Crewe, December 2, 1792.
11. Burney, *General History* Vol. 4, pp. 517–18.
12. Burney to Mrs. Crewe, February 19, 1784, *The Letters of Dr. Charles Burney*, Vol. 1 (1751–1784) (Oxford: Clarendon Press, 1991), p. 410.
13. Burney to Mrs. Crewe, February 19, *Le H/D*, Vol. 1, p. 264.
14. Gluck, Letter to *Mercure de France*, (p. 182) Feb. 1773, in *Le H/D*, p. 115.
15. Ranieri de' Calzabigi and C. W. Gluck, "Preface to *Alceste*, (1769)," in *Fubini*, pp. 364–5.
16. Charles Burney, *The Present State of Music in Germany, the Netherlands and United Provinces* (2nd edition), edited by P. Sehaler as *Dr. Burney's Musical Tours* (Oxford: Oxford University Press, 1959). The language of one of Burney's few direct comments on a political event some years later suggests that he retained his judgment of factionalism, although his remark in this case could have just been in response to the occasion. During clashes between Protestants and Catholics ("the Gordon Riots") over religious toleration Burney remarked sourly on "the pusillanimity of one party and the malignity of another." Burney to Thomas Twining, June 11, 1780, *The Letters of Dr. Charles Burney*, Vol. 1, p. 301. On the British elections of 1784 see W.A. Speck, *A Concise History of Britain 1707–1975* (Cambridge: Cambridge University Press, 1993), pp. 42–3.

17. Michael Kelly, *Reminiscences of Michael Kelly, of the King's Theater and Theatre Royal Drury Lane* Vol. 1 (London: Henry Colburn, 1826), p. 210. For the summary of Calzabigi's life, see Patricia Howard, *C.W. Gluck, Orfeo* (Cambridge: Cambridge University Press, 1981), p. 16 and Brue Alan Brown, *Gluck and the French Theater in Vienna* (Oxford: Oxford University Press, 1991), p. 46, 361.
18. See Howard, *C.W. Gluck, Orfeo*, p. 16.
19. See Brown, *Gluck and the French Theater*, especially pp. 3–19.
20. Quoted in Howard, p. 68. Gluck made the comment in *Mercure* in February 1773.
21. Burney, *Present State of Music in Germany, the Netherlands and United Provinces* (2nd edition), pp. 81–82.
22. Metastasio to Giacomo Martorelli, August 19, 1771 in Burney/Metastasio, Vol. 3, pp. 110–111.
23. Quoted in Derek Beales, "Christians and Philosophes," in his *Enlightenment and Reform in Eighteenth Century Europe* (London and New York: I.B. Tauris, 2005), p. 74.

Chapter 14: From Crete to Rome

1. For "general theme," Giorgio Pestelli, *The Age of Mozart and Beethoven* (Cambridge: Cambridge University Press, 1990), p. 80. "Musical effects" quoted by John Eliot Gardiner, "Idomeneo: A Reappraisal," in the booklet accompanying *Idomeneo* (Hamburg: Deutsche Grammophon Ghbh/Archiv Recording, 1991), p. 13.
2. See "Nachschrift Mozart and Seine Schwester," Wolfgang Amadeus Mozart, *Briefe und Aufzeichnungen*, Band I (Kassel: Bärenreiter-Verlag, 2005), p. 388. It is dated September 8, 1770.
3. W.A. Mozart and Giambattista Varesco, *Idomeneo* in *Seven Mozart Librettos: A Verse Translation by J.D. McClatchy* [Hereafter: *SML*] (New York and London: Norton, 2011), pp. 43, 53, 49. These citations for the libretto follow McClatchy's translation, which I have found satisfying poetically and intelligent although I modify or amend it where I think more literalness captures political or other resonances in the original. I do likewise for *La clemenza di Tito*.
4. *Idomeneo*, pp. 93, 97.
5. *Idomeneo*, p. 117.
6. *Idomeneo*, p.123.
7. *Idomeneo*, p. 127.
8. *Idomeneo*, p. 127.
9. *Idomeneo*, p. 129.
10. Quoted by Beales in "Philosophical Kingship and Enlightened Despotism" in his *Enlightenment and Reform*, p. 41.
11. John A. Rice, *W.A. Mozart: La Clemenza di Tito* (Cambridge: Cambridge University Press, 1991), p. 13.
12. Cited in Rice, *W.A. Mozart: La Clemenza di Tito*, p. 11.
13. "Domenico de Guardusoni's Contract with the Bohemian Estates, 8 July, 1791," Document 107 in *New Mozart Documents: A Supplement to O.E. Deutsch's Doc-*

umentary Biography (London: MacMillan, 1991), p. 67. See Rice, *W.A. Mozart: La Clemenza di Tito*, p. 11 and H.C. Landon, *1791: Mozart's Last Year* (London: Thames and Hudson, 1999), p. 97.

14. On Mazzolà and Mozart's transformation of Metastasio's text, see especially, Rice, pp. 35–7. On action ensembles, also see *W.A. Mozart, Don Giovanni*, p. 140. For a useful discussion with a different emphasis, see Anthony Arblaster, *Viva la Libertà* (London and New York: Verso, 1992), p. 95–9.

15. Rushton, p. 99.

16. For details on the opera's reception, see Rice, *W.A. Mozart: La Clememza di Tito*, pp. 1–9. Also see Daniel Heartz, "Mozart and his Italian Contemporaries: La Clemenza di Tito," *Mozart-Jahrbuch*, 1978–79 (Basel, Tours, London: Bärenreiter Kassel, 1979); Marita P. McClymonds, "Mozart's 'La Clemenza di Tito,' and Opera Seria in Florence as a Reflection of Leopold II's Musical Tastes," *Mozart-Jahrbuch*, 1984–1985 (Basel, Tours, London: Bärenreiter Kassel, 1989).

17. Stendhal, *Life of Mozart*, (Montreal: Guernica, 1991), p. 72.

18. W.A. Mozart and Caterino Mazzolà (adopted from Pietro Metastasio), *La Clemenza di Tito* in *SML* [Hereafter: *Tito*], p. 885.

19. *Tito*, p. 887.

20. Rice, *W.A. Mozart: La Clememza di Tito*, p. 83.

21. *Tito*, p. 924.

22. See Rice, p. 63 and Donald Heartz, *Mozart's Operas*, edited with contributing essays by Thomas Bauman. (Berkeley, Los Angeles, London: University of California Press, 1990), pp. 325–29.

23. *Tito*, p. 939.

24. *Tito*, p. 945.

25. *Tito*, p. 947.

26. *Tito*, p. 951.

27. Cicero, "Laelius, or On Friendship," in Cicero, *On Living and Dying Well* (London and New York: Penguin Books, 2012), p. 89.

28. Cicero, "Laelius, or On Friendship," p. 98.

29. *Tito*, p. 487.

30. *Tito*, pp. 954–7. He wonders, then, about "*ingiuria del giusto*" as a problem for justice, not only "injury to the law," as the translation reads.

31. *Tito*, p. 957.

32. *Tito*, p. 973.

33. *Tito*, p. 490.

Chapter 15: Masters and Servants

1. Solomon, *Mozart*, p. 9

2. Leopold Mozart, *Versuch einer gründlichen Violinschule* (Vienna: Carl Stephenson, 1922; facsimile of the original 1756 edition), p. 5.

3. On Mozart in Salzburg, see Cliff Eisen, "Mozart and Salzburg" in Simon P. Keefe, ed., *The Cambridge Companion to Mozart*, (Cambridge: Cambridge University Press, 2003) and the same author's "Salzburg under Church Rule,"

in Zaslaw, ed., *The Classical Era* (Englewood Cliffs, NJ: Prentice Hall, 1989), pp. 166–187.

4. Mozart to Leopold Mozart, May 9, 1781, in *The Letters of Mozart and his Family* [Hereafter: *LMF*], Vol. 2, 2nd ed., Emily Anderson, ed. and trans. (London/New York: MacMillan/St. Martin's Press, 1966), pp. 727–8.

5. Mozart to Leopold Mozart, June 9, 1781, in *LMF*, Vol. 2, p. 741. Mozart's words are "*einem Tritt im Arsch.*" *Mozart, Briefe und Aufzeichnungen*, Vol. 3, p. 127.

6. Mozart to Leopold Mozart, July 12, 1783, in *LMF*, Vol. 2, p. 856.

7. Mozart to Leopold Mozart, August 8, 1781, in *LMF*, Vol. 2, pp. 757–8.

8. Derek Beales, *Joseph II*, Vol. 2 (Cambridge: Cambridge University Press, 2009), p. 469.

9. Johann Pezzl, *Pezzl's Sketch of Vienna, Part 1, 1786*, translated in H.C. Robbin Landon's *Mozart and Vienna* (New York: Schirmer Books, 1991), p. 129–30.

10. Pezzl, pp. 65–8.

11. Steven Beller, *A Concise History of Austria* (Cambridge/New York: Cambridge University Press, 2006), p. 99. On the Masons in Mozart's Vienna, see also Beales, *Joseph II*, Vol. 2, pp. 526–43, and Till, *Mozart and the Enlightenment*.

12. See Solomon, *Mozart*, pp. 321–35.

13. Pezzl, p. 70.

14. Pezzl, p. 72.

15. Pezzl, p. 77.

16. Mary Hunter, *The Culture of Opera Buffa in Mozart's Vienna* (Princeton: Princeton University Press, 1999), p. 6.

17. Carlo Goldoni, "The Author to the Reader" of "Off to the Country," *The Holiday Trilogy* (New York: Marsilio, 1992), p. 4.

18. Pezzl, pp. 147–9.

19. Pezzl, pp.110, 114.

20. Pezzl, p. 97.

21. Pezzl, pp. 100–101.

22. Pezzl, p. 162.

23. See Thomas Bauman, *W.A. Mozart, Die Entführung aus dem Serail* (Cambridge: Cambridge University Press, 1987), p. 18.

24. For an easily accessible reproduction of the original, see Christophe Willibald Gluck and J.H. Dancourt, *La Rencontre imprévue ou les Pèlerins de la Mecque: Opéra en trois actes* (Caen: Théâtre de Caen/Actes Sud, 1998).

25. See Neal Zaslaw's "Notes" in the booklet accompanying *Zaide*, recorded by the Academy of Ancient Music (Harmonia Mundi, France 1998), pp. 8 and 53.

26. Hermann Abert, *W.A. Mozart*, Vol. 2 (New Haven and London: Yale University Press, 2007), p. 736.

27. Pierpaolo Polzonetti, "Opera as Process," in Anthony R. DelDonna and Pierpaolo Polzonetti, eds., *The Cambridge Companion to Eighteenth Century Opera* (Cambridge: Cambridge University Press, 2009), p. 5.

28. Nicholas Till, *Mozart and the Enlightenment*, p. 57.

29. Mozart to Leopold Mozart, June 16, 1781, *LMF*, Vol. 2, p. 746.

30. W.A. Mozart, *Die Entführung aus dem Serail, Text von Chr. F. Bretzner in der Bearbeitung von J.G. Stephanie D.J.* [Herefter: *Serail*] (Stuttgart: Philipp Reclam, 2003),

p. 26. (I often make use of McClatchy's poetic translations but modify them where the original German has more of a political edge or nuance). *SML*, pp. 183, 185.

31. *Serail*, p. 27. (*SML*, p. 185).
32. Mozart to Leopold Mozart, October 19, 1782, in *LMF*, Vol. 2, p. 828.
33. *Serail*, p. 27. McClatchy uses "free" to translate "*zur Freude geboren*" but while the assertion of freedom is a persistent theme for Blonde including in this scene, *Freude* here means happiness or joy. (*SML*, p.187). Freedom and happiness are thus united.
34. *Serail*, p. 27. (*SML*, p. 187).
35. *Serail*, p. 32. (*SML*, p.199).
36. For an influential and insightful discussion of the characterization of Osmin and its implications see Peter Kivvy, *Osmin's Rage: Philosophical Reflections on Opera, Drama, and Text* (Ithaca and London: Cornell University Press, 1988).
37. Mozart to Leopold Mozart, Sept. 26, 1781, in *LMF*, Vol. 2, p. 769.
38. Hector Berlioz, "Review of Abu Hassan and the Abduction from the Seraglio," in *The Art of Music and Other Essays* (Bloomington and Indianapolis: Indiana University Press, 1994), pp. 167–8.
39. Mozart to Leopold Mozart, Sept. 26, 1781, in *LMF*, Vol. 2, p. 769.
40. *Serail*, p. 16. (*SML*, pp. 154–5).
41. *Serail*, pp. 16–17. (*SML*, pp. 154–5).
42. *Serail*, p. 54. (*SML*, p. 261); *Serail*, pp. 36–7. (*SML*, pp. 211–13).
43. *Serail*, pp. 23–4. (*SML*,174).
44. *Serail*, p. 31. (*SML*, p. 197).
45. *Serail*, p. 44. (*SML*, p. 235).
46. *Serail*, p. 52. (*SML*, p. 255).
47. *Serail*, p. 55. (*SML*, p. 263).
48. The term "orientalism" as a deprecating classification was made prominent by Edward Said's *Orientalism* (New York: Vintage, 1978), based significantly on Michel Foucault's critique of the Enlightenment. Said makes Napoleon's invasion of Egypt in 1798 into a basic turning point, but this results in misunderstandings of seventeenth- and eighteenth-century European views. It is also misleading in its presentation of the Middle East since it brackets effectively centuries of interaction between the Ottomans and the West and the Ottomans and the larger Middle East (for example, with the Persians).
49. Sometimes the translations were wobbly or expurgated and usually abridged.
50. On race and slavery in Islam, see Bernard Lewis, *Race and Slavery in the Middle East* (Oxford and New York: Oxford University Press, 1992). He discusses *The Thousand and One Nights* on pp. 19–20. Steps to ending slavery in Turkey began in 1830. Throughout the nineteenth and twentieth centuries slavery was eradicated in most of the Middle East (p. 79).
51. Quoted in W. Daniel Wolfson, "Turks on the Eighteenth Century Operatic Stage and European Political, Military and Cultural History," *Eighteenth Century Life*, Vol. 9, No. 2, 1985, pp. 79–80, 89. The librettist of *Der Serail, oder unvermüthete Zusammenkunft in der Sclaverey zwischen Vater, Tochter, und Sohn* was Joseph Sebastini and its composer was Joseph von Freiberth. *Adelheit von Veltheim*'s composer, the Saxon Christian Gottlob Neefe, a member of the Illuminati, was a future mentor of Beethoven. The librettist, Friedrich Wilhelm Grossman, was from Berlin and headed the court theater in Cologne.

52. Charles Rosen, *The Classical Style* (New York: W.W. Norton, 1997[1971]), p. xxiii and p. 25.
53. See Rosen, *Classical Style*, p. 226 and Thomas Schmidt-Beste, *The Sonata* (Cambridge/ New York: Cambridge University Press, 2011).
54. Rosen, p. 81.
55. Rosen, pp. 100–101.
56. Rosen, pp. 153–4.
57. Rosen, p. 301.
58. Quoted in John Irving, "Sonata (2)," *The Grove New Dictionary of Music and Musicians*, 2nd ed., Vol. 23 (London: Macmillan, 2001), p. 677.
59. Mozart to Leopold Mozart, October 13, 1781, *LMF* Vol. 2, p. 773. The original: *"bey einer Opera muss schlechterding die Poesie der Musick gehorsame Tochter seyn."* Mozart, *Briefe und Aufzeichnungen, Gesamtausgabe*, Vol. 3, p. 167.
60. Mozart to Leopold Mozart, October 13, 1781, *LMF*, Vol. 2, p. 773.
61. Bauman, *W.A. Mozart, Die Entführung aus dem Serail*, p. 18.
62. Da Ponte, *An Extract from My Life*, quoted in Hodges, p. 13.
63. Mozart to Leopold Mozart, October 13, 1781, *LMF*, Vol. 2, p. 773.

Zwischenspiel (II)

1. Mozart to Leopold Mozart, May 7, 1783, *LMF*, Vol. 2, p. 848.
2. Mozart to Leopold Mozart, November 24, 1781, Vol. 2, p. 780. Mozart moved into the Judenplatz in 1783, and he knew and was friendly with Jewish bankers, court Jews, and converted Jews.
3. I cull from John Julius Norwich, *A History of Venice* (New York: Vintage, 1989), pp. 595–596.
4. Quote in Charles Diehl, *La République de Venise* (Paris: Flammarion, 1985), p. 265 and Norwich, pp. 596–600.
5. Kelly, *Reminiscences of Michael Kelly*, pp. 131–3. These memoirs were ghostwritten, apparently, from Kelly's notes.
6. Kelly, *Reminiscences of Michael Kelly*, pp. 127–130.
7. Quoted in Joseph Louis Russo, *Lorenzo Da Ponte* (New York: Columbia University Press, 1922), p. 37.
8. Andrew Steptoe, *The Mozart-Da Ponte Operas* (Oxford: Oxford University Press, 1988), p. 100.
9. Kelly, *Reminiscences of Michael Kelly*, pp. 235–6. Awkward gaits and lisps were characteristics often ascribed to Jews at this time.
10. For many details of Da Ponte's early years, I am indebted to Sheila Hodges, *Lorenzo Da Ponte* (London: Grenda, 1985).
11. *"Se gli uomini per le leggi e per le distribuzioni della civil società abbiano il sentiero della felicità umana appianato o ristretto o se per queste leggi medisme sienu in rapporto alla loro nel primiero stato rimasti?"*
12. For an exploration of the relation between Italian opera and events in the "New World," see Pierpaolo Polzonetti, *Italian Opera in the Age of the American Revolution* (Cambridge: Cambridge University Press, 2011).

13. Lorenzo Da Ponte, *Memoirs* (New York: New York Review of Books, 2000), p. 52. Da Ponte's poems were long forgotten. The manuscripts were found in the Treviso Archives and published by his first biographer, Angelo Marchesan, *Della vita e della opera di Lorenzo Da Ponte* (Treviso: Turazza, 1900).
14. Anthony Holden's translation in his *The Man who Wrote Mozart* (London: Weidenfeld and Nicolson, 2006), pp. 27–9.
15. Da Ponte, *Memoirs*, pp. 52, 55.
16. For overviews of Da Ponte's periods in Portogruaro, Venice, and Treviso, his trials and stay with Memmo, see the various biographies, including Russo, *Lorenzo Da Ponte*, pp. 21–35; Hodges, pp. 9–15, and pp. 22–5; Holden, *The Man Who Wrote Mozart*, pp. 11–45; Rodney Bolt, *The Librettist of Venice* (New York: Bloomsbury, 2006), pp. 14–63.
17. Russo, p. 37.
18. Russo, p. 36.
19. Da Ponte, *Memoirs*, p. 69.
20. Hodges, pp. 31–2. For its translation, see Holden, p. 36–8.
21. Da Ponte, *Memoirs*, p. 70.
22. Norwich, *History of Venice*, pp. 601, 636.
23. Diehl, *Venise*, p. 265.
24. Holden's translation, pp. 37–8.
25. Da Ponte, *Memoirs*, p. 71.
26. Hodges, pp. 40–3.

Chapter 16: Gaits of History

1. Louis XVI quoted in Jacques Guicharnaud, "Pre-Revolution (a Comedy)," in Denis Hollier, ed., *A New History of French Literature* (Cambridge and London: Harvard University Press, 1989), p. 549. For Goethe's comment: Johann von Goethe, *Conversations with Eckermann*, April 10, 1829 (San Francisco: North Point Press, 1984) p. 263.
2. Pierre-Augustin Caron de Beaumarchais, *Le Mariage de Figaro*. (Paris: Gallimard, 1999), p. 206.
3. Da Ponte, *Memoirs*, pp. 128–9.
4. Da Ponte, *Memoirs*, pp. 129–30.
5. Daniel Heartz, "Constructing *Le Nozze di Figaro*" in Daniel Heartz, *Mozart's Operas* with contributing essays by Thomas Bauman (Berkeley and Los Angeles: University of California Press, 1990), p. 137, 16.
6. Lorenzo Da Ponte, *"Le Nozze di Figaro"* [Hereafter: Da Ponte, *Nozze*] in Da Ponte, *Libretti Viennesi*, Vol. 1 [Hereafter: *LV, 1*] Parma: Fondazione Pietri Bembo/Ugo Guanda Editore, 1999), p. 240–1. In English: Wolfgang Amadeus Mozart, *The Marriage of Figaro* [Hereafter: *Marriage*] in *Three Mozart Libretti* [Hereafter: *TML*] (New York: Dover, 1993), p. 17.
7. Tim Carter, in his *W.A. Mozart: Le Nozze di Figaro* (Cambridge: Cambridge University Press, 1987), p. 51. My discussion of music and dance in this opera is often indebted to Carter and Wye Jamison Allanbrook, *Rhythmic Gesture*

in Mozart (Chicago and London: University of Chicago Press, 1986). Special thanks to Richard Kramer for pointing me to Allanbrook's remarkable book.

8. My thanks to Pierpaolo Polzonetti for pointing out the suggestiveness of tumbling here.

9. Da Ponte, *Nozze*, p. 253; *Marriage*, pp. 32–3.

10. Quentin Skinner, "Meaning and Understanding in the History of Ideas," in *Visions of Politics, Vol. 1: Concerning Method* (Cambridge: Cambridge University Press, 2002), p. 84.

11. Its history in France has been outlined extensively in Alain Boureau, *Le droit de cuissage: La Fabrication d'un mythe (XIIIe-XX siècle)* (Paris: Editions Albin Michel, 1995).

12. Quoted in Robert Kann, *A Study in Austrian Intellectual History* (New York: Prager, 1960), p. 125, Henry J. Strakosch, *Absolutism and the Rule of Law: The Struggle for the Consolidation of Civil Law in Austria, 1753–1811* (Sydney: Sydney University Press, 1967), p. 37, pp. 152–3.

13. See Julian H. Franklin, "Sovereignty and the Mixed Constitution: Bodin and his Critics," in Burns and Goldie, *The Cambridge History of Political Thought, 1450–1700*, pp. 309, 312.

14. For her views and on general issues of status and law, particularly in the Habsburg empire, see especially Strakosch, *Absolutism and the Rule of Law*, pp. 60–4, 152–3.

15. Strakosch, pp. 152–3.

16. In addition to Strakosch, my summary of law in France and Austria follows closely, draws on, but also simplifies the discussion in Peter Stein, *Roman Law in European History* (Cambridge: Cambridge University Press, 2000), pp. 83–5, 110–15.

17. See David Sorkin, *The Religious Enlightenment* (Princeton: Princeton University Press, 2008), pp. 217–40.

18. Quoted in Kann, *Austrian Intellectual History*, pp. 180–1.

19. Heather Morrison, *Pursuing Enlightenment in Vienna, 1781–1790* (Ph.d. Diss., Louisiana State University, 2005), pp. 17, 30.

20. Mozart to Leopold Mozart, March 20, 1784, *LMF*, Vol. 2, p. 871.

21. Da Ponte, *Nozze*, pp. 283; *Marriage*, p. 75.

22. Da Ponte, *Nozze*, pp. 284–4; *Marriage*, p. 75.

23. Da Ponte, *Nozze*, pp. 243–4; *Marriage*, pp. 17–19.

24. Da Ponte, *Memoirs*, pp. 138–40.

25. Da Ponte, *Nozze*, 243–44; *Marriage*, p. 19–21. They do a kind of dance in some stagings.

26. See Carter's summary, p. 58, and Allanbrook, *Rhythmic Gestures*, pp. 60–2.

27. Allanbrook, p. 77.

28. Allanbrook, p. 81, 60.

29. Allanbrook, p. 81.

30. Allanbrook, pp. 81.

31. Nino Pirrotta, *Don Giovanni's Progress* (New York: Marsilio, 1991), pp. 11–12. Most of the details that I present of the prehistory of *Don Giovanni* come from this study.

32. Lorenzo Da Ponte, *Il dissoluto ossia il Don Giovanni* [Hereafter: *DG*] in *LV, 1*, p. 691. Also *Don Giovanni* in *TML*, p. 137.

33. *DG*, p. 659. *Don Giovanni* in *TML*, p. 135.
34. Quotations in my discussion of these particular scenes from later productions come from the literal translations of them by N. Platt and L. Sarti in W.A. Mozart, *Don Giovanni*, English National Opera Guide No. 18 [Hereafter: *DGENOG*] (London/New York: Calder and Riverrun Press, 1995), pp. 107–109. Some suggest that Casanova assisted in the libretto here. On the Prague and Vienna versions and their differences see especially Julian Ruston, *W.A. Mozart: Don Giovanni* (Cambridge: Cambridge University Press, 1981), pp. 21, 53–56, 142, footnote 5.
35. *DGENOG*, p. 109.
36. Aristotle, *Eudemian Ethics*, (Oxford/New York: Oxford University Press, 2011), p. 120
37. *DG*, p. 709. *Don Giovanni* in *TML*, p. 159.
38. He calls it "pure" in *Eudemian Ethics*, p. 121. On bad men being friends, see p. 121. Aristotle believed laws were needed to sustain the exchanges of utilitarian friendship. It is possible to imagine them as feudal rules governing relations between lord and servant, but Mozart and Da Ponte have added another, powerful psychological dimension in Leporello's longing to be like the Don combined with his need and desire for pay. There is, then, a kind of rule, psychology and cash bound nexus.
39. Aristotle, *The Politics* (Cambridge: Cambridge University Press, 1988), pp. 3, 79; and *Eudemian Ethics*, p. 112.
40. *DGENOG*, p. 109.
41. Allanbrook, *Rhythmic Gestures*, 220–3.
42. Allanbrook, 81.
43. David Wyn Jones, "Music and Action in 'Don Giovanni,'" in *DGENOG*, p. 24.
44. For a somewhat different analysis of class in *Don Giovanni*, see E.J. Dent's description of the minuet as aristocratic, the contredanse as bourgeois, and the waltz as "proletarian." The problem with this proposition is that Don Giovanni and Zerlina are not bourgeois, and Massetto and Leporello are not proletarian, even if they come from lower classes. See E.J. Dent, *Mozart's Operas* (Oxford: Oxford University Press, 1947), pp. 163–4.
45. *DG*, p. 747; *Don Giovanni* in *TML*, p. 211.
46. *DG*, p. 750; *Don Giovanni* in *TML*, p. 215.
47. Till, *Mozart and the Enlightenment*, p. 212.
48. Rosen, *Classical Style*, pp. 94–95. On "*società*" see Rushton, pp. 29–31.
49. *DG*, p. 752; *Don Giovanni* in *TML*, p. 219.
50. Lorenzo Da Ponte, *Così fan tutte ossia la scuola degli amanti* [Hereafter: *Così*] in Da Ponte, *Libretti viennesi*, Vol. 2 [Hereafter: *LV, 2*] (Parma: Fondazione Pietri Bembo/Ugo Guanda Editore, 1999), p. 1051. *Così fan tutte* in *TML*, p. 261.
51. *Così*, p. 1095; *Così fan tutte* in *TML*, p. 307.
52. *Così*, p. 1033; *Così fan tutte* in *TML*, p. 245.
53. *Così*, p. 1092; *Così fan tutte* in *TML*, p. 303.
54. *Così*, p. 1084; *Così fan tutte* in *TML*, p. 295. The latter translation leaves out Don Alfonso's important words that nature makes no exceptions.

55. *Così*, p. 1089. *Così fan tutte* in *TML*, p. 295.
56. For discussions of the disputes see Bruce Alan Brown, *W.A. Mozart: Così fan tutte* (Cambridge: Cambridge University Press, 1995), pp. 57–81 and John Stone, "The Background to the Libretto," in *W.A. Mozart: Così fan tutte*, English National Theater Guide 22 (Paris, London, New York: Calder Publications and Riverrun Press, 1991), pp. 35–45.
57. The poem is translated in Holden, *The Man Who Wrote Mozart*, pp. 113–16.
58. See Holden, p. 116.
59. Da Ponte, *Memoirs*, pp. 175–6 and Hodges, pp. 109–111.
60. Da Ponte to Casanova, March 1, 1793 in *Mémoires suivis de Lettres inédites de Lorenzo Da Ponte à Jacques Cassanova* (Paris: Jonquières, 1931), p. 295. For his conflicts in London see the "Préface" by Raoul Vèze. On Da Ponte's reaction to the French events also see his letter to Casanova of May 10, 1793, p. 298.

Chapter 17: Looking for Enlightenment

1. Quoted in H.C. Robbins Landon, *1791: Mozart's Last Year* (London: Thames and Hudson, 1999), pp. 133–34. Also see Paul P. Bernard, *From the Enlightenment to the Police State: The Public Life of Johann Anton Pergen* (Urbana and Chicago: University of Illinois Press, 1991). Pergen was not alone in his fear of conspiracies. His employers worried too. But conspiracy theories were widespread then in Europe. See, for example, the well-known text by John Robinson, *Proofs of Conspiracy against all the Religions and Governments of Europe carried on in the Secret Meetings of Free Masons, Illuminati, and Reading Societies* (New York: Forman, 1798). The author, a professor of natural philosophy in Edinburgh, saw the Illuminati as "accessory" to the Masons. See p. 89.
2. Quoted in Landon, *1791*, p. 134
3. Andrew Michael Ramsay, "A Discourse upon the Theology and Mythology of the Pagans," in Ramsay, *The Travels of Cyrus to which is annexed A Discourse upon the Theology and Mythology of the Pagans* 6th ed. (London: Bettenham, 1734), p. 275.
4. Margaret C. Jacob, *The Origins of Freemasonry* (Philadelphia: University of Pennsylvania Press, 2006), pp. 21–3.
5. Margaret C. Jacob, *Living the Enlightenment: Freemasonry and Politics in 18th Century Europe* (Oxford and New York: Oxford University Press, 1991), p. 151.
6. Gotthold Ephraim Lessing, "Ernst and Falk: Dialogues for Freemasons," in *Philosophical and Theological Writings* (Cambridge and New York: Cambridge University Press, 2005), pp. 187–91. Perhaps Falk's words crossed Friedrich Engels's mind when he proposed that the transcendence of capitalism would bring about the "withering away" of the state and its replacement by a commune. The phrase "experimental stage" comes from Reinhart Koselleck, *Critique and Crisis* (Cambridge: MIT Press, 1988), pp. 87. Koselleck's book, which has an insightful discussion of Lessing's dialogue, seems also to defend the odd thesis that a politically inexperienced utopianism derived from the Enlightenment, Free Masons, Illuminati, and eighteenth-century reading societies was responsible not only for the excesses of the French Revolution but for the rise

of Nazism later. Somehow German nationalism and romanticism don't participate in this history.

7. W.A. Mozart and Emanuel Schikaneder, *Die Zauberflöte* [Hereafter: *Zauberflöte*] (Stuttgart: Reclam, 1991), p. 37. My thanks to Richard Kramer for stressing this point to me. I follow Schikander's original German republished in this text.

8. Peter Branscombe, *W.A. Mozart: Die Zauberflöte* (Cambridge: Cambridge University Press, 1991), p. 138.

9. Mozart and Schikander, *Zauberflöte*, p. 16.

10. Branscombe, *W.A. Mozart: Die Zauberflöte*, pp. 20–1, 23; See Solomon on the Zoroaster "Fragments," pp. 337–8. The translation of the proverb is Solomon's.

11. Branscombe, p. 4.

12. On these sources, see especially Branscombe, pp. 17–18, 20–5. On the relation between Mozart's music and the Masons, see especially pp. 137–8.

13. August Jacob Liebeskind, *Lulu oder die Zauberflöte* (Frankfurt am Main: Insel Verlag, 1999), p. 7. I have followed the spelling of places and names in this edition, with some Anglicization.

14. Liebeskind, *Lulu*, p. 12.

15. The inventory of Mozart's library can be found on the website of the Mozart Foundation in Salzburg at www.mozarteum.at.

16. Kurt Honolka, *Papageno: Emmanuel Schikaneder* (Portland: Amadeus Press, 1990), p. 167.

17. I summarize and at times paraphrase from Books 2 and 5 of Fénelon.

18. Thanks to Thalia Magioglou for helping me decipher possible implications of "Termosiris."

19. See Book 8 of *Telemachus*. This kingdom is in Spain.

20. Andrew Michael Ramsay, *The Travels of Cyrus*, pp. 89, 92–4, 104.

21. Honolka, *Papageno*, pp. 37–8.

22. Jean Terrasson, *Séthos, Histoire ou vie Tirée des monumens et Anecdotes de l'Ancienne Egypte traduit d'un manuscript Grec*, Vol. 1 (Amsterdam: Aux Dépans de la Compagnie, 1732). On Osiris, see the first chapter. On the author's purposes and on *Telemachus* and *Cyrus*, see pp. xi, xv–xvi.

23. See Pascale Mormiche, *Devenir prince: L'école du pouvoir en France XVIIe-XVIIIe sièles* (Paris: CNRS Editions, 2009), p. 262 and Louis XVI's statement, quoted in Timothy Tackett, see *When the King Took Flight* (Cambridge and London: Harvard University Press, 2003), p. 29.

24. "Die ihr des unermesslichen Weltalls Schöpfer ehrt" (K. 619) ["You who honor the creator of the Boundless (Infinite) Universe"]. See Solomon, p. 329. Text translation in booklet of Wolfgang Holzmair, *An die ferne Geliebte: Songs by Mozart, Hayden, and Beethoven* (New York: Phillips, 2000), pp. 36–41. Trans. modified.

25. Mozart to Constanze Mozart, June 11, 1791, *LMF*, Vol. 2, p. 953.

26. Tackett, *When the King Took Flight*, p. 65.

27. Kelly, *Reminiscences*, Vol. 2, pp. 25–7.

28. See Strakosch, *Absolutism*, p. 178 and Kann, *Austrian Intellectual History*, pp. 214–15, 222. On Franco-Habsburg relations at this time I draw from Georges

Lefebvre, *The French Revolution*, Vol. 1 (London and New York: Routledge and Columbia University Press, 1962), especially pp. 191–5, 210–12.

29. Tackett, *When the King Took Flight*, p. 41.

Chapter 18: Tamino's Wonder

1. *Zauberflöte*, p. 10.
2. *Zauberflöte*, p. 10.
3. *Zauberflöte*, pp. 10–13.
4. Lessing, "Ernst and Falk," p. 210.
5. *Zauberflöte*, p. 19.
6. *Zauberflöte*, p. 30.
7. *Zauberflöte*, p. 28.
8. *Zauberflöte*, p. 71.
9. *Zauberflöte*, p. 37.
10. *Zauberflöte*, p. 34.
11. *Zauberflöte*, p. 30.
12. Jacob, *Living the Enlightenment*, p. 135. See especially her discussion of women in Freemasonry on pp. 127–9 and p. 141 and in *Origins of Freemasonry*, pp. 24, 93, 109, 125.
13. Ritchie Robertson, "Freemasons vs. Jesuits," *Times Literary Supplement* (*TLS*), October 12, 2012, p. 14.
14. One of the Order's principal figures, Thomas von Schönfeld, a Jew who was born Moses Dobruska in Brünn, Moravia, and converted to Christianity, was closely linked to and had family ties with Jacob Frank, leader of a Sabbatian offshoot, who lived, until his death in 1791, in Brünn. Dobruska, who later re-named himself Junius Frey, became a Jacobin, and was guillotined in the French Revolution in 1793. See Jacob Katz, *Jews and Freemasons* (Cambridge: Harvard University Press, 1970) and Gershom Scholem, *Du Frankisme au Jacobinisme: La vie de Moses Dobruska alias Thomas von Schönfeld alias Junius Frey* (Paris: Hautes Etudes/Gallimard/Le Seuil, 1981). My thanks to Maurice Kriegel for pointing me to the Asiatic Brethren.
15. *Zauberflöte*, p. 36.
16. See Mozart and Emanuel Schikaneder, *The Magic Flute* (London and New York: John Calder, the English National Opera, and Riverrun, 1997), p. 79.
17. *Zauberflöte*, p. 50.
18. *Zauberflöte*, p. 21.
19. *Zauberflöte*, pp. 45–6.
20. *Zauberflöte*, pp. 39–40.
21. *Zauberflöte*, p. 71.
22. There are structural interrelations among these keys and their movements as well. I follow here Mozart biographer Hermann Abert and observations about his list by Branscombe, W.A. Mozart: Die Zauberflöte, p. 130.
23. See Heartz, *Mozart's Operas*, p. 294.
24. *Zauberflöte*, p. 58.

25. *Zauberflöte*, p. 33.
26. *Zauberflöte*, p. 34.
27. *Zauberflöte*, pp. 29–30.
28. *Zauberflöte*, p. 7.
29. *Zauberflöte*, p. 11.
30. G.W.F. Hegel, *Aesthetics*, Vol. 1 pp. 279–80; Jean Starobinski, *1789: The Emblems of Reason* (Cambridge and London: MIT Press, 1988), p. 95.
31. Hegel, *Aesthetics* Vol. 2, pp. 945–6.
32. Isaiah Berlin, "The Temple of Sarastro" in "Two Concepts of Liberty," in Henry Hardy ed. *Liberty*, (Oxford: Oxford University Press, 2002) pp. 166, 190–1, 193.
33. Berlin, p. 200.
34. Starobinski, *Emblems*, p. 95.
35. Quentin Skinner, "Meaning and Understanding in the History of Ideas," *Visions of Politics*, Vol. 1 (*Regarding Method*) (Cambridge and New York: Cambridge University Press, 2007), p. 2.
36. Their claims compare to mid-twentieth-century interpretations of Hegel as a proto-Nazi nationalist proponent of an all-powerful state because the Third Reich depicted him that way. When Hegel saluted the state in the 1820s it was to advocate constitutional monarchy, the idea of a reformed Prussia, and the rationality of rule by law against the irrational bonding and nationalist emotionalism that characterized contemporary student extremism.
37. *Zauberflöte*, p. 37.
38. *Zauberflöte*, p. 37.

Sarastro's Sabbatical: This Is Not a Finale

1. G.W.F. Hegel, "The Positivity of the Christian Religion," in *Early Theological Writings* (Philadelphia: University of Pennsylvania Press, 1971), p. 152.
2. *Der Zauberflöte. Zweyter Theil unter dem Titel: Das Labyrinth oder der Kampf mit den Elementen. Eine grosse-heroische Oper in zwey Aufzügen von Emmanuel Schikaneder. In Musik gesetzt von Herrn Peter Winter* (Vienna: Verlegt Bein Hans Schneider, 1992), p. 24. [Hereafter: *Labyrinth*.]
3. *Labyrinth*, p. 25.
4. *Labyrinth*, p. 55.
5. *Labyrinth*, p. 36. The revival at the Salzburg Festival in 2012 took real efforts to portray Monostatos in ugly racial terms. He and the other Moors have ape-like shapes and were in blackface with white lips. This abridged version can be seen on an Arthaus Musik DVD.
6. *Labyrinth*, p. 50.
7. Johann von Goethe, *The Campaign in France*. (London: Chapman and Hall, 1849) p. 302.
8. Why this is especially so in Goethe's case becomes evident when his *Magic Flute* is linked to *Conversations among German Refugees*, a text he completed in close temporal proximity. It concludes with a famously allusive "Fairy Tale." *Conversations*

begins with a procession of German aristocrats by the Rhine in flight from the French army. While resting they debate. Passionate young Karl is unhappy at crossing the river. He is pro-French and "seduced" by a "dazzling beauty." She is "liberty," who retains admirers even when she mistreats them. But "Love is blind. . . ." Johann Wolfgang von Goethe, *The German Refugees*, Mike Mitchell, trans. (Langford Lodge, UK: Daedalus, 2006), p. 19. Karl is challenged by an old privy counselor, "a stickler for principle" for whom "liberty" is "despotism" disguised. The masses remain "true" to themselves, he thinks, when they take violently "the word for the deed, appearance for reality." (*Refugees*, p. 23) An idealistic quest for a new end must end badly. This position captures succinctly a traditional—particularly German—critique of the Revolution, close to Goethe's own, although he was open-eyed to the Old Regime's failures. His ambiguous "Fairy Tale," which might make for a great opera, presents worlds separated by a river—a dangerous if allusive ideal on one side and on the other, statues of old and new kings (deep in a cave).

9. An intellectual historian might situate this Wanderer's sojourn in a temporal domain between Kant and Hegel. When Goethe wrote his fragment it was toward the end of Kant's career and just before the latter's rise. It is, however, not only a matter of timing. Kant tried to delineate categories of understanding that all people share. Hegel insisted that using such tools changes them and consequently they don't remain historically chaste. Goethe's Wanderer returns with a pure stone to add to Enlightenment after engaging the world, but the world should have changed the stone. The same issue would arise if we envision the Wanderer as a man bound on imperial adventure. But the setting of *The Magic Flute* is more Egyptian than European. Exotic locales were, as we have seen, used in opera and literature to make statements about Europe. Perhaps, however, there is a wish here: Europeans should go out into the world and still remain pure.

10. J.W. Goethe, "The Magic Flute: A Comic Opera Fragment," in *Tales for Transformation* (San Francisco: City Lights Books, 1987), p. 116.

11. The exception was an elected military commander.

12. Goethe, "Magic Flute," p. 117.

13. I have often used "Priests" and "Brothers" interchangeably and have not tried to correct for gender neutrality in ways that would have been alien to eighteenth-century language and other librettos of the time. Moreover, in this case, the terms also suggest the sanctification of community members and (sometimes) a hierarchy within it reminiscent of Masonry.

14. J.W. Goethe, *Conversations with Eckermann*, entry of February 12, 1829 (San Francisco: Northpoint Press, 1984) p. 237. Goethe added that he thought Giacomo Meyerbeer might have been able to compose music for it but found him then too preoccupied with Italian musical styles. In another sense, however, Goethe's comments here are especially keen: they were made before he could have seen and heard Meyerbeer's portrait of satanic motifs in his opera *Robert le Diable* of November 1831. For Goethe's attendance at a Mozart concert, see the entry of February 3, 1830 in *Conversations with Eckermann*, p. 281.

15. Goethe, *Conversations with Eckermann*, entry of March 11, 1828.

16. When Orpheus leads Eurydice out of hell, Jupiter throws a thunderbolt that causes the startled musician to turn around and lose his love. It is not Orpheus's fault and much to the glee of all except "Public Opinion." See Jacques Offenbach, *Orphée aux Enfers*. Livret d'Hector Crémieux et de Ludovic Halévy, (Marseille: Opéra de Marseille et Actes Sud, 1993).

Appendix: "Backstage"

1. For a sympathetic overview resting on postmodernist premises, see Nicholas Till, "Introduction: Opera Studies Today" and various essays in Till, ed., *The Cambridge Companion to Opera Studies* (Cambridge: Cambridge University Press, 2012). For an especially trenchant critique of postmodern approaches, see Richard Taruskin, "Introduction: History of What?" in Taruskin's *Music in the Seventeenth and Eighteenth Centuries (The Oxford History of Western Music)* (Oxford and New York: Oxford University Press, 2010).
2. Theodor W. Adorno with the assistance of George Simpson, "On Popular Music," in Adorno, *Essays on Music* (Berkeley and Los Angeles: University of California Press, 2002), p. 441.
3. Theodor W. Adorno, *Minima Moralia* (London: New Left Books, 1974), p. 86.
4. Taruskin, "Introduction: History of What?", p. xix.
5. Theodor W. Adorno, "Bourgeois Opera" [1955] in *Opera Through Other Eyes*, ed. David J. Levin (Stanford: Stanford University Press, 1994), p. 27.
6. Adorno, "Bourgeois Opera," p. 37.
7. Adorno, "Bourgeois Opera," pp. 31–5 and p. 29.
8. Siegfried Kracauer, *Jacques Offenbach and the Paris of His Time* (New York: Zone Books, 2002), pp. 23, 25.
9. Theodor W. Adorno to Walter Benjamin, May 4, 1937 in *Walter Benjamin and Theodor W. Adorno: The Complete Correspondence 1828–1940* (Cambridge: Harvard University Press, 2001), p. 184.
10. Carl Dahlhaus, *Foundations of Music History* (Cambridge: Cambridge University Press, 1993), p. 106 on Monteverdi; p. 101 on Offenbach.
11. Dahlhaus, *Foundations*, p. 3.
12. Dahlhaus, *Foundations*, p. 3 and 35.
13. Dahlhaus, *Foundations*, p. 1.
14. For an overview of the German circumstances, see Anne C. Shreffler, "Berlin Walls: Dahlhaus, Knepler and the Ideologies of Music History," *Journal of Musicology*, Vol. 20, No. 4, 2003, pp. 498–525.
15. Dahlhaus, pp. 93–4.
16. Collingwood, *An Autobiography*, p. 31.
17. See Lucien Goldmann, *Le Dieu caché: Étude sur la vision tragique dans les "Pensées" de Pascal et dans le théâtre de Racine* (Paris: Gallimard, 1955), p. 27. On Goldmann, see Mitchell Cohen, *The Wager of Lucien Goldmann: Tragedy, Dialectics and a Hidden God* (Princeton: Princeton University Press, 1994).
18. Jean-Paul Sartre, *Critique de la raison dialectique* précédé de *Questions de méthode*, Texte etabli et annoté par Arlette Elkaim-Sartre, Tome 1, Theorie des ensembles

pratiques. Vol. 1 (Paris: Gallimard, 1985 [1960]), p. 53. Taruskin captures this point too although with a different edge and concerning music and composers. He praises Béla Bártók's statement that Kodály's *Psalmus Hungaricus* "could not have been written without Hungarian peasant music" and then remarks, "Neither, of course, could it have been written without Kodály." See Taruskin, "Introduction: History of What?" p. xviii.

19. Skinner has, in fact, made many since the initial appearance of his work.
20. Dahlhaus, *Foundations*, p. 9.

SELECT BIBLIOGRAPHY

Abbate, Carolyn, and Roger Parker, *A History of Opera* (New York and London: W.W. Norton and Co., 2012).

Abert, Hermann, *W. A. Mozart*, Vol. 2 (New Haven and London: Yale University Press, 2007).

Adorno, Theodor W., *Essays on Music* (Berkeley and Los Angeles: University of California Press, 2002).

_____, *Philosophy of Modern Music* (New York: Continuum, 1985).

Allanbrook, Wye Jamison, *Rhythmic Gesture in Mozart* (Chicago and London: University of Chicago Press, 1983).

Anthony, James R., *French Baroque Music* (Portland: Amadeus Press, 1997).

_____, "Jean-Baptiste Lully," in *French Baroque Masters* (New York and London: W.W. Norton, 1986).

_____, "The French-Ballet Opera in the Early 18th Century: Problems of Definition and Classification," *Journal of the American Musicological Society*, Vol. 18, No. 2 (Summer 1965).

Arblaster, Anthony, *Viva la Libertà* (London and New York: Verso, 1992).

Aristotle, *The Politics* (Cambridge: Cambridge University Press, 1988).

_____, *Eudemian Ethics*, (Oxford and New York: Oxford University Press, 2011).

_____, and Horace, Longinus, *Classical Literary Criticism* (London: Penguin, 1965).

Arnold, Denis, *Monteverdi* (Oxford: Oxford University Press, 1990).

Barbier, Patrick, *Jean-Baptiste Pergolèse* (Paris: Fayard/Mirare, 2003).

Batteux, Charles, *Principes de littérature. Nouvelle édition*, Vol. 1 (Gottigue and Leide: Elie Luzar Fils, 1755).

Baudson, Émile, *Charles de Gonzague, Duc de Nevers, de Rethel, et de Mantoue, 1580–1637* (Paris: Librairie Académique Perrin, 1947).

Bauman, Thomas, *W.A. Mozart, Die Entführung aus dem Serail* (Cambridge: Cambridge University Press, 1987).

Bayle, Pierre, *Dictionnaire historique et critique*, [5th edition], Vol. 1 (Amsterdam: P. Bunel, 1740).

Beales, Derek, *Enlightenment and Reform in Eighteenth Century Europe* (London and New York: I.B. Taurus, 2005).

_____. *Joseph II*, Vol. 2 (Cambridge: Cambridge University Press, 2009).

De Beaumarchais, Pierre-Augustin Caron, *Le Mariage de Figaro* (Paris: Gallimard, 1999).

Beaussant, Philippe, *François Couperin* (Paris: Fayard, 1980).

_____, *Lully ou le musicien du soleil* (Paris: Gallimard, 1992).

Beller, Steven, *A Concise History of Austria* (Cambridge and New York: Cambridge University Press, 2006).

Berlin, Isaiah, *Liberty*, Henry Hardy, ed. (Oxford: Oxford University Press, 2002).

_____, *Against the Current* (New York: Viking Press, 1979).

Berner, Samuel, "Florentine Political Thought in the Late Cinquecento," *Il Pensiero Politico*, Vol. 3, No. 2, August 1970.

Bermbach, Udo, *Wo Macht ganz auf Verbrechen ruht: Politik und Gesellschaft in der Oper* (Hamburg: Europäische Verlagsanstalt, 1997).

Bianconi, Lorenzo, *Music in the Seventeenth Century* (Cambridge: Cambridge University Press, 1987).

Bireley, Robert, *The Counter-Reformation Prince* (Chapel Hill and London: University of North Carolina Press, 1990).

Blanning, T.C.W., *The Culture of Power and the Power of Culture: Old Regime Europe, 1660–1789* (Oxford: Oxford University Press, 2002).

Blow, Douglas, *Doctors, Ambassadors, Secretaries: Humanism and Professions in Renaissance Italy* (Chicago and London: University of Chicago Press, 2002).

Boccalini, Traiano, *Advices from Parnassus* (London: L. Stokoe, 1727).

Bodin, Jean, *Les six livres de la république* (Paris: Librairie Iuré Samaritain, 1577).

Bolt, Rodney, *The Librettist of Venice* (New York: Bloomsbury, 2006).

Du Bos, Jean-Baptiste, *Réflexions critiques sur la poesie et sur la peinture*. Vol. 1 (Paris: P-J Mariette, 1733).

Bouisson, Sylvie, *Jean-Philippe Rameau* (Paris: Fayard, 2014).

Bossuet, Jacques-Bénigne, *Politique tirée des propres paroles de l'Écriture sainte* (Geneva: Librairie-Droz, 1967).

———, *Maximes et réflexions sur la comédie* (Paris: Annison, 1694).

Botero, Giovanni, *The Reason of State* (London: Routledge and Kegan Paul, 1956).

Boureau, Alain, *Le Droit de cuissage: La Fabrication d'un mythe (XIIIe-XX siècle)* (Paris: Editions Albin Michel, 1995).

Bouwsma, William J., *Venice and the Defense of Republican Liberty* (Berkeley, Los Angeles, London: University of California Press, 1984).

Brand, Peter, and Lino Pertile, eds., *The Cambridge History of Italian Literature* (Cambridge: Cambridge University Press, 1999).

Branscombe, Peter, *W.A. Mozart: Die Zauberflöte* (Cambridge: Cambridge University Press, 1991).

Brooke, Christopher, *Philosophic Pride: Stoicism and Political Thought from Lipsius to Rousseau* (Princeton: Princeton University Press, 2012).

De Brossses, Charles, *Lettres familières sur l'Italie*, Vol. 2 (Paris: Firmin-Didot, 1931 [1753]).

Brown, Bruce Alan, *W.A. Mozart: Così fan tutte* (Cambridge: Cambridge University Press, 1995).

———, *Gluck and the French Theater in Vienna* (Oxford: Oxford University Press, 1991).

Brown, Horatio F., *Venice: An Historical Sketch of the Republic* (London: Rivington, Perival and Co., 1895).

Brown, Peter, "Lionardo Salviati and the 'Discorso sopra le Prime Parole di Cornelio Tacito,'" *Italian Studies*, Vol. 15, 1960.

Bujic, Began, "Rinuccini the Craftsman: A View of L'Arianna," *Early Modern Music*, Vol. 18, 1999.

Burke, Edmund, *A Philosophical Inquiry into the Sublime and Beautiful and other Pre-Revolutionary Writings* (London and New York: Penguin, 1998).

Burke, Peter, "Tacitism, skepticism, and reasons of state," in J.H. Burns, ed. with the assistance of Mark Goldie, *The Cambridge History of Political Thought, 1450–1700.* (Cambridge: Cambridge University Press, 1991).

Burney, Charles, *A General History of Music from the Earliest Ages to the Present Period,* Vol. 4 (London: Becket, Robson, and Robinson, 1789).

_____, *An Eighteenth Century Musical Tour in France and Italy* (Oxford: Oxford University Press, 1959[1773]).

_____, *Memoirs of the Life and Writings of the Abate Metastasio in which are Incorporated Translations of his Principal Letters,* 3 vols. (London: Robinson, 1796).

_____, *The Present State of Music in France and Italy* [2nd edition] (London: Becket, Robson, Robinson, 1773).

_____, *The Present State of Music in Germany, the Netherlands and United Provinces* [2nd edition], ed. P. Sehaler as *Dr. Burney's Musical Tours* (Oxford: Oxford University Press, 1959).

_____, *The Letters of Dr. Charles Burney, (1751–1784)* (Oxford: Clarendon Press, 1991).

Busenello, Gian Francesco, *Sonetti morali ed amorosi, di Gian Francesco Busenello,* Testo critico per cura di Arthur Livingston (Venice: Prem. Stab. Grafico G. Fabbris di S., 1911).

_____, *A Perspective of the Naval Triumph of the Venetians over the Turk,* (London: Henry Harringman, 1658).

_____, *L'incoronatione di Poppea: Opera Musicale Rapressentata nel Teatro Grimano l'anno 1642* (Venice: Andrea Giulini, 1646).

_____, *La Didone: Opera Rappresentata in Musica nel Teatro di San Cassiano* (Venice: Giulini, 1641).

Buti, Francesco, *Orfeo* (Montpellier: Opéra de Montpellier, 1990).

Campra, André, *Cantatas* Vol. 2 (New York and London: Garland Publishing, 199).

Carter, Tim, "Composing Opera from Dafne to Ulisse Errante," *Pratica Musica* 2 (Crakow: Musica Iagellonica and Katedra Historii I Teorii Muzyki UJ, 1994).

_____, "Jacopo Peri (1563–1633): Aspects of his Life and Works," *Proceedings of the Royal Musical Association,* Vol. 105 (1978/79).

_____, *Monteverdi's Musical Theatre* (New Haven and London: Yale University Press, 2002).

_____, and Richard Goldwaithe, *Orpheus in the Market Place: Jacopo Peri and the Ecnomy of Late Renaissance Florence* (Cambridge: Harvard University Press, 2013).

_____. *W.A. Mozart: Le Nozze di Figaro* (Cambridge: Cambridge University Press, 1987).

Cavalli, Pietro Francesco, *La Didone* (Deutsche Harmonia Mundi/BMG Classics, 1998).

Chambers, David, *Venice: A Documentary History, 1450–1630* (Oxford: Blackwell, 1992).

Charlton, David, *Opera in the Age of Rousseau* (Cambridge: Cambridge University Press, 2013).

Christensen, Thomas, *Rameau and the Musical Thought of the Enlightenment* (Cambridge: Cambridge University Press, 1995).

Cicero, *On Living and Dying Well* (London and New York: Penguin Books, 2012).

Clarke, Jack A., *Gabriel Naudé: 1600–1653* (Hamden, Conn.: Archon Books, 1970).

Clark, Peter, ed., *The European Crisis of the 1590s* (London: George Allen and Unwin, 1985).

Cochrane, Eric, "The Failure of Political Philosophy in Seventeenth Century Florence: Lorenzo Magalotti's 'Condordia della Religione e del Principato,'" in Anthony Molho and John A. Tedeschi, eds. *Renaissance Studies in Honor of Hans Baron* (DeKalb, Ill.: Northern Illinois University Press, 1971).

_____. *Florence in the Forgotten Centuries: 1527–1806* (Chicago: University of Chicago Press, 1973).

Cohen, Mitchell, *The Wager of Lucien Goldmann: Tragedy, Dialectics, and a Hidden God* (Princeton: Princeton University Press, 1994).

Collingwood, R.W., *An Autobiography* (Oxford: Oxford University Press, 1991 [1939]).

Collins, James B., *The State in Modern France* (Cambridge: Cambridge University Press, 1999).

Collins, Michael, and Elise K. Kirk, ed., *Opera and Vivaldi* (Austin: University of Texas Press, 1994).

Corp, Edward T., "The Exiled Court of James II and James III: A Centre of Italian Music in France, 1689–1712," *Journal of the Royal Musical Association*, Vol. 12, No. 2, 1995.

Couperin, François, *Oeuvres complètes de François Couperin, II, 1; Pièces de Clavecin* (Monaco: Éditions de L'Oiseau-Lyre, 1980), p. 10.

_____. *Oeuvres complètes de François Couperin, IV, 2; Musique de Chambre* (Monaco: Éditions de L'Oiseau-Lyre, 1988).

_____. *Oeuvres complètes de François Couperin, IV, 3; Musique de Chambre* (Monaco: Éditions de L'Oiseau-Lyre, 1987).

_____. *L'Art de toucher le clavecin*, in *Oeuvres complètes de François Couperin, 1, Oeuvres didactiques* (Paris: Éditions de L'Oiseau-Lyre, 1933).

Cowart, Georgia J., *The Triumph of Pleasure* (Chicago: University of Chicago Press, 2008).

Cox-Rearick, Janet, *Destiny and Dynasty in Medici Art* (Princeton: Princeton University Press, 1984).

Cranston, Maurice, *Jean-Jacques: The Early Life and Work of Jean-Jacques Rousseau, 1712–1754* (Chicago and London: University of Chicago Press, 1982).

Cremer, Albert, "Les théoriciens de la raison d'état, juges de Jean Bodin," *Revue d'histoire diplomatique* Vol. 89, (1975).

Curtis, Alan, "La Poppea, Impasticciata or, Who wrote the Music to L'incoronazione (1643)," *Journal of the American Musicological Society*, Vol. 42, No. 1, Spring 1989.

Cusick, Suzanne, " 'There was not One Lady who Failed to Shed a Tear': Arianna's Lament and Construction of Modern Womanhood," *Early Music* Vol. 22, No. 1 (February 1994).

Da Ponte, Lorenzo, *Libretti viennesi*, 2 vols. (Parma: Fondazione Pietri Bembo/Ugo Guanda Editore, 1999), p. 1051.

_____. *Memoirs* (New York: New York Review of Books, 2000).

Da Ponte, Lorenzo L., *A History of the Florentine Republic and of the Age and Rule of the Medici* Vol. 2 (New York: Collins and Hanny, 1833).

Dahlhaus, Carl, *Foundations of Music History* (Cambridge: Cambridge University Press, 1993).

D'Alembert, Jean, *Preliminary Discourse to the Encyclopedia of Diderot* (Chicago: University of Chicago Press, 1995).

Dallington, Robert, *A Survey of the Great Dukes of the State of Tuscany* (London: Eduard Blount, 1605).

Danchet, André, "Approbation," in François Couperin, *L'Art de Toucher le Clavecin* in *Oeuvres complètes de François Couperin*, 1, *Oeuvres didactiques* (Paris: Éditions de L'Oiseau-Lyre, 1933).

Dancourt, J.H., *Le Rencontre imprévue ou Les Pèlerins de la Mecque: Opéra en trois actes* (Caen: Théâtre de Caen/Actes Sud, 1998).

Dante, *The Divine Comedy: 1. Inferno* (New York: Oxford University Press, 1981/82).

Darnton, Robert, *Poetry and the Police: Communication Networks in Eighteenth Century France* (Cambridge and London: Harvard University Press, 2010).

Davis, James Cushman, *The Decline of the Venetian Nobility as a Ruling Class* (Baltimore: Johns Hopkins University Studies in Historical and Political Science, Series LXXX, No. 2, 1962).

Decroisette, Françoise, Françoise Graziani, Joël Heuillon, eds., *La naissance de l'Opéra: Euridice 1600–2000, Collection Arts 8*, sous la direction Françoise Decroisette, Françoise Graziani, Joël Heuillon, (Paris: L'Harmattan, 2001).

DelDonna, Anthony R., and Pierpaolo Polzonetti, eds., *The Cambridge Companion to Eighteenth Century Opera* (Cambridge: Cambridge University Press, 2009).

Della Corte, Andrea, *Drammi per musica dal Rinuccini allo Zeno*, 3 Vols. (Turin: Unione Tipografico-Editrice Torinese, 1958/1978).

Dent, E.J., *Mozart's Operas* (Oxford: Oxford University Press, 1947).

de Vivo, Filippo, *Information and Communication in Venice: Rethinking Early Modern Politics* (Cambridge: Cambridge University Press, 2007).

Diderot, Dénis, *Les Bijoux indiscrets* (Paris: Gallimard, 1981).

_____, *Écrits sur la musique* (Paris: J.C. Clattès, 1987).

_____, *Political Writings* (Cambridge and New York: Cambridge University Press, 1992).

Diehl, Charles, *La République de Venise* (Paris: Flammarion, 1985).

Dill, Charles, *Monstrous Opera: Rameau and the Tragic Tradition* (Princeton: Princeton University Press, 1998).

Dupavillon, Christian, *Naissance de l'opéra en France, Orfeo, 2 Mars 1647* (Paris: Fayard, 2010).

Feldman, Martha, *Opera and Sovereignty: Transforming Myths in Eighteenth Century Italy* (Chicago and London: University of Chicago Press, 2007).

Fénelon, François de, *Oeuvres* 1 (Paris: Gallimard, Pléïade, 1983).

_____. *Telemachus, Son of Ulysses*, Patrick Riley trans. (Cambridge: Cambridge University Press, 1994).

Fenlon, Iain, "Music and Spectacle at the Gonzaga Court," *Proceedings of the Royal Musical Association* (London), Vol. 103 (1976–77).

Finley, M.I., *The World of Odysseus* (New York: New York Review of Books, 2002).

Freitas, Roger, *Portrait of a Castrato: Politics, Patronage and Music in the Life of Atto Melani* (Cambridge: Cambridge University Press, 2009).

Fubini, Erico, ed., *Music and Culture in Eighteenth Century Europe: A Sourcebook* (Chicago and London: University of Chicago Press, 1994).

Fumaroli, Marc, *L'Âge de l'éloquence* (Geneva: Droz, 2009 [1980]).

Fuzelier, Louis, "Avertissement," *La Reine des Péris, Comédie persane, représenté par l'Académie Royale de Musique L'an 1725* (Paris; Ribous, 1725).

_____. "Avertissement," *Les Indes galantes: Ballet heroique représenté pour le premier fois par l'Académie Royale de Musique. Le Mardy, Vingt-troisème d'Août 1735* (Paris: Ballard, 1735).

Galilei, Vincenzo, *Dialogue on Ancient and Modern Music*, trans. and introduction by Claude V. Palisco (New Haven and London: Yale University Press, 2003).

Gardiner, John Eliot, "Idomeneo: A Reappraisal," in W.A. Mozart, *Idomeneo* (Hamburg: Deutsche GrammophonGhbh/Archiv Recording, 1991).

Girdlestone, Cuthbert, *Jean Phillippe Rameau* (New York: Dover Publications 1969).

Glixon, Jonathan, "Was Monteverdi a Traitor?" *Music and Letters*, Vol. 72, No. 3, August 1991.

Glover, Jane, *Cavalli* (London: B.T. Batsford, 1978).

Gluck, Christophe Willibald, *Le Rencontre imprévue ou Les Pèlerins de la Mecque: Opéra en trois actes* (Caen: Théâtre de Caen/Actes Sud, 1998).

Goçek, Fatma Murge, *East Encounters West: France and the Ottoman Empire in the 18th Century* (New York: Oxford University Press, 1987).

Goethe, Wolfgang von, *Campaign in France* (London: Chapman and Hall, 1849).

_____, *Conversations with Eckermann.* (San Francisco: North Point Press, 1984).

_____, *The German Refugees* (London: Dedalus, 2006).

_____, *Tales of Transformation* (San Francisco: City Lights Books, 1987).

_____, *Unterhaltungen deutscher Ausgewandertren* (Stuttgart: Reclam, 1991).

Goldmann, Lucien, *Le Dieu caché: Étude sur la vision tragique dans les Pensées de Pascal et dans le théâtre de Racine* (Paris: Gallimard, 1959).

Goldoni, Carlo, "The Author to the Reader" of "Off to the Country," *The Holiday Trilogy* (New York: Marsilio, 1992).

Gôrce, Jérôme de la, *Jean-Baptiste Lully* (Paris: Fayard, 2002).

Gordon, Bonnie, "Talking Back: the Female Voice in Il ballo delle ingrate," *Cambridge Opera Journal.* Vol 2, No. 1, March 1999.

Gronda, Giovanna and Paolo Fabbri, eds., *Libretti d'opera italiani dal seicento al novecento* (Milan: Arnoldo Mondadori, 2007).

Grout, Donald Jay, *A Short History of Opera* [3rd edition] (New York: Columbia University Press, 1988).

Guicciardini, Francesco, *Maxims and Reflections (Ricordi)* (Philadelphia: University of Pennsylvania Press, 1992).

Hale, J.R., *Florence and the Medici* (London: Phoenix Press, 2001).

Hanning, Barbara Russano, "Apologia pro Ottavio Rinuccini," *Journal of the American Musicological Society* (Summer 1973).

_____. "The Ending of L'Orfeo: Father, Son, and Rinuccini," *Journal of Seventeenth Century Music* Vol. 9, No. 1 (2003), http://sscm-jscm.press.uiuc.edu/v9/no1/hanning.html.

_____. *Of Poetry and Music's Power: Humanism and the Creation of Opera* (Ann Arbor: UMI Research Press, 1980).

Hathaway, Baxter, *The Age of Criticism: The Late Renaissance in Italy* (Ithaca, NY: Cornell University Press, 1972).

Hawkins, John, *A General History of the Science and Practice of Music*, Vol. 2 (London: Novello, 1853[1776]).

Heartz, Daniel, and Bruce Alan Brown, "Galant," in *The New Grove Dictionary of Music and Musicians*, [2nd edition] Vol. 9 (London: MacMillan, 2001).

_____. *Mozart's Operas* with contributing essays by Thomas Bauman (Berkeley and Los Angeles: University of California Press, 1990).

Hegel, G.W.F., *Aesthetics* 2 vols. (Oxford: Oxford University Press, 1998).

Heilbron, J.L., *Galileo* (Oxford: Oxford University Press, 2010).

Heyer, J.H., ed., *Jean-Baptiste Lully and the Music of the French Baroque: Essays in Honor of James R. Anthony* (Cambridge: Cambridge University Press, 1984).

Holden, Anthony, *The Man Who Wrote Mozart* (London: Weidenfeld and Nicolson, 2006).

Hollier, Denis, ed., *A New History of French Literature* (Cambridge and London: Harvard University Press, 1989).

Homer, *The Odyssey*, Robert Fagles, trans. (New York: Penguin, 1996).

Honolka, Kurt, *Papageno: Emmanuel Schikaneder* (Portland: Amadeus Press, 1990).

Howard, Patricia, *C.W. Gluck, Orfeo* (Cambridge: Cambridge University Press, 1981).

Howe, Irving, *Politics and the Novel* (Columbia University Press, 1992[1957]).

Hunter, Mary, *The Culture of Opera Buffa in Mozart's Vienna* (Princeton: Princeton University Press, 1999).

Le Huray, Peter and James Day, eds., *Music and Aesthetics in the Eighteenth and Early Nineteenth Centuries* (Cambridge and New York: Cambridge University Press, 1988).

Irving, John, "Sonata (2)," *The New Grove Dictionary of Music and Musicians*, [2nd edition] Vol. 23 (London: Macmillan, 2001).

Isherwood, Robert M., *Music in the Service of the King: France in the 17th Century* (Ithaca and London: Cornell University Press, 1973).

Jacob, Margaret C., *Living the Enlightenment: Freemasonry and Politics in 18th Century Europe* (Oxford and New York: Oxford University Press, 1991).

Joly, Jacques, *Les fêtes théâtrales de Métastase à la cour de Vienne (1731–1767)* (Clermont-Ferrand: Université de Clermont-Ferrand II: Faculté des Lettres et Sciences humaines, 1978).

de Jonquière, Le Vte, *Histoire de l'empire ottoman*, Vol. 1 (Paris: La Hachette, 1914).

Kann, Robert, *A Study in Austrian Intellectual History* (New York: Prager, 1960).

Katz, Jacob, *Jews and Freemasons* (Cambridge: Harvard University Press 1970).

Keefe, Simon P., ed., *The Cambridge Companion to Mozart* (Cambridge: Cambridge University Press, 2003).

Kelly, Michael, *Reminiscences of Michael Kelly, of the King's Theatre and Theatre Royal Drury Lane*, Vol. 1 (London: Henry Colburn, 1826).

Keohane, Nannerl O., *Philosophy and the State in France* (Princeton: Princeton University Press, 1980).

Kerman, Joseph, *Opera and Drama* (Berkeley and Los Angeles: University of California Press, 1968).

Ketterer, Robert, *Ancient Rome in Early Opera* (Urbana and Chicago: University of Illinois Press, 2009).

Kimbell, David. *Italian Opera* (Cambridge: Cambridge University Press, 1994).

Kintzler, Catherine, *Jean-Philippe Rameau: Splendour et naufrage de l'esthétique du plaisir à l'Age classique* (Paris: Le Sycamore, 1983).

Kirkendale, Warren, *The Court Musicians of Florence during the Principate of the Medici* (Florence: Olschki Editori, 1993).

Kivvy, Peter, *Osmin's Rage: Philosophical Reflections on Opera, Drama, and Text* (Ithaca and London: Cornell University Press, 1988.)

Kosellek, Reinhart, *Critique and Crisis* (Cambridge: MIT Press, 1988).

Kologlu, Orhan, *Le Turc dans la presse française des débuts jusqu'a 1815* (Beirut: Maison d'Editions al-Hayat, 1971).

Kracauer, Siegfried, *Jacques Offenbach and the Paris of His Time* (New York: Zone Books, 2002).

Kristeller, Paul Oskar, *Renaissance Thought and its Sources* (New York: Columbia University Press, 1979).

⸻, *Renaissance Thought and the Arts* (Princeton: Princeton University Press, 1990).

Lahontan, Baron Louis-Armand, *Dialogue de Monsieur Baron de Lahontan et d'un Sauvage dans l'Americque* (Amsterdam: Chez Veuve de Boeteman, 1704).

Landon, H.C. Robbins, *1791: Mozart's Last Year* (London: Thames and Hudson, 1999).

Lattarico, Jean-François, *Busenello: Un théâtre de la rhétorique* (Paris: Classiques Garnier, (2013).

⸻, *Venise incognita* (Paris: H. Champion, 2012).

Launay, Denise, ed., *La Querelle des Bouffons: Textes des pamphlets* avec introduction, 3 vols. (Geneva: Minkoff, 1973).

Lederer, Josef-Horst, "Scipio as a Historical Figure," in the booklet accompanying Mozart, *Il Sogno di Scipio, Complete Mozart Edition* (Philips: London, 1979).

Levinson, J. ed., *Aesthetics and Ethics* (Cambridge University Press, 2001).

Leopold, Silke, *Monteverdi: Music in Transition* (Cambridge: Cambridge University Press, 1991).

Lessing, Gotthold Ephraim, *Philosophical and Theological Writings* (Cambridge and New York: Cambridge University Press, 2005).

Levin, David J., ed., *Opera through Other Eyes* (Stanford: Stanford University Press, 1994).

Lewis, Bernard, *Race and Slavery in the Middle East* (Oxford and New York: Oxford University Press, 1992).

Lipsius, Justus, *Politica: Six Books of Politics or Political Instruction*, trans. Jan Waszink (Assen, the Netherlands: Royal Van Gorcum, 2004).

⸻, *Ivsti Lipsi Epitolae*, Vol. 13, J. Papy, ed. (Brussels: Palais des Academiën, 2000).

Litchfield, Burr, *Emergence of a Bureaucracy: The Florentine Patricians, 1530–1790* (Princeton: Princeton University Press, 1986).

Livingston, Arthur, *La vità Veneziana nelle opere di Gian Francesco Busenello* (Venice: V. Callegap, 1913).

Lully, Jean-Baptiste, *Armide*, Lois Rosow, ed. in *Oeuvres complètes*, Série III, Vol. 14 (Hildesheim, Zurich, New York: Georg Olms Verlag, 2003).

_____, *Acis et Galatée, Pastorale heroïque en musique répresentée pour la premiere fois dans le Châteu d'Anet devant Monsieur le Dauphin. Par l'academie Roiale de Musique* (Paris, 1690).

Machiavelli, Niccolò, *The Discourses* (Harmondsworth/Baltimore: Penguin, 1970).

_____, *The Prince* (London and New York: Penguin, 1981).

Maland, David, *Culture and Society in Seventeenth Century France* (New York: Scribner, 1970).

_____, *Europe in the Seventeenth Century* (London: MacMillan, 1977).

Marchesan, Angelo, *Della vita e della opera di Lorenzo Da Ponte* (Treviso: Turazza, 1900).

Martines, Lauro, *Lawyers and Statecraft in Renaissance Italy* (Princeton: Princeton University Press, 1968).

Mathiesen, Thomas J., "Problems of Terminology of Ancient Greek Theory: 'APMONÍA,'" in *Festive Essays for Pauline Alderman; A Musicological Tribute* (Provo, Utah: Brigham Young University, 1976).

Ménestrier, Claude-François, *Des représentations en musique anciennes et modernes* (Paris: 1681).

De'Medici, Lorenzino, *Apology for a Murder* (London: Hesperus Press, 2004).

Mellers, Wilifred, *François Couperin* (London: Dobson, 1950).

Mellors, Ronald, *Tacitus* (New York and London: Routledge, 1993).

Miller, Peter N. and Ian Fenlon, *The Song of the Soul: Understanding Poppea* (London: Royal Musicological Association Monograph 5, 1992).

Miller, P.N., "Friendship and Conversation in Seventeenth Century Venice," *Journal of Modern History*, Vol 73, No. 1 (March 2001).

Miller, Stephen, "Why Cato Had to Die," *Times Literary Supplement*, October 1, 1999.

Moindrot, Isabelle, *L'opéra seria ou la règne des castrats* (Paris: Fayard, 1993).

Monson, Craig A., "The Council of Trent Revisited," *Journal of the American Musicological Society* Vol. 55, No. 1 (Spring 2002).

Monteverdi, Claudio, *L'incoronazione di Poppea*, Alan Curtis, ed. (London and Sevenoaks, Novello, 1989).

_____, *The Letters of Claudio Monteverdi*, Revised edition, Denis Stevens ed. (Oxford: Oxford University Press, 1995).

_____, *The Operas of Monteverdi: Orfeo/ Il ritorno d'Ulisse in patria/L'incoronzione di Poppea* (Paris/London/New York: Calder and Riverrun, 1992).

_____, *Orfeo: Nouvelle édition et restitution*, Edward H. Tarr, ed. (Paris: Editions Costallat, 1974).

_____, *Il ritorno d'Ulisse in Patria*, libretto by Giacomo Badoaro, edited by Alan Curtis (London: Novello, 2002).

Moote, A. Lloyd, *Louis XIII: The Just* (Berkeley, Los Angeles, and London: University of California Press, 1989).

Moretti, Pietro Yates, "Busenello and his Composers," (New Haven: Ph.d. Diss., Yale University, 2010).

Morrison, Heather, *Pursuing Enlightenment in Vienna, 1781–1790* (Ph.d. Diss., Louisiana State University, 2005).

Mormiche, Pascale, *Devenir prince: L'école du pouvoir en France XVIIe-XVIIIe siècles* (Paris: CNRS Editions, 2009).

Motte, Houdar de la, *Pigmalion, Acte de Balet Représsente pour le premier fois par l'Académie Royale Musique* (Paris: L'Academie, 1748).

_____, *L'Europe galante: Ballet en musique* in *Oeuvres de Monsieur Houdar de la Motte*, Vol. 6 (Paris: Prault, 1754).

Mozart, Leopold, *Versuch einer gründlichen Violinschule* (Vienna: Carl Stephenson, 1922; facsimile of the original 1756 edition).

Mozart, Wolfgang Amadeus, *Briefe und Aufzeichnungen*, Band I-3 (Kassel: Bärenreiter-Verlag, 2005).

_____, *Così fan tutte*, Libretto by Lorenzo Da Ponte, English National Opera Guide 22 (Paris, London, New York: Calder Publications and Riverrun Press, 1991).

_____, *Don Giovanni*, Libretto by Lorenzo Da Ponte. English National Opera Guide No. 18 (London/New York: Calder and Riverrun Press, 1995).

_____, *Die Enteführung aus dem Serail*, Text von Chr. F. Bretzner in der Bearbeitung von J.G. Stephanie D.J. (Stuttgart: Philipp Reclam, 2003).

_____, *The Letters of Mozart and His Family* 3 Vols. [2nd edition], (London/New York: MacMillan/St. Martin's Press, 1966).

_____, *The Magic Flute*. Libretto by Emanuel Schikaneder (London and New York: John Calder, the English National Opera, and Riverrun, 1997).

_____, *Seven Mozart Librettos: A Verse Translation* by J.D. McClatchy (New York and London: Norton, 2011).

Muir, Edward, *The Culture Wars of the Late Renaissance* (Cambridge and London: Harvard University Press, 2007).

Nagel, Ivan, *Autonomy and Mercy* (Cambridge and London: Harvard University Press, 1991.)

Nagler, Alois M., *Theatre Festivals of the Medici, 1539–1637* (New Haven and London: Yale University Press, 1964).

Neville, Don, "Moral Philosophy in Metastasian Drama," *Studies in Music from the University of Western Ontario* Vol. 12, 1982.

_____, "Metastasio" in *The New Grove Dictionary of Opera* Vol . 3 (London: Macmillan, 1982).

Norwich, John Julius, *A History of Venice* (New York: Vintage, 1989).

Nosow, Robert, "The Debate on Song in the Accademia Fiorentina," *Early Music History*, Vol. 21 (2002).

Ovid, *Metamorphoses* (New York and London: Norton, 2005).

Pagden, Anthony, *Lords of the World: Ideologies of Empire in Spain, Britain and France c. 1500–c.1800* (New Haven and London: Yale University Press, 1995).

Palisca, Claude V., "The Alterati of Florence: Pioneers in the Theory of Dramatic Music," in *New Looks at Italian Opera: Essays in Honor of Donald J. Grout* William Austin, ed. (Westport: Greenwood Publishers, 1968).

_____, *The Florentine Camerata: Documentary Studies and Translations* (New Haven and London: Yale University Press, 1989).

_____, "Girolamo Mei, Mentor to the Florentine Camerata," *The Musical Quarterly* Vol. 40, No. 1 (January 1954).

_____, *Humanism in Italian Renaissance Musical Thought* (New Haven and London: Yale University Press, 1985).

_____, "Musical Asides in the Diplomatic Correspondence of Emilio de' Cavalieri," *The Musical Quarterly*, Vol. 49, No. 3 (July 1963).

Parisi, Susan Helen, *Ducal Patronage of Music in Mantua, 1587–1627: An Archival Study* (University of Illinois, Urbana-Champaign, Ph.d. Diss., 1989).

Parrott, David, "The Mantuan Succession, 1627–31: A Sovereignty Dispute," *English Historical Review* Vol. 112, No. 445 (February 1997).

Peri, Jacopo and Ottavio Rinuccini, *Euridice* edited by Howard Mayer Brown from the first edition [Florence: G. Marescotti, 1600] (Madison: A-R Editions, Inc./Recent Researches in the Music of the Baroque Era, Volumes 36 and 37, 1981).

Pestelli, Giorgio, *The Age of Mozart and Beethoven* (Cambridge: Cambridge University Press, 1990).

Pezzl, Johann. *Pezzl's Sketch of Vienna*, Part 1: 1786, translated in H.C. Robbin Landon's *Mozart and Vienna* (New York: Schirmer Books, 1991).

Pirrotta, Nino, *Don Giovanni's Progress* (New York: Marsilio, 1991).

_____, "Metastasio and the Demands of his Literary Environment," *Studies in Music from the University of Western Ontario*, Vol. 71, No. 1 (1982).

_____, "Temperaments and Tendencies in the Florentine Camerata" in Pirotta, *Music and Culture in Italy from the Middle Ages to the Baroque* (Harvard: Harvard University Press, 1984).

Pitou, Spire, *The Paris Opera* (Westport, Conn.: Greenwood Press, 1983).

Plaisance, Michel, "Littérature et censure à Florence à la fin du XVe Siècle: Le Retour du Censuré," in *Le Pouvoir et la Plume: incitation, contrôle et répression dans l'Italie du XVI siècle: Actes du Colloque international* (Paris: Université de la Sorbonne Nouvelle,1982).

_____, "L'Académie des Alterati au travail," in *La Transmission des Savoirs au Moyen-Age et à la Renaissance* Vol. 2 (2005).

Plato, *The Collected Dialogues of Plato*, Edith Hamilton and Huntington Cairns, eds. (Princeton: Princeton University Press, 1961).

Plutarch, *The Lives of the Noble Grecians and Romans*, Vol. 2, John Dryden, translator. (New York: Modern Library, 1992).

Polzonetti, Pierpaolo, *Italian Opera in the Age of the American Revolution* (Cambridge: Cambridge University Press, 2011).

Prunières, Henry, *Monteverdi* (New York: Dover, 1972).

_____, *Cavalli et l'Opéra vénitien au XVIIe siècle* (Paris: Les Éditions Rieder, 1931).

Pullan, Brian, ed. *Venice: A Documentary History, 1450–1630* (Oxford: Blackwell, 1992).

Raccamadoro-Ramelli, Francesco, *Ottavio Rinuccini* (Fabriano: Stab. Tip. Gentile, 1900).

Raguenet, François, *Paralele des Italiens et des François ce qui regarde la musique et Les Opéra* (Paris: Moreau, 1702) [Geneva: Minkoff reprint, 1976].

Rameau, Jean-Philippe, *Complete Theoretical Writings*, Vol. 5, Edwin R. Jacobi, ed. (N.P.: American Institute of Musicology, 1969).

_____, *Treatise on Harmony*, (New York: Dover, 1971).

Ramsay, Andrew Michael, *The Travels of Cyrus to which is annexed A Discourse upon the Theology and Mythology of the Pagans* [6th edition] (London: Bettenham, 1734).

Ravel, Jeffrey S., *The Contested Parterre: Public Theater and French Political Culture, 1680–1791* (Ithaca and London: Cornell University Press, 1999).

Rice, John A., *W.A. Mozart: La Clemenza di Tito* (Cambridge: Cambridge University Press, 1991).

Riley, Patrick, *The General Will before Rousseau: The Transformation of the Divine into the Civic* (Princeton: Princeton University Press, 1986).

Rinuccini, Ottavio, "Dedication of Euridice" (1600), in Oliver Strunk, ed., *Source Readings in Music History* (New York: W.W. Norton, 1950).

Robertson, Ritchie, "Freemasons vs. Jesuits," *Times Literary Supplement (TLS)*, October 12, 2012.

Robinson, Paul, *Opera and Ideas* (Ithaca and London: Cornell University Press, 1985).

Rosand, David, *Myths of Venice: Figuration of a State* (Chapel Hill and London: University of North Carolina Press, 2001).

Rosand, Ellen, "Seneca and the Interpretation of L'incoronazione di Poppea," *Journal of the American Musicological Society* Vol. 38, No. 1 (Spring 1985).

_____. *Opera in Seventeenth Century Venice* (Berkeley, Los Angeles, London: University of California Press, 1991).

_____. *Monteverdi's Last Operas: A Venetian Trilogy* (Berkeley, Los Angeles, London: University of California Press, 2007).

Rose, C.J., "Marc Antonio Vernier, Renier Zeno and the Myth of Venice," *The Historian*, Vol. 3, No. 36 (May 1974).

Rosen, Charles, *The Classical Style* (New York: W.W. Norton, 1997[1971]).

Rosow, Lois, "Power and Display: Music in Court Theater," in T. Carter and J. Butt, eds., *The Cambridge History of Seventeenth Century Music* (Cambridge: Cambridge University Press, 2005).

Rousseau, Jean-Jacques, *The Confessions* (Harmondsworth: Penguin, 1953).

_____. *"Le Devin du Village"* in *Oeuvres complètes*, Vol. 3 (Paris: Gallimard, 1964) and *Le Devin du Village, Intermède, Represésenté à Fontainebleau avant le Roy les 18 & 24 Octobre 1752 & à Paris par L'Académie Royale de Musique, Le Jeudy premier Mars 1753* (Paris: V. Delformel & Fils, 1753).

_____. *Oeuvres complètes* Vol. 5, *Écrits sur la musique, la langue et le théâtre* (Paris: Gallimard, 1995).

Rushton, Julian *W.A. Mozart, Don Giovanni* (Cambridge: Cambridge University Press, 1981).

_____. *W.A. Mozart, Die Entführung aus dem Serail* (Cambridge: Cambridge University, 1987).

_____. *W.A. Mozart, Idomeneo* (Cambridge: Cambridge University Press, 1993).

Russo, Joseph Louis, *Lorenzo Da Ponte* (New York: Columbia University Press, 1922).

Sanders, E.K., *Fénelon: His Friends and Foes* (London: Longmans, Green, and Co., 1901).

Sartre, Jean Paul, *Critique de la raison dialectique*, précédé de *Questions de méthode*, Texte établi et annoté par Arlette Elkaïm-Sartre, Tome 1, Théorie des ensembles pratiques. Paris: Gallimard, 1985 (1960).

Saslow, James M., *The Medici Wedding of 1589* (New Haven and London: Yale University Press, 1996).

Schreffler, Anne C., "Berlin Walls: Dahlhaus, Knepler and the Ideologies of Music History," *Journal of Musicology* Vol. 20, No. 4 (2003).

Starobinski, Jean, *1789: The Emblems of Reason* (Cambridge and London: MIT Press, 1988).

Schellhase, Kenneth C., *Tacitus in Renaissance Political Thought* (Chicago and London: University of Chicago Press, 1976).

Schmidt-Beste, Thomas, *The Sonata* (Cambridge and New York: Cambridge University Press, 2011).

Scholem, Gershom, *Du Frankisme au Jacobinisme: La vie de Moses Dobruska alias Thomas von Schönfeld alias Junius Frey* (Paris: Hautes Études/Gallimard/Le Seuil, 1981).

Scholes, Percy A., *The Great Burney* (London and New York: Oxford University Press, 1948).

Scott, R.H.F., *Jean-Baptiste Lully* (London: Peter Owen, 1973).

Skinner, Quentin, *The Foundations of Modern Political Thought*, 2 vols. (Cambridge: Cambridge University Press, 1978, 1979).

_____. *Machiavelli*, (Oxford: Oxford University Press, 1991).

_____. "Meaning and Understanding in the History of Ideas," *Visions of Politics, Vol. 1 (Regarding Method)* (Cambridge and New York: Cambridge University Press, 2007).

_____. "Surveying *The Foundations*: A Retrospect and a Reassessment," in Annabel Brett and James Tully, eds., with Holly Hamilton-Bleakley, *Rethinking The Foundations of Modern Political Thought* (Cambridge: Cambridge University Press, 2006).

Smith, Patrick J., *The Tenth Muse: A Historical Study of the Opera Libretto* (New York: Knopf, 1991).

Solomon, Maynard, *Mozart: A Life* (New York: HarperCollins, 1996).

Sorkin, David, *The Religious Enlightenment* (Princeton: Princeton University Press, 2008).

Stein, Peter, *Roman Law in European History* (Cambridge: Cambridge University Press, 2000).

Stendhal, *Life of Mozart*, (Montreal: Guernica, 1991).

Sternfeld, F. W., *The Birth of Opera* (Oxford: Oxford University Press, 1995).

Steptoe, Andrew, *The Mozart-Da Ponte Operas* (Oxford: Oxford University Press, 1988).

Strakosch, Henry E., *State Absolutism and the Rule of Law: The Struggle for the Codification of Civil Law in Austria 1753–1811* (Sidney, Australia: University of Sydney Press, 1967).

Stradling, R.A., "Mantua Preserv'd or the Tragicall Historie of Count Olivarez, Great Favorite of Spayne," *The Seventeenth Century*, Vol. 4, No. 2, Autumn 1989.

_____. "Prelude to Disaster; the Precipitation of the War of the Mantuan Succession, 1627–29," *The Historical Journal* Vol. 33, No. 4 (1940) December 1990.

Strong, Roy, *Splendor at Court: Renaissance Spectacle and the Theater of Power* (Boston: Houghton Mifflin Co., 1973).

Strunk, Oliver, ed., *Source Readings in Music History* (New York: W.W. Norton, 1950), Revised edition, Leo Treitler, ed., 1997.

Suetonius, *The Twelve Caesars* (London and New York: Penguin Books, 1989).

Syme, Ronald, *Tacitus*, Vol. 1 (Oxford: Oxford University Press, 1958).

Tacitus, *The Annals of Imperial Rome* (London and New York: Penguin Books, 1996).

_____. *The Agricola and the Germania* (London and New York: Penguin, 1970).

_____. *Agricola, Germania, Dialogue on Orators* (Indianapolis: Bobbs-Merrill, 1967).

_____. *The Histories* (London and New York: Penguin Books, 1995).

Tackett, Timothy, *When the King Took Flight* (Cambridge and London: Harvard University Press, 2003).

Taruskin, Richard *Music in the Seventeenth and Eighteenth Centuries* (*The Oxford History of Western Music*, Vol. 1) (Oxford and New York: Oxford University Press, 2010).

Terrasson, Jean, *Séthos, Histoire ou vie tirée des monumens et anecdotes de l'Ancienne Egypte traduit d'un manuscript grec, Vol. 1.* (Amsterdam: Aux Dépans de la Compagnie, 1732).

_____. *Dissertation critique sur l'Iliade d'Homer* (Paris: F, Fiunier and FA. U.-Coustelier, 1715).

Tierney, Brian, "'The Prince is not Bound by the Laws': Accursius and the Origins of the Modern State," *in Comparative Studies in Society and History*, Vol. 5, No. 4 (July 1965).

Till, Nicholas, ed., *The Cambridge Companion to Opera Studies* (Cambridge: Cambridge University Press, 2012).

_____. *Mozart and the Enlightenment* (New York: Norton, 1992).

Tomlinson, Gary, *Monteverdi and the End of the Renaissance* (Berkeley and Los Angeles: University of California Press, 1990).

Toscani, Bernard, "La Serva Padrona: Variations on a Theme," in F. Degrada, ed., *Studia Pergolesiani*, 2 (NP: La Nuova Italia Editrice, 1988).

Towneley, Simon, "Early Italian Opera," in Gerald Abraham., ed. *The New Oxford History of Music, Vol. IV: The Age of Humanism, 1540–1630* (Oxford: Oxford University Press, 1968).

Treadwell, Nina, *Music and Wonder at the Medici Court* (Bloomington: Indiana University Press, 2008).

Tuck, Richard, *Philosophy and Government: 1572–1651* (Cambridge: Cambridge University Press, 1993).

Virgil, *The Aeneid*, trans. Robert Fagles, (London/New York: Penguin Books, 2006).

_____, *The Georgics* (London and New York: Penguin Books, 1982), p. 140.

Voltaire, *Le Siècle de Louis XIV* (Paris: Le Livre de Poche, 2002).

Walker, D.P., ed., *Les Fêtes du Marriage de Ferdinand de Médicis et de Christine de Lorraine, Florence 1589: Musique des Intermèdes de 'la Pellegrina'* (Paris: Éditions du Centre National de la Recherche Scientifique, 1958).

Warburton, Ernest, "Introduction," to *Catone in Utica: Opera Seria in Three Acts. Libretto after Metastasio , The Collected Works of Johann Christian Bach, 1735–1782* Vol. 2 (New York and London: Garland Publishing Inc., 1987).

Weinberg, Bernard, "The Accademia degli Alterati and Literary Taste from 1570 to 1600," *Italica*, Vol. 31, No. 4 (December 1954).

_____. "Argomenti di Discussione Letteraria Nell'Academia degli Alterati (1570–1600)," in *Giornale storico della lettarature italiana* Vol. 131 (1954).

Weiss, Piero, ed., *Opera: A History in Documents* (New York and Oxford: Oxford University Press, 2002).

Weiss, Piero and Richard Taruskin, eds., *Music in the Western World: A History in Documents* (New York: Schirmer Books, 1984).

Whenham, John, *Claudio Monteverdi: Orfeo* (Cambridge: Cambridge University Press, 1986).

Whenham, John and Richard Wistreich, eds, *The Cambridge Companion to Monteverdi* (Cambridge: Cambridge University Press, 2007).

Wolff, Hans Julius, *Roman Law* (Norman, Oklahoma: University of Oklahoma Press, 1976).

Wolfson, W. Daniel, "Turks on the Eighteenth Century Operatic Stage and European Political, Military and Cultural History." *Eighteenth-Century Life* Vol. 9, No. 2 (1985).

Wooton, David, *Paolo Sarpi: Between Renaissance and Enlightenment* (Cambridge: Cambridge University Press, 1983).

Zagorin, Perez, *Ways of Lying: Dissimulation, Persecution and Conformity in Early Modern Europe* (Cambridge: Harvard University Press, 1990).

Zaslaw, Neal, ed., *The Classical Era* (Englewood Cliffs, NJ: Prentice Hall, 1989).

INDEX

Page numbers in italics indicate illustrations.

XIV and, 145, 146, 159–61; Molière
and, 145, 159, 160, 169; pastorals of,
160; portraits of, *147*, *162*; Quarrel
of Ancients and Moderns and, 168;
Quinault and, 145, 159–63; Raguenet
on, 185; Rameau and, 190–1; recitative of, 145, 161, 163–4; *Acis and
Galatea*, 144–50, 163, *164*, *191*, 219;
Armide, 162–4, 170; *Atys*, 160–1; *Le
bourgeois gentilhomme*, 169; *Cadmus
and Hermione*, 160; *Festivals of Love
and Bacchus*, 160; *Phaëton*, 169; *Te
Deum*, 145
"lyric drama," 152
"lyric tragedies," 145, 148, 169, 176–9

Machiavelli, Niccolò, 9–10, 76, 123,
375; Botero on, 40–1; Cato and, 238;
Metastasio on, 231; Tacitus and, 26,
41; Titus and, 259–60; on Venice,
87; on *virtù*, 75, 87, 139–40, 263;
Discourses on Livy, xxii, 13, 138–9;
The Prince, xxi–xxiii, 13, 40–1, 76, 223
madrigals, 15, 18, 22; of Monteverdi, 55,
56, 65, 86
"madrigal-opera," 395
Maintenon, Madame de, 163, 170, 181
Manelli, Francesco, 96
Manni, Agostino, 34
Mantua, 55–6, 64, 79–83, 396; Holy
Roman Empire and, 60, 65, 82–3, 85;
Sack of, 98, 119; War of Succession
of, 81, 153
Margherita of Savoy, 71, 73
Marguerite of Valois, 8
Maria Theresa of Austria, 226–9, 242–3,
274; death of, 251, 268; Freemasonry
and, 339; law code of, 306–7
Marie Antoinette, Queen of France, 249,
251, 259, 264, 302; Da Ponte and,
333; flight of, 349, 351; on her hus-
band, 352; Leopold II and, 350
Martini, Karl Anton von, 307–8
Marx, Karl, 118, 326, 399, 401, 403
Masons. *See* Free Masonry
Maternus, Curiatius, 31–2

Mazarin, Jules, 151, 153–8
Mazzolà, Caterino, 256, 259, 261, 300
Medici, Alessandro de', 11, 42
Medici, Catherine de', 32, 33, 152
Medici, Cosimo I de', 11, 12, 18; Botero
on, 44; as "Father of Florence," 47; as
Florence's Augustus, 42; reign of, 48
Medici, Ferdinando I de', 4, 11; Botero
on, 44; Henri IV and, 3–4; marriage
of, 33–5; reign of, 49
Medici, Francesco I de', 18, 20, 26, 30;
Botero on, 44; marriages of, 32–3, 48
Medici, Maria de', 6, 152–3; marriage of,
3–4, 34; Rinuccini and, 71–2
Mei, Girolamo, 14–16, 18, 48; Bardi and,
19; Galilei and, 21; Monteverdi and,
65
Melani, Atto, 154, 158
melody, 15; Hegel on, xv–xvi; Monteverdi
on, 69; Rameau on, 194; Rousseau on,
150, 163–4, 194, 198–9, 250. *See also*
monody
Memmo, Bernardo, 297, 298
Ménestrier, Claude-François, 169, 171
Mersenne, Marin, 150
Mesmer, Franz Anton, 330
Messala, Vipstanus, 31–2
Metastasio, Pietro, xviii, 229–37, 291; Da
Ponte and, 292; death of, 251; Gluck
and, 250; on government, 236–7,
247–8; Hasse and, 249; legacy of,
273; on Machiavelli, 231; portrait of,
235; *La Betulia liberatà*, 229; *Catone in
Utica*, 237–42, 260; *La clemenza di Tito*,
225–6, 228–31, 256–64, 373, 378–9; *Il
sogno de Scipione*, 228, 231, 260
Meyerbeer, Giacomo, 389, 446n14
Michelangelo Buonarroti, 182
Milton, John, 245–6
mimesis, 15, 25–6, 185–6, 200
minuet, 212; in *Don Giovanni*, 323–4; in
Marriage of Figaro, 304, 311, 312, 314
Mirrors for Princes, 12–13, 76, 127
Mocenigo, Girolamo, 86
Molière, 205, 316; Lully and, 145, 159,
160, 169

Nevers, Duc de (Charles Gonzaga), 82–4
"new music," 5–6, 17, 25; of Caccini, 24, 49; of Cavalieri, 34, 49; of Monteverdi, 55, 63, 65–6, 68–9; of Schönberg, 394
"new musicology," 393–4
noblesse de robe (legal nobility), 154–5, 402–3, 423n40
Le nozze di Figaro. See under Mozart, Wolfgang Amadeus

Octavia (play), 124
Offenbach, Jacques, 389, 397–8, 447n16
One Thousand and One Nights, 200, 287–8, 341
opera-ballet, 181–3
opera buffa, 230, 251, 274, 301; as "counter-genre," 273; development of, 233; Durazzo and, 249–50; "heroic," 344; Mozart and, 278, 302; of Piccini, 252
opera seria, 222, 230, 251, 273; Gluck and, 248; Leopold II and, 255–6; Metastasio and, 234; Mozart and, 253, 256, 278; Stendhal on, 257
operetta, xxiv
Oran (Algeria), 286
Orfeo (Monteverdi and Striggio), 69–70, 185, 373–4, 395–8, 405; narrative of, 6, 55–62, 67–8; popularity of, 63; *Il ritorno d'Ulisse in patria* and, 107–8
Orfeo (Rossi and Buti), 153, 155–8
Orléans, Anne-Marie-Louise of, 151, 158
Orléans, Duke of, 188–9
Orléans, Gaston of, 151
Orphée aux enfers (Offenbach), 389, 447n16
Orpheus, 344–5; as Apollo's son, xxiii, 9, 63; death of, 62–3; in *Euridice*, 4, 49–52, 57–60; in Gluck, 250; Horace on, 7; *Magic Flute* and, 359, 366–7, 374, 385; in *Orfeo*, 55–62; in Ovid, 6–7, 63, 374–5; Pluto and, xxiii, 7, 51–2, 57–61, 155; Poliziano on, 8; Rinuccini on, 49–52; Scipio Africanus and, 228; Theseus and, 76; Virgil on, 6–7, 63
Osman, Topal, 205–6, 209

Ottoboni, Pietro, 124–5, 231
Ottoman Empire, xxi, 64, 65, 181; Habsburgs and, 183–4, 204, 205, 275, 276, 283; Thirty Years War and, 81; Venice and, 92, 100; Voltaire on, 215
Ovid, xix, 8, 38, 98, 112, 374–5, 405; Astraea in, 174; Galatea in, 146; Lully and, 160–1; Orpheus in, 6–7, 63, 374–5; Ulysses in, 105

Paine, Tom, 349–50
Paisiello, Giovanni, 301, 303
Palestrina, Giovanni Pierluigi de, 17
Parma, Duke of, 119, 207
Pascal, Blaise, 401–2, 423n40
pastorals, 8, 146, 159, 160, *164*
Patrizi, Francesco, 25
Paul V, Pope, 60, 91
Pellegrin, Simon-Joseph, 178–9, 197
Pergen, Johann Anton von, 335–6
Pergolesi, Giovanni Battista, 216–18; *La serva padrona*, 148–50, 165, 218, 273, 303
Peri, Jacopo, 5; Monteverdi and, 6, 398, 405; *Dafne*, 4–5, 24, 46–7, 49. *See also* Corsi, Jacopo; *Euridice*; Rinuccini, Ottavio
Pernucio. *See* Couperin, François
Perrin, Pierre, 159
Petrarca, Francesco, 14
Pezzl, Johann, 271–4
Pfitzner, Hans, 17
philosophes, 186–7, 189, 192, 196
Piaget, Jean, 401
Piccini, Niccolò, 252
Pisani, Giorgio, 299
Pizarro, Francisco, 207
Plankenstern, Raimund Wetzlar von, 293
Plato, xvii, 7, 43; Aristotle and, 14–15, 25; on harmony of the spheres, 7, 20, 35–8; on justice, 37, 405; on mimesis, 15, 185; on music's dangers, 180, 291; Neoplatonism and, 7, 25, 79, 152; on rhythm, 39, 69; *The Laws*, 38–9; *The Republic*, 9, 37–9, 131, 190, 225
Platonic Academy (Florence), 7